SCOTLAND
The Making of the Kingdom
James V-James VII

THE EDINBURGH HISTORY OF SCOTLAND

General Editor
GORDON DONALDSON, D.Litt.

—————————

Vol. I.   *Scotland : Making of the Kingdom*

II.   *Scotland : Later Middle Ages*

III.   *Scotland : James V to James VII*

IV.   *Scotland : 1689 to the Present*

SCOTLAND

James V - James VII

Gordon Donaldson

Volume 3

MERCAT PRESS

1990

MERCAT PRESS
James Thin Ltd.
53–59 South Bridge
Edinburgh EH1 1YS

Hardback edition first published, 1965
Reprinted (with corrections) 1971, 1976
First published in paperback, 1978
Reprinted in paperback 1987, 1990

ISBN 0 901824 85 2 *paperback*

Printed and bound in Great Britain
by Billing & Sons Limited, Worcester.

PREFACE

The period of almost two centuries with which this volume has to deal was a period crammed with incident, and it embraces many of the most familiar, as well as the most significant, episodes in Scottish history. Besides, partly as a result of conspicuous events but largely because of more subtle and less perceptible changes in the constitutional, ecclesiastical and economic structure, the period was one in which Scotland was transformed, and there emerged in the end institutions and ways of life more akin to those we know today than to those of 1513. So far as the general history of the period is concerned, I have aimed at recounting only enough detail to explain what happened and—so far as the evidence permits—why it happened, but even to do this takes up a very large proportion of the space available. Consequently, I am only too conscious that I have been able to do little more than indicate some themes, especially in the development of society and its relationship to church, state and economy, which are deserving of far more extended treatment.

I have profited greatly from the comments and suggestions of my fellow-authors in this series—Professor A. A. M. Duncan, Dr W. Ferguson and Dr R. G. Nicholson—who have all read parts of the work in typescript. I am much indebted also to Dr J. W. M. Bannerman, who read the book with a critical eye when it was in the proof stage. Authors are apt to take the work of their publishers for granted, but I should be guilty of rank ingratitude if I failed to record my appreciation of the way in which Mr I. R. Grant and his colleagues in the house of Oliver and Boyd have encouraged me by the great personal interest they have taken in the making of this book.

G. D.

NOTE TO SECOND IMPRESSION

The opportunity of a second impression has been taken to make a number of corrections and amendments throughout, and also to insert a list of Addenda at the end of the Bibliography.

G.D.

CONTENTS

Preface   v

List of Abbreviations   ix

Part I

DIPLOMATIC AND ECCLESIASTICAL CRISES

1 The Structure of Society and Politics   3

2 The International Setting   17

3 Albany, Arran and Angus   31

4 The Policy of James V   43

5 The Minority of Queen Mary   63

6 The Revolution Against France and Rome   85

7 The Personal Reign of Mary   107

8 The Church Before and After the Reformation   132

Part II

THE NEW MONARCHY

9 " Uproar " and " Repose "   157

10 Discordant Policies and a *Via Media*   171

11 Two Kingdoms or One Kingdom?   197

12 King James's Peace   212

13 The Economy of Jacobean Scotland   238

14 The Culture of Jacobean Scotland   256

15 The Constitution in the Seventeenth Century   276

CONTENTS

Part III

REVOLT AND REACTION

16   The Policy of Charles I   295

17   The Revolution of the 1640s   317

18   The Cromwellian Interlude   343

19   The Reigns of Charles II and James VII   358

20   Scotland in the Later Seventeenth Century   385

Bibliography   402

Genealogical Table   423

Maps showing the location of all places mentioned in the text   424-6

Index   427

LIST OF ABBREVIATIONS

Particulars of the volumes referred to will be
found in the Bibliography

A. P. S.	= *Acts of the Parliaments of Scotland.*
B. O. E. C.	= *Book of the Old Edinburgh Club.*
Baillie	= Robert Baillie, *Letters and Journals.*
B. U. K.	= *Acts and Proceedings of the General Assemblies.*
Calderwood	= David Calderwood, *History of the Church of Scotland* (Wodrow Soc.).
Cal. S. P. Scot.	= *Calender of State Papers relating to Scotland and Mary, Queen of Scots.*
E.H.R.	= *English Historical Review.*
E.R.	= *Exchequer Rolls.*
Foedera	= Thomas Rymer, *Foedera* [etc.], London 1704.
H. M. C.	= Historical Manuscripts Commission.
Keith	= Robert Keith, *History of the affairs of Church and State in Scotland* (Spottiswoode Soc.).
Knox	= John Knox, *History of the Reformation* (ed. Dickinson).
L. and P.	= *Letters and Papers of the Reign of Henry VIII.*
Lesley	= John Lesley, *History of Scotland* (Bannatyne Club).
Nicoll	= John Nicoll, *Diary of public transactions* (Bannatyne Club).
Public Affairs	= *Acts of the Lords of Council in Public Affairs.*
R. P. C.	= *Register of the Privy Council of Scotland.*
Reg. Ho.	= General Register House.
R.M.S.	= *Registrum Magni Sigilli Regum Scotorum.*
R. S. S.	= *Registrum Secreti Sigilli Regum Scotorum.*
Rothes	= John, Earl of Rothes, *A relation of proceedings concerning the affairs of the Kirk of Scotland.*
Row	= John Row, *History of the Kirk of Scotland* (Wodrow Soc.).

Part I

DIPLOMATIC AND ECCLESIASTICAL CRISES

1

THE STRUCTURE OF SOCIETY
AND POLITICS

When the fifth successive James became king of Scots, in 1513, the nation was habituated to the rule of the house of Stewart, which had held the throne since 1371. While Plantagenet, Lancastrian, Yorkist and Tudor had contested the English throne, in Scotland the crown had passed undeviatingly from father to son. It is true that the Stewarts had been elevated to kingship only through a fortunate marriage, and that the Balliol and the Bruces who had preceded them had gained the throne only through unexpected deaths and the complications of Anglo-Scottish relations. Men who had become kings by accident could hardly be " hedged " by any " divinity," and the Stewart succession had initially been defined by statute, with a destination to the heirs male of Robert II and the express exclusion of females. Yet, when the male line became extinct, with the death of James V in 1542, the crown was to go, without challenge, to an infant girl.

The monarchy was sustained by attachment to a long and largely mythical line of " Scottish kings," who already in 1320 were said to have numbered one hundred and thirteen. But the belief was not in the inviolable rights of one particular family; it was in the inviolate independence of the kingdom and in the identification of a Scotland embracing all the lands north of the Tweed with an ancient Scotia in the Celtic west. Allegiance to the monarchy was therefore one of the few features in Scottish life which over-rode the geographical, racial and linguistic divisions of the country. The most important physical hindrance

3

to cohesion lay less in natural obstacles to communication than in the sharp contrast between the large proportion of high and infertile land, representing a mainly pastoral economy, and the sparser low-lying lands suited to arable farming. And, although there is much high land in southern Scotland and some low land in the west, the bulk of the low land forms an eastern coastal plain, while the bulk of the high land is in the centre and west; thus the geographical division largely coincided with the racial division between Teuton and Celt and the linguistic division between English and Gaelic. The " Highland Line " separated the barren mountains of the centre and west not only from the Forth-Clyde plain and the southern uplands but also from the strip of fertile land which runs south from Caithness along almost the whole eastern seaboard. That the boundary separated one way of life from another is at once apparent if burghs, royal castles, monasteries, cathedrals or sheriffs' seats are plotted on a map, for the area within the Highland Line is in every case almost blank. The Lowlander considered himself to be racially, linguistically and socially distinct from the Highlander, and, as lists of the inhabitants of any Scottish district very readily show, there was hardly any intermingling of the two peoples. The monarchy was one of the few things shared by the races on both sides of the Highland Line, and belief in its antiquity helped to give cohesion to the country.

Apart from its significance as a symbol of national integrity, the monarchy gave Scotland most of the institutional unity which it possessed, and was, for entirely practical reasons, little short of a necessity in the life of the nation. The crown was an essential element, for which no alternative had yet been considered, in the legal system; it was indispensable in the system of land tenure; and it was the source of patronage. All along, the crown had granted lands, pensions and feudal casualties, and had made appointments to offices which conferred both power and profit. Latterly, crown patronage had been extended to the church, for in 1487 the pope had given an undertaking that he would consider the king's recommendations for appointments to benefices above a certain value, and James IV had in practice nominated to bishoprics and abbeys.

The nature of the monarchy was such that a vigorous king, exercising in person the powers, privileges and patronage of his

office, could make his rule effective: but during a minority or
the rule of a weak king, those powers, privileges and patronage
were a prize to be competed for by individuals or factions. Each
minority thus meant a set-back for the monarchy, and the ground
gained by one king was apt to be lost before his successor came of
age. This was especially true in relation to finance. Taxation
was not yet a normal instrument of government, and some of
the sources of revenue were almost static. The ferms paid by the
royal burghs were by this time a negligible item even in gross,
they were so heavily burdened by assignations and pensions that
hardly anything came to the crown, and they were not capable
of any appreciable increase, since most important burghs, if not
all, had feu charters and paid a sum fixed in perpetuity. The
yield of the customs could be improved only by the slow process
of fostering trade.[1] Although the justice ayres held intermittently for criminal cases could produce worth-while sums, the
proceeds from fines in local courts were negligible, because only
small compositions were made over. It was, therefore, principally
by the acquisition of land that the king could hope to improve
his financial position. The intention, declared in 1455, that
certain lands and revenues should remain inalienably with the
crown, was not fulfilled, and the revocations of grants made
improperly during minorities were not effective, but some
progress was made: in the reign of each king from James I to
James IV earldoms and lordships had been forfeited to the crown,
and over the period the landed wealth of the crown did increase,
until the king was unquestionably superior in resources to even
the greatest of the nobles.

Somewhat similarly, the king was the fount of justice, but
jurisdiction as well as land had been alienated by the charters
which created baronies and regalities. A regality possessed a
system of legal administration reproducing in miniature that of
the kingdom; its courts might have power to deal with all crimes
except treason; forfeitures and escheats accrued to its lord; its
tenants could be " repledged " from the courts of royal justiciars
and sheriffs. The sheriff himself was often a local magnate,
holding his office in heritage. All in all, the activities of baron
courts, burgh courts, regality courts and hereditary sheriff courts

---

[1] The customs, which had been £2,400 gross in 1471, rose to £5,300 gross in
1542, an increase which did little more than offset the depreciation of money.

were of far more account than the judicial powers exercised by royal officials. Besides, many branches of law were administered not by secular courts at all, but by the ecclesiastical courts, which had competence in executry and matrimonial cases and in proceedings for the fulfilment of obligations, and were able to use excommunication or " cursing " to enforce their decisions. Yet a vigorous king could still do much to extend royal justice, by regular justice ayres for criminal cases and by permanent " sessions " of judges appointed by either parliament or council to hear civil cases. While attempts to curb the granting of regalities did not succeed, and the central as well as the local courts were still in the hands of amateur, part-time judges, the period from James I to James IV on the whole showed an increase of royal justice.

There was not much that was tangible or visible to make men aware of the central government. The only officials to be seen permanently in the localities were local magnates, in whom, even when they were disguised as sheriffs, delegated royal authority was not immediately obvious. There was no habit of obedience to royal officers who came on occasional errands, for it was their common fate to be " deforced." The royal castles were in the custody of local magnates as keepers or captains. The monarchy was now making its impress less by its castles than by its palaces, for the king was no longer content to reside in a fortress or to accept the hospitality of a religious house, and domestic ranges for the royal household were going up at Holyrood, Stirling, Linlithgow and Falkland. In general the sense of unity symbolised by the monarchy could best be strengthened by the king in person on his progresses throughout the country. While there were hindrances in plenty to transport, there were no serious obstacles to the movement of the king's household, his councillors, and the handful of officials who constituted the central administration: rivers of any size were not ill-supplied with bridges and ferries; individuals on horseback could ford the lesser streams and pick their way through mountain passes with little more difficulty than they had in following the rough tracks which in more level country did duty as roads; firths, lochs, and coastal waters were natural highways for traffic. The unresting movements of James IV, from Whithorn to Tain and from Aberdeen to the Firth of Lorne, " brought him into contact with every class of his subjects, in every part of his kingdom, and enabled them to recognise and admire . . . his sympathy, his generosity, and his strong sense of justice, evident in little things as in great."[2]

Such personal loyalty, valuable aid though it was to the authority of an energetic king, was no substitute for the permanent cohesion which could have come about either through the dominance of a succession of adult monarchs possessed of the instruments of coercion or through the habit of obedience to an administrative machine. In so far as a legal system and institutions of government helped to hold Scotland together they did it less through their formal association with the monarchy than through their association in practice with the social structure of the country, for administration was mainly in the hands of the great landholders. It was power and influence, rather than pecuniary wealth, that a noble derived from his landed property. His rents (largely in kind) afforded him ample food and fuel, and he had no difficulty in staffing his household and his estates with men and women who would serve in return for the free quarters which could so readily be provided. Indeed, it was a feature of Scottish life that at almost every social level, down to that of very small farmers, there was an abundance of " servants.' Even in the middle of the seventeenth century, when Cromwellian justices of the peace drew up an assessment of wages, a farm labourer or a herd was to have only a house, arable ground and pasture, with quantities of oats and pease, but no money wage, and servants who did receive money had to be content with sums ranging from 40 merks down to 10 merks.[3] The mere fact that the property of a landed magnate was supporting an army of retainers made it impossible to convert the produce of the land into cash, but it is equally true that neither transport nor markets existed to make such produce readily saleable. What, for example, could Huntly do with his 1,389 capons and his 5,284 eggs?[4] There were, on the other hand, few sources from which a sixteenth-century Scottish noble could obtain much cash, except the tenure of office under the government or, in the generation before the reformation, English or French pensions. There is every reason to accept the truth of the following contemporary comment:

This realme is puyr and the greit men can na way beyr greit exspens of thar awn leving. All greit men in this realme has, and

---

[2] R. L. Mackie, *James IV*, p. 127.   [3] *Scotland and the Protectorate* (S. H. S.), pp.
[4] Chambers, *Domestic Annals*, I. 314.   406-8.

utheris efter thair greis has, folkis to serve tham in thair awn boundis but [*i.e.*, without] ony mone[y], bot allanerly gud tretyng and greit houss to be haldin of daly exspens ordynar of meyt and drynk.⁵

It could be said with a certain amount of truth that the crown, not being possessed of the means to dominate the feudatories, could maintain the government only by coming to terms with them. James III's reign, after all, had ended with a campaign in which the royal forces were defeated by a coalition of magnates. Such a clash was, however, most exceptional: only once in the whole sixteenth century did a Scottish sovereign have to yield to an army in the field, when Mary surrendered (without bloodshed) at Carberry in 1567. More often rebellions were half-hearted affairs which tended to peter out when the sovereign took the field in person. At the same time, even the strongest of kings knew that he ignored at his peril the opinions of his more influential subjects; a wise monarch therefore avoided conflict and sought to rule by conciliation, consent and co-operation.

The king had instruments of such co-operation in his privy council and in the parliaments and general councils in which the three estates of prelates, barons and burgesses assembled, but none of those institutions necessarily provided an opportunity for free discussion and criticism. During a minority, unless one faction had made its domination so complete that its opponents felt it useless or dangerous to attend, the privy council might represent all who wanted a voice in affairs, and policy might be debated. But when the king was of mature years the composition of the privy council—which usually contained, besides the leading officials, a number of prelates and peers—was determined partly by the king's choice, partly by the willingness of the magnates to co-operate. In parliament and in general council, the baronial estate consisted in theory of all who held of the crown, and occasionally included one or two barons below the rank of peers, but in practice it was almost wholly made up of earls and lords. There were burgess members, coming almost entirely from the royal burghs, of which there were about forty at the beginning of the sixteenth century, but only a handful of the burghs were regularly represented and some were seldom or never represented.⁶

⁵ *Scottish Correspondence*, p. 242.
⁶ By 1460 only eleven burghs had been represented; a hundred years later the number which had been represented *at one time or another* had risen to thirty-five.

Decisions vital for the fate of the country were sometimes made by a parliament or a general council, especially during minorities when parties were delicately balanced, though even then the opposition was apt to absent itself rather than attend and be outvoted. More often, especially as the king's subjects were not accustomed to take the initiative in framing policies in parliament, the decisions were made elsewhere, either by the king or by the faction in control, and any bargaining and consultation between the government and its influential subjects took place outside the parliament house.

The face of the country showed, more clearly than constitutional machinery, the social and economic structure of Scotland and the location of wealth and power. Generally throughout the countryside the " touns," or little groups of cottages and huts, were inconspicuous in comparison with the tower houses of lairds and the castles of nobles. The noble's castle had earlier been a demonstration of his ability to defy the crown, but with the introduction and improvement of artillery that day was passing and the last instance of serious resistance by a noble in his castle was to be by the Earl of Angus at Tantallon in 1528. The castle was now mainly symbolic. Nor were the tower houses of any importance for serious military operations. They were places of security for men and their movable goods against casual lawlessness which was apt to render both persons and goods unsafe unless they were behind stone walls. An act of parliament of 1535 ordained that each man possessed of lands valued at £100 " in the inland or upon the bordouris " was to build a barmkin or enclosure " for the ressett and defens of him, his tennentis and their gudis, in trublous tyme, with ane toure in the samyn for himself gif he thinkis it expedient," and men of less substance were to build " pelis and gret strenthis " for the same purpose.[7] The contrast between the very numerous castles and towers on one hand and humbler dwellings on the other may have been sharpened if the former were already surrounded by enclosed parkland and woodland,[8] for the farmers' fields were unenclosed by dykes or hedges and their boundaries were generally defined only by natural features or boundary stones. Many of the substantial stone towers of the lairds are still to be seen,

---

[7] *A. P. S.*, II. 346.
[8] That they were so surrounded by 1600 is shown on Timothy Pont's maps.

either complete or in ruins, whereas the homes of the common folk—the tenant farmers and the cottars who laboured on the farms in the hands of the lairds—have left no visible trace above ground. These houses were mainly of turf or of wood, and one or at the most two apartments were generally thought to suffice for the accommodation of livestock as well as human beings. Some observers thought that the poor quality of tenants' houses was the result of the prevalence of short leases, for men were unlikely to build or improve houses which they might not long enjoy. The only other buildings in the countryside which could vie with—and often surpass—the castles and tower houses were the ecclesiastical buildings, monuments of a wealthy institution. Small and poor though the parish churches often were, they overshadowed the squalid huts of the ordinary parishioners, and a great abbey was more impressive than many a castle.

The burghs were in the main so small as to be inconspicuous in the setting of dispersed rural settlement. Within a burgh, the indications of ecclesiastical wealth were more notable than they were even in most country parishes. The massive burgh church dominated the houses, overshadowed the only other public building in the town centre, the tolbooth, and at least rivalled, sometimes surpassed, the buildings of the nearby castle. Something of the pattern which held good in the sixteenth century may still be seen in a burgh where a cathedral remains intact and the population has remained small: Kirkwall, for example, still dominated by its cathedral, may give some impression of what Dundee, dominated by the church of St Mary, or Glasgow, dominated by its cathedral, looked like in the sixteenth or seventeenth century. But, while some burgh houses were already comfortable enough to be fit to house James IV, on the whole their simplicity was such that the contrast between church and dwelling-house was sharper then than it can be in any town to-day. Besides, as there were no industrial premises and as each house usually had a long yard behind it, even a burgh did not present a wholly urban appearance. In addition to the cathedral or parish church, there were in many towns one or more establishments of friars, each set in spacious gardens.

Though the burghs were small, they were numerous in some parts of the country: Buchanan said of Fife, " frequentibus oppidulis praecingitur,"[9] and Andrew Fairservice later likened its south coast to " a great combined city." Few additions were now being made to the roll of royal burghs, which had a monopoly of much external trade, but there was a sharp increase in the number of burghs of barony, seventy-six of which were founded between 1450 and 1560, with authority to house craftsmen and to hold markets and fairs for internal trade. Most of these baronial burghs were mere villages, but there were some non-royal burghs of longer standing, especially the ecclesiastical burghs of St Andrews and Glasgow, which were more important than all but the largest of the royal burghs and which shared with them the privilege of parliamentary representation and the duty of paying taxes. There was any number of ports, both on the east coast and the west, capable of accommodating the small vessels of the time, but from the strategic point of view special importance attached to Dunbar and Dumbarton, each easy of access from the open sea, each an entrance to the heart of Scotland, and each commanded by a castle the holder of which could ensure or deny the use of the harbour.

In the sixteenth century Edinburgh's assessment for taxation sometimes equalled the combined figures for the next three burghs—Dundee, Perth and Aberdeen—and its proportion of the total burgh taxation usually amounted to a fifth or a quarter, while its proportion of the total customs might amount to a half or even more. Its pre-eminence among the burghs was such that any government apprehensive about its own security thought it worth-while to insist on having its nominee elected as provost. The list of provosts is some index of the state of the country: when the office was held by a douce burgess or a local laird, it usually meant that Scotland was in a settled state, but if the provost was a Douglas, a Hamilton or a Stewart, it is a sure sign that factions were engaged in a contest for power; thus the rivalry of Douglases and Hamiltons in the early years of James V's reign is reflected in the fact that the provost of Edinburgh was a Douglas in 1513, 1517 and 1519 and a Hamilton in 1515 and 1518. But even in this important burgh, although there were some substantial houses belonging to nobles and prelates as well as to the wealthier burgesses, ecclesiastical establishments were the most conspicuous buildings: there were, in and about the town, no less than four

[9] *Rerum Scoticarum Historia* (1582), fo. 7.

of the collegiate churches on which money was now being lavished, as well as three friaries, an abbey, and several other churches.

Apart from the evidence of ecclesiastical wealth in burghs, it would not be wholly untrue to say that burghal institutions were to some extent a mere façade, concealing the domination of the nobility and gentry. Many a burgh was, generation by generation, under the sway of a local peer or laird. Besides, a burgess who prospered was apt to acquire a landed estate and so himself pass into the ranks of the gentry: the Napiers, in Edinburgh, had done this in the fifteenth century, and there were many more instances in the sixteenth.

Wherever one looked, in the Scotland of 1500, there was evidence that wealth and power lay with the nobility and the church. But these were not two distinct or competing social elements, for bishops and dignitaries were drawn largely from the noble and landed families and formed one social group with them. Nobles were not likely to be jealous of " clerical influence " when the clerics were their own kinsmen. They were much more jealous of the elevation to political influence of men of lower social rank and of their own exclusion from what they conceived to be their proper place as the natural councillors of their sovereign.

Yet, while a common social status might be a bond joining noble with noble or noble with prelate and setting them apart from lesser men, there were other powerful links which defied social distinctions. Blood relationship joined together men of very different social status, and the practice was for men of the same surname, whether or not they were demonstrably related by blood, to act together. In the Lowlands, where surnames had become all but universal before the end of the fifteenth century, the evidence of the cohesion of families and of bearers of the same name is overwhelming. Again and again it is plain that Hamiltons, or Stewarts, or Douglases, stood or fell, were forfeited or rehabilitated, en bloc. For example, the Hamiltons, as a body, opposed the marriage of Queen Mary to Lord Darnley, and supported the rebellion raised on that occasion—the rebellion suppressed in the Chaseabout Raid. A few months later they were pardoned en bloc: there is a remission mentioning by name 37 Hamilton lairds and 120 Hamiltons of lower rank.[10]   A man

10 R. S. S., v. 2523.

could not be expected to fight against his kin: when James V was besieging the Earl of Angus in Tantallon, Douglas of Glenbervie was exempted from service in the royal army because he was " tender of blude " to the rebels.[11]

The idea that kinship was a more important element in Highland society than in Lowland society is debatable. From the documents of the sixteenth century, when as yet very few Highlanders had surnames, it is impossible to determine how far blood relationship was involved in the composition of a " clan " and in the relationship between a chief and his followers; but the more ample evidence for later times shows that, beyond the inner circle of the chief's family and the cadet branches of his house, neither kinship nor a common surname was an important element in a clan. Nor should the difference in land tenure between Highlands and Lowlands be exaggerated. In the Highlands, as in the Lowlands, the holding of land, whether in property or in superiority, was in historic times vested in individuals by charters. Equally, however, in both Highlands and Lowlands many tenants who had no legal rights to security of possession did enjoy a customary continuity of tenure, as " kindly " or hereditary tenants, and considered themselves to have rights which should not be challenged.

In any event, purely Highland families played hardly any part in national affairs in the sixteenth century. After the suppression of the Lordship of the Isles by James IV, the two families in the Highlands which were most important politically were the Campbells, headed by the Earl of Argyll, and the Gordons, headed by the Earl of Huntly. The Earl of Argyll's original seat was in mid-Argyll, but he was extending his power and property both north and south and into the Islands, and his cousins, the Campbells of Glenorchy, were by this time supreme throughout Breadalbane. Besides, Argyll himself had lands in the Lowlands, as the name Castle Campbell in Clackmannanshire reminds us; the Campbells of Loudoun had long been established in Ayrshire; at the beginning of the sixteenth century a cadet of the Argyll family acquired the Cawdor property, in Nairnshire, by marriage; and by the middle of the century we find a Campbell abbot of Coupar and a Campbell bishop of Brechin. While the Campbells thus expanded from the

[11] Fraser, *Douglas Book*, III. 228.

Highlands into the Lowlands, the Gordons, who were of Lowland origin and retained lands in Berwickshire, acquired northern estates in Angus and in the lowland as well as in the highland portions of Aberdeenshire and Banffshire: but Huntly's brother became Earl of Sutherland by marriage, and Huntly himself, as sheriff of Inverness, had some authority in practically all the country north and west of that town. No Highland chief was of much importance in comparison with those two semi-lowland families.

Apart from " the kin " or " the name " as a link between man and man, there was the formal " bond of manrent " which pledged service in return for protection. Moreover, although no reference to a servile status of tenants is to be found after the fourteenth century, tenants and other men of humble rank were habituated to hereditary service to some great house. John Knox declared that he had a " good mind " to the Hepburns of Hailes, Earls of Bothwell, because his great-grandfather, grandfather, and father had served them;[12] and George Buchanan allowed his similar attachment to the Earls of Lennox to influence his political views. A classic expression of the same kind of loyalty, though at a different social level, was the remark of Home of Wedderburn that " if his chief should turn him out at the fore door, he would come in again at the back door."[13] It was not a one-sided or dishonourable relationship, and in this feature of Scottish life there may lie the explanation of the remarkable fact that, whatever the faction in control, the legislation of parliaments and general councils was not infrequently in the interests of the lower classes. In the second half of the fifteenth century " no fewer than ten separate acts were passed at brief intervals for the benefit of a class of the community described as ' the puir tennentes ' or ' the puir people that labouris the grund . . . whose heavy complaintes has ofttimes been maid '."[14] Reading the legislation, one would never guess that a baronial clique was in control of affairs. This reciprocal relationship may explain why, if there was any serious social unrest in Scotland before the Reformation, it never issued in such peasants' revolts as were known in France and England. It may also explain how it came about that although Scotland was, and still is, a more egalitarian country than

---

[12] Knox, II. 38.   [13] Hume of Godscroft, *House of Douglas* (1743), II. 260.
[14] Lord Cooper, *Supra Crepidam*, p. 4.

England, the Scot could combine his lack of class-consciousness with a sincere respect for the representatives of the ancient noble houses. Peers themselves were not ashamed of a tradition of hereditary service, for the Lennox Stewarts could describe themselves as " natyf born servandis to Sant Mongow and to that kyrk [of Glasgow]."[15]

The links of the kin, the bond, and hereditary service, which went a long way to obviate a horizontal division into classes, also gave cohesion to the whole nation when there was no discord at the top: but they intensified vertical divisions, for the whole of society became involved whenever political disagreement arose. And there was freedom to disagree, for Scotland, which had escaped turmoil like that of the Wars of the Roses in the fifteenth century, also escaped brutal repression like that under Tudor rule in the sixteenth. Parties were freely formed, often by the drawing up of formal bonds pledging the signatories to act in concert, and appeals were made to self-interest, traditional alignment, and personal inclination, as well as to political opinions. One example may be given here, from among the many which the century offers. In 1544 the Earl of Arran and Cardinal Beaton were engaged in a contest with Mary of Guise, the queen mother. Arran, who was governor, had political patronage at his disposal, and ecclesiastical patronage was shared between him and the cardinal: Huntly, for example, could be controlled through the candidature of one of his kin for the bishopric of Aberdeen[16] as well as by the cardinal's ability to grant him feu charters of coveted lands. The partisans of Mary of Guise, on their side, with fewer financial inducements to offer, had to use more finesse, and a letter to her, though over-optimistic about her prospects, anticipates the technique which was to be used to " make interest " in eighteenth-century parliamentary elections: she was to intervene in the disputes between Lord Ruthven and Charteris about the affairs of Perth in order to win one of them to her side; Argyll, Glencairn and Cassillis could be relied on for the west; undertakings by Huntly, Marischal and Errol would secure the north-east; " gef ye haif the Lord Graye ye haif fra Taye north "; she was to use Lord Erskine to prevail on his son-in-law, Douglas of Lochleven, to have an interview with her, for he was a man that " well kyp that he promissis "; the

15 Fraser, *Lennox*, II. No. 192.   16 *Scottish Correspondence*, p. 118.

laird of Raith was to be her agent with the gentlemen of Fife to " mak tham yowrs "; on the other hand, Rothes " well be the cardenellis," if only because he would take the opposite side from Lochleven.[17]

Political decisions were quite commonly the result of a contest between two parties, and reflected, in the ultimate analysis, the preference of individuals to support this policy or that, to adhere to this party or that. The ascendancy of one party or another was not normally established either by parliamentary debate or by violence: a demonstration in force usually sufficed to bring about a bloodless *coup d'état*, for the government had no standing forces and might easily be surprised before it could muster men to put up resistance. No doubt the parties did consist of groups of families, each massed under the head of the kin, but it was party government of a kind, and the contests did not constitute " baronial strife " any more than eighteenth-century British politics—with which they have much in common—constituted baronial strife.

[17] *Scottish Correspondence*, pp. 112-13.

2

THE INTERNATIONAL SETTING

Scotland had been at war with England intermittently since 1296 and her "auld ally" was France. But this alignment had become traditional in a period when England threatened to conquer France, whereas in the sixteenth century the threat to France came less from England than from the house of Hapsburg. Through the fortunate marriages of that house, four separate inheritances—the Austrian dominions, most of the Netherlands, the kingdom of Castile, and the kingdom of Aragon with its Italian dependencies—fell to a single prince, who in 1519 succeeded his grandfather, Maximilian, as the Emperor Charles V. To meet the threat represented by this concentration of power, France from time to time sought the alliance, or at least the neutrality, of England, and in order to court the English France did not hesitate to sacrifice her ancient allies, the Scots.

This was first demonstrated only a few months after James IV had fallen at Flodden (9 September 1513), in a campaign undertaken in the interests of France. To the Scots, Flodden was only one of many heavy defeats suffered in the course of their wars with England, and they saw in it neither an irretrievable disaster nor a reason for a change in their diplomacy: the league with France was to stand, the war was to go on. A new king, James V, was crowned at Stirling on 21 September and a month later a council of regency was nominated to act with the queen mother, who, in terms of James IV's will, was tutrix to her son during her widowhood. But the queen mother was Margaret Tudor, sister of King Henry VIII of England, and some may have seen a danger in entrusting her with authority. In any event, there were Scottish representatives at the French court, for the Earl of Arran and Lord Fleming had reached France in September with the Scottish fleet, and when they learned of Flodden they supported or initiated a proposal that the office of governor of Scotland should be claimed by John, Duke of Albany. This duke (1481-1536) was the son of James III's brother Alexander, who had been forfeited and exiled and who, after divorcing his first wife in 1478, had married again in France, where he died in 1485. Duke John, though in effect a Frenchman, who had served with distinction in the French army, had already shown that he was not unaware of his position and prospects in Scotland as next in succession to the crown after James IV and his issue. When Arran and Fleming returned home in November they were accompanied by Albany's agent, Antoine d'Arces, seigneur de la Bastie sur Melans, who had visited Scotland at least twice during the previous reign. On 26 November a general council agreed that Albany should come to Scotland with men and munitions and acceded to the request of King Louis XII that the league should be renewed. Lord Fleming was sent back to France before the end of 1513, obviously to work out plans for continued Franco-Scottish co-operation, in anticipation of a renewed attack on France in the spring by England and her continental allies.[1]

However, the spring brought no renewal of the war, but an Anglo-French truce (13 March 1513/4), and negotiations for a definite peace began in April. Fleming was therefore kept waiting until June, when Louis announced that he would send 8,000 men to Scotland with Albany, but at the same time commended to the Scots a policy of peace. France was coolly preparing for either contingency, peace or war, and Albany, although already addressed as " governor " by the pope and by Louis himself, remained in France. Peace was made between Henry and Louis in August 1514, and, after Louis's death, was confirmed by Francis I in the following April. Scotland was included in the peace, but without her consent and with an offensive condition: should any party of Scots raid England with the consent of the government, or should a party numbering 300 or more raid England without such consent and fail to make restitution, then Scotland's comprehension in the treaty was to be

[1] *A. P. S.*, ii. 281-2; *Analecta Scotica* (ed. J. Maidment), i. 41; *Public Affairs*, pp. 5, 9-11; cf. *Edinburgh Burgh Recs.*, i. 146.

null—but there was no corresponding provision for the protection of the Scottish frontier. The Scots resented an arrangement which permitted provocative English raids but promised to check Scottish retaliation, especially as, in the raiding which had gone on intermittently since Flodden, they had been doing their share in the mutual infliction of damage. Henry himself did not believe that the Scots could observe the conditions of the treaty, and the Scottish council, in August 1514, made a fresh appeal to Albany on the ground that " the condiciouns of the comprehencioun ar undirstand to contene rather weir than pece."[2]

Henry had exacted a promise that Albany should be kept in France, but the duke arrived in Scotland on 16 May 1515. He had not, however, been released to fulfil the purpose for which the Scots had invited him, for instead of bringing men and munitions to resume war he brought advice to keep the peace. The Scots felt more than ever frustrated after the French victory at Marignano (September 1515). Albany instructed them to celebrate it by bonfires,[3] and they thought it a signal for renewed Franco-Scottish action against England, but their requests for a renewal of the league and for a French bride for their king were very coldly received in France.[4] Albany must have been converted to the Scottish point of view, for by the early summer of 1517 he approved a policy of threatening that if France would not agree to a league and a marriage alliance the Scots would look elsewhere for support against England. If Albany thus initiated the policy, later to be pursued by James V in person, of raising Scotland's price by inviting bids in more than one market, he was successful up to a point, for after leaving Scotland for France on 8 June 1517 he brought about the formulation of the treaty of Rouen (26 August). This provided that France and Scotland should give mutual assistance in the event of hostile action by England against either of them, and offered James certain hypothetical prospects of a French bride: Louise, the first-born daughter of Francis, was already pledged to Charles of Spain, and her younger sister Charlotte (born on 23 October 1516) was designed as a substitute in the event of the death of Louise, but James was to have the reversion of Charlotte, and failing her a younger sister should one be born. However, Louise died in September 1517, and the treaty remained unratified.

[2] *Public Affairs*, p. 21.   [3] *Treasurer's Accounts*, v. 47.   [4] *Letters of James V*, p. 33.

Not only so, but Albany, who had undertaken to return to Scotland in four months, was detained in France for over four years. In 1518, when the Anglo-French understanding was renewed, England evidently exacted a promise that Albany would be kept in France, though no such clause appeared in the formal treaty;[5] and, despite Scottish protests, a fresh undertaking of this nature was given in June 1520, when Francis and Henry met on the Field of Cloth of Gold. However, before and after that meeting there were two meetings between Henry and the Emperor Charles, who in 1521 agreed to make a joint attack on France. Francis was thus free from his undertakings to Henry, and was now disposed to revert to the traditional policy of looking to Scotland to provide a distraction for English forces. Albany therefore returned to Scotland on 19 November 1521. Scotland ratified the Treaty of Rouen on 28 December, and Albany, in approaching Francis for his ratification, reminded him that the Princess Madeleine, born on 10 August 1520, was now available as a bride for King James. Francis did ratify the treaty on 13 June 1522, and to that extent encouraged Albany to prepare an expedition against England.

On 24 July 1522 there was an act, on the lines of one passed before Flodden, granting concessions to the heirs of those who should lose their lives in the forthcoming campaign.[6] The host which the governor mustered at Roslin and led towards the Solway must have been unusually large, for the English professed to believe that it numbered 80,000 and was well equipped with artillery and hand-guns. Albany prepared to attack Carlisle, but received clear intimation that the Scots would not invade England for the sake of France, and a truce was made on 11 September. Before the campaign had been mounted, Albany had pleaded with Francis for military help as a necessary condition of effective Scottish action in the field, but Francis had excused himself on the ground of his other commitments; thus, when the Scots refused to advance in the cause of France they must have been aware that France did not propose to do much for them. Albany left Scotland on 25 October 1522, to appeal personally for French support. Early in the following summer,

5 *L. and P.*, ii (2). 4471; *Foedera*, xiii. 624, 631.
6 *A. P. S.*, ii. 284. For an analysis of this and other similar acts, see *R. S. S.*, vi, Intro. p. viii.

Francis sent a token force of 500 men, which suffered in an encounter with English ships on approaching the Firth of Forth, and he promised substantial help later in the year; and on 18 June, in presence of a French ambassador, the Scottish council ordered preparations for war. Albany himself, evading an English naval force, landed in Scotland once more on 24 September. He brought with him forces variously estimated but probably numbering 4,000 foot and some arquebusiers, with 500 or 600 horses, artillery, money, and supplies. Possibly because of the expense of maintaining his troops, he decided on an immediate campaign, late though the season was. Elaborate and widespread preparations were made for a muster on 2 October: the burghs were to furnish horses, victual and pioneers, religious houses were to provide oxen for the artillery and food for men and beasts, and the roads were to be put in order.[7] But, despite the French help now given, the adventure turned out to be a dismal repetition of that of the previous year. There was some reluctance to join the host, there was a certain indiscipline on the march,[8] and when the Tweed was reached (at the end of October) there was an almost superstitious dread of crossing it. An attack on Wark Castle, where the French seem to have borne the brunt of the fighting, was so discouraging that Albany, faced with the approach of winter, in danger of being caught with a flooded Tweed in his rear, and alarmed by reports of the approach of a large English force, had no choice but to withdraw. The Scottish parliament soon insisted that the French troops should leave the country, and Albany himself departed once more on 20 May 1524.

Clearly, the Scots, who had clamoured for war in 1514 and 1515, had now lost their appetite for anything beyond defensive operations[9] and would not even take action across the border to avenge the burning by the English of Kelso and Jedburgh in June and September 1523. They had not forgotten Flodden, but it now represented an occasion when the " auld alliance " had led to a war which Scotland herself would not have sought, and no appeal was ever again to prevail on the Scottish nobles to cross that fatal frontier in the interests of France and risk a repetition of the disaster of 1513. But thoughtful Scots were also beginning to reflect that an Anglo-Scottish understanding

7 *Public Affairs*, pp. 180-1.   8 *Ibid.*, pp. 187-8, 190.
9 *Ibid.*, pp. 169-74.

promised not only to save their country much loss and suffering but also to keep profitable markets open to Scottish wool and fish. In John Major, whose *Greater Britain* (1521) was a plea for Anglo-Scottish union, a pro-English or " unionist " policy gained perhaps its first pamphleteer. Already, too, as a result of the marriage of James IV to Margaret Tudor, the Scottish queen mother and her heirs were close to the English succession, especially as the first of Henry VIII's children to survive infancy had been Mary, born on 18 February 1516, and she was his only surviving child until 1533. There were plenty of motives for the growth of a party opposed to war with England.

Albany's departure for France in May 1524, though it was that of a disappointed man, may have been for personal rather than political reasons, for his wife died in the following month. So far as the situation in Scotland was concerned, he might have returned yet again and still enjoyed powerful support, but international relations once more determined the course of events. England, which had already in 1524 been contemplating a change of alliance, took up negotiations with Francis seriously after he suffered his great defeat at Pavia in the spring of 1525, and Anglo-French treaties were concluded in April 1527. Once again, therefore, it was not to the interest of France to intervene in Scotland.

During James V's personal rule, beginning in 1528, the history of Scotland continued to be shaped as much by developments in other countries as by events at home, and one of those developments was now the Reformation, which affected Scotland both directly and indirectly. Soon after Luther's revolt started in 1517 there came to Scottish east-coast ports, especially Dundee and Leith, " merchants and mariners, who, frequenting other countries, heard the true doctrine affirmed,"[10] and they brought Lutheran books, against the import and circulation of which parliament legislated, without lasting effect, in 1525. Patrick Hamilton, commendator of Fearn, who was put to death for " heresy " in 1528, had propagated the Lutheran emphasis on justification by faith. Contacts with Germany, the Low Countries and Denmark were not the only channels through which novel doctrines came in, for a Frenchman who had been in Albany's train was charged with spreading Lutheran teaching, and from England there came copies of Tyndale's translation of the New Testament.

[10] Knox, I. 25.

Several German princes, and also the kings of Denmark and Sweden, were giving their protection to Lutheranism and were appropriating ecclesiastical wealth, but the Scottish government in 1527 expressed its preference for supporting orthodoxy—at a price: opposition to the reform movement must be rewarded by favours from the church. After James began to direct affairs, he followed up a letter to the pope in which he expressed his anxiety " to banish the foul Lutheran sect " with another in which he demanded that the pope should preserve the privileges of the Scottish kings in consideration of James's consistent " loyalty to the orthodox faith."[11] The argument was one which the pope, as he watched the defection of continental princes, found it hard to resist, and it became even more cogent when Henry VIII's proceedings for divorce from Catharine of Aragon led him to reject papal authority. In February 1531 Henry obtained recognition from the convocation of Canterbury as their " supreme lord and, as far as the law of Christ allows, even supreme head," and in 1533 he married Anne Boleyn. The pope was now resolved to retain the allegiance of Scotland, at the cost of conceding whatever boons the king of Scots might crave.

The European political situation, too, was favourable to a Scottish government which wanted to bargain, and any proposal for a continental marriage for James V was bound to induce counter-bids. The Emperor Charles, guided mainly by his rivalry with France, was alienated also from Henry VIII, since the discarded Catharine was his aunt, and he therefore seemed cast for the part of papal champion against the schismatic English. He was too heavily committed against the Lutherans in Germany and the Turks in Central Europe to be enthusiastic for a crusade against Henry, but he was willing enough to see Scotland detached from her traditional association with France and used against England. The requisite bride for King James could be found among imperial princesses: in 1527 the emperor's sister Mary, widow of the King of Hungary, had been suggested, and in 1528 the emperor's brother-in-law, the deposed King of Denmark, offered one of his daughters. Besides the prospects of a Hapsburg bride and her dowry, Charles had another bait for the Scots, in that a commercial treaty relating to Scotland and the Low Countries, made in 1427 for a hundred years, was due for renewal

[11] *Letters of James V*, pp. 134, 161, 167.

and the town of Middelburg, to which Albany had promised the Scottish staple, had appealed to the emperor against Campvere, with which James was in negotiation.   In June 1529 a Scottish envoy to the Low Countries, sent nominally to complete the renewal of the commercial treaty, was authorised also to enquire about the Queen of Hungary and inspect that lady. After Queen Mary made it clear that she thought a marriage to James abhorrent, the Scottish government, in May 1530, consented to the marriage of their king to one of " the emperor's nieces of Denmark." This was agreeable to Charles, who responded by confirming the treaties between Scotland and the Low Countries (July 1531), sending ordnance and ammunition to Scotland (September), conferring on James the order of the Golden Fleece (May 1532) and—so at least James claimed— promising to recognise him as heir presumptive to England. Talk of a marriage with a Danish princess went on until the beginning of 1536—concurrently with many other proposed matches.

France, allied with England since 1527, made peace with the emperor in 1529 but was still active in diplomacy against him and therefore did not want to see Scotland go over to the imperial side.   The threat of an imperial marriage could always be relied on to stimulate Francis into an acknowledgment of his obligations to Scotland, but at the same time he dared not offend his English ally by fulfilling the Treaty of Rouen and arranging for the marriage of James to the Princess Madeleine.   Consequently, the French message to Scotland, sent for the first time in December 1528 and again and again in later years, was almost stereotyped —the Princess Madeleine was too young, or too frail, for marriage. All that Francis could offer as a counter-attraction to an imperial princess was the hand of some more remote kinswoman.

As England did not want King James to contract either an imperial or a French marriage, she also made offers to Scotland. Henry's marriage to Anne Boleyn, who might have male issue, was prejudicial to James, but Henry offered to recognise James's place in the English succession if he would acknowledge Anne as queen, while James on his side—simultaneously with one of his applications for Madeleine—raised the question of a marriage to the Princess Mary.   Henry was not at this point willing to concede so much, but he took other steps to steer James away from his attachment to the emperor.   He conferred the Garter on James

(February 1534/5) and invited him to come to England and proceed to a meeting with Francis in France, all at England's expense. In June and July 1535, however, Bishop Fisher and Sir Thomas More were executed for their refusal to acknowledge Henry's ecclesiastical supremacy, and in the same year the London Carthusians suffered death with the customary brutality of English treason law. Scottish opinion was shocked, especially as refugees from Henry's reign of terror found safety in Scotland, and Henry's proceedings could hardly be reconciled with James's own orthodoxy. The Scottish king was therefore unmoved by English blandishments.

The year 1536 brought a diplomatic revolution which altered the setting of Scottish policy. As the Anglo-French alliance had broken down and a fresh war between France and the emperor had started in 1535, Charles was inclined to seek an alliance with England, and the opportune deaths of Catharine of Aragon (January 1535/6) and Anne Boleyn (June 1536) removed obstacles to an understanding. Thus, for France and Scotland the way was clear for a renewal of the old league. Negotiations between Scotland and England did continue, but the motive on the Scottish side can have been only to put further pressure on France. In the autumn of 1535 James had been sending hawks as a present to Henry, listening to English advice to renounce the pope's authority and seize the church's wealth and receiving English representations against a French match. Even in the spring of 1536, James—against the wishes of his own council as well as of the pope—consented to a proposal that he should meet Henry in the autumn. But by the autumn James was on his way to France and he was at last united to the Princess Madeleine on 1 January 1536/7. A few days later the pope sent James a sword and cap with an intimation that he hoped for Scottish co-operation with France against England in the cause of orthodoxy. Madeleine died in June 1537, but James found a second French bride in Mary of Guise.

Scotland was thus again tied to France, and in circumstances which seemed peculiarly menacing to England. Neither Charles nor Francis had hitherto given much countenance to papal schemes against Henry, but the treaties which they made in 1538 and 1539 were seen in conjunction with the actions of the pope, who since 1537 had been proclaiming a general council and who in December 1538 ordered the execution of his bull of excommunication against Henry. The danger of an invasion of England was taken very seriously in the spring of 1539,[12] and Henry's position had been shaken by troubles in Ireland, where Fitzgerald intrigued with the emperor, and in England itself, with the Pilgrimage of Grace (October 1536) and a conspiracy to which descendants of the Yorkist line were parties (December 1538). Even should Scotland not become a base against Henry, it was at least a focus of elements hostile to him, for refugees from his fury continued to find asylum there, and the brutalities following the Pilgrimage of Grace disposed some Englishmen to look to James for help.[13] Henry was therefore more than ever concerned to bring James over to his side, and although he could make less use of James's prospects in England since the birth of Prince Edward in October 1537, he had a new argument in the advantages which would accrue to James should he follow his uncle's example and dissolve the monasteries. Henry's persuasive tactics reached a new intensity in 1540 and 1541.

But the coalition against England soon dissolved. By 1541 Francis and Charles were at loggerheads again and both were seeking Henry's aid, so that when the Scottish government, faithful to its engagements to France and Rome, sent Cardinal David Beaton to France in July 1541 to ask for help against England, his mission proved fruitless. All that came of the grand design for a crusade against England was an Anglo-Scottish war in which Scotland was not only unaided, but divided. While those Scots who were attached to the ecclesiastical *status quo* adhered to the French alliance and favoured action against the schismatic English, the progress of the Reformation in England had augmented the number of friends to reform in Scotland and had added them to the party preferring Anglo-Scottish amity. In the existence of those two parties lies part of the explanation of the disaster of Solway Moss (November 1542). When James mustered his army on Fala Muir, some attended " to show their obedience, against their hearts,"[14] but many did not attend, and among the absentees was a significant proportion of lairds from Angus, Mearns and Aberdeenshire who either had been, or were

12 *Trans. Roy. Hist. Soc.*, Ser. V, x. 48-9.
13 *S. P. Henry VIII*, v. 79. The Pilgrimage of Grace is a convenient term to cover a series of risings in northern England in 1536/7.
14 Sir James Melville, *Memoirs*, p. 79.

to be, associated with reforming opinions.[15] James also found, as Albany had done, that his nobles would not cross the Border, but their hesitation now had a religious as well as a political motive: in their eyes, Scotland was now adventuring on behalf of the pope, just as in 1513 she had adventured on behalf of France.

After the death of James V (December 1542), the pro-English and reforming party came into power and pledged itself to an English marriage for the infant Queen Mary. But, simultaneously, Henry concluded an alliance with the emperor against France, so that the " auld ally," which had done nothing to help Scotland before Solway, was again ready to intervene against England, and it was partly as a result of French machinations that before the end of 1543 the Scots broke off their negotiations with the English. Henry's plan to make Scotland a kind of satellite state, and thereby secure his northern frontier while he went to war with France, had thus come to nothing, and it made matters worse for him when the emperor deserted him in 1544 and when the forces of the counter-reformation rallied at the opening of the Council of Trent in 1545. It was out of fury at his disappointment, rather than out of policy, that he launched on Scotland the devastating invasions of the Earl of Hertford in 1544 and 1545 which are known as the " Rough Wooing."

Henry's violence could not prevail on the Scottish government to resume negotiations for the English alliance, but it was equally true that it did not destroy the pro-English party. The combination of political, ecclesiastical and economic considerations on which anglophile opinions were based was well illustrated in the very years of Hertford's invasions, when the reformer George Wishart came from England to preach in Montrose, Dundee, Perth, Fife, Leith, " the westland," and East Lothian. His labours were in areas which had long been reforming centres, for the east-coast burghs had felt the impact of the Lutheran reformation and the people of Leith had already been pronounced " all good Christians,"[16] while the " gentlemen of Kyle "[17] who welcomed Wishart may have been sons or grandsons of those Ayrshire lairds who had professed Lollard tenets fifty years earlier. Besides, the merchants in the burghs had a distaste for English wars which disrupted their trade, and lairds in Angus, like Wishart of Pittarro and Erskine of Dun, and lairds in East Lothian,

[15] E.g., R. S. S., III. 395, 820. [16] L. and P., XVIII (1). 974. [17] Knox, I. 61.

like Crichton of Brunstane, Douglas of Longniddry and Cockburn of Ormiston, welcomed Wishart, as they had opposed the Solway expedition, partly because they were conscious of the economic advantages of peace with the southern neighbour.

The interaction between Scottish affairs and the international situation was illustrated once more when, in the summer of 1546, a party of pro-English Scots, mainly Fife lairds, murdered Cardinal Beaton and seized the castle of St Andrews. As England and France came to terms in June, England was able, without any risk of French intervention, to take up the cause of the " Castilians " at St Andrews, who sent emissaries to London in November. Henry VIII died on 28 January, but there was no change in English policy, for the protector under the young Edward VI was Scotland's old enemy Hertford, now Duke of Somerset, and, as a Scottish observer in London ruefully remarked, " I see na thing bot as the ald kyng wer levyng, and ilk day I heir of our infelicite."[18] On 7 February the English council voted pensions amounting to over £1,000 to the " Castilians."[19] But before England could act, the death of Francis I (31 March) brought about a change in the French attitude. Henry II, the new king, was eager to move against the English, in the hope of recovering Boulogne, held by them since 1544, and if possible Calais as well. Moreover, the Guise family, to which the Scottish queen mother belonged, established an ascendancy at the French court: it was reported to Mary of Guise that " your freyndis ar gret consalouris and reularis," and it was almost at once rumoured that France would seek " the mariaig of owr maistres."[20] A French force was therefore sent to clear the friends of England out of St Andrews Castle.

England had not moved to save St Andrews, but shortly after its fall English policy towards Scotland entered—for the last time—on a militant and aggressive phase. The Scots were heavily defeated at Pinkie (September 1547) and English garrisons were established in many strongholds in south-eastern Scotland. As a divided Scotland was incapable of reducing those garrisons, the only escape from English occupation could be French occupation, and French help was given, on condition that Queen Mary should be sent to France as the prospective bride of the dauphin.

---

[18] *Scottish Correspondence*, p. 180.   [19] *L. and P.*, xxi (2). 524n.; cf. *Foedera*, xv. 132-3.
[20] *Scottish Correspondence*, pp. 180, 183.

In 1548 and 1549 Scotland became a battleground for English and French forces, but the country was finally cleared of the English only by virtue of a peace not made in Scotland. In August 1549 successful attacks on Boulogne by the French caused the English to relax their hold on Scotland, and in September they abandoned their principal stronghold, Haddington. Warwick, now protector in England, wanted peace, and by the Treaty of Boulogne (24 March 1550) he ceded Boulogne and undertook to relinquish every foothold in Scotland. Thus it was by the " lawboris " of " the kyngis mageste " of France that " the boundis of Scotland " became again " als fre as thai war in ony of ouris dayis."[21]

The last phase of the operation of the " auld alliance," which France had consistently exploited for her own purposes, came in the 1550s. The marriage of Mary Tudor to Philip II of Spain (25 July 1554) led England into participation in a war in which France was defeated by the Spaniards at St Quentin (10 August 1557) and Paris itself menaced. Scotland acquired fresh importance to France as an instrument by which English effort could be diverted from France and by which, while the French threatened Calais, an attack could be made against that other relic of England's medieval conquests, Berwick-on-Tweed. The Scots again reacted against the use of their country as a tool of France, and this time the outcome was the political and ecclesiastical revolution of 1559-60. Scotland then finally renounced the French alliance as well as the pope, but she was able to liberate herself from French domination only with the help of Elizabeth of England. It was the exact counterpart of the situation twelve years earlier, when the Scots had called in the French to rid the country of the English, but this time, by the Treaty of Edinburgh, both French and English troops withdrew from Scotland. It is a curious fact, significant of the dependence of Scottish affairs on the international situation, that at this crisis in the nation's history the settlement was made by an agreement between two foreign powers.

When the English army crossed the Border in 1560, to be for the first time welcomed as a deliverer, it meant the end of an Anglo-Scottish war which had gone on intermittently since 1296. The diplomatic revolution of 1560 proved permanent, for after it, although there were still vicissitudes in Anglo-Scottish relations,

[21] *Scottish Correspondence*, p. 353.

Scotland never again feared English conquest or had to appeal to France for help against England, and the two countries drew ever closer together in amity until in 1603 they were joined peacefully in a personal union. Such a union had long been looked for. For two generations there had seldom been more than one life between the Scottish royal line and the English succession, and with the death of Mary Tudor in 1558 the heir presumptive to the crown of England, by right of blood if not by the will of Henry VIII, was Mary, Queen of Scots. Mary at first claimed Elizabeth's throne, she then sought acknowledgment as Elizabeth's heir, she later strengthened her claim by marriage to another claimant. But it was not merely a matter of Mary's personal ambitions: those who, in 1560, thought of superseding her and finding a protestant sovereign in the house of Hamilton, proposed to secure union in another way, by marrying James Hamilton, Earl of Arran, to Elizabeth, and when that plan fell through there were those who thought that the marriage of Mary to Arran was the best way to make her acceptable as heir to England. The possibility of a union of the two realms had come to dominate Scottish political calculations.

The effect of generations of hostility and suspicion could not be at once extinguished, but the forces making for amity were powerful. When John Knox remarked to William Cecil in June 1559 that the perpetual concord of the two realms would be effected by the preaching of Jesus Christ[22] he indicated the importance of a common religion as the most powerful force fostering a consciousness of common aims and a common destiny. Next to religion, it was language that was uppermost in men's minds as a link between the two peoples. In a letter which the English privy council proposed to send to the Scottish insurgents in 1559, the hope was expressed that " this famous isle may be conjoined in heart as in continent, with uniformity of language, manners and conditions."[23] There were other links, in literature, education, and other cultural fields, as well as in commerce.[24] Dynastic accident could unite the two states, but it could not have united the two peoples without the conjunction of other developments which brought them into partnership.

22 *Cal. S. P. Scot.*, I. 218.   23 *Cal. S. P. Scot.*, I. 234-5.
24 See in general " Foundations of Anglo-Scottish Union," in *Elizabethan Government and Society* (edd. S. T. Bindoff *et. al.*), pp. 282-314.

3

ALBANY, ARRAN AND ANGUS

When James IV fell at Flodden, he was survived only by a son seventeen months old, born at Linlithgow on 10 April 1512; and another son, born posthumously on 30 April 1514, died before he was two years old. The heir presumptive was John, Duke of Albany, who was invited to come over from France and assume the office of governor. Albany was childless, and after him stood James Hamilton, first Earl of Arran, a son of James II's daughter Mary by Lord Hamilton. Arran, as next in succession after the duke and a native Scot, was a potential rival for the governorship, but he did not claim it and was, except for one brief defection, loyal to Albany. The challenge to Albany was to come rather from families which had no interest in the succession but were notorious for unreliability, especially the Douglas earls of Angus. The fifth earl of the line had gained his nickname of Bell-the-Cat by taking the lead in a conspiracy against James III, he had opposed that king again at the end of his reign and twice in the reign of James IV he had been under suspicion. Bell-the-Cat's son was killed at Flodden, and his grandson Archibald, who succeeded as sixth earl in 1514, was to be the ultimate beneficiary in James V's minority.

It was this Earl of Angus whom Queen Margaret, a widow of twenty-four, married on 6 August 1514. On 18 September the council ruled that she had thereby terminated her right to be tutrix to the king, and urged Albany to " come home " with all possible haste.[1] But Margaret and her sons were in Stirling Castle, the keeper of which was Lord Drummond, Angus's grand-

1 *Public Affairs*, p. 20.

father, and the Douglases supported her in challenging the council's authority; the chancellor, Archbishop James Beaton of Glasgow, found himself with a competitor in Gavin Douglas (Angus's uncle), and in November rival parliaments were summoned. There was also a clash over the archbishopric of St Andrews, vacant since Flodden. The Scots had been unanimously resolved to support the candidature of Elphinstone, Bishop of Aberdeen, but when he died, in October 1514, Margaret and her brother, Henry VIII, recommended Gavin Douglas, who seized St Andrews Castle. However, the faction favourable to Albany frustrated the Douglas bid for power: Gavin was driven out of St Andrews, after a siege, by John Hepburn, the prior, who had been elected to the archbishopric by the chapter; and by the beginning of 1515 affairs seem to have been conducted mainly by the Earl of Arran, Lord Home and James Beaton, who were all in favour of Albany's assumption of the governorship.

When Albany at last arrived, in May 1515, he received an enthusiastic welcome, if only because of expectations that a governor of his blood and distinction would supply effective government. Margaret was compelled to give up her children, and Angus and she were easily driven out of the country. More serious trouble was made for Albany by the defection first of Lord Home, then of Arran. The Home family had a dubious record: the first Lord Home and his kin had taken a lead in overthrowing James III; now the third Lord was said to have played a suspicious part at Flodden and was even alleged to have murdered James IV after the battle. Home had warmly supported the invitation to Albany to accept the governorship, but he may have been disappointed that Albany was not prepared to be his tool or he may have been offended at Albany's restoration to his father's earldom of March, in a region where the Homes were now dominant; on the other hand, the Homes' record could in itself have aroused Albany's suspicions. It was to Albany's disadvantage that he could be accused of designs against the king and his brother, who alone stood between the governor and the crown, and the growth of mutual suspicion would be all the easier in that Albany was ignorant of the Scottish tongue. At any rate, Home and Arran signed a bond for the removal of the king from the governor's custody, and they were apparently joined by the Earls of Lennox, Glencairn and Eglinton. Also in concert with them were various Highland chiefs, including Sir Donald MacDonald of Lochalsh, who, in the months after Flodden, had joined with MacLean of Duart and MacLeod of Dunvegan in seizing royal castles. There was thus a serious coalition against Albany, and an armed clash near Glasgow, in which, however, the governor had the advantage. Much of the opposition to the governor was encouraged, if not inspired, by Henry VIII, who claimed for himself the office of protector of Scotland[2] and demanded the dismissal of Albany. Henry was always ready for intrigues with disaffected Scots, especially if he thought that he might thereby gain possession of King James and his brother.

Albany showed considerable skill in maintaining his position. He was unquestionably loyal to the young king, and declined to send James's brother to France as Francis desired. He showed a real solicitude for the punishment of lawbreakers, and almost his first action was to summon parliament to meet for the administration of justice on 12 July 1515, only two months after his arrival. But, in spite of the picturesque account of a temper so irascible that when he was crossed he would throw his bonnet into the fire, he does not seem to have been vindictive by nature and he seems to have been aware of the fact—which Scottish rulers ignored at their peril—that vindictiveness was an unprofitable policy. Margaret was no sooner gone than he offered terms whereby she could return to Scotland if she would be " ane gud Scottis weman,"[3] and later he gave an undertaking that she could enjoy her own property if she would return what belonged to the king. Angus, Lord Drummond and Gavin Douglas were soon pardoned; Arran and Lennox were not long out of favour; and in the Highlands a policy of conciliation was pursued with some success. Of the coalition of lords who had taken up arms, Home alone—and then only after being once pardoned—was executed, along with his brother (October 1516). In ecclesiastical affairs, Albany took a strongly nationalist line which satisfied Scottish sentiment. After Flodden, when James IV died under sentence of excommunication, the pope had claimed the disposal of Scottish prelacies, and had designed the archbishopric of St Andrews for his own nephew, but Albany defied the pope[4] and was thereby

---

[2] *Public Affairs*, p. 40.   [3] *Ibid.*, p. 57.

[4] A reading of the *Letters of James V* leaves no doubt that " defied " is not too strong a term. The complete renunciation of papal authority seems to have been contemplated (cf. *L. and P.*, XIV (1) No. 843; *Letters of James V*, pp. 65-6).

able to use the crown's rights in ecclesiastical patronage as an instrument of appeasement. Thus, at St Andrews, where the archbishopric ultimately went, on Albany's recommendation, to Andrew Forman, James IV's diplomat and a faithful servant of the French connexion, Prior Hepburn was consoled with very substantial revenues and privileges, and two of his kinsmen became bishops. All in all, Albany seems to have gone a long way to make his regime acceptable and to draw together dissentient elements into some kind of concord. His own position as second person of the realm was formally acknowledged in November 1516, when parliament ordered the registration of his father's divorce from his first wife and expressly bastardised her surviving son.[5]

From 1517 until 1521 Albany was in France, but even as an absentee he was able to render Scotland some services. In approaching the pope for confirmation of the indult whereby the Scottish crown had been guaranteed the right to have its recommendations heard in the disposal of prelacies, Albany was supported by Francis I, who had exacted from Rome the Concordat of Bologna (1516), whereby the pope undertook to accept the French king's nominees for promotion; and it was also to Albany's advantage that his wife's younger sister married Lorenzo de Medici, the pope's nephew. On 5 January 1518/9 the pope, at Albany's instance, issued a bull renewing the indult.[6] Complaint was also made to Rome about England's contraventions of the peace and her opposition to Albany's return, and the pope on 19 June 1520 issued a further bull, taking Scotland and its king under his protection and affirming Albany's authority as governor.[7] From Francis himself, Albany obtained a concession freeing Scottish traders from the duties to which foreign goods were subject at Dieppe.[8] He also intervened in the dispute over the location of the Scottish staple port in the Netherlands, and prepared the way for the agreement reached with Middelburg in 1522.[9]

Before Albany left Scotland, in May 1517, a commission of regency had been given to the two archbishops, the Earls of Angus,

[5] *A. P. S.*, II. 283.   [6] Reg. Ho. Bulls, No. 45.
[7] *Letters of James V*, p. 79.
[8] M. W. Stuart, *The Scot who was a Frenchman*, App. C; this and other privileges granted to Scots in France, down to 1646, are printed in *Miscellanea Scotica*, IV.
[9] *Book of the Old Edinburgh Club*, IX. 51.

Huntly, Arran and Argyll, and Albany's agent, De la Bastie. Argyll had special responsibility for the west Highlands and Isles, Huntly for the remainder of the Highlands and the north-east, and De la Bastie for the Merse and Lothian; after the murder of De la Bastie, in a feud with the Homes, in September 1517, Arran appears as lieutenant for the Merse. There were French garrisons in Dunbar, Dumbarton and Inchgarvie, and De la Bastie seems to have been president of the council—and certainly an assiduous attender—until his murder. After that, Arran was undoubtedly at the head of affairs. He was supported by Argyll, Huntly and Archbishop Beaton (whose niece Arran had recently married), but Angus, who seems soon to have wearied of co-operating in the administration, preferred to associate with the Homes and other disorderly elements in the south-east and to exploit, to the embarrassment of Arran's government, the popularity which he and his Douglas kinsmen enjoyed in Edinburgh. In July 1517 there had been " ane inordinat motioun of the people " in that town; there was an " actioun and debait betuix my lord of Arane and the toun " in November 1519; and in March 1520 Arran declared that " he sould nocht cum within the toun quhill my Lord Chancellar [Beaton] maid ane finall concord betuix him and the nychbouris thairof."[10] This was the background to the " Cleanse the Causeway " incident, assigned to April 1520, when the Hamiltons were driven out of Edinburgh by the Douglases. In October it was decided that the provost of Edinburgh should have four halbardiers " becaus the warld is brukle and trublus."[11] The absent governor characteristically suggested that neither a Douglas nor a Hamilton should hold the provostship of Edinburgh and that the daughter of Angus should marry the son of Arran, but stability was not restored until Albany's personal influence was again exerted after his return to Scotland in 1521.

It was Albany's misfortune to be out of tune with Scottish sentiment in each of his periods as active governor: between 1515 and 1517 it had been his business to restrain the Scots from the warlike acts against England to which they were inclined; between 1521 and 1524 it was his business to stimulate them into aggression to which they were not disposed. But the opposition

[10] *Public Affairs*, pp. 97, 121; *Edinburgh Burgh Records*, i. 192, 196.
[11] *Edinburgh Burgh Records*, i. 201.

in the second phase was more serious, for whereas men compelled to hold their hands from vengeance on their traditional enemies might grumble, those asked to run the risks attaching to war on foreign soil might mutiny, and it was something hardly short of mutiny that Albany had to face in 1523. Besides, Albany's French companions were always unpopular, and in the autumn of 1523, when serious friction arose over the presence in Scotland of a large French force, there were complaints that the Frenchmen lodged in Edinburgh were wasting the fuel stored for the winter and were burning furniture.[12] It had also become apparent on Albany's first visit that his household was far more expensive than the country could afford, and he was probably guilty of the mismanagement of crown property,[13] though when Gavin Douglas described Albany's comptroller as " a very pirate and sea reiver "[14] he was under-rating the undoubted financial ability of Robert Barton of Over Barnton. Considering the grounds for criticism, it is creditable to Albany that his personal influence usually sufficed to preserve harmony, and when he went to France in 1522 he was able to entrust the administration once more to Argyll, Huntly, Arran and Beaton, again with a French associate, this time Gonzolles. Only during the campaign against England in 1523 (when it was said that he was disclosing his plans to no Scot) and in the few months which remained to him in Scotland thereafter is there any reason to believe that he was losing the support of some of the influential men who habitually took part in the management of affairs, perhaps especially Arran and Lennox. But to the very end Albany was not without friends, and Scots who contrasted his record with that of the administration during his absence between 1517 and 1521 had good enough reason to implore him to remain in the country.[15]

What the evidence does not reveal is how far the opposition to Albany of a " pro-English party " had a genuinely political foundation. Between 1515 and 1517, English intrigues with disaffected Scots, English readiness to foment disturbances in Scotland, an action like the granting of asylum to the murderers of De la Bastie, had merely followed an old pattern. Then, between 1517 and 1521, while Arran's administration was admittedly upholding the French connexion and the governorship

12 *Public Affairs*, pp. 186-7.   13 Cf. *A. P. S.*, II. 287; Pinkerton, II. 195-6.
14 *L. and P.*, III (2). 1898.   15 *L. and P.*, IV. (I). 382.

of the absent Albany, it would be going too far to see an " English party" in Angus, the Homes, and the "rebels and broken men "[16] who consorted with them. It is true that in the next stage, after Albany's return, Henry constantly strove to undermine Scottish allegiance to the governor: when a truce expired, in February 1521/2, Henry demanded from the Scottish estates the removal of Albany as a condition of its renewal;[17] and almost a year later Henry more intelligently offered a truce for sixteen years, the hand of his daughter Mary for King James and the cession of Berwick, on condition that the Scots would repudiate Albany and the French alliance. But few responsible Scots were even now ready to further Henry's policy, and the conduct of those who were his agents was not such as to command respect. Angus as yet showed so little capacity for statesmanship that he was described by his uncle as " a young witless fool."[18] Queen Margaret, again, was merely capricious. By 1517 she was contemplating a divorce from Angus and had ceased to be a member of his faction; in 1521 she was for a time Albany's ally, possibly because she hoped for his influence at Rome to further her divorce suit, though the worst construction was put on their relations by English observers and by King Henry himself; soon she reverted to the role of English agent, and in 1522-3 she was trying to influence the young king against Albany. The English cause was commended far less by the actions of Angus and Margaret, or even of Henry himself, than by the growth of a critical attitude towards France for her vacillations and lack of generosity towards Scotland;[19] but even in 1522 and 1523, when Albany twice failed to carry the Scots with him in aggressive action against England, it is hard to disentangle the pro-English party from the Douglas faction. Thus, although Angus himself was compelled to withdraw to France, it was Gavin Douglas, his uncle, who went to England in December 1521 to remind Henry that as Albany had exceeded his agreed period of absence the legality of his governorship could be contested; and the spokesman against the French alliance in 1523 was the Master of Forbes, who was married to Angus's niece.

The events after Albany's withdrawal show, more clearly than anything which had happened before, the existence of what can truly be called an English party and a French party. An old

---

[16] *Edinburgh Burgh Records*, I. 205.   [17] *Foedera*, XIII. 762.
[18] *L. and P.*, III (2). 2007.   [19] Cf. pp. 20-2 above.

pattern was followed to the extent that Henry brought Angus across from France and prepared him for renewed intervention in Scotland, but others besides the Douglas faction now took part in changing Scottish policy. Already in 1523, as the date for the limit of Albany's permitted absence drew near, the idea of " erecting " the king and securing the return of Margaret to power had been suggested by England,[20] and little time was lost in putting such a plan into effect after Albany's departure in May 1524. The Earl of Arran, whose position as the native-born Scot nearest to the throne had been strengthened by Albany's withdrawal and by the death of the Duchess of Albany without surviving children, came to terms with Margaret and, with the support of other nobles, invested the king in person with the symbols of sovereignty (26 July). On 1 August James was present at the council, when many of the officers of state resigned their offices into his hands (most of them to be almost at once reinstated). This " erection " of the king brought Albany's governorship to an end. The foreign policy of the new administration was made clear in a letter signed by James on 5 August, to his " derrest and richt inteirlye weilbelufit uncle, the king of Inglande," intimating that he had put an end to the authority of Albany, " under quhais governans oure realme and lieges hes bene richt evill demanyt ";[21] and early in September arrangements were made for an embassy to England to conclude a treaty. Henry paid for two hundred men-at-arms as a bodyguard for James, and sent north two English agents to be residents at the Scottish court. They believed James to be completely captivated by their advice to eschew French influences and trust " his good uncle of England," but the reader of their reports may suspect that James was a shade too ostentatious in giving " wholly his young heart " to Henry.[22]

The *coup d'état* had still to be authorised by the estates, and, although Albany had left on the understanding that if he did not return by 1 September his governorship would be at an end, they found it impossible to reach a unanimous decision. Archbishop Beaton (now of St Andrews) urged loyalty to Albany and France, and he had the support of five bishops, as well, apparently, as Argyll, Lennox and Moray. The party of Arran, who argued

20 *L. and P.*, III (2). 3339.

21 *S. P. Henry VIII*, IV. 95-6; facsimile in *National Manuscripts from William the Conqueror to Queen Anne*, II, No. 14.

22 *S. P. Henry VIII*, IV. 115, 139, 209, 243, 308.

for the material advantages of a treaty with England, included
two bishops, Lord Home and the Earl of Cassillis, but it may
well have been the less numerous, and it was reported that it
was by a show of force that Arran gained compliance with the
decision that Albany had lost office (16 November).[23] Beaton,
who was regarded by the English as the principal obstacle to
their cause, was, along with the Bishop of Aberdeen, imprisoned
for a time, and was in danger of being kidnapped and removed
to England, but his captivity did not last, and the great seal was
restored to him early in the following spring. In any event, the
French cause was not lost, for David Beaton, the archbishop's
nephew, came from France in December 1524 with reassuring
messages from Francis; Albany was still heir presumptive; Dunbar continued to be held for him; and anti-English feeling was
stimulated by sympathy for the French after their heavy defeat
by the emperor at Pavia in the spring of 1525.[24]

Yet once again it was not only because of political differences
that the realm was so "marvelously divided"[25] that in February
1524/5 Arran and Margaret were holding the castle of Edinburgh
while Angus and Lennox held the town.[26] The explanation is to
be found in the activities and position of Angus. In February the
estates named him as one of the queen's counsellors, on 6 March
he reappeared on the council and began to attend with unwonted
assiduity, and from this point he, with Lennox and Argyll,
formed the core of the administration. But there was no possibility of holding Margaret in any combination which contained
her husband and, as Angus was the premier English agent, who
would serve England "better than five earls of Arran,"[27] Margaret
was thrown once more on to the side of France and Albany,
while Arran, neglected by England, became her ally. On 3
August the estates declared that Margaret would lose her authority within twenty days unless she would resume co-operation
with the lords,[28] and an appeal to arms which Arran and she made
in the following January proved fruitless.[29] She married Henry
Stewart, afterwards Lord Methven, in March 1526.

It had been arranged in July 1525 that the king should
remain in the custody of each of the leading nobles in turn,

23 *A. P. S.*, II. 286.   24 *S. P. Henry VIII*, IV. 406.   25 *Ibid.* pp. 288-9.
26 *Edinburgh Burgh Records*, I. 221; *L. and P.*, IV (1). 1088, 1113.
27 *S. P. Henry VIII*, IV. 198.   28 *A. P. S.*, II. 298.   29 *L. and P.*, IV (1). 1908.

but, when it fell to Angus to give up the king in November, he declined to do so. On 14 June 1526 there was a kind of fresh " erection," when authority was declared to be in the king's hands—a device to deprive anyone save Angus of any power. In July Beaton was deprived of the great seal, and it was retained by Angus, who ultimately himself became chancellor (August 1527). Not only did Angus appoint his uncle, Archibald Douglas, as treasurer, and have him made once more provost of Edinburgh, but he appointed his brother, George, as master of the household, James Douglas of Drumlanrig as master of the wine-cellar and James Douglas of Parkhead as master of the larder, so that, in a household dominated by Douglases, the king was secluded from lords who might have served him, and, constantly under observation, was really a prisoner.

As Angus progressively appropriated offices to his own kin he alienated the nobles who had helped him to power: Lennox, Argyll, Cassillis and Glencairn disappeared from the council in August 1526, and Arran, with whom Angus had come to terms in the summer of 1526, was hardly ever present after October of that year. There was thus ample foundation for a coalition against Angus. The first attempt to liberate the king had been made on or about 25 July, by Scott of Buccleuch, near Melrose, but it may reflect no more than Scott's antagonism to the Kerrs and Homes who were with Angus. Lennox remained neutral in that engagement, but the king had entered into a compact with him on 26 June,[30] and presently he took the lead against Angus, whom he accused of holding the king in captivity. He had the support of Queen Margaret, Argyll, Moray, Glencairn, Cassillis, Home, Ruthven and the two archbishops, as well as lesser men like Scott of Buccleuch and Cranston of Smailholm,[31] but he was killed in an attempt to rescue James near Linlithgow on 4 September. By 1528 not a single earl was in regular attendance at the council, but, however powerful might be the coalition against Angus, it was impossible to overthrow him as long as the king was in his hands, and George Douglas, Angus's brother, declared that should the king's body be torn apart in a rescue attempt, the Douglases would still keep one part of it.

However, in 1528 the king reached a secret agreement with his mother which put Stirling Castle at his disposal, and, escaping

[30] Fraser, *Lennox*, I. 357.   [31] *E.g.*, *R. S. S.*, IV. 1114, 1249, 1329, 2274.

from Edinburgh between 27 and 30 May, he made his way there. On 6 July he entered Edinburgh, at the head of a party including Bothwell, Home, Arran, Moray, Argyll, Eglinton, Rothes, Montrose, Marischal and Maxwell, some of them men not habitually involved in public affairs but evidently prepared to rally to the sovereign in this crisis. Angus had withdrawn from Edinburgh on 2 July, on 13 July he was summoned for treason and when parliament met in September he was put to the horn. But the royal forces did not succeed in taking his stronghold of Tantallon in a twenty days' siege, and on 5 December it was agreed that if the Douglases yielded up their castles they might retire to England; Scottish commissioners were to represent to the English government that the latter should take responsibility for any evil the Douglases might do in Scotland in the future. The king, now in his seventeenth year, had emerged from tutelage.

The prominence, during this minority, of the manoeuvres of a handful of magnates like Home, Angus, Arran and Lennox obscures the importance of other men whose record was different. In particular, the third Earl of Argyll, whose tenure of the title exactly spans the period, and the third Earl of Huntly (1501-24) seem on the whole to have supported the administration whatever faction was in power, for they were consistent attenders at the council, and between them they were able to maintain stability in the whole of the west and north, especially after the troublesome Donald of Lochalsh died without male heirs in 1519—though no doubt they were serving their own interests rather than the crown's. While criminal justice was unquestionably weak, and English observers described Scotland as a land where there was "no justice" but "continual murders, theft and robbery,"[32] it is noticeable that most of the recorded disturbances were in the country south of Forth, especially the south-east. Besides such lay magnates as Argyll and Huntly, there were influential clerics. It is not true that the casualties among the nobility at Flodden delivered the country to the rule of ecclesiastics, for, while much political experience had gone with those who fell at Flodden, the survivors and the heirs of the fallen were most of them men of mature years and some of them veterans, and it would be hard to demonstrate that churchmen were any more powerful now than they had been in some earlier periods. At

[32] S. P. Henry VIII, IV. 289.

the same time, the importance of James Beaton, Archbishop of Glasgow until 1523 and then of St Andrews, chancellor from 1513 until 1526 and without exception the most assiduous attender at the council until Angus established his power in 1526, cannot be ignored. It is noticeable, too, that laymen of humble origin— Robert Barton and Adam Otterburn—attained office as comptroller and lord advocate and that Sir Thomas Erskine of Haltoun, secretary under Angus, was the first layman to hold that office for a century. There was also remarkable continuity in the tenure of office, not least in the continuance or reappointment, after Angus's fall, of men who had been in office under him, notably Erskine, the secretary, Sir James Colville, the comptroller, and Otterburn, the advocate.[33]

Not only did such holders of offices keep their places, but the official, non-noble element on the council was stable, and it was actually in the 1520s that the court of session reached an important stage in its evolution. The development of a body of lords of session, differentiated from the privy council, had gone a long way under James IV, but was retarded after 1513, and there is evidence that in 1517 central civil justice was in a state of confusion and congestion for which the council could not provide an effective remedy. In the spring of 1526, however, eight persons, four spiritual and four temporal, whose only function was " to sit continually upoun the sessions," were appointed to join with the lords of the privy council and the " ministers of court " to deal with civil causes. Among the persons named were Alexander Myln, Abbot of Cambuskenneth and a future lord president of the court of session, three ecclesiastical " officials " who were professional lawyers, Scott of Balwearie, one of the lairds who were now beginning to make the law a profession, and two other lairds who held heritable sheriffdoms. In 1528 the men not specifically appointed for the sessions were excluded therefrom. Most significantly, out of the fifteen judges who were to be named as members of the college of justice in 1532, no less than eleven had already been acting as judges on " the session " in 1527. It seems plain that the administration of Angus, deserted by the magnates, had given an unusual opportunity to lesser men.

[33] Both Barton and Otterburn have found biographers—the first Scots laymen of this type to do so: W. Stanford Reid, *Skipper from Leith* (1962) and J. A. Inglis, *Sir Adam Otterburn of Redhall* (1935). Barton was comptroller 1516-25 and 1529-30, Colville was comptroller 1525-9 and 1530-8; Otterburn was lord advocate 1524-38.

4

THE POLICY OF JAMES V

The financial position of the Scottish crown can seldom have been weaker than it was when James V began his personal rule. The resources of the royal household had had no chance to recover from the strain imposed by the costly visits of Albany, for neither Queen Margaret nor Angus felt any restraint in their intromissions: between 1525 and 1528 there were repeated complaints that the household was more expensive than ever and that, even if its needs had priority, funds were still inadequate.[1] As well as extravagance, there was improvidence, for customs were frequently remitted out of favour, casualties which fell to the crown were given away instead of being disposed of for a suitable composition, and there was no strict control over gifts of crown property. In the southern parts of the country, revenue from crown lands must have fallen off because of the intermittent disorder, while in the north and west Huntly and Argyll collected the rents but found excuses for not remitting them to the exchequer: for instance, Argyll's tale in 1522, that the lands of Kintyre had yielded nothing since 1511 because they had been wasted since Flodden,[2] though unconvincing, was sufficient to excuse him from paying anything. The total ordinary revenue, which had reached nearly £30,000 under James IV, hardly exceeded £13,000 in 1525-6.[3] The comptroller, who had the management of the income from property, was carrying a

1 *Public Affairs*, pp. 221, 227, 234-5, 246, 260, 262.   2 *Exchequer Rolls*, XIV. 419.
3 Athol L. Murray, "The Exchequer and Crown Revenues in Scotland, 1437-1542" (Edinburgh Ph.D. Thesis), Appendix K. Much information about the state of the finances is usefully brought together in W. Stanford Reid, *Skipper from Leith*, pp. 127-8, 137, 142, 160, 175, 201, 204, 209, 233, 241.

heavy deficit in the last years of the minority and was able to operate at all only with the help of subventions from the treasurer (who managed casualty) and by the expenditure of " his awin geir," and from time to time lamented that he could " sustene na forrar."[4] Taxation for the normal needs of government was still out of the question, but in the course of the negotiations about the location of the Scottish staple in the Netherlands the government was able to collect contributions from the Scottish merchants as well as from the towns which competed for the privilege of serving as the channel for Scottish trade. Recourse was also had to the benevolence of private individuals: Huntly lent 2,000 merks in March 1530, though the example of Archbishop Beaton, who had advanced £860 in 1525 and was not repaid so late as 1538, was not encouraging.[5] The time was one when the value of money had begun to fall catastrophically: during the century prices in England rose by over 500 per cent, and the Scots pound was all the time declining even in relation to sterling.

The history of James V's reign consists very largely of the repercussions caused by the exploitation of three new and extraordinary sources of revenue—the wealth of the church, the dowry which might be expected with the king's marriage, and the forfeitures and compositions which might result from proceedings in relation to the nobles. While the third source was a domestic concern, except in so far as treasonable dealings with England might be the reason or pretext for forfeitures, the first required negotiations with the pope and involved a relationship with an ecclesiastical reformation which had become an international movement, and the second was a matter of foreign policy, because while James not infrequently (even so late as 1536)[6] contemplated marriage with one of his mistresses, only a foreign princess would bring the necessary dowry.

James had been educated by Gavin Dunbar,[7] who had been promoted to the archbishopric of Glasgow at Albany's instance and who was James's chancellor from 1528 for the remainder of the reign. The king was, besides, the relentless enemy of his

---

4 *Public Affairs*, pp. 281-2, 304, 306, 344; *A. P. S.*, II. 296.

5 *R. S. S.*, II. 601: *Public Affairs*, pp. 221, 464.

6 *L. and P.*, x. 1229; *Letters of James V*, pp. 320, 324.

7 That he *was* educated, and that accounts of his illiteracy are exaggerated, is the conclusion of D. E. Easson in *Gavin Dunbar*, pp. 29-32.

former gaolers, the Angus Douglases, who represented English influence, and he had, on the other hand, been much attached to Lennox, a victim of Angus who had close ties with France. The king's personal preference was almost certainly for a French marriage, and although his irritation at the reluctance of France to concede him a bride occasionally led him to seek " honourable grounds " for departing from his obligations to France, if only because Scotland could not wait indefinitely for an heir,[8] his frequent negotiations with the emperor and with England[9] were mainly designed to stimulate France into the fulfilment of the Treaty of Rouen. Moreover, the Duke of Albany, still heir presumptive, acted as a Scottish agent on the continent until his death in 1536, and his attitude was coloured by Henry VIII's invincible dislike of him and by his relationship to Pope Clement VII, as well as by his many associations with France.

Albany's ideal was a Franco-Scottish-papal combination against England and the emperor, and, while this was impracticable as long as there was an alliance between England and France and an alliance between the pope and the emperor, he was determined at least to counter the imperial match for James which was under consideration in 1529. He therefore revived a proposal which he had first made in 1527, for the marriage of James to his niece, Catharine de Medici, the kinswoman and ward of Clement VII. In April 1530 James sent Erskine, the secretary, with authority to apply to the pope for Catharine. King Francis was at first prepared to support this application, but Henry VIII, who foresaw the possibility of Albany's return to Scotland as a papal agent in the train of a Medici queen, prevailed on Francis to request the hand of Catharine for a French prince—a proposal which appealed to the pope, who was all along opposed to the departure of Catharine for remote Scotland. When Erskine arrived at Rome in February 1531 and discovered the double-dealing of Francis, he was persuaded to revert to the project of an imperial match, which would satisfy both pope and emperor. Albany, who had conveyed French opposition to the Medici marriage, could hardly refuse to support this alternative scheme and was thus, for once, in sympathy with a Scottish understanding with the emperor as well as the pope.

The entire pattern of the next stage of the negotiations has

[8] *Letters of James V*, p. 201.   [9] Cf. pp. 23-5 above.

never been determined. As the emperor was now making King James something of a *protégé*, imperial influence on the pope was in Scotland's favour, and the pope himself, aware that a crisis was approaching in England, thought it desirable to cultivate James. It may also be conjectured that Scottish candour in admitting that James's interest was less in Catharine than in her dowry suggested a means to console James for the refusal of his bride, and that with money which did not come out of the pope's own pocket. At any rate, on 9 July 1531 Clement wrote to the Scottish prelates asking their opinion on a proposal for a tax of £10,000 per annum for the defence of the realm, and only a week later he imposed on the Scottish church a levy of one tenth for three years, payable by all benefices worth more than £20. To look for a subvention from the church required little originality, but only a sense of crisis could have stimulated the pope to action on this scale. The levy of the three tenths was with a view to strengthening and protecting the Scottish state, and a fresh pretext had to be advanced to justify the permanent tax of £10,000 a year. That pretext was the establishment of a college of justice.

At a time when laymen generally were inclined to challenge ecclesiastical pretensions and to contemn " the process of cursing,"[10] churchmen were finding it difficult to collect their revenues and the church courts were becoming ineffective. There would therefore be no injustice should the church be made to contribute to the endowment of a strong civil court, especially as many of the judges on " the session " were ecclesiastical lawyers. It was that " wise councellar and chancellar,"[11] Archbishop Gavin Dunbar of Glasgow, who had presided over the session in 1527 and had been, by all accounts, the architect of the development of the court in succeeding years; Albany, at Rome, was experienced in laying Scottish requests before the pope; and Erskine, the secretary, who had studied at Pavia and knew of that city's college of justice, may have reflected that Italian ears would be impressed by a plan to set up a " college of justice " in Scotland.

On 13 September 1531 the pope issued a bull, relating representations by Albany that King James desired to establish a college of justice for civil causes, with half of its members churchmen, and ordaining that the Scottish prelates should contribute annually 10,000 ducats, gold of the *camera* (about £10,000

Scots) for its endowment. A year later the pope conceded that no Scottish case falling under ecclesiastical jurisdiction was to be called to Rome in the first instance but was to be judged by ecclesiastics appointed by the king, provided that he remained obedient to Rome. In May 1532 the Scottish parliament played its part by passing two closely related statutes, which satisfied the nuncio whom the pope had sent to see that James earned his money. The first remarked—with truth—that, while earlier popes had been generous, " Pape Clement, now pape of Rome, has bene mair gracius and benevolent till his grace than to all his forbearis," and recorded the king's resolution to defend " the auctorite, liberte and fredome of the sete of Rome and halikirk." The second act related the king's intention to "institute ane college of cunning and wise men . . . for the doing and administracioun of justice in all civile actionis," and nominated the abbot of Cambuskenneth as president, with seven clerics and seven laymen as judges.[12]

There was much dissatisfaction among the prelates, possibly led by Archbishop Beaton of St Andrews, who could not look favourably on a development which owed so much to his rival of Glasgow. In September 1532 it was reported that all the Scottish prelates were hostile to the king except Glasgow, Dunkeld and Aberdeen, and it was those three who, in 1533, were named as commissioners for the trial of Beaton when he was accused of treasonable dealings with England.[13] But even Dunbar did not carry his enthusiasm so far as to keep up to date with his payments of taxation, and in 1541 was 1,000 merks in arrear. There was an understandable reluctance to face a burden of £10,000 per annum in perpetuity, while the king, on his side, can never have had any intention of spending anything like that sum on the salaries of fifteen judges. An agreement was therefore reached whereby £72,000 was to be paid in four years as a composition and certain benefices in the patronage of the prelates were to be assigned for judicial salaries, apparently on the understanding that the crown would also make a contribution. In March 1534/5, Paul III, in the course of concessions to the Scottish crown which included a recognition of the right of

12 *A.P.S.*, II. 335-6.
13 Beaton was subject to James V's bitter animosity (Teulet, *Relations politiques*, I. 81 ff.).

nomination to vacant prelacies and the extension of the period for nomination from eight months to a year, ratified the erection of the " college " and imposed a tax of £1,400 from the assigned benefices, along with not more than £200 from benefices in the crown's patronage. The prelates were in no hurry to pay their £72,000 (to which the pope did not refer), and the benefices assigned to the judges were to become available only as they fell vacant. In 1541 parliament ratified the " erection of the said college," and its endowment, in general terms.[14]

All that had happened was the inadequate endowment of the " session " of semi-professional and specialist judges which had already been taking shape: of the fifteen judges named in 1532, all but one had been on the session in 1531. Nothing at this stage did much to accelerate or complete the separation of " session " from " council ": only after 1540 did separate registers appear for the proceedings of the privy council on one hand and the acts and decreets of the court of session on the other; and not until 1554 did a separate register of deeds emerge for the court of session.

It remained to be seen whether the course of Scottish diplomacy, which had thus been directly profitable in one way, would also produce a well-endowed bride for the king. The negotiations which went on from 1532 to 1536 were tortuous, and in so far as they were inconclusive they hardly affected the course of Scottish history.[15] What matters is that James in the end won his French bride. In the summer of 1533, King Francis, genuinely reluctant to part with his delicate daughter Madeleine and also unwilling to offend his English ally, turned to the offer of some more remote kinswoman. At the end of 1534 he made a definite offer of Mary, daughter of the Duke of Vendôme, with a dowry of 100,000 crowns;[16] James, after seeing a portrait, stipulated also for a pension of 20,000 livres, the order of St Michael, the surrender of Dunbar, and the extension to other ports of the privileges already enjoyed by the Scots at Dieppe. In July 1535 a Scottish commission was appointed to treat for this marriage and Francis confirmed the marriage settlement on 29 March 1536; a month

14 *A. P. S.*, ii. 371.

15 The account in Bapst, *Les mariages de Jacques V*, though it can be elaborated, is still substantially accurate.

16 A crown was equated with 2.25 livres or francs and a franc was equated with 9s. Scots (*Treasurer's Accounts*, vi. 412, 467-8; cf. *Letters of James V*, p. 325).

later he sent James the collar of St Michael. James sailed from Leith near the end of July 1536 and proceeded north-about, but ran into a storm in the North Channel which made the ship turn back. He sailed again, from Kirkcaldy by the east coast, on 1 September, and landed at Dieppe on 10 September. The marriage which took place in France was not, however, to Marie de Vendôme, whom James (after inspection) rejected in favour of the oft-refused Madeleine. The contract was signed on 26 November, providing for a dowry of 100,000 livres on the marriage day and annualrents on a sum of 125,000 livres. The marriage took place on 1 January 1536/7.

Death next intervened, for Madeleine, who returned with James on 19 May 1537, died on 7 July. There seems to have been no question but that another French queen should take her place. Negotiations were entrusted to David Beaton, nephew and coadjutor to the Archbishop of St Andrews and ultimately his successor. Beaton's experience as an envoy to France had begun many years before, and he seems never to have been in any doubt as to where Scotland's interest, or duty, lay. He was to become Bishop of Mirepoix, in France, in 1537, and a cardinal in December 1538—rewards for his services to France and the papacy. Beaton now agreed to the nomination by Francis of Mary, daughter of Claude of Guise-Lorraine, Duc d'Aumale. James had made her acquaintance when he was in France, and she had become a widow through the death of her first husband, the Duc de Longueville, in June 1537, just a month before the death of Madeleine. After some interruption caused by a proposal that Henry of England, recently also a widower through the death of Jane Seymour, should marry Mary, the marriage contract between her and James was prepared in January 1537/8. Her dowry was 150,000 livres. The marriage took place by proxy on 18 May, she landed at Crail probably on 10 June and was married to James at St Andrews a few days later.

The foreign policy to which Scotland was committed by James V's French marriages was to lead directly to the disaster with which his reign closed. But it was not the only cause of that disaster, for the king's domestic policy also played its part.

During a minority when trouble was made largely by Homes and Douglases, who by property and kinship had their following in the south-east and south, there had been little rule in the

Borders. Angus had sided with the lairds of the middle and east marches against the more turbulent men of the western dales, and had led ineffective expeditions against the Armstrongs of Liddesdale, but his fall may actually have increased the instability.[17] In 1530 there came forceful royal action, first against the Armstrongs. The accounts of the execution of Johnnie Armstrong, in the spring of 1530, agree that, if there was not actual treachery, the king at least took advantage of Armstrong's readiness to put himself in the royal power. Armstrong was accused of treasonable dealings with England, and no doubt his family, like other Borderers, could fairly be said to have " agreit with Ingland and keipis thar merkat in Ingland,"[18] but the Armstrongs were credited with doing as much damage in England as in Scotland. James, however, disdained the policy of *divide et impera* which Angus's proceedings might have suggested, and lairds from all parts of the Borders were in ward at one time or another— Lord Maxwell, although he had been at enmity with Armstrong; Bothwell and Home, although they had been lieutenants of the Border in 1529; Buccleuch, Fernihurst, Polwarth, Johnstone and others.[19] Indications of a conciliatory policy are very infrequent,[20] and the effect of the strong royal action seems to have been that after 1531, although members of the Armstrong family were in trouble again in 1535 and 1536, overt disaffection was extinguished for the rest of the reign.

In the west Highlands and Islands, the death at the end of 1529 of the third Earl of Argyll, who had been all-powerful as lieutenant, was an opportunity to reconsider crown policy, but also offered prospects of revenge to all who had suffered from Campbell aggrandisement. In 1529 Alexander MacDonald of Islay and the MacLeans ravaged Campbell lands, and the Campbells retaliated by attacking Mull, Morvern and Tiree. In 1530/1 there are signs of vacillation or of conflicting counsels in the government: on one hand, MacLean of Duart (who, as he had tried to drown his Campbell wife, was the especial enemy of

17 The famous " cursing " of Border reivers belongs to 1525 (*St. Andrews Formulare* [Stair Soc.], I. 264-71); the reivers' boast of destroying fifty-two Scottish parish churches belongs to 1529 (*L. and P.*, IV (3). 5289).

18 *Public Affairs*, p. 124.

19 It is significant of James's high-handed attitude that Hay of Yester was deprived of his heritable sheriffship of Peebles in 1530, to be restored in 1543.

20 *Public Affairs*, p. 345; *R. S. S.*, I. 4072, II. 745, 753.

Argyll) was given protection against Argyll and had a safe-
conduct to come to the council " for making of gud wayis anent
the reule of the cuntre ";[21] on the other hand, the new Earl of
Argyll, along with the Earl of Moray, was entrusted with action
against troublesome western Highlanders and Islesmen.   Argyll
was certainly going to resent the diminution of his family's power,
for in a memorial presented to the council in June 1531 he undertook to compel the inhabitants of the southern Isles to pay their dues
to the comptroller or drive them from the country, and continued:

> How the saidis ilis sal be reulit and governit in tyme to cum, I desyr
> that the kingis grace wald geif command to his counsale that I
> may consort with thame in the addressing tharof, becaus I and
> my frenndis hes als gret experience in the danting of the ilis . . . as
> ony uthiris of the realme, and specialie for the distructioun of
> thaim inobedient to the kingis grace and in the rewarding of
> thame that makis gud service to his hienes.

He therefore asked for a lieutenancy over the south Isles ; and
Moray made a somewhat similar offer in respect of the north
Isles.[22]   But Argyll was in fact eliminated from his position, he was
out of favour for several years and he was brought to renounce
some lands in the Isles which he did not recover until after James's
death.[23] His rival, Alexander of Islay, who represented that Argyll
had deliberately fomented mischief to give him an opportunity to
destroy " the inobedient," was commissioned to secure the
adherence of lesser chiefs and the payment of rents and duties
from the south Isles and Kintyre, and Alexander's son was taken
to be educated at Edinburgh under the king's eye. James paid
a number of visits to the west, and the whole area seems to have
remained on the whole peaceful until 1539, when Donald Gorm
of Sleat rose in rebellion but was fatally wounded in besieging
Eilean Donan Castle.   In 1540 came the king's most ambitious
venture—a cruise, with Beaton, Huntly and Arran and twelve
ships well provided with artillery, to Orkney and then down the
west coast, where he succeeded in apprehending several chiefs,
who submitted to kidnapping as readily now as they had done
under James I and were to do again under James VI.[24] The Earl
of Huntly seems to have retained his dominating position in the

---

21 *R. S. S.*, II. 1030, 1083.
22 *Public Affairs*, pp. 356-8.   23 *L. and P.*, XVIII (1). 88.
24 Nicholas d'Arville's account of King James's " Navigation " is printed in
Miscellanea Scotica, III.

north, but in the west the delegating of authority to persons who were not local magnates seems to have continued, for in the last years of the reign Archibald Stewart and the Master of Glencairn were in charge of Islay and Kintyre.[25]

Apart from policy in the Borders and the Highlands, there are indications of a solicitude for order and of a determination to have the laws obeyed. James is said to have held justice ayres regularly and to have been often present at them in person, and he was certainly not remiss in criminal justice.[26]   Many of the sentences passed by the courts continued, however, to be nullified by remissions and respites, although in 1534 it was agreed that for five years no respites or remissions for slaughter or mutilation should be granted, and in 1536 the justice clerk was instructed to ignore any letters which had been granted by the king " in hurt of justice."   Other gaps in the defence against crime arose from the privileges of the clergy and the right of " sanctuary." Among the evidence that the criminous and even homicidal clerk was not an unfamiliar figure is the trial in 1530 of the treasurer of Caithness, a parson, a vicar, and half a dozen chaplains for the slaughter of the laird of Duffus. In 1535, accordingly, the king asked the pope not to grant dispensations to clergy suspected of homicide, and he suggested to parliament that there should be some restriction on the abuse of sanctuary " girths " by criminals.

To judge where firmness ended and severity began was not easy, but there is some reason to believe that James was not only severe, but vindictive.   First among the unpardonable were Angus and his kin.   The crime of communicating with them was often an exception when a remission or a respite was granted, and among prosecutions for this offence were those of Colville of East Wemyss, the comptroller, and Adam Otterburn, the lord advocate.   Lady Glamis, the sister of Angus, was under the king's suspicion as early as 1531, in 1532 she was accused of poisoning her husband, and she was burned in 1537 on a charge of conspiring against the king.   Five days after her execution, the Master of Forbes, whose wife was a niece of Angus, was put to death on a charge of plotting to shoot the king.   The suspicion attaching to the whole Douglas name may explain why James Douglas of Parkhead was summoned for treason in September 1540.

25 *R. S. S.*, ii. 4628, 4631.
26 This is borne out by both *Treasurer's Accounts* and *R. S. S.*

Unrelenting severity towards possible trouble-makers could explain the king's proceedings against the Earl of Bothwell, who, after two periods in ward, was banished in 1537 and compelled to resign Liddesdale, and against Scott of Branxholm, who was condemned for treason and imprisoned during the king's lifetime. The same explanation could hold good of the proceedings against the " wicked master " of Crawford, son and heir of the eighth earl, who, on the ground of crimes against his father, was ultimately compelled to renounce the succession to the earldom. But those proceedings cannot be dissociated from the king's dealings with the " wicked master's " father, the earl, who was mulcted in such large sums for nonentry that he had to mortgage many of his lands.[27] So regarded, the attitude of the king to the Crawfords falls into line with his pursuit of the Earl of Morton, who had no male heir and was relentlessly harried until in 1540, under fear of death, he agreed to resign his lands in favour of Douglas of Lochleven, who made them over to the king. In such a case there would seem to have been no motive save the " covitousse [covetousness] " to which, it was reported in 1539, the king " inclynethe daylye more and more."[28]

Equally, regard for financial efficiency could easily pass into cupidity. To forbid the granting of letters of legitimation *gratis* was a reasonable measure to prevent the loss to the crown of the estates of bastards who died intestate and without heirs of the body. But was it so reasonable that in 1541 the king demanded from the Earl of Bothwell, as sheriff of Berwick and Haddington, the castlewards of those sheriffdoms for the past twenty-eight years?[29] And proceedings for alleged crimes could be undertaken merely with a view to the sale of remissions: Colville of East Wemyss paid £1,000 for one. The king's acquisitiveness may also explain his act of revocation, made at Rouen in 1537 and confirmed by parliament in 1540.[30] A revocation was nothing new, but this one was used as an instrument to exact large sums by way of compositions: Lord Gray was owing 10,000 merks and did not pay the balance of 7,000 until 1543; Colquhoun of Luss owed £1,000, and paid the final instalment in 1546.[31]

---

[27] S. P. Henry VIII, iv. 598.   [28] Ibid., v. 160.
[29] Public Affairs, pp. 414-5, 502-3.
[30] A. P. S., ii. 357-8.   [31] R. S. S., iii. 398, 1884.

James's dealings with the church fall into the general pattern, for they reflect his desire for financial advantage and his severity in executing the law. Throughout the 1530s there was intermittent prosecution of heretics, and a few executions—David Stratoun of Lauriston and Norman Gourlay in 1534, two friars, a canon regular, a secular priest and a layman in 1539;[32] other critics of the ecclesiastical establishment found safety—and sometimes distinguished careers—in England or on the continent. In 1541 there was an act of parliament generally against heresy and iconoclasm. James may, like his father, have combined a private life which was scandalous by any standards with genuine respect for those whose lives were more austere, and he certainly commended the Observant Friars, who were the strictest churchmen of the time. Yet no respect for character or zeal prevented his making appointments to bishoprics and abbeys which were, with hardly an exception, disreputable. He seems, too, to have practised the traditional devotion to shrines and relics which some now called superstition, for we find in the *Treasurer's Accounts* such an item as a payment for " ane relique to ane bane of Sanct Mahago."[33] But, however inconsistently, he also appreciated the attacks on relics—as well as those on clerical immorality and other abuses—in Sir David Lindsay's *Three Estates*. One motive behind James's prosecutions of heretics was, of course, to impress on the pope that he was earning the financial concessions which in themselves did much to weaken the ecclesiastical system. His policy was in the main marked by a cynical disregard for the wellbeing of the church.

No Scottish king could have pursued such courses without alienating many of his subjects. As early as December 1531 the Earl of Bothwell, in an interview with the Earl of Northumberland, complained that he had been deprived of his Teviotdale lands and had been imprisoned for half a year, and he enlarged on the treatment of other nobles: in view, he said, of the banishment of Angus, the " wrongful disinheriting " of Crawford, the " sore imprisonment " of Argyll, the " little estimation " of Moray and Maxwell, and the " simple regarding of Sir James Hamilton for his good and painful service," he had no doubt

---

[32] The brief account in Knox, I. 24-6, can be supplemented by Pitcairn and by many references in *R. S. S.*, II.

[33] *Treasurer's Accounts*, VII. 395.

that, with his own power and the support of Angus, he could crown Henry of England in Edinburgh " within brief time."[34] Bothwell, if not merely lying, was at least an over-optimistic *émigré*, and the English on their side were over-credulous, yet his statement did anticipate a situation which actually developed as the years went on.

Again, the remark of an English ambassador in 1536 that " the whole council " consisted of " none else but the papistical clergy,"[35] and another, in 1540, that the king depended on the clergy,[36] appear to be supported by the extant evidence, for the sederunts of the council show a preponderance of lords of session, with churchmen in a majority.[37] After about 1532 the earls seem almost to disappear from the council, and at the parliament of 1541 only one earl is named among the *Domini electi ad articulos et sessionis* and only three among the *Domini electi ad articulos et concilii.* It is true, too, that James, in whose reign non-hereditary " lords of council and session " were established, did not create any hereditary lords of parliament. It must, however, be said that the earls attended parliament regularly enough, that some of them were on the regency appointed when the king went to France and that others accompanied him on his voyage. As for the clergy, who were said in 1536 never to have been so ill-content,[38] they might well fear a king who could threaten to send six of the proudest of them to his uncle of England,[39] but they had little cause to love him. The probability is that the permanent nucleus of " lords of council and session " merely found that conciliar as well as judicial business was left very largely to them. Yet it remains a significant fact that James did not love the nobility and relied on lesser men. Thus, in 1532 it was reported that state secrets were known only to the Archbishop of Glasgow, the Bishop of Aberdeen, Henry Kemp and Davie Wood[40]—that is, Henry Kemp of Thomastoun, who seems never to have held any office but who received many favours from the king, and David Wood of Craig, who became comptroller in 1538 and was likewise the recipient of many gifts. The nobles may well have felt that they

[34] *S. P. Henry VIII*, IV. 597-8.   [35] *Ibid.*, V. 36.   [36] Sadler, *State Papers*, I. 47.
[37] The Acta Dominorum Concilii et Sessionis are, however, almost entirely concerned with judicial business, and the question remains whether a record of conciliar business has been lost.
[38] *L. and P.*, X. 536; *S. P. Henry VIII*, IV. 667.
[39] *L. and P.*, XV. 114.   [40] *Ibid.*, V. 1246.

had lost influence and office which they considered theirs by right, and looked jealously on the " minions " who surrounded the king. There is, all in all, a great deal to substantiate the report of 1537 about the situation under James: " so sore a dred king and so ill beloved of his subjectes was never in that londe: every man that hath any substance fearyng to have a quarrell made to hym therfore."[41]

The counterpart of James's neglect of the nobles could be his activities as " the poor man's king." He certainly mixed freely with subjects of low degree, but his personal relations with his people, and his not infrequent acts of kindness and consideration, can in the main be paralleled in the reign of his father. It is true, too, that the parliaments of 1535 and 1541 confirmed many old acts and passed new ones for the benefit of the whole community; but such blocks of well-intentioned legislation can likewise be paralleled more than once in the fifteenth century. Yet James's very severity to malefactors may have made him loved by the law-abiding; he passed acts for the improvement of justice in sheriff and other courts and for order among notaries; he revived the appointment of an advocate for the poor; he issued letters for the protection of tenants against eviction; and his proposals for the abolition of the detested mortuary dues, levied by the church, and for the reform of the teind system, were in the interests of the smaller men. One near-contemporary writer remarked that James earned goodwill because his people " lived quietly and in rest, out of all oppressioun and molestacioun of the nobility and riche persones."[42]

James's greatest success, though it was not one to endear him to his people, was his own enrichment. Fines and forfeitures were profitable, and to that extent there was an ulterior motive behind the administration of criminal justice. The revenues of the crown lands, thanks to forfeitures and the increase of rents and duties, rose from £5,300 in 1535/6 to £9,300 in 1539/40 and over £15,000 in 1542. But although the total revenue from ordinary sources rose to some £46,000 in 1539/40,[43] this was far below the king's requirements. Taxation contributed little, though in 1535 there was a tax of £20,000 for the king's expenses in France. The exploitation of the royal mines by German

41 *S. P. Henry VIII*, v. 109.   42 Lesley, p. 167.
43 The statistics come mainly from Athol L. Murray, *op. cit.*

experts can hardly have produced spectacular profits, but James's activities as a flockmaster,[44] significant as indicating his versatility, brought a worth-while return, and his manipulation of the coinage yielded several thousands of pounds in his last years. The marriage with Madeleine brought not only a lump sum and a pension, but also, it is said, plate, apparel and jewels worth more than 100,000 crowns, as well as two great ships[45] and munitions; and Mary of Guise brought a second dowry. The levies on the church, despite evasion and inefficient collection, represented immediate gains and set a precedent for future exactions. Besides, the fruits of the abbeys of Melrose, Kelso and Holyrood and the priories of St Andrews and Coldingham, to which the pope appointed the king's illegitimate infants, came into the royal coffers.[46] The upshot was that if James did not enrich " his realme " as well as " himselfe," he certainly had " gold and silver, all kinde of riche substance, quhairof he left greyt stoir and quantyte in all his palices at his departing,"[47] for there is record evidence of his " tresour, pois and boxis " in Edinburgh Castle and his personal fortune was reputed to be 300,000 *livres*.[48]

The money levied from the church, instead of going to the purposes for which it had been ostensibly raised, went largely to the king's building schemes, and even part of the tax for the visit to France was diverted in this way.[49] Between 1529 and 1541 the expenditure of the master of works is shown, in a series of accounts which is not complete, to have exceeded £26,000, and upon two occasions the annual sum was over £5,000.[50] In his building activities, James was to some extent following the example of his father, and also that of Albany (who employed French workmen in building at Holyrood and in making improvements in David's Tower at Edinburgh Castle). But James was far more ambitious, especially in the palace block at Stirling and the courtyard façade at Falkland, and at Linlithgow he raised a noble palace which Mary of Guise thought worthy of comparison with those

44 *Exchequer Rolls*, xvii. lii-lv; *R. S. S.*, iii. 12.
45 After the king's death two ships of his were sold for £5,500.
46 Their total revenues amounted to at least £30,000 in 1561.
47 Lesley, p. 167; cf. *L. and P.*, xvii. 1214.
48 *R. S. S.*, iii. 383; *Missions of de la Brosse* (S. H. S.), p. 19.
49 E.g., *R. S. S.*, ii. 1935, 2147; *Public Affairs*, pp. 490, 493.
50 *Masters of Works' Accounts*, i.

of France. James was lavish in expenditure on other conspicuous luxuries, and there may be some truth in the report that he had learned expensive tastes in France and introduced to Scotland customs " moir superfluous and volupteous " than the nation could sustain.[51] He kept what seems an enormous domestic staff, the household expenses reached new records and £10,000 a year from the clerical taxation were diverted to help to meet them.[52] The expenditure on the furnishing of the ship in which the king sailed round the islands in 1540 shows that the expedition was something of a luxury cruise. And in 1542 new crowns were made for the king and queen, absorbing gold worth £718, no doubt some at least of it from the royal mines.[53]

The sense of insecurity among the king's subjects must have become more acute as his " covetousness " became more pronounced. According to Buchanan, " the different factions pointed out the riches of their opponents, as a booty ready for [the king] whenever he chose; and he, by agreeing alternately with either, kept both in a state of suspense between fear and hope."[54] There are certainly grounds for believing that the clergy emphasised to James the financial advantages which would accrue from action against those disaffected to the church and that there was a " black list " of nobility and gentry whose estates might be confiscated on this ground.[55] Confidence may have been finally shattered by the fate of Sir James Hamilton of Finnart, the master of works. Finnart had been in favour under Angus, and continued to have gifts bestowed on him until so late as December 1539. He seems to have been connected in some way with the tension between the clergy and the reforming party; he was commissioned to act as a justice, possibly against " heretics," and, while the clergy can have had no love for the master of works, they may have welcomed action by Finnart which would lead to the confiscation of the estates of their opponents, but such action would of course earn him the hatred of the reformers. He was executed on 16 August 1540, on a charge of plotting to kill the king and corresponding with the Douglases, but contemporaries suggest that

51 Lesley, p. 154.

52 A. P. S., II. 424.

53 Entries in the Treasurers' Accounts relating to James's personal and household expenditure are printed in Pitcairn, Criminal Trials, I. i, 287 ff.

54 Buchanan, Rerum Scoticarum Historia (ed. J. Aikman), II. 318.

55 Knox, I. 34, 42; Sir James Melville, Memoirs, p. 60; Sadler, State Papers, I. 47.

his real crime was his wealth, and with his death the king acquired his heritage and his movables, including a hoard of gold.[56]

It was, however, international events which brought the final crisis. James was sufficiently impressed by Henry VIII's persuasive tactics[57] to agree to a meeting at York in September 1541, but the council declined to let him go. There were good grounds for refusing, as Henry had been contemplating the kidnapping of James on Scottish soil, and the king's person was especially precious since the deaths of his two infant sons in the spring,[58] but it was alleged that the real obstacle was the attitude of the clergy, who, fearful lest James would agree to copy Henry's church policy, offered to pay for an army should war ensue. Henry, who—for the only time in his life—made the long journey to York, and made it in vain, was justifiably indignant.

The breakdown of negotiations caused Henry to mobilise a force in the north, and in August 1542 Sir Robert Bowes crossed the Border, to be defeated at Haddon Rig; but another English army was sent into Scotland and Henry prepared a statement of the English claim to suzerainty over Scotland.[59] At the end of October James was at Lauder, and the English expected him to cross the Border in a day or two, but very soon they learned that the Scottish force was retiring and dispersing. Reports ran that victual had been scarce, that the soldiers' spoliation of their own country had caused complaints, that the many " Irish " in the army had been unpopular. But it soon emerged that the trouble was more deep-rooted: " the lords would not agree " with the king's proposal to invade England; Huntly, the victor of Haddon Rig, had been blamed by the king for subsequent inaction and had been superseded by Moray; James charged the lords with being " faint-hearted."[60] The angry monarch succeeded in exacting an undertaking that a further effort would be made " before the light of this moon ended," but it was made under new guidance. The disgraced nobles were excluded from the king's counsels, and the only earl consulted seems to have been Moray. James resigned the direction of affairs to Cardinal Beaton, who was reported to be thinking in terms of a crusade

---

[56] *Treasurer's Accounts*, VII. 383-5.   [57] P. 26 above.

[58] In 1536, when James proposed to meet Henry at York, the council had refused to let him go beyond Newcastle (*Letters of James V*, pp. 316-7).

[59] *S. P. Henry VIII*, v. 212-3; *L. and P.*, XVII. 1033.

[60] *S. P. Henry VIII*, v. 213, 215; *L. and P.*, XVII. 1039, 1100, 1117.

during which he would proclaim England to be under interdict, and to Oliver Sinclair of Pitcairns, who was " the most secret man living with the king of Scots."[61]   Sinclair, who had become keeper of Tantallon early in 1540 and had received many gifts since, including a tack of Orkney and Shetland, was a cadet of the almost princely house of Caithness and Roslin, but ranks as the last of James's " minions."[62]

The king, with the cardinal and Moray, left Edinburgh on 21 November and advanced towards the west march, with an army variously estimated at between 14,000 and 20,000 men. Beaton and Moray retired to Haddington, the king took up his station at Lochmaben with part of his force, intending to proceed across the Solway sands with an ebb-tide, while the remainder, under Oliver Sinclair, advanced from Langholm on a more easterly route.   The latter force encountered Wharton, the English deputy warden, near the River Esk and was driven back in a disorderly rout at Solway Moss (24 November).[63]   Few Scots were killed, but 1,200 were captured.   Some Borderers —the Liddesdale men—slew some of the Scots, took everything of value from others and, it was said, seized some nobles and turned them over to the English.[64]   Lord Maxwell was reported to have caused the rout and the capture of himself and others by galloping with other nobles to the rear and inducing a panic in the rearguard.[65]   It would be in keeping with the effects of James's policy if there was in fact disaffection among the Borderers; and equally if Scottish nobles were not unwilling to become prisoners, rather than die in the service of a king in whom so many of his subjects had completely lost confidence.

James withdrew by Peebles to Edinburgh and then spent a week with his queen at Linlithgow before retiring to Falkland.[66] There, broken in spirit rather than in body, he took to his bed, and he died on 14 December.   The narrators have much to say about his last hours: how he moaned, " Fy, fled Oliver?   Is Oliver tane?   All is lost ";   how he received the news of his daughter's birth with the words, " It came with a lass, it will pass with a lass ";   and how he turned his back to his lords and

61 L. and P., XVII. 1130, 1136, 1140, 1157.
62 G. A. Sinclair, " The Scots at Solway Moss," in S. H. R., II. 372-7.
63 L. and P., XVII. 1117, 1121, 1140, 1142, 1175.
64 Ibid., 1157; Diurnal of Occurrents, p. 25.
65 L. and P., XVII. 1207.   66 S. H. R., III. 382.

his face to the wall.[67] But contemporary report had it that in his extremity the king realised the errors of his policy and recommended that Angus should be recalled, prisoners liberated, forfeited estates restored, and the Borders committed to men whose heads he had recently proposed to cut off.[68]

Some contemporary and near-contemporary writers, like Buchanan, Pitscottie and Lesley, speak well of James V as acute and prudent in understanding, strong and courageous in body and spirit, sparing in food and drink, opposed to pride, and an enthusiast for order and justice. Nothing in the evidence which has been transmitted to later generations is specifically at variance with the virtues thus claimed, and yet the overall picture of James is far less favourable than the one those narrators had in mind. Their assessment may do no more than reflect the glamour which attached itself to James retrospectively and fortuitously. His personal rule had given the country a stability which contrasted sharply with the disorders of the long minority which followed, and after his death Scotland did not again have an adult king for nearly half a century. It may also be true that modern psychology might find, in the circumstances of James's upbringing, something to explain, if not extenuate, his defects. The background of his childhood and adolescence was the " dull and squalid intrigues of a selfish, sensual termagant "[69]—his mother—and implacable hostility between his mother and his stepfather, a stepfather whom James himself came to detest as his gaoler. It also seems that the prostration which led to James's death when aged only thirty indicates a tendency to excessive nervous or mental stress. With all we know of the effect of his policy on his subjects' loyalty, the political situation in itself is not adequate to explain the dismal death-bed scene at Falkland, and behind that scene there must lie more than the disgrace of Solway Moss. The king's character may have been shaken by personal as well as political tragedy, and it is said that he became over-confident with the births of his two sons (May 1540 and April 1541) and was plunged into melancholy by their deaths. Yet, however far the views of sixteenth-century narrators and modern psychologists might go to explain James V's character, they do little to lessen the revulsion with which he must be regarded. The vindictiveness

[67] Knox, I. 39; Pitscottie (S. T. S.), I. 407.
[68] *L. and P.*, XVII. 1209, 1225, 1233.   [69] Andrew Lang, *History of Scotland*, I. 409.

which made his later years something of a reign of terror went so far beyond what was politic that it suggests a streak of sadistic cruelty in his nature.   Apart from the punishments meted out to those who were his victims for political or financial reasons, there are instances of brutality towards lesser men.   The author of the *Diurnal of Occurrents*, whose pages are at this point very largely a catalogue of convictions and punishments, says that James ordered that a certain thief should be " brynt quick, quhilk was done, byndand him to ane staik, and was brynt;   quhilk deid was never sene in this realme of befoir, nor will be heireftir ";   he also notes that Simon Armstrong was drawn, hanged and quartered, and that the Master of Forbes was drawn, hanged and beheaded[70]—a form of execution familiar in England but startlingly strange in Scotland.   Perhaps James V is not to be judged by Scottish standards.   He was, after all, half a Tudor by birth and perhaps a Tudor rather than a Stewart in character. He combined in his own person the acquisitiveness of his grandfather, Henry VII, the lust and ruthlessness of his uncle, Henry VIII, and the unrelenting cruelty of his cousin, Bloody Mary.

[70] *Diurnal*, pp. 15, 20, 22.

5

THE MINORITY OF QUEEN MARY

Mary, the daughter of James V, had been born at Linlithgow on 8 December 1542, only six days before her father's death. Evidently in accordance with his wishes, the direction of affairs was assumed by the Earl of Arran (who was proclaimed governor on 3 January),[1] Cardinal Beaton (who was appointed chancellor on 10 January),[2] and the Earls of Moray, Huntly and Argyll. The cardinal and Arran were cousins, Argyll was married to Arran's sister and Moray to Argyll's sister, but recriminations over responsibility for the recent disaster must have separated Beaton and Moray from the other lords, and harmony was hardly possible between Beaton and Arran, whose name had headed the " black list " of heretics in the late king's reign. A fortnight after the king's death, Arran was reported to have drawn his sword on the cardinal as a " false churle," who told many lies " in the king's name."[3] The suspicion was that the cardinal had extorted a disposition in his own favour from the dying king, or had even caused " a dead man's hand " to " subscribe a blank,"[4] and an instrument actually drawn up, naming Moray, Huntly and Argyll, but not Arran, as the cardinal's colleagues in the government, was challenged on the ground that the acting notary was not qualified.

The issue was decided not by the rights and wrongs of James V's testamentary dispositions, but by a political revolution which put the control of affairs temporarily into the hands of a pro-English faction. Already before James's death it had been

---

[1] *L. and P.*, xviii (1), Nos. 4, 13; cf. xvii, No. 1225.   [2] *R. S. S.*, iii. 21.
[3] *L. and P.*, xvii. 1249; *H. M. C. Report*, xi, App. vi, pp. 219-20.   [4] Knox, i. 40.

evident that some at least of the prisoners taken at Solway Moss were likely to be used in the English interest, and on 29 December they were released on terms: they agreed to serve Henry by furthering the marriage of Mary to his son and heir, and ten of them—including Cassillis, Glencairn, Maxwell, Fleming, Somerville and Gray—undertook in addition to help Henry to secure the sovereignty of Scotland in the event of Mary's death.[5]   These lords were reinforced by Angus, an exile in England since 1528, who had been summoned before Henry on 12 December[6] and who soon returned to Scotland with his brother, Sir George Douglas, and the Earl of Bothwell, another exile. A day or two after these friends to England were received by Arran (25 January) the cardinal was arrested and threatened with deportation to England.[7]   Arran declared that for five years he had considered the pope to be no more than a bishop " and that a very evil bishop," and he commissioned a friar to preach in favour of the vernacular Bible.[8]   On 18 March, Sadler, Henry's envoy, arrived in Edinburgh to further his master's aims.

On 13 March parliament rescinded the forfeitures of Angus and other victims of James V's suspicion or cupidity,[9] and also acknowledged Arran as second person of the realm, heir presumptive to the crown, and governor, with full power, until the queen's " perfect age." Commissioners were appointed to negotiate for a treaty with England and a marriage between the infant queen and Prince Edward, aged five. An act, introduced by Lord Maxwell, one of the lords sworn to Henry, and passed in spite of a protest from the clerical estate, permitted the lieges to possess the scriptures in the vernacular. In accordance with advice from the south to " let slip amongst the people " the English Bible, preaching of " the true word of God " was officially encouraged, there was said to be a great thirst for copies of Bibles, primers and psalters, and the Bible was so much in fashion that it was to be seen " almost upon every gentleman's table."[10]   The effect was to stimulate radical tendencies, for later in the year there were outbreaks of violence against religious houses in Perth,

5 *L. and P.*, XVII. 1128, XVIII (1). 22; *Acts of the Privy Council [of England]*, 1542-7, p. 69.

6 *A. P. C.*, p. 62.   7 *L. and P.*, XVIII (1). 88 (28 Jan.).

8 *L. and P.*, XVIII (1). 324.   9 *Ibid.*, 281, 286.

10 *L. and P.*, XVIII (1). 324; *Hamilton Papers*, I. 445; Knox, I. 45; *Extracts from records of burgh of Aberdeen*, I. 189.

Dundee and Edinburgh, and an opportunity was given to acquisitive laymen like the Earl of Bothwell, who confined the prioress and nuns of Haddington and made free with the possessions of the house. But the act authorising the vernacular scriptures had itself forbidden disputation and a warning came from King Henry, who had recently imposed severe restrictions on Bible-reading.[11] In June, therefore, when " bills, writings, ballads and books " defaming " all estates both spiritual and temporal " were in circulation, the Scottish council forbade the possession of heretical literature and legislated against unorthodox opinions on the sacraments.[12] Officially, it is plain, the model was not protestantism, but the Henrician one of non-Roman catholicism, and Anglo-Scottish conformity was demonstrated when Arran and the English envoy received Holy Communion together.

Beaton had been warded successively at Dalkeith, Seton and Blackness. But before the end of March he had been removed to his own castle of St Andrews, a step towards the recovery of liberty which enabled him to renew clerical opposition to the English alliance and to lead the clergy in making an offer of money and plate for the defence of the realm against England.[13] He could count on the support of the queen mother, who had from the first been trying to sow mistrust between Arran and the English and to encourage Henry to make excessive demands which would antagonise the Scots,[14] and France, like England, was ready to send Scottish exiles home to act in her interest. One of them was Matthew, Earl of Lennox. Arrangements for his return to Scotland, bringing supplies, were made with promptitude, care and secrecy, and by 5 April he was with the queen mother at Linlithgow. As Arran's father had married his mother only after a divorce from a previous wife, there was doubt about his legitimacy, and the advent of Lennox, who stood next to him in the succession, reminded the governor that he was at the mercy of the cardinal, as head of the ecclesiastical authority which had jurisdiction in matrimonial causes. Lennox, besides, though a man of twenty-six, had the advantage of being a bachelor, and could therefore be regarded as a possible consort for the infant queen. As important as Lennox was another

11 34 & 35 Henry VIII, c. 1; *L. and P.*, xviii (1). 364.
12 *Public Affairs*, pp. 527-8.
13 Robertson, *Statuta Ecclesiae Scoticanae*, pp. cxlii-cxliii.
14 *L. and P.*, xviii (1). 313, 355.

returning exile—John Hamilton, Abbot of Paisley, the governor's half-brother and the brains of the house. This ambitious church-man, always alive to the interests of his family, was convinced by the arguments which Beaton put before him in an interview about the end of March: there could be promotion for John himself, and, should the English alliance be abandoned, Queen Mary would be available for Arran's own son, the Master of Hamilton—a possibility which had been in some minds almost from her birth.

The Hamilton proximity to the crown had been a factor in Scottish history ever since the death of James IV, and since the death of Albany in 1536 Arran had been heir presumptive. From this period until 1707 the house of Hamilton again and again had the crown almost within its grasp, but its head never had ability to match his birth and the outstanding characteristic of the family was irresolution. At this stage, when contrary influences were brought to bear on the inconstant Arran, it was said that " What the English lords decide him to do one day, the abbot [John Hamilton] changes the next."[15] But the pro-English policy had in fact been all along opposed by others besides " the abbot," the cardinal, the dowager and Lennox. Argyll, Moray and Huntly had disapproved of the admission of the Douglases to the council and of the confinement of the cardinal, and, while the March parliament had been attended by twelve earls and eighteen lords—one of the biggest attendances between 1513 and 1567—as well as by a clerical membership only slightly below the average, it had been boycotted by Argyll, Bothwell, Eglinton and Sempill, who even talked of a rival convention. Nor were " the English lords " unanimous: Fleming, although he had attended the parliament, was soon on Beaton's side. By 6 July, Huntly, Bothwell and Argyll were allied " contrair the gover-nour,"[16] and before the end of the month Beaton had enough support to be able to engineer the removal of the queen and her mother from Linlithgow to Stirling, where Mary was safer from seizure on behalf of Henry. Some thought the association of the dowager with the cardinal and Bothwell a curious one, for both were gentlemen with whom she was suspected of " over great familiarity."[17]

Anxiety over the fate of the queen had arisen in the course of

15 *L. and P.*, XVIII (1). 425.   16 *Diurnal of Occurrents*, pp. 27-8.
17 *L. and P.*, XVIII (2), 255; cf. Knox, I. 40, 322.

the negotiations with England. Demands that the marriage should not involve the absorption of Scotland into England were on the whole conceded: Scotland was to remain a separate realm under a native governor, with its own parliament, courts, laws and liberties; should Mary be left a childless widow, she was to return to Scotland unconditionally, and should there be no children of the marriage Mary's heirs were to succeed in Scotland. But the impatient Henry, who had already been tried by the failure of his Scottish clients to produce quick results, wanted Mary to cross the Border almost as soon as she could leave the care of her mother. The Scots knew that if the queen passed into English hands prematurely, all the safeguards for the integrity of Scotland might be nullified, and they wanted her to remain in Scotland until she could " complete marriage." In the Treaties of Greenwich, concluded on 1 July, it was arranged that the marriage should be contracted by proxy before she reached the age of ten, at which age she was to leave for England.[18]

Henry encouraged the wavering Arran by offering Princess Elizabeth as a bride for the Master of Hamilton and promising that if Arran encountered resistance to the ratification of the treaties he would have 5,000 men, while, if the opposition arranged another marriage for the queen, Scotland would be conquered and Arran made king beyond the Forth. Arran had his doubts, for, as his own lands lay in southern Scotland, he did not consider a northern kingdom attractive, and he thought that £5,000 would be more useful than 5,000 Englishmen,[19] but he was brought to the point of ratifying the treaties, at Holyrood on 25 August. Henry's ineptitude, however, soon nullified the transaction. Only a degree less unpopular than his attempts to secure the young queen's person was his demand that the Scots should break their alliance with France; even pro-English Scots appreciated that if Arran were to introduce 5,000 Englishmen he would lose the support of 20,000 Scots; the English government seized some Scottish ships which had put to sea trusting that the peace had become effective; and, finally, Henry failed to ratify the agreements of 1 July within the prescribed period of two months. The English king had disregarded the warnings of Sadler, who, though professing to marvel that any Scotsman could refuse Henry's

[18] *A. P. S.*, II. 411-3, 425-6; *Foedera*, XIV. 786-96; *L. and P.* XVIII (1). 402, 664.
[19] *L. and P.*, XVIII (1). 395, 482, 509; (2). 9, 22, 46.

" reasonable and beneficial " desires, had not been two days in Edinburgh when he reported that Henry's insistence on the custody of the queen would throw Arran on to the other side, and he repeatedly told his master that the situation was a delicate one, in which excessive demands would hazard all.[20]

Little more than a week after Arran had ratified the agreements he capitulated to the cardinal and his party. He was taken to Dundee to deal with the persons who had attacked the friaries and so demonstrate his change of front, his son was placed in the cardinal's castle of St Andrews as a kind of hostage, and he was in future to be advised by a council of which Beaton and the dowager were to be members. Beaton was reinstated as chancellor, John Hamilton became treasurer. On 11 December the Scottish parliament, on the grounds of the English seizure of Scottish ships and delay in ratifying the agreements, denounced the treaties with England and confirmed those with France; and an act was passed urging proceedings against heretics and affirming the governor's readiness to do his part.

The change of policy did not bring unity any nearer, but hardened divisions along different lines. France and the papacy came to the support of an administration which was commited to their interests: the Patriarch of Aquileia, sent by the pope to collect the last ecclesiastical subsidy solicited by James V and to spend it on the defence of the realm and the faith, arrived early in October, in company with French envoys who brought money, artillery and other supplies and who were present at the December parliament; and Beaton was appointed legate in January 1543/4. England, on the other hand, in losing the support of Arran, inevitably gained that of Lennox, who, no less than Arran, had dynastic interests, for he was thinking of a marriage to Margaret Douglas, daughter of Angus by Queen Margaret Tudor, and of English support for his claim to be second person in Scotland. Likewise, Arran's administration, in gaining the lords who had opposed the anglophile policy, lost at least some of those who had supported it, for Angus, Morton, Errol, Marischal, Cassillis, Rothes and Glencairn, who had been present at the March parliament, were absent in December.

Lennox left Stirling immediately after taking part in Mary's coronation on 9 September 1543, and aligned himself with those

[20] L. and P., XVIII (1). 325, 425, p. 174; (2) 127-8, 154, 176.

who adhered to Henry. At Dumbarton he received the munitions and money brought by the French envoys, who were unaware of his change of front. Angus and his brother made a
demonstration against Edinburgh, and by the end of the year the
pro-English party assembled a large force in Leith. Beaton was
believed to have a scheme for all-round reconciliation: Arran
was to be divorced and marry the dowager and was to remain
nominally governor, while Lennox was to be contracted to Mary
and was to be effective ruler as lieutenant-governor.[21] This was
over-ingenious, and an agreement made at Greenside on 13
January 1543/4, whereby Lennox, Angus and their associates
agreed to be true to the queen and to assist the governor in the
defence of the realm and the church, was quite insincere.[22] Far
from being won over, the Angus-Lennox faction was soon in
arms again, utilising the French supplies which Lennox had
appropriated, and with the additional support of Lord Ruthven
and his son. Lennox, after taking Glasgow and Paisley, stood a
siege in Glasgow by the governor in April, but had to surrender.
Angus was warded, Lennox left Dumbarton for England at the
end of May.

Henry's first reaction to the Scottish *volte-face* had been to try
direct force, for in September 1543 he had spoken of burning
Edinburgh and seizing Arran and Beaton, but he had been
advised that such violence would only further alienate the Scots.
He next planned to work through Lennox, Angus, Cassillis and
Glencairn, who agreed in March to cause the Word of God to be
preached, to endeavour to put Mary into his hands and to have
him made protector during her minority; he would send an army
to co-operate with them, and on their victory Lennox was to be
governor.[23] But by 10 April he had come to realise—what more
acute observers had told him months before[24]—that his Scottish
auxiliaries could not fulfil their undertakings, and, returning to the
policy of force, he drafted instructions for an invasion of Scotland
by the Earl of Hertford, who was not to attempt to hold territory
but to do the maximum amount of destruction and especially
to " turne upset downe the cardinalles town of St. Andrews,
... sparing no creature alyve within the same."[25] When the attack

---

[21] *Hamilton Papers*, II. 151; *L. and P.*, XVIII (2). 364.   [22] *L. and P.* XIX (1). 33.
[23] *L. and P.*, XIX (1). 243; *S. P. Henry VIII*, v. 363-5, 386-7.
[24] *E.g.*, *L. and P.*, XVIII (2). 414, 424.   [25] *Hamilton Papers*, II. No. 207.

was launched, in May, it took the Scots by surprise. Hertford was able to disembark one force near Edinburgh, while another came overland, and together they burned and looted from Leith to the Borders. English propaganda possibly exaggerated the number of buildings, including churches, which were destroyed, but there is some supporting evidence for the destruction of churches,[26] and what such an invasion meant in human misery can only be guessed.

The work of Hertford, apart from indicating the incompetence of the administration of Arran and Beaton, caused some to have second thoughts about the wisdom of their anti-English policy. Besides, they had not improved their position by vindictiveness against some leaders of the pro-English faction or by their action against heretics, for the time had come when no ecclesiastical policy whatever could command universal support. From all those who felt aggrieved at their proceedings there came an attempt, in the summer of 1544, to supersede Arran by Mary of Guise, in whom more confidence was clearly felt. At a convention at Stirling, in June, Arran was suspended and Mary appointed to act in his place. The dowager's adherents were a hetero-geneous group, including some bishops, Angus and the lords of the English faction, as well as Huntly, Moray and Argyll. They hardly formed a party, for, on the central issues of ecclesiastical and foreign policy, there was neither agreement among the members of Mary's group nor any real breach between her and the cardinal. Moreover, no foreign support could be expected. France, whose interests were supported by the cardinal and by Arran, was not likely to countenance opposition to them. Henry of England, for his part, was committed to the Lennox wing of the pro-English faction. On 26 June Lennox undertook to hand over Dumbarton and Bute to Henry in return for lands in England and the governorship of Scotland; on 6 July he married Margaret Douglas, which made him Angus's son-in-law but also placed him in the English succession as well as the Scottish; and on 8 August he was proclaimed by Henry lieutenant for the north of England and southern Scotland. He met with little success, for although he devastated the shores of the Firth of Clyde in August he failed to take Dumbarton, and he was no more fortunate later in the year when he operated from Carlisle against the south-western Border. Yet as long as Henry had Lennox at his disposal

26 *E.g.*, *R. S. S.*, IV. 641, 752; and see Donaldson, *Scottish Reformation*, pp. 21-2.

he was not likely to support the French dowager and her rather equivocal partisans. The test between the two Scottish factions came in November, when rival parliaments were summoned. Arran anticipated the dowager, and in his parliament, which met at Edinburgh on 6 November, charges of treason were made against all who should attend Mary's parliament, which had been summoned to Stirling on 12 November. An appeal was made for unity in the face of " our auld inymeis of Ingland,"[27] a reconciliation was effected and remissions were granted to those who had been charged with treason.

For the next eighteen months Beaton was in control and was not unsuccessful in the difficult task of keeping Arran and Mary of Guise in double harness and in winning the less militant of the English party to support the administration. Although Mary, as well as Arran, now sat regularly on the council, Beaton was not capitulating to France, for the young queen was kept in Scotland and Arran had so much success in gaining signatories to a bond pledging support for her marriage to his son that he was said to enjoy the favour of " the maist part of bayth temporall and spirituall astait."[28] Besides, the policy of resistance to England commanded considerable support. An English invasion at the beginning of 1545, when the Douglas tombs at Melrose were desecrated, was credited with turning Angus into such a good Scot that he led his countrymen to a resounding victory at Ancrum (27 February), but he had actually been serving against the English since November. The Kerrs and the Scotts entered on a mutual bond of lawborrows, or reciprocal assurance, so that their feud should not weaken the defence of the Border.

Henry had no new policy. It was over optimistic to expect the Scots, in April 1545, so soon after Ancrum, to agree to a suggestion that they should re-open negotiations on the basis of the Treaty of Greenwich, and the only alternative Henry could think of was military action on a still larger scale. In May 1545 it was reported that the English were planning to send forces overland by both the east and west Borders and by sea both up the east coast and into the Firth of Clyde, with a total strength of 36,000 men, including landsknechts and other foreign auxiliaries. The Scots received French help, for in June 1545 the seigneur de

27 *A. P. S.*, II. 448.
28 *Scottish Correspondence*, p. 147; cf. *H. M. C. Report*, XI. pt. VI. 36.

Lorges arrived with French troops, who as usual proved unpopular, and French pressure for an invasion of England provoked the customary opposition, led by Angus, Glencairn, Gray and Glamis. Yet the Scots were not idle in their own defence, for there were five musters in twelve months, besides the raising of a special force of 1,000 horse, to be maintained by an extraordinary tax, for service in the Merse and Teviotdale. In September 1545 Scotland experienced the second of Hertford's destructive invasions of the south-east—at a time deliberately chosen as suitable for the burning of the corn cut in an early harvest. In the west, too, Lennox was joined by many clans in a raid on Bute, Arran and parts of Argyll; a " rebel council " included the MacLeans of Duart and Lochbuie, the MacLeods of Harris and Lewis, Mackinnon of Strathardle, MacNeil of Barra, MacIan of Ardnamurchan, and Clanranald;[29] even a " Lord of the Isles " appeared, in the person of Donald Dubh, the son of Angus (himself the son of Lord John) who had been killed in 1490; and there was something like an English-sponsored (and pensioned) administration in the west. However, on the death of Donald, although there were candidates for the reversion of his English pension, there was no obvious or agreed successor, and the insurrection petered out. In any event, the fate of Scotland was not to be determined in the West Highlands.

The general effect of the " Rough Wooing " of 1544 and 1545, with its appeal to force and fear, had not been to nourish affection for England. Henry still had one or two aristocratic supporters in addition to the now expatriated Lennox—Maxwell, for example, who had allowed himself to be captured by the English in May 1544 and had subsequently surrendered the castles of Lochmaben and Caerlaverock (which the Scots recovered at the end of 1545). But on the whole Henry's policy of tampering with the allegiance of the Scottish magnates had failed to maintain a party, if only because others could counter his financial bids. In 1543, Sadler had pointed out the benefits which might accrue to the Scottish nobles should the abbeys be suppressed, but Arran and Beaton were able to offer commendatorships and pensions within the framework of the existing system.[30] Again, Sadler, remarking that there were " none rich here to speak of but kirkmen," had

29 Cf. R. W. Munro, *Dean Munro's Description of the Western Isles*, p. 144.
30 *L. and P.*, xviii (2). 424.

promised sums ranging from £100 to £200 to Cassillis, Glencairn, Maxwell, Somerville and Marischal;[31] but the Scottish government could offer inducements in the shape of tacks of crown property, while the cardinal could grant feu charters and offer ecclesiastical patronage, and in the background there was France, whence pensions could come to the well-affected.[32] Even when prices rose, as they did with an English offer to Glencairn of a pension of £1,000 in May 1544, English bids could still be countered: in December Angus was granted a Scottish pension of £1,000—possibly a more cogent argument than the spoliation of Melrose in causing him to lead the Scots at Ancrum—and his brother one of £500; Bothwell committed himself to Mary of Guise for a pension of £1,000.[33] Angus continued to bargain with both sides, but by the beginning of 1546 he and his brother, along with Argyll, Bothwell, Home and the captain of Dumbarton, were French pensioners.[34]

Henry was undoubtedly beaten at his own game of bribing the Scots. Far and away his greatest asset lay not in the unreliable manoeuvrings of Scottish magnates, but in the spread of reforming and pro-English views among men of less influence than the magnates but of greater stability. Probably ecclesiastical discipline was never completely restored after 1543, and popular resentment against the church continued to find expression in iconoclasm. Then the deliberate destruction of ecclesiastical buildings by the English in 1544 and 1545 must have led to dislocation of church life, and a self-seeking clergy and a partly secularised church lacked the zeal to make losses good by rebuilding. At any rate, the law against heretics was no longer being generally enforced, and in or about April 1545 one of the dowager's correspondents advised her that heresy " is now dowtsum to punes by the law."[35] It is also true that, while the reforming preachers were constantly extending the scope of their attacks, the conservatives laboured under the difficulty that until a council met and carried out some theological definition they did not know exactly what teaching they were trying to defend. The whole situation, political and religious, was illustrated in the

[31] *L. and P.*, xviii (1). 395, 482, 509.
[32] *Ibid.*, (2). 424, 443; *Missions of de la Brosse*, pp. 31, 35, 45.
[33] *R. S. S.*, iii. 987-8; Reg. Ho. State Papers, 38a.
[34] *Balcarres Papers*, i. 124-5.
[35] *Scottish Correspondence*, p. 133.

mission of George Wishart, who was transparently an English agent, for he had spent some time at Cambridge before returning to Scotland in 1543 in company with the commissioners empowered to negotiate the Treaties of Greenwich. In 1544 and 1545 he was preaching in churches with comparative freedom and was attracting a large following. The preaching of Wishart and others made friends for Henry VIII, who, often foolish in his tactics towards Scotland, was sounder on long-term strategy, with his clear concept of Anglo-Scottish union or amity based on ideological conformity.

Henry's one short-term success was the elimination of Cardinal Beaton. Between April 1544 and July 1545, there were plots against the cardinal, with Henry's approval, involving Sir James Kirkcaldy of Grange (who had been superseded as treasurer by John Hamilton), Norman Leslie (son of the Earl of Rothes), Crichton of Brunstane, the Earl Marischal and the Earl of Cassillis.[36] Another conspirator had been "a Scottish man called Wishart." He may or may not have been identical with George Wishart the preacher, but the readiness of Roman catholic writers to make the identification and the abhorrence with which protestants regard it are alike pointless, for the century was one in which popes countenanced massacres and John Knox approved of murders. At any rate, it was as a heretic and not as a would-be assassin that Wishart was arrested and executed (1 March 1546). There is no evidence that the murder of the cardinal eight weeks later was directly connected with the earlier plots against him, though the band who broke into St Andrews Castle early in the morning of 29 May 1546 included Norman Leslie, John, his uncle, and William Kirkcaldy, son of Sir James Kirkcaldy. It was another Fife laird, James Melville of Carnbee ("a man of nature most gentle"),[37] who urged Beaton, at the point of the sword, to repent of the shedding of Wishart's blood, and then despatched him—"which is a very compendious kind of bringing men to repentance."[38] The desire to avenge Wishart was no doubt one motive, and the ecclesiastical and political implications of the removal of the cardinal were manifest. Yet personal motives may have been uppermost in the minds of those Fife lairds, and at the highest they may have been anticipating action which the

[36] E.g., L. and P., XIX (1). 350.   [37] Knox, I. 77.
[38] Mathew Sutcliffe, Answere unto . . . Job Throkmorton, fo. 47.

cardinal, knowing of their plots, planned against them.[39] At any rate, the conspiracy does not seem to have been broadly based or to have enjoyed sufficiently influential support either within Scotland or outside it to issue in a revolution. The conspirators themselves could agree to further the marriage of Mary to Prince Edward,[40] but the treaty of Greenwich did not commend itself to many Scots and its rejection was reaffirmed by the council on 11 June; and the murderers, some of whom were so notorious for their evil lives as to be, even in protestant eyes, " men without God,"[41] represented radical elements for which moderate reformers, let alone conservatives, may well have felt distaste.

The murderers seized and held the castle of St Andrews, Lennox and his brother the Bishop of Caithness almost simultaneously seized Dumbarton Castle, and violence was here and there offered to ecclesiastical properties, but that was all. Had it been possible for the government either to come to terms with the " Castilians " or to recover the castle of St Andrews, as it recovered Dumbarton, by prompt action, the episode might have had no effect on the situation. But Arran, although the death of the cardinal to some extent restored his freedom of action, was in a difficult position. His brother John, bishop-elect of Dunkeld, could hardly condone the murder of the primate; and the Hamilton dynastic interest forbade capitulation to a faction which proposed to marry Mary to Edward. On the other hand, Arran did not want to call in French help, for with France also there might well be disagreement over the destination of the queen; nor could he press the " Castilians " too hard, for his son was still in the castle. All he could do was to conduct an ineffective siege and try to win by negotiation a castle " unhable to be gottin bot be hungir quhilk will nocht be haistelie done."[42] By armistice terms, suggested in August and concluded in December, the garrison agreed to surrender on receipt of an indemnity and an absolution from Rome, but when the absolution came, in the following year, it contained the phrase *remittimus irremissibile* and was therefore rejected.

The prolongation of the siege turned it into an international incident.[43] In the spring of 1547 there was some reason to believe

[39] Cf. *R. S. S.*, iv. 152, 715, 1877.
[40] *Foedera*, xv. 132-3.
[41] Knox, I. 97.
[42] *R. P. C.*, I. 58.
[43] See p. 28 above.

that England would intervene,[44] and it was apparently in this hope that at Easter (10 April) John Knox, a priest who had previously been associated with Wishart when he preached in East Lothian, entered the castle. The armistice still held, and Knox began his career as a preacher in the pulpit of the parish church of St Andrews. But, to his dismay and indignation, France anticipated any action by England, and the castle fell to a French expedition on 31 July. The " principal gentlemen" were put in prison in France, and the others, including Knox, were consigned to the galleys, to remain there until 1549.

England acted only after St Andrews had fallen. At the beginning of September the Protector Somerset crossed the Border at the head of an army of some 16,000 men, well furnished with artillery and heavy cavalry and supported by a fleet. At Pinkie, on 10 September, it was met by a Scottish army which was more numerous but was poorly equipped and very weak in cavalry. There was some courageous fighting, but the engagement ended with mismanagement, confusion, and ultimately panic, in which thousands of Scots, hemmed in between the sea and the Esk, were killed and about 1,500 taken prisoners.[45]

Somerset withdrew his army after the victory, but the previous holding of St Andrews by a band of English supporters seems already to have suggested to the English, as a substitute for mere raiding, the occupation of strong points " quhar thai think best in Fiff or Lothiane and quhar thai have moniest fauveraris."[46] English garrisons held Inchcolm, Broughty Castle, Inchkeith and Dundee for various periods between the end of 1547 and the summer of 1549. Above all, in the spring of 1548 the English took possession of Haddington, so that, besides dominating the Forth and Tay estuaries, they were able to terrorise the Lothian countryside up to the very gates of Edinburgh. The only success of the Scots was the repulse of an attempt by Lennox, with English help, at Dumfries, in February 1548.

The divisions among the Scots were such that they were no longer unanimous even against an invader on their own soil. For one thing, the coalition which Beaton's astuteness had built up had disintegrated. A fortnight after the cardinal's murder

[44] There were preparations against an expected English invasion on 20 May.

[45] The most recent account of Pinkie is by Sir James Fergusson in *The White Hind*, pp. 14-32; cf. C. W. C. Oman in *Archaeological Journal*, xc. 1-25 and his *Art of War in the sixteenth century*.   [46] *Scottish Correspondence*, p. 188.

Arran had formally released the signatories of his marriage bond from their undertaking,[47] and, while he tried to secure allies by making Huntly chancellor and by designating a kinsman of Angus for the abbey of Arbroath, he was mainly concerned to exploit the situation in the interests of his own kin: John Hamilton was nominated for translation to St Andrews; and for Glasgow, after the death of Gavin Dunbar in April 1547, there was nominated James Hamilton, another natural brother of the governor, with pensions to David and Claud, Arran's sons. The governor had forfeited any claim to confidence in either his competence or his integrity, and, although Angus led the van at Pinkie, lack of trust between him and Arran may have contributed to the disaster. Of course, pro-French and clerical opinion was bound in any circumstances to continue to oppose England—and a significant number of clergy fell at Pinkie, fighting under a banner inscribed " Afflicte sponse ne obliviscaris."[48] There were also those who thought that the English, in spite of their reputation for wisdom, " gane nocht the rycht way to mak union off thyr twa realmis."[49] But there were others in whose minds sympathy with the Reformation now proved stronger than patriotism. In November 1547, less than two months after Pinkie, the English governor of Broughty reported that there was much desire in Angus and Fife to have Bibles and Testaments and " other good English books."[50] Lord Methven, puzzled to find an explanation why " Inglis men is fawvorit and the authorite nocht obeyit nor servit," could think of four " prynsipall caussis ": three of them were material considerations—the desire for security, profit and stable government—but he gave priority to the fact that " part of the legis has tayn new apoynzionis [opinions] of the scriptour and has don agan the law and ordinance of haly kirk."[51] Henry VIII's fostering of reforming opinions was now yielding fruit, and it was reinforced by Somerset's own propaganda. Before Pinkie he denied that he intended to threaten Scottish independence and declared that he sought only to deliver the Scots from bondage to the pope and to fulfil that " godly and honourable purpose," the marriage contract of 1543,[52] and English manifestos drew attention to the

---

[47] *R. P. C.*, I. 27.   [48] Teulet, *Relations politiques*, I. 155.
[49] *Scottish Correspondence*, p. 214.
[50] *Cal. S. P. Scot.*, I. No. 74.   [51] *Scottish Correspondence*, p. 241.
[52] William Patten, *Expedicion into Scotland* (1548), sig. d i *v* (reprinted in Dalyell, *Fragments of Scottish History*.).

material advantages which would accrue from the " godly purpose."[53] At any rate, whatever the motives, the English had any
number of supporters. Among the nobles, Lord Gray delivered
Broughty Castle, the Master of Ruthven was prepared to bargain
for the surrender of Perth, Argyll abandoned his operations
against the English in Dundee and had visions of the governorship,
and Bothwell, three weeks after Pinkie, was negotiating for a
marriage to an English princess as the price of the delivery of
Hermitage Castle.[54] Fife lairds like Balfour of Mountquhanie and
the Melvilles of Raith were on the English side, while Kerr of
Cesford and other Border lairds took part with the lieutenant of
the north of England.[55] Especially active as collaborators were
East Lothian lairds, who already had a record of plotting against
Beaton, supporting Wishart and harbouring Knox: Heriot of
Trabroun, Broun of Colstoun, Cockburn of Ormiston, Crichton
of Brunstane and Douglas of Longniddry joined Somerset after
Pinkie and assisted the occupying forces by surrendering their
own houses and helping the English garrisons in Hailes and Haddington. Hundreds of Scots were subsequently found guilty of
" taking of assurance with oure auld inymeis of Ingland, fortyfeing
and assistance geving to thame."[56]

At the time of the Pinkie campaign, Mary was sent for a brief
space to the safety of the island priory of Inchmahome, and
within a few weeks the Scottish council discussed the possibility
of her going to France. Henry II, it was clear, would not give
effective help to Scotland except on his own terms, and the discredited Arran was too vulnerable to resist, partly because his
plans to entrench his kinsmen in the prelacies were being obstructed by the pope, apparently under direction from France,
and partly because of French offers of material inducements.
On 27 January 1547/8 he promised that, in return for a French
duchy, he would secure the consent of the Scottish parliament to
the marriage of Mary and the dauphin, the conveyance of the
queen to France, and the delivery of strongholds into French
hands. Blackness and Dunbar were handed over to the French
at this stage. On 28 April Arran obtained a guarantee that when

[53] *An exhortacion to the Scottes to conforme them selfes to the . . . union betweene the two
realmes* (1547) and *An epistle or exhortacion . . . from the Lorde Protectour to the inhabitantes
of the realme of Scotlands* (1548); cf. *Cal. S. P. Scot.*, I. Nos. 285, 357.

[54] *Cal. S. P. Scot.*, I. 14, 22   [55] *Public Affairs*, p. 573.

[56] *E.g.*, *R. S. S.*, III. 2679, 2692, 2847; IV. 338.

his governorship expired he would be held clear of all financial claims[57] and a promise that his heir would marry the elder daughter of the Duke of Montpensier.[58] Arran's heir sailed for France in May or early June, before the arrival of the French galleys which brought a force to assist the Scots and landed it at Leith. A joint Franco-Scottish force then laid siege to Haddington, and at the nunnery near to that town a treaty was made on 7 July 1548 whereby the Scots agreed that Mary should marry the dauphin, while an undertaking was given on behalf of the king of France, in general terms, to maintain the realm and lieges of Scotland in their customary freedom, liberties and laws. The French ships proceeded from Leith to Dumbarton, where at the end of July they took on board Queen Mary and the " four Maries " —Beaton, Seton, Fleming and Livingston. After waiting for a favourable wind and then making a circuit by the west of Ireland, the party reached Roscoff, near Brest.[59] Two of Mary's half-brothers were also removed to France.[60] Arran was rewarded by the completion of his half-brother's appointment to St Andrews, and in February 1549 he became Duke of Châtelherault.

The French forces which had been introduced were indispensable for their military skill, especially as the English were so firmly established and the war became largely a matter on both sides of holding territory by the erection or occupation of strong points, such as Inveresk, Luffness, Dunglass, Eyemouth, Home Castle, Lauder, Jedburgh and Old Roxburgh. Yet in the end it was not military effort in Scotland, but attacks by the French on the English garrison in Boulogne, which compelled England to abandon Haddington (September 1549).

The problem facing France and her supporters was to reconcile the Scottish nation to the policy of capitulating to France. Mary of Guise did her share by bringing about the release and rehabilitation of the gentlemen who had been imprisoned in France after the fall of St Andrews Castle.[61] Honours were available—Angus, Argyll and Huntly were admitted to the order of St Michael[62]—but Arran himself was not satisfied with empty

---

[57] *Balcarres Papers*, II. xxxvii.   [58] *Ibid.*, I. 197.

[59] On 13 August; but the ship may have proceeded to St Pol and landed the passengers there on 15 August (W. M. Bryce, " Mary Stuart's voyage to France in 1548," in *E. H. R.*, XXII, 43-50).

[60] *Public Affairs*, pp. 575-6.   [61] Cf. *Scottish Correspondence*, p. 241.

[62] *Balcarres Papers*, II. 281 *n.*; Knox, I. 103.

honours, for his duchy of Châtelherault was worth 12,000 livres a year, and French gold was, now as earlier, a powerful argument. In 1550 Mary of Guise went to France, accompanied by a remarkable group of Scottish notables—Huntly, Glencairn, Marischal, Cassillis, Maxwell, Fleming, Lord James Stewart (a natural son of James V and commendator of St Andrews Priory), John Winram, subprior of St Andrews, John Spottiswoode, parson of Calder, James Sandilands of Torphichen, Robert Stewart, Bishop of Caithness, and others. Nearly all of them were men committed to, or with leanings towards, the English and reforming side, and the aim was to subject them to French influence and expose them to French offers. The king of France, it was reported, " bought them completely."[63] Home had 2,000 livres and, with Glencairn, another pensioner, received payment in Paris;[64] Lord John Stewart was nominated to one French abbey,[65] Lord James to another;[66] 2,000 francs were to go to Maxwell;[67] the Master of Ruthven was due to receive money in Paris from Villemore, a member of the dowager's household, but complained that when he demanded " gud money " Villemore only " cuist out ane pursfull of auld sousis."[68]

The important part which Mary of Guise had to play in French plans must explain why she had remained in Scotland at all after her daughter left for France, and why she returned after her visit to France, as she did in November 1551. She had been cut off already from her kinsfolk, though constantly reminded of them by regular correspondence; she had been separated also from her son (by her first marriage), who wrote frequently to his mother, on one occasion enclosing a piece of string to show how tall he had grown; and now she was severed from her daughter as well. The office of governor of Scotland cannot of itself have appealed to her, and, while she may well have enjoyed the political game for its own sake, she must have been moved mainly by a sense of duty to her country, her family, her church, and her daughter's rights. She now had to play for support not only for France against England but for herself against Arran, for as early as February 1550/51, when she was in France, it had

[63] *R. S. S.*, IV. 879-93; Knox, I. 116; *Cal. S. P. Venice*, v. 361.
[64] *Scottish Correspondence*, pp. 346 n, 347; *Balcarres Papers*, II. 164.
[65] *Scottish Correspondence*, p. 343.
[66] Robertson, *Inventaires de la royne descosse*, p. xxxix n.
[67] *Scottish Correspondence*, pp. 349-50.   [68] *Ibid.*, pp. 346-7.

been rumoured that the French meant to " prevein the tyme of the governouris office afoir the quenis cuming to perfite age."[69] Châtelherault's continued tenure of the office of governor became little more than camouflage: French troops garrisoned Dunbar, Blackness, Broughty and Inchkeith; it was said in 1551 that D'Oysel, the French resident in Scotland, wielded almost sovereign authority;[70] a treaty between England and Scotland on 10 June 1551 was signed by commissioners who included M. de Lansac, who had been sent by Henry to Scotland in January as a mediator in Border controversies; and the French ambassador in Flanders acted in Scottish negotiations with the emperor.[71]

Resistance to French policy might conceivably have been organised. The French troops in Scotland proved as unpopular as ever;[72] the Scots themselves had become more than weary of the incessant musters, attendance at which it was difficult to enforce;[73] when war between France and the empire started again, in 1552, the Scots declined to comply with the French request to declare war and even a project to raise a force for the French service had to be abandoned because of opposition.[74] Châtelherault himself lacked the ability, the credit and the resolution to organise and head resistance, and such a Hamilton policy as there was at this stage reflects rather the ideas of his abler brother, the archbishop, for it was ecclesiastical as much as political. In May 1551 the governor gave a formal undertaking in parliament to be faithful to the church,[75] and this brought its reward, for Gavin Hamilton became coadjutor of St Andrews and the governor's son, John, was provided to Arbroath[76] (though the bulls for the latter were not yet released). In 1549 and 1552 two councils of the Scottish church passed a whole code of reforming statutes, designed to check such irregularities as concubinage, pluralism, non-residence, the tenure of benefices by unqualified men, and the neglect of church buildings. There was to be regular visitation by bishops in person, and it was to extend

[69] *Scottish Correspondence*, p. 344.   [70] *Cal. S. P. Spanish, 1550-2*, 339.

[71] *Scottish Correspondence*, p. 354.

[72] E.g., *Scottish Correspondence*, NO. CCI; Teulet, *Relations politiques*, I. 207; R. P. C., I. 100.

[73] *Scottish Correspondence*, pp. 263, 321; R. S. S., IV. *passim*.

[74] R. P. C., I. 120; *Treasurer's Accounts*, X. XXXV, 154.   [75] A. P. S., II. 482.

[76] These provisions were made on the same day (4 September 1551) as James Beaton—and not the governor's candidate James Hamilton—was promoted to Glasgow.

to monastic houses, to which apostate monks were to be recalled; the system of oversight was to be intensified by the activity of archdeacons and rural deans.   There were also schemes for the better education of the clergy, and Hamilton completed the organisation of St Mary's College at St Andrews, projected by James Beaton and partly endowed by David Beaton.   Arrangements were made for preaching, and provision was made for the better instruction of the people by the issue of a new Catechism, in the vernacular.   While the council of 1549 denounced those who followed Zwingli in denying a real presence of any kind in the Eucharist, and Adam Wallace, who represented a radical line of reforming thought, was burned in 1550, the Catechism went a long way towards conciliating moderate reformers and was even capable at points of a Zwinglian interpretation, though in the main its doctrine more resembles that of Luther.   It was also noticeable that the Catechism nowhere mentioned the pope. Now, Archbishop Hamilton was legate *a latere*, and his association with his brother, the governor, inevitably recalls the association of the English legate, Wolsey, with Henry VIII; in Scotland, too, the way was being paved for a breach with Rome, and at this point the whole trend of the thought of Scottish churchmen, however conservative their views on other matters, was to ignore papal authority.   Politically viewed, the design was to commend the Hamilton interest to those who had the welfare of the church at heart, but at the same time to draw the teeth of the protestant opposition and also to open the way to a *rapprochement* with England.   The nobles and the less scrupulous clergy, who had everything to gain by the continuance of the old ecclesiastical system, might well have looked askance at a policy of reform had they taken it at face value, but Hamilton was too wary to say anything about endowment and no one can have believed that there was any possibility of real changes in ecclesiastical morals as long as the existing hierarchy remained in office.   That the Hamilton policy attracted some support is suggested by the action of parliament, in May 1552, in ratifying the agreement made in 1544 rescinding the dowager's action for the supersession of Arran,[77] but the obvious weakness was Arran's inability to resist should France choose to exert real pressure.

There was in fact only one obstacle to the formal removal of

[77] *A. P. S.*, II. 489 c. 29.

the governor: although England was weak and France strong, as long as Edward VI lived the possibility could not be ruled out of an appeal to England, based on the Hamiltons' dynastic interest, Scottish irritation against the French, and religion. In 1553 it was actually rumoured that Arran had asked for the assistance of the king of England "on the ground of the new religion."[78] But after Edward VI died (6 July 1553), the new Queen of England, Mary, was the daughter of Catharine of Aragon, and there could be little doubt about the direction of her policy. The possibility was now eliminated of English help for an anti-French party in Scotland, since such a party would necessarily also be anti-papal. The duke could safely be displaced.

His term of office was not due to expire until the Queen of Scots reached her "perfect age," which was understood in Scotland to mean the completion of her twelfth year, at which age a girl was entitled in law to choose her own curators. But in December 1553, when she had only entered her twelfth year, the *parlement* of Paris gave its opinion that she was now of age to dispose of the regency.[79] This decision, however, though it showed the drift of French policy, was not used except possibly as a threat. The less high-handed course was followed of inducing the duke to a voluntary resignation in exchange for financial advantages. Already on 11 December 1553 the bulls providing John Hamilton to Arbroath had been executed (at Paris); on 9 December Archbishop Hamilton had resigned Paisley in favour of his nephew, Claud; on 20 February 1553/4 the dowager pledged herself to secure for the duke a complete discharge for all intromissions since 1543;[80] the archbishop, who had been treasurer since 1543 and whose arrears amounted to over £31,000, was compensated by the assignation to him of the arrears and by a series of gifts, and laid down his office; the question of the marriage of Châtelherault's heir was again taken up and various French ladies of high rank suggested.[81] On 1 March 1553/4 Mary of Guise gave an assurance that Scotland would continue to be governed by its own laws and customs and that if Mary had no children the duke's claim would be supported.[82] At the parliament of April 1554, when the transfer of the regency to Mary of

78 *Cal. S. P. Span.*, XI. 42.
79 Teulet, *Relations politiques*, I. 274-6 (placed in 1552).
80 *Public Affairs*, pp. 629-31.
81 *Balcarres Papers*, II. 247, 256.   82 *Public Affairs*, p. 630.

Guise was effected, the Scottish estates were emphatic that the transaction had taken place " before the queen's perfect age."[83]

Of Châtelherault it was said that by this time " all the lordis of Scotland wer aganis him,"[84] and Knox's comment was that his deposition was "justly by God but most unjustly by men."[85] Contempt for the ex-governor was not a sufficient foundation for the stability of a new administration, but Mary of Guise had skilfully played for support by her policy of conciliating anglophiles and by the distribution of French gold, and, while reformers distrusted Arran and could look for no help from England, the conservatives in both politics and religion were bound to welcome the closer link with France.

[83] *A. P. S.*, ii. 600 ff.
[84] *Diurnal of Occurrents*, p. 51.
[85] Knox, i. 116.

6

THE REVOLUTION AGAINST FRANCE
AND ROME

The Reformation had its antecedents in economic and religious unrest,[1] but when revolution came it was a revolt against France as well as Rome and its course was determined primarily by the political situation. From the assumption of the regency by Mary of Guise in 1554 it was French policy to reconcile the Scots to the rule of their country in the interests of France and to woo them into co-operation in war against England. Conciliation involved a leniency towards the reformers which was congenial enough to Mary of Guise, who was probably by inclination neither a zealot nor a persecutor. Besides, when Mary Tudor ruled in England, the activities of reformers in Scotland did not represent a political danger at home and might stimulate disruptive elements in England itself. It is significant that one of the reformers who preached with impunity in Scotland in 1555 was John Willock, who had been associated in 1554 with a rebellion against Mary which had the countenance of French diplomats. Another of those preachers was William Harlaw, who, like Willock, had been in England under Edward VI. Yet another was John Knox, who, like so many English protestants, had fled to the continent on the accession of Mary Tudor, but now ventured back to Berwick to marry the Englishwoman Marjory Bowes, and, to avoid the perils of England, visited Scotland. There he expounded to John Erskine of Dun and William Maitland of Lethington his view that it was not

1 These are dealt with in Ch. 8.

permissible to attend mass, and he gained the support of Argyll, Lord Lorne (Argyll's son), and Lord James Stewart. No action was taken against Knox, even when he was in Edinburgh, and the burning of his effigy after his departure was a harmless demonstration. If the governor for her part was disposed to leniency, Archbishop Hamilton could not injure the prospects of his family by a display of severity, and the·competitive mildness of the two enabled the reformers to develop their organisation unmolested. Leniency to preachers was only one aspect of the policy of appeasement practised by the regent, who was by this time expert in the " management " of Scotland. With some of the burghs and some of the merchants she established a relationship of understanding on her part, confidence on theirs; protestant and anglophile lairds like Brunstane, Grange and Ormiston were rehabilitated in 1556; Cassillis, who had a record as a friend to England and an acquirer of church property, was chosen to succeed John Hamilton as treasurer. As the years passed, Mary made a special effort to win back peers who were inclined to the reforming side: in November 1557 she secured a bond of manrent from the Earl of Morton; in December she recommended one Campbell for the bishopric of Brechin and another (a natural son of Argyll) for the reversion of the abbey of Coupar;[2] and in 1558 she asked for a pension of £900 from the abbey of Kelso for a son of Glencairn.[3]

On the other hand, specific concessions to individuals or groups were largely nullified because the evidence of French domination was an affront to national sentiment. For example, Huntly, the chancellor, was in effect superseded by the Frenchman De Roubay, as vice-chancellor. The resident French ambassador, D'Oysel, was so prominent and influential that in 1555, and again in 1556, when Edinburgh gave a " propyne " to Mary, he had to have one as well.[4] Villemore, formerly a member of the dowager's household, became comptroller; another Frenchman, Bonot, was bailie of Orkney; and John Roytell, also a Frenchman, was appointed " principal master mason to all her highness's works " in March 1556/7.[5] The presence of French troops as garrisons of Scottish fortresses like Broughty, Dunbar and Inchkeith would

[2] *Highland Papers* (S. H. S.), IV. 211.   [3] Pollen, *Papal Negotiations*, p. 30.
[4] *Edinburgh Burgh Records*, II. 208, 227, 257.
[5] *Master of Works Accounts*, I. xxxiv.

in any event have been unpopular, but delay in paying their wages led to relaxed discipline and abnormal friction with the natives. As early as 1555 there had to be an act against " speaking evil of the queen's grace and of Frenchmen."[6]

Besides, money had to be raised for military operations which Scots could not regard as defensive. From the Hamilton administration Mary of Guise had inherited a deficit of £30,000. She had a long experience of financial difficulties, for payments from France had reached her only irregularly, and she had not been sparing of her own resources, for she had sacrificed plate to pay soldiers; she now gave up her French pension of 20,000 livres to help maintain her daughter's establishment in France (though, even so, another 25,000 livres had to be furnished from Scotland),[7] and she had some supporters who were equally ready to expend their own substance, for the Bishop of Dunblane lent her £4,400 in 1555.[8]   But if means were to be found to pay off the deficit, meet current expenses and provide for the erection of fortifications at Kelso and Eyemouth as well as for the wages of French troops, exceptional measures were necessary.   In January 1555 the council resolved on a " grete extent "[9] of £20,000, specifically to meet the cost of the Kelso fort.   In February Mary approached the pope for a subsidy.   The case was much weaker now than it had been when defence of the faith against Henry VIII had been an appropriate pretext, and the remarkable proposal was made that as the monasteries were over wealthy and of little use the crown should have control over transactions in ecclesiastical property. This did not commend itself to the pope, but he granted a twentieth of ecclesiastical revenues in 1556 and again in 1557. By far the most startling of the financial proposals was a scheme in 1556 for a perpetual tax to be raised on a new assessment: on 2 May the lords of the articles proposed that returns be made to the treasurer not only of the " auld extent " of all lands, but also of the names of all freeholders, feuars, tenants and other parishioners, including craftsmen and cottars, " with the qualities and habilitie of everie manis person and quantitie of thair substance and gudis movable and immovabill."[10]   The nobles, we are told, withstood this, " affirming that they meant not to put their goods in inventory, as if they were to make their last wills

6 A. P. S., II. 499-500.   7 Balcarres Papers, II. xlviii, li-liii.   8 Ibid., xlix.
9 Edinburgh Burgh Records, II. 214-5.   10 A. P. S., II. 604.

and testaments,"[11] and the mere suggestion must have been enough to destroy confidence in a sixteenth-century government. The taxes which were imposed were collected only with " danger, grudge or murmour of the pepill."[12] Yet pressure continued, with a tax of £60,000 for the queen's marriage, another of £48,000 to pay 1,000 men and an assessment on Edinburgh for the fortification of the burgh. A crisis was reached in the autumn of 1557, when an army marched to the Border and the nobles declined to " hazzard batle furth of thair countrey."[13]

Scottish recalcitrance may have prompted the French to hasten the marriage of Mary to the Dauphin Francis and thereby undermine Scotland's independence. At any rate, on 14 December 1557 the Scottish estates acceded to the request of Henry II that commissioners should be sent to France to conclude the marriage agreement. Châtelherault protested that nothing should be done to prejudice his rights,[14] and the commissioners did secure a recognition of the liberties of Scotland and the claims of the Hamiltons. But, by documents signed secretly three weeks before the marriage (which was celebrated on 24 April), Mary bequeathed Scotland to the King of France failing issue of the marriage, put her kingdom in pledge to him for sums spent on its defence and on her education, and annulled any promises which might be made contrary to the first and second undertakings.[15] The belief in France was that the sovereignty of Scotland had, quite simply, been transferred to the French royal house.[16] The deaths of four of the eight Scottish commissioners before they left France raised the suspicion that they had been pressed to make further concessions, and their deaths, if not natural, may possibly indicate that they had learned too much. The surviving commissioners obtained from the Scottish parliament, on 29 November 1558, its consent that the queen might " honour hir spous . . . with the crowne matrimoniale . . . during the mariage, . . . and this crowne to be send with twa or thre of the lordis of hir realme," and the estates also granted a privilege, reciprocal to one already granted by the French king to Scots, whereby French subjects

[11] *Cal. S. P. Scot.*, i. No. 411.
[12] *Scottish Correspondence*, p. 403; cf. *Treasurer's Accounts*, x. 288-9.
[13] Lesley, p. 260-1; Keith, i. 365-6; Knox, i. 125.
[14] *A. P. S.*, ii. 605.
[15] Hay Fleming, *Mary, Queen of Scots*, pp. 22-4.
[16] Teulet, *Relations politiques*, ii. 121-2; cf. J. E. Phillips, *Images of a Queen*, 13-15.

enjoyed the same rights as native Scots.[17]   The conferring of the
" crown matrimonial " was to be without prejudice to Mary's
Scottish heirs, and no crown was ever sent to France, but the
prospect for Scotland was rule by Francis and Mary and their
descendants, under whom Scotland could hardly fail to be
governed as a province of France.

Mary of Guise, in her anxiety to win the Scots to support
the marriage agreement, had continued her policy of conciliation,
and three supporters of the Reformation—Cassillis, Lord James
and Erskine of Dun—had been among the commissioners sent to
France.   It was a complex situation, for some may have reflected
that if Mary married the dauphin and remained in France a
revolution in Scotland would be facilitated by her absence.
Equally, the dowager was still presumably willing to countenance
the activities of reformers for the sake of their possible effect
in England.   Thus, when some protestant lords sent for Knox in
the spring of 1557, they were inviting a representative of the
left wing of English protestantism, whose return to this island
might awaken a movement against Mary Tudor.   Later in the
year the lords seem to have had second thoughts, or perhaps there
were conflicting opinions among them.   At any rate, in the
autumn, when Knox had reached Dieppe, he was told to come no
farther, and a bond on behalf of the Reformation, prepared in
December, seems to have misfired.   This " First Band," drawn
up in the month when commissioners were sent to France to
conclude Mary's marriage contract, pledged the signatories to
work for the recognition of the reformed church.   But, although
it was signed by Argyll, Glencairn, Morton, Lord Lorne and
Erskine of Dun, it failed to attract the support of the many
others for whose signatures ample space was provided.[18]   On
the other hand, about the beginning of 1558 the " lords and
barons professing Christ Jesus " went so far as to draw up definite
proposals for reformed worship and for preaching.[19]   There was
still a strong English flavour about the whole thing, for, although
Knox did not come to Scotland, that other notable Anglo-Scot,
Willock, was again among the preachers active in Scotland, and
it was in faithful imitation of English example that in some of
the eastern burghs, and perhaps elsewhere, regular congregations

---

[17] *A. P. S.*, II. 506-7; Teulet, *Relations politiques*, I. 312-7.
[18] The original is in the National Library of Scotland.   [19] Knox, I. 137-8.

of protestants began to meet for worship, using the Prayer Book
and electing elders and deacons in the same way as the congregations which English refugees had recently founded on the
continent. This might be all very well as viewed, politically, by
the government, but the hierarchy now concluded that the
situation was getting out of hand. Archbishop Hamilton ex-
postulated officially with Argyll for entertaining a preacher, and
it may have been the primate's knowledge that he was being
criticised for being remiss[20] which led him to make an example of
Walter Myln, who was burned in April 1558.[21]

The reformers continued to press the advantage given them
by the wariness which the regent showed as long as negotiations
over the marriage and the crown matrimonial proceeded: in
July 1558 a summons of the preachers was withdrawn after a
vigorous demonstration in their favour by the gentlemen of
" the westland,"[22] and iconoclasm led to the first signs of disaffection in the capital, where the image of St Giles was destroyed
in the summer and a riot broke out when a substitute was carried
in procession on 1 September. In response to petitions for the
authorisation of services in the vernacular and for reform of the
lives of the clergy, Mary of Guise directed Archbishop Hamilton
to summon yet another provincial council, which sat in March
and April 1559. It set itself against drastic changes, though it
did issue a vernacular " godlie exhortation " to communicants
which in its general tenor resembled the exhortations in the
vernacular Order of Communion authorised in England in 1548.
The council also passed another batch of well-intentioned statutes
along the lines of those of 1549 and 1552. The suggestion sometimes made that this legislation, on its third appearance, caused
defection from the church on the part of immoral clergy, and on
the part of laymen who had acquired ecclesiastical property and
feared for its security, is merely comic, for the interests of the
immoral and the greedy alike were the maintenance of the
status quo and not the inauguration of a reformed church which

[20] Knox, II. 248.
[21] This impolitic action by Hamilton (if it was his) is quite out of character, but
the circumstances are obscure. If it is true that Hamilton won the support of the other
prelates to oppose the sending of the crown matrimonial to France, while Mary won
the protestants to support it, the execution was a demonstration of political differences.
But Knox in one place blames the Bishop of Moray for the death of Myln (I. 190).
[22] Knox, I. 126.

would be far more exacting than any archbishop's council. It is true that steps were taken to reinforce the council's legislation by regulations made at diocesan level, but it must have been obvious that bishops who showed no sign of reforming their own lives were no more likely now than they had been earlier to take effective action against delinquent clergy.

This council represents the final instalment of Mary's policy of conciliation, for the international situation had wholly changed. Mary Tudor had died on 17 November 1558 and had been succeeded by her sister Elizabeth. Although the convocation of Canterbury, at the end of February in the next year, was as hostile to drastic changes as the contemporary Scottish provincial council, the English parliament had begun in January to repeal Mary's legislation, and Elizabeth's administration, with William Cecil as secretary, began to take on a protestant complexion. Mary and Francis, on the ground that by canon law Elizabeth was not legitimate, assumed the arms and style of sovereigns of England, and the English, still not resigned to the loss of Calais (7 January 1558), were more apprehensive than ever about Berwick, especially when their ally Spain came to terms with France, first in a truce (October 1558) and then in the Treaty of Cateau-Cambrésis (March and April 1559). England and Scotland were comprehended in the treaty, and no clause bound France and Spain to joint action against the Reformation, but the English feared that their new and untried regime might have to face, in isolation, at least an attack by France, now free from her commitments against Spain.

Mary of Guise had achieved the concession of the crown matrimonial, there was no longer any question of countenancing Scottish protestantism with a view to embarrassing the English government, and France was no longer in any military danger. It was therefore French policy that she should turn against the reformers exactly as Henry II now did in France. Knox says that from Easter 1559 (26 March) she " appeared altogether altered."[23] But the opposition, as well as the government, " altered," in the direction of a new militancy: on 1 January, if not earlier, there had appeared on the doors of Scottish friaries the " Beggars' Summons," warning the friars to quit their houses in favour of the poor and infirm at the next Whitsunday term; in

[23] Knox, I. 159.

January Châtelherault was conferring with Sir Henry Percy on the Borders—the first indication of a revival of a type of Anglo-Scottish understanding which had been in abeyance during Mary Tudor's reign but which would be the obvious retort to the use of Scotland as a base for a papalist attack on England;[24] and such an understanding was unofficially furthered by Maitland of Lethington, in the course of his official duties as secretary in connexion with the Treaty of Cateau-Cambrésis. Contemporaries held that the beginning of the revolution was to be dated on 6 March 1558/9,[25] a date on which nothing of significance is known to have occurred in Scotland but which may have marked the point at which the abstinence from war between England and Scotland became operative.[26]

The series of events within Scotland which comprise the revolution did not, however, begin until May. Knox, in common with the rest of the Marian exiles, had regarded Elizabeth's accession as a signal for his return, but the queen declined to have in her realm the author of *The first blast of the trumpet against the monstrous regiment of women*, especially as Knox was unwilling to countenance Elizabeth unless she would acknowledge that she was queen by a special dispensation of God and not by any law of man. Had he been acceptable in England he might have picked up the threads of his earlier life there and never seen Scotland again. As things were, however, he had to content himself with announcing to Cecil from Dieppe on 10 April that " England, in refusing me, refuseth a friend."[27] He then made for Leith, where he arrived on 2 May, just in time for a crisis which coincided, suitably enough, with the news that Elizabeth had given assent to legislation restoring the English Prayer Book and the royal supremacy over the church (on 8 May). The Beggars' Summons was due to become operative on " flitting Friday " (12 May), and the regent, perhaps to anticipate its fulfilment, prepared for action in Perth and Dundee, which had now publicly embraced the Reformation, and summoned the protestant preachers to compear at Stirling on 10 May. The townsmen of Dundee and the gentlemen of Angus and Mearns prepared to accompany

24 *Cal. S. P. Scot.*, I. No. 441.
25 *E.g.*, *R. P. C.*, I. 162-3. The date at which marriage within the hitherto forbidden degrees became legal was 8 March 1558/9.
26 Cf. Tough, *The Last Years of a frontier*, p. 188.   27 Knox, I. 286-7.

their preachers, and she persuaded Erskine of Dun to " stay "
the company, whereupon the preachers were outlawed for failure
to appear. Knox made first for Dundee and then for Perth, where
a " multitude " of burgesses and lairds was assembled, ready to
defend the preachers. In St John's Church at Perth, on Thursday,
11 May, Knox preached a sermon " vehement against idolatry,"
which led to a riot in which church ornaments and furnishings
were destroyed and the houses of the Black and Grey Friars and the
Carthusian monks were despoiled. The looting continued on
" flitting Friday."[28] Within ten days the town council of Ayr, on
the other side of the country, had stopped the celebration of mass.

The " congregation " in Perth made it clear that they would
fight if the governor persisted in her attempt to suppress the
Reformation, and appealed by letter to " all brethren."[29] Thus,
when the government appointed a muster at Stirling on 24 May,
" the brethren from all quarters "[30] came flocking into Perth, and
Glencairn hastened with a force from the west. An armistice
was made on 29 May on the understanding that the people of
Perth would not be molested and that a French garrison would
not be placed in the town. Argyll and Lord James now committed themselves to join the opposition should the terms of the
appointment be infringed, and when the mass was restored in
Perth and the town garrisoned with Scots soldiers in French pay
they left the regent, along with Ruthven and others of lesser
note—not only lairds from the Lothians, but Campbell of Glenorchy from the Perthshire highlands. Huntly's brother, the bishop
of Galloway, joined the congregation, Huntly himself was wavering, and Patrick Hepburn, Bishop of Moray and commendator
of Scone, presently promised his support. D'Oysel remarked on
14 June, " You cannot tell friend from enemy, and he who is
with us in the morning is on the other side after dinner."[31]

The insurgents mustered at St Andrews, partly to make " reformation " at the ecclesiastical headquarters but partly to await
the English help for which they were urgently asking. The government forces were weaker in numbers and, after moving from
Perth to Falkland and Cupar, were compelled to evacuate Fife
and even Edinburgh and fall back on Dunbar, where they in
turn might await reinforcements from overseas. The insurgents

28 Knox, I. 161 ff.; see also S. H. R., XXXIX. 175-6. 29 Knox, I. 166.
30 Ibid., p. 172. 31 Teulet, Relations politiques, I. 319.

were therefore able to occupy Perth on 25 June and to advance, by Stirling, to Edinburgh, where they arrived at the end of the month. At Perth the mob had got out of hand and sacked the abbey of Scone,[32] and in the course of their march the " congregation " treated the friaries in Stirling, Linlithgow and Edinburgh as they had treated those in Dundee and Perth; parish churches were " purged " of the apparatus of medieval worship and the services of the Prayer Book were introduced. At Edinburgh, the town council, fearing for the safety of the burgh property, hired sixty men to protect the church of St Giles, but their concern was more for the preservation of the fabric than for the retention of the old ceremonial, and John Knox was appointed minister of the capital on 7 July. As the damage and looting took place before the insurgents claimed to be the government of Scotland, the Scots' proceedings were not strictly parallel to the destruction wrought in England, where an act of parliament had authorised the destruction of rood lofts, and Queen Elizabeth's injunctions authorised the abolition of " things savouring of superstition." But in England the pillage went far beyond what was authorised, and it may be doubted whether a " *furor* of vandalism "[33] was avoidable in either country.

The insurgents' success was not lasting, for their volunteers soon drifted away, enabling the standing forces of the dowager to re-occupy Leith. By a truce made on 24 or 25 July, the capital was to choose its own religion and was not to be garrisoned, there was to be an indemnity (pending a parliament in January), and attacks on churches were to cease, while, on the other hand, " idolatry " was not to be restored in places where it had been suppressed. Châtelherault and Huntly promised to leave the regent if she did not observe those terms. The lords of the congregation now dispersed, arranging to reassemble at Stirling on 10 September.

The reformers, however, retained the Edinburgh churches, in which they even celebrated Holy Communion, and they declined to submit to a plebiscite, on grounds which were to have a long

---

[32] Knox had attributed the earlier looting at Perth to " the brethren " in a letter he wrote at the time and to " the rascal multitude " in his *History*, written some time later. But the sack of Scone cost the reformers the support of Commendator Hepburn, and the episode does show that the mob took action which no responsible leader would have countenanced.

[33] Black, *Reign of Elizabeth*, p. 33.   [34] *Edinburgh Burgh Records*, III. 47.

run in Scottish church life: they could not consent that " oure religioun . . . sall be subject to the voiting of men, . . . for . . . the maist pairt of men hes ever bene aganis God and his treuthe."[34] Their lack of confidence in public opinion was not groundless, for on 4 August the town council ordained that payment should be made as usual to the prebendaries of St Giles,[35] and Knox, with his customary prudence, decided that, as Edinburgh was " dangerous," he would hand over his charge there to Willock.[36] The regent arrived at Holyrood and had her mass there, and she soon started to garrison and fortify Leith, a port of which the French had long realised the significance, and which Mary had wooed by promising to erect it as a royal burgh. On 10 July Mary, Queen of Scots, had become Queen of France also, with the death of Henry II and the accession of her husband as Francis II, and this ensured the fuller co-ordination of French and Scottish policy. In August 1,000 French troops arrived, and in September another 800, giving the dowager in all at least 3,000, probably 4,000, trained professional soldiers who were not likely to be overcome by any Scottish force.[37]

The increased threat to the " congregation " stimulated a renewed appeal to England[38] and proposals to depose Mary, who was now unlikely ever to return to Scotland. On 13 August the Scots let Cecil understand that as soon as they had an agreement with England they would depose their queen, and Cecil prepared a memorandum indicating his opinion that God might be " pleased to transfer " from Mary the rule of Scotland " for the weal of it."[39] Cecil, who saw the French hold on Scotland and Mary's claim to England as threats to the English reformation and to Elizabeth's throne, also arranged to confer with Knox. Elizabeth, however, was hard to move: in her own insecure position, she feared that to countenance rebellion in Scotland might encourage trouble at home, and, although she permitted Sadler to go north early in August with £3,000, she thought she could not afford military action. Nor did Knox improve matters by exhorting her to " forget her birth and all title which thereupon doth hang."[40] Negotiations, however, continued, though

35 *Edinburgh Burgh Records*, III. 50.   36 Knox, I. 211.
37 Cf. *Cal. S. P. Scot.*, I. No. 566.
38 19-20 July (*Cal. S. P. Scot.*, I. Nos. 493, 494, 507).
39 *Ibid.*, Nos. 525, 537.   40 *Ibid.*, No. 496.

Elizabeth disclaimed any knowledge of them, and Cecil proposed to overcome his queen's scruples by cultivating Châtelherault, as second person in the realm and heir presumptive. The duke's adherence would make the Scottish rebellion respectable if not legal, and an internal revolution in Scotland would be cheaper than an English expeditionary force. The difficulty, as both Cecil and the lords of the congregation realised, was that Châtelherault could not commit himself as long as his son was in France;[41] but, should that young man return and Mary be superseded, he might marry Elizabeth and ensure the Anglo-Scottish amity on which the security of the English reformation depended. Young Arran, whose prospects of marrying Mary seemed finally closed by her marriage to Francis, had adopted the reformed religion and was now disposed to negotiate with Elizabeth. In May, the appearance of an English resident in Paris, following the conclusion of peace, had opened a means of communication, and through his agency Arran's escape was arranged in June. Henry II, alarmed by an illness of Mary, had sent for Arran, and, finding him already gone, had ordered the Channel ports to be watched. English agents arranged a circuitous journey by way of Geneva and Friesland, and Arran, brought secretly to Cecil's house in London on 28 August, had an interview with Elizabeth, who, characteristically, did not commit herself. From London, Arran proceeded by night and in disguise to Berwick and thence to Hamilton. He was at Stirling on 16 September, in time to join the convention which had met there on the 10th, and the leading lords then conferred at Hamilton with the duke, who had begun to negotiate with them as soon as he had heard that his son was on the move. On 19 September Châtelherault joined the congregation and on the 24th, along with " the remanent of the nobility and council," authorised Maitland to treat with England.[42] The duke had an interview with his brother, the archbishop,[43] who decided to adhere to Mary of Guise, but Gavin Hamilton, coadjutor of St Andrews, followed the duke to the other side,[44] so that the Hamiltons at least ensured their position in the metropolitan see.

The insurgents, mustering in Stirling on 15 October with

---

[41] *Cal. S. P. Scot.*, Nos. 487, 525; p. 79 above.
[42] *Cal. S. P. Scot.*, I. No. 543.   [43] *Scottish Correspondence*, pp. 424, 427.
[44] He signed the treaty of Berwick in the following February.

Châtelherault as their figurehead, marched on Edinburgh and occupied it. They had plenty of arguments to justify a transfer of " the authority." For one thing, they had repeatedly appealed to Mary of Guise to further the reformation, but, as she had failed in what they conceived to be her duty, other constitutional organs must now take her place, because " the reformation of religion . . . doth appertain to more than to the clergy or chief rulers called kings."[45] There was also a political argument, for it was contended that the regent, by restoring the mass in Holyrood and introducing fresh French troops, had violated the agreement made in July, that in her proceedings she had ignored Scottish advice and that in particular she had fortified Leith without consulting the council or nobility. The inference, argued by Knox and Willock, was that the nobility and baronage, as the " born councillors " of the realm, could transfer the sovereignty.[46] And, after an ultimatum demanding that Mary should desist from fortifying Leith, the lords proceeded, on 21 October, to " suspend " her from the regency. The action was taken in the name of the king and queen (though of course without any commission from them) and on the ground of the dowager's acts of oppression, but it was in reality the transfer of power from an " ungodly prince " to what may be called a " godly council "—a " great council of the realm," under the duke's presidency.

This step did nothing to contribute to the success of the revolution. It took time for a provisional government to raise money,[47] and some thousands of pounds[48] on their way from England were intercepted on 31 October by the Earl of Bothwell. The volunteer forces of the insurgents, mutinous for lack of pay, began to " steal away,"[49] and, after an assault on Leith proved a fiasco, the lords had to evacuate Edinburgh (6 November) and retire in disorder to Stirling. In Edinburgh the mass was restored and the church of St Giles re-consecrated. The castle was held, in a kind of neutrality, by Lord Erskine, who had not been active on the reforming side but declined to surrender his charge to the dowager.

The despondent " congregation," at Stirling, heard a sermon from Knox, disdaining reliance on the arm of the flesh, but others

[45] Knox, I. 134; Donaldson, *The Scottish Reformation*, p. 134   [46] Knox, I. 250.
[47] Edinburgh agreed to grant 2000 merks to the lords " for raising of men of war " (*Burgh Records*, III. 58-9).
[48] The amount is uncertain (Teulet, *Relations politiques*, I. 380n).
[49] Knox, I. 264.

saw things differently, for on 8 November Maitland of Lethington, who had openly joined the reformers towards the end of October, was despatched to apprise Elizabeth of the position.[50] This diplomat, who saw the whole situation primarily in political terms, was more likely than Knox to move Elizabeth to open intervention. It was certainly hard to see how the strife could end decisively without intervention from abroad. The lords might muster a force again, and take the initiative, but the French could then simply withdraw to Leith, which was impregnable to native forces, and await the renewed dissolution of their opponents' army.[51] Meantime, although the French could hardly hope to hold all Scotland unless they, on their side, received reinforcements, they continued their offensive: they occupied Stirling at the end of December and caused the lords to withdraw, one section of them to St Andrews and the other to Glasgow. The French forces, based on Leith and holding Inchkeith, were admirably placed not only to await reinforcements, but also to carry on operations in Fife, where they occupied Kinghorn and, though harassed by guerilla tactics, prepared for a further advance. Châtelherault, whose meagre stock of resolution had begun to fail even in November, wrote to France offering to return to his allegiance,[52] and Mary of Guise—so it was said—exclaimed triumphantly, " Where is now John Knox's God? My God is stronger than his, yea, even in Fife."[53] On the morning of 23 January the French were on the march north-east from Dysart, and had crossed the River Leven, when ships appeared in the Firth. They turned out to be not reinforcements from France but an English fleet under Admiral Winter, sent north ostensibly to seek out pirates, actually to cut the communications of the French base with France and with Fife. The French troops had to retire by way of Stirling. This intervention saved the reforming party, but the French had still to be dislodged from Leith.

Provision for the further English help which was so obviously necessary was made by the treaty of Berwick, on 27 February, negotiated by Norfolk, as lieutenant of the north of England,

---

[50] *Cal. S. P. Scot.*, I. No. 589.   [51] Cf. *Ibid.*, No. 619.

[52] Teulet, *op. cit.*, I. 406; cf. II. 143-4. This letter may have been the forgery alluded to in *Cal. S. P. For., 1559-60*, No. 906. Cf. W. L. Mathieson, *Politics and Religion*, i, 60n.

[53] Knox, I. 277. This assertion of Knox is the more improbable in that his name is never mentioned in the volumes of the correspondence of Mary of Guise.

with Scottish commissioners representing the duke and the lords associated with him " for maintenance and defence of the ancient rights and liberties of the country." Nothing was said about religion; England was to intervene only for the preservation of the Scots " in their old freedom and liberties," the treaty was to stand only for the duration of Mary's marriage and a year thereafter, and the duke and his associates were not to withdraw obedience from their lawful sovereigns, provided that the liberties of the subjects were not infringed.[54] English troops under Lord Grey entered Scotland at the end of March and established their headquarters at Restalrig. Although Mary of Guise left Holyrood on 1 April and was received by Lord Erskine into the castle,[55] she had been advised that the invaders could not long maintain themselves and she declined to treat on any terms except the dutiful return of the lords to their obedience.[56] The siege of Leith was therefore pressed, but the French conducted successful sallies and made such a stubborn resistance that the operations were indecisive. It was by no means clear that the fortress would be reduced even by famine, for reinforcements and supplies might yet come from France. However, one French expedition had been dispersed by a storm in January, with the loss of ships and men,[57] and the political and religious opposition to the Guises, culminating in the tumult of Amboise in March, made further French military effort impossible. Instead, two envoys—the bishop of Valence and M. de Randan—had arrived in London, the first of them in April, the second in May, on their way to mediate in Scotland. As they proceeded northwards, Sir William Cecil and Dr Nicholas Wotton were sent to confer with them, first at Newcastle, then at Berwick. While their discussions were going on, the queen regent died (at 1 a.m. on 11 June), and this removed an obstacle to the conclusion of hostilities. The English and French commissioners proceeded to Edinburgh, where they concluded a treaty on 6 July. It was agreed that the English troops and the French troops (save 60 in Inchkeith and 60 in Dunbar) should withdraw from Scotland, and that Mary, by

[54] Knox, I. 304-7.

[55] On the same day the church of St Giles was once more " purged of idolatry " (*Wodrow Soc. Misc.*, I. 83).

[56] Knox, I. 317; *Cal. S. P. Scot.*, I. No. 750.

[57] Teulet, *Relations politiques*, II. 139; *Cal. S. P. Foreign, 1559-60*, No. 575; *Cal. S. P. Spanish, 1558-67*, No. 82.

giving up the use of the English arms, should implicitly recognise Elizabeth's title. Simultaneously with the treaty, certain " Concessions " were granted to the Scots in the name of their king and queen: the sovereigns were to ratify the summons of a parliament, and the estates were to draw up a list of twenty-four names, from which seven or eight were to be chosen by Mary and five or six by the estates, to form a council. On 15 July the English army moved off to Musselburgh, the French troops started to embark, and the dismantling of the fortifications of Leith commenced, to the relief of those who reflected " how hurtfull the fortificatioun of Leith hes bene . . . and how prejudiciall this samyn salbe to the libertie of this haill cuntre in cais strangearis sall at ony tyme heireftir intruse thameselffis thairin."[58]

The part played in the preceding military operations by the Scots themselves had not been glorious, and indeed between Scots and Scots there had been little bloodshed at all. Among them the battle had been fought less by weapons than by propaganda. The insurgents made the most of the danger from France, and already in June 1559 claimed support in the interests of national integrity, threatened by the marriage of Mary and Francis.[59] The arrival of French troops in August, with their wives and families, gave some ground for alleging that Frenchmen were to be planted " in your native rooms," and " the just possessors and ancient inhabitants " to be ejected.[60] At the end of September, Argyll was reported to be spreading the idea that the French " ar cumin in and sutin down in this realm to occupy it and to put furtht the inhabitantis tharoff "; and, it was added, " he makis the exampill of Brytanny," which had been absorbed into France through marriage half a century earlier. By such appeals to patriotic fears as well as to apprehensions about the security of Scottish property, " the myndis of the common pepill " were raised against the regent.[61] In the following month young Arran was appealing to Lord Sempill on the ground that patriotism should outweigh the latter's ecclesiastical conservatism: " albeit peradventur ye be nocht ressolut in your conscience towartis the religioun, yit nevertheles for the commoun wealth and libertie

---

[58] *Edinburgh Burgh Records*, III. 69.
[59] Knox, I. 188.
[60] Knox, I. 216, 224.
[61] *Scottish Correspondence*, p. 427.

of this your native cuntray."[62] Appeal was made for support also on the ground of excessive taxation, the fear of a new assessment on "all your goods, movable and immovable," along the lines of the proposal of 1556,[63] and the debasement of the coinage.[64]

Mary of Guise, on her side, had a distinctly weaker case, but she knew how to appeal to the common people over the heads of the nobility, and she had not lost her tactical skill. She tried to win over the craftsmen of Edinburgh and secure them a vote in burgh elections, though her nominee as provost, Lord Seton, was too unpopular to keep his place. She made personal appeals, to the duke and others, as long as she thought they might avail. But her most effective propaganda line, on Knox's own admission,[65] was the accusation that the reforming party's purpose was to overthrow "the authority" and transfer the crown, for the whole drift of the lords' proceedings seemed to contradict their claim that they contended only for "the evangell" and did not aim at "inobediance of the prynce or usurping of hiear powaris."[66] It may have been partly to counter Mary's allegations, though it was also partly to conciliate Elizabeth, that from the time of the Treaty of Berwick the Scottish insurgents put their emphasis more on religious and less on political objectives. Faced with an attitude which was expressed by the burgh of Aberdeen when it agreed to support "the congregation" only provided that it did not "interpryss ony purpos aganis the authorite,"[67] the lords thought it well to disavow any intention of renouncing their allegiance, and at the end of April and the beginning of May a fresh bond, committing its signatories to the reformation of religion and the end of French domination but proferring future obedience to the lawful sovereigns, was signed by about a dozen peers, some sons of peers, and about thirty lairds.[68] Among the signatories was Huntly, who had still been hesitant at the time of the Treaty of Berwick. To judge from the prolonged resistance which was to be made when the crown was later, in 1567, actually transferred from the lawful sovereign, the assurance given by the insurgents in 1560 may well have been a decisive factor in their

[62] *Scottish Correspondence*, p. 429. The manifesto of the lords of the congregation to the princes of Christendom, composed probably in October 1559, has as its theme the threat to Scottish independence (Teulet, *Relations politiques*, II. 1-14).

[63] Knox, I. 221.   [64] Cf. *A. P. S.*, III. 92.

[65] Knox, I. 237.   [66] *Edinburgh Burgh Records*, III. 46.

[67] *Aberdeen Burgh Records*, I. 322 (11 March 1559/60).   [68] Knox, I. 314-5.

success. The outstanding fact is the novel appeal of both sides to a public opinion. The opposition at this point represented a coalition of men whose personal and dynastic interests were at variance, whose ecclesiastical sympathies ranged widely, and who were held together by political agreement. In this revolution Scotland had found a new political maturity.

In the spring of 1560, when the lords were putting their emphasis on ecclesiastical issues, they had commissioned some ministers to prepare a " Book of Reformation," and this book, which was completed by 20 May, must be presumed to have contained a part, though only a part, of the matter which constitutes the document known as the first Book of Discipline. Moreover, by the end of May it had been decided that a parliament should be proclaimed for July.[69] The parliament, authorised by the " Concessions " granted in July, met in August, to accept a reformed Confession of Faith (17 August), abrogate papal authority and forbid the celebration of mass (24 August). According to the " Concessions," the parliament was to be one at which it was to be lawful " for all those to be present who are in use to be present " and which was not to deal with religion; but it was attended by a large number of lairds or " barons," below the rank of lords of parliament, who were not " in use to be present," and it did deal with religion, in legislation which the queen never ratified. Moreover, the " Book of Reformation " was apparently not considered, and nothing was done either to establish an organisation for the reformed church or to transfer to it the existing ecclesiastical endowments. Whatever the ministers might think, the interest of the dominant faction lay in maintaining the *status quo* so far as the patrimony of the church was concerned.

While the bishops, or some of them, suffered unauthorised expropriation at the hands of certain lords, the social and personal situation was decisive against any action to make them conform or deprive them if they refused. The Archbishop of St Andrews was the duke's half-brother; there was another Hamilton in Argyll; there were close kinsmen of Huntly in Aberdeen and in Galloway; there was a royal Stewart in Caithness and a Hepburn of the line of the Earls of Bothwell in Moray. Such men could not be coerced, especially by a provisional government based on a precarious coalition. The parliament of August 1560 did no

[69] *Cal. S. P. Scot.*, i. No. 799.

more than forbid the bishops to exercise jurisdiction in virtue of authority derived from Rome, and in practice, besides retaining their places in parliament and controlling most of their revenues, they continued to give collation to benefices and to exercise juris-diction in matrimonial causes. Certain of the bishops did volun-tarily join the reformers, but most of them did not. St Andrews, Dunkeld and Dunblane, at whom persuasive efforts were especially directed, admitted the need for reforms and even for doctrinal modifications, but declined to give at any rate an im-mediate assent to the Confession of Faith.

Consequently, apart from the work of three bishops who took it into their own hands to carry through the reform of their dioceses, the reformed church had no regional organisation. In one see only does the experiment seem to have been made of at once appointing a substitute for a recusant bishop: the Arch-bishop of Glasgow had gone off to France, and John Willock, it was reported, became " bishop of Glasgow " in his place.[70] But no more was done at this stage. The congregational organisation which had appeared here and there in the previous two or three years was spreading, kirk sessions were showing signs of assuming some of the functions of the old church courts, and quite a number of ministers and readers were at work, but they had no author-isation save from their flocks, and all that existed as yet was a church which we should now call congregationalist.

The victorious insurgents had little to fear from active opposi-tion within Scotland, but they resolved to secure their gains and anticipate a possible counter-offensive. Therefore, besides sending Lord St John to ask Mary and Francis to ratify the treaty of Edinburgh, they also made a renewed appeal to England.[71] Although the recent emphasis on obedience to the lawful sover-eigns had pushed into the background the idea of transferring the crown to the Hamiltons, and although there was another candidate in the person of Lord James, whom Cecil thought " not unlike either in person or qualities to be a king soon,"[72] Maitland resumed his pressure for the marriage of Elizabeth and Arran.[73] He secured a large measure of unity on this point. Even ecclesi-astical conservatives like the bishops of Dunkeld and Dunblane supported a reaffirmation of the Hamiltons' right of succession

[70] Keith, III. 10.
[72] Cal. S. P. Scot., I. No. 821.
[71] Teulet, Relations politiques, II. 147-50.
[73] Ibid., 871, 874, 877, 908, 926.

and the despatch of an impressive embassy in October, to crave a permanent league with England and to propose Arran for Elizabeth's hand.[74]

The whole situation changed when the death of Francis II, on 5 December 1560, " made great alteration in France, England and Scotland."[75] In France, it brought to an end the power which the house of Guise had exercised through Mary as queen-consort, and since the regency for the new king fell to Catharine de Medici, the queen mother, it seemed likely that Mary, now no more than a widowed queen, would have to fall back on Scotland. In England, Queen Elizabeth, three days after the death of Francis, though apparently in ignorance of that event, rejected the suit of the Earl of Arran.[76] In Scotland, the news of Elizabeth's decision, brought when the ambassadors returned from England at the beginning of January, caused " many to enter on new discourses,"[77] but some did not even wait for the disclosure of this news: as soon as Knox received private intelligence that the illness of Francis was mortal, he set off to confer with Châtelherault, and it was in accordance with their consultations that young Arran himself, " not altogether without hope that the queen of Scotland bore him some favour, . . . wrote unto her, and sent for credit a ring which the queen our sovereign knew well enough."[78] Elizabeth and Knox, for once in agreement, visualised Mary, returning to Scotland and married to Arran, as committed to the reformed cause.

But the possibility had also to be faced that the queen's return might mean the overthrow of the Reformation, and the reforming party had to try to strengthen the *de facto* position of their church. Discussion of the " Book of Reformation " may have gone on, if only informally, since the parliament, but the crisis of December accelerated matters. A convention of the nobility was summoned for January, but on 20 December a convention of representatives of some of the reformed congregations met and probably remitted the revision and expansion of the book to committees, whose work was approved, without careful co-ordination, when the ecclesiastical convention reassembled, after an adjournment, on 15 January. In the Book

[74] *A. P. S.*, II. 605; Keith, II. 6-7n.   [75] Knox, I. 350.

[76] *Cal. S. P. Scot.*, I. No. 927; cf. Henderson, *Mary, Queen of Scots*, I. 144.

[77] *Cal. S. P. Scot.*, I, No. 948.   [78] Knox, I. 351; cf. *Cal. S. P. Scot.*, I. No. 945.

of Discipline, as it had now taken shape, the monastic temporalities were not mentioned, but practically all other revenues were claimed for a system based on the needs of the parishes. The funds derived from the parishes were to be used in the parishes, where a competent ministry was to be maintained on comfortable stipends, the churches kept in repair, the poor cared for, and the children educated. The lands which had previously belonged to bishoprics and cathedrals were earmarked to support the universities, where the ministers would be trained, and to pay superintendents, whose task it would be to supervise the work of the ministers. The compilers of this programme ignored all competitors except the holders of monastic lands and disregarded the fact that a large proportion of other church property was also gone beyond hope of recovery. The convention of nobility and lairds, to which these proposals were submitted in January, declined to approve of schemes which threatened their own hold on ecclesiastical wealth and which would have reduced to pauperism their numerous kinsmen who held benefices. On 27 January a considerable number of nobles and lairds did subscribe the book, but only on condition that clergy of all ranks who supported the reformation should enjoy their livings for life, provided that they contributed to the support of ministers.[79]

This approval of the Book of Discipline, though qualified in respect of finance, did give the reformed church the authorisation it craved, and made it possible to set up something more than a congregational organisation: the machinery provided in the book was operated in March and April to install superintendents in Lothian and Fife, and other appointments were made later. The superintendents acted " in the name of God and of the secret council, our present and lawful magistrates," under mandate from the lords of council who had issued licences for their election. A little earlier, it had been " the commissioners of burghs, and some of the nobility and barons " who had appointed and allocated ministers.[80] This practice was in accordance with the Confession of Faith, which had acknowledged that the " conservation " as well as the " purgation " of religion pertained to kings, rulers and magistrates. Besides, the Book of Discipline had been a report to the great council of the realm which had commissioned its compilation, and it was therefore

[79] Knox, I. 344-5, II. 324. [80] Donaldson, *The Scottish Reformation*, pp. 134, 136-7.

logical that the affairs of the reformed church should be directed by the " godly ·magistrates " in the shape of the council.   The Book of Discipline had indeed spoken, in wonderfully vague terms, of a " council of the church," apparently subordinate to the prince or council of the realm, and such an ecclesiastical council may be represented by a body which met in December 1560 and again in May 1561, in each case in association with a convention of the nobility.   But it is not clear whether anything was done to give the reformed church a central authority, independent of the state, which would operate should the rule of a " godly " council be replaced by the rule of an " ungodly " princess.

7

THE PERSONAL REIGN OF MARY

It was a divided nation, with diverse hopes and fears, which awaited the return of its queen. Militant opposition to the revolution had been negligible in 1560, but the successful coalition was now disintegrating. There were those, like Huntly, whose ecclesiastical preferences had been conservative and who were ready to accept Mary unconditionally now that she had ceased to be Queen of France and to represent French domination. Among those who were unwavering in their attachment to the Reformation, extremists favoured the policy of coercing Mary into marriage with Arran and membership of the reformed church, but others thought such a policy an infringement of her sovereign rights and were ready to give their obedience provided that Mary came without foreign help and did not take positive action to reverse the ecclesiastical change. The moderate policy was defined by Maitland, who saw the whole situation primarily in the context of Anglo-Scottish relations: in his view the concomitant of tactful handling of Mary in Scotland must be the " allurement " of her into friendship with England through her recognition as heir to Elizabeth in return for renunciation of her claim during Elizabeth's life.[1] At the convention which met in January 1560/1, the division of opinion was clear, but Lord James, who was commissioned to go to France and prepare Mary for her return, rejected extremist counsels:

> He was plainly premonished, that if ever he condescended that she should have mass publicly or privately within the realm of

---

[1] *Cal. S. P. Scot.*, 1. Nos. 963, 966.

> Scotland, then he betrayed the cause of God. . . . That she should
> have mass publicly, he affirmed he should never consent; but to
> have it secretly in her chamber, who could stop her?[2]

Lord James did not leave until 18 March, and he was back in Edinburgh on 29 May, in time to report to another convention. In the meantime, ambassadors had come from France to urge the renewal of the old league, but the convention declined to renew it, and, taking up a supplication from the reformed church, agreed on proceedings for the suppression of " idolatry."

If Mary received a suggestion that on leaving France she should make for Aberdeen and join forces with Huntly, she rejected it; inevitably she wanted to avoid falling into the clutches of Arran's faction, which represented constraint in both matrimony and religion; and her choice was to rely on the middle party of the Lord James and Lethington. She applied to Elizabeth for permission to travel through England, but Elizabeth had no desire to admit to her realm a rival who in June had declined to ratify the Treaty of Edinburgh and thereby lay aside her claim to England, nor had she any desire to hasten a journey which might revive an anti-English faction in Scotland; the safe-conduct therefore reached France only after Mary had left to make the journey by sea. English ships were sent out, not with a view to challenging a French fleet or capturing Mary, but perhaps to prevent a landing in the north of England and perhaps to try to force Mary to take the west-coast route to Dumbarton and the Hamiltons, with whom Elizabeth was in close touch.[3] Mary left Calais on 14 August, and the oarsmen of her two galleys made a swift passage through fogs to reach Leith, on 19 August, a week before she was expected.

There was no question of attempting an ecclesiastical reaction, for the great majority of Mary's privy council were of " the congregation," prelates were excluded and although Huntly was a member, not even he could be reckoned an unequivocal papalist.[4] A few days after the queen's arrival a proclamation was issued forbidding meantime any " alteration or innovation of the state of religion . . . which her majesty found public and universally

---

2 Knox, I. 354-5, cf. II. 5. Knox wrote some years later, but events demonstrate that there was disagreement on the subject of the queen's mass.

3 *Cal. S. P. Foreign*, VI. No. 337n; *Cal. S. P. Scot.*, I. No. 992.

4 *R. P. C.*, I. 157-8, XIV. 16-7; cf. Knox, II. 20.

standing at her majesty's arrival in this her realm."[5]   It may
not have escaped notice that one of Elizabeth's first public acts
had been a somewhat similar proclamation,[6] and there was plenty
of ground for optimism among the reformers.   On the other
hand, Mary's proclamation did insist on the safety of her French
servants and companions, and on the first Sunday after her
arrival mass had been celebrated in her chapel.   When certain
of the zealous clamoured that " the idolater priest should die
the death,"[7] the Lord James kept the door and two of his brothers,
also communicants of the reformed church, protected the priest.

Arran, the lay leader of the extremists, made a public protest
against the queen's proclamation, and refused to come near the
court as long as Mary had her mass.   His ambition to marry the
queen had become an obsession, and hopes repeatedly deferred
led to mental instability.   He engaged with the Earl of Bothwell
in a plot to seize the queen's person and overthrow Lethington
and Lord James, but, while the plot led to Bothwell's imprisonment and exile, Arran's insanity became so obvious that from
1562 until his death in 1609 he was in confinement.   Thus
Châtelherault, head of the house of Hamilton, had in the end
" not only lost his game, but lost it in a manner pitiable almost
beyond words."[8]   The extremists, however, had an abler man
than any Hamilton in their clerical leader, Knox.   A sermon
against the queen's mass led to his first interview with Mary,
when—according to his own account—he enlarged on the right of
subjects to resist.   His mind seems to have been made up from
the outset that there could be no co-operation with the queen;
he was even to decline to pray that God would enlighten her,
except with the qualifying phrase " if Thy good pleasure be,"
because, as he explained, he had learned to pray only in faith,
and he had made up his mind that Mary's heart was " indurate
against God and His truth."[9]   It was caustically observed in
1563 that Knox was as full of distrust of the queen as if he were
" of God's privy council " and knew her destiny.[10]

Knox was not without popular support, and he was a master
at stirring violent passions: the town council of Edinburgh
issued a proclamation which classed mass-mongers with whore-

[5] *R. P. C.*, I. 266-7.   [6] Strype, *Annals*, I (2). 391.
[7] Knox, II. 8.   [8] Henderson, *op. cit.*, I. 231.
[9] Knox, II. 20, 112.   [10] *Cal. S. P. Scot.*, I. 672-3.

mongers, and when Mary went on progress there were local disturbances because of her mass. But Knox did not speak for all. Many thought his sermon against the queen's mass untimely, and, especially as a sovereign's court at Holyrood was a novelty to all men under middle age, Mary had ample opportunity to win sympathy and support.[11] There were, too, repeated arguments between Knox and milder men who were not convinced that it was permissible to use force to deprive the queen of her mass or even to resist an " ungodly prince " at all. The breach between Knox and Lord James, with whom he ceased to be on speaking terms in 1563, was notorious, and reformers who sat on the council thought that the preacher went too far when, in December 1563, he convoked the lieges in support of men accused of breaking into Holyroodhouse when mass was said in the queen's absence. In Knox's view, the " servants of God " were fighting a " double battle," against " the idolatry and the rest of the abominations maintained by the queen " and also " against the unthankfulness of such as sometime would have been esteemed the chief pillars of the kirk."[12] But there were " servants of God," like Superintendents Winram, Willock and Spottiswoode and John Douglas, rector of St Andrews University, who had come under Lutheran or Anglican influence and had never been near Geneva. There was no need for Mary or anyone else to split the reformers, for there were all along differences of emphasis, which emerged not only in their attitude to the queen but also in liturgical matters and in an issue like the propriety of anointing a sovereign at his coronation.[13]

Mary could not come to terms with Knox, but neither could Elizabeth, and any assessment of Mary's policy must largely discount Knox's abuse. Nor should too much significance be attached either to the fair words with which she periodically reassured the pope or to her occasional intervention to check some individual instance of the persecution of a Roman catholic. The main lines of her policy suggest an opportunism and self-interest which dictated that she should endeavour to make herself acceptable to both parties in Scotland, to both parties in England, and to continental princes. While she kept her own mass, she frequently issued or reaffirmed a proclamation[14] in virtue of which

11 Knox, II. 23-4.
13 P. 131 below.
12 *Ibid.*, II. 105.
14 *R. P. C.*, I. 208-9, 267, 268, 355-6.

several priests were prosecuted for saying mass. She also acknowledged that if her recognition of the reformed church meant
anything some financial provision must be made for the ministers.
The initiative in this matter seems to have come from the lairds,
stimulated by the preachers, but all could see that some action
must be taken if the property of the church was not to be wholly
appropriated by enterprising laymen. After some weeks of
negotiations, it was ordained in February 1562 that, while in
general two-thirds of their revenues were to remain with the
existing holders of benefices for their lifetimes, the other third was
to be collected by the government and divided between it and the
reformed church; certain classes of revenues were to be wholly
devoted to hospitals and schools. Apart from the fact that a good
many thirds were " remitted " on various grounds, the principal
weakness of the scheme was that the share of the reformed church
was not defined and that year by year the crown's share tended
to increase, but the plan was not unstatesmanlike in its attempt
to reconcile conflicting interests. Besides, the crown's financial
interest in the thirds was a disincentive to a conservative reaction,
and had such a reaction come it could have come, as in England
under Mary Tudor, only with reservations in respect of church
property.

It tells equally against Mary's devotion to the church of
her fathers that in 1562 she took part in a campaign which led
to the defeat and death of Huntly and the weakening of the conservative cause in one of its centres. Religion, it is true, was not
the issue on which the strife arose, though Huntly may have
disapproved of the queen's concessions to the reformed church as
well as of the anglophile policy of Lord James and Maitland.
The real source of Huntly's resentment was more probably a
grudge against Lord James, for Huntly had been administering
the earldoms of Mar and Moray, and gifts of them in favour
of Lord James were drawn up at the beginning of 1562 (though
the grant of Moray was not made public until September).
Besides, Sir John Gordon, Huntly's third son, had designs on
Mary, and was even believed to have contemplated seizing her
person. When Mary set out on a northern progress in August
1562, she was apparently resolved to take action against Sir
John for an assault on Lord Ogilvie and for the acquisition by
doubtful means of certain lands which should have been inherited

by Ogilvie of Cardell. When she reached Inverness, the captain of the castle, on the orders of Lord Gordon, Huntly's heir, refused her admission, and was punished by death. Huntly assembled his forces, but did not contest Mary's passage back to Aberdeen. Then, put to the horn for refusing to appear before the privy council, Huntly marched on Aberdeen but was defeated at Corrichie (28 October 1562) and died suddenly after his capture. Lord Gordon, Sir John Gordon and the Earl of Sutherland (Huntly's cousin) were condemned to death and Sir John was executed. Huntly was forfeited posthumously by parliament on 28 May 1563. The whole affair had represented no movement of disaffection, for although Huntly had tried to rally Châtelherault (to whose daughter Lord Gordon was married), no peer had sided, at least openly, with the Gordons.[15]

In 1563 Mary went still farther in her policy of appeasing the reformers. When parliament met, statutory recognition for the reformed church was implied in acts providing that ministers should have the use of manses and glebes and that churches should be repaired. In the same year, there were several prosecutions for saying mass, and Archbishop Hamilton was imprisoned for a time. Moreover, the queen had given little encouragement to the Jesuit de Gouda, who came to Scotland in 1562, and, although the Archbishop of Glasgow and the Bishop of Ross were on the continent in 1563, Mary did not arrange for Scottish representation at the final session of the Council of Trent, when Romanism and protestantism were finally divided by rigid boundaries. The drift of Mary's policy was disappointing to militant papalists, and some zealous protestants alleged that she was in truth ill-pleased at Huntly's overthrow, but a good impression was made on those whose minds were not closed. Cecil shrewdly observed in 1562 that Mary was " no more devout towards Rome than for the contentation of her uncles,"[16] but even that was not the whole story, for in the France from which Mary had come there was a good deal of non-papal catholicism, and one of her uncles—the Cardinal of Lorraine—was in favour of Communion in both kinds and the authorisation of the Bible and service-books

15 The army which defeated Huntly was led by the new Earl of Moray, who prudently obtained a commission which absolved him from any charge of levying war on his own behalf (*R. P. C.*, I. 222-3).

16 *Cal. S. P. Foreign, 1562*, p. 82.

in the vernacular. A year or two later Mary's policy was to change for a time, but only for personal and political reasons, and towards the end of her reign she again showed herself ready enough to conciliate the reformers. It was no devout Roman catholic who handed over precious church vestments to her lover Bothwell and who married that same Bothwell by reformed rites. Mary was ultimately to lose her throne not because of her fidelity to Rome but because she entered into a scandalous marriage, and when, on the most dismal day of her life, she was insulted by the women of her capital, it was not " Burn the papist " that they shouted, but " Burn the whore."

Mary's equivocal policy was a conspicuous political success, for she was able to engineer a unity among the Scottish magnates which had hardly been paralleled since 1513. Yet a queen who went to mass could not be supreme governor of the reformed church. The " general assemblies " which met to direct its affairs before her return seem to have been purely ecclesiastical conventions, though each of them was closely associated with a civil convention meeting at the same time. But, when there was no longer any guarantee that civil conventions would be dominated by the " godly," a different pattern had to be followed, and an organ of ecclesiastical government was devised which was in effect a full convention of estates with both the spiritual and temporal elements in one house. The normal general assembly of the 1560s, therefore, was composed of, first, the " godly baronage," including both peers and " commissioners of shires "; second, commissioners of burghs, chosen by town councils; and, third, the superintendents, commissioners [17] and bishops, with ministers whom they selected. It thus represented the control of the entire community over the church, exactly as the three estates, assembled in parliament, might have done. It met in the tolbooth of Edinburgh like a parliament, and sometimes co-operated with the privy council, but its legal position was indeterminate, if not precarious.

It has been said that, to Mary, Scotland was nothing more than an " interlude between the France of her memories and the England of her dreams." [18] But in the earlier years after her return the interlude was one which permitted the " joyousity " to which she had been accustomed in France, though some of

[17] See p. 141 below.   [18] S. T. Bindoff, *Tudor England*, p. 206.

her subjects thought it verged on indecorum. Running at the ring, shooting at the butts, hawking, hunting and golf were recreations which this tall, athletic young woman took part in or saw as a spectator; indoors she had needlework, music, dancing, cards and dice; she enjoyed masques; and after dinner she would read some Livy in company with George Buchanan. Buchanan, who had a culture derived from a long exile, mainly in France, partly in Portugal, was congenial to the queen, and, although he had earlier been suspected of " heresy " and later presided over a general assembly, he was in truth a humanist rather than a Christian.

Yet the dreams were all the time of England and of matrimony, and the success of the policy of Moray and Maitland demanded the co-operation of Elizabeth and Mary's recognition as heir to England. Besides, Mary's prospects in England would react on the situation at home, for if she would not renounce her mass for Scotland she might do so if she became convinced that it would improve her prospects in England.

Within a fortnight of Mary's arrival, in 1561, Lethington had been sent to England, *inter alia* to negotiate about the succession. Elizabeth expressed her unwillingness to name her successor, and in her turn demanded the ratification of the Treaty of Edinburgh, which, as it committed Mary to abstain " henceforth " from styling herself Queen of England, might be held to mean renunciation of Mary's right to the English crown for all time. Mary's answer suggested that a ratification might be forthcoming in return for a promise of the English succession, and she said so more explicitly in January 1562, when she suggested a personal meeting with Elizabeth. Arrangements were made for a meeting, at Nottingham on 3 September 1562, but Elizabeth intimated in July that she could not associate with a daughter of the house of Guise at a time when persecution of the Huguenots had been resumed in France, following the return of the duke of Guise to power in the spring. In September, instead of meeting Mary, Elizabeth made a treaty with the Huguenots.

Statesmanship might well have reconciled the interests of the two queens, which were not necessarily divergent, but it could hardly have reconciled the attitudes of the two women. Elizabeth, with all her occasional brilliance in tactics, had no notion of long-term strategy except to let events take their course, and she could never bring herself to face the fact that she must some day have a successor. Her only interest in the Scottish claim was its potential value as a lever with which to influence Scottish policy, and it was nothing to her that her death might be followed by a war of succession. The attitudes of the two women to matrimony were also divergent. It was probably repugnant to Elizabeth that Mary should find a husband while she herself, nine years Mary's senior, remained unmarried; but the longer she remained unmarried, the more likely it became that Mary would succeed her and the more urgent that Mary should herself marry and have issue to carry on the succession.

The marriage of a queen regnant posed serious problems, for the consort of a queen normally became king. Thus the choice of a foreign husband raised complications with which England and Scotland alike had recently been familiar, and it was no easier to marry a subject and raise him to sovereignty. Mary had many continental suitors—her brother-in-law the King of France, the King of Sweden, the King of Denmark, the Archdukes Charles and Ferdinand (sons of the Emperor Charles V), the Duke of Ferrara and the Duke of Nemours—but the most serious negotiations were those with Don Carlos, the son and heir of Philip II of Spain. There was nothing fanciful about such a proposal, for after all Mary had been the wife of the King of France and Mary Tudor had been the wife of the King of Spain. But the considerations involved were complex. Moray and Maitland approved of negotiations which, by threatening England with the Spaniard on her northern frontier, might end Elizabeth's procrastination, and in June 1563 Elizabeth was stimulated into telling Lethington that if Mary married Don Carlos she would be her enemy, whereas if she married to please her she would be made heir to the English throne. Certainly if the primary consideration was the acknowledgment of Mary's right to succeed in England, she could hardly afford to marry without Elizabeth's approval. But, on the other hand, marriage to Don Carlos did offer the chance of gaining the English throne, with Spanish and papal help, without waiting for Elizabeth's death in the course of nature, and to that extent was more attractive than the policy of conciliating Elizabeth and the reformers. The negotiations with Spain went on until April 1564, when

Philip closed them because the insanity of his son could no longer be concealed, but the marriage had ceased to be practical politics before the end of 1563.

The Scots were entitled to ask whether Elizabeth could be other than obstructive and whether she would herself choose a husband for their queen. If Elizabeth cared at all for the future welfare of England, she had an interest in the choice of Mary's consort, who might be the father of her own successors. But Elizabeth's suggestion, mentioned in general terms in March 1563 and taking definite form a year later, was the barely credible one that Mary should marry Robert Dudley (created Earl of Leicester in September 1564), the man whose relations with Elizabeth, before and after the suspicious death of his wife, had come near to the degree of scandal later associated with Mary and Bothwell. It is hard to believe that even Elizabeth was vain enough to think that Dudley would be acceptable, or that she ever wanted to relinquish her favourite to Mary, and easier to believe that her aim was to drive Mary to some incautious or reckless course. Yet Mary and her advisers were prepared to consider even this match if it brought a guarantee of the English succession, and negotiations went on until the beginning of 1565.

But supposing that Mary were to abandon continental prospects and "let fall her anchor between Dover and Berwick,"[19] there was another possible suitor—Henry Stewart, Lord Darnley, grandson of Margaret Tudor and son of Matthew, Earl of Lennox, who had been forfeited in 1544 for his treasonable association with Henry VIII and had now been in England for twenty years. Darnley stood next to Mary in succession to the English throne, and some thought that his English birth and upbringing made his claim stronger than Mary's. He had been spoken of more than once before as a possible husband for Mary, and it was not difficult to see the implications of Lennox's return to Scotland in September 1564 and his rehabilitation by parliament in December. Little time elapsed before a request was made that Darnley should follow his father, and when he arrived in Scotland at the beginning of 1565 Mary took an immediate liking to him, as "the lustiest and best proportionit lang man that sche had seen."[20] And Elizabeth, with what in anyone else would be

---

19 *Cal. S. P. Scot.*, ii. No. 71.
20 Sir James Melville, *Memoirs*, p. 134.

regarded as ineptitude, chose this moment to intimate that she would not proceed to make any declaration about the succession until she herself had either married or had announced her intention never to marry. This made it plain that Mary had nothing to gain from trying to please Elizabeth, and was tantamount to an invitation to Mary to go her own way. It was contrary to Elizabeth's interest to permit the combination of two claims to the English succession, and it is not the least of the riddles of the period why she let Darnley go to Scotland, even though she may have calculated that, as his mother was in England and his family had property there, she still had a hold over him. It was characteristic of her that, after giving Lennox permission to go, she tried to withdraw it at the last minute and that, after the damage was done which her own action had made possible, she intimated her disapproval of Mary's marriage to Darnley and sent Lady Lennox to the Tower. From the English point of view, however, Darnley was preferable to a continental Roman catholic, and Elizabeth may have known enough of his character to be aware that the marriage would bring Mary no lasting happiness.

Mary, professing her willingness to defend " the Catholic religion,"[21] applied to the pope for the requisite dispensation, and the marriage (on 29 July 1565) was by Roman catholic rites, but it was celebrated before any dispensation had arrived. Darnley was thought by some to be " indifferent " in religion. His mother, who seems to have had that warm attachment to Rome which was characteristic of more women than men in both this century and the next, had done her best to make her son acceptable to English Roman catholics and had even at one point brought her husband as well as herself under suspicion for trafficking with papists. But Lennox himself had been Henry VIII's agent against the French and papalist faction in Scotland in the 1540s, he was later to become one of the protestant regents in the minority of James VI, and his brother, the Bishop of Caithness, was a faithful adherent of the reformation. Darnley had professed the reformed religion in England, at his marriage he did not attend the nuptial mass, he had no scruples about sitting under John Knox in the church of St Giles, and the last recorded act of his life was to sing a metrical psalm from the

21 Robertson, *Statuta*, clxix.

" psalm book " in which the metrical psalms were bound with the reformers' Book of Common Order.[22]

In any event, Mary was ready to make concessions to the reformers to win approval of a match on which she had set her heart. She professed to be ready to hear conference and disputation on the scriptures and even to attend public preaching, she was present at a baptism according to the reformed rite, she issued a proclamation assuring the reformed church that its members would not be "inquietit" for religion,[23] and she later reissued her original proclamation forbidding alteration in the state of religion. The Darnley marriage, therefore, did not of itself injure Mary's prospects with either ecclesiastical party, whether in Scotland, England or the continent, or necessitate any departure from the ecclesiastical policy which she had pursued since 1561. But it was the ruin of the other branch of the Moray-Maitland programme, for it meant the end of the possibility of an understanding with Elizabeth. It also meant the loss by Moray of the influence which he had wielded and of the position to which he had raised himself while Arran, Bothwell and Huntly had successively been eliminated from political power. Policy apart, Moray could expect support from other noble families, especially the Hamiltons, who resented the elevation of the heir of the house of Lennox.

In March Moray had made a bond with Argyll and Châtelherault, in May he left the council, and in July he and his associates asked Elizabeth for support, which she promised. Open rebellion started in August, after the conspirators had been put to the horn for failing to answer repeated summonses. It was easy to appeal to protestant suspicions, whether they had any foundation or not, and it was reasonable to oppose the breach with Elizabeth and the elevation of Darnley to the kingship without parliamentary sanction. Yet what Moray hoped to achieve by rebellion is far from clear, unless he aimed at another revolution which, with English help, would satisfy his ambitions by at least putting Mary under his tutelage. But Moray completely failed to re-create the favourable circumstances of 1559/60. He now had the support of only some of the former lords of the

---

[22] Henderson, *op. cit.*, II. 657; according to a report in Teulet, *Relations politiques*, II. 259, Darnley " avoit tousjours monstré estre protestant " until he started to attend mass at Christmas 1565.   [23] *R. P. C.*, I. 338 (12 July 1565).

congregation, and he had to deal not with a middle-aged dowager and foreign troops but with a young queen, of personal charm and considerable political intelligence, who relied on the loyalty of native Scots. Mary, besides reassuring the reformed church and thereby weaning many protestants, like Morton, Cassillis, Lindsay and Ruthven, from Moray's side, also appealed to Moray's rivals: the heir of Huntly was released from custody on 3 August and soon restored to his titles and estates; Bothwell, recalled in July, was back in Scotland in September and on the council in October, although, like many other supporters of the queen, "he went not to mass."[24] Mary also showed spirit and resolution in the conduct of the campaign. While the malcontents gathered at Ayr, she ordered a muster (22 August) and pledged her jewels to pay soldiers. On 26 August she left Edinburgh for the west, and although the rebels evaded her and entered Edinburgh on 31 August, they met with such a cool reception that they withdrew on 2 September, and on 5 September were in Dumfries. Mary had meanwhile returned to Edinburgh to raise a larger force, but it proved to be unnecessary. The English help for which the rebels waited was refused on 24 September, and on 6 October Moray crossed the Border, to learn that although Elizabeth had given him asylum she had no welcome for unsuccessful revolutionaries.

This misjudged effort, called the Chaseabout Raid, was highly damaging to the cause which it had been intended to serve. As Elizabeth was now the declared enemy of the Scottish regime and as Mary's assurances to the reformed church had not averted rebellion, neither anglophiles nor protestants could expect to be countenanced. Archbishop Hamilton was liberated and the administration of the thirds was taken out of the hands of Wishart of Pittarro, an "earnest professor," and committed to Murray of Tullibardine, who was more complaisant to the demands of the crown.[25] The challenge from the protestant lords provoked Mary into asking aid, on religious grounds, from

[24] Knox, II. 174. It should be remembered that Darnley, a Lennox Stewart on his father's side, was an Angus Douglas on his mother's. In May 1565 his mother renounced her claims to the earldom of Angus (*H. M. C. Report* III. 394; cf. *Cal. S.P. Scot.* IX. 522)—a gesture to reassure Morton, who, as tutor to the young Earl of Angus, was temporarily head of the house. It was because of this renunciation that James VI's claim to be heir general of the Earls of Angus was dismissed.

[25] *Accounts of the collector of thirds* (S. H. S.), xxvi-xxvii.

Philip of Spain, and the Bishop of Dunblane went to Rome to ask for men and money on her behalf, while she, on her side, professed an intention to do something in parliament for " the auld religion."[26] It is true that Mary benefited no more from her appeals abroad than Moray did from his, but protestants who had been loyal to her in the crisis were now alienated.

One of the grievances mentioned by Moray and his party had been Mary's " leaving the wholesome advice and counsel " of her nobles and barons, and following instead that " of such men, strangers, as have neither judgment nor experience of the ancient laws and governance of this realm " and were " of base degree, and seeking nothing but their own commodities."[27] It was now true that almost the only peers about the queen were Huntly, Bothwell, Atholl and Lennox, while there was much activity on the part of foreigners and others who were not of noble birth—David Riccio, Francisco de Busso, Sebastian Danelourt, an Englishman called Fowler, and the Scottish lawyer James Balfour, parson of Flisk[28]—and it had not been forgotten that the " Concessions " of 1560 forbade the appointment of foreigners to offices.[29] This development would of itself have gone a long way to bring disaster, but it was accompanied by differences between the king and the queen. Darnley, only nineteen years of age, was both morally and intellectually worthless, and it did not take Mary long to see that he was unfit for a real share in power or for the grant of the crown matrimonial, which would have given sovereignty to him and his heirs should Mary predecease him. Thus both the Scots lords and the king consort felt that they were being neglected; and they both felt that they were being supplanted by the same individual—David Riccio.

Riccio had arrived in Scotland in 1561, in the train of the ambassador from Savoy, and his musical accomplishments won Mary's favour. While he never became secretary of state, he was a secretary on Mary's French establishment,[30] he was said to have much influence and to be haughty towards the nobles. The protestant suspicion that he was a papalist agent is not supported

26 Keith, II. 412-3.   27 Calderwood, II. 572-3.
28 Cf. Teulet, *Relations politiques*, II. 232-3.
29 P. 100 above; cf. *R. S. S.*, VI. 13.
30 *Cal. S. P. Scot.*, II. No. 153, cf. 124; Teulet, *op. cit.*, II. 266-7, 272. The idea that Morton was dispossessed of the seal and that it was intended to confer it on Riccio seems to be unfounded.

by the evidence, and the other suspicion, that there was a scandalous relationship between him and the queen and that it was of his child that Mary became pregnant in the autumn of 1565, is barely credible, though several contemporaries and near-contemporaries professed to believe it. The removal of the Italian was, however, an objective on which a coalition could be engineered between Darnley and those who represented aristocratic, religious and political disaffection. But there were other elements in the bargaining which led to Riccio's murder. Of the persons involved in the Chaseabout Raid, large numbers of lesser men had received remissions, and Châtelherault had been pardoned on condition that he would go into exile for five years, but Moray, Argyll, Glencairn, Rothes, Ochiltree, Boyd, Kirkcaldy of Grange and others were summoned to stand trial by parliament on 12 March 1566. In association with other protestant lords, like Morton, who had not joined them in their rebellion but had been alienated by Mary's proceedings since, they offered to support Darnley's claim to the crown matrimonial on condition that he would prevent action against them[31]—a striking commentary of their lack of principle, for Darnley was the man whose elevation to kingship had led to their rebellion. The actual attack on Riccio, carried out on 9 March 1566 in Mary's presence with needless brutality, was designed to endanger the lives of the queen and her unborn child: it had been reported on 13 February that something was intended against Mary as well as Riccio, and after the crime it was rumoured on the continent that Darnley had murdered his wife.[32] Morton, Lindsay and Ruthven were the ringleaders, and showed their protestant zeal by murdering also a Dominican friar whom Mary had been harbouring, but Moray and his associates were ready to enter Edinburgh as soon as the deed was done.

Darnley, whose dagger was carefully left in Riccio's corpse, carried out his part of the bargain by cancelling the session of parliament, Moray arrived and negotiated with Mary for a pardon, but that was all the conspiracy achieved. Not only did Mary survive, but she outwitted the conspirators by detaching the pliable Darnley, who rode off with her to Dunbar early on 12 March. His discomfited allies, disappointed of their pardon,

31 *Cal. S. P. Scot.*, II. No. 351; *Maitland Club Misc.*, III. i, 188; Keith, III. 262.
32 Pollen, *Papal negotiations with Queen Mary* (S. H. S.), p. 473.

retaliated by sending Mary the bond which proved Darnley's complicity in the murder, but thought it wise to leave Edinburgh on the morning of 17 March; and John Knox, who had warmly applauded the crime, departed the same afternoon for the safety of Ayrshire.[33]

Mary, still guided by her non-aristocratic familiars like Sir James Balfour (who became clerk-register), had been joined at Dunbar by Huntly, Atholl, Bothwell, Fleming and Seton. She now split the opposition by offering pardons to the leaders of the Chaseabout rising as distinct from the murderers of Riccio. She was back in Edinburgh on 18 March, with a considerable force, and on 19 March the privy council summoned Morton, Ruthven, Lindsay and more than sixty other persons to appear within six days; but they were already across the Border. Moray, Glencairn and Argyll were restored to favour and reconciled to Huntly, Bothwell and Atholl, with whom they formed the core of the council for almost a year.

The reconciliation between Mary and Darnley had been short-lived; they were known to be on such indifferent terms that before the end of April there was a rumour of a mission to Rome for a divorce.[34] After the birth of Prince James on 19 June,[35] Darnley did come to see the child, whom Mary solemnly announced to be his, but the queen's loathing for her husband was patent to all, and it was soon accompanied by a growing partiality for James Hepburn, the thirty-year-old Earl of Bothwell. His family—the Hepburns of Hailes—were among the greatest magnates of south-eastern Scotland and the Border country and held the office of hereditary High Admiral. Another element in the Hepburn heritage was what was called " kindness " to widowed queens, for since the death of James I there had not been a royal relict whose name had not been linked with the lord of Hailes of her day, and when Earl Patrick, in 1543, procured a divorce with a view to marrying Mary of Guise he was setting an example to his more notorious son. Earl James, though on the reforming side, had been a trusted supporter of Mary of Guise, and " as mortal an enemy to " the English " as

33 Subsequently Knox paid a visit to England, where his sons were being educated, and he did not return to Edinburgh until the eve of Mary's overthrow.

34 *Cal. S. P. Scot.*, II, No. 375.

35 The recurrent myth that remains found in Edinburgh Castle in 1830 were those of Mary's child was disposed of by Frank Gent, *The Coffin in the Wall* (1944).

any man alive."[36]   After Mary recalled him in 1565 he put his
ability and resolution at her disposal, and raised a force of
Borderers on her behalf after the Riccio murder. He ultimately
held the sheriffships of Edinburgh and Haddington, the bailiary
of Lauderdale and the wardenship of all three marches, and was
master of the castles of Borthwick, Crichton, Hailes, Dunbar and
Hermitage. There were sound political reasons why Mary should
regard him as a reliable and useful servant, but the fact seems
to be that after her experience of maternity Mary was more
moved by sexual passion than she had ever been before, and
subsequent events make it seem likely that her relations with
Bothwell, some time before the death of Darnley, were not
innocent.[37]

The picturesque incidents which are supposed to demonstrate
Mary's infatuation for Bothwell were, however, detailed by George
Buchanan, whose hereditary attachment to the house of Lennox
made him an apologist for Darnley and a detractor of Mary.
For example, Buchanan has his account of what happened in
October 1566, when Mary was at Jedburgh holding a justice
ayre and Bothwell was seriously wounded in a Border skirmish
and taken to his castle of Hermitage. But the narrative of the
queen's impulsive and hasty ride to visit her lover, with disreputable company and in wintry weather, to " display her out-
rageous lust in an inconvenient time of the year,"[38] is demonstrably false, for five or six days elapsed between Mary's receiving
the news of Bothwell's wound and her visit to him. The ride
to Hermitage and back did, however, bring on the most serious
of Mary's many illnesses, and on 25 October she was thought to
be dead. After recovering and making a circuit of the eastern
Border, Mary spent a fortnight, from 20 November, at Craigmillar, and then a few days at Holyrood before going to Stirling
for the baptism of Prince James on 17 December.

Darnley had withdrawn to Stirling in September and had
been talking of going abroad. He did not accompany Mary on
her tour in the south, and although he ultimately came to her
sick-bed at Jedburgh, Bothwell had anticipated him by several
days. Mary and Darnley met again on two or three occasions

---

[36] *Cal. S. P. Scot.*, I. p. 679.   [37] P. 125 below.
[38] George Buchanan, " Ane detectioun," in *Appendix to the History of Scotland* (1721),
p. 11.

within the following few weeks, but neither of them made any attempt to conceal that their estrangement was complete. Darnley did not attend the baptism, and the ceremony was organised by Bothwell. During Mary's stay at Craigmillar, Bothwell, Huntly, Maitland, Argyll and Moray had conferred in her presence about her relations with her husband. Mary was opposed to a dissolution of her marriage, lest it should render her son illegitimate, and Lethington hinted at "other means" whereby she might be quit of Darnley. Mary stipulated that nothing should be done contrary to her honour and conscience, and Lethington assured her that she would "see nothing but good and approved by parliament," but it must have been clear to all that, whereas if Darnley were first divorced he might then be charged with treason and, with some show of legality, killed in resisting arrest, it was hardly possible to proceed against him as long as he was king except by irregular means.[39]

Darnley felt safer in Glasgow, a centre of his family's influence in the west. It is not impossible that he meditated a counter-stroke whereby he could bring about the imprisonment of his wife and the coronation of his son with himself as regent. He wrote letters to the pope and the King of Spain, he showed an unwonted devotion to the mass, and the idea may have flitted through his mind that Mary's equivocal policy made it possible for him to pose as a champion of the Roman catholic cause, to which Mary had been so disappointing. If, as a party to the murder of Riccio, he had tried to encompass the death of his wife, he was unlikely to be more scrupulous now. But Mary may have been threatened by more serious dangers than anything Darnley could contrive. The birth of the prince had done nothing to strengthen her position, for she was no longer the only bulwark against a disputed succession, and her removal would now mean a minority, with all the opportunities it offered to those—whether scrupulous or unscrupulous—who counted on being able to mould an infant sovereign. Besides, the baptism of the prince by Roman catholic rites[40] suggested the prospect of a succession of sovereigns under whom the position of the reformed church would still be precarious. And it may have added to Mary's

39 Hay Fleming, *Mary Queen of Scots*, pp. 142-3, 422-3.
40 Omitting, however, the spittle, on the insistence of Mary, who would not have "a pocky priest" (Archbishop Hamilton) spit in her child's mouth.

insecurity that in December 1566 she entered on her twenty-fifth year, the year in which sovereigns were accustomed to make an act of revocation, always dreaded by acquisitive nobles.[41] There were many who stood to gain should Darnley be eliminated by a plot in which Mary's participation would be so patent that her own downfall would follow.

To all appearances, however, it was Mary who was taking the initiative, by moves which seem to put beyond any doubt her complicity in schemes against Darnley. The reformed church, which had already received an important concession in October, by an ordinance that benefices worth less than 300 merks should go to ministers, now on 20 December received from the queen a direct gift of £10,000 in money, with victual probably worth almost as much again, and in succeeding months ecclesiastical properties in burghs were assigned to town councils. On 23 December the Archbishop of St Andrews was formally restored to jurisdiction which would enable him to pronounce decrees of nullity between Mary and Darnley and between Bothwell and his wife. On 24 December Mary pardoned the Riccio murderers, and to let them loose was a fairly certain way of ensuring Darnley's death. The subsequent revocation, before 9 January, of the commission to the archbishop[42] may suggest that a plan other than divorce had by that time been selected to deal with Darnley.

But Mary's next actions are most easily explained by the theory that she changed her design because in January she suddenly feared that she was pregnant of a child which could not be her husband's.[43] This made it imperative to achieve a reconciliation with Darnley, who since Christmas Eve had been ill, probably of syphilis. Mary therefore left for Glasgow on 20 January and spent five days there before returning, with Darnley in her company. Far from luring him to his doom at Kirk o' Field, her interest now was to preserve his life[44] at least long enough

---

[41] Cf. Sir James Melville, *Memoirs*, p. 148.   [42] *Cal. S. P. Scot.*, ii. No. 461.

[43] By 15 June 1567 Mary was said to be five months pregnant (*Cal. S. P. Spanish*, i. 649). The twins of which she miscarried on 24 July must have been conceived long before her marriage to Bothwell in May (Dan McKenzie, " The obstetric history of Mary, queen of Scots, at Lochleven," in *Caledonian Medical Journal*, xv. 2-6). Only two months after her marriage to Bothwell Mary admitted to being " seven weeks gone with child " (*Cal. S. P. Scot.*, ii. p. 355).

[44] He would not have been safe in Glasgow, for Lennox was attacked there.

to allow her to resume marital relations with him—which she had promised to do on the very night after his murder took place.[45]

The truth about the murder continues to elude historians, possibly because there was more than one conspiracy and, as no individual was privy to more than one, no contemporary knew the whole truth. There were certainly different groups of conspirators, and it is not clear how far they acted in concert. There were the Riccio murderers, headed by Morton, with their essentially personal grudge against Darnley. There were the politicians who proposed to rid Mary of her husband, and it cannot be doubted that both Moray and Maitland had foreknowledge of a design against Darnley at Kirk o' Field. Both of those groups had reason to believe that they stood to gain should Mary's reign, as well as Darnley's, come to an end. Then there was Bothwell, who wanted to open the way to his own marriage to the queen. He was in touch with representatives of the first and second groups, although he had never been in sympathy with them before, and he discussed with them ways and means of doing away with the king, but it is not proved that he collaborated with them in the actual crime and it is more likely that he would be playing for his own hand. There is, finally, the theory[46] that the main plot in February 1567 was one, to which Darnley was privy, against Mary, but it is hard to believe that a convalescent, from his sick-bed, concocted a large-scale gunpowder plot in the ten days between his arrival in Edinburgh and his death (on 10 February), especially as he had not himself elected to remove to Kirk o' Field and as he had no party or faction to support him.

The plain difficulty is to find any theory which fits all the facts, not only of what happened at Kirk o' Field but of all that preceded and followed it. There was nothing suspicious in the choice of Kirk o' Field as a place of convalescence, for it was on the edge of the country and much more healthy than low-lying Holyrood. But the choice of this site, in preference to Craigmillar, where Mary had proposed to lodge Darnley, may have been that of Sir James Balfour, who was universally believed to have been a principal actor in the crime, although he must have been

---

45 This theory is not incompatible with the genuineness of the " Long Glasgow Letter," on the likely assumption that Bothwell was in Mary's confidence in her repulsive task.

46 This is the theory of Major-General Mahon, in *The tragedy of Kirk o' Field.*

the agent or confederate of one of the groups of conspirators. And it was thought strange that Darnley was accommodated not in Hamilton House, which stood on that part of the site where the Court Room of Edinburgh University is now, but in the old provost's lodging, adjacent to a building belonging to Balfour's brother, at the south-east corner of the present Old Quadrangle. This house can hardly have been as " ruinous " as Buchanan alleges,[47] for Mary herself more than once spent the night there, sleeping in the room under Darnley's, but it was assuredly no place of security.

Statements that the gunpowder was introduced into the room where Mary normally slept, on the evening before the murder, are clearly wrong, though a small amount may have been some-what ostentatiously put there to draw suspicion on her. The powder, or most of it, must have been stored, in considerable quantity, in cellars on a lower level, or in a mine, for only so could the house have been as completely destroyed as it was. And had it been only a matter of removing Darnley, poison would have aroused no more suspicion than hung around many death-beds in that period; Darnley's illness had already, indeed, been attributed to poison. One reason for blowing up the house may have been to put it beyond doubt that the king's death was no accident, and so to draw suspicion on others—presumably on Bothwell and on Mary herself. If the explosion was designed to remove all traces after Darnley had been killed, then the murderers bungled it, for his dead body was found in the garden. These are all possibilities based on the assumption that the victim aimed at by the main plot was Darnley.

If, however, the main plot was aimed at Mary, the explosion would be explained by preparations to kill the queen, with her councillors and courtiers, at one stroke. Some features in the affair can undoubtedly be explained most easily on the assumption that Darnley knew of the presence of the powder and met his fate when attempting a hurried escape after fire had started. But was it then sheer coincidence that in the garden he encountered a second band of murderers, who despatched him? It is usually accepted, on the evidence of Darnley's dying exclamation, " Have mercy on me, kinsmen, for the sake of Him who had mercy on all the world,"[48] that the actual slayers of this son of Margaret

[47] Buchanan, *op. cit.*, p. 18.   [48] Pollen, *op. cit.*, p. 369.

Douglas were Douglases, henchmen of Morton. The somewhat desperate suggestion has even been made that there were a first, a second, and a third band of murderers—Darnley's agents, who introduced the powder, Bothwell, who found the powder and put a match to it, and Morton's men who happened to meet the fleeing king in the garden and smothered him.[49]

The fact of most political importance was and is that the circumstantial evidence permits no reasonable doubt about the guilt of Mary, not as an accessory to the Kirk o' Field crime, but as an unfaithful wife and a party to schemes against her husband. The question of the authenticity of the Casket Letters is of only secondary importance. It is a fair guess that some genuine letters from Mary to Bothwell were tampered with and that some of the papers were written to Bothwell not by Mary but by another woman to whom he had been betrothed and whom he had abandoned. And, if the circumstantial evidence against Mary was strong before the death of Darnley, it mounted thereafter.

Mary was shaken beyond measure by the murder, and the only course open to her, in her desperation, was an early marriage to the man whose child she was carrying. He had first to be acquitted of the Darnley murder, of which he was universally regarded as guilty. On 28 March the privy council ordered his trial for 12 April, but threw the onus of the prosecution on Lennox instead of on the crown, and on the day appointed for the trial Edinburgh was so packed with Bothwell's supporters that Lennox could not safely appear. Mary had next to make a bid for support, and she did so when parliament met in April. On 19 April she formally took the reformed church under her protection, and the estates ratified gifts to Lethington, Morton, Moray, Lord Robert Stewart and Huntly, as well as to Bothwell. Bothwell, on his side, obtained influential support for his candidature for the queen's hand, in a bond signed on 19 April by eight bishops, ten earls and eleven lords; the signatories may have seen the proposed marriage as a means of bringing about the ruin of both Bothwell and the queen, but some of them may have been genuinely convinced that Bothwell was the strong man who could restore the situation.[50] The next step was one which

49 Robert Gore-Browne, *Lord Bothwell*, pp. 316-22.
50 The " Ainslie's Tavern Bond " is in Keith, II. 563-6 and elsewhere; cf. Sir James Melville, *Memoirs*, p. 177.

had been foreseen by the end of March—the divorce of Bothwell: on 3 May his countess obtained sentence against her husband, on the ground of adultery, in the commissary court of Edinburgh, which had been set up in 1564 to supersede the old church courts in matrimonial causes; and on 7 May the earl procured from the court of the Archbishop of St Andrews[51] a decision that his marriage had been null for lack of a dispensation—although a dispensation had been granted by the archbishop himself.[52]   On 15 May Mary married Bothwell at Holyrood in the presence of a small group of notables who were nearly all on the conservative side in religion, and on the same day she wrote to the pope, professing herself his "most devoted daughter";[53] yet the ceremony which joined her to the protestant Bothwell was according to the reformed rite and was conducted by the reforming Bishop of Orkney.   Mary's sole concession to respectability had been to state that she had turned down Bothwell's suit[54] and to submit, on 24 April, to be seized by Bothwell and carried off to Dunbar. Bothwell was quite capable of a genuine abduction, and the action was impolitic to the extent that it simply invited a movement to " liberate " the queen, but contemporaries regarded it as a pretence and unanimously condemned Mary.   The pope declared on 2 July that it was not his intention to have any further communication with her " unless in times to come he shall see some better sign of her life and religion than he has witnessed in the past,"[55] and it has been remarked that "all her censors agree . . . that Mary's marriage with Bothwell admits of no defence, that it was a shame and a disgrace."[56]

Mystery did not end with the Bothwell marriage, for before the ceremony there had been half a day of " great unkindness " between the pair, and during the honeymoon Mary asked " for a knife to stick herself, or else, said she, I shall drown myself."[57]

[51] Since 1560 the archbishop had from time to time exercised his consistorial jurisdiction, but its legality became more questionable after the establishment of the commissary court of Edinburgh in 1564.   It may be that although the commission of 24 December 1566 had been revoked, he received another such special commission for the Bothwell case.

[52] Hamilton (who did not, however, preside in person over the court) may have been a willing party to the suppression of the dispensation, since its production later would enable him to bastardise any issue of Mary and Bothwell.

[53] R. P. C., xiv. lxxii.   [54] Keith, ii. 592-601.

[55] Pollen, op. cit., p. 397.   [56] Ibid., p. cxxxii.

[57] Cal. S. P. Foreign, viii. 229; Sir James Melville, Memoirs, p. 180; Teulet, Relations politiques, ii. 297.

On the assumption that their relations had been innocent before marriage, or that Mary had married Bothwell either under compulsion or for political reasons, the explanation might simply be that she found him unendurable as a husband. It is not easy to believe that the trouble was his infidelity, his jealousy or his coarse talk, for of all these Mary must already have been aware. Some of her defenders have ventured to suggest that only after her marriage did she discover Bothwell's part in Darnley's murder. On the whole, however, the most reasonable explanation of Mary's misery is that Bothwell made some other disclosure which shocked her. Was it something about her mother? It has been suggested that Bothwell's reported remark that " the queen " had been " the cardinal's whore " referred to the relations of Mary of Guise with David Beaton and not to those of Mary herself with one of her cardinal uncles.[58] Even more revolting would have been disclosures about the relations of Bothwell's father with Mary's mother, for scandalous relations between them, which had been hinted at earlier, seem to be the only possible explanation of the remark, " Some saye that [Bothwell] is nere sybbe unto her grace."[59]

Already before the marriage, opposition had been organised, for on 1 May a bond was prepared pledging the signatories to set the queen at liberty and to defend her and the prince.[60] Once the marriage had taken place, the proclaimed purpose of the confederate lords was to dissolve it, but some thought that their real aim from the outset was to set up James as king.[61] When they assembled in arms, Mary and Bothwell left Holyrood for Borthwick, but they were almost surprised there and had to make for Dunbar. They raised an army of a kind, but they had the support of few nobles—Huntly and Crawford were the only earls to appear at council meetings after Mary's marriage. On 15 June the two forces confronted each other at Carberry. There were negotiations over a proposal for a single combat between Bothwell and a champion of the confederate lords, and in the course of them Mary's army began to melt away. Finally, after seeing

[58] *Cal. S. P. Scot.*, ii, Nos. 161–2; Gore-Browne, *op. cit.*, pp. 184–5.

[59] *Cal. S. P. Scot.*, i. p. 563; "nere sybbe" = closely related. Knox (who is at his most scurrilous when he writes of Mary of Guise) is almost alone in casting doubt on Mary's paternity (i. 322). Cf. 66 above.

[60] *R. P. C.*, xiv. 315; cf. the later bond (11 June), *Ibid.*, i. 519.

[61] *Cal. S. P. Spanish, 1558/67*, p. 639.

Bothwell safely off the field, Mary surrendered, to be brought to Edinburgh in disgrace and sent to Lochleven, where on 24 July she was constrained to abdicate in favour of her son and to nominate as regent the Earl of Moray, whom failing, Morton. King James VI was crowned at Stirling on 29 July; Knox preached the sermon, but his objections to unction were disregarded and the king was crowned and anointed by Adam Bothwell, Bishop of Orkney. Moray, who had left for the continent two days before Bothwell's trial in April, returned on 11 August. He had an interview with his sister in which he seems to have left the impression that she was in danger of execution and in which he obtained a " voluntary " confirmation of his nomination as regent. He was proclaimed regent on 22 August.

8

THE CHURCH BEFORE AND AFTER
THE REFORMATION[1]

The sixteenth century brought to an end that period of upwards of four hundred years during which *Ecclesia Scoticana* had been one of the churches of western Europe which were associated in a common allegiance to the Roman see. The church was the catholic church in Scotland—Scottish to the extent that it enjoyed a measure of autonomy in its day-to-day administration and in the regulation of its worship and that it could identify itself with the cause of national independence even against the pope, catholic in the sense that its doctrinal accord with the other western churches was unquestioned. Within Scotland, a variety of institutions had been introduced or developed—territorial dioceses and parishes, cathedrals, houses of monks and nuns, friaries, collegiate churches—and the whole had been vitalised and sustained by communication with the continent. The piety of generations had lavished on the church wealth in the form of lands, rents and other dues, it was legally entitled to teinds of the produce of Scotland's arable land, pasture, rivers and seas, and it exacted offerings, fines and fees from all who required its offices. It has been argued that because the church bore half of a taxation[2] it possessed half the national wealth, and, although that particular argument is not sound, there are some

---

[1] Documentation for the material in this chapter is to be found in Donaldson, *The Scottish Reformation.*

[2] The traditional proportion had been two-fifths from the church, but in 1522, 1524 and 1535 the church's share was a half. In 1536 there was a reversion to two-fifths, but from 1545 onwards the ecclesiastical proportion was always a half.

telling comparisons: the annual revenue of the church in 1560 was in the region of £400,000, at a time when the total revenues of the crown amounted to no more than £40,000; and that sum of £400,000, although a fair amount of it was actually going into lay hands, represented nominally the income of some 3,000 clergy in a population of perhaps 800,000. The institutional, material and cultural achievements of this opulent corporation were very considerable, and many of the dignified buildings which adorned a poor country still survive, despite the ravages of time, the weather, pre-reformation neglect and post-reformation demand for building stone. Judgment on the spiritual and moral effectiveness of all the enormous effort and expenditure could be made only in relation to the comparative importance of theory and practice, because, while standards of Christian conduct were constantly upheld in principle, the medieval mind was not perturbed when practice was at variance with principle, and it was accustomed, in church and state alike, to laws and ordinances which were no more than pious aspirations.

In the sixteenth century this organisation encountered a threefold challenge. There was, first, the doctrinal revolt, repudiating the priesthood in its existing form, denying the sacrificial character of multiplied masses as in themselves propitiatory for the sins of the living and the dead, and asserting, by contrast, faith in the Bible and trust in the one sacrifice of Calvary as alone efficacious for the remission of sins. Stage by stage the reforming preachers extended the scope of their attack: in the 1540s they were condemning sacramental penance, the invocation of saints, and masses for the dead, as well, of course, as the papacy, and with the mission of Wishart (1544-5) the idea was introduced that all practices should cease for which scriptural warrant could not be adduced. In the end, however, it was the sacrificial mass which became the focus of the reformers' attack, as at once idolatrous (since it involved the worship of a wafer) and blasphemous (since it derogated from the redeeming work of Christ). A second challenge to the church was the economic and financial one, demanding a redistribution of the ecclesiastical endowments, partly in the interests of the church's work among the people but partly also in the interests of lords and lairds who now regretted the munificence of their ancestors. And there was, thirdly, the humanist criticism. Those whose practice was not in accordance with their profession were now regarded with cynicism or scorn. While the theologians of the Reformation were confident that they were redressing the balance between faith and works in favour of faith, the new outlook demanded that works should be in keeping with faith. And, apart altogether from any challenge on theological or moral grounds, there was only too much in the existing church system which could be condemned on grounds of mere common sense.

There were parts of the church system which still had considerable vitality and retained the attachment of a good many people. In the burghs, both gilds and individuals were still endowing chaplains to serve at the numerous altars in the town churches. Lairds were still showing an interest in the endowment of collegiate churches, though few of those were completed on the scale which a more fervent or more munificent generation had planned. Behind those endowments lay a continued belief in the efficacy of private masses. The interest in education, too, which had led fifteenth-century bishops to give Scotland three universities, was stimulated by the challenge of the Reformation, with the result that at St Andrews the new college of St Mary was established.[3] The friars, again, were still conspicuous as theologians and preachers, their moral standards were high, and the fidelity of the Observant Franciscans, in particular, to their obligations, including the rule of poverty, made them outstanding among the religious orders.

On the other hand, it may be doubted whether the members of a single Scottish monastery, with the exception of the Carthusians at Perth, were any longer conscientiously performing all the functions for which the house had been founded. Some houses did something to encourage crafts and trade,[4] and the monks seem in the main to have been of reputable private life, but the vitality which may be detected here and there, notably at Cambuskenneth and Kinloss, was directed mainly towards fostering the intellectual rather than the spiritual life of the community. Besides, the head of the house was as often as not a commendator who was not necessarily a cleric of any kind and whose interests were mainly financial, while the monks lived in comfort and at leisure, each on his individual " portion " and in

[3] See p. 82 above.   [4] *Essay on the Scottish Reformation*, pp. 216-17.

his own chamber, and attempts to restore the ideal of community of property were strongly resisted. Neither the commendator nor the monks had any interest in maintaining buildings other than their domestic quarters, so that the church decayed or, if damaged in military operations, was imperfectly repaired. Some commendators were so preoccupied with finance that they were averse from admitting recruits, and where this happened the life of the house in every sense was grinding to a standstill.

What especially crippled the church and weakened its impact on the mass of the people was its persistent neglect of the parishes, their clergy and their churches. By 1560 the bulk of the revenues of nearly 90 per cent of the parishes of Scotland was being diverted to religious houses, cathedral chapters, collegiate churches and universities,[5] leaving only a slender residue for local use. Very few of the vicars serving the parishes had a living wage and the buildings where they served were often bleakly utilitarian, sometimes devoid not only of ornament and of the necessary apparatus of worship, but even of windows and roofs. No doubt many a parish priest, ill-equipped as he and his church were, was faithfully imparting the essentials of Christianity in a quiet and simple way; but the fact remains that contemporaries of every school of thought were seriously exercised about the intellectual and moral standards of the parish clergy.

Not only did ambitious careerists, whose sole interest was material gain, become commendators of abbeys or priories or accumulate a plurality of benefices, especially the wealthier canonries and dignities in cathedrals. There were even means whereby Scottish families could acquire heritable rights to ecclesiastical wealth. The sovereign's right to nominate to vacant prelacies had been finally conceded by the pope in 1535, and by 1560 the crown, which now regularly exercised the right of disposing of the temporality of vacant abbeys and bishoprics and claimed to be able to dispose of their spirituality as well, had ingeniously extended its authority to the extent that it could give effective possession without reference to Rome at all. The acquisitions of the royal house were outstanding, for six of James V's illegitimate sons ultimately held abbeys as commendators, and the entrenchment of the Hamiltons was perhaps the closest parallel: one of Châtelherault's half-brothers became Archbishop

5 I. B. Cowan, *The parishes of medieval Scotland* (S. R. S.).

of St Andrews, another Bishop of Argyll, one of his sons obtained Arbroath, another obtained Paisley in succession to his uncle the archbishop, and in the archbishopric itself the succession was secured to Gavin Hamilton. But instances could be multiplied of benefices, great and small, which passed from one member of a family to another and were recognised as " kindly " or heritable property, and quite conscienceless bargaining was the rule.[6] Some magnates who did not gain the title to a benefice exercised effective control over its properties as bailies, like Huntly in the bishopric of Aberdeen and the Kennedys of Cassillis in the bishopric of Galloway and the abbey of Glenluce. The strong arm of a lay bailie became indispensable to the clergy as ecclesiastical authority weakened, but the bailies acted in no altruistic spirit, and bailiaries, like commendatorships, became hereditary.[7] Indefeasible heritable rights in church property were constituted also by the feu charters so frequently granted by churchmen in the generation before 1560. The " great tax " which the pope permitted James V to impose in 1532, and later impositions, similar in principle though smaller in scale, could be met only out of capital, and had to be borne by the prelates at a time when the growing disregard for ecclesiastical censures was making it difficult enough for them to collect their ordinary revenues. Canon law forbade them to alienate their property by simple sale in return for cash, but the feu charter (by which lands were conveyed for an initial payment and a fixed duty in perpetuity), though in effect alienation, could be brought within the scope of permissible transactions. The practice of feuing was accelerated, and was adopted by churchmen of all ranks, as the sense of insecurity increased, for it enabled them to raise capital sums as an insurance against dispossession: the five friars of Wigtown, by setting their property in feu, secured £1,000 down and £80 a year.[8] The popes, who had already virtually abdicated their control over appointments, also relinquished control over feu charters, which could be confirmed by Archbishops David Beaton and John Hamilton, as legates *a latere*, and were sometimes simply confirmed by the crown. Thus secularisation was facilitated in every possible way. It was mainly the nobility who benefited, and attempts after 1560 to annex the monastic property to the

[6] *E.g.*, R. S. S., IV. 2893, 2902.   [7] *E.g.*, R. P. C., I. 291.
[8] *Wigtownshire Charters* (S. H. S.), pp. 132-3.

crown met with resistance and in the end with failure. The lands of many Scottish religious houses still remain with the descendants of those who established themselves as commendators before 1560.

The curious idea persists that Scottish nobles and lairds supported the Reformation because they hoped to gain church property, whereas the truth is that they were already firmly entrenched and their economic interest would seem rather to have been the maintenance of a *status quo* which had proved so profitable. They may conceivably have feared that their titles, though good in law, might be challenged should there be an effective recovery within the church, whereas a revolution might convert their feus into superiorities, but they can hardly have been so naive as to suppose that an aggressive reformed church would not want to recover ecclesiastical property from lay hands. Nor can the idea be entertained that the nobles were won to the reforming cause by English pensions, for those who received such pensions often did little enough in return, and pensions were taken indifferently from England and France. When one recalls the persistent aristocratic opposition, ever since Flodden, to adventures across the Border, one suspects that the prospects of peace with England may well have been the dominant secular consideration with the nobles as with others.

It is not clear that lairds, either, had much to gain financially by an ecclesiastical change within Scotland. Nor is the fact that lairds in the Lothians, Fife and Angus could discern political and economic advantages in alignment with England an adequate explanation of their attitude. The conclusion seems to be in-escapable that the lairds, many of them enriched as tacksmen of teinds and feuars of kirk lands, were attaining a new self-esteem: their names begin to find their way into the narrative of the main stream of Scottish history during the 1540s and 1550s, they were to assert their right to seats in parliament in 1560, and their growth towards political consciousness may have been accompan-ied by a readiness to demand that the clergy and the management of the church should be subordinated to the laity.

In such anti-clerical tendencies the lairds were at one with the burgesses, who had been influenced by reforming thought from the continent since the 1520s. Although the burgesses had given lavishly of their substance to their local churches, in which they exercised proprietary rights and were dictatorial towards the clergy, they had no reason to cherish the ecclesiastical system as a whole. Prelates, the monastic orders and the Roman court were "idle bellies," that is, consumers and not producers of the material wealth which never came to Scottish laymen of the middle class without hard work. Besides, to the burgesses the Reformation and the English alliance offered a guarantee against the recurrence of destructive invasions.

There were, however, those lower in the social scale with whom economic motives were an incentive to revolution. It can hardly be doubted that in sixteenth-century Scotland life was so precarious for the mass of the people that there were always many who were on or near the level of poverty or even starvation, and the numerous paupers are often alluded to in legislation and in contemporary writings. Whatever the record of the church in earlier times, there is no reason to believe that the care of the needy was now a serious concern of many ecclesiastical institutions, and even before reforming preachers pointed to the contrast between apostolic poverty and prelatical wealth the poor cannot have been well disposed to bishops, abbots or dignitaries, or even to monks; their bitterest resentment seems, however, to have been reserved for the friars, some of whom, though professing poverty, were living in comfort and engrossing alms which might have relieved more genuine needs. On the other hand, the lowest class in the social scale was least likely to be attracted to new theology and new ways of worship, and most likely to be satisfied with the ministrations of the average parish priest. Nor was this class of any weight constitutionally, but its numbers made it an element to be reckoned with should it be stirred up by demagogues, who could hold out prospects that a reformation would liberate revenues which could be devoted to poor relief.

The tenants on ecclesiastical estates appear on the whole, in earlier generations, to have enjoyed moderate rents and a security of tenure which was often in practice hereditary. But when feuing began to prevail, the clergy, in their desire for large lump sums, which many tenants could not afford, too often found feuars in nobles and lairds who proceeded to recoup themselves by rack-renting or evicting the tenants, who bitterly resented the disregard of their traditional claims. Besides, all tenants, whether on church lands or not, had grievances in connexion with teinds, especially when the clergy began to exact larger sums from those to whom they granted teinds in tack and the tacksmen tried to pass on the increase to the farmers. The reformers, on their side, took up the cause of " the poor labourers of the ground " and proposed to reform the teind system. Tenants who had lost their substance or had been economically depressed would be even more inflammable material than paupers who knew only despair.

Whatever inferences may be drawn about economic and political motives, it is harder to assess the force of religious opinions. Belief in the direct dependence of the sinner on Christ, without the need of any intermediary, had evidently never been wholly effaced, for some of the devotional literature of the late fifteenth century discounted, both implicitly and explicitly, the value of the intercessions of the Blessed Virgin and the saints.[9] In the sixteenth century such a belief was reinforced first by the Lutheran doctrine of justification by faith and then by the Calvinist doctrine of the divinely pre-determined salvation of the elect. The new theology was expounded by educated men like Patrick Hamilton, the martyr of 1528, and Alexander Seton, a Dominican friar who had to flee to England about 1536, but the populace, too, was soon stirred, and, although the agitation in the 1530s was mainly against images, the abuse of " cursing " or excommunication, pretended miracles, and the evil lives of churchmen, verses were circulating[10] which demonstrate in moving language that the spiritual needs of men were being satisfied by the new theology. It is to be assumed that by 1560 the reformed teachings were heard in all the more accessible parts of the country, and the reason why they made more impact on some groups than on others is clearly to be found in non-theological factors. There is, for instance, no ground for believing that the new doctrines made a peculiar appeal, on spiritual grounds alone, to the Lowland lairds. Apart, however, from the strictly theological content of the reformers' programme, its emphasis on discipline, of clergy and laity alike, had a moral appeal to all who shared in the critical and cynical attitude to the clergy which had been encouraged for two decades by satirical literature like the works of Sir David Lindsay.

9 *Devotional pieces in verse and prose* (S. T. S.), pp. 213; cf. pp. 252, 261, 264.
10 In the *Good and godly ballads*, which belong to the Lutheran phase of the reformation.

The humanist, moral and commonsense criticism of the ecclesiastical system fastened on the fact that irregularities like concubinage, the tenure of benefices by unqualified men, non-residence, pluralism, the neglect of church buildings, were all contrary to canon law and to statutes repeatedly passed by provincial councils. But the machinery which should have enforced the law was weak at every point. Bishops were too often themselves in need of reform; the crown, on appointing bishops, habitually burdened the revenues with " pensions " which might amount to the greater part of the fruits; some sees were held for years by unconsecrated " administrators "; and the concern of such titulars as well as of some genuine bishops was to maladminister the revenues in the interests of themselves and their families. Besides, should a bishop be conscientious, or should the crown attempt to intervene against irregularities, they were frustrated owing to the practice of obtaining dispensations from the pope which set aside salutary laws and regulations. Thus, even apart from the difficulty of countering the reformers' arguments from scripture and primitive practice, and the persistence in Scotland of a belief in the superiority of general councils over the pope, it was hard to make a case for the papacy when it was so obviously a major obstacle to good government.

In so far as the Reformation represented a moral revolt and a reaction against the relaxed discipline of the late medieval church, it had been anticipated by James V's threats that he would make the prelates reform themselves, and had begun to find expression before 1560 not only in the legislation of provincial councils but also in the legislation of parliament : the administrations of Châtelherault and Mary of Guise passed statutes against the holding of markets and fairs on holy days, against adultery, against profanity, and against the traditional May-day festivities.[11] To carry this further, and to make discipline effective within the church, the reformers were disposed to put an end to the frustration and depression of the episcopate through papal action and to the entanglement of bishops in politics and secular affairs. They were ready enough to use the services of bishops who joined them, but as part of their general scheme of reorganisation they proposed that regional administration should be in the hands of ten superintendents, each with the oversight

[11] *A. P. S.*, II. 500; Hamilton, *Catechism*, pp. 68, 91; cf. *R. P. C.*, I. 296, 298.

of approximately a hundred parishes. Only five superintendents were ever appointed, because there were political and financial difficulties in the way of implementing the scheme, but three dioceses were supervised by their conforming bishops and the remaining two or three areas were in charge of " commissioners." The commissioner differed from the superintendent in that he was appointed by the general assembly and not by the state, he received a much smaller stipend, he normally served a parish as a minister and his commission was for a term and not for life. The superintendents, bishops and commissioners took the leading part in the examination of ministers and their admission to charges; in the course of their tours of inspection they examined the life and work of the parochial clergy, whom they had power to suspend or deprive; they controlled the machinery for summoning the members of a general assembly, and one of them normally presided over its sessions. " My lord superintendent " was a great dignitary, but he was himself answerable to the general assembly for the conscientious discharge of his duties.

The emphasis on discipline, and its expression in more efficient supervision, were among the novel features of the Reformation. But in many of its aspects the Reformation did no more than continue trends already discernible in the late medieval system. Even the rejection of the papacy was no more than a logical sequel to the steady growth of royal control over the church before 1560; and, more generally, a critical attitude to external authority, the weakening of the international ideal and the strengthening of national and local feeling, had been reflected already in the greater interest taken in collegiate and burgh churches, locally controlled, than in religious orders with their headquarters overseas. Equally, the stress of the Reformation on the authority of the laity, and its anti-clericalism, had been foreshadowed in the responsibility of town councils for their churches, so that it was no great innovation when a town council ordered the cessation of the old ways of worship and continued to superintend the use of its church in the new system.

The Reformation carried the anti-clerical tendency farther, because it was also anti-sacerdotal. With the use of the vernacular, the composition of metrical psalms, the introduction of a Book of Common Prayer or a Book of Common Order, the congregation was able to take part in the services. With the invitation of the people to communicate at every celebration of the Eucharist, the restoration of the cup to the laity and the setting up of a table around which minister and communicants assembled, the sacrament ceased to be something done by the priest at the altar and became a corporate action in which the participation of the congregation was essential. In baptism, too, the emphasis was not on a priestly rite but on the reception of the child into the Christian community. In short, the concept was of a kind of corporate priesthood, belonging to the congregation. It was proposed that congregations should elect their ministers, and the minister was seen as a delegate of the congregation, authorised by them and not by a bishop. Again, for confession to an individual priest, in private, there was substituted a system whereby elders, representing the congregation, examined the members and determined their fitness to be communicants, and whereby the sinner, instead of having penance imposed in private, was publicly denounced before the congregation. It was an important distinction from the practice of later times that those elders were elected annually, and were unquestionably laymen. Yet those lay elders were—so at least the first Book of Discipline proposed—to censure their minister and even, with the superintendent's consent, depose him. Anticlericalism could hardly have gone farther unless to sweep a professional ministry away altogether. Deacons, also annually elected, were intended to control all ecclesiastical revenues, but as things worked out almost the only funds which came to them to administer were the alms for the relief of the poor.

Yet the system was one in which the ministry of word and sacraments was in the hands of men set apart for the purpose— ministers fully qualified to preach and to administer the sacraments, exhorters authorised to preach, and readers permitted to read the service and the homilies. The intermediate office of exhorter disappeared in the early 1570s, and readers were then authorised to administer the sacrament of baptism and to officiate at marriages, as well as catechising children. This was an attempt to assimilate the reader's office to that of the Anglican deacon, and the Scottish church thus had for a time a "threefold ministry," in superintendents, ministers and readers.

The English Book of Common Prayer, which had been used in the " privy kirks " of the 1550s and had been introduced to parish churches in 1560, had a rival in another English service-book—that used by the English congregation which had worshipped at Geneva in Mary Tudor's reign. This book was already in use in some places in Scotland in 1560, and after it had been printed in Scotland, in 1562, the general assembly ordained its use. While this Book of Common Order, as it was called, was not a rigid liturgy, but allowed ministers a certain discretion, some prayers were intended to be invariable and public worship was defined as including " the reading of common prayers "; there was provision for the use of the Lord's Prayer, the Creed, and the Gloria; and there were metrical versions of some canticles —the *Nunc Dimittis* and " the song of Blessed Mary, called *Magnificat.*" The reformers would gladly have made the sacrament of the Lord's Supper a weekly service, but the people had so long been accustomed to communicate only once a year, at Easter, that they declined to communicate frequently, and the normal Sunday morning service could be only the Ante-Communion or first part of the Communion service. Lent continued to be observed, by state ordinance, for economic reasons, but it seems to have retained a certain spiritual relevance, for some preferred to avoid that season for the celebration of marriage. While the observance of the traditional holy days was officially condemned, some of them continued to be recognised not only by the populace but by kirk sessions, and some were retained for legal purposes.

Changes in worship, even a revolution in the character of the ministry and in the internal discipline of the church, could be carried through by a congregational organisation or by a general assembly not authorised by the state. But there were other matters which required the intervention of the civil authority. The first of them was endowment. In the first Book of Discipline the reformers laid claim to the whole of the spirituality, or teinds, and the temporality of bishoprics, cathedrals and dignities, while the temporality of monastic houses was tacitly relinquished. This proposal involved breaking up the existing benefices into their constituent parts, or " dissolving " them, and so disrupting a complex structure which had grown up over the centuries. With the appropriation of parishes, teinds had been taken away from the parish of their origin, sometimes to be distributed among two or more benefices; and, to add to the complication, when a bishopric or a monastery was drawing rents and teinds from the same lands, it might set both kinds of dues in tack for a single payment, with the result that the distinction between rent and teinds, or temporality and spirituality, was lost. There would obviously be immense difficulty in any attempt to extricate the teinds and make them available for the work of the reformed church in each parish. Besides, the proposals of the Book of Discipline ignored the interests of the crown, they offered no alternative to the system whereby the existing benefices bore 50 per cent of the national taxation, and their reception by the nobles[12] showed that the latter had an invincible preference for the old ecclesiastical structure.

The compromise represented by the assumption of thirds[13] therefore satisfied the crown and the nobles by leaving the old structure intact. The prelacies were not " dissolved "; abbots or commendators, along with all other holders of benefices, retained two-thirds of their revenues; the monks retained their " portions " and even their chambers and " yards " in the precincts. Many clergy of all ranks, secular and regular, did agree to serve under the new regime, and in many a parish the pre-reformation incumbent, after being duly approved by the superintendent, continued to minister to his people.[14] But no provision was made to ensure that, as the existing holders of benefices died, they would be succeeded by men able and willing to serve in the reformed church; the old machinery of presentation by a patron, followed by collation by a bishop (and not a super-intendent or commissioner) continued to operate, there was no compulsion to appoint men acceptable to the reformed church, and the whole tendency was towards secularisation.

The survival of the old structure meant, among other things, that feuing could continue. The government intervened to pro-tect the old tenants against eviction and to substitute royal for papal or legatine confirmation. In June 1561 a proclamation for-bade the feuing of church lands,[15] but this was a mere emergency measure; in September, the council, on the ground that the clergy had set most of their lands in feu " to the greit hurt nocht onlie of the quenis majestie bot also of the pure tennentis thairof," forbade application to Rome for confirmation of feus granted since

[12] See p. 105 above.   [13] See p. 111 above.
[14] G. Donaldson, " The parish clergy and the reformation," in *Innes Review*, x.
1-20.   [15] *Treasurer's Accounts*, XI. 55 ff.

6 March 1558/9;[16] in ·December of the same year, and again later, respite was granted to tenants under notice to quit;[17] and in 1563 parliament ordained that no feus were to be given without royal authority.[18] The receipt of compositions for confirmation of feus gave the crown a further financial interest in the Reformation.

Another matter which required the intervention of the state was the provision of a judicature to replace the old church courts, which, although they had not been abolished in 1560, had largely ceased to operate. Theoretically, marriage had hitherto been dissoluble only by decree of nullity, but the law had been so open to manipulation that Scottish husbands and wives were said to be able to repudiate each other " quant ilz ne se trouvent bien ensamble."[19] The reformed church, in this as in so much else, brought theory closer to practice by permitting divorce for adultery and desertion, and its courts began in 1559 to exercise jurisdiction in matrimonial causes. Litigants also began to go to the court of session, on the ground that they could not get justice elsewhere. Confusion was ended in 1564, when the commissary court of Edinburgh was established, with jurisdiction over the whole country in divorce suits and in testamentary cases above a certain value. A subsidiary jurisdiction pertained to local commissary courts which represented a continuation or revival of the courts previously held by bishops' officials or commissaries. These courts dealt with a wide range of cases which had formerly been the business of the old church courts, but in the course of time proceedings for the fulfilment of obligations went increasingly to the civil courts.[20]

The successive acts of parliament and council by which the state intervened in matters of endowment and jurisdiction all amounted, explicitly or implicitly, to recognition that a reformation had taken place and that a reformed church existed. And, although the reformed church deplored the inadequate financial provision made for its needs and tried to halt the drift towards secularisation of ecclesiastical property, it was ready to welcome state intervention in ecclesiastical matters should such action be

16 *Treasurer's Accounts*, XI. 71 ff.; *R. P. C.*, I. 162-3.
17 *R. P. C.*, I. 192, 234; *A. P. S.*, II. 540.
18 *Ibid.*
19 Teulet, *Relations politiques*, II. 299. This was written in 1567, but refers to pre-reformation practice.
20 " The Church Courts," in *Introduction to Scottish legal history* (Stair Soc.).

favourable to the Reformation. Yet the reformed church was in no real sense established as long as Mary was on the throne, and its record had hitherto been, in the main, one of opposition, or resistance, to the crown. Ready enough at the outset to appeal to Mary of Guise for her support, the reformers found it necessary, on her refusal to listen to them, to reconcile the apostolic injunction of subjection to the " higher powers " which are " ordained of God " with the exigencies of their position. Knox had argued that " the authority " which is " God's ordinance " was not necessarily to be identified with the crown and that it could be found in other organs of the constitution. Recourse was therefore had to the estates of the realm, in which the reformers found the authority which carried through their revolution in 1559/60 and which, in the shape of the general assembly, governed their church thereafter. The second revolution, in 1567, had its apologist in the scholarly George Buchanan, whose arguments, in his *De jure regni apud Scotos*, appealed more to precedent than to theology. The Scots, he asserted, had always exercised the right of calling bad kings to account, and had imprisoned, exiled or put to death no less than a dozen out of the hundred-odd Scottish monarchs who were reckoned to have formed the royal line. There was nothing novel in the assertion of the right of deposition, and neither Knox nor Buchanan added much to the political thought of the essentially medieval philosopher and theologian John Major, but they did much to root the theory of resistance to " ungodly " rulers in the thought of the reformed church.

It remained to be seen how the reformed church, with this background, was going to accommodate itself to the new circumstances of the rule of a " godly prince." The general assembly pronounced in 1567 that future sovereigns should promise in their coronation oaths to " maintain and defend and by all lawful means set forward the true religion,"[21] and a few years later it became the practice to exact from all clergy an oath acknowledging the king as " supreme governor of this realm, as well in things temporal as in the conservation and purgation of religion."[22] Some thought that the general assembly should now lapse, and its powers be transferred to crown and parliament, but the view prevailed that it should be retained at least until the sovereignty of King James was unchallenged.

[21] *B. U. K.*, I. 108-9.   [22] *Ibid.*, I. 220.

The immediate practical result of the political change in 1567 was that the general assembly's demands were now more likely to be implemented by crown and parliament. Those demands were no longer for the policy of the Book of Discipline, for since 1563 the assembly had repeatedly craved not that the benefices should be dissolved but that they should be filled by men qualified to serve in the reformed church. It now, in 1567, became the law that patrons must obtain approval of their nominees from the superintendents, and in succeeding years the regular practice was to appoint to the lesser benefices men qualified to serve as ministers or readers. Arrangements for applying a similar practice specifically to the prelacies were not made until 1572. In the bishoprics Mary's policy had vacillated between gifts to lay titulars and nomination to Rome for papal provision, and to the abbeys and priories she had appointed lay commendators; the ultimate step towards which the developments in the abbeys pointed—the formal creation of heritable temporal lordships— was taken only in the case of the preceptory of Torphichen. The reformed church came to see the logic of filling the bishoprics, like other benefices, with qualified men, but it would obviously be necessary to ensure that the men appointed would be acceptable to the crown as well as to the church. However, the question was not at once acute after 1567, for there was no outstanding vacancy and the regents acting in the name of the infant James VI were not likely to risk alienating support by attempting to deprive bishops or even by appointing successors to bishops who were forfeited for supporting the deposed Queen Mary. The matter might have remained dormant until the final triumph of the king's party had it not suddenly become acute when Archbishop Hamilton was hanged in April 1571.[23]

In August 1571 the government nominated archbishops for St Andrews and Glasgow, but the church, which had not been consulted, insisted that the qualifications of persons appointed to bishoprics must be approved by some ecclesiastical authority. After some months of wrangling, a settlement was reached in January 1571/2. Ministers were now to succeed to the bishoprics, just as, since 1567, they had succeeded to lesser benefices. The bishoprics were to remain in being, and the diocesan boundaries were not to be altered in the meantime. On a vacancy, the crown

23 P. 164 below.

was to make a nomination, and its nominee was to be elected or rejected by a chapter, composed of ministers. Formal admission or " inauguration " was to be by the imposition of hands of superintendents, commissioners and conforming bishops. As part of a comprehensive settlement of the problems of endowment, it was agreed that the persons appointed as commendators of abbeys should also be approved by the church and that lesser benefices like prebends and chaplainries were to go to students. The structure of the benefices, in short, was to be retained in its entirety, and the reformed church was to have access to every part of it.

As the bishops were to have the same powers as superintendents and were to be subject to the general assembly, church government was neither more nor less " episcopal " now than it had been since 1560; the change was merely in endowment. That being so, there were no grounds for objection on principle, but there was criticism of some details, such as the retention of the old diocesan boundaries, the arrangement for election by chapters rather than by the whole clergy and laity of the dioceses and the recognition of some unscriptural titles like archbishop and dean. The generally favourable, though not wholly uncritical, attitude of the church as a whole was also that of the individual ministers whose views are recorded, including John Knox, who urged emphatically that the new arrangements should be faithfully and fully carried out.

One step remained to complete the association of the reformed church with the benefices—the dispossession of existing holders who could not or would not serve in the reformed church. A statute of 1573 provided that all beneficed men must subscribe the confession of faith and take the oath of supremacy, or else suffer deprivation. This eliminated the very small number of determined recusants, and the likelihood now was that at no distant date the reformed church would be in full possession of the ancient polity with all its benefices and offices.

The prospects of stability on the basis of the retention of the old structure proved illusory, owing to the emergence of the novel ideas of Andrew Melville. Melville (1545-1622), the son of an Angus laird, had studied at St Andrews and then proceeded to Paris and to Poitiers, where he taught in the university. In 1568 he had moved to Geneva, where for six years he taught humanity. On his return to Scotland in 1574, Melville became principal of the college of Glasgow, and in 1580 he was transferred to St Andrews. As an author, Melville never wrote in the vernacular, even his Latin output hardly went beyond occasional verses and epigrams, and he never committed to paper his thoughts on civil or ecclesiastical politics. His status in the church was that of a " doctor," and as such he claimed the right to sit in the general assembly, but he never acted as a full-time parish minister and it is doubtful if he was ever ordained. His remarkable influence over a kind of ecclesiastical intelligentsia was exercised by personal contacts and through his work as a university teacher and organiser, which made him the dominant figure in the education of Scottish divines. The logic in his thought undoubtedly appealed to the Scottish mind, but both his personality and his teaching quite lacked the warm evangelical fervour of the reformers.

Melville contended that the parity of ministers must not be violated, and that therefore the church must be governed not by superintendents or bishops but by committees of ministers, known as presbyteries. But he raised other issues. In his view, church and state were separate entities—" two kingdoms." Central ecclesiastical authority, he held, must therefore lie with a general assembly not now consisting of the three estates but having as voting members only " ecclesiastical persons," by which he meant ministers, " doctors " like himself and elders of a novel kind—quasi-clerical elders, appointed for life and possessed of an office which was " a spiritual function, as is the ministry."[24] Neither crown, parliament, council, nor any other body with lay members should have ecclesiastical authority. On the other hand, " ecclesiastical persons " were no longer to hold office in the civil government. Yet the application of the doctrine of the " two kingdoms " meant in practice the domination of the church: on the definition of the respective spheres of church and state everything depended, and Melville would accept no definition but his own, so that ministers were to be permitted to pronounce from the pulpit on state policy but were not to be answerable to any civil tribunal for what they said. A church which claimed the allegiance of every man, woman and child in the country and which asserted its exclusive right to the teinds, paid by every

[24] *B. U. K.*, II. 496.

farmer, could not, in the sixteenth century, be permitted to exclude the generality of the people or their representatives from all voice in its affairs, and the crown and parliament could not surrender their rights. The fact is that Melvillianism cut at the whole concept of establishment as it is usually understood. Melville's proposals about finance were almost as embarrassing as his ideas about church-state relations, for he aimed at reversing the whole trend of recent developments. Not only was the structure of the benefices to be scrapped and patronage to be abolished, but all ecclesiastical property, temporality as well as spirituality, was to be administered by deacons on behalf of the reformed church.

Melville's new concepts initiated a period of controversy within the Church of Scotland, but they did nothing to hinder progress towards the achievement of most of the reformers' ideals. The more effective supervision of the clergy which came in with the Reformation succeeded almost at once in eliminating the old scandals, and within a generation or so the educational standards of ministers had been so raised that a non-graduate minister was all but unknown. As the financial position of the reformed church gradually improved—though without any such violent upheaval as both the first reformers and Melville had proposed—it was possible to expand the parochial ministry, until by about 1620 there was hardly a parish without a minister. As the number of ministers increased, readers ceased to have charge of parishes, but their office was not abolished as Melville had proposed and they continued to perform useful functions as assistants. A substantial measure of ecclesiastical authority continued to rest with laymen, instead of being confined to " ecclesiastical persons ": town councils exercised their traditional powers, and nobles and lairds could still play their parts in the affairs of rural parishes, for the elder remained a genuinely lay officer, appointed for only a term. The discipline of the kirk sessions was extended throughout the country along with the parish ministry, until by the second or third decade of the seventeenth century there can have been few parishes without a session. Thus the people were being exhorted, instructed and disciplined as never before.

The ministry, as well as having its moral and educational standards raised, attained a higher social status. Before the

Reformation, while the episcopate and other dignities had been largely staffed by members of noble houses, the rank and file of the clergy can hardly have had other than the humblest social origins. After the Reformation, the social range became more restricted. It becomes rare to find even a bishopric held by a member of a noble family, and, while a certain number of ministers were related to peers, this element in the ministry is hardly conspicuous; on the other hand, not many ministers now came from the lowest social range. At the outset, in the 1560s, few ministers had stipends which could make a clerical career financially attractive even to men of middle-class origin, but from the 1570s there was a steady improvement. As early as 1574 the general assembly had to forbid ministers and their wives to deck themselves out in fine clothing, to adorn themselves with jewellery or to wear silk hats; this suggests that some clergy were already so far above the poverty line as to be open to the temptation of luxurious living. The church never again offered a highly remunerative career to the younger sons of noble houses, but in the seventeenth century ministers were so well paid that a clerical career would appeal to the younger sons of lairds, and ministers, as their testaments show, were often better off than the smaller lairds. Thus in the seventeenth century both the episcopate and the ministry generally were recruited largely from the families of the landed gentry. The Reformation, by transferring abbatial property and rights to laymen, greatly extended lay patronage and in this way contributed to the integration of the clergy with the landed classes. One thing that the Reformation did not eliminate was the traditional strength of " the kin." Hereditary succession in the church was now respectable, in that illegitimacy was no longer involved, and the qualifications of ministers' sons were presumably as searchingly examined as were those of other candidates; but the fact remains that there were many clerical dynasties, just as there were legal dynasties, and it is not altogether rare to find three generations of the same family serving in a parish and holding it with little intermission from the Reformation to the Revolution. Apart from such cases, however, the proportion of ministers who were themselves sons of the manse was very high—comparable to the proportion of them who were the offspring of lairds, and, in some districts and at some periods, actually higher. Besides, a significant number

of families were both clerical and landed. The number of ministers drawn from burgess stock is not insignificant in the early
part of the century, especially in the Borders and the south-west,
but this element nearly everywhere diminished as the century
went on.   Apart from that change, much the same pattern
prevailed throughout the whole period, though a significantly
smaller proportion of men of gentle origin were appointed during
the few years when patronage did not operate (1649-62). There
is no doubt as to where the clergy fitted into the social structure,
for not a few ministers were able to acquire landed property by
purchase, while others married into the families of landed gentlemen.   To a very large extent the ministry was upper-middle-
class.

The developments from 1560 onwards strongly suggest that
much of the population had been fairly receptive to the reformed
faith and that most were prepared at least to acquiesce in its
adoption. Many of the clergy may have had no better principles
than the Vicar of Bray, but, even so, instructive comparisons
can be made: when, in 1573, it at last became impossible to
retain a benefice without acknowledging the reformed faith,
a mere handful of clergy were deprived, whereas in 1662, when
a presbyterian system was superseded by an episcopalian system,
nearly 300 ministers were deprived, and when the episcopalian
system in turn gave way to presbytery in 1690 over 600 ministers
were deprived.   If sincerity is to be measured by a readiness
to incur financial loss, the conclusion is inescapable that there
was far less attachment to the pre-reformation system in and
after 1560 than there was to either of the two competing reformed
systems in the seventeenth century.

There had, in and after 1560, been many men who, either
actively or passively, challenged the Reformation, at least in the
form which it had taken. Quentin Kennedy, Commendator of
Crossraguel, whose *Compendious Tractive* (1558) appealed to the
traditions of the church and to the authority of the early general
councils against the reformers' appeal to the scriptures and to
private judgment, challenged John Knox to debate.   Ninian
Winyet, a Linlithgow schoolmaster, in *Certane Tractatis* (1562)
posed questions which searched out the weaknesses and inconsistencies in the reformers' position and resolutely upheld the concept of a personal succession in the ministry from apostolic times.

Three or four peers had voted against the Confession of Faith
at the parliament of 1560. Numerous priests were prosecuted
for saying mass in 1563[25] and 1569,[26] and no doubt many others
had said mass but escaped prosecution. And there may have
been an uncounted multitude who could say, " my hart gevis me
to the mess and thairfor I can nocht come to the commonion."[27]
But nothing was done to rally such men and make their challenge
effective. Archbishop Beaton of Glasgow, who should have led
them, went off to France in 1560, never to return; the bishops
who declined to approve of the Confession of Faith when it came
before parliament were either conscientiously hesitant or pusil-
lanimous; the definitions of the Council of Trent (1563) came too
late to help the Scottish conservatives by at last making it clear
what doctrines the papacy approved. Leaderless, and despondent
about prospects at home, the more intransigent, including
Winyet, followed Beaton to the continent. With their retreat,
the steady reduction by death of the number of recusant priests
remaining in the country, and the lack as yet of any measures
to mount a counter-offensive from the continent, the prospect
facing Scottish Romanism in the 1570s was the prospect of
extinction.

[25] Pitcairn, *Criminal Trials*, I. ii, 428.
[26] *R. P. C.*, II. 40.
[27] *The buik of the kirk of the Canagait* (S. R. S.), p. 38; cf. *Essays on the Scottish Reformation*, pp. 229-30.

PART II

THE NEW MONARCHY

9

"UPROAR" AND "REPOSE"[1]

Mary's deposition raised almost as many problems as it solved, and the unity of the confederate lords did not endure for long, if indeed it had ever existed. Their professed purpose had been merely to punish the murderers of Darnley, to preserve the person of the prince and to deliver the queen from " bondage and captivity."[2] When Mary surrendered at Carberry (15 June 1567), she was not told that within forty-eight hours she would be in genuine bondage and captivity in the castle of Lochleven. There was, of course, a case for her confinement, because her captors, who must have recalled how she had slipped through their fingers after the murder of Riccio, now found that she reaffirmed her fidelity to Bothwell, who was still at large and in touch with other nobles opposed to the confederates. But when Bothwell withdrew northwards, first to the household of his uncle the Bishop of Moray at Spynie and then to his dukedom of Orkney, he ceased to be at any rate an imminent danger. Moreover, although the Casket Letters had been discovered on 20 June, they were not—and it is a significant fact —used to justify sterner measures against the queen. Consequently, the further actions of the confederates in extorting Mary's abdication (24 July) and crowning James (29 July) did not command the support of all who had taken up arms in June, and only five earls and eight lords are named as being present at the coronation. When Moray returned, to assume the regency,

1 " Tempore ultime perturbationis et uproris " (R. S. S., vi. No. 2715); " this time of repose which God has granted us after our long troubles " (Wodrow Soc. Misc., p. 289).   2 R. P. C., I. 519.

his rigorous attitude to his sister did nothing to commend him to more moderate men, and his upbraiding of her " like a ghostly father "[3] came unfittingly from the leader of a party which had pledged itself to the punishment of Darnley's murderers and which yet was relying on the support of men who had themselves been implicated.

Among those who had never joined the confederacy were Huntly and Lord John Hamilton (Châtelherault's second son), who had been on their way to join the queen when the encounter at Carberry had taken place. The opinion of the Hamiltons was that the regency, should there be one, belonged of right to their own head, as heir presumptive to Mary; besides, the supersession of Mary by James weakened their claim to the succession, for it was arguable that, as Darnley had been king, James's heir was Darnley's younger brother, Charles. Châtelherault had been in exile since the Chaseabout Raid, and did not return until February 1568/9, but the Hamilton interest was, as so often, ably advanced by the archbishop, and there was an idea that should Mary be released and separated from Bothwell she might marry Lord John. Apart from those who had never joined the confederates, there were deserters from them, like Argyll, who aligned himself with the Hamiltons about a week after Carberry. Argyll thought of his own brother, and not Lord John, as a candidate for Mary's hand, but this did not prevent his working with the Hamiltons and Huntly. There were also " secret favourers of the queen "[4] among the confederates, such as Maitland of Lethington and Kirkcaldy of Grange, who were of opinion that what Mary had conceded under duress could not prejudice her rights. Kirkcaldy, who felt a particular responsibility as he had received the queen's surrender at Carberry, did continue to co-operate with those who may now be called the king's party, but his next piece of service was to lead an expedition which pursued Bothwell to Shetland in the hope of bringing him to justice and ensuring that the queen would be finally quit of him. Bothwell escaped to Norway, but there he was unlucky enough to fall into the hands of the kinsfolk of a Danish girl he had seduced and he entered on a captivity which ended only with his death in 1578.

At first, not much came of the opposition to Moray, and it seemed that he would consolidate his power. The Hamiltons

[3] Keith, II. 737.   [4] Melville, *Memoirs*, p. 190.

and their associates were scattered in September; Dunbar, which had been held for Bothwell, surrendered; and Gavin Hamilton, coadjutor of St Andrews, went to France to try to win over Châtelherault. A parliament in December was attended by Argyll and Huntly, and as time passed more peers and others took their places in Moray's council. His regency might well have continued to attract increasing support had it not been interrupted by the escape of Mary from Lochleven on 2 May 1568. She made for Hamilton, but the nine earls, nine bishops, twelve commendators and eighteen lords who pledged their support[5] included men who had sat in Moray's parliament and council as well as those who had not, and the rapidity with which a force of some 5,000 or 6,000 men was raised suggests that sympathy with her was widespread. The escape had caught Moray at Glasgow, in a district where his opponents were strong, and his force was outnumbered. The queen's army decided to make for Dumbarton, which was held by the friendly Lord Fleming, but it was outmanoeuvred by Moray as it passed Glasgow and was defeated at Langside on 13 May. Mary fled, by Sanquhar and Terregles, to Dundrennan, and crossed the Solway to England on 16 May.

It had all along been evident that Moray had failed in 1567, as in 1565, to reproduce the circumstances of 1560, for there was neither unity in Scotland nor English support for his party. After Carberry, Elizabeth had sent Throckmorton to deal for Mary's release on condition that she repudiated Bothwell, and although, when he succeeded in communicating with Mary at Lochleven, he found that she would not contemplate divorce, Elizabeth still refused to acknowledge Moray's administration. Mary had therefore some grounds for regarding Elizabeth as a friend, but the latter found the presence of the fugitive in England to be an embarrassment. For one thing, as Mary had never renounced her claim to England, she was still a rival for Elizabeth's throne. For another, Elizabeth had always been reluctant to support rebellion, and to detain Mary implied English countenance for those who had dispossessed her. Convenience and policy alike thus suggested negotiations for Mary's restoration. Almost immediately, on 8 June, Elizabeth wrote to Mary, promising to restore her on certain conditions, one of which was that Moray

5 Keith, II. 807-10.

was to be called on to answer for his rebellion, but he was also to have the opportunity to produce his evidence against the queen. Mary agreed to this, though it meant that she, as well as Moray, was to be on trial. And Moray had no alternative but to take the risk of submitting his case to Elizabeth, for to refuse would have deprived him of any chance of English recognition and would have made it hard for Elizabeth to do otherwise than insist on Mary's restoration.

A tripartite conference representing Moray, Mary and Elizabeth met at York in early October, reassembled at Westminster on 25 November, and finally met at Hampton Court on 16 December. The prolonged and tortuous nature of the proceedings arose from the fact that no party was single-minded. Mary's representatives, including Lord Herries and John Lesley (whom Mary had appointed to the bishopric of Ross) do not seem to have been wholly convinced of her innocence. Moray's supporters were not unanimous, for some of them felt that they could not afford to take irrevocable action against one who might again be their sovereign and have their lives and fortunes at her disposal. Besides, Maitland of Lethington, who was one of the regent's delegation, still cherished the idea of Anglo-Scottish union through the recognition of Mary as Elizabeth's heir, and was possibly moved by distaste for the revolutionary proceedings of 1567 as well as by a reluctance to see disclosures which might prejudice his own safety. He therefore favoured Mary's restoration on terms which would not be detrimental to her rights in England, and found that he had much ground in common with the Duke of Norfolk, who headed Elizabeth's delegation at York. It would have suited them both that Mary should divorce Bothwell and be restored with Norfolk as her consort. However, when proceedings were resumed at London and an assurance was forthcoming that the English commissioners were authorised to find Mary guilty, Moray formally accused her of murder and the Casket Letters (which had been shown privately to Norfolk at York) were publicly produced as evidence.

On 10 January 1569 Cecil delivered Elizabeth's judgment: nothing had been said which impaired Moray's honour and allegiance, and he was to return to Scotland in " the same estate " as he had been in when he left; on the other hand, nothing had been said to induce Elizabeth to think ill of Mary. If there was any policy, and not merely constitutional irresolution, behind this inconclusive finding, it was that it did not drive Mary's supporters, in despair of English help, to appeal to a foreign power. It is true that Moray was the immediate gainer, for he went home with a loan of £5,000 and a measure of recognition for his government, and some of the Marians, including Huntly and Argyll, were so discouraged that between March and May 1569 they acknowledged the regent and entered on a kind of armistice. Elizabeth also sent a little military help, which was used against disaffected elements on the Borders. Châtelherault and Herries were imprisoned in April, and in May Moray toured the north-east, receiving the submission of Huntly's vassals.

Elizabeth saw, perhaps more clearly than some of her critics have done, that both parties in Scotland contained old friends to England and staunch supporters of the Reformation and that there was no conclusive case for supporting one in preference to the other. The king's party, of course, took its stand on the Reformation, and in December 1567 the first parliament of the new reign re-enacted the legislation which had been passed in 1560 but had never been ratified by Mary. It was equally natural that Mary's cause should attract ecclesiastical conservatives like Bishops Crichton of Dunkeld and Lesley of Ross, as well as Atholl, who had voted against the legislation of 1560, and Huntly, whose house always leaned to conservatism in both politics and religion. It is true, too, that Mary's cause was being advanced in France by James Beaton, Archbishop of Glasgow, and William Chisholm, Bishop of Dunblane, who were both on the papal side. But the queen had many supporters whose background was different. The Hamiltons were not primarily interested in one faith or the other, and Châtelherault, whom Mary had appointed as governor on her behalf on 12 July 1568, had, after all, been the figurehead of the insurgents who had received English help in 1560. Argyll, too, who acted as Mary's lieutenant until Châtelherault came back from France, had always belonged to the reforming party and was Moray's brother-in-law. The way in which political principles, conscientiously held, cut across ecclesiastical affiliations is illustrated by the fact that Bishops Gordon of Galloway and Bothwell of Orkney, who had both worked for the reformed church since 1560, were now on opposite sides. The adherence to the queen's party of moderate reformers like Bishop Gordon and of ministers who did not share Knox's violent antipathy to Mary was, perhaps deliberately, encouraged by some of the actions of Mary and Elizabeth: in 1568 and 1569 Elizabeth called on Mary to profess " the manner of religion used in England " as a condition of her restoration,[6] and Mary, in the early years of her imprisonment, went through a kind of Anglican phase, which she discarded only after she realised that continental powers offered better prospects than did Elizabeth. It should also be remembered that Norfolk, to whom Mary's marriage was proposed, was not himself a recusant although he was associated with the English Roman catholic party. The Marian faction, in short, was no narrow group of intransigent papists, and it was not unreasonable that Elizabeth should entertain proposals for Mary's release when they came from such influential men as Argyll, Huntly, Cassillis, Atholl and Archbishop Hamilton, as well, latterly, as that enthusiast for Anglo-Scottish amity, Maitland of Lethington. Elizabeth's attitude was not one that left the Marians without hope.

Moray's last months of power, in the second half of 1569, therefore did not see the consolidation of his authority. At the end of July, a proposal from Mary that a process be instituted for her divorce from Bothwell[7] as a preliminary to her restoration— and also to her marriage to Norfolk—was put before a convention at Perth, attended by nine earls, five bishops, eight commendators and fifteen lords.[8] It was rejected by forty votes to nine, but the minority, to whom this return to the original aims of the revolt of 1567 made its appeal, included Maitland of Lethington, his brother John, Huntly, Atholl and the Bishop of Galloway, while Argyll, Herries and Fleming were not present. In September Lethington was arrested on the charge of foreknowledge of Darnley's murder, but the custody of his person was assumed by Kirkcaldy of Grange, who shared his views, and this pair was to represent an important accession of diplomatic and military skill to the Marians.

The Northern Rising in England, started by Norfolk's allies

[6] *R. P. C.*, II. 1-5; *Cal. S. P. Scot.*, II. Nos. 740, 743, 757; cf. Hill Burton, *History of Scotland*, IV. 343n, 411-4.
[7] It was reported in November 1570 that a bull dissolving Mary's marriage to Bothwell had been issued (*Cal. S. P. Foreign, Eliz.*, IX. No. 1412), but there seems to be no doubt that the marriage was never dissolved until Bothwell's death (cf. *Cal. S. P. Rome, 1572-8*, pp. 216-30).   [8] *R. P. C.*, II. 8-9; cf. XIV. 28.

in November 1569, constituted a threat to Moray as well as to Elizabeth. Moray had recently been much occupied on the Scottish side of the frontier, taking hostages and proceeding against priests, and he was prompt to offer help against the rebels. On their defeat he prepared to deal with them if they crossed into Scotland, and when the Earl of Northumberland fled from England Moray arrested him. The regent then confronted Elizabeth with demands for financial assistance and a guarantee of his regime, on condition of the delivery of Northumberland. But before Elizabeth could reply, Moray's regency had terminated with his murder at Linlithgow, on 23 January 1569/70, by Hamilton of Bothwellhaugh with the foreknowledge of the archbishop. Moray's murder, when he was barely forty, and the troubles which followed his death, helped to form the picture of a "Good Regent," whom some thought Scotland's best governor "sen James in Falkland deit"[9] in 1542, but it is hard to disentangle his services to church and state from self-interest and ambition. Nor had he shown much political acumen, for his manoeuvres had often involved miscalculation and failure, and his rare successes owed at least as much to favourable circumstances as to his own unaided designs.

More than five months elapsed before a successor to Moray was appointed, and during the interregnum the prospects of the king's party did not improve. Elizabeth was still a long way from decisive action, though the papal bull excommunicating her (25 February 1569/70) might have done something to commend support for a Scottish party which was at least a defence against Rome. In April 1570 the Earl of Sussex did carry out a punitive expedition across the Border, burning and destroying the castles of those Borderers who had assisted and harboured fugitives after the late rising, and a few weeks later Sir William Drury was sent from Berwick. The English penetrated to the Hamilton lands in Lanarkshire and Lothian and assisted the king's troops in the siege of Dumbarton Castle. But, while the campaign did material damage to Marians, it did nothing to make friends for either England or King James. The king's party, almost in despair, put itself in Elizabeth's hands in the selection of a new regent. Her choice was Lennox, who had come north in Drury's company in May and was made lieutenant of the kingdom in

9 *Lamentatioun of Lady Scotland* (1572), sig. a iii v.

June and regent in July. The appointment eased relations with England, but Lennox's record did not commend him to patriots, his elevation intensified the hostility of the rival house of Hamilton, and his determination to avenge the murder of Darnley did not increase his popularity. The Marians, encouraged by the death of Moray and resolutely opposed to Lennox, could muster nine earls and thirteen lords. At the suggestion of Maitland, who declined to work for an administration under Lennox, they again appealed to Elizabeth for Mary's restoration, in association with the preservation of the Anglo-Scottish *entente*.[10]

Civil war could not be avoided, and there were operations against Huntly, Argyll and the Hamilton supporters in the west and south-west. On English mediation a truce for six months was arranged in September, but war was resumed when it expired. In April 1571 Dumbarton Castle was taken for the king. This reduced the likelihood that the Marians would receive French help, and it also deprived them of the services of Archbishop Hamilton, who was captured in the castle and hanged.

From this point, although Huntly was still in power in the north-east and the Hamiltons in control of Clydesdale, interest centred on Edinburgh, where Kirkcaldy of Grange held the castle and was joined by Maitland in April 1571. That fortress contained the regalia, the principal store of ordnance, and the Register House where the records of the kingdom were kept. Besides, it commanded the capital, and Kirkcaldy dominated the citizens. In October 1569 the town council had rejected Moray's request for his removal from the office of provost, and he retained it for a year. In April 1570, Huntly, Argyll, Atholl and " the lordis of the west countre " had been made welcome in the town, and in May the council granted Grange £200 to strengthen the castle against the approaching English army.[11] Whatever the opinions of the burgesses, they had no defence against Kirkcaldy, so that he was able to seize the tolbooth and to attend service in the church of St Giles, while Knox found it expedient to withdraw to St Andrews, leaving his pulpit to be occupied by the Bishop of Galloway. In June 1571 the queen's party even held a parliament in the tolbooth of Edinburgh, the traditional meeting place. But, although the duke, Huntly, Home, Maxwell and Lord

10 *Cal. S. P. Scot.*, III. Nos. 184, 822-3, IV. 56-7, No. 410.
11 *Edinburgh Burgh Records*, III. 271.

Claud Hamilton were among those present, the representation was poorer than that at the " creeping parliament " which the king's party had held in May in the Canongate, where they had to assume undignified postures to avoid fire from the castle.

The queen's party was, in fact, breaking up, and in the summer of 1571 Argyll, Cassillis, Boyd and Eglinton went over to the king. At the end of August a parliament met at Stirling which was more fully attended than any had been for years, and although the true regalia were still in Edinburgh Castle, a crown, sword and sceptre were borne before the five-year-old king. Kirkcaldy attempted a *coup*, for he entered Stirling by night and seized the lords, but he failed to get his prisoners away and in the scuffle Lennox was killed (3 September). The next regent was John Erskine, Earl of Mar, who had never been a strong party man and lacked the ruthlessness which the office needed. An attempt on Edinburgh Castle in October was a failure.

The effective leadership of the king's party now belonged to James Douglas, fourth Earl of Morton, although he did not become regent until November 1572, following the death of Mar in October. A nephew of the sixth Earl of Angus, Morton had never wavered from the anglophile and protestant tradition of his house. If anyone in Scotland deserved English support, it was Morton, and in the spring of 1571 he had been in England, pleading strenuously for an alliance on the ground of a common religious cause. The time was opportune, for this was the year of the second Norfolk, or Ridolfi, plot, whereby a Spanish landing was to take place in association with a rising of English Roman catholics, and Mary was to marry Norfolk. Norfolk was arrested on 7 September, and John Lesley, under threat of torture, revealed the whole conspiracy. This was another intimation to Elizabeth, added to that of the Northern Rising of 1569, that the king's party was in effect fighting the same battle as she was, and it further moved her in the direction of intervention in Scotland. Hitherto there had been an obstacle to such intervention in that Elizabeth wanted to avoid a breach with France over her policy towards Mary, but negotiations between England and France issued in April 1572 in the Treaty of Blois, whereby France agreed to support action for the pacification of Scotland. The Anglo-French understanding was disrupted by the massacre of St Bartholomew's Eve (24 August 1572), which brought hope to the Marians, who calculated that if France was going to revert to a militant anti-protestant policy she might come to their aid; but on the other hand it increased Elizabeth's resolution to bring about a settlement in Scotland before France could intervene there.

In September and October Elizabeth toyed with the idea of handing Mary over to Mar, so that she could be dealt with in Scotland, but after his death (28 October), English intervention was directed to securing the king's party without reference to Mary at all. Between August and December, Châtelherault, Lord Claud, Huntly and Seton had left Edinburgh, and on 23 February 1572/3 they were induced by Killigrew, the English envoy, to acknowledge King James, in the Pacification of Perth. The defections from the queen's party had enabled the regent's forces to reoccupy the town of Edinburgh in the autumn of 1572 and Knox to return to his home, where he died on 24 November; but English help was necessary to reduce the castle. After Grange and Lethington refused to surrender, Drury crossed the Border again in April 1573, while siege guns were sent by sea to Leith. The English and the Scots undertook not to grant terms without the consent of their allies, and it was agreed that Kirkcaldy, William Maitland and his brother John, Melville of Murdo-cairny and five others should in any event stand trial by the laws of Scotland. On 28 May, after an eleven days' bombardment, the castle fell. Kirkcaldy, of whom Henry II of France had said, " Yonder is one of the most valiant men of our time " and of whom a fellow-Scot remarked that he was " gentle and meek like a lamb in the house, but like a lion in the fields,"[12] was exe-cuted; Maitland cheated the hangman by dying, possibly by his own hand.

The fall of the castle closed a long contest, with a victory for the section of the reforming and anglophile party which had been more militant politically.   The decisions of 1560, 1567 and 1573 may not have been irrevocable, but no attempt to reverse them was ever again made with any prospect of success. The remarkable fact about the contest which ended in 1573 is that in its last phases the leading magnates—Huntly, Argyll and Châtelherault—had been Marians. Whatever may be said of the revolution of 1559-60, it was no combination of the leading nobles which brought about the final decision against Mary.

12 Melville, *Memoirs*, p. 257.

It seems indisputable that the success of the king's party, in the face of so much aristocratic opposition, was due to the support, not indeed of the lower classes, who were not yet liberated from their ties to the magnates and who hardly cared—or knew— whether they were ruled by a king or a queen, but of many lairds and burgesses. It is in this context that truth is to be seen in the oft-quoted remark which Killigrew made in 1572: " Me- thinks I see the noblemen's great credit decay . . . and the barons, burghs and such-like take more upon them."[13]

It was fitting that power now lay with Morton, for with the deaths of Argyll in 1574 and Châtelherault in 1575 he was the sole survivor of the politicians and men of action who had been prominent at every stage since the revolution started. And for five years there was a political tranquillity which had been unknown for a generation. There was no renewed threat from Mary or from any continental power, and the amity with England endured, though it was strained by the Raid of Reids- wire, in 1575, when a scuffle took place during one of those days of truce when the English and Scottish wardens met to settle disputes. Both before and after that incident Morton applied to the Borders a judicious mixture of severity and conciliation: he exacted hostages, imposed heavy fines and established a stand- ing force for the maintenance of order, but offered " clemencie and pardoun for bigane offencis " rather than " the lyffis of men socht."[14] A similar policy was pursued in the north, where in 1574 the earls and barons undertook to repress disorder.[15] Mary's attempts to hold justice ayres for the punishment of criminals and to check the granting of remissions for crimes had been only intermittent, and Moray's efforts in the same direction had been interrupted by his death, but there was now an opportunity to restore the machinery of justice generally throughout the country. A clear concept of submission and unity lay behind such measures as the restriction of office in the burghs to those who would take an oath acknowledging the king and the reformed faith[16] and the exaction from the clergy of an oath acknowledging the king as " supreme governor of the realm as well in things temporal as in the conservation and purgation of religion."[17]

13 *Cal. S. P. Scot.*, IV. 432; Amos C. Miller, *Sir Henry Killigrew*, p. 158.
14 *R. P. C.*, II. ix ff., 367, 465-7, 572; cf. Tough, *Last years of a frontier*, pp. 222-9.
15 *R. P. C.*, II. 398.   16 *Ibid.*, p. 401.   17 *B. U. K.*, I. 220.

The settlement of ecclesiastical problems in 1572-3[18] must likewise be seen in the context of Morton's whole policy of friendship with England, conciliation of the nobility and insistence on obedience to authority. One element was " conformity with England,"[19] and the *formulae* adopted for episcopal appointments so closely resembled the English *formulae* that, in the words of an English observer, " so far as may be the order of the Church of England is followed."[20] But another motive arose from the fact that part of the strength of the queen's party had lain in the continuing preference of many nobles for the old ecclesiastical system: they " desired again the papistry, not for the love they bear to it . . ., but hoping to have promotion of idle bellies to benefices "; they deplored " the present estate, where (as they say) ministers get all and leave nothing to good fellows"; and

> . . . thay desyre never to se thair Quene
> Bot that thay may in hir name bruik offices
> With power to cleik up the benefices.[21]

It had therefore to be demonstrated that " good fellows " could " cleik " ecclesiastical revenues within a reformed system and that such revenues could at once recompense the king's supporters, like Lennox and Morton, for their expenses and losses and reward deserters from the other side like Argyll and Boyd. Such a plan was part of the business of the parliament of September 1571, which initiated a scheme for the disposal of the bishoprics. In practice, the diversion of episcopal revenues was to be far less unashamed than it had been before 1560, but some of the bishops were nominees of nobles, and after their appointment they lavishly granted feus and pensions to nominees of their patrons.

But it was hard to satisfy both the nobles and the church, and failure to control the financial operations of the bishops was one element in a situation which soon presented a new challenge to the government. The general assembly, which had not withered away after 1567, as some thought it ought to do, became the platform from which Andrew Melville expounded his programme. Morton scoffed at Melville's " oversea dreams, imitation of Geneva discipline and laws," and remarked to him

18 P. 147-8 above. 19 James Melville, *Diary*, p. 45. 20 *Cal. S. P. Scot.*, IV. 133-4. 21 Gatherer, *op. cit.*, 185; *Lamentatioun of Lady Scotland* (1572), sig. a iiii.

that " there will never be quietness in this country till half a dozen of you be hanged or banished,"[22] but he took no action to frustrate the development of the Melvillian movement, and that movement alienated from the regent a powerful section of ecclesiastical opinion, in whose eyes his services to protestantism were eclipsed by his hostility to presbyterianism.

Again, although Morton had secured the submission of the Marians, he was not the man to win their affection, and many of them remained excluded from office. Besides, no one could have pursued a career like his without making many private enemies, and his policy of enforcing respect for the law was unwelcome to those who had profited by disorder. At one stage, his stern attitude to Argyll and Atholl, who had become involved in a feud, led those two nobles to patch up their own differences and combine against him. Nor did Morton's financial policy show far-sighted statesmanship. Mary's personal reign had seen only ineffective attempts to curb the dissipation of the crown's resources, and had in the main been marked by prodigality. A tax of £12,000 for the prince's baptism had been the only tax, but the traditional sources of revenue had been supplemented by the crown's raids on the thirds. Since 1567 the civil war had been detrimental to finance. The treasurer's deficit rose from £33,000 in 1564 to £61,000 in 1569; in 1574 the king was said to be £37,000 in debt; and in 1575 the crown was " unable on the present rents thereof to sustain even now the estate of our sovereign lord and public charges of the realm, much less to bear out his majesty's estate and expenses at his more mature and perfect age."[23] Morton did nothing to restore the national finances. He was reputed to be personally avaricious, and the fact that he owned a ship and exported 35 barrels of salt beef suggests that he was at least enterprising.[24] He was, besides, an accomplished nepotist, whose four natural sons[25] were lavishly provided for, and he abused crown patronage to obtain for his clients church livings and pensions. He was, it is true, capable of insisting on the inviolability of crown property, and he made an enemy of the Earl of Argyll by requiring that the Countess,

---

[22] James Melville, *Diary*, p. 68.
[23] *A. P. S.*, III. 89-90.   [24] R. S. S. (MS.), XLVII. 124.
[25] Morton has been reproached for his private life, but it should be remembered that when his wife died in 1581 she had been insane for twenty-two years.

who was the widow of Moray, should give up certain crown jewels which her first husband had appropriated.[26] But in general he seems to have been too easy-going, for during his regency gifts of feudal casualties were habitually made without the exaction of any composition in return,[27] and his only taxation was one of £4,000 for an expedition to the Borders. One financial device to which he did resort was the debasement of the coinage, and that alienated the burgesses, the commercial classes and the poor.[28] All in all, even when Morton did not make enemies, his policy had little in it to attract active support, and the very success of his regime, in producing stability, induced a false sense of security in which men felt that they could afford to " look through their fingers " at his fall.[29]

[26] *R. P. C.*, II. 330-31.
[27] This is shown in *R. S. S.* After the end of the regency an act was passed that no gift should be disponed *gratis* (*R. P. C.*, II. 683-4).
[28] *Diurnal*, pp. 344-5; Moysie, *Memoirs*, p. 18.
[29] Sir J. Melville, *Memoirs*, p. 266, cf. p. 260.

10

DISCORDANT POLICIES AND
A *VIA MEDIA*

Morton's power was first undermined, and his overthrow was in the end brought about, not by any challenge on political or ecclesiastical policy, but by mere faction and personal rivalries. In the spring of 1578 the king was approaching the age of twelve—the age at which his grandfather had been formally " erected " as head of the administration—and on 4 March the Earls of Atholl and Argyll, admitted to the royal presence at Stirling, asked James to summon the nobility to pronounce judgment on certain differences between them and the regent. Morton sent a message that he must either have power to punish those who challenged his authority or else be relieved of his office, and his opponents persuaded the king to accept the latter alternative. A council was formed to conduct the government in the king's own name, and Morton's regency came to an end. Morton's supplanters thought themselves secure because they had the support of Alexander Erskine, Master of Mar, who had succeeded his brother, the Regent Mar, as keeper of the king's person. However, the young Earl of Mar, nephew of the Master and one of James's schoolfellows, intrigued with Morton and asserted his hereditary right to the custody of the king, which he obtained on 26 April, whereupon Morton joined him at Stirling. For a time authority was in dispute, but an accord was reached in the autumn whereby Morton retained the direction of affairs, though some of his opponents sat on the council. These incidents in 1578, when control of the king was seized first by one faction, then by another, were the first and second in a series of *coups d'état* which punctuated Scottish history for eight years.

A renewed threat to Morton came about largely through the personal relationships of the king, who first became a factor in Scottish affairs in his early adolescence. From the Countess of Mar, wife of the regent, James possibly received some of the kindness a child needed, and one of his tutors was Peter Young, who " was loath to offend the king at any time, and used himself warily, as a man who had mind of his own weal, by keeping of his majesty's favour."[1]   But the king's principal preceptor, appointed when James was only four, was George Buchanan, an aged bachelor of purely academic interests, a rigorous disciplinarian and a pamphleteer of the king's party who tried to imbue his pupil with his own hatred of Mary and his warm attachment to Darnley's family of Lennox. Although Buchanan nominally retained the office of preceptor to the king until he died in 1582, James was never again completely under tutelage after the spring of 1578. He made his formal entry into Edinburgh on 17 October 1579 and did not return to the seclusion of Stirling until the following February. Then, in the summer of 1580, as he was reaching the age of fourteen, he made a progress through Fife and Angus.

Already in September 1579 there had arrived from France the man who was to become a new influence on the king. He was Esmé Stewart, seigneur d'Aubigny, a nephew of Matthew, fourth Earl of Lennox, and so a first cousin of Darnley. He had ample personal reasons for coming to Scotland at this juncture. Charles, Darnley's younger brother, who had been Earl of Lennox since 1572, had died in 1576, leaving only an infant daughter, Arabella. Robert, Bishop of Caithness, a brother of Earl Matthew, had been created Earl of Lennox in June 1578, when he was a bachelor over sixty years of age, but he married in January 1578/9. Esmé was, after his uncle Robert, the male heir of the house of Lennox, the king's nearest kinsman on his father's side and, failing Arabella, the inheritor of the Lennox interest in the Scottish succession. It is very likely that James invited this near kinsman to Scotland, but Esmé himself may well have wanted to safeguard his prospects, threatened by the elevation of Bishop Robert and his belated marriage. Another fact which may have induced

1 Melville, *Memoirs*, p. 262.

Esmé to return was the action taken in the summer of 1579 against the whole Hamilton kin, culminating in November in the forfeiture of Lords John and Claud for their part in the murders of the first and second regents; the heir of the house of Lennox could expect to profit by the fall of the rival family.

A man in his late thirties, acquainted with the ways of a world wider than the Scottish court, Esmé Stewart completely won the affection of an adolescent king who had never known parental care and whose nature had been warped by those who taught him to hate and despise his mother. It was a familiar enough situation, with a physical, but not necessarily gross, side to it. The devoted king prevailed on old Robert Stewart to resign the earldom of Lennox, on 5 March 1579/80, in favour of Esmé, who in 1581 was made Duke of Lennox. The favourite was also appointed commendator of Arbroath (forfeited by Lord John Hamilton), and keeper of Dumbarton Castle, and he was admitted to the privy council in June 1580. Morton's opponents found an influential leader in the new councillor, and the ex-regent was arrested, on a charge of complicity in Darnley's murder, on 31 December 1580 and executed in the following June. His accuser was James Stewart (a son of Lord Ochiltree), who had become a favourite courtier of the king in 1580. Stewart was admitted to the privy council in February 1580/1 and (on the pretext of his descent from a daughter of the first Hamilton Earl of Arran) advanced to the earldom of Arran on 22 April. Lennox and Arran found colleagues in some former supporters of Mary, like John Maitland of Thirlstane (Lethington's brother), Lord Maxwell (on whom the earldom of Morton was conferred), Lord Seton, Kerr of Ferniehurst and Melville of Murdocairny.

In these two or three years, competing policies had gradually become more important than the mere rivalry of personalities, and forces had emerged which were to shape the pattern of Scottish history for the next sixteen years or so. There was a militant protestantism, political as much as ecclesiastical in its outlook, anxious for complete alignment with England against the papalist threat at home and abroad. This party was the heir of the revolutions of 1560 and 1567 and included the noble and lairdly families of the south-eastern counties and of Ayrshire which had been consistently protestant and anglophile. Its leaders were Lord Ruthven (created Earl of Gowrie in 1581), the eighth Earl of Angus (Morton's nephew and ward) and the sixth Earl of Glencairn. They had the backing of the presbyterians, who were ever ready to use their pulpits for the political propaganda of ultra-protestantism. At the other extreme was a faction associated with the cause of Queen Mary and with the intrigues of continental powers, especially Spain. This faction is called " Roman catholic," but it is as true of this period as of the following century that there was only " a catholic ' interest ', politically conservative, allergic to the ethos of the New Religion, . . . a politico-religious preference which could not issue in regular sacramental practice owing to the great scarcity of priests."[2] The one strong centre of Roman catholic practice seems to have been Dumfriesshire, under the aegis of Lord Maxwell, and it is unlikely that in the late 1570s any other Scottish nobleman, except perhaps Lord Seton, was a practising Roman catholic. Most of the leaders of the " Catholic interest " were characterised not by religious zeal but by a general conservatism, aristocratic lineage and association with the lands north of the Tay—the Earls of Atholl (d. 1579), Caithness (d. 1582) and Crawford (d. 1607) and, in later years, the Earls of Erroll (b. 1564) and Huntly (b. 1562). From 1580 onwards the Roman catholic mission to England began to have secondary effects in Scotland, and the Jesuits who occasionally appeared in the country gave a religious as well as a political stimulus to this party, but even then there were few " Roman catholics " who did not accommodate themselves to the ecclesiastical situation by conforming outwardly. Protestant fears, which seem rather forced in the light of the internal situation, were justified only in relation to the progress of the counter-reformation on the continent and the possibility that France or Spain would intervene in Scotland.

The interlude in the spring of 1578, when Morton had been temporarily excluded from power, had been too brief to permit any effective marshalling of forces, but it had brought hope to Mary, who looked with favour on Morton's temporary supplanters, Atholl and Argyll, and it revived the activities of her advocates on the continent, like the exiled Archbishop Beaton. Partisans of every view had begun to ask themselves what influences

2 David Mathew, *Scotland under Charles I*, p. 20; cf. " William Semple's reports on Scotland in 1588 and 1610," in *E. H. R.*, XLI. 579-83, where the editors comment that " the term catholic is used in a purely political sense."

could be brought to bear on the young king when the great bulwark of the English and protestant interest should be removed with the final displacement of Morton, now in his sixties. Therefore, when Lennox established his ascendancy, he became the focus for foreign intrigues. Lennox's purpose was to advance his own interests and there is no reason to believe that he was a zealous supporter either of the Roman Church or of Queen Mary's cause. In the France from which he came, many influential men supported the reformed faith, and Lennox made no difficulty about professing that religion in Scotland.[3] But the Duke of Guise, leader of the more militant Roman catholics in France, took an interest in Esmé Stewart's departure for Scotland, and Esmé did attract the attentions of those who thought that they could use him in the papal interest.

At the beginning of 1581 Mary proposed through Guise a scheme of " Association " whereby she should be restored as joint sovereign with James. Although James wrote an affectionate letter to his mother in April, neither he nor Lennox received her proposals with any cordiality, and Mary had to look rather to the possibility of armed intervention by Philip of Spain, with whom Guise had already been working in her interest. The intrigues in Scotland in 1581-2[4] were mainly of Spanish origin and were also linked with the Jesuit mission to England, for the English Jesuit Parsons began to work very closely with Mendoza, the Spanish ambassador in London, at the end of 1580. In the latter part of 1581 they despatched to Scotland first William Watts, a secular priest, and then Holt, a Jesuit, who reported that Scottish magnates like Huntly, Argyll, Caithness, Seton and Eglinton, as well as Lennox, would accept Spanish and papal help to bring about James's conversion or, should they fail, to transport him from the kingdom or even depose him. James interviewed these agents secretly and professed to favour Spain, but gave no real ground for hope of his conversion, and another priest reported that Lennox was untrustworthy and " avowedly schismatic."[5] In February 1582 two more Jesuits, William Crichton (who had been in Scotland with de Gouda in 1562) and Edmund Hay, arrived from Rome to join Holt, and in May,

---

[3] Cf. David Mathew, op. cit., p. 200n.
[4] The best account of those intrigues is in Thomas Graves Law, Collected Essays and Reviews, pp. 194-5, 217-43.   [5] Graves Law, op. cit., p. 229.

when Crichton returned from Scotland to Paris and interviewed Archbishop Beaton, Cardinal Allen (head of the English Roman catholic interest), Parsons and Guise, an ambitious enterprise was discussed: Lennox was to have a large Spanish and papal force with which to secure Scotland and then raise the Roman catholics in England. But there was no substantial support, either from Scotland or from the Spanish government, for those fantasies of the priests, which went far beyond what any responsible official could have countenanced and were based upon over-optimistic reports on the situation in Scotland.

While France and Spain were thus intriguing in Scotland, Elizabeth consistently refused to take effective action in favour of the friends of England. Among her officials were many ultra-protestants and puritans, like Francis Walsingham and William Davison, who took the view that Scotland's relationship to England should be that of a " satellite " in the modern sense of that term; that is, not only should Scotland be denied the right to an independent foreign policy, but her government should consist only of men acceptable to England and the two countries should share an ideology—the puritan-presbyterian ideology. Queen Elizabeth took a different view. Scotland was permitted to pursue an independent foreign policy, to the extent that King James could use negotiations with foreign powers to raise his value in the English market, although Elizabeth could at any time have checked these negotiations by conceding Scottish demands for a settlement of the succession and for financial subventions. Nor did the concept of ideological conformity ever appeal to her. There is no indication that in 1560 she had cared, as Randolph, her ambassador, had cared, that there should be uniformity of worship between the two kingdoms; although she later urged the Prayer Book on Mary that was with a view to weaning her from papistry and not to checking radical tendencies in Scotland; and Morton's policy of " conformity with England " did nothing to attract English support for his administration. It is doubtful if Elizabeth was much interested even in a common protestantism, for she could have allied with a Roman catholic Scotland as she allied with a Roman catholic France. Her frigid realism cut her off from the zealots, who " beckoned her in vain to a crusade on behalf of the reformed faith."[6]

6 J. B. Black, *The reign of Elizabeth*, pp. 333-4.

During Morton's regency Elizabeth had declined to listen to suggestions from him and from some of her own advisers that she should enter into a formal defensive league with Scotland and subsidise the administration there.[7] Beyond attempting to reconcile Atholl with Morton in December 1577, she did nothing to prevent the growth of a faction opposed to the regent, and once his position was threatened by Lennox and Arran she limited her action to instructing her envoys to make representations. One of them, Bowes, was told in April 1580 to try to undermine Lennox's credit, to encourage the propaganda of the ministers against him and to convey a threat to James that if he did not abandon Lennox he would lose England's friendship. In January 1580/1, again, Randolph was sent to Edinburgh with instructions to try to save Morton's life by encouraging the opposition to Lennox, but it was too late for anything short of armed intervention to have any effect and although a force was prepared on the Border it never marched and was disbanded in April.

Elizabeth's attitude to Lennox was determined by her relations with France and Spain. The threat to England came not from France, but from Spain, which annexed Portugal in 1580, was in touch with disaffected elements in Ireland and at this time seemed likely to subdue the revolt in the Netherlands. Elizabeth was therefore anxious to preserve an understanding with France, and in 1579 and 1581 there were negotiations for her marriage with the Duke of Anjou, brother of the French king, and leader of the French forces which were intervening against Spain in the Netherlands. Lennox represented France rather than Spain and there was no inherent reason why a French favourite in Scotland should be more dangerous than a French consort in England. Lennox was, in truth, much less dangerous than ultra-protestant Scottish ministers and ultra-protestant English agents professed to believe. To that extent, Elizabeth, who had already resisted ultra-protestant hostility to her marriage negotiations, was justified in refusing to be stampeded by her puritan politicians into intervening in favour of Morton and against Lennox.[8]

Within Scotland, political opposition to Lennox was headed

[7] The fullest account of English diplomacy in this period is in Conyers Read, *Walsingham*, Ch. IX.

[8] The circumstances of Morton's fall and English policy at the time are examined by Maurice Lee in " The fall of the Regent Morton: a problem in satellite diplomacy," in *Jour. Mod. Hist.*, XXVIII. 111-29.

by Angus, but, after the discovery of a plot in which he had been encouraged by Randolph, Angus was imprisoned and then fled to England.   More effective opposition came from many of the ministers, who were so adamant in their refusal to co-operate with Lennox that they may have stimulated him into trying to reach an understanding rather with Roman catholics at home and abroad.   He was denounced as an agent of the counter-reformation, and the fall of Morton and the appearance on the council of old supporters of Mary led to a kind of popish scare. It was in vain that Lennox formally accepted the reformed faith and that the king, in January 1580/1, signed the Negative Con-fession, a document which so vigorously denounced all things papistical that it could hardly be improved on as a test of protest-antism.   Nothing would reassure the presbyterians, who were invincibly opposed to the government because of its refusal to countenance the proceedings of the general assembly, which had recently condemned the office of bishop and prepared a scheme for the erection of presbyteries.   The government, instead of agreeing to make the changes in statute law necessary to authorise such a revolution, took up the presbyterians' challenge by making a fresh appointment to the archbishopric of Glasgow, which had fallen vacant: Montgomery, minister of Stirling, was appointed to the see, under an agreement which gave Lennox a substantial interest in the revenues.   When Montgomery was excomm-unicated by the presbytery of Edinburgh, the sentence was annul-led by royal proclamation, so that a direct conflict arose between the government and the dominant party in the church.

The reaction against Lennox came in a palace revolution called the Ruthven Raid, which took the shape of the seizure of the king's person in August 1582. Lennox withdrew through England to France in December and died in the following May. The motives for the " raid " were in part personal: the Lennox regime had been extravagant—a " King's Guard," under Captain James Stewart, was to cost £1,000 a month—and the deficit carried by Ruthven, Earl of Gowrie, who had been treasurer since 1571, had risen within a few months from £36,000 to £45,000; the Master of Glamis, who took a leading part in the " raid," had a feud with the popishly-inclined Earl of Crawford and had been fined £20,000 at the instance of Lennox;[9] nor should it

9 *Cal. S P. Scot.*, vi. 477.

be overlooked that whereas the Lennox regime had represented
a Stewart ascendancy (when power and profit went to Esmé
Stewart, James Stewart [Arran] and Stewart of Doune), Angus
and other Douglases had been forfeited under Lennox and were
now restored. But the faction which supported Gowrie included
men who, like him, represented the tradition of support for the
Reformation and the English alliance: Glencairn, Lindsay,
Angus, Douglas of Lochleven (Morton's heir), Cockburn of
Ormiston and other East Lothian lairds, as well as the Earl of
Mar, whose family had not been so strongly partisan. The *coup*
clearly had popular support, for Edinburgh decided to concur
with the Ruthven faction and rejected an appeal by Lennox,
from whom the burgesses were alienated because he had banished
from the city one of their ministers, John Dury, for an attack on
the administration.[10] Besides, the general assembly, which found
the ultra-protestant and anglophile character of the new government congenial, referred to the raid as " the late action of the
reformation."[11]

The Ruthven administration found that Elizabeth, who had
given encouragement before the raid and approval afterwards,
was more generous with good advice than with material aid. In
April 1583 an embassy was sent to London to ask that James
should have the English estates of the Lennox family,[12] the sum
of £10,000 as an immediate subvention and £5,000 annually.
Elizabeth declined to rise above £2,500, which the Scots esteemed
" so small that it might not with honour be publicly received."[13]
What was worse, Elizabeth, both before and after the embassy
to London, had been considering the possibility of Mary's release
and her " association " in sovereignty with her son. Such a
plan had much to commend it on paper: it was acceptable to
France, and therefore not contrary to Elizabeth's foreign policy;
to James's government it offered a legality which otherwise his
rule could hardly enjoy as long as his mother lived. But the
interests of the parties concerned were not really reconcilable.
Mary thought of the scheme as nothing less than a step towards
her restoration to full sovereignty; James welcomed the French
ambassadors who arrived at the end of 1582 and the beginning

---

[10] *Burgh Records*, IV. 240, 244-5.   [11] *B. U. K.* II. 594.
[12] A suggestion previously made in June 1578 (*R. P. C.*, II. 707).
[13] *Cal. S. P. Scot.*, VI. 413, 526-7.

of 1583 because they gave him recognition and he hoped that they would foster the opposition to the Ruthven group; and Elizabeth's main concern was to hold the threat of Mary's release over the Ruthven party in order to keep it subservient to her. Although the Ruthven administration obtained no effective English help, its critics made capital out of its English connexion and spread rumours of a scheme to have the king transported to England.

James escaped from the Raiders in June 1583. Magnates like Huntly, Crawford, Argyll, Montrose, Rothes and Marischal—mostly northerners of conservative preferences—rallied to him, but the leading figure in the administration was soon James Stewart, Earl of Arran, who, after an imprisonment during the Ruthven ascendancy, reappeared on the council in August 1583 and was joined by Thirlstane and Murdocairny. Reports that James was in the hands of " favourers of the French and of the king's mother "[14] caused such alarm in England that Walsingham himself, the secretary of state, was sent to Scotland at the end of August 1583. With his ultra-protestant prejudices, his presbyterian sympathies and his unrelenting hatred of Mary, he formed a very unfavourable impression of the situation. But his actions—lecturing James on the iniquity of changing his counsellors without Elizabeth's approval, taunting him with his inexperience and lack of power, and declining to deal with Arran—rather encouraged negotiations with continental powers. James had received a letter from Guise shortly after his escape from the Ruthven Raiders, and in reply he professed to be ready to work for his mother's release and to operate against Elizabeth. Early in 1584 he wrote again to Guise, and also to the pope, at a time when Arran's position was threatened by a conspiracy encouraged by Walsingham and other English diplomats. Mar and Glamis, with Angus and Lords John and Claud Hamilton, actually seized Stirling Castle in April 1584, but they received no material English aid and, when the king gathered a force which would have overwhelmed theirs, they had to flee to England. Gowrie, who had been arrested before the action at Stirling, was executed on 2 May. Thus Arran's position was strengthened, and after this he felt he had no need to seek continental support.

Arran, who had been soldiering in France and Sweden before returning to Scotland in 1579, was a man of education and

14 *Cal S. P. Scot.*, VI. 538, cf. 558.

accomplishments, described as "very wise and learned,"[15] and was, incidentally, the brother-in-law of John Knox. He became chancellor on 15 May 1584 and three days later the office of secretary was given to Maitland of Thirlstane, who resembled his brother Lethington in both his ability and his enthusiasm for amity with England. Although the administration represented a strong conservative reaction against the left-wing extremes of the Ruthven Raiders, it did not go as far as the Esmé Stewart regime, which, alike in its flirtations with papal agents, its flouting of the presbyterians and its disregard of England, had represented a sharp swing to the right. Arran's government was more like a reversion to the *via media* of Morton, who, while he was a protestant, and well disposed to England, was not prepared to accept dictation from England and was resolutely opposed to presbyterianism. The ecclesiastical policy of Arran was determined for him by the presbyterians' association with the Ruthven Raiders. Andrew Melville, summoned to trial for seditious speech in the pulpit, declined to submit to the jurisdiction of the council and, to avoid imprisonment, fled to England in March 1584. In May the "Black Acts" asserted the power of the king over all persons and estates, denounced "the new pretended presbyteries" and reaffirmed the authority of the bishops. Nearly a score of ministers followed Melville to exile in England.

The ultra-protestant English diplomats, influenced by their contacts with the presbyterian exiles, remained invincibly hostile to Arran, but the latter realised that those diplomats spoke neither for the whole of English official opinion nor for the queen, and he had hopes that his anti-presbyterian policy would facilitate an understanding with England if the diplomats could be by-passed. With this end in view, Archbishop Adamson of St Andrews had gone to England in November 1583, partly to represent the Scottish government politically, partly to seek Anglican support for its ecclesiastical policy. The ecclesiastical side of the venture was a failure. Not only did Adamson meet with a very cool reception from Archbishop Whitgift,[16] but the notion of Anglo-Scottish conformity on an Anglican basis still made no appeal to Elizabeth. She had regarded the first successes of the Scottish presbyterians,

---

15 *R. P. C.* III. lxxi.
16 G. Donaldson, "The attitude of Whitgift and Bancroft to the Scottish church," in *Trans. Roy. Hist. Soc.*, 4th ser., XXIV.

between 1581 and 1583, with equanimity, and although she was warned by a Scot in 1584 that the " democratical designs " of the presbyterians were the " enemy to all princes "[17] she was not to reach an appreciation of the political dangers of presbyterianism until so late as 1590, when she had the impudence to " warn " James " that there is risen, both in your realm and mine, a sect of perilous consequence, such as would have no kings but a presbytery."[18] James's, or Arran's, greater foresight had led them to legislate against precisely this peril in 1584, but that had gained them no credit with Elizabeth.

The political side of the approach to England was, however, more successful, for Elizabeth did not share the distrust of Arran which moved Walsingham and Davison, and she chose another agent in Lord Hunsdon, who was favourable to Arran and had a discussion with him in August 1584. There also appeared a new agent of Scottish diplomacy, in the Master of Gray, who had been in France and returned in company with Ludovick, Duke of Lennox, the son of Esmé. Gray had been, and nominally still was, in the service of Mary, who was again proposing the " Association," but he saw the weakness of Mary's plans and also recognised that Philip of Spain would not conquer England to give it to James. He therefore advocated an English alliance, which would ensure the retention of Mary in captivity, and in October 1584, James, who was personally attracted to Gray, sent him to London. He was to ask for the expulsion of the fugitive lords, and he did prevail on Elizabeth to make them retire from Newcastle to the south of England. But Gray was also to work for an Anglo-Scottish alliance, and he was successful in allaying Elizabeth's doubts about the reliability of the Scottish administration. In May 1585, after James had categorically repudiated any intention of approving of the " Association," Elizabeth sent Sir Edward Wotton to Scotland to offer £4,000 down and £4,000 yearly, and on the acceptance of these terms a league was formulated in July.[19]

But although Arran's government had thus achieved a success abroad, his position at home was not secure. The supple Gray was ready to listen to Walsingham's proposals for undermining Arran,

---

17 *Cal. S. P. Scot.*, VII. No. 508.   18 *Ibid.*, x. No. 441.
19 *Cal. S. P. Scot.*, VIII. 43-5. The payments made in subsequent years varied from £2,000 to £5,000 (H. G. Stafford, *James VI of Scotland and the throne of England*, p. 293).

and when Wotton came to Scotland he also conspired with Gray and Maitland against the chancellor, who found himself discredited on all sides. He had gone too far with England to retain the support of the Roman catholic element, but he had not gained the confidence of the ultra-protestants and he had bitter enemies in all who sympathised with the exiled ministers and lords. His opponents tried to sow in the king's mind the suspicion that Arran was not sincere about the league, and when, on 27 July 1585, Sir Francis Russell, son of the Earl of Bedford, was killed in a Border affray by an ally of Arran, Wotton accused Arran of instigating the incident in order to break the league. James was brought to agree to put Arran in ward, but his attachment to the chancellor soon made him relent. Elizabeth, on the prompting of Gray, then decided to release the exiled lords. They returned from England in October and were before Stirling on 2 November. As there was no force to resist them, the king surrendered and Arran fled.

Negotiations with England were soon resumed. At the beginning of March 1586 the veteran Randolph, who had helped to lay the foundations of Anglo-Scottish amity in 1560, arrived in Edinburgh to conclude the league. The Scots had all along wanted not only recognition of James's title to succeed Elizabeth, but the conferring on him of an English peerage and provision for mutual naturalisation of English and Scots in each other's countries. None of those points was conceded in the agreement concluded on 5 July 1586.[20] Elizabeth would not even raise her annual subsidy from £4,000 to £5,000, as she had half promised, and the only undertaking she would give was never to do or suffer to be done anything to the derogation of any right or title that might be due to James, unless she should be provoked by manifest ingratitude. Each country was to give the other certain specified help in the event of an invasion.

The league had not long been made when it was subjected first to one test, then to another. Already in 1585 England's arrangements with Scotland, in July, had been followed by a treaty with the Netherlands in August and the despatch of Drake to attack Spain in September, and the sequence of later events— 1586, league with Scotland; 1587, execution of Mary; 1588, the Armada—has an air of inevitability. As early as August

[20] *Cal. S. P. Scot.*, VIII. 491 ff.

1586, in the month after the conclusion of the league, the Master of Gray reminded Elizabeth that *mortui non mordent*[21] and in September James learned that his mother's life was in danger because of the revelations of her knowledge of Babington's plot against Elizabeth. It was on 11 October that a commission was appointed to try Mary for conspiring against Elizabeth's life, and on 12 November, after she had been found guilty, parliament petitioned for her execution. Elizabeth signed the death warrant on 1 February and it was carried out on the 8th. There was much excited talk in Scotland, both before and after the execution. Nobles and prelates offered to support the king in action to avenge his mother's death, and the Borderers carried out raids into northern England. But James must have viewed with detachment the fate of a parent whom he had never known, whom he had been trained to hate and despise and whose very existence was an obstacle to his position and prospects; any pleas he might make for his mother's life could have no motive save compliance with propriety. His one real fear was that Mary's taint, as a condemned traitor, might be held to descend to him and debar him from the English succession. His attitude therefore involved the possibility of a bargain: his unofficial representative in London, Archibald Douglas, conveyed the impression that should James's title be recognised he would stomach his mother's death and would not break the league; and his official ambassadors, Sir Robert Melville and the Master of Gray—sent after parliament had ratified the sentence on Mary—conveyed a strong appeal for something short of the extreme penalty but at the same time brought a suggestion that James's right of succession should now be publicly recognised. Accounts of his behaviour when news came that his mother had actually been put to death are so conflicting that they can be reconciled only on the assumption that he professed a sorrow which he cannot have felt. All policy was in favour of acquiescence, and Walsingham gave James a reminder, which he cannot have needed, that it would be folly to take up arms alone and that neither France nor Spain would intervene except in their own interests and not in his. James professed himself satisfied with the official explanation that the actual execution had been unintentional on Elizabeth's part, and, just as she made a scapegoat of Davison, the secretary who had sent the death

21 *R. P. C.*, IV. 168.

warrant off to Fotheringhay, so James made something of a scapegoat of Gray, who was imprisoned partly because of the messages which he had conveyed to Elizabeth.

The second test of the league came in 1588. In preparation for the encounter with the Armada, Elizabeth in June limited her subsidy to £2,000, leaving her ambassador free to encourage James by unauthorised promises. There was, of course, the Roman catholic " interest " in Scotland, ready to co-operate with Spain: in 1586 Huntly, Maxwell and Lord Claud Hamilton sent letters to Spain asking for men and money, and in 1588, in association with the Jesuit William Crichton, they were thinking in terms of a Spanish invasion which would be followed by James's conversion. Philip was not very interested in such plans, and a Spanish conquest of England would very likely be followed by that of Scotland. However, as James felt that his pro-Spanish nobles might offer a faint chance of survival should Spain defeat England, he was not prepared actively to discourage their intrigues. Otherwise he was wholly loyal to his league with England, for Scotland was prepared to resist should the Spaniards land. James also took action to curb Maxwell, who alone of the pro-Spanish lords took up arms, and he demonstrated his protestantism by taking action against Jesuits and challenging one of them to a public debate. He was rewarded for his fidelity by a gift of £3,000, which made the unusually high total of £5,000 for the year.

The question of the king's marriage had long been under consideration, and at one stage English diplomats had been concerned lest James should marry into one of the Roman catholic houses. A match with Catharine, the sister of Henry of Navarre, the Huguenot heir to the French throne, had much to commend it politically, but Catharine was eight years older than James and Henry could not offer a large dowry, while James could not provide the armed assistance required by Henry for his war against the papalist party in France and their Spanish allies. A Danish match, which had been suggested as early as 1582, was clearly preferable, for Denmark, though protestant and an old commercial friend of Scotland, was not, like Henry of Navarre, committed to hostility to Spain and, while unlikely to make demands on James, might do something to help him to prosecute his claim to England. In 1585 and 1587 a request had been made for the hand of Elizabeth, the elder daughter of

Frederick II, whom failing for Anne, who was eight years James's junior. A further mission was sent in 1589, with extravagant demands for military help should James require it to make good his claim to England, for a vast dowry and for the surrender of the Danish rights in Orkney and Shetland. In the end Anne's dowry was fixed at 75,000 dollars, equivalent to £150,000 Scots. The marriage took place by proxy at Copenhagen on 20 August 1589, and Anne set out for Scotland, but, driven back by bad weather, had to put into Oslo. The impatient bridegroom embarked at Leith on 22 October and married Anne in Oslo on 23 November. They travelled to Kronborg at the end of the year and remained in Denmark until April. They landed at Leith on 1 May 1590.

Anne was a lively creature, but no suitable mate intellectually for James, though her influence on the culture of the court and the country may have been considerable. James settled into matrimony, and Anne bore him seven children between 1594 and 1606, but after a phase when James played the part of an ardent lover there was little depth in their affection for each other and in later years they were almost estranged. James was probably on the whole disappointed in his marriage and also in his relations with his sons—the energetic, open-hearted and direct Henry and the reserved Charles. In his later years he fell under the domination of male favourites, notably Robert Kerr, Earl of Somerset, and George Villiers, Duke of Buckingham. The attraction was partly physical, but there is no reason to believe that the relationships were scandalous, and the mere fact that the king made so much of his favourites in public suggests that nothing to be ashamed of took place in private. The truth seems to be that James became a sentimental old man, whose genuine fondness for children, coupled with his failure to achieve his ideal relationship with his wife and sons, led him to take vicarious pleasure in the marriages and family life of younger men.

James had attained the age of twenty-one in June 1587, and his gradual emancipation from control by individuals or factions was by that time complete. In his childhood, an attempt had been made to indoctrinate him with the political theories of the reformers, who, after suffering at the hands of two generations of hostile sovereigns, at last had as their prince a child whom they believed they could mould into their ideal monarch. While

George Buchanan was instructing James he was working on his *Rerum Scoticarum Historia* (1582), in which the reigns of real and mythical monarchs are used to illustrate the responsibility of kings to their subjects. Against Buchanan's lessons there was the inevitable reaction as James grew older. The king was not to be moulded by his preceptors, for alike in his attitude to Rome, to his mother, and to his people he took an independent line. So far as statecraft was concerned, he may have been more impressed by example than by precept, and the first example had been that of Morton, who ruled Scotland from the king's seventh to his fifteenth year, a period during which this precocious youth became capable of drawing his own conclusions from what he saw. Since then he had seen the extremist regimes of Lennox and the Ruthven Raiders, and next the more moderate administration of Arran, with which he was in sympathy and during which his own ideas first began to carry some weight. Already in July 1583 he had announced his desire to " draw his nobility to unity and concord and to be known to be a universal king,"[22] above faction and choosing his councillors at will. The administration which had been organised after Arran's fall at the end of 1585 was such a coalition as the king had in mind, for although the leaders of the Ruthven faction—Angus, Mar and the Master of Glamis—had come back from England, and Glamis became treasurer, Lords John and Claud Hamilton also returned from exile, and former members of Arran's administration, such as the Master of Gray and Maitland of Thirlstane, as well as conservative magnates like Huntly, Montrose, Crawford and Marischal, sat on the council. Maitland, appointed keeper of the great seal on 31 May 1586, became chancellor on 29 July 1587 and was at the head of affairs. There could be no question of returning to the ultra-protestant partisanship of the Ruthven Raiders, and the proceedings of this administration were not so different from those of Arran, save that Maitland, who " kept the king of two grounds sure, neither to cast out with the kirk nor with England,"[23] was more conciliatory towards the presbyterians than Arran had been.

The influence of the king, who now very frequently attended the council in person, was always on the side of the *via media* amid discordant policies, and on such a *via media* he was in the end to engineer a large measure of national unity. But in an age

[22] *Cal. S. P. Scot.*, VI. 523.   [23] James Melville, *Diary*, p. 271.

when the instruments of coercion hardly existed and the only weapons available were diplomacy and conciliation, the position of an administration which sought to avoid capitulation to one extremist faction or another was inevitably a precarious one, at least until its policy could win over the less intransigent of the rival partisans. There were, besides, peculiar difficulties in maintaining a coalition under Maitland: his policy of general pacification, economy and efficiency made no positive appeal to the nobility, and they could not look with favour on the elevation to office of new men or on the eminence attained by Maitland himself, who was the first chancellor in the century who was neither a prelate nor a peer. While the conduct of affairs fell more and more to officials who belonged to non-noble families, the peers, with hardly an exception, became infrequent attenders at the council. On the other hand, Maitland's unpopularity to some extent sheltered his master, who was able to ride out one storm, in 1592, because he sacrificed his minister to the extent of prevailing on him to retire from the court and remain in the background for two years. While the disgruntled aristocrats could hardly combine against Maitland, since they were divided by personal and family feuds as well as by ecclesiastical and political differences, his position was challenged from both the right and the left.

The " Roman catholic " interest, headed by the conservative northern earls, had lost some of its purpose since Mary's death, but it figures large in the history of the period partly because of the king's attitude to it. James was always by temperament inclined to conciliation, at least of the powerful, and he had not read Scottish history without discovering that conciliation was politic, but he had other reasons for wishing to avoid an irreparable breach with the friends of Rome. He did not want to give an excuse to some fanatical priest to assassinate him as William the Silent and Henry III of France had been assassinated, and he did not want to incur papal excommunication, which would damage his prospects with the English Roman catholics. They suffered under harsh penal laws, and James's standing was improved in their eyes by his tenderness towards the northern earls, added to the mildness of Scottish law and practice in dealing with recusants. James always sought to maintain lines of communication, direct or indirect, with the pope and with continental princes, and it was partly for this reason that in 1587 he had taken into his favour the exiled Archbishop of Glasgow (whom he commissioned as his ambassador in France) and the exiled Bishops of Ross and Dunblane.[24] Besides, as a matter of domestic policy, the northern earls could be played off against the ultra-protestants. Finally, policy apart, James had personal reasons for his avoidance of severity, because the young and courtly Earl of Huntly in 1588 married a daughter of Esmé Stewart, to whose children the king transferred some of the favour he had given to their father. At any rate, whether out of weakness, policy or favour, James's dealings with the northern earls followed a con-sistent pattern of refusal to proceed to strong measures, and in consequence these troublesome magnates enjoyed what seems an indefensible degree of licence.

Huntly professed conversion to the reformed faith at the time of his marriage, and he was so high in favour at court that he was made captain of the guard. In February 1588/9 there arrived from England letters which had been intercepted there and in which Huntly and others had expressed their regret at the failure of the Armada and had promised Philip of Spain their aid in a future invasion of England. Huntly suffered a brief imprisonment and was dismissed from his captaincy of the guard, but was soon reported to be preparing to march on Edinburgh, along with Errol and Crawford. The king gathered a force from the southern counties and advanced to the Brig of Dee, whereupon the earls' followers lost their courage and the king entered Aberdeen. Huntly and Crawford surrendered, but were merely placed in easy confinement for a few months. Again, after Huntly headed an attack on the house of Donibristle which led to the murder of the Earl of Moray (February 1591/2), he was punished only by a brief nominal imprisonment. Once more, at the end of 1592, George Kerr, a Roman catholic about to sail for Spain, was found to have in his possession certain blank papers signed by Huntly, Errol, Gordon of Auchindoun and the tenth Earl of Angus (who had recently succeeded to the title and broke the protestant tradition of the house). There was nothing expli-citly incriminating in the papers, but colour and force were given to them by knowledge of the letters intercepted in 1589, and this doubtless determined the course of the examination of Kerr, who, under torture, confessed to a plot begun by William Crichton, a

[24] *R. P. C.*, IV. 154, 163-4, 388-9; cf. *S. H. S. Misc.*, I. 51 ff.

Jesuit, whereby the northern earls were to aid Spain in an invasion of the west of Scotland.[25] The king marched on Aberdeen in February 1592/3 and the earls fled to Caithness, but a parliament in July which was expected to forfeit them did not do so, and in November James secured an act of oblivion for the earls, provided that they would submit to the reformed church; if they did not conform they were to go into exile but retain their estates. This was regarded, with some justification, as the peak of the king's policy of concession to the " Roman catholic " party.

On the other side, one of the foundations of the ultra-protestant cause had vanished with the conclusion of the league with England, for the days were gone when the foreign relations of a Scottish government could provide the reason or pretext for action by an English-sponsored party. It is probably true, too, that after the death of the eighth Earl of Angus in 1588 there was no peer who adhered to the ultra-protestant tradition out of strong religious principles,[26] and none of the families with that tradition was led by a man of statesmanlike qualities. At the head of the house of Ruthven, since the execution of the Earl of Gowrie in 1584, there were only young boys, and the feud of this family against the royal house was carried on only by the fifth Earl of Atholl, who had married Gowrie's eldest daughter. James Stewart of Doune, again, who became Earl of Moray by marrying the daughter of the regent, was significant mainly as the inheritor of the purely territorial feud of the house of Moray against Huntly, and he lives in popular memory as " the bonnie earl " who was " the queen's true love." The most militant of the protestants was Francis Stewart, Earl of Bothwell. As nephew of the Regent Moray and brother-in-law of the eighth Earl of Angus, he stood in the protestant tradition, but there was no religious zeal in a character so complex that it was remarked of him that at once

---

[25] This is the view of Graves Law (*op. cit.*, pp. 257-9), who points out that *A discoverie of the unnatural and traiterous conspiracie of the Scottish papists*, published in 1593, is largely taken up with the letters discovered in 1589, and suggests that the protestants made more of the " Blanks " than the evidence warranted. Mr Francis Shearman, in *Innes Review*, III. goes further and suggests that the papers found on Kerr may have been quite innocent. The paper which, according to Calderwood (v. 25), was suppressed because it " touched the king with knowledge and approbation " is identified by Graves Law with James's summing up of the pros and cons of supporting Spain (*H. M. C. Salisbury MSS.*, IV. 214).

[26] James Melville, *Diary*, pp. 185, 315; cf. Calderwood, v. 549; *Cal. S. P. Scot.*, XII. No. 452.

for wickedness, valour and " good parts " he surpassed any three of the other Scottish nobles.[27] His policy was shaped partly by his dual feud with Maitland: the Hepburn Earls of Bothwell had contested the priory of Haddington with Lethington, and Thirlstane was a competitor for the priory of Coldingham, which had belonged to Lord John Stewart, father of Francis.

Bothwell's actions lacked consistency, and his escapades were to all appearances less purposeful and more futile than even the manoeuvrings of the northern earls, but he seems to have believed that he could insult with impunity a king who was his first cousin; he was noted for the education and culture which James respected and he displayed a dash and verve for which the cautious king may have had a perverse admiration. In his impetuous way, Bothwell was moved by revulsion against Elizabeth for her execution of Mary, as well as by his hatred of Maitland, into temporary collaboration with the Roman catholic element, and at the time of the Brig of Dee affair he tried to raise the Borderers against the king, but had to surrender. In January 1590/1 he broke into Edinburgh tolbooth and seized a witness due to appear at the trial of one of his adherents. In April came revelations, in the course of trials for witchcraft, that Bothwell had employed witches to operate against the king on his voyage to Denmark. Bothwell was imprisoned, but escaped in June, and in July the king raised a force with which he pursued the earl to the Borders. He was denounced a rebel and declared an outlaw, but he next appeared in Edinburgh and Leith, publicly defying the law. On 27 December he raided Holyroodhouse itself by night, possibly with the connivance of courtiers who were discontented with Maitland, and made his escape before he could be seized. In June 1592, after being forfeited by parliament, Bothwell almost obtained possession of the king's person at Falkland, but was beaten off. In July 1593, after parliament had reaffirmed his forfeiture, he made his way into Holyroodhouse again and extorted from the king a promise of a fair trial on the old charge of witchcraft, on the understanding that he would meantime retire from the court. In a convention in September, however, the concessions to Bothwell were revoked. He made a final " raid," in April 1594, when James had to retire hastily from Leith to Edinburgh. After that, in his last phase of activity

[27] *Cal. S. P. Scot.*, ix. 655.

as in his first, he was in league with the northern earls, and he finally left Scotland in April 1595.

Such serious political importance as attached to Bothwell arose from his leadership of the protests against James's leniency to the northern earls. Popular sympathy in Scotland was with Moray against Huntly, while the publicity given to the affair of the Spanish Blanks turned English official opinion, too, against King James. The populace, the ministers and Queen Elizabeth all therefore encouraged Bothwell, especially when it seemed that he was being more harshly treated than Huntly and Errol were. Some of the more violent of the ministers were prepared to give their blessing to any of Bothwell's escapades, for he was the Lord's " sanctified plague," appointed to compel the king to " turn to Him."[28] The more sober of the ministers, however, while fully agreeing with the criticism of James, did not approve of the earl: James Melville remarked that he " never lyket the man nor haid to do with him."[29]

The fact is that James was all along less of a partisan than his protestant critics alleged, and he illustrated his concept of " universal kingship " by an attempt, concurrently with his leniency to Huntly and his associates, to reach a *rapprochement* with the presbyterians through concessions which, from the civil point of view, were in non-essentials. There was much to foster amicable relations between the king and the ministers. The Spanish threat of 1588, for example, was a reminder of the benefits accruing from a godly prince, and younger men, who had never known the rule of a sovereign antipathetic to the Reformation, learned something of the fear which had dominated the minds of their seniors. Then, during the king's absence in Norway and Denmark, considerable authority was exercised, with full royal approval, by Robert Bruce, the minister of Edinburgh; and at Queen Anne's coronation Bruce officiated and Andrew Melville recited a Latin poem. At this stage James was out of humour with English churchmen because of reflexions on his sincerity in a sermon published by Richard Bancroft in 1589, and he delighted presbyterians by extolling the perfection of the Church of Scotland and extending favour and protection to refugees from the anti-puritan campaign in England. Meantime the gradual increase of the authority of presbyteries at the expense of that of the

[28] Calderwood, v. 255-6.   [29] J. Melville, *Diary*, p. 315.

bishops was being tacitly permitted, and the Act of Annexation of 1587, which appropriated the ecclesiastical temporalities to the crown, had contributed to the temporary eclipse of the episcopate. In May 1592 parliament at last authorised a presbyterian polity. This concession in a purely ecclesiastical sphere was probably designed, as part of a bargain, to wean the ministers from their political opposition, for the same parliament passed sentence of forfeiture on the Earl of Bothwell. But all James's amiable behaviour did not amount to a single material concession: the acts against clerical interference in politics stood unrepealed and no fresh provision was made for the endowment of the reformed church.

These ecclesiastical concessions may, therefore, have been a mere manoeuvre, but circumstances in the end drove James to align himself with the protestant rather than the Roman catholic interest. For one thing, Elizabeth made her displeasure felt by manipulating her subsidy, which in 1592 and 1594 amounted to only £2,000. Again, any government was bound to appreciate the services which the ministers could render as propagandists, and in 1592, when public opinion was strongly against the king for his suspected complicity in the murder of Moray, he had to take the undignified step of sending for some ministers and requesting them to " clear his part before the people."[30] James seems to have determined to rely on the ministers until he had broken the political threat of Roman catholicism. In the autumn of 1594, after the northern earls had been excommunicated by the general assembly and forfeited by parliament, the king marched against them, accompanied by Andrew Melville and other ministers, in whom he expressed his confidence as trusty subjects. Argyll, a youth of eighteen and a personal rival of Huntly, was sent on ahead and was roughly handled in Glenlivet at the beginning of October, but the earls again declined to face the king in person and fled before him. Huntly and Errol promised to go abroad and did so in March 1595. This display of severity seems to have convinced the earls that they must submit. Huntly and Errol returned secretly in June 1596 and came to terms, first with a convention in August which agreed that they might remain in Scotland if they satisfied the king and the church, and then with the general assembly itself. In June 1597 they were formally

[30] Calderwood, v. 145.

received into the reformed church and in November their forfeitures were revoked by parliament. These proceedings marked
the extinction of Roman catholicism as a political danger.

The extinction of ultra-protestantism as a political danger
was the outcome of a situation in which the triumphant ministers
over-reached themselves. It had been apparent for years that
they recognised no limits to their competence. In 1592 the church
tried to prevent Scottish ships from undertaking charters for
French merchants, and in 1593 the general assembly prevailed on
the convention of royal burghs to suspend trade with Spain. An
attempt was also made to forbid the holding of a Monday market
in Edinburgh, on the ground that preparations for it encroached
on " the Sabbath."[31] The clergy even tried to interfere in English
affairs: in December 1589 the presbytery of Edinburgh had drawn
up a petition in which they proposed to tell Queen Elizabeth
that she was "hielie provoking our patience," to threaten her
with " a fearfull curse within your owen bowells," and to ask
her " to proclaim a public fast out-through your realm, with
preaching and supplication."[32]   Neither the authorisation of
presbyterianism in 1592 nor the settlement with Huntly and
Errol in 1596 allayed fears about the religious soundness of the
government, and 1596 was the peak year of ministerial presump-
tion. There was, for one thing, plain speaking about the habits
of the king and queen: in March the king was rebuked for
" banning and swearing " and the queen for " not repairing to
the word and sacraments, night walking, balling etc.," and in
November the queen was accused of " spending of all time in
vanity."[33] It is only fair to say that the general assembly also drew
up an indictment of the whole nation which would suggest that
Scottish morals had never fallen so low as at this time of presbyterian ascendancy,[34] and even ministers were denounced as " drun-
kards, liars, detractors, flatterers, breakers of promises, brawlers
and quarrellers."[35]   In September of this year Andrew Melville
had that famous interview with the king, at Falkland, when he
lectured "God's silly vassal " on his subordination to the church;[36]
about the same time the minister of St Andrews, when called to

[31] *Edinburgh Burgh Records*, VI. 73-4, 95-6; *History and life of James the Sext*, pp.
254-5; *Convention of Royal Burghs Records*, I. 402; Chambers, *Edinburgh Merchants*, p. 13.
[32] Calderwood, v. 72-7.   [33] *Ibid.*, pp. 408-9, 459.
[34] Calderwood, v. 409-10; *B. U. K.*, III. 873-4.
[35] *B. U. K.*, III. 866.   [36] J. Melville, *Diary*, pp. 370-1.

account for sermons in which he had preached that " all kings are devil's children " and had called Queen Elizabeth an atheist, declined the jurisdiction of the council;[37] in November it was demanded that the king's ministers of state should be called to account for " their negligence in hearing the word ";[38] and in December commissioners of the church insisted on being in constant attendance on the king because of a fear of " the alteration of religion, or the bringing in of liberty of conscience at the least."[39]

At this stage the government retorted by ordering the commissioners of the assembly to leave Edinburgh, declaring their powers illegal, ordaining that ministers must submit to the council when accused of sedition, and reviving an act prohibiting speech against king and council. To that extent ministerial apprehensions may have been genuine enough, but it may have been thought that a popish scare, which had led to an ultra-protestant triumph in 1581-2, might do the same again. At any rate, on 17 December, when the king and the lords of session were sitting in the tolbooth of Edinburgh and the ministers were gathered in a neighbouring church, the cry arose that the papists were up and that king, councillors and ministers were to be massacred. The tumult was stayed, but the king chose to blame the ministers and the citizens. The town council grovelled before the royal displeasure and was ready to comply with almost anything which could contribute towards " pacefeying his hienes wrayth consavet aganis " the burgh.[40] The ministers of Edinburgh were ordered to ward in the castle and the magistrates undertook not to receive them back, or admit other ministers in future, without the king's consent; the burgh was fined 20,000 merks and ceased temporarily to be the seat of government. Thus the king, and not the ministers, had turned the incident to account.

In 1596-7, with the end of the menace of political Roman catholicism and of political presbyterianism, although James's problems within Scotland were not yet solved, the way was clear for him to pass from defence to the policy of aggression which from that point onwards he steadily pursued. The achievement within Scotland contributed in more ways than one to the solution of the dominating external issue, that of the English

---

[37] *R. P. C.*, v. 326-7, 334-6, 340-2. [38] Calderwood, v. 462.
[39] Row, *History*, p. 184. [40] *Edinburgh Burgh Records*, vi. 174.

succession.   In his dealings with foreign powers and in his dealings with parties within England itself—transactions which form no part of Scottish history[41]—James could not appeal to the power of the purse or to any force he was likely to have at his command; as in his internal policy, his only weapon was diplomacy.

[41] For a good account of those negotiations, see H. G. Stafford, *op. cit.*

11

TWO KINGDOMS OR ONE KINGDOM?

The reformed church had started its career in rebellion against the crown and had been associated with a revolution which deposed the sovereign. Before the new monarch reached maturity, Andrew Melville was on the scene, with his doctrine of the " two kingdoms," which denied ecclesiastical authority even to a " godly prince " but authorised ministers to " teach " the king his duty in civil as well as ecclesiastical affairs. The theological challenge was met by a king who was himself a theologian, the first king about whose thoughts and ideals we are adequately informed through his own writings.[1] James was an apologist for monarchy, and for a monarchy responsible to God and not to the people. The laws of Scotland, he explained, did not exist before the monarchy; on the contrary, the king had been and still was the author of the laws, which he made with the consent of his high court of parliament. Even against a bad king, rebellion is not justified, for the people must endure him as a divine discipline, and his punishment is to be left to God, " the sorest and sharpest schoolmaster."[2] Nor had preachers any right to censure their rulers, and ministers who interfered in politics were anti-monarchical and beset with the sins of pride and ambition to which clerics were always prone. James had a strong sense of his own responsibility to God, and remarked that " the highest bench is sliddriest to sit upon,"[3] but he felt no need for the dictatorship of clerical mentors, and he was head of all estates, clerical as well as lay.

[1] See p. 256.   [2] C. H. McIlwain, *Political works of James I*, p. 69.
[3] *Ibid.*, p. 70.

The issues between the king and Melville were largely constitutional and political: James believed that the place where the voice of the church could be heard on political matters was in parliament, where the church's representatives sat as one of the estates; bishops were the obvious agents not only for bringing about the subordination of the ministers but also for ensuring their representation in parliament. But there was an underlying theological difference. Melville claimed that, because Christ was " King and Head of His Church,"[4] therefore supreme ecclesiastical authority should be vested in a general assembly. To James this seemed not only poor logic but a limitation of the kingship of Christ: that kingship, he believed, extended to the state as well as to the church and could as properly be exercised through king and parliament, on behalf of the entire Christian community, as through a general assembly consisting only of " ecclesiastical persons." James did not deny that he was God's vassal, and indeed gloried in the fact, but he believed in one kingdom, of which God was the Head, with the king as His vicegerent.

Although the presbyterian programme had been adopted by the general assembly in 1578, the necessary legislation to authorise the transference of power from bishops to presbyteries had been refused while Morton and Lennox were in control, and even during the more favourable administration of the Ruthven Raiders only slight progress was made towards the displacement of bishops and commissioners by presbyteries, except in a few areas in the central Lowlands. Then, by the " Black Acts " of 1584, presbyteries were denounced and episcopal authority reaffirmed. As kirk sessions and synods were still authorised, administration went on very much as it had done in the 1560s and 1570s, but the bishops and commissioners were now to be responsible to the king and not to the general assembly. Indeed, the intention was to suppress the general assembly, and there was a statute formally asserting the authority of the high court of parliament, " of late years called in some doubt."[5] Here was the royal answer to Andrew Melville.

After Arran's fall, Melville and his associates were disappointed to find that there was no immediate reversal of policy. Not only did the " Black Acts " remain the law, but there was a new

---

[4] Calderwood, III. 628.	[5] *A. P. S.*, III. 293.

statute against criticism of the king, his government and laws,[6] and sentence of imprisonment was passed on a minister who remarked that, whereas he had considered Arran to be the persecutor of the church, he now found that the persecutor was the king himself. However, a compromise in ecclesiastical administration was worked out by councillors in February 1585/6 and accepted reluctantly by a general assembly in May: the erection of presbyteries was permitted and, although bishops were to be permanent moderators of presbyteries and synods, the bishops were to act in administration only with the advice of committees of ministers, they were to be subject to the general assembly and each bishop was to have his own congregation. The scheme did not operate well, for the atmosphere was unfavourable to compromise, and in succeeding years the government tacitly permitted the development of presbyteries and the depression of the episcopate, so that by 1592 bishops had been almost eliminated from ecclesiastical administration.

The statute of 1592 which at last authorised the presbyterian system was, therefore, little more than the recognition of a *fait accompli*. Nor did it do much to increase the effectiveness of presbyteries, for in succeeding years considerable powers were still exercised by individual commissioners, presbyteries were not in operation everywhere, and there were hundreds of parishes without even ministers and kirk sessions. The office of bishop, while certainly eclipsed, was not abolished, and cathedral and diocesan dignities, which it was hard to reconcile with presbyterian parity, likewise survived. Lay patronage, too, was maintained, and on the central issue of ecclesiastical independence there was no capitulation to Andrew Melville. It was conceded that a general assembly was to meet once a year, but, as it was still an offence to convoke ecclesiastical assemblies without the king's authority, the time and place of meeting were to be named by the king or his commissioner at the preceding assembly; the assembly was free to appoint time and place if neither king nor commissioner was present, but no machinery was provided to ensure that a time and place would be appointed should the king or commissioner be present but decline to appoint. The assembly had not been transformed into the clerical body envisaged in the second Book of Discipline, for it still had " barons " and burgesses

6 *A. P. S.*, III, p. 375.

among its members and retained something of the character of a meeting of the three estates. Melville's theories would have been satisfied only by parliament's abdication of its right to legislate for the church, but, while ecclesiastical independence was a convenient cry when parliament ventured to legislate against the presbyterian system, few presbyterians were so doctrinaire as to object to parliamentary action in its favour, and the legislation of 1592 was regarded as the Magna Carta of presbytery.

As soon as the king had eliminated Roman catholicism and ultra-protestantism as political dangers, he was ready to turn on the presbyterians within the church. The mechanics of restoring the office of bishop as a means of providing ecclesiastical representation in parliament and as a device for insinuating royal control over the church were relatively simple. Moreover, the experience of 1584, when the great majority of the ministers, especially north of the Tay, had been prevailed on to submit to the bishops and only a small minority had followed Andrew Melville into exile, had shown that there were within the church two parties, or at least two opinions, one of them not unfavourable to what the king had in mind. It was still true after 1592 that the heterogeneous nature of the church's organisation was paralleled by considerable divergence of opinion on a variety of topics. Discussions in 1597 showed that there was no agreement on such matters as the place of elders in presbyteries, the rights of theological professors to attend church courts and the machinery for electing commissioners to the general assembly.[7] Opinion was sufficiently fluid, and there was enough distaste for Melville's programme, to make it likely that the king could count on the support of many ministers. But a means had to be found of overcoming or circumventing the domination which Melville's resolute party had established in the general assembly. Information about the membership of assemblies is very imperfect, but the sederunt for August 1590 shows that out of 160 members only six came from the country north and west of Angus; there were 15 from Angus itself; and nearly all the others came from south of the Tay, no less than 33 from Fife and 42 from the Lothians. Thus, mainly for geographical reasons—for assemblies met almost invariably in Edinburgh—the opposition to Melville was inadequately represented.

[7] Calderwood, v. 589-91, 598, 601-2.

Within two months of the riot of December 1596 the king opened his campaign with an assurance which suggests that his policy had already been planned. A general assembly met in February at Perth and not, as the previous assembly had appointed, in April at St Andrews. This set the pattern for years to come. It was hard to raise objections if the king chose to bring forward the date of an assembly, but when his right to do this was admitted it was equally hard to challenge his right to postpone an assembly. And if he could postpone an assembly from one date to another, could he not postpone it *sine die*? It was at least as hard to challenge the king's power to name the place of meeting, and year by year he showed a plain reluctance to have an assembly either in Edinburgh, where the burgesses might support the ministers, or in the Melvillian stronghold of St Andrews, and a preference for towns more easily accessible to ministers from the less radical north. But the campaign which opened in 1597 was not confined to the manipulation of times and places: the assemblies of that year, chastened by the aftermath of the December riot, conceded that ministers should not be appointed in the chief towns without the consent of the king, and passed various measures curbing the freedom of ministers, in the course of their sermons, to attack the laws, to censure individuals and to enlarge on politics. The assembly also appointed a commission to advise the king on ecclesiastical matters, and this commission proved a convenient agency by which the king could exert personal influence on leading ministers, and through them on the assembly. Finally, at the end of 1597, a petition was presented that the church should have voice in parliament.

This was a step towards the solution of a problem which had exercised men's minds intermittently since about 1580, and every time it seemed that the bishoprics would finally become extinct the issue had become a live one. Proposals that presbyteries should send commissioners to parliament, in place of the spiritual lords, commended themselves to the church, if only for the practical reason that church representatives might thus be heard in parliament on the question of the patrimony, instead of merely " standing at the door giving in papers."[8] The interests of the king coincided with those of the church to the extent that he too wanted churchmen in parliament as one of the estates,

[8] Calderwood, v. 669.

and in December 1597 there was a statute to the effect that the king should nominate ministers to vacant sees and that they should sit in parliament. But James, besides possibly seeing ecclesiastical representation as a counterpoise to the nobles, wanted it to make a breach in ministerial parity, and the potentialities of his plan were realised by the presbyterians: " Busk him as bonnily as ye can and bring him in as fairly as ye will, we see him well enough; we see the horns of his mitre."[9] There were now in effect rival proposals from church and king, and attempts were made to arrive at an adjustment. An assembly at Dundee in March 1598 overplayed its hand by proposing that the church should have 51 representatives—who might well have swamped the house—and the presbyterians pressed for the annual election of the representatives of the church and for the disuse of the term " bishop." After a decision by the assembly, in March 1600, that there should be annual election, the king turned with his usual dexterity to other instruments. He was accused of having the assembly minutes tampered with, to make it appear that no more was required than the annual submission of commissions for approval, but he had recourse also to the terms of the statute of 1597 and to his undoubted power to appoint prelates by letters patent. Appointments were made in 1600, to the sees of Aberdeen, Ross and Caithness, of " bishops " who were mere titulars, voting in parliament but with no ecclesiastical status other than that of ministers. The consent was obtained first of a convention of delegates of synods—a device to gain ecclesiastical approval when an assembly was recalcitrant—and later of the general assembly itself.

If the imperfections of the settlement of 1592 had provided a reason or a pretext for the appointment of such " parliamentary bishops," they likewise made it easy to find a place for the bishops in ecclesiastical administration. The continued existence of the office of commissioner or visitor, and the failure of presbyterial organisation to become effective throughout the whole country, enabled bishops to be endowed with administrative functions, as commissioners of their dioceses, without causing any dislocation. Apart from this quite unobtrusive development, there was after 1600 something of a lull, while the church was left to digest the " parliamentary bishops " and the way was prepared, by circumstances as much as by deliberate policy, for the king's next

9 Calderwood, v. pp. 680-1; James Melville, *Diary*, p. 437.

campaign. Several incidents either demonstrated the king's ability to override ministerial opposition in minor matters or added to his prestige. Thus, in 1599, when a company of English actors visited Edinburgh, the church condemned their plays as indecent and objected to their performance on Sunday, but the king, who was supported by the burgesses, secured the withdrawal of the objections. In the following year came the Gowrie conspiracy. The third Earl of Gowrie was the inheritor of a feud with the reigning house, for his grandfather, Lord Ruthven, had been one of the murderers of Riccio, and his father, the first earl, had led the Ruthven Raid. He was also the inheritor of a debt by the king of £80,000. As the representative of a house with ultra-protestant traditions, he enjoyed credit with the presbyterian ministers and was popular with the people generally. When King James was decoyed to Gowrie House, in Perth, on 5 August 1600, by the tale of a mysterious stranger with a pot of gold, and when his attendants were informed that he had left the house although he was in fact in a turret room within it, it is not inherently improbable that Gowrie and his brother were planning an ultra-protestant *coup*, on the pattern of the Ruthven Raid and the escapades of Francis Stewart. It undoubtedly suited the king that Gowrie and his brother were slain on the spot by the king's rescuers, but to see the business as a contrivance by James to rid himself of a creditor is unconvincing.[10] James certainly avenged one of the wrongs suffered by his mother, for Mary had said, on the occasion of the Riccio murder, that " if she died of her child, or her commonweal perished, she would leave the revenge thereof to her friends, to be taken of the said Lord Ruthven and his posterity."[11] The main historical significance of the affair is that whether or not the king's version of the happenings in Gowrie House was true, he was able to make the ministers accept it, though some of them were sceptical and were reluctant to condemn a man who was in their confidence. Five Edinburgh ministers at first declined to give thanks for the king's deliverance in the terms he dictated, but four of them soon submitted, and Robert Bruce, who alone held out, was banished to the north. The populace cannot have shared the ministers' misgivings, for when James returned safely to his capital he was welcomed " as

---

[10] The latest account is by W. F. Arbuckle, in *S. H. R.*, xxxvi.
[11] Henderson, *op. cit.*, II. 381.

if he had been new born."[12]   Less than three years after the
Gowrie Conspiracy, James's accession to the English throne
added to his prestige, and a further fortuitous reinforcement of
his position came from the Gunpowder Plot, in 1605, which
cleared him of any suspicion of popish sympathies.   For years
his subjects dutifully gave thanks on 5 August and 5 November
for his dual deliverance.

James's further proceedings showed an able combination of
tenacity and dexterity, for while he moved steadily towards his
objectives he varied his instruments.   Experience had already
shown that he could exert considerable influence in general
assemblies, but he went on to demonstrate that general assemblies
were not indispensable and that other machinery could be used
in their place.   As his tampering with the times and places of
the meetings of assemblies went on, anxiety grew, and when the
assembly appointed for Aberdeen in July 1604 was, in spite of
petitions, prorogued to July 1605 and then prorogued indefinitely,
the opposition felt impelled to make a stand.   Nineteen ministers
insisted on constituting an assembly at Aberdeen in July 1605,
and, when charged in the king's name to disperse, appointed the
next meeting for the following September; ten others, arriving
late, associated themselves with this action.   Fourteen of those
ministers were imprisoned, and six of the fourteen, convicted by
the court of justiciary in terms of the act of 1584 against convoking
ecclesiastical assemblies without the king's authority, were
banished for life.   This piece of terrorisation was followed by
another.   Eight presbyterian ministers, including Andrew Melville, were invited to London at the end of August 1606 for a
consultation with the king.   When Melville arrived, he made a
passionate speech in defence of the imprisoned ministers, denounced the lord advocate in his presence and spoke in favour of a
free general assembly.   The ministers were then forbidden to
return to Scotland without permission and their stay in London
was arbitrarily prolonged.   Melville did not improve matters by
writing an epigram attacking the furnishings of the chapel royal
and by treating the Archbishop of Canterbury much as he had
treated the king ten years earlier, shaking the prelate's lawn
sleeves and calling them " Romish rags."   After a further period
of detention, Andrew Melville was sent to the Tower, which he

12 Calderwood, VI. 50.

left in 1611 to spend his later years, until his death in 1622, at the university of Sedan; his nephew, James, was sent to Newcastle, where he was commanded to remain, and the others were confined under strict conditions in different parts of Scotland.

A suitable atmosphere was thus provided for the king's next moves, designed to fit the bishops into church government very much as they had been fitted in the compromise of 1586, when bishops had been acknowledged as permanent moderators of presbyteries and synods. Ignoring the assembly, James had put his scheme for " constant moderators " of presbyteries before meetings of synods which he convened simultaneously in February 1606, but it had been rejected. In December 1606, however, a nominated assembly, or " convention," of 136 ministers was called to Linlithgow and, under the influence of intimidation as well as of bribery, gave its approval to constant moderators of presbyteries. This innovation was accepted without very serious difficulty, whereupon the king went further and—tampering with the minutes of the Linlithgow convention—declared that consent had been given to constant moderators of synods as well. This, which looked much more like diocesan episcopacy, met with strenuous opposition nearly everywhere before it was accepted.

But the king, not content with turning from one ecclesiastical organ to another, was ready to use a secular organ as well, and in July 1606, before even constant moderators of presbyteries had been approved, he took parliamentary action, with an act " for the restitution of the estate of bishops." This act, which stressed the importance of the episcopate as an essential part of the con-stitution of the kingdom, and annulled the act of annexation of 1587 so far as it concerned the authority, privileges, lands, rents and teinds of the bishoprics, was purely civil and financial in its effects and had no bearing on the ecclesiastical status of the bishops. That status was, however, greatly strengthened by the adoption of bishops as constant moderators of synods, and in succeeding years both privy council and parliament added to the episcopal functions, with the result that by 1609 something like diocesan episcopacy was again in operation.

The final steps were taken in 1610. In a general assembly held at Glasgow, where considerable sums were expended, if not in bribery at any rate in paying the expenses of well-disposed ministers from distant parts,[13] approval was given to the restoration to the episcopate of some of the functions which for the last twenty years or so had more often been performed by presbyteries. In the same year came episcopal consecration. The bishops appointed in and since 1600 had received no spiritual authorisation, merely appointment by the crown, and as there were no consecrated bishops alive in Scotland recourse was had to England, where the succession of episcopal consecrations had not been interrupted by the Reformation. The three Scottish bishops who went to Westminster for consecration on 21 October 1610 were not required to accept Anglican ordination as deacons and priests as a preliminary step, and no English archbishop took part in the rite, to make it clear that all that was conferred was spiritual status, in no sense involving subordination to England.

The location of supreme ecclesiastical authority remained in some doubt. A statute of 1606 had acknowledged the king as governor over all persons, estates and causes, both spiritual and temporal, within his realm,[14] and from 1607 all holders of civil and ecclesiastical offices were required to make a similar acknowledgment. Again, both the act of 1609 restoring the bishops' consistorial jurisdiction and a statement by the king in the same year made it clear that James considered the authority of the bishops to be derived from the crown.[15] The whole concept of preferring parliament to the general assembly had been lost sight of, and the issue came to be one not of assembly *versus* crown-in-parliament, but of assembly and parliament *versus* the royal prerogative. Yet James did not oust the general assembly as a legislative body. In 1610, when for the first time the king chose that a major change in ecclesiastical polity should be sanctioned by the general assembly before it was sanctioned by parliament, the assembly was actually given a position of unprecedented weight. And throughout most of the remainder of the reign, although administration was in the hands of bishops, there was still a general assembly which was recognised as the highest authority in church affairs and which might be manipulated by the king but could not be ignored. At the parliament

---

13 The number of ministers from north of the Tay was almost equal to the number from the south and the total membership was 138. There is no evidence that any ministers of note were deliberately excluded. (G. C. Wadsworth, " The general assembly of 1610 " [Edinburgh Ph.D. thesis, 1930].)

14 *A. P. S.*, IV. 282.   15 *A. P. S.*, IV. 430; *R. P. C.*, VIII. 604-5.

of 1617 an article proposed that the king, with the advice of the bishops, should have power to legislate for the church; but this had to be withdrawn even after it had been conceded, on the bishops' insistence, that the advice of " a competent number of the ministry " should also be taken. After 1618 there were no meetings of assemblies, but even then they were not formally superseded.

So far from the existence of bishops being detrimental to the rest of the presbyterian system, the evidence all suggests that the combination of bishops with presbyteries worked well and that under their joint direction kirk sessions operated more widely and more effectively than ever before. The episcopate had been revived and developed without needlessly offending presbyterian susceptibilities, for there was no general re-ordination of men in presbyterian orders, the office of the ministerial deacon was all but unknown, and the rite of confirmation by bishops was rarely, if ever, practised. The system as a whole can be regarded either as a mere modification of the system which had operated in the 1590s, with a greater uniformity now in the employment of individual visitors or overseers, or as a reversion to the system which had operated in the 1560s and 1570s, modified by the existence now of the presbytery as an organ intermediate between the congregation and the bishop's synod. Howsoever regarded, it was, at least in its constituent parts, no novelty, and it is assuredly misleading to call it " the First Episcopacy "; to style it " the Jacobean compromise " gives suitable credit to its ingenious architect. James had avoided the extreme of the " proud papal bishops " against which he warned his son.[16]

Only a small number of convinced, doctrinaire Melvillians were so attached to unadulterated presbyterianism that they felt really strongly against the compromise which the king had worked out. The great majority, even of the ministers, were acquiescent if not enthusiastic, and the laity generally can have detected little change from the somewhat imperfect presbyterian system which had existed for a few years in the 1590s, while older men would see the compromise as nothing more than a reversion to earlier, pre-Melvillian, practice. Innovations in worship would be another matter, for they would alienate more of the clergy and would touch the ordinary worshipper by affecting

16 *Basilicon Doron* (S. T. S.), 1. 81.

what he saw in his parish church Sunday by Sunday. In 1601 the general assembly, of its own volition, had proposed some alterations in, and additions to, the authorised services, but James did nothing to advance liturgical innovations until he had safely completed his alterations in church government.   There is no reason to believe that, before 1603, James had been sympathetic to Anglican worship, any more than there is to believe that he had then planned the honour and authority to which bishops were later to be advanced.   In the *Basilikon Doron* he had expressed his agreement with some of the puritan strictures on the Prayer Book and had declared himself averse from rigid conformity to a liturgy; and he was probably at that time sincere in professing himself content with the forms of worship to which he was accustomed in Scotland and in declaring his indifference in matters of ceremonial and clerical vesture.   But it is also true that after 1603 James's views changed, under English influence, so much so that his earlier statements could later be quoted against him.[17]

The liturgical policy began in 1614.   A royal proclamation ordered the celebration of Holy Communion at Easter.   In the next year such celebration was ordered to take place in all time coming, the university of St Andrews was ordered to observe the greater festivals of the Christian Year, and all colleges were instructed to use the Prayer Book for certain parts of their services. The question of liturgical improvement was next taken up.   The Archbishop of St Andrews (John Spottiswoode, recently promoted from Glasgow) insisted that the matter must go before a general assembly, and an assembly at Aberdeen in 1616 recommended the preparation of a new liturgy, book of canons, confession of faith and catechism, the examination of children by bishops on their visitations, and the observance of Easter.   Two draft liturgies were prepared, probably in 1616 and 1617.[18]   One was essentially a revision of the Sunday morning service as it stood in the Book of Common Order, with some additional prayers; the old book was still to be used for certain prayers and for the rites and sacraments.   The second provided orders also for Baptism, Holy Communion and marriage, but still relied to some extent on

[17] *B. U. K.*, III. 1161.
[18] The draft of 1616 is printed in *Scottish Liturgies of James VI* (Church Service Society); that of 1617 is printed in *S. H. S. Misc.*, x.

the Book of Common Order. These drafts represented moderate opinion, and proved abortive because the king's policy on other, but allied, matters, outran the progress in liturgical revision.

Clerical and episcopal opposition to more radical changes was strong. In 1616 the bishops had hesitated about accepting proposals for kneeling at Communion, private administration of the sacraments and the observance of the Christian Year. In 1617 they succeeded in persuading the king to countermand his order for the erection of statues of the Apostles in the chapel at Holyrood in preparation for his visit to Edinburgh. During that visit, which extended from 13 May to 4 August, James consulted a meeting of 36 parish clergy in addition to the bishops, and all agreed that only a general assembly could approve the king's proposals, which had now taken shape as Five Articles—kneeling at Holy Communion, the Christian Year, private Communion and private Baptism, and confirmation. An assembly was summoned at St Andrews in November 1617, but in effect rejected the articles. James was furious: " Since your Scottish Church hath so far contemned my clemency, they shall now find what it is to draw the anger of a king upon them."[19] In January 1618, on royal warrant, the privy council proclaimed that Christmas, Good Friday, Easter, Ascension Day and Whitsunday should henceforth be holidays. Later in the year a " national assembly " met at Perth. By means of nomination of members and " management " (through threats to reduce stipends, or to withhold increases), eighty-six supporters were found for the king's proposals, but there was a minority of forty-one. Besides the articles, approval was given to the preparation of a liturgy and canons.

It seems legitimate to suggest that the Five Articles—the high water mark of James's liturgical policy—though a demonstration of " the anger of a king," were a serious tactical error on the part of James, whose sensitivity to Scottish opinion had possibly been dulled by age and absence. He endangered the whole of his ecclesiastical settlement for the sake of " these wretched articles."[20] The greatest hostility was aroused by the requirement of kneeling at Communion, a matter which concerned the laity rather than the clergy. One result of the appearance of the Five Articles was to crystallise opposition to any alterations in the liturgy, for it was clear that any new liturgy would now be framed, under royal

19 *Original Letters*, II. 524.   20 W. L. Mathieson, *Politics and religion*, I. 317.

auspices, by men leaning towards Anglican usage and that it would inevitably include recognition of the Articles.

It is true that not more than about a dozen ministers had to be deprived for obstinate refusal to observe the Articles, and that although laymen were threatened and even sentenced none seem actually to have been punished. But this is no measure of the amount of dissatisfaction. In the synod of Fife, half of the ministers at first declined to conform and, although by the next year the number of recalcitrants was reduced to nine, who promised to reconsider their attitude, there were obviously those who were yielding with reluctance and doing so only because the alternative was to be robbed of their livelihood and secluded from the exercise of their vocation. There would have been more deprivations and other punishments if the king had had his way, but the strongest possible pressure in favour of moderation was exerted by the council and by Archbishop Spottiswoode, who was always a mediating influence between James and his subjects.[21] Even in 1624, after James had issued a special proclamation for the celebration of Holy Communion in Edinburgh at Christmas and had reiterated the requirement that the sacrament be received kneeling, he withdrew it on representations by the town council and the bishops.[22] The Articles were, in practice, widely disregarded, but the king became less concerned with them for their own sake than as a test of obedience, and his sharpest hostility was reserved for the hard core of the non-conformists, who did their best to keep opposition alive and who were active at the parliament of 1621 in trying to influence the members against consenting to ratify the Articles.

But if James's animosity towards the militant resistance was unrelenting, his other actions show that he realised his mistake and learned his lesson. It is true that a new draft liturgy was prepared in 1618 which, unlike the earlier drafts, was based on the Book of Common Prayer.[23] Its orders for morning and evening prayer were similar to Mattins and Evensong, but excluded versicles and responses and some of the canticles and permitted a service which in its structure resembled that of the Book of Common Order. There was a collection of special

[21] Cf. *R. P. C.*, xii. 186n; *Original Letters*, ii. 627.
[22] Calderwood, vii. 622-3; *Original Letters*, ii. 773.
[23] This draft is in *Scottish Liturgies of James VI.*

prayers and thanksgivings, along the lines of the proposals repeatedly made for enriching the existing Scottish service-book. The
orders for Baptism and confirmation were based on the English
rites, but omitted the sign of the cross. The order for Communion
contained much of the phraseology of the English book, but also
omitted much of it and instead added longer prayers. The whole
book represents a reasonable compromise which might, in more
favourable circumstances, have had a chance of general acceptance. As it was, the storm raised by the Five Articles made even
such a moderate liturgical reform quite impossible. A licence
for printing the new liturgy was issued, and an ordinal was
published in 1620, but the revised liturgy itself never appeared.
In the 1621 parliament, James secured the ratification of the
Articles (by a majority of 85 to 59) as part of a bargain in which
he promised that he would make no more innovations, and he
kept his word. Partly because James knew where to stop, and
even when to retreat, but partly also because comparatively few
ministers were intransigent in their opposition and partly because
of the restraint and good sense of the bishops, there was little overt
opposition in the church at the end of the reign.

12

KING JAMES'S PEACE [1]

In Scotland the era of the Reformation had involved no massacres or wars of religion as in France, no wholesale executions or uprisings cruelly suppressed as in England, nothing parallel to the brutalities in Germany and the Low Countries. The revolution of 1559-60 had taken place with little bloodshed and there had been nothing that could be dignified by the name of civil war save the strife between king's men and queen's men which ended in 1573. Since then there had been one or two rather half-hearted rebellions and an occasional demonstration in force, but by the end of the century revolts and even *coups d'état* were things of the past, and the crown was dominant over the groups which had competed for power in past years. From the riot in Edinburgh on 17 December 1596 to another riot in Edinburgh on 23 July 1637 there stretched forty years of unprecedented tranquillity.

The whole concept of monarchy was itself undergoing a change, partly in consequence of the Reformation. The Scottish reformers were as determined as any others that the divine right of kings should be asserted in opposition to papal claims; and, while this emphasis on the responsibility of kings to God could and did lead to the claims of a theocratic clergy to dictate to the king, it could and did lead equally to the king's claim to be answerable to God alone and not to any of his subjects as intermediaries. But there were also more material factors. Until the birth of Prince Henry, in 1594, there was no heir apparent, it

---

1 " This dilectable tyme of peax under your majesteis happie regne and most excellent government " (*R. P. C.*, XIII. 744 [1622]).

was hard to say where the heir presumptive was to be found, and James's own life stood between Scotland and a civil war in which rival claimants might have had the support of foreign powers as well as of factions within Scotland. Henry's birth was received with rejoicing " as if the people had been daft for mirth."[2] James's accession to England increased his prestige and surrounded him with wealth and pomp which more sharply than before marked him off from even the greatest of his subjects. It also gave him personal security: no longer was he liable to be insulted by insolent ministers, no longer could he be surprised in his palace *en deshabille*, as he had been by Francis Stewart, and the Scottish crown was now immune from the aristocratic *coup*. The king was surrounded, instead, by obsequious courtiers, whose flattery was probably responsible for a deterioration in his character and in his political judgment in his later years.

Neither any alternative to monarchy nor any claim on behalf of an alternative branch of the royal line was seriously put forward. The Earl of Menteith was demoted to the earldom of Airth in 1632 for saying, or allowing it to be said, that as the descendant of the second, and unquestionably legal, marriage of Robert II he had better blood than Charles I; and about the same time there was gossip about the claims of the house of Hamilton;[3] but neither Menteith nor Hamilton could be called a pretender to the throne. Even when Scotland, or a large part of it, rebelled against Charles I, the king remained " our sweet prince," misguided and misinformed but still the monarch;[4] and when a Scottish army was led against him, one of its supporters wrote: " We fought no crowns. . . . We loved no new masters. Had our throne been void, and our voices sought for the filling of Fergus's chair, we would have died ere any other had sitten down on that fatal marble but Charles alone."[5] The execution of Charles I by the English horrified the Scots, who at once and without hesitation accepted Charles II as his successor. The attachment to the long line of " Scottish kings " had by this time become the expression of a belief in indefeasible hereditary right. A petition of 1643, from those who opposed Scottish intervention on behalf of the English parliament against the king, referred to

2 David Moysie, *Memoirs of the affairs of Scotland* (Bannatyne Club), p. 113.
3 David Masson, *Drummond of Hawthornden*, pp. 189-91.
4 Baillie, *Letters and Journals*, i. 92, 184, 198.   5 *Ibid.*, i. 215.

the " unparalleled lineal descents of an hundred and seven kings,"[6] and the Marquis of Montrose pled for the cause of " a race of kings who have governed you for two thousand years with peace and justice and have preserved your liberties against all domineering nations."[7]   It was appropriate that the royal line, stretching back to " Fergus I " in 330 B.C., should be visibly represented in the long gallery of Holyroodhouse by command of Charles II, for as the century wore on there was something little short of intoxication with the idea of hereditary monarchy.

The attachment to the reigning sovereign was already in James VI's reign expressed in fulsome terms.   In 1601 the town council of Edinburgh ordained that " for the honour and reverence thai aucht to our soveran lord, his darrest spous and childrein," royal portraits were not to be treated like other chattels, but were to be exempt from pointing and rouping.[8] In 1610 the Scottish privy council advised the English privy council to take care of his majesty's precious person against such a mischance as had just befallen Henry IV of France, who had been murdered by Ravaillac: " As that great jewel, our dread sovereign and gracious lord, shines daily in your sight and eyes, so will his rare virtues no doubt kindle in your minds an ardent zeal to preserve by all possible means his sacred person from all dangers."[9]   The cult of the monarchy was fostered not only by parliament, the council, and the church, but also by the poets: when James died he was mourned by Drummond of Hawthornden in a sonnet which concludes:

> The world which late was golden by thy breath
> Is iron turned, and horrid, by thy death.

But much of the credit for the establishment of the new monarchy belongs to James VI's own personality.   It is true that there was theorising in plenty in James's political writings and in his speeches and letters, and it may have been his theorising which won the *Basilikon Doron* a degree of recognition abroad which no work previously produced in this island had gained.   But there was also a wealth of practical wisdom, derived from shrewd observation of Scottish life and institutions.   James was a man of very remarkable political ability and sagacity in deciding on

[6] Burnet, *Memoirs of the Dukes of Hamilton* (1852), p. 265.
[7] Napier, *Montrose*, I. 288.   [8] *Edinburgh Burgh Records, 1589-1603*, p. 284.
[9] *R. P. C.*, VIII. 626-7.

policy and of conspicuous tenacity in having it executed. He may not have been the ablest of the Stewarts, but he was assuredly the most successful of his line in governing Scotland and bending it to his will. His reign of fifty-eight years, for forty of which he was personally responsible for the direction of policy, would of itself have made a mark on Scotland which none of his predecessors had had an opportunity to make. For rather more than half of his active reign he was an absentee monarch, moving among his various English palaces and hunting seats, but between them and Scotland messengers were constantly going to and fro, and James directed affairs no less effectively when he did so through the post. One of his earliest acts after he reached London in 1603 was the organisation of a postal service between Edinburgh and Berwick,[10] and the construction of a bridge at Berwick, which was at once symbolical and practical, was begun in 1610, though not completed until 1634.

The art of governing Scotland had all along involved the use of patronage to reward support or to anticipate opposition. But the lack of coercive power meant also that the government had to be sensitive to public opinion, within the range of the politically active classes. James continued the old devices, but he also extended the appeal to public opinion. In the course of the revolt against France and Rome, and again during the civil war in James's minority, the king's subjects had become accustomed to have manifestoes and proclamations addressed to them, and it became a regular practice to issue propaganda justifying the government's policy. As early as 1582 there appeared a *Declaration of the king's majesty's will anent religion*, and in 1585 an able *apologia* for the " Black Acts "—a *Declaration of the king's majesty's intention and meaning towards the late acts of parliament*. The king drew public attention to the ambiguities and uncertainties in ecclesiastical opinion by publishing in 1597 certain questions which he submitted to the general assembly. In 1600 there were works stating the king's case against Gowrie and his brother. In 1606 came a *Declaration of the just causes of his majesty's proceedings against those ministers who are now lying in prison*, which was penned, at least in part, by the royal pamphleteer himself. Besides, there

10 *R. P. C.*, vi. 567-71; cf. William Taylor, " The Scottish privy council, 1603-25 " (Edinburgh Ph.D. thesis, 1950). There was already a regular postal service between Berwick and London (H. M. Wallace, " Berwick in the reign of Queen Elizabeth," *E. H. R.*, xlvi. 87).

were works descriptive of the Scottish royal line and the house of Stewart, and the king prescribed for use in schools as well as in private families a manual called *God and the King*, which inculcated passive obedience. The press was, of course, used by the opposition as well: the Ruthven Raiders issued a manifesto justifying their action in 1582, and in 1593 it was the presbytery of Edinburgh which directed the publication of *A discovery of the unnatural and traitorous conspiracy of Scottish papists*, to stir the people against the king for his leniency to the Roman catholic interest. The government had powers of censorship in terms of an act of council of 1612, but in the later years of the reign, with its crises past, the king was too secure to feel much need either to issue propaganda or to curb that of his critics—who could in any event have their tracts printed on the continent.

The king's resolve to commend the monarchy and its policy directly to his people without any intermediary was one of the many facets of the principle of a single kingdom of which he was the head, and this principle, if carried out logically, was fatal to the feudal or baronial character of Scottish society and administration. James conceived it to be in the interests not only of the crown but of the generality of the people that the mutual bond between baron and dependents must be broken down and the law must be administered equitably and without respect of persons. Yet he would not, perhaps could not, use a policy of severity. He remarked in the *Basilikon Doron* that forfeitures should be avoided and that the nobility should not be slighted as they had been by James V, and his policy in the 1590s in relation to the northern earls must be seen in this wider context of winning rather than punishing. The nobles, therefore, unlike the presbyterian leaders, did not suffer repression. Instead, their position was altered by changes, partly political and partly economic, which produced something of a new pattern in Scottish society. The 1590s, in this respect as in others, mark the end of an era, for never again did a faction of nobles of themselves challenge the crown: rebellion, when it came again, was to come from a different and more complex marshalling of forces.

Almost as early as he had declared his intention to be a " universal king " and not the instrument of a faction,[11] James had declared a preference for reliance on men of middle-class

[11] P. 187 above.

origins and an intention to make service, rather than birth, the path to advancement. In 1584 he said that he never wanted to promote any earl or lord, but only simple soldiers and gentlemen like James Stewart (Arran), whom he could put down again at will.[12] And after the death of Maitland of Thirlstane he said that " he would no more use chancellor or other great men in those his causes, but such as he might convict and were hangable."[13] In 1596 he dismissed the Master of Glamis from the office of treasurer, and handed over the management of the crown finances to eight men who, as Queen Anne's councillors, had been conspicuously successful with her revenues. Two of those " Octavians " were younger sons of peers, most were of lairdly stock, but their essential characteristic was that they were professional men.[14] As a body of commissioners for finance they were allowed to operate for less than a year, because the king sacrificed them to an outcry against the curb they imposed on peculation, but individually they continued to hold various offices, and it is remarkable that already, so soon after the death of Maitland, James had selected men who were to serve him for most of the remainder of his reign in the offices of chancellor, secretary, lord president and lord advocate.

Very few new peerages had been created since the reign of James IV, and hardly any for persons not connected with the royal house. The only dukedoms were those of Mary's third husband, Bothwell, and James VI's cousin, Esmé Stewart. Some royal bastards became earls, and an existing earldom was occasionally transferred to a new line, on sound or dubious legal grounds; but the only new earldom created for a man not of royal blood was, perhaps significantly, that of Gowrie, in 1581. Even lordships had been most sparingly bestowed. The development of a new peerage, dating from the lavish creations of the years from about 1600 onwards, amply illustrates that careers in the service of the state were open to talents and that ability as well as wealth or royal favour could earn advancement to high social rank.

[12] H. M. C., *Salisbury*, III. 57.   [13] *Cal. S. P. Scot.*, XII. 117.

[14] They were David Carnegie of Culluthie, *James Elphinstone, Thomas Hamilton*, John Lindsay (parson of Menmuir and secretary), *Alexander Seton*, Sir John Skene (clerk-register), *Walter Stewart*, and Peter Young (formerly the king's preceptor). Those whose names are italicised are the subject of comment in later pages. The commission to them is printed in Purves, *The revenue of the Scottish crown* (ed. D. M. Rose), pp. 8-13.

Courtiers were, indeed, promoted, but not very frequently,[15] and few of the new peers who had a courtly origin left much of a mark on affairs even when they held high office: Sir George Home of Spott, afterwards Earl of Dunbar, was treasurer from 1601 to 1611, although he resided mainly in England, and he was succeeded by Robert Kerr, Earl of Somerset, who was also an absentee; Sir George Hay of Kinfauns, later Viscount Dupplin and Earl of Kinnoull, became chancellor near the end of James's reign (1622); and Sir William Alexander, Earl of Stirling, became secretary after James's death (1626).

Peerages were frequently granted to families in which the legal profession or office in the state had become hereditary, though sometimes only in the second or third generation of distinguished service. The Bellendens of Auchnoule, for instance, established almost a heritable right to the office of justice-clerk, which was held by three of them in succession; the first of the family had been parish clerk of Canongate because he was related to an Abbot of Holyrood, and through their relationship by marriage to a later commendator of Holyrood they acquired the barony of Broughton, but did not attain the dignity of Lord Bellenden of Broughton until 1661. Andrew Murray of Blackbarony (d. 1572), who came of a family of burgesses and lairds, was the father of Sir Gideon Murray of Elibank, who was a privy councillor, a lord of session and treasurer depute (1612-21); but the Elibank peerage was conferred only in the next generation. The MacGills had a similar record. Sir James was provost of Edinburgh in the reign of James V; one of his sons, James, of Rankeillor Nether, was clerk-register from 1554, and another son, David, of Cranston Riddell, was king's advocate in 1582; of David's two sons, one became a lord of session and a privy councillor but died at an early age in 1607, while the other, James, also a lord of session, became Viscount of Oxfuird in 1651. Sir Thomas Hope, again, who came of Edinburgh burgess stock, became lord advocate in 1626 and three of his sons were

15 John Murray, gentleman of the bedchamber, Viscount Annan (1622) and Earl of Annandale (1624); Richard Preston, page and servitor in the royal household, Lord Dingwall (1609); James Maxwell, familiar of the household, Earl of Dirleton (1646); Patrick Maule of Panmure, gentleman of the bedchamber, Earl of Panmure (1646). James Drummond, gentleman of the bedchamber, was created Lord Madertie in 1609, but he was commendator of Inchaffray and that gave him another claim to a peerage.

lords of session, but the family did not acquire its earldom until 1703. One of the most impressive examples of the rise of a family from obscurity, through professional life, to a peerage, is that of the Primroses. Originally burgesses of Culross, one of them, Gilbert, became surgeon to James VI, Peter became a minister, Archibald a writer in Edinburgh and James a servitor to the clerk of the privy council before himself becoming clerk in 1599. Archibald, son of James, was also clerk of the privy council under Charles I and became clerk-register in 1660; only his son, however, achieved the peerage as Earl of Rosebery. The Bothwells had the advantage of burgess-ship in the capital, where William flourished at the beginning of the sixteenth century. One of his sons was canon of Ashkirk, director of chancery and lord of session, another was provost of Edinburgh and also a lord of session. The latter was the father of Adam, Bishop of Orkney and commendator of Holyrood, and Adam's son became Lord Holyroodhouse in 1607.

The most important source of the new peerage in James VI's reign was the erection of ecclesiastical properties into hereditary temporal lordships. There had been a few instances before 1587, but the most significant point of development was in and around 1606: as the complement to the restitution of the estate of bishops, the king undertook not to impugn erections of abbeys and priories, and at this stage there were twelve new erections and five confirmations.[16] By 1625, no less than twenty-one out of thirty abbeys had become lordships. Their holders had a vested interest in the maintenance of the king's government,[17] for they were not likely to forget that the king who had set them up might pull them down, and they were not likely to sympathise with the Melvillians, who would have tried to recover the abbey property for ecclesiastical uses. The experience of the whole century was to demonstrate that ecclesiastical issues alone, and ministers and their followers alone, could never bring about a revolution, and James had succeeded in isolating such ecclesiastical disaffection as existed from the baronial support which might have made it dangerous. And if James so managed matters

16 *A. P. S.*, IV. 321-61.
17 Maurice Lee (*Maitland of Thirlestane*, pp. 141-2) has an interesting argument that the possibilities of using erection as an instrument to gain support occurred to James and Maitland during the parliament of 1587.

that few nobles would support the presbyterian cause, there is also some reason to believe that what has been called his policy of " authoritarian conservatism "[18] made its appeal to something in the ethos of the Roman catholic interest and tended to absorb that interest into the following of the monarchy. None of the king's ministers was a practising Romanist, and they hardly could have been, for in 1605 there was said to be only one priest in Scotland, and he was old and infirm.[19] But the Earl of Montrose, who became chancellor in 1599, had been associated with Huntly and Errol, and his successor, Alexander Seton, although a communicant in his parish church, was also said to go occasionally to Roman catholic confession and Communion. The lord president and the lord advocate also made a favourable impression on visiting Jesuits (who were inclined, however, to be too credulous).[20] It is certainly true that the king's tenderness to Roman catholics meant that the country was not deprived of the services of men who leaned towards Rome, and the influence of the queen, who submitted to the pope in 1602, meant that such men were not out of place at court.

Some of the men who benefited by the erections were already peers or sons of peers. For example, John and Claud Hamilton, sons of Châtelherault, retained Arbroath and Paisley; Deer, which had long been held by the family of the Earls Marischal, was in the end incorporated with that peerage; the abbeys which had pertained *in commendam* to the Erskines were erected into the lordship of Cardross, held by the earls of Mar; and Inchcolm went to Sir James Stewart of Doune, who became Earl of Moray by marriage. But the significant men were those who reached a lordship of erection from humbler social origins and by way of a career in the law or office in the state. As before the Reformation, church property was still used to pay for service to the commonwealth, but the reward could now carry an assurance of heredity. Even within a single family, the tradition might span the Reformation: Edward Bruce, Commendator of Kinloss and first Lord Kinloss (1603), lord of session and ambassador to England, was the nephew of Robert Reid, who had been

18 David Mathew, *op. cit.*, p. 209.   19 *Innes Review*, x. 188-9.
20 Forbes Leith, *Narratives of Scottish Catholics*, pp. 279, 282. The lord advocate had Roman catholic associations in his early days, but there is no evidence that he had popish sympathies.

commendator of Kinloss and president of the court of session before
1560. James's leading officials were all lords of erection. Walter
Stewart, a son of Sir John Stewart of Minto and Commendator of
Blantyre, was appointed treasurer in 1596 and was created Lord
Blantyre in 1604. Alexander Seton, Commendator of Pluscardin
from 1565, was lord president in 1593, chancellor and Earl of
Dunfermline from 1605 until his death in 1622. James Elphinstone, secretary from 1598, became Lord Balmerino in 1603 and
from 1605 was lord president as well as secretary, until, in 1608, he
was made the scapegoat when a letter was revealed which disclosed
James's negotiations with the pope. A later secretary is a better
known figure—Sir Thomas Hamilton, or Tam o' the Cowgate,
who came from a family of small lairds and burgesses. His father
had become a lord of session, as did his brothers Andrew and
John, and Thomas himself, after being lord advocate in 1596 and
secretary from 1612, combined the offices of secretary and lord
president from 1616 to 1626. An ardent supporter of the king's
ecclesiastical policy, he was described by the archbishop of St
Andrews as " my good lord secretare, the fourteenth bischop of
this kingdom."[21] He was created Earl of Melrose in 1626, but
later changed the title to that of Haddington. Another of the
officials who took their styles from religious houses was the comptroller, Sir David Murray of Gospertie, who acquired part of the
property which had been held by the Gowrie family and was
created Lord Scone.[22]

It was men like those, rising to the peerage through their
acquisition of church properties, who served King James, while
the peers of older creation played less and less part in affairs.
Besides, the peerage was all the time being further diluted, by
other creations besides those of courtiers, professional men and
officials, for from about 1600 it seems to have been a matter of
policy to promote to peerages the representatives of families which
had a long history as lairds, as well as to raise to higher rank peers
of old standing.

The bishops fitted into the same pattern as the officials and
the new nobility. Of those appointed by James from 1600
onwards, hardly any were of the same social standing as

21 *Original Letters*, i. 295.
22 Sir Patrick Murray of Geanies, who had served the king in the north, received
an erection of the abbey of Fearn in 1598.

pre-reformation prelates or connected with the oligarchy which had been dominant in the past. The majority came from the families of lairds, and some were of good burgess stock. All of them were men of ability, who either had held university appointments or had been prominent in church affairs before their promotion, and it was clearly the king's policy to appoint " new men ", to an office which he regarded as part of his administrative machine.

James's policy towards the nobility was aimed not only at the aggrandisement of the monarchy, but also at the establishment of such order and such respect for the law as would be beneficial to the generality of his subjects. He was by temperament as well as by policy a peacemaker and constantly exerted his own influence in favour of conciliation, with a view to extinguishing feuds and preventing duels and assaults. To counter feuds, the practice was to bind the parties to keep the peace towards each other, under heavy penalties: for example, in the case of a dispute between Fraser of Muchalls and Keith of Ludquharn, in 1622, the council bound the parties to keep the peace under penalty of 20,000 merks.[23] Should the bond be infringed, the penalty was inflicted or the parties committed to ward, but every effort was made to secure reconciliation and the submission of the disputes to law or to arbitration, under the sanction of the council.[24] When a dispute was submitted to law, the problem arose of eliminating the terrorisation of the courts by the retinues which great men brought with them when they engaged in litigation. The burgesses of Edinburgh had complained in 1580 that they were " trublit and putt in hazard of thair lyffes in the dayes of law betuix pairteis," and decided to muster in arms " upoun ilk day of law betuix greitt pairteis."[25] The king and council therefore adopted the practice of restricting retinues: when the Earls of Cassillis and Wigtown had a suit in the court of session, the council laid down that neither should appear in the streets of Edinburgh with more than six followers. James, who never wearied of extolling the benefits of a " weill governit commounwele," observed of duels that, besides being " prohibite and forbiddin be the lawis of this realme " they were " not authorised, permittit nor allowit in na uther wele governit commounwele "; and in any event, he sensibly remarked, a " singular combat " was

---

23 R. P. C., xii. 652-3, 725-7, 733.   24 E.g., R. P. C., xii. 39.
25 Edinburgh Burgh Records, iv. 157.

unlikely " to settle the trouble and attempt quhairupoun the challenge proceidit and procuir peace to baith pairteis."26 He unhesitatingly demanded the imposition of heavy sentences for violence of any kind. Sharp lessons were taught when, in 1608, Lord Maxwell was executed for the murder of the laird of John-stone, and when, in 1612, Lord Sanquhar was executed for the murder of a fencing master. In 1611 the Earl of Lothian, who had assaulted a burgess and a laird, was committed to ward and the king suggested a fine of 10,000 merks, which on the council's intercession was reduced to 3,000. Fines were imposed also for frauds, evasions of customs dues and the carrying of fire-arms, a practice which the council strove for years to stop but which was still normal when James died.

James made more than one attempt to solve the long-standing problem of the administration of criminal justice. As the court held by the justice general and his deputies in Edinburgh was insufficient for the needs of the country, and as justice-ayres, for the administration of criminal justice in the shires, were only intermittent, too much reliance had been placed on special commissions of justiciary, often granted to magnates with their own interests to serve. In 1587 it was proposed that two justices should be deputed by the justice general for each quarter of the country, to hold ayres twice a year and deal with offences not great enough to come before the central court in Edinburgh, but this seems to have been almost, if not quite, abortive, for different arrangements were planned in 1588 and again in 1594. The real difficulty may well have been financial, and the device which in the end solved the problem was the use, as commissioners of justiciary, of senators of the college of justice, who were already salaried judges. This had been foreshadowed earlier, and in the later 1620s, under Charles I, eight senators were appointed as itinerant justices and a pair of them was made responsible for visiting each quarter of the country. When, in 1671-2, the court of justiciary, in very much its modern form, was finally organised, the principle of utilising senators was followed. The lord justice general remained head of the court, with the lord justice clerk as his lieutenant; but the old-style deputies disappeared, and instead five senators became commissioners of justiciary, each of them having equal powers with the justice general and the justice

26 *R. P. C.*, VI. 65 (quoted above from MS.).

clerk. Circuit courts were to be held annually in certain specified towns by six of the judges in three pairs (the justice general being " supernumerary ").

The work of the court of justiciary was the punishment of offenders. But another question was how to anticipate trouble and prevent the committing of offences. As early as 1579 the magistrates in burghs had been appointed " his majesty's justices in that part " to deal with those who carried firearms, and in the following year the council had proposed that there should be " justices " with powers to execute the acts of parliament against profanity and against behaviour which disturbed public worship or detracted from the reverent observance of Sunday, and also to undertake provision for the relief of the poor.[27] Then the act of 1587, which attempted to reconstitute the justice ayres, provided that the king should appoint in each sheriffdom several " commissioners and justices in the furtherance of justice, peace and quietness," who would investigate breaches of the law, punish minor offenders and turn over the more serious criminals to the justice ayre.[28] There is no evidence that this was more than a proposal, but in 1609 there was another statute, from which the institution of justices of the peace in Scotland is usually dated. This act, after alluding to the sloth of magistrates in neglecting to suppress the first seeds of dissensions, and the feuds which resulted when remedies were not applied at an early stage, gave the justices power to " oversie, trye and prevent all sic occasionis as may breid truble and violence amongis his majesteis subjectis or forceable contempt of his majesteis authoritie and breache of his peace." One of the principal functions of the justices was to bind persons to keep the peace, under penalties, but, should preventive action fail, they were empowered to imprison persons who had broken the peace and those who abetted them. Their comprehensive commission included power to put in execution the laws against masterful beggars, vagabonds, forestallers and regraters, to supervise the maintenance and repair of highways, to control ale-houses, to regulate weights and measures and the quality of goods sold in markets, to fix wages, to make arrangements against the spread of infection, and to provide jails.[29]

This scheme, while not wholly abortive, did not take root. A full complement of justices for the whole kingdom was again

[27] *R. P. C.*, III. 266.   [28] *A. P. S.*, III. 458 c. 57.   [29] *A. P. S.*, IV. 434.

nominated in 1634, but, except during the different circumstances of the Commonwealth period, justices were not effective until after 1707. Probably the principal reason was the inability of the justices to compete with existing jurisdictions. Scotland was very well supplied with sheriff courts, regality courts, baron courts and burgh courts, many of them already trying, however ineffectively, to perform the functions now allotted to justices; the regulation of weights and measures, for example, was a function of the burgh courts. As sheriff, regality and baron courts were a source of profit, the gentlemen who held them had a vested interest in defending them. James VI condemned the heritable jurisdictions,[30] but he was ahead of his time, for they were so strongly entrenched that they were not abolished until 1747. From somewhat similar motives, James endeavoured to secure the observance of an act of parliament against the appointment of noblemen to magistracy in the burghs.

The most important curb on outbreaks of violence may have been provided not by any of the older courts, still less by the new justices, but by the kirk sessions, which had existed here and there since 1560 but which first became generally effective in the early seventeenth century. The sessions are popularly associated with their activities against sexual irregularities, but they took cognisance also of slander (with which serious trouble could often originate), minor assaults and petty theft, besides acting as general watchdogs in the parish and constantly upholding certain standards of conduct. It may well be that one important factor in the reducing of Scotland to order was the persistent work of the kirk sessions in the parishes up and down the country. The kirk session was apt to be closely linked with the secular magistracy in the burghs, where the bailies and council sometimes had the dominant, or even the sole, voice in the selection of elders, and it was decided in 1599 in Glasgow that the persons elected as provost and bailies should always be enrolled among the elders.[31] The king seems to have thought that a similar link should be established between the kirk sessions and the justices of the peace, for we find

30 *Basilicon Doron*, I. 88-9. At one stage the lieutenant of the west march was instructed to act " notwithstanding any privilege of regality " and was to admit no such privilege unless the possessor of the regality would sit with him (*R. P. C.*, v. 450-1).

31 R. H. Story, *The Church of Scotland past and present*, IV. 66-7 (citing Minutes of General Session of Glasgow, 4 Oct. 1599).

that in Elgin he commissioned the elders as justices.[32] We can go further than this, for it is plain that the justices, not least when they are first mentioned in 1580, were intended to carry out functions associated with kirk sessions.[33] James never had any intention of superseding the sessions, and his bishops were fostering them, but he may have felt that a court which was doing such valuable work should be integrated into the state's system of courts. Somewhat similarly, the courts of high commission, which were set up in the year after the justices of the peace (1610) and were designed to strengthen the disciplinary system of the reformed church, had peers and lairds as well as ministers and elders among their members and were to work in conjunction with the privy council and the court of session; they were evidently designed to bond the system of ecclesiastical discipline into the general judicial structure.[34] Both the justices of the peace and the courts of high commission thus represent one facet of the working out of the concept of the " one kingdom." Be that as it may, in all schemes for the settlement of hitherto disorderly areas stress was laid on the repair of churches and the establishment of a settled ministry. No doubt one motive was to defend and foster the reformed faith; but with the kirks and the ministry came the kirk session and its discipline.

While the government of Scotland was in so many ways becoming more intensive, it was also becoming more extensive. Hitherto a sharp demarcation had been acknowledged between the rule of law in the more accessible parts of the country and the lawlessness of the remoter areas. Thus, in 1579, when a Midlothian farmer complained to the council about the slaughter of his horses and oxen and injury to his ploughmen, he remarked that this kind of thing should not happen " in a cuntrie quhilk sould be peciabill, sa neir the seat of justice, and sould rather gif exempill to the far hielandis and bordouris, quhair sic forme of conqueist [forcible seizure] is used."[35] The government's policy now—again part of the concept of a single kingdom—was to efface such distinctions, and the reign of

---

[32] *Records of Elgin* (New Spalding Club), II. 54.

[33] Cf. further provisions in 1589 (*R. P. C.* IV. 419).

[34] In 1592 the king had appointed that the commissioners of the assembly should choose lay " justices and commissioners " to act with them in visitation, and he empowered them to act against papists, beggars, and vagabonds (*R. P. C.*, IV. 753).

[35] *R. P. C.*, III. 109-12.

James VI saw the extension of the power of the central government in the Borders, the Highlands and the western and northern islands.

The Borders were not merely to be integrated into the Scottish kingdom; they were to be transformed into the " middle shires " of Great Britain. The problem was an old one, for we hear much and often in earlier reigns of expeditions for " putting order on the border "—the phrase is Sir David Lindsay's—but, whereas earlier kings had failed, James VI succeeded because he was able to tackle the problem on a new basis. Even before his accession to the English throne, Anglo-Scottish amity had made co-operation on the Borders easier: in 1588 James borrowed guns and gunners from Carlisle for his action against Lord Maxwell, and in 1597, after the episode when the laird of Buccleuch rescued Kinmont Willie from Carlisle Castle, the two governments appointed a joint commission on the Borders and made a treaty for the better administration of justice.[36] In 1605 a body of conjunct commissioners, five English and five Scots, was appointed, and the enforcement of its decisions on the Scottish side was entrusted mainly to Sir William Cranston, whose twenty-five mounted police subjected the Borders to a vigorous disciplining: in one year " above 140 of the nimblest and most powerful thieves in all the Borders " went to the gallows.[37] In 1618 a conjunct commission was again set up, to enforce the old rules and also a new one reducing the number of public-houses. James felt that his work was done, and in 1621 the Border guard, or police force, was disbanded as being no longer necessary. A certain recrudescence of disorder followed, with some concern about vagabonds and " lymmaris " on the Borders,[38] and the migration of thieves and resetters of thieves into England caused difficulties once more. Joint commissions were therefore appointed by Charles I in 1630 and again in 1635, and it may be that the Borders were still not completely settled before governmental authority was once more impaired in 1638. Even after the Restoration, disorder was not unknown, but in essentials the problem of the Borders had been solved by 1609, when the chancellor remarked—with some exaggeration—that " all these ways and passages betwixt . . . Scotland and England " had been rendered " free and peaceable,"

36 Tough, *op. cit.*, pp. 246, 264-9.
37 Balfour, *Annals*, II. 17.
38 *R. P. C.*, XII. xl.

making the Borders " as lawful, as peaceable and as quiet as any part of any civil kingdom of Christianity."[39]

Two of the elements in James VI's Highland policy can be discerned in 1597, when one act ordered all landholders in the Highlands and Islands to compear in the exchequer and bring their titles, and another authorised the creation of three burghs in the Highlands. The question of titles was associated with crown finance, and again and again James reverted to his belief that he ought to draw more revenue from the Highlands than he was actually receiving and that his rents from " the Isles " were being withheld. The other development envisaged in 1597—the creation of burghs—was part of the policy of " plantation " or colonisation by " answerable inlands [*i.e.* Lowland] subjects " among the " utterly barbarous " islanders.[40] After the act of 1597, Lewis was declared forfeit and a number of Fife gentlemen undertook to " plant thameselffis thairin be force,"[41] but after two attempts to establish themselves the colonists had finally, in 1607, to give up in the face of native hostility.[42]

As a piece of strategy, policy in the Highlands and western Isles had a new complexion after 1603. The English problem of north-eastern Ireland and the Scottish problem of south-western Scotland were, in fact, a single problem. As far back as the Treaty of Northampton (1328) the English king promised not to intrigue with the Celtic subjects of the Scottish crown in the western Isles, while the Scottish king undertook not to ally with the Celts of Ireland. The connexion between the lands and peoples on the two sides of the narrow North Channel seems seldom to have been closer than it was in the late sixteenth century. One family—MacDonald or MacDonell of Dunivaig and the Glens— had come, through marriage, to hold land in Antrim as well as in Islay and Kintyre. Highlanders and western Islanders had been exceptionally active in Ireland all through Elizabeth's reign, not only as mercenary troops but as something of an occupying force in certain coastal areas of Ulster. Sometimes they professed to act in name of the king of Scots and to deny the English any right in Ireland, sometimes they professed allegiance to Elizabeth.[43]

39 *Letters and State Papers of James VI* (Abbotsford Club), p. 172.
40 *Basilicon Doron*, I. 70.
41 *Edinburgh Burgh Records, 1589-1603*, p. 221.
42 W. C. Mackenzie, *History of the Outer Hebrides*, Chs. vii-ix.
43 W. C. Mackenzie, *Highlands and Isles of Scotland*, pp. 144, 166.

This problem, therefore, was, like that of the Borders, soluble only through Anglo-Scottish co-operation, and, as in the Borders, there were already signs before 1603 that the two governments would work together. A significant stage was reached in 1608, when an expedition by Lord Ochiltree, which is best known for his *coup* in enticing the island chiefs on board his ship in the Sound of Mull and imprisoning them, coincided with the suppression, by Sir Arthur Chichester, lord deputy of Ireland, of a rebellion in Ulster. Chichester offered assistance to Ochiltree and asked in return that the Scottish council should prevent the Irish rebels from recruiting in Scotland and should deal with defeated Irish who took refuge there. The strategic problem was finally solved when the plantation of Ulster[44] cut off the Scottish Celts from the Irish. Control of Ireland also contributed to the settlement of the Borders, whence criminals had escaped to Ireland; in 1624 it was agreed to station officials at certain points on the Irish and Scottish coasts to apprehend fugitives.

The crown had hitherto relied mainly on the issue of commissions of fire and sword and special lieutenancies, which meant encouraging certain chiefs and clans at the expense of others. After 1600 this policy was still pursued, at least intermittently. In the south, use was made particularly of the Campbells. The Earl of Argyll in 1607 received a charter of the crown lands in Kintyre and the southern isles, from which he was to eject MacDonalds and MacLeans, and he was also commissioned as justiciar and lieutenant for six months. In 1609 he set about the erection of the burgh of Lochhead (Campbeltown). After he had suppressed MacDonald risings in 1614 and 1615, his title to Kintyre was ratified (1617), and the Lowland plantation there went on in earnest. Lowlanders were planted in the burgh of Inveraray as well, and these settlements, though small in scale, are to be seen as a counterpart to the plantation of Ulster. Some ten years after the risings of 1614-15, a commission of fire and sword was issued to Lord Lorne, Argyll's heir, and four other Campbell lairds, to deal with a rebellion of Clan Ian in Ardnamurchan and other parts of north Argyll. The early seventeenth century thus saw the continued aggrandisement of Clan Campbell, which was to be such a menace to the crown later in the century. In the north-western Highlands, the Mackenzies played a part

---

[44] Pp. 252-3 below.

parallel to that of the Campbells in the south-west.   Kenneth
Mackenzie, who had been created Lord Kintail in 1609, was given
a special commission of justiciary to deal with a rebellion under
MacLeod of Lewis, and was granted the island of Lewis, where in
1610 he acquired the rights of the frustrated Lowland adventurers.
A MacLeod attempt to regain Lewis in 1622 was followed by a fresh
commission to Colin, Lord Kintail, who became Earl of Seaforth
in 1624, and to other Mackenzies.   The Mackenzies, with lands
now stretching from Cromarty to Lewis, had acquired an importance comparable to that of the Gordons and the Campbells.

In this period, however, an alternative was found to the policy
of entrusting the settlement of the Highlands to feudal magnates
and of setting up one clan against another.   The man who did
most to extend crown authority in the Isles was the bishop,
Andrew Knox, who was strenuously opposed to the policy which
was leading to Campbell aggrandisement: " Neither can I think
it either good or profitable," he wrote, " to his majesty or this
country to make that name [Campbell] greater in the Isles than
they are already, or yet to root out one pestiferous clan and plant
in one little better."[45]   Behind the bishop stood a commission of
the council which had as its quorum Archbishop Spottiswoode,
Knox himself, Lord Ochiltree and the comptroller, and which
did not include Argyll.   One feature of the policy now followed
was the recognition of the clan as a unit and a disposition to use
each chief as responsible to the government for the behaviour of
his clansmen—something much milder than James had had in
mind earlier, when he characterised the Islanders as " wolves
and wild boars."[46] The principle of the " general bond," whereby
a landowner or chief accepted responsibility for the conduct of
his tenants or clansmen, was not a new one, and had been resorted
to more than once, in the Highlands, the Borders and elsewhere,
on several occasions in the sixteenth century.[47]

Bishop Knox, who had been in company with Lord Ochiltree
on his expedition in 1608, had a meeting at Iona in 1609 with a
group of chiefs more or less identical with those who had in the
past constituted the council of the Isles—MacDonald of Dunivaig
(Islay), MacLean of Duart and MacLean of Lochbuie (Mull),
MacDonald of Sleat and MacKinnon of Strathardle (Skye),

45 *Original Letters*, II 393-4.   46 *Basilicon Doron*, I. 70.
47 *E.g.*, R. P. C., IV. 99 (referring to old acts of parliament).

MacLeod of Harris, MacLean of Coll, MacDonald of Eilean Tioram (the captain of Clanranald) and MacQuharrie of Ulva—who pledged themselves to obey the king and his laws and agreed to the " statutes of Icolmkill." These provided for the extension of the ministry of the reformed church; the establishment of inns; the control of the import and production of alcoholic beverages; the suppression of idle vagabonds, beggars and bards (who kept alive the memory of old feuds) and the limitation of chiefs' retinues; the prohibition of the carrying of fire-arms; and the sending of the heirs of men of substance to the Lowlands for education. It was also agreed that chiefs should arrest and try malefactors, and in the following year the chiefs became bound to appear before the council at stated intervals. The statutes and bond were in substance renewed in 1616, with a new provision, that no one should inherit property in the Isles unless he could read, write and speak English, and in 1624 there was a conference at Edinburgh of thirty-six Highland landowners with twenty-one privy councillors.

Under Charles I essentially the same policies were followed. Bishop Knox's successor was appointed justiciar and commissioner for the west Highlands and Isles, leading chiefs were summoned before the council, and in 1636 the council called for lists of servants and tenants in the Highland area, with the names of their masters and lords. These proceedings had a steady effect, though there are indications that the Highlands had not been permanently pacified before the disturbances beginning in 1638 once more weakened the central government, and even after the Restoration there were isolated outbreaks, to suppress which resort was occasionally had to commissions of fire and sword.

Most clans were settled societies, with a chief whose clansmen were also his tenants, but the term " clan " was used in a derogatory sense, in both the Highlands and the Borders, of bands or gangs of landless men,[48] and there were also " clannis that hes capitanis, chieffis and chiftennis, quhomeon they depend, oftymes aganis the willis of thair landislordis."[49] The most notorious of the last type of clan was the Clan Gregor. The chief had a small estate at Glenstrae, at the head of Loch Awe, but he was acknowledged as chief by men scattered over various other estates, particularly those of Campbell of Glenorchy and Menzies of Weem.

[48] *R. P. C.*, II. 367.   [49] *R. P. C.*, IV. 782.

The MacGregor chief obviously could not take the responsibility for his clan which the government was coming to expect, and his clansmen were strategically placed for plundering raids, through Glenfalloch, Glenogle, Strathtay and Glenlyon, into fertile territory, and for retreat into inaccessible fastnesses on the Moor of Rannoch. Already before James's accession " the wicked and unhappy race of the Clan Gregour "[50] was notorious for its offences, and caused almost ceaseless concern to the government.[51] Their slaughter of the Colquhouns at Glenfruin in 1603 was the immediate occasion of a special campaign against them in 1603-4, and, after a lull for some years, in 1610 a campaign of extermination opened: twenty-eight nobles and lairds who had the followers of MacGregor as neighbours received a commission of fire and sword to " ruit oute and extirpat all that race."[52] The chief's name was proscribed, the price of £1,000 was put on the head of each leading member of the clan, 1,000 merks on the heads of lesser men, and any clansman could earn his own pardon by bringing in the head of another. This drastic policy seems to have achieved its objective, and after some years the clan ceased to be a danger, for about 1627 the chief was in a position to offer to keep it in order.

The problem of the northern isles of Orkney and Shetland was not one of disorder at the lower levels of society, but a question almost of sovereignty, certainly of law—whether the old Norse law or the law of Scotland should prevail. The inhabitants would certainly have resented their association with Highlanders, for in 1604 there was a complaint about the resort to the islands of " beggaris, sornaris and vacaboundis " who had " brokin fra thair companeis and clanis out of the Hilandis and utheris barbarous partis."[53] The trouble, in a sense, was not too little government, but too much government—by potentates who ruled almost as independent sovereigns. In 1564 Queen Mary had set the crown lands and rights in the islands in feu to her half-brother, Robert, commendator of Holyrood, and appointed him sheriff. In 1568 Robert compelled the Bishop of Orkney to accept the abbey of Holyrood in exchange for the episcopal lands, jurisdiction and patronage in Orkney and Shetland, so that crown, earldom and bishopric property and rights were

50 *R. P. C.*, vi. 72.　　51 *E.g.*, *R. P. C* , i. 248-50, 255-8, 269-70, 361.
52 *R. P. C.*, ix. 166.　　53 *Court Book of Shetland* (S. R. S.), p. 123.

concentrated in the hands of Lord Robert, who became Earl of Orkney in 1581. He was disposed to take advantage of the indeterminate international status of his dominions, which had never been formally ceded to Scotland, for he was suspected of treasonable dealings with the King of Denmark, and he also exploited the distinct legal system obtaining in the islands. In 1503, when an act of parliament had abolished laws not in accordance with the law of Scotland, Orkney and Shetland had been excepted, and in 1567 it was still the view of the parliament that the islands should be subject to " their own laws."[54] Thus Lord Robert, and his son, Earl Patrick, were able to maintain such features of older usage as upheld or extended their authority, and they were accused of applying either Norse law or Scots law, whichever better served their " gain and commodity."[55] In any event, the manifold regulations of the old code gave them ample opportunities of imposing fines, sometimes so heavy that the natives were forced to part with their lands to pay them. In 1606, however, James Law became Bishop of Orkney and in 1608 he appealed to the crown against Earl Patrick. The bishop may not have been disinterested, but he was a useful counterpoise to the earl and was a crown agent who would not found a dynasty. Patrick was summoned to Edinburgh, where he was imprisoned, and in 1615, after his son had raised a rebellion in Orkney, he was executed. Bishop Law became the king's " commissioner, sheriff and justice " in the islands, the Norse law was abolished by the privy council (1611), and the castle of Kirkwall was demolished. The earldom thus lost its political significance, and, though many local usages divergent from Scottish legal practice continued to operate, the islands were never again a source of concern to the central government.

The use made of Bishop Knox in the Isles and of Bishop Law in Orkney was paralleled in Caithness, where the earl was held to be incapable of introducing order among an " incivil and barbarous " people and the bishop, Alexander Forbes, received a commission not unlike those given to the bishops of the Isles and of Orkney.[56]

Certain of the achievements of the government of James VI,

---

[54] *A. P. S.*, II. 244, 252; III. 41.
[55] *R. P. C.*, IX. 181-2. Cf. G. Donaldson, *Shetland Life under Earl Patrick*.
[56] *R. P. C.*, IX. 237-8.

in solving problems which had been outstanding for generations, can fairly be described as spectacular. But there were other, less conspicuous, developments which also made for order, unity and uniformity. It is true that the government was not wholly disinterested, for revenues could be more efficiently collected in an orderly kingdom. One of the king's innovations was the establishment, in 1603, of a mounted force called the king's guard, to execute warrants of the council and apprehend offenders; and later, as conditions became more orderly, its specific purpose was to arrest persons who were at the horn for non-payment of taxes.[57] Besides, the fines levied on wrongdoers were a welcome addition to the exchequer, though the amounts which ultimately found their way there were sometimes disappointing. For example, under acts of 1611 the Earl of Argyll was given full powers against the Clan Gregor, and resetters of members of that clan were to be fined, the proceeds to go in the proportions of $77\frac{1}{2}$ per cent to Argyll and the remainder to the crown. The total amount of fines imposed was £115,000. But some of the impositions were abated, some were cancelled, to the amount in all of £38,000, and of the remainder, £32,000 was still " restand auchtand " in 1623. Thus, of the £45,000 which seems to have been actually collected, the crown's share was £10,000.[58]

Yet the manifold activities of the government were prompted partly by a genuine solicitude for justice and equity. A minor illustration was the fixing in 1606 of the tariff to be paid for the issue and sealing of writs in the various offices. A major one was the successful establishment of the register of sasines in 1617. For over a century effort after effort had been made to secure a system whereby transactions in heritable property would be recorded in a public register, and in 1617 machinery was at last devised which has endured, with only comparatively minor changes, until the present day and has endowed Scotland with a unique series of records. It is to this period, too, that the earliest extant registers of baptisms, marriages and burials belong. It is not easy to relate their existence to the legislation which required that they should be compiled, for some—such as the registers of

---

[57] The guard at first numbered forty, and although it was supposed to be reduced to nine in 1611 payment continued to be made to forty, possibly because it was combined with the police force for the borders (W. Taylor, " The Scottish privy council " [Edinburgh Ph.D. thesis], pp. 64-5).   [58] *R. P. C.*, XIV. xc-xcvii.

Dunfermline, beginning in 1560—seem to have anticipated legislation, others to have lagged far behind it; but the mere fact that they have survived from this period indicates the development of orderly habits and settled conditions. In civil justice there was no need for new machinery, but there were reforms of the existing court of session. In 1590 it was ordained that candidates for the bench should be examined by the judges before their appointment, in 1592 that judges were to be at least twenty-five years of age and possessed of a property qualification, and in 1594 that no judge should sit in a case concerning his father, brother or son.

When there was such a passion for order, some of the legislation of an extremely paternal government was of a character quite unknown in the more libertarian eighteenth and nineteenth centuries, though familiar again in the more authoritarian regime of recent times. For example, in 1615 we learn that there had grown up " a most unlawful and pernicious trade of transporting of eggs by avaricious and godless persons, void of modesty and discretion, who, preferring their own private commodity to the common weal, have gone and go throughout the country and buy the whole eggs that they can get, barrel the same and transport them at their pleasure "; penalty, £100.[59] In 1619 there was an act for the prevention of cruelty to animals, relating that the practice in Orkney and Shetland of removing wool by plucking it from the sheep was " grievous and noisome to the poor harmless beasts "; but after enquiries it was proved that the practice was not cruel, and the prohibition was withdrawn.[60] Sometimes the government was concerned with what seem trivialities: an act of parliament of June 1609 settled that judges, magistrates of burghs, churchmen and officials should wear distinguishing dress; it was left to his majesty to design the costumes, and when he had made his decision, after six months, it was embodied in an act of council. And there was frequently legislation against tobacco, in 1616 on the ground that " the use or rather abuse of taking of tobacco is laitlie croppin in within . . . Scotland, ane weade so infective as all young and ydill personis ar in a maner bewitchet thairwith."[61] This came appropriately from a monarch who penned A counterblast to tobacco, in which he complained that smokers of tobacco made " the filthy smoke and stink thereof to

[59] R. P. C., x. 325-6.   [60] R. P. C., xi. 510; xii. 111-2.
[61] R. P. C., x. 516.

exhale athort the dishes and infect the air, when very often men that abhor it are at their repast," and scoffed at the mutually contradictory arguments used in favour of smoking: " It refreshes a weary man, and yet makes a man hungry. Being taken when they go to bed, it makes one sleep soundly, and yet being taken when a man is sleepy and drowsy, it will, as they say, awake his brain and quicken his understanding."

When James extolled the example of " utheris weill governit commounwelthis " it was usually the example of England which he had in mind, and he had laid down in his advice to his son that the two kingdoms should be assimilated to " the fashions of that realm of yours that ye find most civil, easiest to be ruled and most obedient to the laws."[62] Yet he had not before 1603 shown himself a slavish imitator of English ways, and in at least one act, that which ordained that from 1600 onwards the year should begin on 1 January, he was a century and a half in advance of England, where the year continued to begin on 25 March until 1752; he was indifferent to English example, for his act related that " in all utheris weill governit commoun welthis and cuntreyis the first day of the yeir begynis yeirlie upoun the first day of Januare ... and that this realme onlie is different fra all utheris."[63]

As James's difficulties in England multiplied in his later years, he may sometimes have been in doubt as to which of his kingdoms was " easiest to be ruled "; all his experience certainly justified his forecast in 1603 that " the augmentation " would be "but in cares and heavy burdens."[64] But the cares and burdens were not of James's making; they constituted the *damnosa hereditas* left by Elizabeth Tudor, a sovereign utterly careless of the well-being of her kingdom after her own demise, who had allowed unsolved problems to pile up in her later years and whose reign had ended in anti-climax, in decline, almost in failure. James went to a country heading for insolvency, and one in which the whole system of government was already being challenged. He tried to apply in England the same principles of authoritarianism and pacification as he had applied in Scotland. For example, Elizabeth had belatedly seen the danger of puritanism,[65] but it was left to James to redefine Anglicanism and indeed to recon-struct the Church of England on a non-puritan foundation which

---

[62] *Basilicon Doron*, I. 199-200.　　　[63] *R. P. C.*, VI. 63.
[64] *Letters to King James the Sixth* (Maitland Club), p. xxviii.　　[65] P. 182 above.

was to endure. James's reign also brought peace with Spain, the pacification of Ireland and the first permanent English colony in America. His logic and commonsense were not appreciated by his more emotional English subjects, but the fact is that problems which Gloriana never solved were solved by this king from Scotland.

13

THE ECONOMY OF JACOBEAN SCOTLAND

King James's typical subject was a countryman, not a towns-man, for the economy of Scotland continued throughout the seventeenth century to be an essentially rural economy, in every sense of the term. Such concentration of population as there was arose mainly from the fertility of the soil in certain areas, with the result that districts like the lower Tweed valley, the Solway shores and the Laigh of Moray counted for far more than they have done since the eighteenth century. The populous areas were widely dispersed, and it must have been true then, as it still was in 1755, that half the people of Scotland lived in the lands north of the Tay. It is very doubtful if as many as a fifth of the population lived in burghs, and several of the burghs were mere villages, numbering their inhabitants only by the hundred. The genuine townsman, wholly differentiated from the countryman, hardly existed outside the capital and perhaps two or three other burghs, for elsewhere the burgess had his rural interests, to the extent of being a small-holder; it was quite characteristic that in Montrose, for example, a burgess who had shares in two trading vessels and a fishing vessel also grew wheat and bear on his roods in the burgh and possessed a cow, a heifer and a calf.[1]

Conditions were in many ways favourable to Scottish agri-culture in the sixteenth and seventeenth centuries. After the 1540s there were no more devastating invasions from the south, there were no military operations of any consequence between

[1] Cf. Pryde, *Court Book of Burgh of Kirkintilloch* (S. H. S.), lxx.

the end of Scotland's own civil war in 1573 and Scotland's involvement in the English civil war in the 1640s, and disorder of every kind diminished. The farmer could now sow his seed with some confidence that no human agency would prevent him from reaping his crops. Moreover, the changes consequent on the Reformation were on the whole beneficial to agriculture on the ecclesiastical estates. It had been a persistent complaint in the sixteenth century that the feus granted by churchmen too often went not to the sitting tenants but—in return for large initial payments—to middlemen who recouped themselves for their outlay by rack-renting or evicting the tenants. Yet this practice, though common, was far from being invariable, for feus were quite frequently granted to the existing tenants. On the Melrose abbey estates there were many instances where the kindly tenant became the feuar of his own holding, and that without an excessive augmentation of his accustomed rent;[2] on the Kinloss estates, too, it seems to have been the regular practice to feu to the existing tenants.[3] At any rate, proprietorship, at whatever level, was now hereditary, and this meant stability and continuity in management and less likelihood of action prejudicial to future owners. While farmers who now had feus enjoyed the incentive to improvement which is alleged to come from security of tenure, the feuars who were not themselves farmers wanted higher rents which could be paid only by progressive tenants who were prepared to " ryve out the mures, the bestialls gers intak " and so extend arable at the expense of pasture.[4] Farmers whose rents were being sharply increased were of necessity much exercised over methods of improving fertility, and liming was extensively resorted to.[5] A more commercial nexus began to supersede the keeping of " kindly tenants " who paid small rents but rendered services, including so many days' work in harvest— sometimes to the detriment of work on their own holdings. No doubt tenants in general still held only by the much-criticised short lease, but in one collection of family papers after another a series of tacks or long leases does begin in the early seventeenth century—some of them, of course, not to actual farmers but to

2 *Melrose Regality Records* (S. H. S.), III, *passim*, especially pp. 166, 228 ff.

3 This is demonstrated by numerous charters recorded in *R. M. S.* and *R. S. S.*

4 *Lamentatioun of Lady Scotland* (1572), sig. a v v.

5 Lowther, *Our Journal into Scotland* (1894), 35; cf. *East Lothian Antiq. and Field Naturalists' Soc. Trans.*, IX. 1-3.

middlemen. There is also, in the small amount of extant evidence, some slight indication that landlords were insisting on good husbandry and even that action was already being taken, here and there, to consolidate holdings.[6] Finally, the arrangements made by Charles I for the commutation of teinds[7] offered farmers a chance of liberation from a burden which had sometimes been prejudicial to their harvesting.

Possibly the customary view of the older Scottish agricultural system too much reflects the contemptuous attitude of the eighteenth century " Improvers." In their eyes all was inefficient and uneconomic. The infield, in the vicinity of the " toun " of farmhouses, was kept in moderate fertility by the application of all the manure from the steading, but was sown with oats and bear without respite and without rotation; the outfield received no special fertilisation at all and when a portion of it was tilled it was cropped annually for several years, with diminishing returns, and its recovery was then entrusted to nature. As there were no root crops or artificial grasses, and no serious hay-making, winter feeding for cattle was so inadequate that there had to be a slaughter at Martinmas of the beasts which the farmer could not hope to feed. During the winter the only escape from the salt flesh of those " marts " was to be found in fish and in pigeons from the dovecotes; and the temptation, in the spring, to terminate the miserable existence of some of the surviving cattle had to be checked by the maintenance, after the Reformation as before it, of the season of Lent, during which it was forbidden to eat flesh except by licence. Much land in the valleys which could have been brought under the plough lay waterlogged and undrained, and the cultivated land was drained only by open ditches. The resources of Scotland were certainly not being fully utilised.

But the system must be seen in its context. Any exportable surplus was a secondary consideration, for Scottish farming was then essentially subsistence farming, designed primarily to feed the farmers and their families, who were, in effect, the people of Scotland. And this objective it was on the whole achieving. It is quite clear, from numerous examples, that although in years of scarcity corn had to be imported, in years of plenty corn could be exported. In a really good year, the

[6] See in general " Sources for Scottish agrarian history before the eighteenth century," in *Agric. Hist. Rev.*, VIII, PT. II, 82-90.   [7] Pp. 297-8 below.

exports of grain were substantial, and an English visitor of 1618 marvelled at the figures he was given—320,000 bushels in a year from Leith alone.[8] The exports of cattle and other animals fluctuated in a somewhat similar way, for the size of the surplus depended on the weather, but there was always a large exportable surplus of skins and hides. Thus, in 1614, the Scots shipped overseas the skins of 1,944 cattle, 1,092 deer, 240,000 sheep, 162,000 lambs and 16,000 goats, and these exported skins, as well as skins utilised at home, represented carcasses which had presumably been eaten. Supplies of meat cannot have been inadequate, and in the middle of the sixteenth century a French visitor had remarked on the cheapness of meat in Scotland.[9] Besides, the cattle population represented immense stores of butter and cheese, which figure in the rentals of some religious houses: Paisley drew some 700 stones of cheese and Melrose some 100 stones of butter.[10]

The inference from all this must be that on balance the scale of production of foodstuffs in Scotland was roughly what was required and that the level of agriculture was not indefensible. The objectives of the time could be achieved on far lower standards of efficiency than became necessary later, with a rapidly increasing urban population to be fed. As it was, from the products of Scotland's fields and hills, rivers and seas, the inhabitants were fed, clothed and kept warm. The typical Scot was concerned mainly with the provision of the needs of his own household. His crops of oats, bear and flax, his flocks and herds, his wood or peat, his fruit trees, his poultry and fish, all had their obvious uses—as well as some not so obvious nowadays, for horn was made into spoons, hair was used in the masons' mortar, and tallow was made into candles. Judged by the standards of the time, there was nothing radically wrong with Scottish agriculture, and fertile areas like Mid and East Lothian compared well enough with other lands: Oliver Cromwell, who must have known something about agriculture, remarked that " about Edinburgh it is as fertile for corn as any part of England,"[11] and another English visitor described the fields between Berwick and Edinburgh as " replenished with corn and grain of all sorts . . . as plentiful as in most countries in England."[12] The crop grown

8 P. Hume Brown, *Early travellers in Scotland*, p. 112.   9 *Ibid.*, pp. 73-4.
10 *Thirds of benefices* (S. H. S.), 44; cf. *R. S. S.* VII. 826.
11 Carlyle, *Cromwell's letters and speeches*, ed. Lomas, II. 137.
12 *Charles II and Scotland in 1650* (S. H. S.), p. 139.

in greatest quantity was probably oats, but bear must almost have equalled it, and both were universal throughout the length and breadth of the country. Wheat, although it was not thought of as a staple food,[13] was grown in all the east-coast areas from Moray to Berwickshire, as well as in Perthshire, Stirlingshire, Ayrshire and Roxburghshire. Crops of pease and beans, and of rye, were of little account.[14]

It was climatic conditions which mainly determined the prosperity of an essentially rural Scotland. But peace and security certainly, and progressive agriculture possibly, contributed to the steady improvement in the material state of the country discernible after 1600. Before that date there had been bad seasons in 1560, 1562, 1585-7 and 1594-8, all necessitating heavy imports of grain. But, whereas in the 1590s the grain imports from the Baltic had averaged 563 lasts a year, from 1601 to 1610 the average was 211 and from 1611 to 1620 it was only 111.[15] If this is evidence that Scottish agriculture was more sufficient, there is also proof that it was producing more wealth: the average value of the estate of a farmer or small laird about 1600 was little more than £500, by 1640 it was nearly £1,000, and this in a period when there was relative stability in prices.[16] It is true that it was still sometimes demonstrated, as in 1621-2 and 1629-30, that although a good year provided an exportable surplus of corn, a poor harvest still made it necessary to forbid exports and facilitate imports. It is also true that there were often local shortages, so that the people of the south-west might have to come to Leith to buy corn.[17] But " the tentative conclusion is that life in Scotland in the closing years of King James's reign was easier and safer than it had been when he was a boy. . . . There was still poverty, but mass famine and mass destruction were slipping into the mists of memory."[18]

It might be going too far to argue that the " Improvers " of the eighteenth century were to any extent anticipated in the

[13] *R. P. C.*, 2nd. ser., IV. 191.

[14] This impression is based on *Thirds of benefices* (S. H. S.).

[15] Lythe, *The Scottish economy*, p. 32.

[16] These figures are based on an examination of sample batches of testaments, numbering over 400 in all. There is also a significant change in the distribution of the values of estates: in the range up to £2,000, the pattern *c.* 1575 is of a pyramid, *c.* 1600 it is more like a column and in the 1630s it begins to look like an inverted pyramid.

[17] Burnet, *Own time* (1823), I. 74.   [18] Lythe, *op. cit.*, pp. 22-3.

early seventeenth. But one of the interests of improving land-owners—silviculture—had already appeared: Sir James Pringle, in 1629, was compelling his tenants to plant trees; Duncan Campbell of Glenorchy was interested in afforestation, and in 1637 we find the Earl of Lauderdale sending to him for fir seeds; Sir William Mure of Rowallan, who died in 1657, " delyted much in building and planting."[19] Their experiments must have encountered many difficulties. To ensure success, plantations of young trees must be effectively protected from rabbits, hares, deer, cattle and sheep, and at that time the habit of " enclosing " fields was not yet established; again, the possibilities of making extensive use of the higher mountain slopes for afforestation could not be exploited without scientific choice of trees. So far as conservation was concerned, all that was as yet done was the occasional re-enactment of the age-old legislation against the cutting of green wood (for which the penalty was death), and this had no effect in halting the process by which large areas were denuded of trees. It seems clear that the Borders were generally bare of trees, and so was Fife;[20] and one can understand the impression made by the bald wind-swept southern uplands, the Moorfoots and the Lammermoors, on visitors who never pene-trated into more distant parts of the country which were, in fact, well wooded. The Highland area generally may not have been quite " overclad with fir trees,"[21] but there was abundant growth of the native birch, rowan, alder and hazel, and in some places there was timber which constituted an acknowledged asset: John Wemyss of that ilk, who died in 1571, was said to have the right to an action for the destruction of 100,000 birch trees, valued at 6s. 8d. each, on his Perthshire estate of Strathardle.[22] To some extent the trouble was not lack of timber, but difficulty of transport, for, with the exception of Inverness and Perth, to which timber could be floated down by loch and river, Scots burghs found it easier to obtain supplies from Norway than from the Scottish Highlands.

[19] C. Lowther, *Our journall into Scotland* (1894), p. 17; Cosmo Innes, *Early Scotch History*, pp. 346, 519; *D. N. B.* on Mure.
[20] But an oak wood at Falkland was cut down by the English in 1652 (*Diary of John Lamont of Newton*, p. 43).
[21] Hume Brown, *Scotland before 1700*, p. 299.
[22] Edinburgh Testaments, 27 May 1574. For another instance, see *R. S. S.*, VII. 1031.

Improved conditions, in which life could be more than a mere struggle for existence, turned men's minds to the expansion of Scotland's meagre manufactures. The king himself " imbraced all such divises, overtouris, projectis and inventouris as onywayes seemed to be beneficiall," and thought that " the practice of tradis not formarlie knowne " in his kingdom could most easily be encouraged if " stranger craftsmen " were not only permitted, but allured, to settle among his subjects.[23] Another thoughtful Scot was Sir Thomas Craig, who believed that his countrymen had " begun to accustom themselves to occupations and trade " and concurred with the king on the necessity of bringing in skilled workers to give instruction.[24] It was especially important, he added, to develop the manufacture of cloth, without which " we shall find it hard to raise money to pay for our imports."[25] In 1582, 1594 and 1600 there were acts in favour of foreign craftsmen who were to instruct the Scots in various operations connected with cloth-making, and both Flemish and English weavers, spinners, waulkers and dyers are to be found in Edinburgh, at least, in the last years of the sixteenth century and the beginning of the seventeenth.[26] It is not clear that Scottish cloth-making did benefit much from the foreign craftsmen, but it did gain from the use of foreign raw materials, for wool imported from England, and sometimes from Spain, was used to supplement the inferior native wool. Besides being used for cloth, wool had recently come to be used for knitting, especially of stockings; Scottish knitted hose were now highly prized, and by the 1620s 14,000 pairs were being shipped annually from Leith alone.

Another widespread and well established industry, the linen manufacture, was also intended to benefit from foreign experts, for in 1611 some Dutchmen were brought in to give instruction. A German received a patent for the manufacture of paper in 1590,[27] and later in James's reign Venetians were introduced to assist with new glass works and Englishmen to assist in the leather industry. The device in which most confidence was put for the encouragement of manufactures was, however, the grant of patents or monopolies to Scotsmen. The objectives of such

---

[23] R. P. C., XII. xvii; *Basilicon Doron*, I. 93.

[24] Sir Thomas Craig, *De unione regnorum Britanniae* (S. H. S.), p. 417.

[25] *Ibid.*, p. 448.

[26] *Edinburgh Burgh Records, 1573-89*, p. 530; *1589-1603*, pp. 281-2, 287, 289, 290, 293; *1604-26*, App. i.   [27] R. P. C., IV. 452.

grants, ostensibly at least, were to free Scotland from dependence on imports, to encourage and reward skill and to ensure the quality of the product. When a patent for the leather manufacture was granted to Lord Erskine, it was provided that no hides should be sold unless they bore a stamp showing that they had been tanned by the approved method, and the patentee, who was to bear the expense of bringing in expert tanners from England and of stamping the hides, was authorised to collect a levy of 4s. a hide for twenty-one years and 1s. for a further ten years.[28] When monopoly rights were claimed in soap manufacture, the privy council reflected that the imported soap in use was " pestiferous and noisome," and received a favourable report on the soap for which a monopoly was asked, but cautiously arranged that to ensure " the continuance of the said soap in the present fineness " inspectors should periodically " try the sufficiency of the said soap . . . at unawares."[29] The patent for glass making, originally issued in 1610, did have the effect of establishing a new industry for which Scotland had the raw materials, in kelp and sand, and which Sir George Hay (later Earl of Kinnoull) pursued successfully at Wemyss from 1612 onwards. Also notable, as the beginning of an industry which was to have a long history in Scotland, was the grant in 1628 to two London merchants and a Scot of the sole right of refining sugar in Scotland for thirty-one years.[30]

It is to be feared that the readiness of the government to grant patents and monopolies was apt to encourage the over-confident and the mere adventurers, like Nathaniel Udward, who had monopolies of linen cloth, brick and tile making, soap, ordnance, saltpetre and salt, at various dates between 1611 and 1631. At the same time, although agitation in England prompted the king to concentrate on patents for new processes rather than monopolies and perhaps stimulated the setting up of a commission for grievances in Scotland (1623), there is little evidence that the grants were seriously burdensome to the Scots. The criticism of the government's various efforts to encourage crafts arose mainly from the conservatism of the burghs, jealous as they were of the exclusive rights of their own inhabitants. Just as the

[28] R. P. C., XII. 190-93.   [29] R. P. C., XII. 106-7, 505-6, 508, 516-7.
[30] Several extracts relating to patents are assembled in Chambers, *Domestic Annals*, I. 507-8, 512, 514.

royal burghs had, in law, a monopoly of foreign trade, so the making of articles for sale was restricted to burgesses. It had been to placate the burghs that an act had been passed in 1598 for the exclusion of foreign craftsmen, though this was contrary to the general drift of government policy. It was the burghs, too, which petitioned the commission on grievances against monopolies and which described the versatile Udward as " like ane rolling stone, now heir now thair, leiving upoun projects."[31]

There were two other industries which, like the manufacture of woollen and linen cloth, already had a long history—the making of salt by the evaporation of sea water and the closely associated collieries, both of which had flourished, especially on the shores of the Firth of Forth, for many centuries. The government was slow to realise that commodities for which there was a use at home could also with advantage be exported, and King James was for once behind the times, for he was suspicious of merchants who exported " things necessary " in return for " whiles unnecessary things and whiles nothing."[32] The principle of giving priority to home needs is understandable in relation to foodstuffs, for there was a persistent fear that the export of Scottish produce, attracted to England by ample markets and high prices, would lead to dearth at home, but there was less reason behind the repeated discouragement of the export of coal,[33] for, as coal was not easily transported inland, its use as a fuel was restricted to places near the pits or near the sea. Besides, in the sixteenth century the ownership of much land in the coal-bearing areas had passed from unenterprising ecclesiastics to far-seeing laymen who, despite the government, were ready to seize their opportunities to develop the industry and export coal. The beginning of the seventeenth century saw the establishment of Sir George Bruce's under-water mine at Culross, one of the wonders of Scotland, and in 1620 Samuel Johnstone of Elphinstone received a patent for new methods of draining pits and bringing coal to the surface. Scottish exports of coal, very largely to London, rose steadily, until by 1640, it has been estimated, they amounted in a year to 60,000 tons.[34] The export of salt also rose sharply:[35] until the late sixteenth century, the salt used in England came

31 *Edinburgh Burgh Records, 1604-26*, p. 407.   32 *Basilicon Doron*, I. 89.
33 Lythe, *op. cit.*, p. 84; cf. *R. S. S.*, VI. 2173.
34 J. U. Nef, *Rise of the British coal industry*, I. 45, 84.   35 *Ibid.*, I. 177-8.

mainly from the west coast of France, but the wars of religion in France disrupted this trade and reduced production, so affording to salt from north-eastern England and from Scotland a chance to compete with the French product. There are figures for Scottish exports in 1614 to all countries except England, and those show that the value of the salt exported was about a third that of the textiles, while the coal exported was worth more than half the salt; another mineral—lead ore—was nearly equal in value to the coal.[36]

A generation so given to " projects " could hardly have ignored the fisheries. There was no question but that Scotland was bountifully endowed with rich fishing grounds, and fish did figure prominently among Scottish exports—in value some 18 per cent of the 1614 total. But the main harvest of herring, and even of white fish, was reaped chiefly by the Dutch, whose fleet operating in Scottish waters numbered hundreds of vessels. The branches of the industry which were in Scottish hands were the herring fishing in the Firths of Forth and Clyde, some inshore fishing for white fish, and the salmon fishing. The expansion of the fisheries in the more remote parts of the country was hampered by the fact that the export of herring and salmon was a monopoly of the royal burghs, and although burghs of barony were authorised by James VI at Stornoway, Gordonsburgh (Fort William), and Campbeltown, no royal burghs were erected on the west coast until later in the century. It was proposed, with the enthusiastic approval of Charles I, that there should be a great company of Scots, English and Irish, to exploit the fishing all round the Scottish coasts. The Scots objected to the English sharing in the fishing inside lochs and bays and within a fourteen-mile limit, as well as to their settlement on the coasts for curing. Ultimately the fishing in the Firths of Forth, Tay and Clyde was reserved to the local inhabitants, but the whole project was interrupted by the civil war. A " society " or company for fishing set up in 1669 was no more successful, and no inroad was made on the Dutch hold.

The character of Scottish trade generally could be deduced from the nature of Scotland's internal economy. The chief exports were, inevitably, raw materials, the exportable surplus

36 For lead exports, 1585-1590, see *Anâlecta Scotica* (ed. J. Maidment), I. 91-3. The total was over 15,000 stones.

of what was primarily a subsistence agriculture, and this exportable surplus, which came directly from the countryside, far
exceeded in importance the urban products; such manufactures
as were exported consisted largely of goods made from materials
produced in the country and made, as often as not, by country-
dwellers and not by townsfolk. The principal exports were
stated in contemporary documents to be corn, hides, skins, wool,
lead ore, coal, salt, fish, woollen cloth, linen yarn, stockings
and gloves, while others of less importance ranged from beef
to honey and included beer, bonnets, cattle and other livestock.
To France went wool, woollen and linen cloth, and salt fish;
to the Netherlands, skins and hides, with increasing quantities
of coal and salt, as well as cloth, stockings, salmon, butter
and beef; to Scandinavia and the Baltic, cloth, skins, coal, salt
and fish; and to Ireland, linen, cloth, stockings, herring and
coal.

Among the imports, the only significant raw materials were
iron, which came from Spain and Sweden (sometimes in the form
of bars) and timber. Native production of iron was negligible,
and native timber, even when it was available, was not as suitable
as imported timber for the manifold needs of the builders, who
required wood not only for roofing and internal structural work
but also for the wooden galleries and extensions which so often
projected from the main stone structure of town houses. From
Norway especially came prodigious quantities of " deals " or
sawn planks, spars, joists, " tries " or balks of timber, " wain-
scots " and corbels, as well as barrel staves. For the building
and equipping of ships there had to be imported from the Baltic
not only timber, but flax, hemp, pitch, tar, iron and copper.
Most of the other imports—far more important than these raw
materials—were either food and drink or manufactured goods.[37]
Corn was almost the only staple food which ever had to be imported, and when dearth at home required it the source was
chiefly the Baltic, through ports like Danzig and Königsberg.
Wine came to some extent from Spain but mainly from the
Biscay ports, and the Scottish imports of wine have been estimated as of the order of half a million gallons in a year.[38] Some
beer and spirits also came in. The diet of native food was
varied by prunes, walnuts and chestnuts from France and

[37] Cf. Craig, *op. cit.*, p. 448.   [38] Lythe, *op. cit.*, p. 178.

seasoned by the spices which came mainly from the Netherlands. Clothing, of cloth, silk and fur, came chiefly from the Netherlands. Beyond these items there was a wide range of more or less luxury articles, including furniture and utensils, carpets and glass, but extending, according to a contemporary alphabetical list, from alabaster to virginals and including anchovies, dolls and rattles, caviare, carraway seeds, chessboards and chessmen, " elephants' teeth," drugs, guns and armour, ostrich feather fans, harpstrings, paper and parchment, pearls, soap, spectacles, spices, sponges, swords, thimbles and tobacco.[39] A large proportion of these luxury articles came from northern France.

Neither the political nor religious changes of the sixteenth century had disrupted Scotland's traditional trade routes. She had been at war with no continental power since 1266, her alliance with France had been maintained in James V's reign without prejudice to friendly relations with the emperor and his subjects in the Netherlands, and her reformation, although it had in the end aligned her with England, had not involved a rupture with England's enemies. Indeed, the Anglo-Spanish war seems actually to have stimulated the activities of Scottish merchants in Spain, as intermediaries for the English. The French wars of religion did for a time interfere with Franco-Scottish commerce, but they left the Huguenots, with whom the Scots had ecclesiastical affiliations, dominant in some of the seaboard regions where Scotland had the closest trading links, and in any event Scottish trading privileges, especially exemption from customs in Normandy, were confirmed by Henry IV in 1599. Scottish ties with the Netherlands, likewise, were not disrupted by the Reformation, and with the United Provinces they were actually drawn closer by theological affinity. Trade with the Baltic and Scandinavia was never seriously interrupted, but showed a significant increase over the period between the Reformation and the Covenanting troubles. Early in the seventeenth century there was a proposal for a " Muscoviane Indiane companie " or " societie . . . traffiquand in the eist contrey."[40]

---

[39] *Ledger of Andrew Halyburton* (ed. C. Innes, 1867), 289-333. Cf. also the lists of goods imported under " the new inwart customes " of 1597, in *E.R.*, xxiii. 315 ff. No doubt lists could be of potential, rather than actual, imports, but Dr Smout's researches make it clear that, after the Restoration at least, the variety of imports was as great as such lists indicate (*Scottish trade on the eve of union*, pp. 24-5, 172, 192 ff.).

[40] *Edinburgh Burgh Records, 1604-26*, p. 156 and n.

Trade with Ireland, too, was never subject to political interference and was fostered through the plantation of Ulster and
subsequent migration of Scots to northern Ireland.

The character of Anglo-Scottish commerce was not
dramatically altered by the union of the crowns. It is true that
for a few years after 1603 there was the possibility of a customs
union and that certain concessions were made: in 1604 the
English " custom " of 25 per cent of the " subsidy " (itself 4s. in
the £) was no longer levied on goods imported from Scotland;
there was until 1611 virtually free import of English goods into
Scotland; and in 1615 the two countries proclaimed reciprocal
privileges whereby English and Scottish ships were to be treated
alike in both countries. But there were still two administrations
and two parliaments, and it was characteristic of commercial
·legislation to run counter to the natural economic trends.[41] If
Scottish manufacturers were to be artificially fostered, there
had to be restraint on imports from England as well as other
countries; if the English markets drained away Scottish produce
which was needed at home, there must be restraint on exports.
The trade on which there was most legislation was that in wool
and cloth. Scottish interest dictated that the export of wool
across the Border should be forbidden and that the import of
English cloth should be forbidden, while the export of Scottish
cloth and the import of English wool were to be allowed. Between 1581 and 1623 the Scottish parliament at least seven times
passed acts along these lines. The English interest, however,
was directly contrary: England wanted to export her cloth but
not her wool and she was ready to import Scottish wool to be
used in manufacture in England. Scottish wool was always
welcome in England, and English cloth welcome in Scotland,
whatever legislators might say. There were, of course, items of
commerce where there was less conflict of interest than there
was in the woollen trade. Linen yarn and cloth were important:
18,000 ells of linen cloth went to England in 1599-1600 and up
to 73,000 lb. of linen yarn in 1620-1.[42] As already mentioned,
increasing quantities of coal and salt were exported to England
in the early seventeenth century. On the other hand, the Scots
imported some English beer—which, as James VI intimated in

41 Cf. C. V. Wedgwood, " Anglo-Scottish relations, 1603-40," *Trans. Royal Hist.*
Soc., SER. IV. XXXII. 42-3.   42 Lythe, *op. cit.*, p. 222.

1595, had a special appeal to his dearest spouse[43]—and in the course of the seventeenth century luxury articles tended increasingly to come from England. Trade with the English " plantations " across the Atlantic was not officially open to Scots except by occasional licence, but there were Scottish merchants who in one way or another managed to bring tobacco into their home ports from the West Indies.[44]

Under King James's peace Scottish commerce attained unprecedented stability[45] and it was for good reason that the reign saw much activity in the restoration of old harbours and the making of new, at Eyemouth, Dunbar, Leith, Wemyss, Elie, Dundee, Stonehaven, Peterhead, Ayr, and elsewhere. London merchants might refer contemptuously to Scots who " trade after the meaner sort . . . by retailing parcels and remnants of cloth . . . up and down the countries, which we cannot do with the honour of our country," but Scottish operations were adequate to enrich the burgesses of Scottish burghs, some of whom amassed what were by the standards of their time great fortunes, and were handling far larger sums of money than the nobles and landed gentry. Thus John MacMoran, the Edinburgh bailie who is best known because he was shot by a schoolboy when he tried to assert municipal authority over the pupils of the town's High School, was described as " the richest merchant in his time,"[46] and the inventory of his possessions[47] substantiates that description. He had shares in the ships *Anna*, *Grace of God*, *Pelican*, *Merting*, *Gude Fortoun*, *Elspeth*, *Floure Delyce*, *Thomas*, and one unnamed; there lay at Dieppe, in payment for goods sold by him, £3,120, and he had many thousands more in ready cash in Edinburgh; with the valuation of his current ventures at Bordeaux and elsewhere his estate totalled £21,544, 10s. 7d., and the debts owing to him amounted to £16,316, 13s. 2d. MacMoran was outstanding in his generation, but even then, if it was rare for

---

[43] *Cal. S. P. Scot.*, XI. No. 463.

[44] E.g., *Royal burgh of Ayr* (ed. A. I. Dunlop), pp. 197-8.

[45] The figures for the passage of Scottish ships through the Sound show that the figure of 100 was very seldom reached before 1590 and in troubled times was sometimes less than 20; after 1590 the figure was only twice less than 100 until troubles began again in 1638.

[46] Calderwood, v. 382.

[47] The document printed in *Fraser Papers* (S. H. S.), p. 226, is merely an inventory of MacMoran's very ample clothing and furnishing. The full inventory is in Edinburgh Tests., 23 July 1596.

the estates of burgesses to reach five figures, quite a number of them were in the higher ranges of four. King James on more than one occasion lodged in the mansion of Robert Gourlay, and he was repeatedly in debt for thousands of pounds to Thomas Foulis and other wealthy burgesses, as well as to George Heriot, the goldsmith, a man who was already wealthy by Scottish standards before he followed the court to England and prospered still more.[48] And in the next generation burgess fortunes rose even higher. Patrick Wood, an Edinburgh merchant who died in December 1638, had hemp in his rope works worth £30,000; tackle etc. worth £21,000; "made salt" at Cockenzie, Preston-pans, Kirkcaldy, Wemyss, Bo'ness, Tulliallan and Burntisland valued at £14,000; coal (£3,864), herring, butter, wool cards, a coach, and potash; in venture to Bordeaux, £8,000; to Spain, £1,700; to the Canaries, £783; to Königsberg and Danzig, £10,000; and shares in the *William*, the *Gift of God*, the *Issobell*, and the *Dolphing*. The total value was just over £100,000, and indicates what such a merchant was handling, though his creditors were ready to account for nearly all his estate.[49]

The vigour and vitality of Jacobean Scotland expressed itself in expansion, not along the lines of territorial aggression but by migration. Within the bounds of geographical Scotland itself, colonisation of a kind was going on, in the shape of a substantial though gradual infiltration of Lowlanders into Orkney and Shetland, the scheme for the plantation of Lewis and the settlement of Lowlanders in Kintyre. The share of the Scots in the plantation of Ulster was an extension of these developments. The arrival of Lowland Scots in Antrim seems actually to have been a secondary migration of Lowlanders who had been planted by the Earl of Argyll in Kintyre and who crossed to Ireland when conditions in Kintyre became disturbed; to County Down, where the young O'Neill chieftain had to part with his lands, Scots were brought in from 1606 onwards by Hugh Montgomery of Braidstane, who became Viscount of Airds, and James Hamilton, who became Viscount Clandeboye. The more ambitious plantation of the remaining counties of Ulster was the consequence of the flight to the continent of the Earls of Tyrone and Tyrconnel in September 1607 and the forfeiture of their estates. In 1609

---

48 Chambers, *Domestic Annals*, I. 253, 255, 295.
49 Edinburgh Tests., 14 Mar. 1639 etc.

" undertakers " were invited to apply for allocations of land, on which they were to settle English or " inland [*i.e.*, Lowland] Scottish inhabitants." There was such competition, from a few peers and courtiers and many lairds in Ayrshire, central Scotland, Fife, and East Lothian, as well as burgesses of Edinburgh and Glasgow, most of them asking for the maximum allotment of 2,000 acres, that the total demand exceeded the land available, and ultimately 81,000 acres were distributed among 59 Scottish " undertakers." While several of them promptly sold their allotments, others either settled in person or left agents and dependents, and, although progress was slow, the ultimate result was to leave its permanent mark on north-eastern Ireland.[50] In the middle of the century it was believed that 40,000 or 50,000 Scots were settled in Ulster.[51]

There was a quite substantial, though much less obstrusive, migration to England, where Scots of all ranks had been finding employment even before the union of the crowns brought the common nationality[52] for which the Scots had asked in vain in the 1580s. Many Scots were settled in coastal towns around the Baltic, and the number in Poland was put—by a wild guess—at 30,000. The main outlet abroad for Scottish energy was, of course, service in continental armies. From the 1560s onwards it was a common occurrence for the Scottish government to grant licences to individuals for the raising of specific numbers of men for service in Denmark, Sweden and the Low Countries,[53] and after 1600 the traffic increased. In 1609 James King of Birness and Dudwick entered the Swedish service, where he rose to the rank of lieutenant-general, and in the war between Denmark and Sweden (1611-13) the Swedes hired a regiment of Scots, 300 of whom, under Alexander Ramsay, were defeated when they invaded Norway (1612). The Thirty Years' War, beginning in 1618, merely heightened the demand and widened the opportunities. First Christian IV of Denmark, then Gustavus Adolphus of Sweden, kings of countries already accustomed to employ Scots, led the protestant armies. Donald MacKay, the first Lord Reay,

---

[50] George Hill, *The plantation of Ulster*; cf. John Harrison, *The Scot in Ulster*.

[51] Carlyle, *Cromwell's letters and speeches* (ed. Lomas), III. 178.

[52] By a Scottish statute of 1607 and an English judicial decision in 1608 ("Calvin's' [*rectius* Colville's] case ").

[53] *E.g.*, R. P. C., II. 235, 237, 238, 256, 257, 641; III. 23; cf. *Edinburgh Burgh Records, 1589-1603*, p. 158.

raised 3,600 men for Christian IV[54] and subsequently served under Gustavus, and Lord Spynie raised 3,000 men for the king of Denmark in 1627. Among those who served under Gustavus were the eleventh Lord Forbes, Patrick Ruthven (later Lord Ruthven of Ettrick and Earl of Forth), and a brother and a son of Thomas, Earl of Haddington, the secretary.[55] Gustavus is said to have had 10,000 Scots at his command, and there is some reason to believe this an under-statement. When France entered the Thirty-Years' War, on what had been previously regarded as the protestant side, a renewed stimulus was given to the tradition of Scottish service in the French forces. The Earl of Irvine, a half-brother of Argyll, raised 4,500 men for the French service, and in all more than twice that number are said to have contracted for this service. John Hepburn (d. 1636), who had commanded the Scots brigade under Gustavus, transferred to the French service and recruited 2,000 men for it in Scotland,[56] and another notable Scot in the French army was Lieutenant-Colonel James Hepburn, who died in 1637, worth £37,000. In addition, the United Provinces of the Netherlands, constantly in danger from greater powers and possessed of ample means to pay mercenaries, were a steady employer of large numbers of Scots, and after the Restoration, when the United Provinces became the leading protestant power, service in their forces became predominant.

No episode is marked by so many of the characteristics of Jacobean Scotland as the Nova Scotia scheme. Here was a " project "; here Scotland was following the example of "uther weill governit commounwelthis "—and following at no great distance, for England's first permanent settlement on the American continent, in Virginia, had likewise been a Jacobean foundation (1607), the French had founded Port Royal (Nova Scotia) in 1605 and Quebec in 1608, and the Dutch had settled at the mouth of the Hudson River in 1609. The enterprise reflected conditions arising from the union of the crowns, for the grant made to Sir William Alexander, Earl of Stirling—poet, anglicised

---

54 Cf. *Monro his expedition with the worthy Scots regiment (called MacKeyes regiment) levied in August 1626 . . . to which is annexed the abridgement of exercise and divers practical observations*, by R. Monro (London, 1637).

55 In *Spottiswoode Soc. Misc.*, II. 383-4, there is a list of 54 colonels and 20 officers of higher rank who served under Gustavus.

56 *Memoirs and adventures of Sir John Hepburn . . . marshal of France under Louis XIII and commander of the Scots brigade under Gustavus Adolphus.* J. Grant. Edinburgh 1851.

Scot, courtier and secretary of state[57]—is parallel to the grant of part of Newfoundland to Sir George Calvert, an English secretary. Alexander was himself one of the new peers, and part of his scheme was the creation of baronets—a title new to Scotland— who were intended to provide men for the colony, but their obligation was later commuted for money. Pioneering parties went out in 1622 and 1623, but no settlement was made until 1629. Circumstances were temporarily favourable, for David Kirke had sacked the French foundation at Port Royal, and he went on in 1629 to compel Champlain to surrender Quebec. Even then, however, there was no attempt at colonisation on a substantial scale. In 1632 Charles I handed back to France all that Kirke had seized, French sovereignty was formally restored and the Scots had to evacuate. Scots who had landed on Cape Breton Island had made an even shorter stay. Colonisation in America was not to provide an outlet for the superabundant vigour of Jacobean Scotland or employment for men who were too active and energetic to find occupations in the peaceful and settled conditions now obtaining in their homeland.

[57] Alexander produced *An encouragement to colonies* (1625). Cf. Gordon of Lochin-var, *Encouragement for all such as have intention to be undertakers in the new plantation of Cape Breton* (1625).

14

THE CULTURE OF JACOBEAN SCOTLAND

That one of the features of the economic life of Jacobean Scotland was "projects" was appropriate in an age which was fertile in ideas and conspicuous for intellectual activity and cultural achievement. Among the lively minds was that of the king himself. He would not deserve first mention save for his royal status, but that made him an outstanding figure, for few sovereigns have equalled his literary output[1] and no other prince ever carried to the English throne as extensive a knowledge derived from reading and study. His own bent was literary, philosophical and theological, but he did not despise scientific investigation, and on his visit to Denmark, besides presenting a cup to the university of Copenhagen, he visited Tycho Brahe's observatory. Some of the king's subjects equalled him in learning and surpassed him in their spirit of enquiry. The claim that the Scottish nobles were " learned scholars, read in best histories, delicately linguished the most part of them,"[2] was not without foundation: James Stewart, Earl of Arran, was well versed in Latin and Greek; Francis Stewart, Earl of Bothwell, had a command of Latin, French and Italian which was admired by the

---

[1] James's works: Paraphrase of the Apocalypse (1616); Meditations on Apoc. xx. 7-10 (1588); Meditations on Chronicles, xv. 25-9 (1588); Daemonologie; Conjuratio Sulphurea; A Counterblast to tobacco (1604); Basilicon Doron (privately printed, 1599; public edition, 1603); The true law of free monarchies (1598); Apology for the oath of allegiance; Meditation on the Lord's Prayer (1619); Essays of a prentise in the divine art of poesie (1585); His majesties poeticall exercises at vacant hours (1591); " The Psalms of King David, translated by King James " (1631).   [2] William Lithgow, *Totall discourse of the rare adventures* (1632), p. 499.

Dean of Durham; the Earl Marischal founded a university; the third Earl of Gowrie was a patron of music and literature and could write a letter sprinkled with Greek as well as Latin. Outstanding among the king's subjects who had an interest in the sciences was John Napier of Merchiston (1550-1617), who invented logarithms but whose fertile brain also explored the possibilities of tanks and submarines as well as the mysteries of alchemy. Next to Napier comes Duncan Liddell (1561-1613), an astronomer and physician who was professor of mathematics at Helmstadt and who bequeathed his library and instruments to Marischal College. Alexander Seton (d. 1604) was an alchemist of European renown, William Davidson (1593-c. 1665) was professor of chemistry at Paris, and the first Lord Balcarres was " a laborious chymist."[3] James Cargill was the first recorded Scottish botanist. Medical science was developing, with the publication, in 1628, of Harvey's discovery of the circulation of the blood, and Harvey was honoured with the freedom of Edinburgh and Aberdeen, but Scottish medical opinion was conservative. James Primrose, a grandson of an early physician of James VI, argued against Harvey, and Alexander Read, in his *Manuall of the anatomy* (1634), did not mention Harvey. Yet Scottish physicians, like Patrick Dun and William Gordon, were active enough to publish quite a number of works, and some of them attained success outside Scotland: John MacCulloch (d. 1622) was physician to the Grand Duke of Tuscany;[4] John Craig (d. 1620) and his son of the same name were physicians to James VI in England; and James Primrose settled in Hull. David Kinloch was the first Scottish writer on obstetrics. David Ramsay, clockmaker to James VI and Charles I, was a student of the occult and an inventor who received many patents; his son, physician to Charles II, was also an astrologer. Geography was hardly yet a science, and map-making still largely a work of art, but the first Scottish atlas was a product of this period: the basic work was done by Timothy Pont, followed by Robert Gordon of Straloch and his son James, parson of Rothiemay, and a set of maps was published by Blaeu at Amsterdam in 1654, as part of a great atlas.

At a time when the polymath had not yet given way to the

3 J. Read, " Scottish alchemy in the seventeenth century," in *Chymia*, I. 139-51.
4 McKerlie, *Lands and their owners in Galloway* (1877), III. 15.

specialist, some men best known for their literary work shared
also in the current scientific interests. Sir Thomas Urquhart
(1611-60), best known as the translator of Rabelais and as a
hearty royalist who died of laughter when he learned of the
restoration of Charles II, had a plan for a universal language
and wrote also on mathematics.[5] Drummond of Hawthornden,
the poet, patented numerous inventions, one of them " an instrument by which a large quantity of salt water may, at slight
expense, be made sweet and drinkable."[6] Lindsay of Menmuir,
the secretary of state, patented an engine for raising water from
mines. William Welwood, best known as the writer of the *Abridgment of all Sea Lawes* (1613)—the first treatise on maritime law
produced in Britain—also obtained a patent for a new method of
raising water from low ground. This interest in scientific, or
pseudo-scientific, matters, and in supposedly practical inventions,
is obviously associated with the activities of the peers and gentlemen who tried to develop industries. Lord Erskine's leather-
tanning, Sir George Bruce's mine and Sir George Hay's glass-
works have been mentioned, but there were others: the Earl
Marischal was building a breakwater at Stonehaven in 1612;[7]
the Earl of Winton built a harbour at Cockenzie which could take
ships of up to 300 tons, and his son built twelve saltpans there;[8]
Duncan Campbell of Glenorchy had an enormous range of
interests.[9] Even the women were affected: Jean Gordon, sometime wife of Mary's Bothwell and later Countess of Sutherland,
began saltworks at Brora and coal-mining which still goes on to-
day and which has appropriately escaped nationalisation.[10] Some
thought that " numbers of our nobility and gentry " had become
" with idle projects down-drawers of destruction upon their own
necks, their children and their estates,"[11] but the whole thing was
symptomatic of restless energy.

The literary interest and achievements of the period reflected
the increasing predominance of English as the language of the
Scottish people. Not only is it true that even in the central and
western highlands most men of substance were already bilingual,

[5] J. Willcock, *Sir Thomas Urquhart* (1899).
[6] David Masson, *Drummond of Hawthornden*, p. 158.
[7] *Edinburgh Burgh Records, 1604-26*, p. 90.
[8] *House of Seytoun* (Bannatyne Club), p. 75.   [9] Innes, *Early Scotch History*, p. 346.
[10] R. Gordon, *History of earldom of Sutherland*, p. 169.
[11] Lithgow, *op. cit.*, p. 500.

and that elsewhere Lowland Scots had hardly a rival, for Gaelic had died out in Ayrshire and Galloway, and in the three northern counties the Norse dialects were rapidly retreating. The more important point is that Lowland Scots had long been, in the eyes of nearly all who used it, " English " and not " Scots." The Scotland which mattered politically and economically was consciously Anglo-Saxon, and would have indignantly repudiated the suggestion that it was anything else. Any chance there ever was that the peculiarities of Lowland Scots might be fostered and Anglicisms suppressed vanished with the Reformation, which, by giving Scotland a Bible, service-books and a metrical psalter in English, accelerated the displacement of the native vernacular. In any event, so little Scottish vernacular prose was in print that, although the Scots continued to read their vernacular verse—as the editions of Sir David Lindsay and Blind Harry testify—the choice of reading matter in prose lay mainly between Latin and the English of England. While Scots was used for narrative, in the works of Bellenden and Pitscottie, it was extinguished before it had a chance to be adapted for use in the loftier subjects like theology and philosophy, and it must already by 1600 have been regarded as a kind of folk-dialect not suited for serious or formal use. Thus, most scholars, including an historian like Buchanan, continued to use Latin until it was superseded by English, without an intermediate phase of Scots. Even in verse, although there was a native tradition such as there was not in prose, already before 1603 James VI and William Fowler preferred English.

Thus Scots, as a literary language, faded out about the period of the union of the crowns, and the series of Scottish contributions to English literature therefore began in Jacobean Scotland. There was no great genius among the Scottish poets of the time, but Drummond of Hawthornden (1585-1649) is one of the secondary figures of English literature, and others, like Sir William Alexander, not far behind him, while many more were at least competent versifiers. Drummond was the nephew of the poet Fowler, who was secretary of Queen Anne, and was a close friend of Alexander, who became secretary of state in 1626, while Sir Robert Ayton (1569-1638), another poet, was secretary first to Queen Anne and then to Henrietta Maria; so they formed a closely knit group, and a courtly group, given to occasional verse to celebrate royal marriages and deaths and favourably disposed to the royal policies. There were still many composers of Latin verse, and an anthology of their work—*Delitiae poetarum Scotorum hujus aevi illustrium*, published at Amsterdam in 1637— consists of two volumes running in all to some 1,300 pages.

Even before the two countries could be said to share a literary language, Scots were able to read English literature without difficulty, and had been accustomed to do so. Now they could draw on the great output of Elizabethan England. Drummond of Hawthornden, whose reading lists for 1606-14 have been preserved, bought *A Midsummer Night's Dream* and *Romeo and Juliet* in 1611, and the five hundred volumes which he presented to Edinburgh University Library in 1627 included some fourteen plays, two of them by Shakespeare. Dramatic and other works figure in the accounts of a Dundee merchant.[12] It was appropriate that Ben Jonson made a journey to Scotland—on foot, wearing out his first pair of shoes between London and Durham—and that Edinburgh gave him a dinner at a cost of £221 6s. 4d.[13]

The proximity of England possibly militated against the development of a Scottish printing press, which—so far as can be judged from the books which have survived—was still singularly unproductive. Copies survive of no more than thirty books which were printed in Scotland before 1560, and only some 380 items are known to have appeared by 1600. The seven or more booksellers who were in business in Edinburgh in 1592[14] were not making a living by selling books printed locally. It is significant of the poverty of Scottish printing that although a licence was issued to Lekprevik to print the Bible in 1568, such a volume did not appear, from the press of Bassandyne and Arbuthnot, until 1579, and Bassandyne had to call on the expert help of " Salamon Kirknet of Madeburgh," from Flanders, which cost him 49s. a week.[15] Even after 1600 there was no substantial growth in the printing of books in Scotland, though the output was steadier and some work of high quality was produced, not only in Edinburgh but by Raban in Aberdeen. During the troubles which began in 1637, pamphlets and official papers swell the lists, but it was only in the last two decades of the century that expansion

[12] *Compt buik of David Wedderburne* (S. H. S.), xxx.
[13] *Edinburgh Burgh Records, 1604-26*, pp. 182-3.
[14] *Edinburgh Burgh Records, 1589-1603*, p. 80.   [15] *R. P. C.*, ii. 582.

was very rapid. Nor did Scotland achieve an independent periodical press before the Revolution, for almost its only experience of newspapers was the occasional short-lived effort, usually under English auspices and sometimes consisting merely of reprints of English productions.[16] Some Scottish books were printed in Holland, partly because they would not have been approved by the authorities at home—for instance, the royalist Wishart's *Life of Montrose* and two presbyterian church histories, Petrie's *Catholick Church* and Calderwood's *Church of Scotland.*

That much church history should be written at that time was inevitable. Calderwood's work is outstanding as a collection of source material, but the rival *History of the Church of Scotland* by Archbishop Spottiswoode is " as much superior to the historical collections of Calderwood in point of style and arrangement as it is inferior to them in accuracy and variety of materials."[17] Both of those histories were printed posthumously, and posterity has thought less highly of the controversial works which the writers published in their lifetimes, including the enormous *Altare Damascenum* of Calderwood (1623).[18] Both academic and ecclesiastical scholarship lay largely in " the tongues," and few of the classicists of the period deserve recall, but Patrick Young, who graduated at St Andrews in 1603 and became librarian to Prince Henry, James VI and Charles I, was the foremost Greek scholar of the age in Britain. Some Scottish divines did make their mark in theology. According to Thomas McCrie, who was not apt to praise bishops, the sermons of Bishop William Cowper, published in 1619, " are perhaps superior to any sermons of that age,"[19] and among the episcopalian theologians known as " the Aberdeen doctors," John Forbes of Corse won perhaps the widest fame of any Scottish theologian of any age.

Legal studies attracted much attention too. In the 1570s the government was much interested in a scheme for digesting " auld laws," statutes, and decisions of the court of session into a kind of code,[20] and, although no such official compilation ever saw the light of day, Sir James Balfour's *Practicks*[21] was a systematically arranged compendium of this nature, meant to be of

16 W. J. Couper, *The Edinburgh Periodical press.*
17 McCrie, *Andrew Melville* (1899), p. 390.
18 Cf. *Spottiswoode Soc. Misc.*, I. 29-62.   19 McCrie, *loc. cit.*
20 *R. S. S.*, VII. 1070, 1559, 1793.   21 Compiled 1579, published 1754.

practical value to lawyers in their everyday work. Sir Thomas Hope, lord advocate under Charles I, produced his *Major Practicks*[22] and his *Minor Practicks*,[23] less detailed than Balfour's work but more thoughtful and pointing forward to the later institutional writers. Sir John Skene, clerk-register, besides publishing an edition of the " auld laws and constitutions of Scotland " (1609), prepared a little legal dictionary—*De verborum significatione* (1597). Sir Thomas Craig's *Jus feudale* (1603) was a treatise representing a more humane and scholarly approach to one department of law, and his *De unione regnorum Britanniae*[24] is an able tract in favour of Anglo-Scottish union, drawing its arguments both from history and the existing situation. Sir James Balfour of Denmilne (1600-57), an active Lyon King of Arms and a student of antiquities and heraldry, is best known as a collector—and forger—of medieval charters. His *Annales*, which are valuable for his own time, represent a venture into general history unusual in this period, though the poet Drummond wrote a *History of the five Jameses*. There was a good deal of composition of contemporary history, memoirs and autobiographies, but most of it remained unprinted until the advent of the historical clubs in the nineteenth century.

The Reformation had given a new impetus to the church's solicitude for education, which had all along been a creditable feature of ecclesiastical activity. There had been schools attached to several of the cathedrals and other great churches, so that in many Scottish towns there was already a grammar school or a song school, and sometimes both. Such schools, originally under ecclesiastical patronage, had in effect become secularised and were already before 1560 largely the concern of the town councils. While the grammar schools in the larger burghs were no doubt well equipped, it was complained that in many towns there was no school building and in most there was not sufficient payment for the master. It had been held to be a reproach to the gentry of Scotland that they educated their children neither in letters nor in morals,[25] but the evidence is that nobles and lairds could for the most part at least read and write. It is more difficult to prove that much schooling was available for people of lower

22 Published by the Stair Society, 1937-8.   23 Published 1726.
24 Published by the Scottish History Society in 1909.
25 Major, *Greater Britain*, p. 48.

rank, especially in the country districts, where the average priest can hardly have been an effective educational agent.[26]

The reformers, although several of them were men whose interests and sympathies were not primarily academic, had proclaimed the ideal of an educated ministry and an instructed people. According to the first Book of Discipline, in country parishes the minister or the reader was to give the children elementary instruction; in every town there was to be a schoolmaster able to teach Latin; in each of the ten towns where superintendents had their headquarters there was to be a " college," with masters qualified to teach logic, rhetoric and languages; and the universities were to be reorganised. The interest of the reformers in higher education is, of course, explained by the need for training ministers. Even in the 1560s some at least of the ministers were scholarly men, eagerly reading theology and lending and borrowing books,[27] and the programme of the reformers was nowhere more successful than in its insistence, never to be departed from, that ministers should be adequately educated. But the anti-clerical strain in reformation thought, and the elevation of the laity which the reformers envisaged, meant that the people generally were also to be so educated that they could play their part in church and commonwealth and be in no danger of falling under the domination of a new priestly caste. Besides, of course, the reformers aimed at the indoctrination of the whole population with the new theology, and for this reason they wanted not only ministers able to instruct the people in the faith but also schoolmasters who should be approved by the church authorities. Education was not to be free, for the commonwealth was not to be burdened with the cost of educating those who could afford to pay, but lack of means was not to be an obstacle, and from 1567 prebends and chaplainries were ingeniously used as bursaries for schoolboys and undergraduates.[28]

From the earliest days, some ministers and readers not only instilled the Catechism but also taught children to read the Bible and the Book of Common Order and even gave instruction in Latin and French. No legislation to put into effect the ideal of a professional schoolmaster in every parish was passed until

[26] *Essays on the Scottish Reformation*, pp. 146-7, 168.
[27] *E.g.*, Testament of Thomas Cranston, printed in I. B. Cowan, *Blast and Counterblast*, p. 31.　　　　[28] *R. S. S.*, VI. xiii.

1616, when there was an act of the privy council on the subject, confirmed by an act of parliament in 1633 which ordained that the bishops could impose an education rate in any parish with the consent of the heritors and the majority of the parishioners or with the consent of the latter alone if the heritors refused. An act of 1646, passed when the presbyterian party was in power, gave to presbyteries much the same powers as bishops had formerly exercised, and ordained that heritors must provide a schoolhouse and a master's salary. This act was rescinded in 1661, but the act of 1633 then again became operative until it was superseded by another presbyterian act in 1696. Throughout most of the century, therefore, despite the vicissitudes in ecclesiastical polity, there was legislation in force for the establishment of schools. Even before the first of the seventeenth-century acts was passed, however, there were many parish schools in Lowland Scotland: in Fife and Angus, for example, out of twenty-three country parishes, thirteen had schools in 1611, and in that year the synod of Fife actually ordered an assessment for the maintenance of schoolmasters.[29] As the century went on, and the acts of 1616 and 1633 took effect, the number of parish schools greatly increased, until it can be said with some confidence that before the Revolution, if not indeed before the National Covenant, it was the normal thing for a Lowland parish to have its school. In the presbyteries of Perth and Dunkeld and the sheriffdom of Fife, out of eighty-eight rural parishes, at least sixty-eight had schools before 1696.[30] Six of the eight parishes in the presbytery of Ellon had schools by 1638.[31] In Ayrshire the situation seems actually to have been better under Charles I than it was to be a hundred years later.[32] Even so, at the time of the signing of the National Covenant, many of the people were still without schooling, and in the parish of Dundonald, for example, 179 out of

[29] McCrie, *Andrew Melville*, p. 471.

[30] Statistics and authorities are given by J. M. Beale in *Common errors in Scottish history* (Hist. Ass. pamphlet), pp. 17-8. Apart from the impression one gains from kirk session records, the number of references to schoolmasters in the *Diary of John Lamont of Newton* is noticeable; and Lamont once mentions a schoolmistress (p. 153). See also D. J. Withrington, " Schools in the presbytery of Haddington in the seventeenth century," in *East Lothian Antiquarian and Field Naturalists' Society*, IX.

[31] W. R. Foster, " Ecclesiastical administration in Scotland, 1600-1638 " (Edinburgh Ph.D. thesis, 1963), p. 362.

[32] William Boyd, *Education in Ayrshire*, pp. 20, 40. There were seven parishes without schools in 1642 and twelve in 1737.

222 signatories could not write; no doubt more could read, but it is plain that a large number of the signatories were dependent on others for any grasp they had of that long and involved document. In the outlying parts of the country the situation was, of course, very much less satisfactory than it was in the central Lowlands.

In the towns, where some ecclesiastical revenues were put at the disposal of the councils for educational purposes, the grammar schools continued or were revived and new ones seem to have been founded, for already in the 1570s the records give the impression that it was usual for a town of any size to have its grammar school.[33] The teaching of " grammar," otherwise Latin, was still the foundation of a reputable education, and the central government more than once concerned itself to the extent of insisting that grammar teaching should be uniform throughout the country.[34] Song schools, as well as grammar schools, continued, encouraged by an act of parliament of 1579, and some of them taught reading and writing as well as vocal and instrumental music. Edinburgh, as the capital and largest town, was no doubt exceptional: its High School attracted gentlemen's sons from all parts of the country; there were English schools and French schools, reading and writing schools, some of them attended by girls as well as boys; there was a fencing school; and there is any number of references to " vulgar schoolmasters " as distinct from Latin grammarians.[35] But Edinburgh was not alone in having a French school,[36] and there were other burghs where girls were educated alongside boys.[37]

The development of the universities presents similar features to that of the schools—a carry-over from pre-reformation activities, excellent intentions on the part of the reformers, and tardy fulfilment of their ideals. The first Book of Discipline devoted a great deal of space to detailed proposals for the reorganisation of the universities: at St Andrews, for example, each of the three

33 E.g., R. S. S., vi. xviii.

34 R. P. C., ii. 478, ix. 272-3, 275-6; 2nd ser., iii. 596-7, iv. 500-1.

35 E.g., Edinburgh Burgh Records 1573-89, pp. 23, 60, 126, 239, 407, 450, 453, 479, 554; 1589-1603, pp. 30, 103, 106, 109, 282; 1604-26, pp. 60, 143, 157, 180, 210; 1626-41, pp. 20, 80, 85. For the song school of Ayr, see Ayr Burgh Accounts (S.H.S.), p. 49.

36 Aberdeen Burgh Records (Burgh Rec. Soc.), i. 80. For a reference to a French text book, and other schoolbooks, see R. S. S., v. 658.

37 Royal Burgh of Ayr (ed. A. I. Dunlop), pp. 214, 242.

colleges was to specialise in particular departments of knowledge; and it was envisaged that teachers of specific subjects should take the places of " regents " conducting students through their entire courses. A plan was drawn up, probably in terms of a commission appointed by parliament in 1563, but nothing was done effectively to implement the reformers' proposals. At Glasgow, far from any improvement, there was decay: despite a crown grant in 1563, only two regents could be maintained, and for a time the college was closed altogether, until in 1572 the town council bestowed some additional endowments. At Aberdeen the principal was an opponent of the Reformation and was not finally ousted until 1573. It was said that the colleges of Scotland were

> . . . cassin downe and revin,
> The maist part ar bot theikit with the hevin.[38]

It was to the languishing college of Glasgow that Andrew Melville chose to go as principal when he returned to Scotland in 1574. His policy, like that of the first Book of Discipline, was specialisation, and he succeeded in securing the appointment of other teachers for various subjects while he concentrated on divinity and oriental languages. According to his admiring nephew and colleague, Glasgow rapidly became incomparable in Europe " for guid letters, for a plentifull and guid chepe mercat of all kynd of langages, artes and sciences."[39] Following the appointment by both general assembly and parliament of commissions to consider the state of the universities—commissions on which, significantly enough, bishops served side by side with Melville—a new constitution for St Andrews was ratified by parliament in November 1579, and Melville went there as principal in 1580. The intention was that each college should specialise, and, although the scheme was only partially carried out and regenting was in the main reinstated after Melville's time, St Mary's College did become a school of divinity, with one professor for oriental languages, three for Old and New Testament and one for systematic theology. A new library was being built at St Andrews early in the seventeenth century.

Melville had influence at Aberdeen as well, for in 1575 he conferred with Alexander Arbuthnot, the new principal of King's

---

[38] *Lamentatioun of Lady Scotland* (1572), sig. a v.
[39] James Melville, *Diary*, p. 50.

College, and agreed with him on a new constitution for Aberdeen as well as for Glasgow. There was a parliamentary commission on the new constitution in 1581, but the plan seems to have encountered opposition, and this was one reason why the Earl Marischal founded his new college in 1593, with emphasis on " the tongues," including Hebrew and Syriac, and with specialist teachers. In 1597 a new foundation for King's College was at last adopted, but even then not in its entirety, for regenting continued until 1628, the old foundation was ratified in 1633 and controversy was still going on in 1638. However, King's attained a new vitality when Bishop Patrick Forbes began to take action in 1619. He had studied under Andrew Melville, and he founded a chair of divinity to strengthen the theological instruction, though he did not follow Melville in other matters and preferred to adhere to the general arrangements of the old foundation. It was significant of an all-round raising of cultural standards that the first librarian of the college appeared in 1633 and that in 1634 the office of " cantor " was revived and was filled by the master of the music school of Old Aberdeen.

Scotland's fourth university, at Edinburgh, was a post-reformation foundation, but its antecedents can be traced before 1560. In 1556 Alexander Sym had been appointed by the crown as a " lectoure and reidar in the lawis or ony uthiris sciencis at oure burgh of Edinburgh or quhair he sal be requirit " and Edward Henderson was appointed to " teiche and reid within the burgh of Edinburgh ane publict lessoun in the lawis and ane uther in Greik thryis in the oulk."[40] Prospects of endowment for a college at Edinburgh emerged in the will of Robert Reid, Bishop of Orkney, who died in 1558. Reid had shown his interest in education when he had drawn up a new constitution for his cathedral in 1546, for it was then provided that there should be a lecture weekly on canon law and that one of the chaplains should act as master of the grammar school. In his will he left 8,000 merks for the purchase of lands in Edinburgh with a view to the foundation of a college there. The town council began petitioning for a university in 1561, but it was not until 11 April 1582 that the privy council, on application by the town council, decreed that Reid's bequest should be made available. Once again ecclesiastical property was turned over to educational uses,

[40] *R. S. S.*, IV. 3144, 3268.

for the buildings and ground of the church of St Mary in the Fields were appropriated to the new college, which began to operate in the autumn of 1583. Two years earlier a lawyer named Clement Little had left his books to the ministers of Edinburgh, but they were transferred to the college to form the nucleus of its library. The repair of old buildings and the erection of new ones, including a library, went on intermittently for decades, paid for by the town council and encouraged by James VI, who decreed in 1617 that the institution should be known as " King James's College."

Dramatic art was not extinguished by the Reformation, and even received a measure of countenance from the reformed church. Knox himself not only attended a play, but seems even to have had a hand in its making, for when Kirkcaldy of Grange made Edinburgh unsafe for him and he was in St Andrews in the summer of 1571, he attended a wedding at which part of the entertainment was a play in which, " according to Mr. Knox's doctrine," the castle of Edinburgh was besieged and taken and its captain hanged.[41] In 1574 the kirk session of St Andrews gave permission for the performance of " the comedy of the Forlorn Son [the Prodigal] " on a Sunday, provided that it did not interfere with church-going,[42] and in 1589 the kirk session of Perth " gave licence to play the play, with conditions that neither swearing, banning nor any scurrility be in it."[43] Court patronage continued, for in 1579 the scholars of the High School of Edinburgh prepared " tragedies " for the king's entry to the burgh,[44] and in 1580, when he visited St Andrews, "the gentlemen of the country had a guise and farce to play before the king," for which " great confluence of people convened."[45] Royal protection was extended to the English players who appeared in Edinburgh more than once in the 1590s and reached Dundee and Aberdeen in 1601.[46] Even the municipal pageants associated with Corpus Christi Day did not disappear, for custom was too tenacious. In 1577 the kirk session of Perth had to fulminate against those taking part in Corpus Christi Day pageants. What is more odd is that in 1599, at Glasgow, participation in a " play

[41] J. Melville, *Diary*, p. 27. [42] *St. Andrews kirk session register* (S. H. S.), I. 396.
[43] *Spottiswoode Soc. Misc.*, II. 264.
[44] *Edinburgh Burgh Records*, IV. 114-5. There are later references to dramatic performances *Ibid., 1589-1603*, p. 223.
[45] J. Melville, *Diary, p.* 81. [46] A. J. Mill, *Medieval Plays in Scotland*, pp. 299-306.

or pastime " was made compulsory, in a proclamation dated 2 June and fixing the day for the performance as " Thursday next," which was Corpus Christi Day. In 1575, however, the general assembly had forbidden " all clerk plays, comedies or tragedies, upon the canonical parts of the scripture " either on Sundays or other days, and later on it prohibited plays of all kinds on Sundays;[47] as weekday festivals were no longer observed by abstinence from labour, and Sundays were the only days when everyone was free, this prohibition was a serious handicap.

The scope of music generally, and assuredly of church music, had been narrowed by the Reformation. Concentration on the metrical psalms was ultimately to have a deplorable effect on both the poetical and the musical tastes of too many Scots, who were taught to confuse poetry with the torture of words and sense for the sake of metre and rhyme and from whose churches musical art was to be exiled for generations. But this had not yet happened in the pre-covenanting era. The musical training and traditions of the unreformed church were carried into the reformed church, for example by some of the canons of St Andrews,[48] and " song schools " continued to fulfil some of their former functions: the master of the song school of Perth " had great travail in teaching the youth of this town in music and in taking up of the psalms ";[49] and in Edinburgh, where the master of the song school was responsible for the " eruditioun of the youthheid in the art of musick,"[50] instrumental as well as vocal music was taught. James Melville relates how he and his fellow-undergraduates at St Andrews played virginals, lute and " githorn."[51] It was realised, and with an enthusiasm which seems to have increased down to 1637, that the metrical psalms did offer scope for musical art, and the considerable achievements of the period came to a climax in the Aberdeen Psalter of 1635. In it, all the Proper and Common Tunes were fully arranged in four-part harmony, and several of them were set " in reports," that is, in arrangements in which one set of voices enters after another; such elaborate settings required trained choirs. Both James and Charles I, too, attempted to popularise " The Psalms of King David translated by King James," largely the work of Sir William

[47] B. U. K., pp. 322-3, 375.   [48] Essays on the Scottish Reformation, pp. 149-50.
[49] Perth Kirk Session Records, 12 Jan. 1578/9.
[50] Edinburgh Burgh Records, IV. 126.   [51] J. Melville, Diary, p. 29.

Alexander; some of the psalms in this version are far superior in literary merit to those used before and since, but the new psalter came into disrepute as one of Alexander's money-making schemes and was finally damned by being printed with the Prayer Book of 1637.[52] James's court had been served by the Hudson family, five English musicians who enjoyed royal patronage as long as James resided in Scotland. Burghs and private families, too, had their " musicians,"[53] and Campbell of Glenorchy had an organ in his chapel at Finlarig and harpsichords at Taymouth.[54] If any secular music was printed in Scotland before 1660 it has not survived, and a continuous tradition can only be inferred for the secular music, both instrumental and vocal, which even to-day can compete with " canned " productions in healthy Scottish communities.

The chapel royal at Stirling had been so neglected by Mary, who was interested mainly in providing Roman catholic worship at Holyrood, that in 1583 " the kingis hienes may nocht weill remain within the same in time of weit or rain."[55] In 1594, however, in preparation for the baptism of Prince Henry, the old chapel was superseded by a new building, which still stands. Apart from the fabric, James did something to recover the endowments of the chapel and use them for the maintenance of musicians.[56] Under Charles I interest reverted to Holyrood, but the constitution of the chapel was reformed and the royal interest in its services maintained. The contemporary emphasis on music emerges in the 1637 Prayer Book, where again and again the " said " of the English book is superseded by " said or sung " in the Scottish.

The history of Scottish portraiture begins in this period with the work of George Jamesone (?1588-1644), nearly two hundred of whose portraits are known. Few Scots of earlier generations are authentically delineated, but portraits of a kind were already in vogue as decorations and as reminders of the heritage of the past: Colin Campbell of Glenorchy paid a German £1,000 for thirty-two portraits of Scottish sovereigns and of the laird's own

52 On the whole subject, see Millar Patrick, *Four centuries of Scottish psalmody*.

53 *Chronicles of the Frasers* (S. H. S.), p. 245; *Edinburgh Burgh Records, 1604-26*, p. 26.

54 *Black Book of Taymouth*, p. 350.

55 Charles Rogers, *History of the chapel royal*, p. lxxxvi.

56 Cf. John McQuaid, " Music and the administration after 1560," *Innes Rev.*, III. 14-21.

predecessors, to be set up in his hall and chamber at Taymouth.[57] There was also a fashion of painting walls and ceilings with Biblical or historical scenes as well as purely decorative designs. But from the time of Jamesone, who in 1635 was doing portraits at 20 merks a piece unframed and £20 framed, the features of most notable Scots are preserved for us,[58] because Jamesone has never wanted successors, beginning with Michael Wright (?1625-1700) and John Scougall (?1645-?1730).

The greatest artistic achievement of the period, and the most significant expression of its character, are to be found in architecture. Until this generation, the characteristic dwelling of a Scotsman of substance was the tower-house, the erection of which, after an intermission from the end of James IV's reign, was resumed about 1570 and went on steadily for another two generations. Many of them now attained a new refinement, elegance and even ostentation which showed that ornament as well as utility was now demanded. Craigievar, completed in 1626, is the finest of them all. But, although the tower house did not fall out of fashion until Charles I's reign, a new and more purely domestic style of architecture had made its appearance. A pointer towards change had appeared, significantly enough, in the regency of Morton, who erected Drochil Castle, which can be classified as a tower house but which represented a concept of building on a larger ground area as opposed to building in height. At Edinburgh Castle, where the medieval fortress almost vanished at and after the siege of 1573, Morton raised the half-moon battery on the ruins of David's Tower—though, characteristically, no Scottish government was ever to turn its guns on the burgh and use it for what seems its obvious purpose of overawing an unruly capital. However, Morton's portcullis gateway at Edinburgh Castle has conspicuous classical decoration, and his own castle at Aberdour shows signs of similar work. It may be that in architecture as in much else King James followed in Morton's footsteps, for classical elements are conspicuous in his work, but it also seems likely that he learned from the example of that great builder, his brother-in-law, Christian IV of Denmark. At any rate, in his new ranges at Edinburgh Castle and Linlithgow and Dunfermline Palaces James left his mark on royal

[57] *Black Book of Taymouth*, pp. 75, 77-8.
[58] John Bulloch, *George Jamesone* (1885).

residences as no other sovereign save James V had done. The highest quality of architecture is, however, to be found in non-royal (if perhaps quasi-royal) building, especially Earl Patrick Stewart's palace at Kirkwall, which is far and away the finest purely domestic Scottish residence of the period. Something of the same tradition is to be seen in the oriels at Huntly. Other notable residences of purely domestic character were those erected by Chancellor Dunfermline at Pinkie (1613) and by the Earl of Winton at Seton. But there was some reluctance to abandon the idea of fortification, for, as one builder sagely remarked in 1632, " the world may change again."[59] Besides, it was an economy simply to add residential quarters to existing tower houses or castles. In a castle, space within the curtain wall could be used for the erection of a new range in renaissance style, conspicuously at Caerlaverock (1634); at Crichton, a generation earlier, Francis, Earl of Bothwell, had inserted a remarkable Italianate façade. In a tower house, the new quarters were sometimes added at the top, so that a seventeenth-century house sprouts from the older tower, as at Preston; elsewhere, the tower was used as the kernel of a more spacious residence, as at Dalkeith. An interesting specimen of non-noble and non-fortified architecture is Heriot's Hospital, in Edinburgh (1627-50), which looks like a development from the style of some of King James's work at Edinburgh Castle and Linlithgow; it blends the turrets of the tower house tradition with renaissance characteristics and also has affinities with Danish building of the period. Around the spacious residences of Scottish gentlemen there were flower and fruit gardens on which the owners lavished much attention and of which they were very proud.[60]

The burghs shared to the full in the building activities of the time, and it is indeed with the burghs of this period that we first have tangible and visible links, because—churches apart—there are practically no buildings extant which belong to earlier periods, whereas almost every old burgh can show at least one or two houses of early seventeenth-century date. In Edinburgh, where the town's main thoroughfare continued to win the praise

[59] *Correspondence of the Earls of Ancram and Lothian*, I. 63.

[60] *E.g., ibid.*, pp. 73-4; *Annals of Banff* (New Spalding Club), I. 41; Gordon, *Earldom of Sutherland*, p. 8; Fraser, *Eglinton*, I. 214; Apted, *Guide to Aberdour*, App. B; *S. H. S. Misc.*, III. 214-5; A. W. Lindsay, *Memoir of Lady Anna Mackenzie*, pp. 50-1; C. Lowther, *Our Journall into Scotland* (1894), p. 18.

of visitors, one of whom called it " one of the fairest streets that ever I saw, excepting that of Palermo, in Sicily,"[61] the good taste and affluence of Bailie MacMoran are still reflected in the fine residence which he erected in Riddell's Court and in which the Duke of Holstein, brother of Queen Anne, was entertained to a banquet.[62] Gladstone's Land, in the Lawnmarket, dates from the 1630s, and a house which was standing in James VI's reign is the much debated building near the extremity of the burgh, which, whether or not it ever housed John Knox, was occupied before 1573. Eastwards from Edinburgh's boundary, at the Netherbow, stretched the Canongate, noted for providing the space, which Edinburgh could not afford, for the extensive mansions, with their fine gardens, which the nobility used as town houses—Moray House, Huntly House and Acheson House are examples still extant. Within Edinburgh, some old churches, like St Giles' and Trinity College, were preserved, others were demolished and their sites turned over to other purposes: the college occupied the site of the Kirk o' Field, the High School was on the site of the church of the Blackfriars, and a new Greyfriars' church arose on the site of the old.

In spite of the good intentions of the reformers, conditions after the Reformation were at first unfavourable to the maintenance of church buildings, for some powerful interests were antipathetic and funds were scarce. A sermon of 1572 denounced the " foul deformity and desolation of your kirks and temples, which are mair like to sheep-cots than the houses of God."[63] But reformed Scotland was not unappreciative of its architectural heritage, for Glasgow Cathedral, for example, was pronounced " ane magnifik work and bigging and ane greit ornament to this realme."[64] Already before 1600 much had been done by way of restoration and preservation, and after 1600 we enter on a period during which, while repair was energetically carried out— as at Dunfermline, Melrose, Holyrood, South Leith, St Nicholas's in Aberdeen, and nearly every cathedral[65]—there was also a considerable amount of building of new churches, like Greyfriars' in Edinburgh, Dairsie, Dirleton, South Queensferry and

---

61 Hume Brown, *Early travellers*, p. 159.
62 This was after the bailie's death (*Edinburgh Burgh Records, 1589-1603*, p. 218).
63 David Fergusson, *Sermons*, p. 73; cf. *Lamentatioun of Lady Scotland* (1572), sig. a v.
64 R. S. S. (MS.), XLVII. 112.
65 *Proc. Soc. Antiq. Scot.*, LXXXV. 130-1.

Anstruther Easter.[66] The unusual design of Burntisland (1592)—a square building which might now be characterised as several centuries ahead of its time—was not followed, and most of the churches of this period were on more or less traditional lines. Official action was taken to ensure the proper equipment of churches, for an act of 1617[67] required every parish church to have its own Communion plate, and there is evidence of the provision of some very fine silver work, as well as of the purchase of bells and the installation of ornamental furnishings like chandeliers. A type of internal adornment not to be overlooked is the burial monument; several impressive examples survive from this period, perhaps the finest of them the tomb of George Home, Earl of Dunbar, in Dunbar parish church. An English visitor in 1629 commented favourably on several Scottish burgh churches.[68]

The interior decoration of churches had to be restrained lest it be condemned as " popish," but there was no restraint about the internal decoration of domestic buildings. Much effort has recently been devoted to the uncovering and restoration of Jacobean painted ceilings, among them those at the " Palace " of Culross, Pinkie House, Huntingtower, Delgatie and Kinneil House (where there are also mural paintings of slightly earlier fashion). The ceiling once at Prestongrange House, dated 1581, has been reconstructed in the medieval Merchiston Tower, which forms the kernel of Napier College in Edinburgh. The subjects of the ceiling-paintings are occasionally scriptural, often classical, and sometimes obscene. Mr Ian Hodkinson, one of the leading authorities on the subject, has remarked that " almost without exception, at this period Scottish houses of any standing were extensively decorated with a gaiety, freedom and confidence which was the outward expression of a nation in the throes of intellectual expansion."

While material prosperity increased and intellectual pursuits flourished, Jacobean Scotland was neither a mirthless country nor one in which the struggle for subsistence or for gain excluded amusement and recreation. The reformers were much less austere than the puritanical covenanters of the following century,

66 George Hay, *The Architecture of Scottish post-Reformation Churches*; cf. also Sinclair Snow, *Patrick Forbes*, p. 113.

67 *A. P. S.*, IV. 534.

68 Lowther, *Our journall into Scotland* (1894), pp. 15, 16, 18, 23, 46.

and even the regulations on Sunday observance were at first concerned only to ensure that there was no interference with public worship. Taverns could be open, markets could be held, except in time of sermon. Even ministers were permitted to keep taverns, provided that they observed decorum.[69] It was only in 1579 that a statute imposed penalties for working (as well as for playing and for failing to attend church) on Sunday, and Sunday markets were not abolished until the end of the century.[70] Weddings were at first held on Sundays, and " caused a great deal of highly unsanctified behaviour ";[71] it was only gradually that " superfluous banqueting " even on a Monday came to be frowned on.[72] Although the old festivals were officially condemned, the people of Ross, Sutherland and Caithness were, according to one visitor, " the best and most bountiful Christmas keepers (the Greeks excepted) that ever I saw in the Christian world," for their feasting extended from St Andrew's day to Shrovetide.[73] Besides, St Valentine's day was observed in the traditional manner.[74] Acrobats were warmly welcomed and generously rewarded,[75] and the king's camel was paraded round the realm, advertised " by towcke of drum or sound of trumpet."[76] The town council of Edinburgh provided a new " playfeild to the toun "[77] in 1606, and less than ten years after the foundation of the university the students were provided with " ane playing place ";[78] the council also protected the swans of the Nor' Loch and supplied oats for them in a hard winter.[79]

[69] *B. U. K.*, I. 378.

[70] *A. P. S.*, III. 138, 238, 507, 548; *R. P. C.*, IV. 419; Chambers, *Domestic Annals*, I. 58, 329; *Ecclesiastical Records of Aberdeen*, p. 28; *Records of Elgin*, II. 71.

[71] *St Andrews Kirk Session Register*, I. xliv, 341.

[72] *Maitland Club Misc.*, I. 104.   [73] Lithgow, *op. cit.* (1632) pp. 500-1.

[74] Chambers, *Domestic Annals*, II. 119.

[75] Chambers, *Domestic Annals*, I. 302.

[76] *R. P. C.*, SER. II., v. 126.   [77] *Edinburgh Burgh Records, 1604-26*, p. 19.

[78] *Edinburgh Burgh Records, 1589-1603*, p. 60.   [79] *Ibid.*, pp. 10, 277.

15

THE CONSTITUTION IN THE
SEVENTEENTH CENTURY

The organs of the Scottish constitution must be viewed not as the embodiment of theories of representation or of rule by consent, but as the machinery by which the government of the country was conducted, as the instruments by which effect was given to the will of the individual or the faction in control. Until James VI attained maturity, as in the reigns of almost all his predecessors for a couple of centuries, the direction of affairs had very often lain with regents or with cliques of magnates who controlled the king. However, from the end of the sixteenth century until the Revolution, except during the covenanting rebellion and the Cromwellian conquest, authority pertained to the king in person and his immediate advisors. The study of the constitution is therefore in this period the study of the means by which the sovereign exercised his authority.

Of the three elements which had long composed a Scottish parliament—clergy, nobles and burgh commissioners—none underwent any revolutionary change until the seventeenth century. The clerical estate, in particular, was not immediately affected by the Reformation. As there was no general dispossession of clergy, the holders of abbacies—whether they were genuine abbots or lay commendators—retained their seats in parliament, and as they died other commendators succeeded, so that the abbatial element in parliament—though increasingly lay and titular—went on without interruption until the erection of abbeys into hereditary temporal lordships had the effect of removing the successors of the abbots from the " spiritual estate " into that of the nobility. The abbatial element had formed a considerable proportion of the total membership: *e.g.*, in 1558, out of some sixty members, there were the heads of sixteen religious houses, and in 1560 there were the heads of twenty-seven religious houses. The bishops, likewise, retained their places in parliament after the Reformation. As bishops died, they were succeeded usually by clergy of the reformed church, occasionally by lay titulars, and those holders of bishoprics, whatever their ecclesiastical status, sat in parliament as part of the spiritual estate. For a time there was talk of increasing the representation of the reformed church in parliament to compensate for the secularisation of the seats formerly held by abbots, but nothing came of it. By the time the office of bishop was first abolished in the established church, in 1638, the general assembly had lost its taste for parliamentary representation, and the clerical estate came to an end for the time being, to be restored from 1661 to 1689.

The nobles, all of whom had the right to attend parliament, so increased their numbers in this period that they came far to exceed, in proportion to the population, the peerage of England. In the sixteenth century an attendance of twenty-five to thirty peers at a parliament was about average, but by 1707 there were 154 Scottish peers and 168 English peers, when the population ratio was about 1:5. One large accession consisted of the lords of erection, who represented a transfer from the clerical estate, but other creations, mainly of the heads of old lairdly families, were numerous from about 1600 onwards. Apparently because there was more restraint about adding to the English peerage, Scottish titles were occasionally conferred on Englishmen who held no land in Scotland. This was felt to be a grievance, for in 1640 it was declared to be improper for anyone not owning land in Scotland to sit and vote as a lord of parliament, and in 1703 an act debarred Englishmen with Scottish titles but without Scottish estates from sitting.

Burgh representation underwent no change in law or theory. It was primarily, as always, of royal burghs, but two or three ecclesiastical burghs were included. There were, however, changes which increased burgh representation. For one thing, new royal burghs were created, so that the number entitled to representation rose from about forty in 1500 to sixty-six in 1700. For another, actual attendances became much greater: before the Reformation there might be only ten or a dozen burgesses in a parliament, in 1560 there were twenty-two, in the seventeenth century there were sometimes fifty. On the other hand, down to 1617 a number of burghs besides Edinburgh sometimes sent two commissioners each—in 1612 five burghs and in 1617 as many as seventeen; but from 1621 the rule was that Edinburgh alone should have two representatives. Commissions to burgess representatives were issued by the town councils for each particular parliament, and the councils normally paid expenses.

Besides the three estates, properly so called, there was an additional element, the officers of state. Before the Reformation minor officials sometimes attended parliament although they were neither prelates nor peers, and after the Reformation, while minor officials ceased to attend, the greater officers of state (many of whom were usually prelates or peers) were recognised as a distinct group, usually eight in number. They ceased to have a place *ex officio* between 1640 and 1661.

To those four elements, all of them already well established in parliament, a fifth was added at the end of the sixteenth century. The legislation of James I, designed first to enforce the personal attendance of all crown tenants and then to secure the representation of the lesser tenants, had been practically a dead letter. The lairds, except for those who happened to be officials, formed a dwindling element in parliaments, and by the middle of the sixteenth century we find parliaments at which no lairds at all were present. Then, in the unusual circumstances of 1560, over 100 lairds flocked to the " reformation parliament," claiming a right to be present on the grounds of the cause of true religion, their capacity to serve in parliament by advice and vote, the principle that valid legislation must have the consent of the governed, and their ancient right to be heard in parliament. The parliament of the now triumphant protestants in December 1567 was again attended by some " barons," though their names do not appear in the official roll, and an effort was made to settle the question of their right by a return to the plan for representation. An " article " which was " approved " provided that when a summons to a parliament went out the sheriffs should be directed to call a special meeting where the barons of the shire were to choose one or two of their number as commissioners. The election was not to be made, as the act of 1428 had proposed, at the " head court," and it was restricted to " barons " instead of being extended also to " other freeholders " as the act of 1428 had proposed. There is no trace of elections in terms of this " article " of 1567, and the small barons who appeared at some of the parliaments during the regencies seem to have been there as individuals and not as commissioners.

In December 1585 parliament received a petition on behalf of the barons, stating that king and parliament should know " the needs and causes " of subjects, especially the commons. In the summons to the next parliament, in 1587, the old obligation of the smaller barons to personal attendance was reasserted, but the crown used this merely as an opportunity to collect money, for the barons were made to pay £40,000 for the privilege of appearing not in person but by representatives. The statute of 1428 providing for representation was now re-enacted; two commissioners were to be elected annually by the freeholders of each shire except the small shires of Clackmannan and Kinross, which elected only one each; these commissioners were to be summoned to parliament and general convention as the members of the other estates were, and were to have equal representation with the burgesses on the committee of articles; their expenses were to be paid by the freeholders. The voting qualification was the tenure of land of the crown of an annual value of 40s. of old extent, and this excluded those holding by feu-ferm tenure, whose lands had not been so valued. Later statutes, however, admitted feuars and further defined the electoral qualification. An act of 1661 acknowledged as voters all heritors holding a 40s. land of old extent of the king, life-renters and wadsetters holding of the king whose yearly rent was 10 chalders of victual or £1,000, and tenants of a like rental occupying church lands which were in the king's hands. An act of 1681 described the freeholders as those " infeft in property or in superiority and in possession " of a 40s. land of old extent held of the crown, so making a bare superiority a qualification. This act also allowed the vote to those holding of the crown by ward tenure or blench tenure on a qualification of £400 of " valued rent," that is, the annual value as assessed for taxation, and the same value was now to stand for feuars.

The qualification for sitting was the same as for voting, but judges, clergy, and some officials could not be elected.

Shire commissioners first appeared in the parliament of 1594, but half a century passed before all the shires were represented.[1] The introduction of such commissioners, in terms of the act of 1587, reflects in a general way the social changes of the period, when the lesser landholders were becoming wealthier and had probably benefited from the break-up of the ecclesiastical estates. But it also reflects more particularly some developments connected with the Reformation. The general assembly, from almost its earliest days, had contained " commissioners of shires," how elected it is hard to say, and there does seem to have been a kind of competition between assembly and parliament for the possession of a broadly based representative character. The crown looked askance at the general assembly, and it would clearly be easier to make a case for suppressing the assembly if parliament contained all the elements which an assembly contained. Besides, in the very year when the act was passed providing for the admission of shire commissioners to parliament there was a statute annexing the ecclesiastical temporalities to the crown. This did not, in the end, make much difference, but it looked for a time as if it might mean the elimination of the prelates—bishops and commendators alike—from parliament, and the question became urgent of providing for parliamentary representation of the reformed church. Had the prelates in fact disappeared from parliament and presbyterial representatives been admitted on the scale which the general assembly proposed, alongside the shire and burgh commissioners, the Scottish parliament would have been transformed and it is hard to see how a case could have been made for the continuance of the general assembly.

All through, in every estate, there was considerable opportunity for the crown to exert influence on the composition of parliament and the attitude of its members. The officers of state, the bishops and the commendators were, quite simply, royal nominees;

[1] Sutherland became a separate shire in 1633, and, as the earl was the only crown tenant there, his vassals were permitted to vote; Caithness became a separate shire in 1641, and the separation of Ross (also from Inverness) became effective in the same year. Tarbertshire was annexed to Argyll in 1633. Following are the dates for the first appearance of commissioners: Orkney, 1612; Argyll, 1630; Sutherland, 1639; Caithness, 1644; Ross, 1649; Kinross, 1681.

the bishops were peculiarly the creatures of the crown, and in the Restoration period bishops who opposed the royal policy were actually deprived. Nobles in the first generation—and there were many of them—were, equally, crown nominees, some of them officials, some of them courtiers. In the shires, the crown had the means of making its wishes known through the sheriffs, who had not been entrusted with election machinery under the act of 1587 but took it over after 1603, and, in Charles I's reign at least, were commissioned to impart " his majesty's royal will and pleasure " to the freeholders and deal " with them to give his majesty satisfaction therein."[2] Burgh commissioners were selected by the town councils, which in their turn were not popularly elected, but usually co-opted, with the consequence that any crown influence over the composition of the councils was reflected in the burgess representation in parliament. At various stages there were provisions which in effect restricted office in burghs to those well affected to the government of the day: in 1622 James VI signified that none should bear office in burghs who did not accept the Five Articles of Perth; in 1625 Charles I insisted that Edinburgh should not have councillors who would not " conforme themeselffis to the ordour established in the churche ";[3] in 1660 the convention of royal burghs decreed that none who had been disaffected should be eligible for a place in the burghs; from 1662 all office-holders had to declare against the covenants; the Test Act of 1681 demanded unconditional acceptance of the royal supremacy from all in public office.

The position in the burghs was complicated because the crown was not alone in attempting to dominate the councils. It is true that there was ample precedent for crown interference in the affairs of particular burghs. It was almost regular procedure for the government to insist on the election of its nominee as provost of Edinburgh, and what could be done in the capital could be done elsewhere. Thus, in 1528 the Master of Ruthven was chosen as provost of Perth at the royal command; the Regent Morton compelled Haddington to accept John Douglas as provost; Graham of Claverhouse was made provost of Dundee in obedience to a letter from James VII—who, however, went farther than his predecessors by nominating town councils in

---

[2] Rait, *Parliaments*, p. 225. [3] *Edinburgh Burgh Records, 1604-26*, p. 275.

all the royal burghs. But very often a burgh was dominated by
a local landed gentleman: *e.g.*, Sir George Ogilvy of Dunlugus
was provost of Banff for at least thirty years and his son was
also provost; the Learmonths of Dairsie were almost hereditary
provosts of St Andrews. Such lairds not infrequently represented
their burghs in parliament, despite intermittent attempts to
enforce a rule that commissioners should be chosen only from
genuine resident burgesses. It was characteristic of the opportunism of royal policy that Charles II tried to exclude country
gentlemen from the estate of burgesses but that James VII wanted
to rescind the rule about residence with a view to finding lairds
who were more docile than burgesses.

Government influence on the actual conduct of elections was
supplemented by some control over the decision of disputed
elections. Before the civil war period the convention of royal
burghs took cognisance of disputed burgh elections, the privy
council of those of the counties. During the civil war period the
estates decided such disputes, but after the Restoration the king's
commissioner nominated a committee for controverted elections,
though the opposition tried to have such disputes referred to the
whole house. Such a committee inevitably made its decisions
purely on political grounds.

Crown control and management extended into the procedure
of the house. Down to the reign of Charles I the estates sometimes met for discussion, if only informally, as separate entities,
but they were forbidden to do so in 1633 and, although the
practice was revived during the civil war period, it ceased once
more after the Restoration. It is true, too, that the burghs, with
their own convention, had a corporate character not possessed
by the nobles or the shire commissioners, and could therefore to
some extent be managed as a unit: Lauderdale acted for years
as the agent at court of the convention of royal burghs, knowing
that watching over their interests " would secure him that third
estate of parliament."[4] In the main, however, the government
was concerned either with the whole house or with individual
members, rather than with estates as such. It was the exceptional
individual who was prepared to brave the royal displeasure which
would be the consequence of voting against the crown's measures,
and there were means of swaying individual members: the vote

4 Sir George Mackenzie, *Memoirs*, p. 227.

of a particular burgh commissioner, for example, might sometimes be secured by the threat of the crown to refuse to sanction an act in favour of his burgh.

So far as the house as a whole was concerned, there was management of parliamentary time. Under James VI and Charles I there was hardly any opportunity for debate at all, because the business of the house was simply the acceptance *en bloc* of the legislation prepared by the government. After the Restoration, although this practice could not be restored, matters were so arranged that opportunity for adequate discussion of some measures was impossible. For example, in 1663 an act asserting the king's prerogative in the ordering and disposal of trade with foreigners, which allowed the imposition of customs and the grant of monopolies, was brought in only an hour before the parliament rose. In the 1681 parliament, measures were brought to the house late in the afternoon and put to the vote that day.[5] It was a weakness in the Scottish parliament that it never had a second chamber and that until its last years it did not even have a procedure of reading bills more than once. The haste with which its proceedings were conducted meant that there was little time for an opposition to organise itself or for divergent interests to combine.

Before 1603, on occasions when the king or the regent did not " hold the parliament " in person, a commission had been appointed to do so, and after 1603 a body of commissioners was regularly appointed for this purpose, including among them a " high commissioner " to act as the king in person would have acted had he been present. From the Restoration it was the practice to appoint only a single commissioner. The president of parliament had in the past been the chancellor, but the high commissioner began in the seventeenth century to perform presidential functions, and his office, from being one of honour rather than authority, increased in importance at the expense of that of the chancellor. Thus, under James VI and Charles I the chancellor had been virtually prime minister, but under Charles II and James VII the high commissioner became the effective as well as the titular head of the government in Scotland and it was the chancellor's office which became largely honorific.

As the estates sat in one chamber and voted in one body,

[5] Rait, *op. cit.*, pp. 78, 86, 383.

it is plain that in a full house the burgesses and the shire commissioners could have outvoted the clergy and the nobility,
for the admission of shire commissioners and the increased attendance of burgh commissioners more than counterbalanced the
Jacobean and Caroline peerage creations. Thus in 1633 there
were present 12 bishops and 66 peers (including proxies), nine
officers of state, 46 shire commissioners and 52 burgh commissioners,
a total of 185; in 1661 there were 74 peers, 55 shire commissioners
and 61 burgh commissioners, a total of 190 without bishops. But
this numerical preponderance of shire and burgh commissioners
was neutralised by the fact that on the committee of the articles,
where alone members of parliament could hope to shape the
legislation to be passed by the house, each estate had equal
representation. In the act of 1587 admitting shire commissioners
it had been laid down that each estate should have the same
representation, with from six to ten members, and in practice the
number was usually eight. Thus a dozen or fewer bishops had
equal weight with either the burgesses or the shire commissioners,
and in the committee the bishops and nobles, with the officers of
state, who also had places, always outnumbered the remainder.
In any event, the ratio between the committee of articles and the
full house had completely changed. In the parliaments of the
sixteenth century sixty had been a fair total membership, and in
such a parliament half the members could be on the committee,
whereas in the seventeenth century only a quarter or less of the
total members would be on it.

The method of election which operated from 1621 went far
to ensure that the committee of articles would consist mainly
of those well disposed to the government and its policy. There
appears to have been a variety of precedents in earlier practice,
and it seems never to have been acknowledged that each estate
had the right to choose its own representatives, though they sometimes did so—as late, apparently, as 1617, when there was opposition to nomination by the king. It had not been unknown
for the nobles and the prelates to choose each other's representatives, and in one way or another it had been possible to exert
royal influence; thus, in 1612, the bishops chose the nobles
whom the king designated, and the burgesses were presumably
chosen by the bishops and nobles. From 1621, however, the
bishops selected eight nobles, who in turn chose eight bishops,

and those sixteen then chose the barons and burgesses. This represented a triumph for the crown, because, since the bishops were the king's creatures, they necessarily chose the nobles whom he recommended, and those nobles, in choosing bishops, had only royal nominees to choose from. This device, which secured the selection of the men " best affected to his majesty's service,"[6] was used in other parliaments before the covenanting revolution. In the first restoration parliament, when there were no bishops, each estate chose its own representatives, without prejudice to the future, and in 1663 the method of 1621 was revived. Royal control was again complete, and in 1669 Lauderdale wrote of the articles, " If they be amiss, blame me, for I wrote the lists and not a man was altered."[7]

Royal influence in the selection of the committee made it possible to achieve a close association with the privy council,[8] and the presence of officers of state on the committee further helped to identify it with the government's policy. Thus the work of the committee, including as it did experienced administrators, in drafting acts and preparing the government's programme for submission to the house, had great value, especially in a single-chamber parliament where acts passed on a single vote. But the work of the committee must be seen, too, against the background of the earlier practice of the Scottish parliament—continuing down to 1543—of handing over its full powers to a commission, which " held " the parliament in the absence of the other members. A parliament therefore met, elected the committee of articles to prepare the statutes, adjourned or was prorogued, and met again only to give formal assent to those statutes, without debate. The full house had no power to initiate measures, for only those brought forward by the committee could be considered; nor had the house any power of amendment, for the acts stood as prepared by the committee. And even the committee itself, as a parliamentary organ, had little or no independence, for the articles must have been in an advanced state of preparation—no doubt at the hands of privy councillors who would sit on the committee of articles—before parliament even met to elect the

---

[6] Rait, *op. cit.*, p. 370.   [7] *Lauderdale Papers*, II. 142.

[8] An analysis by W. Taylor in " The Scottish Privy Council 1603-25 " (Edinburgh Ph.D. thesis, 1950), shows that councillors all but invariably formed a majority of the committee.

committee. This is clear from the time-tables of the parliaments: that of May 1584 sat on only two days (19 and 22 May) and passed 49 acts, and it is inconceivable that the intelligently framed " Black Acts " were thought out *ab initio* in that brief period; in 1633 parliament met on 20 June to elect the committee of articles, and when it met again on 28 June it passed 168 statutes *en bloc*.

Already in the reign of James VI the committee of articles was the sole channel through which measures could come before the house, and it remained so. An attempt in 1669 to " bring in things in plain parliament, without bringing them first to the articles," was rebuked by Charles II as an endeavour to " undermine the very foundation of his authority," for he looked on the articles " as the securest fence of his government."9 Lauderdale described the situation thus: " Nothing can come to the parliament but through the articles, and nothing can pass in the articles but what is warranted by his majesty, so that the king is absolute master in parliament both of the negative and the affirmative."10

Yet, with all the machinery by which the crown could dominate parliament, there might still be opposition strong enough to demonstrate that the powers of the crown were not unlimited. Parliament was by no means useless as an instrument for expressing public opinion. When the highly controversial Five Articles of Perth came up for parliamentary ratification in 1621, there was opposition within the committee of articles, and when the house divided, eleven clergy, thirty-five nobles, twenty shire commissioners and twenty burgesses voted in favour, while fifteen nobles, nineteen shire commissioners and twenty-five burgesses voted against. No government could ignore such figures. After 1660, something of the tradition of free debate survived from the period of the rebellion, and the extent of opposition was brought home to the government.11 Finally, when the critical issue of toleration came up in 1686, the Scottish parliament actually defied and defeated the crown. On that occasion the committee of articles itself accepted the government's proposal by a majority of only 18:14—two officers, two bishops, six nobles, seven lairds and one burgess in favour, and four

9 Mackenzie, *Memoirs*, pp. 263-4.
10 *Lauderdale Papers*, I. 173-4.   11 Pp. 377-8 below.

bishops, two nobles, one laird and seven burgesses against.   It
was remarked that the burghs were " the brazen wall the papists
found hardest,"[12] and their estate does seem all along to have
been the least manageable, at least on religious issues.

The estates met in parliament, on a summons of forty days'
notice, for judicial as well as legislative purposes.   But they
met also, with less formality and without judicial powers, in a
convention, as they had met earlier in a general council.   The
general council had been an afforced meeting of the ordinary
council, of necessity sometimes summoned urgently and at short
notice and including only those members of the estates whose
attendance could most conveniently be secured.   The convention
likewise was in the sixteenth century still sometimes a relatively
small body with a selective membership, but in the seventeenth
century selection gradually came to an end, so that the membership of a convention came to approximate to that of a parliament.
For example, the representation of burghs had hitherto depended
partly on the number to which the king addressed an invitation,
partly on the appeal which the business to be discussed made to
the burgesses.   But the total burgh members rose from seven in
1602 to 31 in 1630, at a time when there were 45-50 in parliaments.   Shire representation, provided for under the act of 1587,
increased from 15 in 1625 to 20 in 1630, as against 27 in the
parliament of 1633.   The revolutionary period marked the
final assimilation of the two bodies in membership, and at the
same time the formality of the convention was increased by the
practices of giving 20 days' public notice of summons and of
proclaiming its acts like those of a parliament.   The convention
thus had virtually parliamentary status.   Its powers in legislation
and in taxation seem to have been equal to those of a parliament,
but it was usually called for certain specific purposes, defined in
the royal letters calling it, and it could not proceed to other business.   Moreover, already in 1617 and 1625 conventions met
solely for the grant of taxation, and under Charles II this became
their only function; thus the estates could be called together to
grant supply without there being any risk that they would
embarrass the government by discussing other matters.

The convention, then, was an organ of government which
came to have highly specialised functions.   The privy council,

12 Fountainhall, quoted by Rait, *op. cit.*, p. 93.

by contrast, was an organ with legislative and judicial, as well as administrative, powers. The supreme authority of parliament as a legislative body may not have been in doubt, and time and again parliamentary confirmation was given to measures already in operation, apparently because parliamentary confirmation was believed to confer a quality of permanence. It is true, too, that the council had special importance for temporary or provisional legislation in the intervals between sessions of parliament. But the line of demarcation between the legislative powers of council and those of parliament is hard to find. The council certainly did some very important things: for instance, the system set up in 1562 to administer the church property was entirely the work of a series of acts of council; although parliament had earlier declared in favour of the retention of the Norse law in Orkney and Shetland, the privy council decreed its abolition, in 1611; the first measure to give effect to the demand for a school in every parish was an act of council in 1616, anticipating parliamentary action by seventeen years.

The judicial functions of the council, again, overlapped with those of the court of session in civil justice and the court of justiciary in criminal justice. In a case before the privy council in 1576, the defence pleaded that by the institution of the college of justice all cases should be tried there, but the lord advocate appealed successfully to an act of James III whereby the king could decide any case, notwithstanding any privilege granted to another judge.[13] It is not easy to see why certain cases came to the council and not to the court of session or the court of justiciary, though it seems that the council was less bound by rules and set forms of procedure than they were, so that its response to the many complaints which came before it was flexible and prompt.

Plainly, the privy council, with its wide residual powers in legislation and justice, was the real heir of the old undifferentiated council—the council which had at one time been the one and only legislative, judicial and administrative body—and it is hard to see what limits, if any, there were to its competence. It is clear that, while the differentiation of institutions was complete by the middle of the sixteenth century, the differentiation of functions in legislation, administration and judicature was never

[13] *R. P. C.,* II. 517.

quite complete as long as Scotland was an independent kingdom. All in all, the council, in almost permanent session, with usually two meetings weekly, was far more important than parliament in the life of the nation, and its proceedings consequently far more informative for the historian. The acts of the parliaments of Scotland are contained in twelve printed volumes, from the earliest times to 1706; the register of the privy council, beginning in 1545, extends to 36 volumes down to 1690, the point which printing has at present reached.

But, although the bulk of the council's business demonstrates its importance, it must not be thought that the council was necessarily a policy-making body on important issues. Informally, no doubt, councillors—some councillors—advised the king in the taking of decisions, but in general the council was very often merely putting into effect policies shaped elsewhere. This is especially true after 1603, when the council no longer had immediate personal access to the king and the king was no longer present at the council as he had often been before. In every matter of real importance and in many matters which can be regarded as trivial, the council received the king's instructions and merely executed his will. In his letters to the council, James VI writes as an imperious master addressing his underlings. He rates and lectures them for negligence, delay, carelessness, inability to proceed wisely and boldly, and threatens them with dismissal, and they, on their side, receive with the utmost respect his " most sacred cogitations," especially if written in his own princely hand. Occasionally the council did venture to oppose the king and succeeded in restraining him: for example, when he pressed for the trial of eight more ministers besides the six condemned for treason in 1605, the council told him how difficult it had been to bring about the conviction of the six and pointed out the impracticability of proceeding against others. Much more often the council acquiesced, with whatever reluctance, in the royal policy. James selected an appropriate metaphor when, in 1608, he decreed that votes should not be merely by an unrecorded show of hands but that division lists should be sent to him, " so that we may discern the goats from the true sheep."[14]

The king was more likely to be influenced by those who did have personal access to him, and from time to time a Scottish

[14] *R. P. C.*, VIII. 97, 504.

council met in London. In the early years of Charles II's reign a council for Scottish affairs, with English as well as Scottish members, was of real importance in shaping the broad lines of Scottish policy. The scheme was that of Clarendon, the English chancellor, who was himself a member, and Lauderdale, although he acted as secretary, was opposed to it. The influence of such a council does not alter the fact of the impotence of the privy council in Edinburgh.

The nominal membership of the council was as a rule very large. Between 1605 and 1607, for instance, 93 councillors in all attended at some time, but only 40 of them were in any degree active. In 1610 James decided that the council was too large and unwieldy and he reduced the nominal membership to 35. The number tended to rise again and throughout the 1620s was between 45 and 50. The effective membership, however, was a mere fraction of the nominal, and attendances were mostly very small. James fixed the quorum at seven, and ordered that irregular attendance should lead to dismissal, but he secured attendance usually of only from eight to ten members, though sometimes as many as 20. In this reign the council always included a considerable number of the old hereditary peers, but they were conspicuously among the least active members. The strength of the council lay elsewhere—in state officials like the chancellor, comptroller, treasurer, secretary, lord president and justice clerk and in senators of the college of justice, who were still in practice as well as in title " lords of council and session " and were always privy councillors. Of the 35 nominated in 1610, about 16 were officials or lords of session, 13 were old hereditary peers and three were bishops. In succeeding years it was still the case that the most regular attenders were the officials, judges or lawyers, while peers like Cassillis, Mar, Glencairn and Hamilton were among the least frequent attenders. The bishops were inconspicuous in the council under James and in the early years of Charles, but from about 1634 they played a much more important part.[15]

On the accession of Charles I, no less than 17 councillors, including those most assiduous in attendance, were also judges. The king proposed that the office of judge should in future be incompatible with membership of the council; in nominating a

[15] P. 299 below.

new council he omitted most of the judges, and afterwards laid down that no peer or state officer should be a judge of session. The 47 persons named by him in 1626 were largely old peers, bishops and officials, with, of course, no judges, and the quorum was to be eight in addition to the chancellor or president and the officers of state. This was quite impracticable, for the peers did not respond to the king's invitation to resume active participation and the reconstructed council often found it difficult to form a quorum. In 1627 the quorum was reduced to nine in all, and subsequently to seven, the figure which had obtained under James. It continued to be the case that only a quarter or less of the members attended even half the meetings, and a handful of officials continued to form the core of the council.

Even when the council is added to the parliament and the convention, the tale of legislative organs is not complete, for there were other bodies exercising the right of legislation for one aspect or another of the life of the nation. The royal burghs had their monopoly in foreign trade, which was convenient to the crown in that it facilitated the collection of customs and which was regarded as a fair equivalent for the burden of taxation borne by the burghs, and they also had privileges and exclusive rights in crafts. The regulation of commerce and manufactures was therefore in part a matter for the convention of royal burghs, which met every year to discuss the common interests of the burghs and to legislate for their affairs. The legislation of the convention could, however, be set aside by parliament. Whether the legislation of a somewhat similar body, the general assembly of the church, could be set aside by parliament was one of the central issues of the time, and the presbyterians' claim for the sovereignty of the assembly in ecclesiastical matters was a serious infringement of the competence of parliament. There was yet another legislative body of a sectional nature, for the court of session, in its acts of sederunt, in effect legislated not only on court procedure but on various matters connected with the legal profession. The Scottish constitution cannot be understood unless the concept of the unchallenged sovereignty of an omnicompetent parliament is set aside.

PART III
REVOLT AND REACTION

16

THE POLICY OF CHARLES I

By dying in his bed, at peace alike with his subjects and with foreign powers, and passing on his royal authority, unimpaired, to a son of adult years, James VI did something done by few of his predecessors. Under his peace, lairds and burgesses had become wealthier, life was less precarious for the poor, inroads had been made on the political influence of the nobility, there were everywhere signs of vitality. The future of the country depended on whether the traditional institutions and political structure would accept modification to fit the changes in economy and society, on the manner in which Scotland's vitality was to find outlets, and on the readiness of private individuals to allow the diversion of some of the growing wealth of the country to public ends.

In Charles I the Scots had a king who was not prepared to regard either the traditional repositories of power or the rights of private property if they conflicted with the public ends which he had in view, and those public ends were the aggrandisement of the crown in wealth and influence, the emancipation of lesser men from the power of the magnates and, perhaps mainly, the material wellbeing of the church. Charles wanted to see the sacred edifices renovated and adorned, the clergy enriched and elevated to that influence to which he thought them entitled, and divine service rendered with greater splendour. To him, more suitably than to David I, can be applied the title of " sair sanct for the croun," because, whereas David's enrichment of the church was carried through with success, Charles's policy led to the temporary eclipse of the monarchy. While the wisdom of

Charles's aims might be debated, there is no room for controversy about his methods, which were consistently ill-advised. Though a native of Scotland, born at Dunfermline on 19 November 1600, he had been brought up in England, he did not know the " stomach " of his Scottish subjects, he underestimated the strength of their interests and underrated the force of their prejudices. He failed to assess the opposition which his schemes would encounter and, completely lacking his father's dexterity and sublety or any regard for expediency, his only policy to meet opposition was obstinate resistance.

There were few issues on which Charles I agreed with Andrew Melville, but one was the claim of the reformed church to all the old ecclesiastical revenues. This doctrinaire solution had never appealed to the cautious James, who saw too clearly the need to conciliate the conflicting interests involved and who had not only confirmed the monastic temporalities to the lords of erection but had consistently deferred a comprehensive settlement of the teinds, a large proportion of which was still tied up with the abbey property. A workmanlike scheme for the extrication of the teinds from the prelacies had been drawn up in 1596, but did not get beyond paper. In 1617 and 1621 commissions were at last appointed which achieved a good deal by means of bargains whereby the tacksmen of teinds were burdened with additional payments towards stipends and compensated by the prolongation of their tacks. Use seems to have been made of the operations of the 1617 commission to influence the clergy to accept the Five Articles of Perth, but otherwise the quiet and piecemeal nature of the work was not such as to raise any dissatisfaction.

Charles I was determined on something more comprehensive. His act of revocation (1625), besides cancelling all grants made of crown property since 1540, also rescinded all dispositions of ecclesiastical property and the erections of such property into temporal lordships. Such a revocation, involving an assertion of a right to dispose of the teinds, would enable the king to provide an adequate endowment for the ministry and also to make arrangements which would relieve farmers from the inconvenience and loss they sometimes suffered in the process of the collection of the tenths of their crops. The king invited the holders of church property covered by the annexation to make voluntary surrenders in return for compensation, but when no such surrenders were made it was announced that the crown would proceed to actions of reduction to invalidate the charters by which the revoked properties were held, and all concerned were summoned to produce their titles. This stimulated a petition for a fresh commission to receive surrenders, and one was appointed in February 1627. The commissioners were empowered to treat with the possessors of ecclesiastical properties " unlawfully acquired by any of them and yet fitting to be secured unto the present possessors upon reasonable conditions "[1]—a phrase which really sums up the scope of the king's intentions.

In practice, it turned out, church lands were to remain with the present owners, but were to be held of the crown. Houses, or " places," too, were secured to the present owners, to be held of the crown for a nominal feu-duty. But, while the lords of erection thus retained their " own proper lands," they were to lose their feudal superiorities should the crown choose to redeem them. Terms of composition were fixed at ten years' purchase—a reasonable figure when interest was usually 10 per cent. As it happened, the crown was never financially in a position to take much advantage of this arrangement, though Hamilton and Lennox appear to have been induced, it is said by English money, to give up Arbroath abbey and St Andrews priory (which went to the Bishop of Brechin and the archbishop, respectively) and Charles purchased some of the properties which went to endow his new bishopric of Edinburgh in 1633. In general, therefore, the monastic temporality, both property and superiority, remained with the existing holders, as the first Book of Discipline had long ago tacitly conceded it should.

But the lords were threatened with the loss of their teinds. In the second commission to receive surrenders it was stated that the king intended " that every man may have his own teinds upon reasonable conditions "[2]—as had been proposed by the first Book of Discipline, and, even earlier, by James V. The intention was that a farmer, instead of being required to yield up the tenth sheaf of his actual crop, could retain the entire yield of the ground in his own hands and pay, in lieu of teind, a fixed proportion of the rent of his land, either in money or meal. Where teinds had previously been paid separately from the rent, they could now be

[1] *R. P. C.*, ser. II., 1.510.   [2] *R. P. C.*, ser. II, I. 228.

valued in proportion to the value of the rent; where they had been combined with the rent, one-fifth of the rent was reckoned as teind. Moreover, after a heritor had had his teinds valued, he could bring an action compelling the titular to sell to him, at nine years' purchase, the valued teinds, except such proportion of them as had been allocated to stipend. Finally, the crown was to draw from the teinds an annuity of 6 per cent, though it was possible to have this burden, too, commuted for a lump sum.

Most of the arrangements were permissive rather than compulsory, and the central fact is that the Caroline settlement provided machinery for the valuation and commutation of teinds and for the provision of stipends—machinery which was to endure, with only minor changes, until 1925. The minimum stipend was fixed by Charles I at 800 merks, and in later times, when augmentations proved necessary, funds were obtained by assessing the heritors in proportion to the rentals of their lands.

The statesmanship of the final arrangements is attested not only by their endurance until modern times but also by the fact that in the course of the revolution against Charles I's government no attempt was made to overturn them. Yet, in the words of a contemporary annalist, the revocation was " the ground stone of all the mischief that followed after, both to this king's government and family."[3] The discontent was a consequence of mismanagement and of the king's emphasis on principle rather than practice. A revocation, far from being a novelty, was a normal proceeding, to be expected in a king's twenty-fifth year, but this was no ordinary revocation. It was introduced with a secrecy which aroused suspicion and apprehension and gave opportunities for exaggerated rumours and the formation of ill-informed criticism. At the next stage, the threatened actions of reduction put the holders of ecclesiastical property in a state of alarm. It is not at all clear, and it is really most unlikely, that the king ever seriously intended to deprive the lords of erection of their lands, and certainly not to take them away without fair compensation. But a sweeping act which put at his disposal the entire ecclesiastical property, in lands and teinds alike, induced a sense of insecurity in nearly every landholder in Scotland, and startled even the churchmen who were intended to benefit. Besides, no pecuniary compensation would be a substitute for the power

3 Balfour, *Annals*, II. 128.

and influence which their feu-duties and teinds had given to the lords.

The influence of the nobles was undermined by other proceedings, some of them reckless extensions of the policy of James. Charles aimed at " drawing back into our crowne all the heritable offices,"[4] and nobles like Rothes, Loudoun and Lorne, as well as Huntly and Hamilton, had to resign heritable sheriffships or similar offices, while the circuit judges for criminal cases[5] were thought by some to infringe the rights of regalities. Further, Charles, as a devout churchman of sacerdotal views, had a rare veneration for the clergy and especially for bishops, and was ready to accord them a position which their lay contemporaries generally were not disposed to concede. The Archbishop of St Andrews was given precedence as the first subject of the realm, and in 1635 was elevated to the office of chancellor, which had been in lay hands since the Reformation; the appointment bred the more displeasure as the archbishop's son was already lord president. The bishops also began to play such an important part in the council that they seemed likely in the end to dominate it.[6] Lay councillors and laymen generally may have been irked by the powers exercised by the bishops on the court of high commission and by the appointment of justices of the peace from lists furnished by the bishops.[7] It made matters worse that some of the bishops whom Charles appointed were out of sympathy theologically with the majority of their fellow-countrymen,[8] and others were without the social background and family connexions which had made so many of their predecessors acceptable to the aristocracy.

The nobles' attitude amounted to something more than jealousy, class-consciousness, or even anti-clericalism, for they had honourable grounds for complaint in the political influence which the bishops enjoyed through their membership of the committee of the articles and their part in its election. This in turn was only one aspect of a wider unrest, or at least uneasiness, on constitutional matters and of the feeling that the manipulation of parliament was an abuse. The king's critics began in 1633 to speak of

---

[4] *Stirling's Register of Royal Letters*, I. 269-70.   [5] P. 223 above.

[6] Miss Elizabeth Rutherford, one of my students, has worked out that the average attendance of bishops before 1630 was 1.8 and that in 1636 it was 3.5, while the average number of lay officials present dropped from about 6 to just over 3.

[7] *R. P. C.*, SER. II, v. 228, 658; VI. 496-7.   [8] Pp. 305-6 below.

a " free parliament," and the existence of discontent on constitutional grounds may be inferred from the actions of the revolutionary party after it achieved power—the abolition of the clerical estate, the abolition of the committee of the articles, the elimination of the officers of state, as such, from parliament, the passing of a triennial act whereby parliament was to meet at least every third year, and the subjection of both executive and judicature to the control of the estates.[9]

However, even allowing for the threats to the property, prestige and political influence of the nobles, it is not too easy to account for their hostility to Charles's government. There seem to have been certain more subtle factors at work, factors psychological rather than material. Since 1603 the king and his court had been in England, and this had two consequences: the nobles were neglected by their sovereign and without a focus in Scotland; and they were somewhat at a loss to find a substitute for the traditional methods of bringing pressure to bear on the king. Charles had none of his father's familiarity with the Scottish nobles, as he had none of his father's familiarity with any of his subjects. The only Scottish peers who were intimate with their king were men who, like Hamilton and Lennox, were deracinated and anglicised, or who, like Roxburgh and Ancram, were courtiers, not likely to tell their master unpleasant truths. Among the lay councillors in Scotland itself it is doubtful if a single one knew the king's mind and understood his motives. And behind these facts lay the great changes which had been coming over the life of the nation as Scotland became more orderly and the feuds which had formerly taken up a good deal of the nobles' time were ruthlessly suppressed. In a later age the nobles were to find alternative occupations like estate management, afforestation, building, patronage of the arts, parliamentary management. But at this stage the widespread and somewhat nebulous resentment against the government of Charles I may have been partly the consequence of under-employment: the Scottish nobles had too little to do.

If the nobles had certain grievances peculiar to their own order, they also shared a resentment at a fiscal policy which was heightening among all the king's subjects a sense of the insecurity of their property. The traditional methods of financing

9 P. 327 below.

Scottish government had finally become hopelessly inadequate towards the end of the sixteenth century. The application of feuing to most of the crown lands meant that income could not increase, and as inflation proceeded the real value of this source of revenue dwindled sharply. The profit accruing to the crown after the Reformation, from the thirds of benefices and from the compositions taken for the confirmation of feus of church lands, was only temporary, and efforts to annex ecclesiastical property to the crown on a large scale brought few permanent gains. In the 1590s James had been driven to various expedients: the bulk of Queen Anne's dowry, amounting to 54,000 thalers, was lent out to certain royal burghs for a return of 10 per cent, Edinburgh's share being £40,000; there was some retrenchment and more efficient administration, notably under the Octavians; the king constantly appealed to Edinburgh for help, and the burgh, besides undertaking the renovation of Holyrood for Anne's reception, at a cost of £1,000, and fitting out a ship to bring the king and his bride home, made many loans to James, though often only of half or less of what he asked.[10] None of those expedients led to any real improvement, for in 1599 Home of Wedderburn, the comptroller,[11] absconded rather than face his undertakings. Guests at royal banquets to celebrate weddings and baptisms continued to be required to bring their own food[12] and in 1603 the king had to borrow 10,000 merks from Edinburgh to pay for his journey south. One regular source of revenue which could be much more effectively exploited was the customs, and their yield rose spectacularly in James's later years. So late as 1583 the customs had been set in tack for so little as £4,000 and thirty tuns of wine—a rate which must have been very beneficial to the tacksmen[13]—but within little more than twenty years, thanks to the increase of trade, the imposition in 1597 of a general import duty of 1s. in the £, and more efficient collection, the tacksmen were paying 115,000 merks.[14] Thereafter a revised book of rates was introduced, and by 1616 the rent of the customs had risen to £140,000. Even with this increased revenue, the government could not be carried on without much heavier and more regular taxation. The frequency of taxation had increased since 1580,[15] and, although the

---

[10] *Edinburgh Burgh Records*, IV. 198, 200, 478; *Ibid., 1589-1603*, p. 16.

[11] *R. P. C.*, v. lxxxvii-lxxxviii.

[12] Lee, *Maitland of Thirlestane*, p. 200n; *Source Book of Scottish History*, III. 291-2.

[13] *E. R.*, XXI. 561-4.   [14] In 1609.   [15] 1581, 1583, 1585, 1586.

amounts were at first small, taxes granted in 1588, 1593 and 1597 ran into six figures,[16] and they set a precedent: in 1607 the amount voted was 400,000 merks.   In 1611 the control of the finances was committed to a body of eight " New Octavians," and the ablest of them was probably Sir Gideon Murray of Elibank, who, as treasurer depute from 1612 to 1621, managed things so well that it was possible to defray the cost of the king's visit in 1617 and to carry out a programme of repair and rebuilding at royal residences.   But it was now inevitable that the subjects must become habituated to steady taxation and that a larger proportion of them must help to carry the burden.

In the early years of Charles's reign there were several complaints of financial difficulty, and one reason for the delay of the king's long-promised visit to Scotland until 1633 was the lack of means to make good the ruinous and decaying state of the royal residences, at a time when " your majesty's coffers are so emptied and your majesty's exchequer so exhausted."[17] The need to augment the revenues was, of course, one motive for the act of revocation, but any hope there may have been that the crown would benefit substantially was disappointed. The only remedy could be heavier taxation. Taxes were still granted only at irregular intervals—1606, 1612, 1617, 1621, 1625, 1630 and 1633 —but as the grant in 1625 was for four years, that in 1630 for four years and that in 1633 for six years, the country was now really being taxed annually. Moreover, taxation was now being imposed on a larger proportion of the people. In 1621, after the nobility had pointed out that, as many lands were affected by bonds and reversions, it was inequitable that proprietors alone should bear the burden of a taxation,[18] the estates offered, in addition to a levy of £400,000 on land, the twentieth penny (i.e., 5 per cent) on all annualrents, including the interest on personal bonds. This was characterised as " the greatest taxation that ever was granted in Scotland heretofore in any age."[19] In 1625, when the experiment of taxing annualrents was repeated, there was considerable opposition, and the fear that the device was going to be permanent was justified, for it was adopted again

16 The tax of £100,000 in 1593 was for the birth of the prince. The taxation for James's baptism in 1566 had been only £12,000.
17 *R. P. C.*, ser. II, II. 386, cf. p. 227.   18 *R. P. C.*, ser. I, XII. 379.
19 Balfour, *op. cit.*, II. 84; cf. *R. P. C.*, ser. II, I. 153.

in 1630 and 1633. In the latter year the rate of tax was raised
from one-twentieth to one-sixteenth, and at the same time the
amount by which any interest exceeded 8 per cent was appropriated to the crown. There was no tradition in Scottish constitutional practice of bargaining over taxation and using demands
for taxes as opportunities for securing concessions, but there was
much grumbling at levies on an unprecedented scale and incidence
and with unprecedented frequency. There was another financial
irritant when Charles gave to the Earl of Stirling the right to
mint copper tokens to the value of £100,000 in order to provide
small change, for these " turners " were ultimately condemned as
worthless. It is not clear how far some of the complaints against
the economic controls imposed, and privileges granted, indicate
serious discontent, but it is worth noting that in 1632 the convention of royal burghs ordered that every burgess, on his admission, should swear not to accept any monopolies, and that the
commission of grievances which the king proposed to set up in
1626 was denounced as " nothing els bot the star-chamber courte
of England under ane other name, come doune heir to play the
tyrant."[20]

For years there was friction between the king and his capital:
in 1630 Charles demurred at some of the privileges granted to
Edinburgh in its charter of 1603; his proposal, in 1631, that the
court of session should sit only from October to April, instead
of the customary two terms, was much opposed by the burgh,
which feared loss of business; and in 1636 Charles recommended
that there should be a " constant counsall " for the government
of the burgh because " the frequent chainge of persounes in
publict effaires does breid inconstancie."[21] The taxation of
annualrents bore heavily on the burghs, and Edinburgh's composition for each of the taxations of 1621, 1625 and 1629 was
more than double the amount payable under the old method of
taxation; and in 1633, with the new exaction on interest, the
composition went up to £100,000. In addition, the king made
special demands on Edinburgh which were manifold and costly.
In 1632 he insisted on a new parliament house, to provide accommodation for parliament, the court of session and other courts.
It was an expensive piece of construction, for the site was a
steeply sloping one and the new building involved the removal

[20] Balfour, *Annals*, II. 131.

of three ministers' manses, which had to be replaced. The total cost was £127,000. In 1633 came the king's visit, which cost the town £40,000. Immediately afterwards Charles founded his new bishopric of Edinburgh, and the Dean of Edinburgh was sent to Durham to obtain a plan for the adaptation of the church of St Giles as a cathedral. The partition walls which had divided the building into three churches had to be demolished and new church accommodation had to be found to house the congregations whose places of worship were thus merged in the cathedral: two new churches were projected, one of them at the Castle Hill, but only that at the Tron was completed (at a cost of £14,000). As part of his policy of enriching the clergy, Charles put pressure on Edinburgh to increase the ministers' stipends, although they had been raised at the very end of his father's reign, and, in order to pay the four senior ministers 2,000 merks each and the others 1,300 merks, it was arranged in 1635 that there should be a new assessment on house rentals, to raise 10,000 merks yearly. All these demands left an unmistakable mark on the burgh accounts. Before 1625 the expenditure had only once exceeded £51,000; in 1635-6 it reached nearly £150,000, and year after year the deficit ran into five figures. The burgh did not consider it adequate compensation that in the charter founding the bishopric of Edinburgh Charles made the burgh a city and formally designated it the capital of the kingdom. It was not that the burgesses lacked money. At a time of general increase of prosperity, church collections, in Edinburgh as elsewhere, had risen sharply,[21] the capital was always ready to raise substantial sums when charitable contributions were called for, and a few years later the citizens were to finance military operations against the king. The trouble was reluctance to part with money for purposes unpopular in themselves. There was so little enthusiasm for building the two new churches that the king had to put pressure on the burgh by threatening to enforce statutes against the export of bullion and impose the penalties which had been incurred by their violation. And when, in 1641, Edinburgh was recompensed with part of the revenues of the bishoprics of Orkney and Edinburgh, one of the charters referred

---

[21] Collections at Trinity College were £1,034 in 1626, £2,423 in 1636; at Belhelvie, £31 in 1624, £80 in 1637; at Elgin, £93 in 1614, £184 in 1636 (W. R. Foster, " Ecclesiastical Administration in Scotland," p. 154).

to the expenses borne by the city in the cause of true religion, policy, letters and public works, " especially of late in the erection of a very costly building for the use of the parliament . . ., in the foundation of churches for divine service, as well as in amplifying the academy of King James, and maintaining the professors therein, whereby the public estate of the said burgh was grievously burdened."[22]

The history of the opposition to Charles is almost as long as the history of his reign. The convention of 1625 refused some of the king's demands, made protests against some alleged proposals of his, and discussed subjects not in the official programme of business.[23] When the actions of reduction were threatened a deputation started for London but was stopped at Stamford, whence there was forwarded to Charles a memorial which he denounced as "too high for subjects."[24] It was said, too, that when in 1628 the king sent Lord Nithsdale to negotiate with the lords of erection the latter were prepared to murder the envoy if argument failed.[25] Protests were again made in the convention of 1630, one of them relating to " the great feare the leigis hes conceaved anent his majesteis revocatioun."[26] As early as 1626 the king had been advised to call a parliament as the only means to " settle the fears and jealousies of his subjects,"[27] but although one was summoned for 1628 it was prorogued again and again and did not meet for business until 1633.

At that time ecclesiastical grievances arose alongside the financial and constitutional grievances. During the earlier years of the reign, while the Five Articles of Perth remained the law, they were not enforced, and there were no ecclesiastical innovations. But the atmosphere was changing. For one thing, it was a time of doctrinal re-definition. In Scotland, as in England, Calvinist theology had prevailed in the later sixteenth century and the beginning of the seventeenth, and the Scots Confession of 1616 had reiterated the rigid Calvinist theories of election and reprobation. But in the second and third decades of the seventeenth century the Arminian reaction against Calvinism began to

[22] *Edinburgh Burgh Records, 1626-41*, pp. 335 ff.
[23] The material is to be found in both *A. P. S.*, v. 166, 184 ff., and *R. P. C.*, SER. II, I. 156, 169-70, 173-4, 178.
[24] William Forbes, *Treatise on church lands and tithes* (1705), pp. 261-2.
[25] Burnet, *Own time* (1823), I. 35.
[26] *A. P. S.*, v. 219-20; Row, pp. 350-1.   [27] Balfour, *Annals*, II. 151-2.

attract a number of the younger clergy, in Scotland as in England. With Arminianism there developed a taste for the readoption of practices and ceremonial which had been laid aside at the Reformation, and, while this movement was more conspicuous in England, where it was led by William Laud, in Scotland too there were " Laudians " or " Canterburians," out of sympathy with the still predominant ultra-protestantism but encouraged by the king. Their enemies' accusations of a leaning towards Rome were almost wholly unfounded,[28] and even among the bishops promoted by Charles I there was only one—William Forbes of Edinburgh—who was prepared to go some way in the direction of accommodation with Rome. Jacobean and Caroline bishops alike were in truth very moderate men, seeking a *via media* which would appeal to Lutherans and Calvinists as well as Anglicans, but their moderation did nothing to commend them to contemporaries who condemned ecumenical efforts as tending to " reconciliation with popery."[29]   The discontent aroused by the Five Articles was still smouldering, and any proposals for changes in ceremonial would certainly fan it into flame. Viscount Kenmure, on his deathbed in 1634, said of " the ceremonies " that they were " idolatrous and antichristian, and come from hell," and added, " It is plain popery that is coming among you."[30]

It was, therefore, in changing conditions that the conduct of public worship once more came under consideration. In 1629 the king asked to see the almost forgotten draft liturgy of 1618, but no decisions were reached until after his visit to Scotland in 1633. On that visit he ordered the use of the English Prayer Book in certain places, and his coronation, in the abbey church of Holyrood, was conducted with a splendour of ornament and vesture unfamiliar in Scotland. Hitherto the Scottish clergy had worn black gowns, and when Spottiswoode was in London for King James's funeral he gave up his place in the procession rather than agree to dress like an English bishop. Now, however, parliament passed an act reaffirming the 1606 acknowledgment of the royal prerogative and the 1609 act empowering the king to prescribe apparel,[31] and the king used it to ordain that ministers should wear surplices and bishops should wear rochets. The structure of this piece of legislation was seen as a snare, because

28 Cf. Sinclair Snow, *Patrick Forbes*, pp. 142-4.   29 Grub, II. 371.
30 Wodrow Soc., *Select Biographies*, I. 397.   31 Pp. 206,235 above.

the innovation could not be rejected without a denial of the royal prerogative, and a contemporary annalist—perhaps forgetting that he had said the same thing of the revocation—described it as " the very groundstones of all the mischiefs that hath since followed."[32] Several members of the parliament signed a remonstrance, expressing their apprehension about the measures being prepared by the committee of articles and asking for free discussion of their details by the whole house; but the session was over before the document was ready for presentation.[33] The king was present in the house, to check discussion and to note how members cast their votes, but even so the division figures were challenged by the Earl of Rothes, who alleged that the negative votes equalled the affirmative. The king made his displeasure felt by the opposition through the withholding of honours: a patent for an earldom for Campbell of Loudoun, though it had actually passed the great seal, was not issued. Thus the proceedings in 1633 were even farther than usual from being those of a free parliament.

The opposition, thus thwarted in parliament, turned its attention to approaching the king by way of an extra-parliamentary supplication. Emphasis was laid on Charles's innovations, and his father's government in church and state was implicitly approved by pointed, if hardly tactful, allusions to the wisdom of " blessed King James." Reference was made to the act on the apparel of the clergy and also to the " multiplying of taxations " (though not to the revocation). The manipulation of the late parliament was " contrary to the constitution of a free parliament." Special mention was made of the place of the bishops in the machinery for the election of the lords of the articles and on the use they made of their power to select noblemen " fittest only for the clergy's mystical ends "—a phrase pregnant of the anti-clericalism of the nobles and their distrust of those sacerdotal, seemingly Romanising bishops whom the king was thrusting upon them.[34] The king declined to receive the supplication, and indicated that he thought it improper for his subjects to approach him in this way on such matters. Not only so, but Lord Balmerino, who had revised the supplication, was found guilty of treason,

[32] Balfour, *Annals*, II. 199-200.   [33] Row, p. 364.
[34] The supplication is in Cobbett, *State Trials* (1809), III. 603-4, and Row, pp. 376-81.

by eight votes to seven, in a trial which caused great popular excitement, and was saved from death only by a royal pardon. It seemed that Charles was determined to disregard any attempt by an opposition to state its case and that there was no constitutional means left of making representations which would halt him.

Thus frustrated a second time, the opposition must have decided that only very drastic action indeed could bring the king to his senses and that their only hope was to make an appeal to the people at large. Possibly they reflected that to raise a religious issue, and in particular to appeal to the popular fear of Rome, would be the easiest means to attract wide support. They were certainly conscious that a general assembly, could one be summoned, would provide a better platform for their party than parliament, and might be manipulated by them as the king manipulated parliament. In June 1627 some of the clergy had proposed to petition the king for a general assembly,[35] and at the time of the parliament of 1633 a remonstrance from a group of ministers recalled that a general assembly had been part of the constitution of the church.[36] No assembly had met since 1618, but in the interval, as no general change had been made in the church save the act on apparel in 1633, which could be held to be covered by the acts of 1606 and 1609, there had been no occasion for an assembly; a reason or pretext for demanding the recall of the assembly would, however, arise should further ecclesiastical changes be proposed. If these were the thoughts of the opposition, the king, by his next measures, played directly into their hands.

After the royal visit the question of a new prayer book had been taken up seriously. Churchmen south of the Border, including Laud, were insistent that Scotland should accept the English Book, but the Scottish bishops were equally determined that a book for Scotland must be distinctive. The king, inclined to the English view, in 1634 ordered the Scots to scrap the draft of 1618 and draw up a liturgy on the basis of the English Book. The work was to be that of the Scottish bishops, but they were to follow certain directions from the king and to submit their proposals to him, while he, on his side, had to consult his English church advisers. Thus three, if not four, points of view were involved—those of the older and the younger Scottish bishops,

35 Row, pp. 344-5.   36 Row, p. 358; Balfour, *Annals*, II. 210-6.

those of the king, and those of certain English bishops—and it was only after three years of correspondence and much coming and going between Edinburgh and the court that the liturgy was completed.

Before it was completed, a code of canons was approved by the king in May 1635 and published in January 1636. This code embodied the Five Articles, went a long way towards forbidding extempore prayer, made no explicit mention of general assembly, presbyteries or even kirk sessions, and gave directions about the furnishing of churches. The canons also required acceptance of a liturgy not yet published—and, as we now know, not yet even in its final form. In addition to canons and liturgy, an ordinal was prepared which provided for the creation of ministerial deacons of the Anglican type as well as of presbyters and bishops.

The liturgy itself appeared in 1637. It was by no means devoid of concessions to Scottish practice and prejudice, inserted mainly on the insistence of the Scottish bishops: the Authorised Version of the Bible was used throughout instead of the Prayer Book version; most of the lessons from the Apocrypha were eliminated; the term " presbyter " was used instead of " priest "; a new and well-chosen set of Offertory Sentences was inserted; the consecration prayer in the Communion Office contained the epiclesis or invocation of the Holy Spirit which the Scots had been in the habit of using but which was absent from the English Book. But the effect of those concessions was nullified by other features which alienated Scottish opinion and for which Charles personally had the main responsibility. It was on the king's instructions that a proclamation was prefixed to the book, commanding its use by royal prerogative alone. The king rejected Scottish pleas for a drastic simplification of the Kalendar, and the version ultimately printed contained not only the great festivals but numerous saints' days. Again, the king obstinately insisted on the inclusion of a dozen specified chapters from the Apocrypha. The preface to Morning and Evening Prayer contained a sinister reference to " ornaments to be prescribed." At the consecration prayer in the Communion Office, the rubric permitted the celebrant to stand with his back to the people in front of a communion table placed altar-wise against the east wall. This in itself, even had there been no other grounds for criticism, would have lent colour to the idea that the book was popish. The very physical appearance of the handsome volume, with its pictorial capitals and other decorations and its red as well as black type, was offensive to the austere.

Alarm about Romanising tendencies of King Charles, though wholly unfounded, went back to the very beginning of his reign and to his marriage to a daughter of the French king.[37] There is little evidence that there had been any growth of Romanism in Scotland itself, apart from the work in the west Highlands, from 1619 to 1637, of Irish Franciscan missionaries, who claimed spectacular numbers of converts (most of whom subsequently "lapsed"); elsewhere there were few priests at work save as private chaplains, and their services were mainly in demand by the female members of the families.[38] But the fear of Rome was perhaps all the greater because of the air of mystery and obscurity which surrounded its agents. Next to popery, the second major complaint was the manner of the introduction of the canons and the Prayer Book, which had no constitutional authority behind them. In Scotland, canons and service-books had previously been made or authorised by general assemblies, in England canons had been made by convocations and service-books authorised by parliaments in which the lay people of England could and did speak their minds. The king's action in introducing canons and service-book by his mere *fiat* was not designed to bring Scottish practice into line with that of England; it was an unprecedented example of arbitrary rule.

The events which followed the introduction of the Prayer Book must be related to the state of opinion which had been reflected at the parliament of 1633 and in the supplication of 1634, but since then discontent had been intensified, for in 1636 the country was swept by extravagant rumours of the king's intention to restore so much property to the church that it would possess a third of the wealth of the kingdom, to appoint forty-eight "abbots" who would give royal nominees a preponderance in parliament,[39] and to promote the Bishop of Ross to the office of

37 *R. P. C.*, SER. II, I. 91.
38 David Mathew, *Scotland under Charles I*, pp. 152, 161, 166, 174, 210-1, 216, 238.
39 It was reported that preparations were made to present a minister to the abbey of Lindores in 1636 (Baillie, I. 6; Row, p. 389; Burnet, *Hamiltons* [1852], p. 38), but neither the Register of the Privy Seal nor the Register of Presentations to Benefices gives any support to the fantastic rumours.

treasurer, as the Bishop of London had recently been promoted in England. The rumours may have been deliberately propagated in order to inflame feeling, but they show the dual concern of the nobility for the security of their property and for their constitutional position. Aristocratic opinion was voiced in 1637 in a protest against the " pride and avarice of the prelates seeking to overrule the haill kingdom."[40] There are indications that something like an organised opposition, comprising both peers and ministers, already existed and that it fastened on the introduction of the Prayer Book in the cathedral of St Giles on 23 July 1637 as a most suitable occasion to rouse feeling against the government.[41] It was no difficult matter to incite some of the women of the Edinburgh streets—or apprentices disguised as women—to make a disturbance at the appropriate time. The Jenny Geddes of history is known only as a disturber of the peace on a different occasion—the festivities to celebrate the Restoration of Charles II in 1660—and there is no contemporary support for the picture of her as a devout Scotswoman whose religious susceptibilities were offended by the theology of the Prayer Book of 1637.[42] The real initiative had come from men like Balmerino and Rothes, whose record of resistance to the crown went back to the parliament of 1621, and religion was no qualification for leadership, for Rothes was a man of dissolute life.

Petitions for the withdrawal of the liturgy came pouring in to the council, and crowds from Fife and the Lothians began to gather in Edinburgh. No doubt the petitions, which were all much to the same pattern, were concerted, but they did represent an opinion which was all but unanimous. By 20 September, after only two months, sixty-eight petitions had been received, as well as a lengthy supplication signed by nobility and clergy stating that " this new Book of Common Prayer is introduced and urged in a way which this kirk hath never been acquainted with, and containeth many very material points contrary to . . . the religion and form of worship established . . . since the reformation."[43] The king's response was to issue proclamations which ordered

[40] Spalding, *History of the troubles* (Bannatyne Club), I. 47.

[41] *Ibid.*, pp. 46-8; Guthry, Memoirs, pp. 20-1; " An ' Advertistment ' about the service-book," in *S. H. R.*, XXIII; Burnet, *Hamiltons* (1852), p. 39. The correspondence of Samuel Rutherford discloses communication with Loudoun, Cassillis and Balmerino, Alexander Henderson and David Dickson.

[42] Hill Burton, *History of Scotland*, VI. 150-2*n*.   [43] *R. P. C.*, SER. II, VI. 699.

the petitioners to leave Edinburgh within twenty-four hours and removed the law courts to Linlithgow. When these proclamations were received, on 17 October, there was another riot, directed against Lord Treasurer Traquair, the Bishop of Galloway and the magistrates of Edinburgh—a disturbance more broadly based than the riot of 23 July. The proclamations also caused four of the leaders among the petitioners—Lords Balmerino and Loudoun and two ministers, David Dickson and Alexander Henderson—to produce a supplication (18 October) which craved that the bishops, as the evil counsellors of " so good a king " and as the authorisers and enforcers of the canons and liturgy, should, being interested parties, be removed from the council while the grievances were under consideration.[44] This petition was at once signed by twenty-four nobles and two or three hundred lairds and was fairly well received among ministers also.

This attack on the bishops as a constituent element in the council was only one of many indications that the opposition was already thinking in terms of the estates of the realm and of machinery for expressing the views of the estates and not merely of individuals. Some of the petitioners had come not as individuals but as representatives of burghs, some as " commissioners " of groups of ministers,[45] and one supplication had been drawn up at a meeting of " the small barons of Strathearn." On 15 November, when the approach of winter presumably made it desirable for the general body of the petitioners to disperse and it was decided to elect " commissioners to eschew multitudes," choice was made of two of the gentry for each " province," one minister for each presbytery, one commissioner for each burgh, and six nobles.[46] These delegates, who eventually took more formal shape in the body known as " the Tables," insisted in December on being acknowledged by the council as representatives of the estates and gained a status which made them almost a rival administration.[47] When the representatives of the petitioners again insisted that the king should receive the supplication against the service-book (17 December), the council sent Traquair to explain matters to the king, and when they approved the supplication against the bishops (21 December), the latter thought

---

[44] Ogilvie, " The national petition," *S. H. R.*, XXII. 245; Rothes, p. 50.
[45] Ogilvie, *op. cit.*, p. 242.   [46] Rothes, pp. 4, 19, 23.
[47] *Ibid.*, p. 37; Baillie, I. 40.

it prudent to retire from the council. When Traquair came back, on 15 February, with another proclamation which was quite unyielding, the opposition organised protests and issued a kind of general invitation to the country at large to convene in the capital.

The next stage was marked by the National Covenant, drawn up by Alexander Henderson and Archibald Johnston of Wariston and revised by Rothes, Loudoun and Balmerino, between 23 and 27 February. Henderson (?1583-1646), minister of Leuchars, was to emerge as one of the most statesmanlike of presbyterian ministers. Of Johnston, an advocate (1611-63), it has been said that he was no mere religious fanatic but a man " walking on the dizzy verge of madness."[48] The Covenant was first subscribed at the end of February—on 28 February in Greyfriars' Church by leading nobility and barons, on 1 March by ministers and burgesses. It was soon decided that every burgh and parish must have a copy, that lists should be returned of those who refused to sign and that the Covenant should be " pressed " on the universities.

This great manifesto reflected the underlying causes as well as the immediate occasion of the revolt. In the forefront was an appeal to the anti-popery of the multitude, designed to give the impression that the whole drift of recent policy had been in a popish direction. But the Covenant was not the work of hysterical ultra-protestants; the hand of shrewd lawyers is plain in it. It was an ingenious stroke to begin with a recital of the old anti-popish covenant of 1581, which King James had signed, for this might deceive the uncritical into believing that nothing new was involved. A large part of the Covenant consisted of nothing more than long lists of statutes, favourable to the reformed religion, which the king was held to have violated, and the king was also reminded of his coronation oath. Here was something more than anti-popery, for this was an appeal to the rule of law, against the royal prerogative and the king's arbitrary courses, an appeal to history and to precedent. Here, too, was an assertion of parliamentary authority, for the list of statutes implied that parliament made the laws and that only parliament could change the laws. This was something new in Scottish history, and reflects English influence, for it had never been

[48] C. V. Wedgwood, *The King's Peace*, p. 185.

Scottish doctrine that a statute remained binding until it was formally repealed. But the rule of law meant not only a check on the king in a legislative sense; it meant also security for the material possessions of the king's subjects. While there was much talk of the " liberties " of " kingdom," " subjects " and " people," there was also an assertion of the interdependence of the king's authority, parliament's authority, and the security of the people in " their lands, livings, rights, offices, liberties and dignities." Here again there was probably influence from England, where the familiar contention that property could not be taken from a subject without his consent save by parliament had been reiterated in the Ship Money Case, heard in December 1637. In the Covenant, therefore, it was revealing, if hardly dignified, to assert that the ecclesiastical innovations tended to the subversion of " our liberties, laws *and estates.*"·

Some of the thought of the Covenant had been anticipated in the supplication of 1634; but the Covenant was no mere supplication—it was a call to action. The signatories pledged themselves to disregard the changes recently made by the king until they had been tried and allowed in free assemblies and in parliaments. They specified " the novations lately introduced in public worship, the corruptions of the public government of the kirk and the civil power and places of churchmen "—that is, the Prayer Book, the canons and the recent promotions of bishops to civil offices. They took good care not to condemn episcopal government, which had, of course, been approved long ago by assemblies and parliaments, though some at least of them had it in mind to subject bishops to " caveats," as in 1610; nor could any candid reader of the phraseology hold that it covered the Five Articles of Perth, which equally had parliamentary sanction.[49] Appeal was made not to ecclesiastical independence, or to the legislation of general assemblies (with which the framers of the document were probably at this time unacquainted), but to statute law. It was obviously the intention to revert to the moderate episcopalian regime which had existed during most of the period between the Reformation and King Charles's innovations.

[49] The guarded phraseology of the covenant must be interpreted in the light of the more specific statement made about the same time by Rothes, who, however, included the high commission in the scope of the attack (Rothes, pp. 43, 59, 61).

The Covenant pledged the signatories to mutual defence "against all sorts of persons whatsoever," which might include the king, and to defend the religion " to the utmost of that power that God hath put into our hands." The signatories were thus in a hopeless position from the start, pledged as they were to defend the ecclesiastical system as it had existed before the late innovations, but pledged at the same time to defend the person and authority of the king—who, in the proclamation just brought by Traquair, had taken personal responsibility for the said innovations. At this point the Covenant over-reached itself in its design to be all things to all men; it was at best a formula into which different men could read different meanings, and the appearance of unity which it produced was quite deceptive.

To some of the signatories the Covenant was far more than a judicious piece of constitutionalism, for it focussed concepts and ideals which had their roots deep in the national consciousness. As a bond, it was in the tradition of the innumerable bonds for political, religious—and criminal—purposes in past generations.[50] As a confession of faith, binding a people to a repudiation of popery, it was a further renewal of the Negative Confession originally adopted in 1581 and produced on more than one occasion since; and as a " covenant " it had its context in the " federal theology " which had been fashionable for a generation. But it appealed to convictions more profound. The notion that the Scots were a chosen race, in some ways comparable to the people of Israel, already had a long history: it is to be found, for example, in the Declaration of Arbroath, in 1320, where the Scots claimed that Christ had selected as their missionary St Andrew, the first apostle whom He had called, and where the Scottish leader, Robert I, was likened to Joshua and Judas Maccabeus, those leaders of the Chosen People. Belief in the exceptional purity of the Scottish reformed church strengthened this particular form of national conceit: Knox claimed that all other churches retained " some footsteps of Antichrist and some dregs of papistry," whereas " we (all praise to God alone) have nothing within our churches that ever flowed from that Man of Sin ";[51]

---

[50] Cf. S. A. Burrell, " The Covenant Idea as a revolutionary symbol in Scotland," in *Church History*, XXVII. 338-50; G. D. Henderson, " The idea of the covenant in Scotland," in *The Burning Bush*, pp. 61-74. There was an English parallel in the " Association " of 1584 against the rights of any person on whose behalf Elizabeth might be assassinated.   [51] Knox, II. 3.

and James VI, so it seems, pandered to a presbyterian audience
by making a similar claim.[52] But it was left to the era of the
Covenant to provide national conceit with a theological foundation.   Samuel Rutherford had written in 1633: " Scotland,
whom our Lord took off the dunghill and out of hell and made a
fair bride to Himself. . . .   He will embrace both us, the little
young sister, and the elder sister, the Church of the Jews."[53]
Johnston of Wariston, though responsible for the legalism and
antiquarianism of the Covenant, yet considered the day of its
signature to be " that glorious marriage day of the kingdom with
God," he saw the parallel between Scotland and Israel, " the only
two sworn nations to the Lord," and he could even write of
" Scotland's God."[54]   The claim was carried no higher when a
covenanter later in the century remarked that " Scotland is the
betrothed Virgin: We were espoused to Jesus Christ, and joined
to Him, by a marriage covenant, never to be forgotten."[55]   Essentially the covenanting movement was, and as its history unfolded
it long continued to be, an aristocratic and conservative reaction.
But the concept of the Covenant as a perpetual undertaking by
the people of Scotland and as a contract between them and God,
was one which was to harness the vitality of a nation.

[52] Calderwood, v. 106.
[53] Rutherford, *Letters* (1894), No. xxviii, pp. 87-8.
[54] Wariston, *Diary*, I. 265, 322-3, 334-5, 344.
[55] Alexander Shiels, *Hind let Loose* (1744), p. 742.

17

THE REVOLUTION OF THE 1640s

The king's choice of a representative to deal with his covenanted subjects was the Marquis of Hamilton, appointed commissioner on 8 May 1638. Hamilton (1606-49), who had married a niece of the royal favourite, Buckingham, had seen little of Scotland and its people save when he had been sent from the court to negotiate the details of the taxation of 1633, and he lacked stability and consistency. It would, however, have been hard to find a leading peer in Scotland who was detached from the opposition but was at the same time free from any taint of association with Roman catholicism, and Hamilton had the advantage that, although his mother was a militant ultra-protestant of the Glencairn family, he was personally uncommitted. The commissioner brought a proclamation conceding the suspension of the Prayer Book and canons, but the demand for an assembly and a parliament was to be granted only on condition that the Covenant was repudiated. Charles did not have it in mind to make permanent concessions, for he authorised his commissioner " to flatter them with what hopes you please . . . until I be ready to suppress them."[1]

In any event, it was doubtful if the suspension of the Prayer Book and canons was now enough, for some of the covenanters had moved on to criticism of episcopal government. So late as July Rothes was trying to reassure the episcopalians of Aberdeen that no more was being demanded than " bishops limited by all strait caveats,"[2] but in April, when presbyteries were here and

[1] Burnet, *Hamiltons* (1852), p. 70.
[2] Rothes, p. 216; cf. *Hamilton Papers* (Camden Soc.), p. 5.

there carrying out ordinations without consulting the bishops,[3] Johnston had begun to look for " the bishops' destruction," and in May he expounded a concept of the development of revolutionary thought until nothing less would serve than " the utter overthrow of episcopacy, that great-grandmother of all our corruptions, novations, usurpations, diseases and troubles."[4]

The Covenant had been signed by the great majority of the nobles and also by many lawyers who, if only from timidity or ambition, would not resist the general drift. To deal with a movement so strong in hereditary leadership and legal skill would have taxed any administration, but most of King Charles's councillors were either sympathetic to the opposition or unwilling to make a stand against public feeling. Even the bishops were not all resolute, for Archbishop Spottiswoode was heard to remark that the only course should be to lay aside the liturgy and not to press the subjects with it any more,[5] and the last of the many acts of mediation in his long career was a proposal for a qualification of the Covenant which would make it acceptable to the king.[6] The actions of other councillors look like treachery, but it was not then accepted that men should decline office, or resign, rather than be associated with a policy of which they did not approve. On the occasion of the initial riot in Edinburgh, although it had been understood that the councillors should be present at the first reading of a Prayer Book authorised by their own proclamation, Lord Lorne and Treasurer Traquair contrived to be absent; this pair were associated, too, with the protest against the " pride and avarice of prelates,"[7] and Traquair declared in December that he would lay down his treasurer's staff rather than practise the liturgy.[8] When, in February 1638, the council met at Stirling to issue a proclamation just brought by Traquair from the court, Lorne was again an absentee and Sir Thomas Hope would not concur. Hope, who had been counsel for the ministers tried for treason in 1605, had not laid aside his sympathies when he became Lord Advocate in 1626. He now interpreted the law to suit the opposition: his denial that the Covenant was illegal made it impossible for Hamilton to denounce the signatories as traitors, and later in the year he gave his opinion that episcopacy was

3 Burnet, *op. cit.*, p. 53.   4 Wariston, *Diary* (S. H. S.), I. 332, 338, 347.

5 *R. P. C.*, SER. II. VII, 7.   6 Burnet, *op. cit.*, p. 74.

7 P. 311 above.   8 Rothes, p. 43.

contrary to the laws of church and kingdom.[9] From a council so composed, resolute action could not be expected.

It was difficult to see how the situation could be restored except by external force. The opposition prepared to anticipate any such attempt. As early as February 1638 they began to raise funds for the purchase of arms and ammunition on the continent; they kept a close watch to prevent the strengthening of Edinburgh Castle; and throughout the summer they were mustering and drilling. The government on its side provisioned Dalkeith Castle, the lieutenants of the northern counties of England were instructed to muster their trained bands, and the king prepared for action by sea as well as land. It was soon clear, too, that if there was going to be war there would be action over a distinct issue in the west. Kintyre, which had been held by the Argyll Campbells for a generation, was now claimed by Randal Mac-Donnell, Earl of Antrim, who had been brought up at court and had married the widow of the Duke of Buckingham. To meet this threat, Lord Lorne, who was to succeed his father as Earl of Argyll in the late autumn of 1638, made his own military preparations, while the protestant settlers in Ulster, who were now signing the covenant, were also ready to take a hand.

Hamilton returned to England in late July, and on 10 September the king conceded the revocation of the Prayer Book, canons, high commission and Five Articles, agreed to the calling of a general assembly and authorised the signing of the Negative Confession of 1581, without the additions made to it in the National Covenant. Of this " King's Covenant " the opposition was bitterly critical, though for contradictory reasons—Hope pronounced that the document condemned episcopacy, Wariston characterised the subscription of it as " atheism and perjury."[10] It was, however, signed by some, especially in Aberdeenshire, where the covenanters were encountering the most serious opposition. In Aberdeen city and university, the episcopalian cause had been fostered by a succession of able and high-minded bishops and had been soundly based on theology by the academic " doctors." The Marquis of Huntly, too, was loyal to the episcopalian establishment, as were his wife and children (although his mother was a practising Roman catholic). It was in vain that the covenanters tried to win him over by offering money to relieve his

---

[9] *Hamilton Papers*, pp. 8, 9, 50-1.   [10] Wariston, *Diary*, I. 392-3.

financial embarrassment. To Aberdeen, therefore, there went in July a mission consisting of James Graham, Earl of Montrose (1612-50), some other covenanting notables and three ministers. The ministers were refused access to the city pulpits and were worsted in their debates with the theologians of the university, who fastened on the undertaking in the Covenant to " resist all " (including, by implication, the king) and on the interpretation put on the Confession of 1581, which the covenanters now held to have condemned episcopacy and (by anticipation) the Five Articles.

The general assembly was summoned by proclamation to meet at Glasgow in November 1638. There had been no assembly for twenty years, and even those who were honestly resolved to follow precedent can hardly have been clear about the composition of an assembly and the method of electing its members. According to an assembly act of 1597, each presbytery was to send three ministers and one " baron," and each royal burgh to send a commissioner, but this act had not been invariably, if at all, observed. Rothes told Hamilton in June 1638 that a " free assembly " should have two ministers and one " elder " from each presbytery. The question of " barons " was thus entangled with that of " elders." According to the second Book of Discipline, elders were to be " ecclesiastical persons " and not laymen, but elders were not yet being ordained for life and in any event non-ministerial members of any kind had not yet become a constituent element in presbyteries. Nor had elders, as such, ever yet sat in general assemblies. Yet a protest made in 1638, against elders as voters in the election of commissioners of presbyteries and as members of a general assembly, was overruled, on the false ground that it was contrary to the custom of the church.[11] The fact was that the covenanters were determined to pack the assembly. It was decided that the ministers and " gentlemen " of every presbytery should consider who were best fitted to be commissioners to the assembly, and that " the ablest and best affected gentlemen in ilk paroch be put on the kirk session that so they may be in optione to be commissioners from the presbitries."[12] Thus lay supporters of the Covenant were mustered as

---

[11] *Edinburgh Burgh Records, 1626-41*, p. 321.

[12] Rothes, p. 169. As elders were usually nominated or co-opted and not elected, it was easy to manipulate the non-ministerial membership.

" elders," so that they could attend presbyteries; then, if an elder from each parish turned up at the presbytery, the chances were that laymen would be in a majority, since some parishes might be vacant and some non-covenanting ministers had already been deprived.[13] The covenanters therefore controlled the elections to the assembly. The " elders " who came to Glasgow consisted of seventeen peers, nine knights, and twenty-five lairds, and there were also forty-seven burgh representatives.[14] " Not a gown was among them all, but many had swords and daggers about them."[15] It is true that there were also 142 ministers, but all who had been members of chapters, who had sat on the court of high commission, who had accepted the canons and Prayer Book or who had been justices of the peace, were disqualified, and others were excluded on various pretexts. The bishops, too, although they had a place in the assembly according to unvarying practice ever since the Reformation, knew that they dared not attend. All in all, the presbyterian system proved admirably adapted to be an instrument of the aristocracy and gentry. The covenanters had challenged the freedom of parliament, but it was now the turn of the king's commissioner to challenge the freedom of the assembly: " You have called for a free general assembly; . . . let God and the world judge whether the least shadow or footstep of freedom can be discerned in this assembly."[16]

Despite the manipulation of the " elections," the opposition came to Glasgow still talking merely of " cautions " and " limitations " of prelates. After all, a complete presbyterian system had never yet existed, a generation had now come to maturity knowing no system of church government other than one in which bishops had had an important part, and few were aware that the office of bishop had ever been condemned. The decisive event, therefore, was the masterly stroke of Johnston of Wariston, as clerk, in producing the old registers of the assemblies, with their acts condemnatory of bishops. This, he said, gave " a solid foundation " to his party, without which, he admitted, they would have " buildit upon sand," and it " cleared all their minds that

---

[13] Burnet, *Hamiltons* (1852), pp. 130-1.

[14] N. Meldrum, " The General Assembly of 1638 " (Edinburgh Ph.D. thesis, 1924). It appears that the rule was to send three ministers from each presbytery, as the assembly of 1638 was itself to ordain.

[15] Burnet, *Hamiltons* (1852), p. 119; *Hamilton Papers*, p. 59.

[16] Burnet, *Hamiltons* (1852), pp. 128-9.

episcopacy was condemned in this church."[17] When the assembly proceeded to vote itself capable of judging the bishops, Hamilton ordered the moderator to dissolve it, but the moderator was intimidated into disregarding the order, whereupon the commissioner left the house (28 November). The assembly went on to annul the canons, liturgy and Five Articles, to abolish the high commission court and to depose the bishops. Such actions, in defiance of statute law, could be justified only by highflown claims for ecclesiastical independence, and talk about " the prerogative of the Son of God "[18] implied that a majority in the assembly could disregard parliament, king and country alike.

The assembly thus ended (on 20 December) in an open breach, and both sides prepared more seriously for an appeal to arms. At the end of 1638 and the beginning of 1639 the covenanters went on with their systematic recruiting and accumulation of supplies, and they were in touch with the disaffected in England. Trained officers were available among Scots who had been engaged as mercenaries on the continent and who were now seeking new paymasters, as the Thirty Years' War no longer offered steady employment. Outstanding among them was Alexander Leslie (?1580-1661), a marshal in Germany, who had been in Scotland in 1635 and had married his son to the daughter of the Earl of Rothes, an opposition leader who happened to be head of the house of Leslie. The marshal, who had kept abreast of developments at home in 1638 and had organised the signing of the covenant by Scots soldiers abroad,[19] arrived in Scotland again at the time of the Glasgow assembly. Among other returning soldiers who joined the covenanters were Livingston of Brighouse, Alexander Hamilton, brother of the first Earl of Haddington, and the third Earl of Lothian. Some sided with the king—James King, later Lord Eythin, Patrick Ruthven, later Earl of Forth, and Donald Mackay, Lord Reay—but the covenanting side, with its aristocratic leadership, made the stronger appeal to men who were either themselves conscious of kinship with noble families or accustomed to fighting under captains with long pedigrees. The army which the covenanters ultimately sent against the king comprised the majority of the peerage, and the thoughts of its officers were as far from austerity as they were

[17] Wariston, *Diary*, I. 402.   [18] *A Large Declaration*, p. 239.
[19] Baillie, I. 111; Spalding, I. 87-8.

from any intention to transfer power to a new social group: " I must trouble your lordship," wrote one, " to desire that I may have two nightcaps and two pair of slippers, one grass green, the other sky colour, with gold or silver lace upon them."[20] The colonels were nobles, the captains were lairds of substance, the lieutenants were experienced soldiers, and the general's bodyguard consisted of lawyers; the privates were mainly " stout young ploughmen " accustomed to obey their lairds.[21] The part of the burgesses was to provide funds: William Dick of Braid, provost of Edinburgh, lent 200,000 merks in the spring of 1639 to " the nobility, gentry and commissioners of burghs."[22] The estates of Scotland were arrayed behind the Covenant.

The king planned a fourfold attack: he left London on 27 March for York, whence he was to cross the Border with the main army; Hamilton, with the fleet, was to land 5,000 men at Aberdeen to co-operate with Huntly, who at Christmas had shown himself an unrepentant episcopalian; Wentworth, the king's lieutenant in Ireland, was to send an Irish force to Dumbarton; and Antrim was to invade Kintyre. But the grand strategy hardly got beyond paper, partly because the royal forces were so badly equipped and supplied that they were demoralised and almost mutinous, and partly because the covenanters took action which anticipated and nullified the king's. Before the royal forces could reach Scotland, the covenanters had taken possession of the castles of Dalkeith and Dumbarton and had placed a boom across the harbour of Leith. In the north-east, Montrose acted in February to prevent a gathering of the Gordons and shortly afterwards decoyed Huntly to Edinburgh. The local covenanters were far too weak to hold Aberdeen, and one of the ships from Hamilton's fleet was able to land there—the sole success of the entire naval venture; otherwise Hamilton could do no more than cruise ineffectively off the east coast. Montrose finally recaptured Aberdeen on 19 June. The king's forces had advanced to Berwick at the end of May, and some of them crossed the Tweed, but had to withdraw in face of Leslie, who encamped on Duns Law on 5 June. Peace negotiations were conducted in the king's camp from 11 to 18 June, leading to the pacification of

---

[20] *Correspondence of the Earls of Ancram and Lothian*, i. 117.   [21] Baillie, i. 211-2.
[22] *Edinburgh Burgh Records, 1626-41*, p. 214. The public debt to Dick ultimately amounted to £500,000, and he was ruined for lack of re-payment.

Berwick, whereby Charles agreed to come to Scotland in the early autumn for meetings of parliament and assembly, and both sides undertook to disband their armies.

But the covenanters did not disband their army, and the king soon showed that he had no real intention of giving way. First he referred to the Glasgow assembly as a " pretended " assembly, and announced that bishops were to sit in the new assembly, but later he decided not to summon bishops to assembly or parliament, so that he would be able to repudiate the meetings as irregular. Meantime, Hamilton, who resigned the office of commissioner, was appointed to intrigue with the covenanters, while the king invited fourteen of their leaders to meet him at Berwick. He gained nothing: five accepted the invitation, including Montrose, but intimated that if bishops were not abolished in Scotland the Scots would join in the attack on the episcopate in England. Charles retaliated by deciding not to attend the assembly or the parliament, and on 3 August he left for London. On 12 August, at Edinburgh, Traquair opened the assembly, which not only re-enacted the legislation of the Glasgow assembly and reiterated the condemnation of episcopacy as contrary to the constitution of the Church of Scotland, but declared the office of bishop to be contrary to the law of God—an assertion which the king, as king of England, could not possibly accept. The parliament, opened on 31 August, was " free " only in the sense that it was controlled by the covenanters instead of by the king, and it gave the assembly's legislation the force of law.

By the beginning of 1640 the king had in his hands a letter from the covenanting leaders to the King of France, and he hoped to use it to rally England to him, but when the Short Parliament met (13 April) it ignored the king's appeal for supply and concentrated on English grievances, leaving Charles worse off than before, for the fact that he had called a parliament had shaken the whole structure of his administration. It was harder than ever to raise and pay an army, and the troops who were embodied, suspecting that their officers were engaged in some popish project, were not enthusiastic for a " Bishops' War " against the protestant Scots. On the day the king left for York (20 August), the Scots crossed the Tweed, headed by Montrose. Ignoring Berwick, which had been fortified against them, they advanced to the Tyne, routed the English at the ford of Newburn, above Newcastle, and occupied that town (30 August). While Charles was still at York, consulting a council of peers and being advised that he must call another parliament, a truce was signed, whereby the covenanters were to occupy the six northern counties of England and to be paid £850 a day. Negotiations proceeded at Ripon[23] and then at London. The English parliament which Charles had been forced to call participated in framing the peace terms and the Scots commissioners furthered political and ecclesiastical co-operation between the king's enemies in the two kingdoms. Peace was not finally concluded until June 1641. The king then undertook to ratify the latest legislation of the Scottish parliament and to remove his garrisons from Berwick and Carlisle. Consultations were to be held on the reform of the English church and the Scots were to receive an indemnity of £300,000, of which the first instalment was to be paid before they would evacuate England.

The estates of Scotland, in arms for the Covenant, had won a complete and almost bloodless victory over the king, and, through the effect of their proceedings on events in England, had contributed to his ultimate downfall. Charles did little to win, or to form, a royalist party, concerned as he was rather with vain attempts to appease the insatiable opposition. Yet his concessions were always too little and too late, for he granted " today that which would have abundantly satisfied yesterday, and the next day that which would have satisfied this day ";[24] in the end he conceded all, but " it was ever his constant unhappiness to give nothing in time."[25] There is little doubt that, given leadership, an effective royalist party could have been formed earlier than it was. Besides the general resistance at Aberdeen and in other traditionally conservative areas, like Angus and Moray, the universities of St Andrews and Glasgow had opposed the Covenant at first. Academic and ministerial opposition might have expected leadership from the bishops, but both the archbishops were over seventy, and Spottiswoode, lamenting that " now all that we have been doing these thirty years past is thrown down at once,"[26] had fled to England, where he died on 26 November 1639. The

23 *Notes on the treaty carried on at Ripon* (Camden Soc.).
24 Kirkton, *Secret and True History of the Church of Scotland*, p. 47.
25 Baillie, II. 373.   26 Spottiswoode, I. p. cx.

only bishop to show real spirit was Brechin, who went into his cathedral with a service-book and a brace of pistols. Among laymen, too, there were active opponents of the covenant, like Sir Robert Spottiswoode, the lord president, and Sir John Hay, the lord clerk register, as well as men of a more detached cast of mind, such as Drummond of Hawthornden, who in September 1639 lampooned the revolutionary party's disregard of experience and authority:

> Bickering upon the Sunday shall be lawful against coaches in the High Street, provided there be either bishop, new councillor, or non-covenanter, in them. . . . It shall be lawful . . . to choose a dictator, providing he can neither read nor write. . . . The books of the Apocrypha being taken away from the Bible, [Buchanan's] *De jure regni* be in place thereof insert. . . . It shall be lawful for the schoolboys . . . to take the schools against the masters, put them out and in their places appoint new . . . masters, for the space of twenty days, in perpetual remembrance of our happy and blessed relief from the ecclesiastic and episcopal government.[27]

But there was not a potential lay leader of the first rank, for Huntly was too reserved and aloof. The king's enemies, by contrast, were all the time strengthening their hold: ministers had to conform or be deprived, the people were controlled through the pulpits and the machinery for excommunication, and local committees, set up by the covenanters, usurped many of the functions of administration.[28]

Opposition to the prevailing faction did become militant not because of the rallying of anti-covenanters but because of the disruption of the unity of the covenanting movement itself. The abrogation of the Five Articles, the overthrow of episcopal government and the abolition of the court of high commission, though going beyond the grievances which had occasioned the revolt and beyond the letter of the National Covenant, had not been illogical. But the victors went on to constitutional changes, alliance with the English parliament and ultimately the destruction of the monarchy—none of them in accord with even the spirit of the Covenant. Divisions therefore arose between those who considered that when the initial aims of the revolt had been achieved the revolt itself should come to an end and those who

27 David Masson, *Drummond of Hawthornden*, pp. 325-7.
28 This is shown in the *Minute-book kept by the war committee of the covenanters in the stewartry of Kirkcudbright in 1640 and 1641* (Kirkcudbright, 1855).

became so obsessed with means that they lost sight of ends—those, it might almost be said, who were determined to keep the revolt going for its own sake. The Covenant itself had been only a means, but it was elevated into an end when the assembly (in August 1639) and later the parliament agreed that acceptance of the Covenant should be enforced. It was hard to reconcile this with the " liberty " of which the Covenant had spoken. At each stage in the development of covenanting policy beyond its initial aims, the support which that policy commanded diminished.

The first matters to cause disputes were constitutional, arising from the novel situation in the parliament of 1639, when, for the first time, a spiritual estate was wholly lacking. The royal commissioner nominated the nobles for the committee of articles, but was unable to find nobles who would put the king's cause before that of the Covenant. Montrose, Huntly and others were uneasy at the prospective elimination of royal influence, and felt that the king should be compensated for the loss of the bishops, if only by the admission to parliament of fourteen laymen of his own nomination. Consequently, when it was proposed, on the motion of Argyll, that in future each estate should choose its own representatives on the committee of articles, the resolution was carried by only one vote. Even more revolutionary conditions obtained in June 1640, when, although some had their misgivings, parliament reassembled in defiance of a royal prorogation, elected its own president and formally asserted the legality of its meeting. The clerical estate and the committee of articles were now alike abolished; such committees as should be necessary were in future to be freely elected. A triennial act provided that parliament should meet every three years at least and that it was to assemble automatically, without special summons, at the time and place appointed by the preceding parliament, unless the king should summon it earlier. The constitutional revolution went still farther in the autumn of 1641, when the king had to grant that councillors, officers of state and senators of the college of justice should be chosen with the advice of parliament, or, if parliament was not sitting, of the privy council, and were to hold office not *durante beneplacito* but *ad vitam aut culpam*. This was an outrage to those who believed in a balanced constitution, and constitutionalists now found themselves in opposition not to the king but to the prevailing party.

A second cause of division among the covenanters arose from suspicions that some individuals, particularly Argyll, were putting their private aims before the general good of the cause. Argyll's record had all along been a curious one. He went to the Glasgow assembly as a privy councillor, but remained after the commissioner withdrew, although he was not an elected member and had not at that time taken the covenant. From that point he showed a tendency to exploit the covenant in the interests of his own aggrandisement. In 1639 he acquired claims on lands in Lochaber and Badenoch in security for some of the debts of his brother-in-law, Huntly, and both in those areas and Angus, while acting as an agent of the covenanters, he interpreted his commission in the interests of his house, dealing harshly with clans and families which happened to be its hereditary enemies. There was also a suggestion that he should take charge of the whole country north of the Forth, while Hamilton superintended the south. Opposition to Argyll centred more and more around Montrose, who protested against the direction of affairs by " a few " and in August 1640, along with seventeen other nobles and gentlemen, signed the Cumbernauld Bond, a pledge to promote the " public ends " of the covenant in opposition to the " particular and indirect practising of a few."[29] In the summer of 1641 he wrote to the king to offer, on his own initiative, counsels of moderation, and when a royal reply was intercepted he was imprisoned (11 June).

The proceedings of the king, before and during his visit to Scotland in the autumn of 1641 (14 August-17 November), still did little to help the growth of a royalist party, though he was active enough in intrigue. He worked at first for an understanding with Rothes, who had come to share in the distrust of Argyll, and Rothes tried to detach Loudoun also from Argyll's side.[30] On the other hand, Hamilton, who had temporarily pursued a policy of mediation, but now saw reconciliation impossible, had gone over to Argyll. After the death of Rothes at the end of August closed one of the king's schemes, he encouraged some of his entourage to intrigue with the covenanting armed forces. These intrigues were evidently connected with the " Incident," an alleged plot to kidnap Argyll, Hamilton and the Earl of Lanark (Hamilton's brother), who had been secretary

29 *Memorials of Montrose* (Maitland Club), i. 254-5.　　　30 Rothes, p. 225.

for Scotland since the death of the Earl of Stirling. It suited Argyll and Hamilton to appear to be in danger from the king's machinations. The name of Montrose, who had recently offered to prove Hamilton a traitor, was linked with the plot, though without justification. The king in the end made nothing of his schemes. He heard many fine speeches, but gained neither popularity nor confidence. He was forced to appoint Loudoun as chancellor, while the treasury was put into commission with Argyll as chief commissioner. Several nobles who had not already signed the Covenant were now compelled to do so, and, before leaving Scotland, Charles included Balmerino and Cassillis in a new list of councillors, knighted Wariston and appointed him a lord of session, created Leslie Earl of Leven, and promoted Henderson to the deanery of the chapel royal, with 4,000 merks a year. He had done much for his enemies, nothing whatever for his friends, except to secure the release of Montrose.

Much more serious division of opinion arose over the question of alliance with the English parliament when its war against the king started in August 1642. A political alliance could have been justified on the prudential ground that should Charles be victorious in England he would probably try to reverse the verdict in Scotland. It is also true that the Scots had for some time been alive to the possible advantages of an economic alliance which would enable them to share in English trade.[31] But the primarily ecclesiastical league which was in the end concluded reflected the international character of presbyterianism and the close relations which had existed between the English and Scottish presbyterian parties ever since those early days when Cartwright and Travers, the leaders of Elizabethan presbyterianism, had been invited to chairs at St Andrews.[32] In contrast to presbyterianism, however, the Church of England had a national, insular character, noticeable as early as Mary Tudor's reign, when English exiles had been resolved to have " the face of an English church,"[33] and this was enough to make the prospects for Scottish interference in England no more promising now than they had been in the 1590s, when a critic of English puritanism wrote of

[31] E.g., *Edinburgh Burgh Records, 1626-41*, p. 253 (Dec. 1641); cf. *S. H. R.*, XLI. 84-6.

[32] Cf. " Scottish presbyterian exiles in England, 1584-88," in *Scot. Church Hist. Soc. Records*, XIV.

[33] Arber (ed.), *A brief discourse of the troubles at Frankfort* (1908), pp. 54, 62.

" English Scottizing for discipline."[34] Besides, while the Londoners and some others in England were as vocal against bishops as any Scots, it was doubtful if they spoke for the majority of the English people and it was even more doubtful if English anti-episcopal sentiment was predominantly presbyterian. The Scots were repeatedly warned of the growth of independency, which was as hostile to presbyteries as it was to bishops. Undeterred, the assembly of 1642, which had received a letter expressing the desire of the " most godly and considerable part " in England for conformity in doctrine, government and worship, appointed a commission to consider the reformation of the church throughout Great Britain and sent John Maitland, son of the Earl of Lauderdale, as a representative to Westminster.[35]

At the end of 1642 the Scots received appeals from both parliament and king. Hamilton, who had arrived in Scotland in June to try to prevent Scottish intervention on behalf of parliament, was working along intelligent lines which were in the end to bring about a real reaction against the zealots: he tried to undermine the position of Loudoun, the chancellor, who favoured intervention, and to muster opposition which would outvote Argyll in parliament, on the understanding that the king would guarantee the continuance of presbyterianism in Scotland. The privy council actually decided, though by the narrowest majority —eleven to nine—that only the king's appeal should be published. Thereupon the council received rival petitions, one demanding that the parliament's appeal should be published, the other— " the cross petition "—that the Scots should do nothing to prejudice the king's honour or the peace of Scotland.[36] The cross petition was condemned by the general assembly and denounced from the pulpits, while presbyteries were instructed to proceed against persons who tried to obtain signatures to it. The council ultimately yielded to the demand for the publication of parliament's message, but there were now clearly two parties in Scotland, one of them strong in the council, the other dominant in the general assembly.

In the spring of 1643, Loudoun and Henderson visited Charles

34 Richard Bancroft, *Daungerous positions and proceedings*, headings of Books ii, iii and iv.
35 Peterkin, *Records of the kirk of Scotland* (1838), pp. 295-6, 329-30. Maitland (1616-82) succeeded as Earl of Lauderdale in 1646.
36 Burnet, *Hamiltons* (1852), pp. 263 ff.

at Oxford and told him that he could prevent Scottish intervention only by agreeing to the reform of the Church of England. Although parliament was not due to meet again until 1644, the party favourable to intervention called a convention, without royal warrant, for 22 June 1643. Montrose and his associates did not attend, many others attended only to protest. Offers were sent to England, and on 7 August English commissioners arrived, to crave an alliance which would give parliament the immediate military assistance which it desperately needed and also assure London its supplies of Scottish coal. By this time the general assembly had met (2 August), and nobles were attending the latter in the morning and the convention in the afternoon. In the Solemn League and Covenant, drafted by 17 August, only ten days after the arrival of the English commissioners, provision was made for the preservation of the reformed faith in Scotland, the reformation of religion in England and Ireland in doctrine, worship, discipline and government, " according to the Word of God and the example of the best reformed churches," the assimilation of the churches in the three kingdoms, the extirpation of popery and prelacy, the preservation of the rights and privileges of the parliaments and liberties of the kingdoms, and the " firm peace and union " of England and Scotland. The phrase "according to the Word of God " was inserted on the insistence of the English, who also decided that the clause was for " limitation " and not merely for " approbation "; but on the Scottish side there was no doubt as to where the best reformed church was to be found or as to what the Word of God dictated. The English accepted the Solemn League on 25 September and a military bargain was concluded in November, when it was agreed that 18,000 foot and 2,000 horse from Scotland should serve the English parliament. Loudoun, Maitland and Wariston went to London as commissioners at the beginning of 1644 and in February a " committee of both kingdoms " was set up.[37]

The Solemn League and Covenant, as distinct from the military agreement, was of negligible importance so far as the English partner was concerned; but its effects on Scotland were to be profound. That it was Scotland's mission to presbyterianise England became an obsession with many Scots—for a brief space

[37] *Correspondence of the Scots Commissioners in London, 1644-6*, was edited by H. W. Meikle for the Roxburgh Club in 1917.

actually with a majority—and as long as this obsession lasted harmonious Anglo-Scottish relations were impossible. Besides, the concept of Anglo-Scottish conformity was to leave its enduring mark on Scottish presbyterianism, through the work of the Westminster Assembly. As early as 12 June 1643 the English parliament proposed to undertake the reform of the Church of England in such a way as would be " most agreeable to God's holy word and most apt to procure . . . nearer agreement with the Church of Scotland and other reformed churches abroad," and decided to take the advice of an assembly of divines. The Scots were invited to send representatives, and on 19 August, accordingly, the Scottish general assembly commissioned five ministers and three elders (the Earl of Cassillis, Lord Maitland and Johnston of Wariston) to take part in discussions to further " the union of this island in one form of kirk government, one confession of faith, one catechism, one directory for the worship of God." These Scots were not members of the assembly, which consisted of over a hundred Englishmen, but the Confession, Larger and Shorter Catechisms, Directory of Public Worship and Form of Church Government, which were prepared by " the assembly of divines at Westminster, with the assistance of commissioners from the Church of Scotland," were adopted by the Scottish general assembly and parliament. There was little chance, even at the time, that these documents would receive equal recognition in the country of their origin, for the Westminster Assembly itself revealed deep differences and outside the assembly English opinion was even more strongly against the Scottish model. In England there was far more concern for the power of the laity in the church, whether as members of local congregations who would elect their ministers and support them with their own contributions or as members of a parliament which would be sovereign under a presbyterian system as under an episcopalian. The Scots, who were far more clerical and far less democratic, thought the English preference was for " a lame Erastian presbytery."[38]

The Scottish government did its best to strangle opposition to the English alliance by enforcing subscription to the Solemn League by severe penalties, and in January 1644 an army crossed the Border, led by Alexander Leslie (who had sworn never

[38] Baillie, II. 362.

to take arms against the king again) and with the cavalry under David Leslie, also trained in the Swedish army. But division of opinion in Scotland was now so deep as to lead to civil war. Months before, the king had been urged by Montrose to authorise action in Scotland to anticipate intervention on behalf of parliament, but at that time he had preferred to listen to Hamilton (created a duke on 12 April 1643), who assured him that a guarantee of presbytery in Scotland would suffice to keep the Scots neutral. Events had now demonstrated the failure of Hamilton's schemes, and he left Scotland in November 1643 for Oxford, where he found himself under arrest. At length, on 1 February 1644, Montrose (now created a marquis) was appointed lieutenant general of the king's forces in Scotland. It was intended that he should have the co-operation of the Marquis of Newcastle, the king's commander in the north of England, and that there should be a simultaneous descent on Scotland from Ireland. There was also the prospect of collaboration with a royalist movement in Aberdeenshire, where in March Gordon of Haddo stimulated Huntly into acting against his son, Lord Gordon, who was holding Aberdeen for the covenanters. In April Montrose invaded Scotland with a mainly English force of about 1,000 men, but found the Borders hostile or at best lukewarm, and had to withdraw. The defeat of the king's northern forces at Marston Moor, on 2 July—when a charge by David Leslie's cavalry and the stubborn resistance of a part of the Scots infantry were decisive—was fatal to the plan for effective English help; and in the north-east, after Huntly had retired in the face of an advance by Argyll, Haddo was executed. The wider royalist strategy thus collapsed, and all that Montrose could salvage from the wreck was some Irish co-operation. Alasdair MacDonald, a near kinsman of the Earl of Antrim and a son of MacDonald of Colonsay (who bore the name of Coll *Ciotach*, or " left-handed "—a name sometimes given to the son), had landed in Ardnamurchan early in July at the head of 1,600 men raised by Antrim from among exiled MacDonalds and MacLeans. When, in August, Montrose made his way to the Highlands, in disguise and with only two companions, his first objective was to effect a junction with this force.

A victory at Tippermuir (1 September) opened Perth to Montrose. Less than a fortnight later he fought his way into

Aberdeen and—provoked by the killing of a drummer boy who had accompanied his messenger to the garrison—permitted his troops to sack that city. Victorious again at Fyvie (24 October), he made a circuit of the central Highlands, followed by an army under Argyll. Mustering the hereditary foes of Clan Campbell, he was in Inveraray in December and sent the Campbell chief off in flight down Loch Fyne. On moving north into the Great Glen, he found himself between one army under Seaforth to the north and another under Argyll to the south, but, turning back to Inverlochy over mountains considered impassable, he routed the Campbells and Argyll scurried off down Loch Linnhe (2 February). On another northward circuit, he won Seaforth temporarily to his side and was joined by Lord Gordon. At Dundee in April he was surprised by an army under Baillie but succeeded in drawing off his plundering troops and, eluding the enemy, was off to the north again, by way of the central Highlands. After two further victories, at Auldearn (9 May) and Alford (2 July), Montrose succeeded in carrying a substantial army into central Scotland, where he won his final success at Kilsyth (15 August). All the covenanting armies in Scotland had been annihilated, and Argyll, escaping by water for the third time, was at Berwick. The covenanters, already disappointed that their intervention in England had not produced spectacular results, were frankly incredulous that their God should thus " make us fall " time after time,[39] while He vouchsafed victory over the king at Naseby (14 June) to an English army which was not predominantly presbyterian.[40]

After Kilsyth Montrose entered Glasgow, and, as lieutenant governor of Scotland, summoned a parliament for 20 October. But his Highlanders began to disperse, as they had done after each of his victories, and this time Alasdair took away most of the Irish for a campaign against the Campbells in Kintyre, while the Aberdeenshire contingent also withdrew. Disdaining retreat when the king's cause was desperate, but disappointed of recruits in the Borders, Montrose was surprised by David Leslie at Philiphaugh on 13 September. The covenanters, at last given victory by their Old Testament Deity, thought it His will that they

[39] Baillie, II. 304.
[40] Cf. C. V. Wedgwood, " The covenanters in the first civil war," S. H. R., xxxix. 1-15.

should massacre the women and children who followed Montrose's camp and prisoners who surrendered on promise of quarter.[41] Montrose escaped, to make yet another attempt to come to terms with Huntly, but the negotiations were still indecisive when the king, in June 1646, ordered them both to disband.

Montrose had been unable to bind together divergent interests. He gained the support of some lowland royalists, but most of them would have nothing to do with a man who turned " Irish and popish rebels and cut-throats against his own countrymen."[42] Huntly, too, had not forgotten Montrose's action against him in 1639, and, apart from constitutional indecision, found it hard to accept the leadership of a man his junior in years and his inferior in rank. As was to be shown again in 1689 and 1745, the fate of Scotland was not to be decided by the successes of a Highland army. Montrose himself never lost sight of the original ends of the National Covenant, but he considered that those ends had been gained and that they did not justify intervention in England. Just before his execution, in 1650, he said, " The covenant which I took, I own it and adhere to it. Bishops, I care not for them. I never intended to advance their interests." Nor did Montrose believe in the king's prerogative, but in " the fundamental laws of the country " and in a balance, or inter-dependence, between the king's authority and the subjects' liberties—an inter-dependence to which the Covenant itself had paid lip-service.[43] It could well be argued that Montrose remained a covenanter and that his opponents were " solemn-leaguers," who adopted policies to which the Covenant had not committed them and which were in the end irreconcilable with the Covenant. The real tragedy of Montrose was that he took up the sword too soon, for within three years of his campaign the majority of Scots had come round to his way of thinking.

The situation which finally split the main body of the covenanters developed after the king, in May 1646, slipped out of beleaguered Oxford and surrendered to the Scottish army, lying

[41] Mathieson, *Politics and religion*, II. 70-73.

[42] Wodrow, *Analecta* (Maitland Club), I. 160-1.

[43] Napier, *Memoirs of Montrose*, II. 787; *Memorials of Montrose*, I. 270. There is an interesting parallel in the thought of Strafford: " The prerogative of the crown and the propriety of the subject have such mutual relations that this took protection from that, that foundation and nourishment from this " (quoted C. V. Wedgwood, *The King's Peace*, pp. 414-5).

before Newark. The Scots almost at once withdrew to Newcastle, there to consider, in greater security, the fate of their prize. The king had come unconditionally, and anyone less optimistic would have realised that he would obtain no help from the Scots except on their terms. There was, however, a case for a bargain between the king and his Scottish subjects, who had long ago attained their own original objectives and had recently discovered that English views on the terms to be imposed on the king, should he surrender, diverged from theirs.[44] In June the Scots did agree with the English parliament (which was still largely presbyterian in sympathy) that Charles must sign the Solemn League and give up control of the armed forces for twenty years; but the two requirements were mutually incompatible, for the English army, in which independency predominated, would not now be an instrument for enforcing Anglo-Scottish conformity, and the hollowness of the agreement was surpassed only by the unlikelihood that the king would agree to either requirement. Charles did go so far as to offer the establishment of presbyterianism in England for three years, but this would not suffice.[45] The question next arose, what was to be done with the king on his refusal of his captors' terms, for in Scotland he would be a focus for disaffection. The Scottish estates would have preferred to see him conveyed to London with " honour, safety and freedom,"[46] but they were in no position to press terms on the English parliament, from which they were attempting to extract payment of money owing to them, and after the financial negotiations were concluded (23 December) the Scots withdrew from Newcastle (30 January), leaving Charles a prisoner in English hands.

It was almost at once apparent that this had been a grave mistake, for, as the English army was growing ever stronger at the expense of the parliament, the prospects for presbyterianism in England were becoming ever fainter; and apprehension soon arose as to the ultimate fate of the king, who was seized by the army in June 1647. This dual anxiety led to the Engagement, concluded on 26-27 December between three Scottish commissioners—Loudoun, Lanark and Lauderdale—and the king, who had regained a measure of freedom at Carisbrooke. This compact represented the policy of Hamilton, who had long before sought

[44] *S. H. R.*, XLII. 86-8.
[45] Burnet, *Hamiltons* (1852), p. 383.   [46] *Ibid*, p. 389.

to win a majority for the king in the Scottish parliament and who, after his liberation in April 1646, had advised Charles to buy off the Scots by ecclesiastical concessions. It also represented something very like the policy of Montrose, who was not an " Engager " simply because it was felt that his association with the enterprise would be damaging. In the Engagement, the Scots expressed their desire that the king should be allowed to go to London in safety, honour and freedom and undertook to intervene on his behalf, in return for the establishment of presbyterianism in England for a trial period of three years and participation in the commercial privileges of English subjects.[47] This compromise showed some sense of realism, and in a way foreshadowed the settlement which was in the end to be made in 1690: Scotland was to be presbyterian, but the Scots acknowledged (though as yet very grudgingly) that the people of England might have some say in the choice of a constitution for their own church.

Behind the Engagement lay the awakening of the Scottish aristocracy to the fact that in appealing to religious fanaticism they had conjured up a force which they could not control; and the reaction against the rule of the " solemn-leaguers " had an appeal to lay people generally. Fully two-thirds of the members of the estates favoured the Engagement—all but ten of the nobles, more than half of the lairds, and almost half of the burgesses. Contrasted with the overwhelming support given to the National Covenant, the Engagement represents the biggest turn-over of opinion in the century. On the other hand, obsession with the Solemn League still swayed the majority in the general assembly. While parliament exhorted the presbyteries to further the national effort on behalf of the king, the clergy tried to win over to their opinion the troops already under arms and they obstructed the levy of fresh forces. Scotland was a country divided as it had hardly been since Pinkie, a hundred years before.

Yet it was not lack of support in Scotland which caused the failure of the moderates at this point. It was military disaster in England. The expedition was inadequately prepared, for although it numbered fully 20,000 men and the cavalry were well mounted, the army as a whole was ill-trained, it was without artillery and short of ammunition. Leven and David Leslie

[47] Cf. p. 357 below.

declined the command, which fell to Hamilton; Callendar, who had commanded a regiment in Holland, was lieutenant-general, Middleton was commander of the horse, Baillie of the foot, and Hurry, who like Baillie had been routed by Montrose, also served. The record of those officers was at best undistinguished, and to make matters worse they could not agree. The only excuse for such an ill-considered venture was that the Scottish force was intended to be a rallying-point in England for former royalist officers and men, for the presbyterians, and for those who were alarmed by the radical social demands now being put forward by agitators in the army and by the confusion caused by sectarianism. The Scottish army, which crossed the Border on 8 July, was allowed to straggle through Lancashire and was defeated in detail at and near Preston between 17 and 19 August, with the loss of 2,000 killed and 8,000 or 9,000 prisoners. Hamilton surrendered on 25 August.

The defeat of the moderates was the opportunity for the extremists of the south-west. That area had a tradition of radical protestantism going back to the Lollards of Kyle; Knox had considered Ayrshire a refuge for the persecuted saints; in the 1620s the district of Cunningham could be called " the academy of religion, for a sanctified clergy and a godly people ";[48] most of the dominant families there had been ultra-protestant, and two local earls—Eglinton and Cassillis—were among the handful of peers who declined to support the Engagement. In this area the " slashing communicants " of Mauchline, who before Preston had formed themselves into an armed force but had been dispersed by government troops, now rallied and marched on Edinburgh in " the Whiggamore raid." The committee of estates fled, and the Engagers, on an assurance that they would not be challenged for their lives and property, agreed to submit to the church and to withdraw from public office. Those notables who had declined to support the Engagement, including Argyll, were joined by Loudoun, a deserter from the Engagement, and a new government was formed, but even with the support of the westland " whigs " it could not hope to command the country. Thereupon these extreme presbyterians, although opposed to toleration and sectarianism, secured their position by an unnatural alliance with Cromwell, based only on a joint detestation of the Engagers.

48 Lithgow, op. cit. (1632), p. 495.

Cromwell entered Edinburgh on 4 October, insisted that all
supporters of the Engagement should be excluded from public
office and, on departing, left a force under Lambert to protect
the " rump " of the Scottish parliament.   In these circumstances
there was passed the act of classes (23 January 1649), ordaining
the exclusion from public office, either in the state or in local
government, of persons who came within four specified classes:
the prominent Engagers and the promoters of Montrose's rebellion; lesser Engagers and all who had been previously censured
as royalists or malignants; all who had shown sympathy with the
Engagement or had not, when opportunity offered, protested
against it; and persons guilty of immorality or neglect of family
worship.   Those of the first class were disqualified for life, those
of the second for ten years, those of the third for five, and the non-
political offenders in the fourth class for only one; and readmission
was in every case to be preceded by satisfaction to the church,
so that the clergy had a veto on all public appointments.   The
ministry, as well as civil office-holders, were brought to conformity,
for eleven ministers were deprived in Perth and Stirling and eighteen in Angus and Mearns because they had refused to preach
against the Engagement.

As the majority of the laity, especially the influential laity,
were opposed to the government now in office, and as the revolution had thrown up no non-aristocratic leaders, either clerical
or lay, the government had to rely on the corporate power of the
ministers.   The rise of clericalism is to be seen in Edinburgh,
where the town council, which in 1648 had refused to consult
the kirk sessions in appointing ministers and in choosing commissioners for the general assembly, had evidently given way by
1650.   It was more significant that on 30 January 1649, seven
days after the passing of the act of classes, the assembly petitioned
for the abolition of patronage, and parliament passed an act in
that sense on 9 March.   The intention was to lessen the
dependence of the ministers on the nobility and gentry, who were
now in the main out of sympathy with the church's policy, and to
strengthen the demagogic powers of the clergy.   It was alleged that
the ministers also ousted nobles and gentry from the kirk sessions,
replacing them by " inferior people ... who depended on them,"[49]
but investigation is required as to whether this was done and also

[49] Burnet, *Own Time* (1823), I. 57.

as to the growth of the practice of keeping elders in office for life instead of making them subject to election each year.[50]   At any rate, the rule of a clerical oligarchy came closest to realisation in this situation, which was always looked back on by extreme presbyterians as the achievement of their ideal.[51]

The beheading of Charles I (30 January 1649) was a shock to the Scots, most of whom were prepared to accept Charles II, but the solemn-leaguers who were in control would " espouse the king's cause " only if he would first " espouse God's cause."[52] Charles at first refused their demands, for he had hopes of a royalist success in Ireland until Cromwell's campaign there in the autumn of 1649 and then had hopes that the Scottish royalists would rally to Montrose, who landed in the Orkneys in March 1650 and crossed to the mainland with a few hundred men.   But Montrose was unable either to raise a substantial force in the far north or to reach the central Highlands, and on 27 April he was routed at Carbisdale.   The king, though pressed to repudiate Montrose, had secured an indemnity for him if he would lay down his arms, but had left it to Montrose to decide whether or not to disband. Montrose was hanged on 21 May.   Two other royalists, with different records, had preceded him to the scaffold, Hamilton on 9 March and Huntly on 22 March.   It was appropriate that a slaughter of royalists should preface the venture now to be undertaken, for all who had fought for Charles I were disqualified, in terms of the act of classes, from fighting for Charles II.   In negotiations conducted at Breda in April 1650, Charles still avoided capitulation to the " solemn-leaguers," who possibly hoped to secure his authority without incurring the risks inseparable from his presence in Scotland.   If so, they were worsted, for he deferred a decision until he was on board ship and did not finally sign the Covenants until he was off the mouth of the Spey on 23 June.   He was forced in August to sign a humiliating declaration denouncing his parents,[53] but some of the zealots thought—rightly—that his submission was insincere, and the strict supervision of his private life did nothing to endear presbyterianism to him.   Both the rejection of the services of proved

50 Cf. Donaldson, *Scottish Reformation*, p. 222n.

51 Cf. " We are only endeavouring to . . . reduce our church and state to what they were in the years 1648 and 1649 " (Apologetic Declaration, Lanark, 1682, in *Informatory Vindication* (1744), p. 96).

52 Baillie, III. 75.   53 Wodrow, I, app. 1.

royalists and the coercion of the king were unstatesmanlike, but it is some extenuation that even the Engagers, when they thought of bringing Charles to Scotland before Preston, stipulated that he must leave Prince Rupert behind and must not bring an Anglican chaplain.

Cromwell led an army north to deal with his late allies. He was at Musselburgh on 29 July, while David Leslie lay on a fortified line between Leith and Edinburgh, where he was secure even although his army was weakened by a purge of men and officers whom the ministers considered unreliable. Cromwell marched and counter-marched in vain attempts to induce Leslie to fight, and ultimately had to fall back on Dunbar at the end of August. There, with about 11,000 effectives, he was trapped between Leslie's army of 23,000 men on Doon Hill, and the North Sea. The tactical error of descending from the hillside to meet Cromwell on the plain, on 3 September, has, like the earlier purge, been attributed to the ministers, but the season was advancing, the weather was bad, and Leslie could not lie out indefinitely on those exposed uplands. Complete victory went to Cromwell, whose warcry was " The Lord of Hosts," and the Scots, who rallied to the call of " The Covenant," lost 10,000 prisoners and 3,000 killed. Cromwell remarked that " There may be a covenant made with death and hell."[54]

Military failure was again, as after Preston, decisive in determining party ascendancy. Cromwell presciently observed, on the day after Dunbar, " Surely it's probable the kirk has done their do. I believe their king will set up upon his own score now; wherein he will find many friends."[55] There was a royalist force in the Highlands, commanded by Middleton, and the king attempted to join it when he made a brief escape in an episode known as " The Start." The significant development, however, was not the king's relations with his old friends, but his making of new friends, for Argyll was presently at the head of a section of comparatively moderate men who decided to co-operate with the royalists. At the end of October the committee of estates granted an indemnity to Middleton, although he had been incapacitated by the act of classes and was excommunicated

<hr>

[54] Carlyle, *Cromwell's Letters and Speeches* (ed. Lomas), II. 79. It is a curious fact that a few months earlier he had used exactly the same phrase to the Irish papists (*ibid.*, p. 7). [55] *Ibid.*, p. 112.

by James Guthrie, leader of the most extreme among the ministers. It was soon clear that the general assembly itself was now divided: the extremists, who held that the act of classes had not been strictly enough applied and that hope should be placed in an army still more rigorously purged, were called remonstrants, because they defined their policy in the western remonstrance, drawn up at Dumfries on 17 October; but a moderate majority in the commission of assembly, on 14 December, passed the " first public resolution," in favour of permitting all persons to fight who were not excommunicated, forfeited, notoriously wicked or obstinate enemies of the covenant.[56] The " resolutioners " were prepared to co-operate with the committee of estates, which on 25 November condemned the remonstrance.

There were now four armies in Scotland—the official army which had survived Dunbar, the "holy army " of the remonstrants in the west, the " malignant army " of cavaliers under Middleton, and the " sectarian army " of the English.[57] The " holy army " was crushed by a detachment of the " sectarian army," under Lambert, in December. On 1 January 1651, at Scone, the king received the crown from the hands of Argyll. On 24 May the commission of assembly passed a " second public resolution," in effect agreeing to the rescinding of the act of classes,[58] and the act was rescinded in June. It was thus possible to incorporate " malignants " in a national levy for the defence of king and country. Cromwell had received the surrender of Edinburgh Castle in December 1650 and had taken up his quarters there, while the Scottish army lay at Stirling. The English made themselves masters of the country south of the Forth and Clyde, crossed to Fife after defeating the Scots at Inverkeithing on 20 July, and entered Perth on 2 August. The Scottish army, to the number of about 15,000, thus found the way south open to it and was in Carlisle by 6 August, but it attracted no support in England and met with disaster at Worcester (3 September 1651).

[56] *Consultations of the ministers of Edinburgh* (S. H. S.). 1. 301.
[57] Nicoll, *Diary*, p. 39.
[58] *Consultations of the ministers of Edinburgh*, 1. 301.

18

THE CROMWELLIAN INTERLUDE

Since 1603 England and Scotland had been under one sovereign, but with two parliaments and two administrations.
This personal union had operated without serious friction
as long as the crown, the unifying factor, had been sufficiently
dominant to prevent the two parliaments from pursuing irreconcilable policies. In the 1640s, however, the crown was eclipsed in
both England and Scotland, and the English and Scottish governments began to follow incompatible courses in both religion and
politics. Ultimately the English declared a republic, the Scots
acknowledged Charles II as successor to his father. Thus the
union had been dissolved, and the consequence for Scotland was
its conquest by Cromwell.

Stirling had surrendered to the commonwealth forces on 14
August 1651 and Dundee was taken by storm on 1 September;
Dumbarton held out until January 1652, the Bass until April,
and Dunnottar until 26 May. The public records fell into English
hands with the capture of Stirling, and the regalia escaped that
fate only because they were removed from Dunnottar before its
fall and buried under the floor of the church of Kinneff. Not
only was Scotland a conquered country, but it was a country
without a legally constituted government. The committee of
estates had been captured at Alyth a few days before the battle
of Worcester, and although an attempt was made to summon a
new parliament to meet at Finlarig, it could be proclaimed only
at Killin, since there was no access to any more important centre,
and only three members appeared. The commonwealth government, in appointing commissioners for the administration of
Scotland in October 1651, announced that England and Scotland

were henceforth to be one commonwealth and on 19 November
the conqueror forbade all public meetings " of any persons for
the exercise of any jurisdiction other than such as is or shall be
from the parliament of England."[1]

The union, therefore, could not be made by negotiation between equals, and Scottish consent was a mere formality.   In
January 1652 the commissioners of the commonwealth charged
the burghs and shires to elect representatives to signify their
assent to the union.   Not only were these representatives to be
elected at the behest of the English government, but it was made
clear that they must be plenipotentiaries unable to refer back
to their constituencies, and when they met, at Dalkeith, they
had no option but to intimate their consent.   Representatives
came from only eighteen shires and twenty-four burghs, and the
only shires which showed any enthusiasm for union were Dunbar-
tonshire and Wigtownshire, but assent was ultimately given by
29 out of 31 shires and 44 out of 58 royal burghs.   If there was
thus no real opportunity for Scottish opinion to express itself
on the principle of union, there was no serious consultation of
Scottish opinion on the details either.   In April 1652 the burghs
and shires were called on to elect representatives who would choose
twenty-one deputies to discuss the terms of union.   Only 23
shires and 37 burghs sent representatives, and when the deputies
proceeded to London, in October, they found that their function
was simply to supply information.

There was clearly some truth in the remark that the embody-
ing of Scotland with England was " as when the poor bird is
embodied into the hawk that hath eaten it up."[2]   Union with a
republic in which power rested nominally with the English house
of commons, really with the English army, involved not only the
abandonment of the concept of government by the estates of the
Scottish realm but also the abandonment of the ancient monarchy,
which the signatories of the National Covenant and the Solemn
League had been pledged to maintain.   Such fundamental constitutional changes were made, not by the " full and free deliber-
ation of the people in their collected body,"[3] or by any assembly
meeting " according to the liberty, laws, practice and consuetude

---

[1] *Scotland and the Commonwealth*, p. xxi.
[2] *Life of Robert Blair* (Wodrow Soc.), pp. 291-2.
[3] *Cromwellian Union*, p. 74.

of Scotland," but merely by delegates who, at a time when Scotland was " under the power and force of the army of the pretended commonwealth of England," were required to meet only " by virtue of and according to the warrant . . . of the pretended parliament of . . . England."[4] Apart from this issue, and apart from the royalism of nearly all Scots which lay behind it, there was fundamental disagreement on ecclesiastical matters. The Scots as a nation were officially pledged to the principle that no form of church government other than the presbyterian was to be permitted, in either Scotland or England. The English commonwealth, however, under the sway of the Independents and pledged to the toleration of all except prelatists and papists, insisted that official protection and encouragement were to extend not only to ministers " whose consciences oblige them to wait upon God in the administration of spiritual ordinances according to the order of the Scottish churches," but also to others " not being satisfied in conscience to use that form."[5] In the eyes of the Scots this meant " a vast and boundless toleration of all sorts of error and heresies, without any effectual remedy for suppressing the same."[6]

Although union was effective from 1652, Cromwell's quarrels with successive parliaments put obstacles in the way of its receiving legislative sanction. The original bill of union had not been passed when the Long Parliament was dissolved in April 1653, and another bill, read in the nominated " Barbones' Parliament " in October 1653, had not been passed when that body was dismissed in December. The Instrument of Government, which set up the Protectorate, was followed by an ordinance of union (April 1654), but the first parliament of the protectorate was dissolved before it had passed an act of union. The act at last became law in the second protectorate parliament, in April 1657. Scotland was represented after a fashion in all those parliaments and also in the parliament which met in 1659, when Richard Cromwell was protector, but the representation was thought by the Scots to be inadequate in respect of numbers and it was certainly inadequate in respect of the character of the members, who were preponderantly nominees of the government. Scots who had been in arms against the parliament of

---

[4] *Scotland and the Commonwealth*, pp. 211-2.
[5] *A. P. S.*, vi (2). 809.   [6] *Cromwellian Union*, p. 35.

England or who had abetted war against it were in general disfranchised.[7]

Parliamentary representation could in any event have been no more than a facade, for Scotland remained throughout the period an occupied country. It was inevitable that it should be so, for the initial conquest had not been long completed when a rebellion broke out, and a royalist force maintained itself in arms for the better part of a year. The Earl of Glencairn obtained a commission from King Charles as commander in chief in Scotland and, landing in the west Highlands in August 1653, raised a force, largely from Atholl and Lochaber, amounting ultimately to about 5,000 men. John Middleton, who was a more experienced soldier, later took over the command. Considerable support was received, from Lowland peers like Balcarres as well as chieftains from the centre and north like Campbell of Glenorchy and Mackenzie of Tarbat, but the leaders were not of one mind on strategy, none of them had the dash of Montrose or the ability to keep a Highland force together and lead it into the Lowlands. Middleton, after a reverse at Dalnaspidal, near the head of Loch Garry, on 19 July 1654, seems to have left the leadership once more to Glencairn, though he lingered in Scotland for a time before returning to the exiled court. Glencairn had one minor success, against a party of dragoons at Dumbarton, but the end of war between England and Holland, in April, had ended hopes of continental help, and the royalist army soon dispersed.

The occupying army, which had been reduced from 36,000 in 1652 to 10,000 or 12,000 in the following year, was increased to 18,000 in the face of the rising. Thereafter it was reduced once more, but the effective force on which the government of Scotland was based was now demonstrated by the erection of five

---

[7] In " Barbones' Parliament" of 140 members there were only five Scottish representatives, and although under the Instrument of Government and the terms of union Scotland was to have thirty representatives, there were 30 in only the second protectorate parliament, and no more than 21 in the first protectorate parliament and in Richard Cromwell's parliament. Officers of the army and government officials (only some of them Scots) numbered nine in the first protectorate parliament, nineteen in the second and fourteen in the third. The presence of the Scottish members in the third protectorate parliament was actually challenged on the ground that they were government nominees. Scotland was assigned four seats in the house of peers set up in 1657, and three sat in Richard Cromwell's parliament—Cassillis, Lockhart of Lee and Wariston. For the arrangements made to group the Scottish shires and counties, see *Cromwellian Union*, pp. lii-liv, and *A. P. S.*, vi (2). 823. Paul J. Pinckney, " The Scottish representation in the Cromwellian parliament of 1656 " (*S. H. R.*, xlvi. 95-114), reaffirms the preponderant influence of the government.

large forts—at Leith, Inverness, Inverlochy, Perth and Ayr—
and the occupation of about a score of subsidiary stations in the
more remote parts of the country. Monck was in command from
1654. The regime was inevitably an authoritarian one, with
many restrictions on personal liberty, such as the need for
permits to move about the country, but the soldiers were under
strict discipline[8] and the occupation, though it must have been
obtrusive enough, was hardly in itself oppressive.

The essentially military character of commonwealth rule in
Scotland was apparent, too, in the personnel of the administration.
The eight commissioners " of the parliament of England for
ordering and managing the affairs of Scotland," who were appointed in October 1651 and who commenced their operations in
January 1652, included three generals, a colonel and a major.
Under the protectorate, a council of state of nine members, which
began to operate in September 1655, included two Scots—
William Lockhart and John Swinton—but the English members
included Monck and four colonels. The court of session did not
meet after July 1650 and justice was for a time obtainable only at
the hands of a committee of English officers at Leith and perhaps
from similar tribunals elsewhere. In 1652, however, the commissioners for the administration appointed four Englishmen
and three Scots as commissioners for justice and nominated
sheriffs for all the counties. Ultimately ten or eleven judges
formed a supreme court of justice, and most of them were Scots.
Half of them acted as a high court in criminal causes, and half
formed a court of exchequer. The admiralty court had three
judges, all English. The offices of the signet, the great and privy
seals, hornings, sasines and apprisings were revived much as
they had been during Scotland's independence, and those of the
public records which were primarily of legal value were returned
from England in 1655. Latin was superseded for legal purposes
by " playne significant Englische Ianguage "[9] from 1652 until
the restoration of the monarchy.

In 1654 an ordinance abolished the baron courts hitherto
held by landlords. New " baron courts " were to be set up on
a popular basis, with power to determine in suits concerning
sums up to 40s. In the burghs, the election of councils and of
magistrates was suspended from 1652 until 1655, but from

---

[8] Cf. " Dundee court martial records," in *S. H. S. Misc.*, III.   [9] Nicoll, p. 96.

September 1655 burgesses recovered the right to hold elections, though persons with a record of disaffection to the commonwealth and those who declined to take an oath to the protector were necessarily excluded from office. At the beginning of 1656 justices of the peace were appointed in every sheriffdom, with jurisdiction in cases of assault, trespass, poaching and riot, powers to suppress begging and vagabondage, to arrange for the repair of roads and bridges, to take action in time of plague, to fix wages and set prices on craftsmen's work, to maintain and erect jails, and to punish fornication, swearing and the breaking of the Lord's Day—but also to provide for the brewing of wholesome ale and beer.[10] One motive, as in the similar Jacobean experiment, was to transfer functions from ecclesiastical to civil tribunals, but it sprang now from a desire to break the power of the church and the dependence of the people on their ministers.

The general testimony was that both the executive and the judicature operated with unwonted efficiency. It is true that there were complaints that the sheriffs were merely " English sojours " and the judges of the supreme courts " a few English,"[11] and that in the later years of the protectorate legal processes became inordinately expensive.[12] It is true, too, that the old baron courts, with their ready jurisdiction in disputes among tenants, had satisfied a real need as none of the new courts did. Yet it was pointed out that the military tribunals gave sentences in cases which had depended without decision before Scottish courts for periods of up to sixteen years, and it was freely admitted that justice was administered with efficiency and impartiality.[13] Both in the Borders and in the Highlands well-affected landowners were allowed to keep arms for the defence of themselves and their tenants, and chiefs were made responsible for the conduct of their clansmen and the production of offenders. Lochiel, for instance, undertook that whenever robbery was committed by any of his tenants or servants he would produce the robbers or else give satisfaction to the people injured; and the chief of Glencoe was empowered to act against robbers in his area. Should a chief fail to keep his clan in order, neighbouring chiefs were given power to bring them to book, and even individual Highlanders of doubtful reputation were employed to catch malefactors

---

10 *Scotland and the Protectorate* (S. H. S.), pp. 403-5.   11 Baillie, III. 288.
12 Nicoll, *Diary*, p. 223.   13 Cf. Nicoll, pp. 65, 75.

of their own or other clans, on the principle, " set a thief to catch a thief."[14] Particularly influential was the fort at Inverlochy, from which a police force worked with such effect that it was said in 1658 that " there is not one robbery all this year, although formerly it was the trade they lived by to rob and steal."[15] One of the governors at Inverlochy was Hill, who returned to duty there a generation later, under William of Orange, when his understanding of highland problems and the effectiveness of his earlier rule were highly praised.[16] It seems that Major-General Deane, another of the Cromwellian commanders, anticipated Wade by having a vessel transported to Loch Ness for patrol duty. All in all, a degree of order seems to have been introduced, after the disturbances of the 1640s and of 1653-4, which would have rejoiced the heart of James VI. " At no time were the highlands kept in better order than during the usurpation," wrote one;[17] and another remarked, " A man may ride all Scotland over with a switch in his hand and £100 in his pocket, which he could not have done these five hundred years."[18]

But the extinction of resistance to the commonwealth, the defeat of a rebellion, the suppression of disorder and the maintenance of effective government, could not be achieved without a good deal of injury to the finances and interests of many Scotsmen. The estates of those who had supported the Engagement and the Worcester campaign were forfeited, and after the rising the estates of twenty-four persons, mostly peers, were confiscated and fines ranging from £14,000 down to £500 were imposed on seventy-three others.[19] Many peers and gentlemen were already heavily in debt because of their outlays during the campaigns from 1639 to 1651, and not well placed to face new financial burdens; many of the fines had to be reduced by a half or more because of the sheer impossibility of exacting payment in full. To make matters worse, the efficiency and impartiality of the commonwealth courts enabled creditors to make their actions effective. Financial ruin was widespread: Lord Cranston, on being restored in 1656 after forfeiture, found that he had an

---

14 *Scotland and the Protectorate*, pp. xxxv-xxxviii
15 Thurloe, *State Papers*, IV. 401.
16 Hugh Mackay, *Memoirs* (Bannatyne Club), p. 90.
17 Burnet, *Own Time* (1823), I. 104.
18 Thomas Burton, *Diary*, IV. 168.   19 Cf. Nicoll, pp. 125-6.

income of £600 per annum and a debt of £10,000; the losses of
the Dalyells of Carnwath were estimated at £188,000, of the Earl
of Perth at £150,000 and of the Earl of Queensberry at £235,000;
the estates of the Earl of Home, the Earl of Lothian and Campbell
of Loudoun were among many estates apprised to creditors; the
Earl of Morton had to dispose of his Dalkeith property. A contemporary mentioned other instances:

> Our noble families are almost gone; Lennox has little in Scotland
> unsold; Hamilton's estate, except Arran and the barony of
> Hamilton, is sold; . . . the Gordons are gone; the Douglases little
> better; Eglinton and Glencairn on the brink of breaking; many
> of our chief families' estates are cracking.[20]

A nameless multitude of lesser men also suffered, and financial
desperation lay behind some of the support given to the Glencairn-
Middleton rising and to royalist plots.[21]

The government's policy was not vindictive towards even the
royalist leaders, though some of the notable prisoners taken at
Worcester remained in captivity until 1660 and there were several
exceptions from an act which in May 1654 cancelled forfeitures
and other penalties. The leaders of the rising, too, received an
amnesty if they found security for their keeping the peace. Men of
lower rank were not in general harshly treated either, though at
least 500 were transported to Barbados, many to be released
or to escape later. Some of the royalist leaders were given permission to raise regiments for foreign service, though none did so.
The government was less concerned with punishment than with
liberating lesser men from the domination of the magnates and
breaking down feudal and hereditary ties.[22] Thus, the vassals
and tenants of forfeited estates were allowed to retain their lands
if they would accept the commonwealth; heritable jurisdictions
were abolished; tenure by military service and feudal casualties
like ward and marriage were eliminated; and creditors were
encouraged to accept land instead of money. Such a policy had
been anticipated, in intention, by James VI, and was to be finally
implemented only in the middle of the eighteenth century. Cromwell himself believed that " the meaner sort " or " the middle
sort " of the people of Scotland prospered under his rule,[23] but

20 Baillie, III. 387.   21 Cf. Nicoll, *Diary*, p. 122.
22 *The Cromwellian Union*, p. xxiii.
23 Carlyle, *Cromwell* (ed. Lomas), III. 179.

whether they could do so depended on the extent to which his government was able to make good its general intention:

> The Lord Protector, . . . being desirous that the mercies which it hath pleased God to give to this nation by the successes of their forces in the late war in Scotland should be improved for the good and advantage of both nations, and the people of Scotland made equal sharers, with those of England, in the present settlement of peace, liberty and prosperity, with all other privileges of a free people.[24]

The fact was that economic conditions were such that no section of the community had much opportunity to prosper during the brief period of commonwealth rule. Several years of peace would have been necessary to undo the disastrous effects of the years since 1638—interruption of trade with England, the losses suffered by Scottish ships at the hands of royalist privateers, the raising within little more than three years of the armies which met with disaster at Preston, Dunbar and Worcester, the destruction caused by Montrose's campaign, the Cromwellian invasions and the operations in 1653-4. A reading of the records of the burgh of Edinburgh suggests that at no time in its history had the town council been so preoccupied with military matters as it was in 1650, and the diversion of interest from normal trading concerns is illustrated in the figures for Baltic commerce: there was a sharp fall in 1638-40, a partial recovery in 1641-3 and then a fairly steady decline until in 1651 a low record for all time was reached, for only nine Scottish ships passed through the Sound; subsequent years, except 1655, did not show a very marked improvement. Edinburgh complained that its resources were at an end;[25] Aberdeen lamented that " our traid is gone, our shipps taikin, our people are turning bankrout ";[26] Glasgow, which suffered from a great fire in 1652, said to have burned 1000 houses, made a rapid recovery, but its efforts to trade across the Atlantic proved unprofitable for merchants with such limited capital that they could not afford to keep their ships at sea on long voyages.

For the people of Scotland to be " equal sharers with those of England " was a doubtful benefit when " the privileges of a free people " involved legislation designed to suit the English,

---

24 *Acts and Ordinances of the Interregnum*, ed. Firth and Rait, II. 875 (12 April 1654).
25 *Edinburgh Burgh Records, 1642-55*, p. 273.   26 *Aberdeen Council Letters*, III. 290.

but not the Scottish, economy. Thus the export of wool and hides (of which Scotland, but not England, had an exportable surplus) and the import of French wines, were prohibited, and the export of coal was hampered by duties (though these were modified after protests).[27] On the other hand, free trade allowed the import to Scotland of English manufactured goods, more cheaply produced than those of Scotland, and they went a long way to drive Scottish manufactures off the market. Overseas trade was interrupted by Cromwell's wars with Holland and Spain. Besides, the Scots had lost so many ships in the course of the wars—and more by a storm in 1656—that they were short of vessels to carry on their trade, and the effect of the shortage was aggravated by the English Navigation Act, which forbade the use of foreign ships for importing goods to Britain. Trade with England and English colonies was, it is true, now open to the Scots as never before, but the opportunities could not be exploited by a country which was, on Cromwell's own admission, " a very ruined nation."[28]

" The privileges of a free people " included the carrying of financial burdens such as King Charles had never laid on his subjects. To maintain an army against the king had proved to be more expensive than the king's government had been. The expense of maintaining troops had been continuous since 1639 and had worked up to a climax between 1648 and 1651: in 1648 Edinburgh compounded for £40,000 in place of men for Hamilton's expedition; in the same year it had to find another £60,000 as the normal payment for " maintenance " and " quartering "; and in 1650 the city was maintaining 575 men at a cost of £72,000. From 1639 onwards, hundreds of thousands of pounds were expended on the purchase of arms and ammunition on the continent. All this outlay could be met only by new financial devices. In 1640 the scope of taxation was defined as " the yearly worth of every man's rent, in victual, money or other wages," and was based on a valuation of " everything whereby profit or commodity ariseth,"[29] and this was going far beyond the taxation of land and annualrents. But the incidence of the land tax, too, was greatly extended. For many years, barons and freeholders had been allowed to reclaim proportions of their

[27] Nef, *British coal industry*, II. 228-9.
[28] Lomas, III. 179.   [29] Rait, *Parliaments*, p. 495.

assessments from their sub-vassals, but no land tax had as yet been directly imposed on others than crown tenants-in-chief. From 1643, however, taxation was on all land, and thus originated the general land tax known to later generations. Another innovation was the excise, introduced in 1644 and consisting of imposts on ale, beer and whisky, imported wine, tobacco and textile materials and exported coal.

These new financial devices, or something like them, were to be among the few enduring achievements of the covenanting revolution. During the Cromwellian occupation there were monthly assessments on personal and real estate. Scotland's quota was at first £10,000, to be raised by valuations in counties and burghs, but in 1654 only £4,000 was being collected and in 1657 the target was reduced to £6,000 (sterling). After the restoration of the monarchy, this monthly quota was revived as a taxation unit, to become familiar as the " cess " or assessment. The excise likewise survived under the commonwealth and after the Restoration.[30]

In the midst of economic and financial stress, Scotland suffered also from the effects of ecclesiastical divisions. The rallying of patriotic sentiment in the campaign which led to Worcester had done much to strengthen the moderate and royalist party of resolutioners, who claimed the support of about 750 out of some 900 ministers. The remonstrants, however, undaunted by lack of numbers, protested (so earning the name of " protestors ") against the general assemblies of 1651 and 1652 and would not agree to acknowledge any general assembly in which the " plurality " was "corrupt."[31] In some areas they even declined to acknowledge presbyteries with a resolutioner majority and formed their own schismatic courts. This was something new in the history of the reformed church in Scotland, and reflected a bitterness of party feeling in comparison with which the presbyterian-episcopalian controversy—which had never yet threatened schism—had been mere friendly rivalry. Lord Broghill, president of the Scottish council set up in 1655, commented:

> It might be no very difficult thing to get either party to acknowledge our government, if you would put the power therefrom into their hands to suppress the others. . . . To accomplish that end they would think nothing too dear.[32]

---

30 P. 360 below.   31 *Consultations of the ministers of Edinburgh* (S. H. S.), I. 351.
32 Thurloe, *State Papers*, IV. 49.

The effect of the strife on the religious life of the country was deplorable. An English observer in 1650 drew up an indictment of the nation, in which he states, in detail, how each of the Ten Commandments was violated: for example—

> Instead of having no other God but one, the generality of people . . . do idolise and set up their ministers. . . . All must fall down before this golden calf and submit to this government. . . . I have not known any of them to spend [the Lord's Day] in religious exercises, only in a bare cessation from labour and work . . ., spending their time in laziness and vanity. . . . Whoredom and fornication is the common darling sin of the nation. . . . [33]

Before this is discounted as a mere caricature, reference should be made to the " solemn and seasonable warning " in which the general assembly castigated the sins of the nation, and even of the covenanted army, in 1645,[34] to the kirk session records which lament the growth of sin of all sorts,[35] to the diary of an Edinburgh citizen who several times adverted to the number of " offences of a horrible and unnatural kind " (as Victorians called them),[36] and to the minutes of the synod of Fife, which in 1650 ordained a day of humiliation for "the general contempt of the grace of the gospel, . . . mocking of piety, gross uncleanness, intemperance, breach of Sabbath."[37] The sacrament of Holy Communion, celebrations of which had become relatively frequent in the 1630s, was almost completely neglected: in Edinburgh, despite repeated appeals from the town council, the ministers would not consent to a celebration between 1648 and 1655. Witch-hunting, too, which had been on the wane before 1638, when some restraint had been imposed by the bishops (who cannot thereby have added to their popularity), broke out with renewed zest as one manifestation of the cruelty which the strife of the 1640s engendered.

The Cromwellian occupation had, however, its compensations. The toleration which was so detestable to presbyterians was a relief to those who reflected on " the bloodie and barbarous inconvenientis quhich hath alwayis accompanied the presbiteriall government," with its " tyrannous persequuting of mens

---

[33] *Charles II and Scotland in 1650* (S. H. S.), pp. 137-9.
[34] Peterkin, *Records of the kirk of Scotland* (1838), pp. 423-7.
[35] Chambers, *Domestic Annals*, II. 198.
[36] *Ibid.*, II. 243 ; Nicoll, *Diary*, pp. 4, 15, 106, 107, 174, 185, 202, 212, 215, 227; cf. Lamont, *Diary*, pp. 46-7.
[37] *Selections from minutes of Synod of Fife* (Abbotsford Club), pp. 168-75.

consciences,"[38] and to those who had the temerity to consider the presbyterian system " but a human invention."[39] Witch-hunting was curbed—though with the result that arrears had to be made up after the restoration. And when, in 1653, the general assembly was forcibly dissolved by the Cromwellian government, which took care that there should be no more contentious gatherings of ministers, some thought it no bad thing, for the assembly " seemed to be more sett upon establishing themselves than promoving religion."[40] It was beneficial that some ministers now preached " nothing but the Gospel, and had left off to preach up parliaments, armies, leagues, resolutions and remonstrances."[41]

The government tried hard to reach an understanding with first one, then the other, of the two ecclesiastical parties. The more likely allies, at first sight, were the remonstrants, hostile as they were to the king. The English had no more respect than the remonstrants themselves for the will of the majority, and characteristically held that in the appointment of ministers, regard was to be had " to the choice of the more sober and godly part of the people, although the same should not prove to be the greater part."[42] This meant the intrusion of remonstrants, at the instance of the government and sometimes by military force, on unwilling congregations. In 1654 the church courts were in effect denuded of their powers in the admission of ministers, and matters were so arranged that appointments should be in the hands of groups of protestors. It was intended, too, that resolutioners should be ousted from the universities and the control of education given over to the minority. But, while some protestors were ready to co-operate—like Patrick Gillespie, whom Cromwell made principal of Glasgow and who was the first Scottish divine to pray publicly for the protector—too many of them were, as Broghill tartly commented, " bitterly averse to your highness's authority, if not to any."[43] In the long run the resolutioners were found to be more tractable, and, thanks largely to the diplomacy of James Sharp when representatives of both factions were summoned to London for consultation, they latterly received more official countenance. Their whole position had been based on loyalty

---

[38] Nicoll, *Diary*, 91; cf. *Spalding Club Misc.*, III. 205.

[39] *Diary of Alexander Jaffray* (ed. John Barclay, 1833), 45. The writer later became a Quaker.

[40] Kirkton, *Secret and true history*, p. 54. [41] Robert Law, *Memorials* (1818), p. 7.

[42] *A. P. S.*, VI. 832. [43] Thurloe, *State Papers*, IV. 557.

to the king, and they kept in close touch with Charles and his agents. Many preached sermons in favour of the rising of 1653-4 and prayed for its success; Middleton was provided with a form of prayer for the king's forces, but, in deference to scruples about government direction in such matters, it was left to his discretion whether he should use it or not. The king knew of other clerical scruples, and wrote in suitable terms to reassure those who doubted whether his way of life befitted a covenanted king:

> I doubt not but the memory of my conversation and behaviour amongst you will preserve me from the scandals of all kinds which my enemies will not fail to raise against me and that you will prudently consider how necessary it is for me . . . to become all things to all men, never forgetting to walk always as in the sight of the Most High. I pray God this heavy exercise of our afflictions may produce that good spirit in us all that we may be as sensible of our sins as of our sufferings.[44]

In August 1655, however, the resolutioners agreed that ministers should give an undertaking to live peaceably under the government, and in October, on threats that they would not only lose their stipends but be forbidden to preach, they gave up praying for the king by name—though they continued to convey to their congregations their intention to pray for him: " Lord, remember every distressed person and every distressed family, and the lower their condition be and from how much higher the station they are laid low, so much the more remember them in mercy."[45] As the years passed, the principle of acknowledging the government came to be ever more generally accepted. Even an uncompromising protestor like Johnston of Wariston was in the end won over, although Cromwell had at one time despaired of ever reaching agreement with him; he was restored to his office of lord clerk register in 1657 and sat in protectorate parliaments in 1658 and 1659.

All in all, the years from about 1644 to 1660 might compete for the description once applied, with far less justification, to the period after 1660—" the most pitiful chapter of the national history."[46] Yet one outstanding fact, which is a significant commentary on what went before and on what was to follow, was that a union with England was not in itself unpleasing to the

---

[44] *Scotland and the Protectorate*, p. 198.　　　[45] *Ibid.*, p. 322.
[46] Hume Brown, *History of Scotland*, II. 379.

Scots. A communication of trading rights had been in the minds of the covenanters almost from the outset; the Solemn League had foreshadowed a union;[47] the continued interest in trading opportunities was reflected in a scheme, in 1647, for a Scottish plantation in Virginia;[48] and even in the stress of the negotiations for the Engagement Scotland's economic needs were not forgotten, for that agreement provided that

> his majesty, according to the intention of his father, shall endeavour a complete union of the kingdoms, so as they may be one under his majesty and his posterity; and if that cannot be speedily effected, that all liberties, privileges, concerning commerce, traffic and manufactories peculiar to the subjects of either nation, shall be common to the subjects of both kingdoms without distinction; and that there be a communication of mutual capacity of all other privileges of the subject in the two kingdoms.[49]

The union achieved under Cromwell was regarded by some Scots as the logical culmination of earlier proposals and as something which should be maintained. Therefore, when the Long Parliament was recalled in July 1659—the first step towards the recovery of constitutional legality in England—a bill of union was introduced, on Scottish initiative, but the dissolution (in October) supervened before the third reading. In the following year, too, when Monck was on the point of leaving for England on a march which was to lead to the restoration of the monarchy, he was petitioned by commissioners of shires and burghs to maintain the union, though with safeguards for the Scottish economy and for Scots law. Union was not one of the enduring achievements of the period: but there was clearly a disinclination to see it go.[50]

[47] P. 331 above. [48] *Edinburgh Burgh Records, 1642-55*, p. 129.
[49] S. R. Gardiner, *Constitutional Documents of the Puritan Revolution*, 351.
[50] The restoration of the two separate parliaments, in 1660, soon demonstrated afresh the difficulties inseparable from rival economic policies, and, after the failure of a scheme for a commercial treaty between England and Scotland, Charles II recommended to his English parliament, in October 1669, the consideration of union. Both parliaments appointed commissioners, who met at Westminster on 14 September 1670. Scottish demands for equal representation of the two countries in the united parliament were refused by the English representatives, and the conference was adjourned and then dissolved. The journal of the proceedings is printed as an appendix to *The Cromwellian Union*. See also Sir George Mackenzie, *Memoirs*, pp. 193-211.

19

THE REIGNS OF CHARLES II
AND JAMES VII

The application of the term " restoration " to the period after 1660 misrepresents the nature of Scottish political and ecclesiastical life in those years. The monarchy was restored and the machinery of government in parliament, privy council and the judicature was again much as it had been before the outbreak of the covenanting revolt. But behind those externals, many essentials were different from what they had been under Charles I, and in so far as the revolt against that monarch had been aristocratic and anti-clerical it found its fulfilment rather than its negation under Charles II. The nobility and gentry, like the king, were now to enjoy their own again.[1] Office and power lay with nobles, some of them the very men who had been active against Charles I: the Earl of Lauderdale, who became secretary, had been one of the Scottish commissioners to the Westminster Assembly; the ninth Earl of Glencairn, of a long line of ultra-protestants, was chancellor from 1661 to 1664; the seventh Earl of Rothes, president of the council in 1661 and chancellor in 1667, was the son of the Rothes who had headed the malcontents in 1638 and inherited his father's licentiousness without his gift for commending himself to the godly; the seventeenth Earl of Crawford was restored to the office of treasurer which he had held under the covenanting government from 1644 to 1649; the Earl of Tweeddale (eighth Lord Hay of Yester), although he had sat in Cromwell's parliaments, became a privy councillor, as did the ninth Baron Sinclair, who had been a

1 Cf. Nicoll, *Diary*, p. 322.

member of the general assembly of 1638 and of covenanting committees of estates. The one holder of high office who was not an aristocrat was Middleton, an able soldier who had fought against Montrose but had taken part in the Preston and Worcester campaigns and now, raised to an earldom, was king's commissioner to the Scottish parliament—an appointment which incurred aristocratic jealousy. The councillors of Charles II were not the kind of men who had been the agents of Charles I.

Nor was there any revival of the political influence of the clergy: although the Archbishop of St Andrews retained his precedence, and the two archbishops sat on the council, no other prelate was admitted as a councillor throughout the reign of Charles II except the Bishop of Galloway in 1678. The bishops consecrated in Scotland in 1662 were expressly warned " not to encroach upon the nobility " as their predecessors had done,[2] and the act of supremacy of 1669 had the effect, so Lauderdale said to the king, that it " makes you sovereign in the church; you may now dispose of bishops and ministers and remove and transplant them as you please . . . . This church, nor no meeting nor ecclesiastical person in it, can ever trouble you more."[3] The men now in control were as hostile to the pretensions of bishops as to presbyters. Sir Robert Moray remarked that a protest by the Archbishop of Glasgow " shows bishops and episcopal people are as bad on this chapter as the most arrant presbyterian or remonstrator,"[4] and Lauderdale commented that " the old spirit of presbytery did remain with some of the bishops: so unwilling are churchmen, by what name or title soever they are dignified, to part with power."[5] Resistance by any bishop to the government's measures was futile, for it would lead only to his deprivation and his replacement by a more compliant prelate.

The parliament of the " restoration " period, like the council, had a different complexion from the parliaments of James VI and Charles I. Parliamentary sessions were much longer, the work of parliament was not now confined to acceptance of the report of the committee of articles en bloc, and for the first time something like a regular opposition began to use parliament as a debating ground from which to challenge the king's ministers—an opposition which, no less than the government, was

2 Nicoll, *Diary*, p. 365.   3 *Lauderdale Papers*, II. 164.
4 *Lauderdale Papers*, II. 138-9.   5 *Ibid.*, p. 163.

headed by aristocrats of old family.[6] In fiscal policy, too, there
was no restoration. Only once (1665) was taxation apportioned,
as of old, on the estates and assessed according to the "old
extent"; otherwise, valued rent was used as the basis for taxation
and proportions were appointed for every shire and royal burgh.
The covenanting innovation of the excise was also retained:
in 1661 parliament voted the king £480,000 yearly for life—
£98,000 from the customs and the remainder from an excise on
malt brewed and sold within the kingdom, whisky distilled at
home, and (at a higher rate) whisky and beer imported from
abroad. The effect of these arrangements was to spread the
financial burden over the whole nation, to the proportional
benefit of the landed class—whose property, incidentally, was
never again threatened by a revocation.

The church policy of Charles II's government had to meet a
situation in which the Scots were a deeply and bitterly divided
nation.[7] The protestors remained convinced of the truth of their
own interpretation of the covenants as undertakings perpetually
binding on the whole people of Scotland, and convinced that
the clerical domination of 1648-9 represented perfection in
church-state relations.[8] The whole concept of government by a
majority was repudiated: the protestors had already objected to
the choice of ministers by a popular vote which might go against
their party;[9] the church, it was soon to be said, was not to be
governed "after a carnal manner, by plurality of votes";[10]
"church government" was not "seated in the people and from
them derived unto the pastors and elders," but "cometh from
Christ . . . and by him immediately conferred upon the rulers and
officers of his house."[11] The refusal of the protestors to acknowledge any general assembly later than that of 1650 (which they
had dominated) and even to acknowledge presbyteries in which—
so they argued—the majority was not a majority of "the godly,"
meant that the presbyterian system of government was inoperable.
The resolutioners, on their side, were determined to use their
weight of numbers to eject the protestors from their parishes as

6 Some account of this is given later (pp. 377-8).

7 The situation was assessed by J. Willcock, "Sharp and the restoration policy
in Scotland," *Trans. Roy. Hist. Soc.*, new ser., xx. 149-69.

8 *Informatory Vindication*, p. 96.

9 [James Guthrie], *Protesters no subverters*, p. 90.

10 Wodrow, ii. app. xlvi.   11 *Informatory Vindication.* p. 85.

soon as the restraint of the Cromwellian regime was withdrawn, and it was even suggested that they would in the end have deprived nearly as many ministers as were actually deprived when episcopacy was restored. Had a general assembly been permitted to meet in 1660 it could only have broken up in disorder, if not in violence, and at this point, as again after the revolution, a settlement by vote of a representative general assembly was impracticable.

While there could be no settlement by consent and no settlement without a dissenting minority, yet toleration was repudiated as vehemently as democracy: one of the benefits expected in 1660 was the end of the " late sinful toleration,"[12] and rigid " solemn-leaguers " were later to refuse to accept toleration when it was offered to them, because it was inconsistent with " presbyterian principles."[13] The elements of compulsion and repression were at once apparent in 1660. A body of protestors met in Edinburgh and proposed an address to the king deprecating the trend towards episcopacy in England and reminding him of his obligations to the Covenants. They were seized by order of the committee of estates and next day a proclamation appeared forbidding all unauthorised meetings without the king's consent; this was, of course, parallel to the policy pursued by the government of the commonwealth and protectorate. Guthrie, the leader of the protestors, was executed, and this was a novelty, for even the most seditious of preachers had never before incurred a worse penalty than banishment. The Marquis of Argyll, who had been associated with the protestors, and had in 1659 been pressing for a return to their ascendancy, was found guilty of complying with the English occupation and of aiding the army which opposed the royalist rising of 1653/4, and was also executed. Johnston of Wariston fled to France, was condemned in his absence, and finally executed in 1663.

Those who thought the Solemn League practicable in 1660 were infatuated, for if England had not agreed to presbyterianism in the 1640s she was not likely to accept it at a time when the whole trend was towards the revival of old institutions. But, while protestors would have accepted nothing less than presbyterianism throughout Great Britain, others might have been satisfied with presbyterianism in Scotland alone, and they were encouraged by a letter from the king to the ministers of Edinburgh

---

12 Wodrow, i. vi, cf. p. li.   13 *Hind let loose*, pp. 184, 192.

(10 August 1660), designed to allay anxiety raised by the drift of events in England: Charles promised to maintain the church government in Scotland " settled by law."[14] It cannot have been forgotten that the policy of presbyterianism in Scotland alone had been envisaged in the Engagement, to which several of the politicians now in power in Scotland had been parties. But Charles II cannot have been encouraged by the earlier experiences of Charles I, for the conceding of the demand for presbytery in Scotland in 1639 had not prevented the Scots from sending an army to help the king's English subjects against him. The fact is that political unity without ecclesiastical uniformity presented difficulties which Charles I had detected when his position as king of England made it impossible for him to accede to the Scottish demand that he should agree that episcopacy was contrary to the Word of God; and after all Charles II himself had been compelled by the covenanters to promise a uniform church system in England, Scotland and Ireland. The notion that a British sovereign might have a presbyterian conscience in Scotland and an episcopalian conscience in England had not yet emerged.

The character of the settlement of both church and state which was made by Charles II's first parliament was indicated in a general way by the Act Rescissory (March 1661), which annulled all the legislation of the parliaments since 1633, although some of those parliaments had been authorised by the king, and if they had been defective in their composition in that they lacked the spiritual estate that was a defect which they shared with the " restoration parliament " itself. Yet the Act Rescissory did not define the legal position under which the church was to operate, for the act of 1633 empowering the king to prescribe the apparel of the clergy and the act of 1621 confirming the Five Articles of Perth, though they were not rescinded, were ignored. Thus, in so far as the church settlement of 1661 was a " restoration " it was a restoration of the moderate episcopalian regime of James VI's middle years, without the ritualistic accretions and the arbitrary interference with canons and liturgy which had occasioned the outbreak of 1637 and which alone had been denounced in the National Covenant. In practice, most earlier legislation was disregarded, and the position of the church was defined in a code

[14] Wodrow, I. 13.

of statutes passed in the summer of 1662, formally restoring epis-copal government, reviving lay patronage, declaring the covenants unlawful and forbidding private conventicles.

It was not a time for a policy based on principles, since principles were unseasonable and, after Scotland's recent ex-periences, discredited. The believers in a divine right of presby-tery and the believers in a divine right of episcopacy were equally disregarded. The settlement must be seen in practical terms. What existed at the time was a kind of beheaded and imperfect remnant of presbyterianism, a system in which the general assembly had been in abeyance since 1653 and in which synods and presbyteries had been operating under the limitations imposed by the Cromwellian government and by the strife between resolu-tioners and protestors. Now, synods and presbyteries were retain-ed, but for the general assembly there were substituted bishops under conciliar and parliamentary control and without any real independence in shaping policy.

In the normal course of administration, the bishop exercised his authority within a framework in which the rights of both presbyters and congregations were substantially safeguarded. Legislative power and appellate jurisdiction lay with the bishop in synod, executive authority was shared between the presbytery and the bishop. Presbyteries conducted visitations, examined candidates before their ordination by the bishop, censured mini-sters (but could not suspend or deprive them without the bishop's consent), and sometimes voluntarily submitted difficult questions to the bishop. Both the bishops and the government stressed the need for the discipline of the kirk session, and the session's power was unrestricted save that it could not proceed to excommuni-cation without the bishop's consent. While the law was in favour of the lay patron, the will of the people was often taken into account when ministers were appointed, and presbyteries did not normally proceed to induction without the congregation's assent. In general, ecclesiastical administration was very much as it had been throughout most of the period between 1560 and 1638, and just as contemporaries could speak of returning to the good old form of government by privy council,[15] so they might have spoken of returning to the good old form of government by bishop and synod.

15 *Lauderdale Papers*, I. 172.

There was little that could offend presbyterian susceptibilities. As only one of the pre-covenanting bishops survived,
recourse was again had to England for consecration, and this
time two of the four candidates, who had not been episcopally
ordained, were required to accept ordination as deacons and
priests before their consecration. But within Scotland ordination
to the diaconate was rare, and there was no general or compulsory
reordination of men in presbyterian orders, for—although some
were persuaded to accept reordination and others sought it
voluntarily—the official view was that by presbyterian ordination
a man could properly have been "admitted to the holy ministry."[16]
The rite of confirmation by bishops was not reintroduced, and
services generally reflected a determination not to repeat the
blunder which had occasioned the rebellion against Charles I,
for there was no altar against the east wall, no surplice, no kneeling
at Communion. Although the Prayer Book was used by individual
ministers in public worship and by many clergy and laity in their
private devotions, there was no compulsory liturgy, but the reading
of the scriptures in church, the doxology, the Lord's Prayer and
the Apostles' Creed were reintroduced. There are indications
that some of the changes made in worship by the covenanters
had not been popular, and the revival of pre-covenanting practice
would commend the " restoration " settlement to many.[17]

The extent of the approval given to this settlement is not
easy to determine. To some, the presbyterian system was one
feature of a revolutionary interlude which was best forgotten:

> From covenants with uplifted hands,
> From remonstrators with associate bands,
> From such committees as governed the nation,
> From church commissioners and their protestation,
>   Good Lord, deliver us.[18]

The extravagant rejoicing which marked the restoration of the
monarchy contributed to acquiescence in the measures of the
king's government,[19] and one point of view was expressed by a
peer who wrote, " I judge myself bound in conscience to defend
episcopacy with my life and fortune so long as his majesty and the

16 *Ecclesiastical records of Aberdeen* (Spalding Club), p. 269.
17 This is the inference from several references by Nicoll and Lamont in their
Diaries, especially Nicoll, p. 382.   18 Kirkton, p. 127.
19 For recently published accounts of the celebrations in Edinburgh, see *Diurnal
of Thomas Rugg* (Royal Hist. Soc., 1961), pp. 95-6, 180.

laws are for it."[20] It is clear, too, that the disturbances of the 1640s and the excesses of the protestors in 1649-50 had led by 1660 to a strong reaction against the Covenants and even against presbyterianism. Protestors and resolutioners alike remarked on the growing " hatred " of the covenants;[21] protestors were the more pessimistic, noting that " presbyterian ministers begin to incline to prelacy," that " there are as many now against the covenant as was for it in 1643," and that " the bulk of the nation was turned . . . against . . . presbyterial government."[22]

Some indication of clerical opinion is, of course, given by the deprivations of ministers who declined to comply with the requirements of the new establishment. It is true that the issues on which the deprivations took place were narrow. One arose from the statute restoring patronage: in order to regularise the position of ministers instituted since 1649, they were required to obtain presentation from the patron and collation from the bishop, and the council decreed that if they did not obey by 1 November 1662 (subsequently extended to 1 February 1663), they would forfeit church and stipend. The other arose from the attitude of the presbyterians to the church courts: much was made of the somewhat academic point that synods and presbyteries now met in virtue of authorisation by the crown and the bishops,[23] and many ministers who declined to attend those courts were deprived.[24] All in all thirty-two ministers were deprived in the synod of Galloway (thirty-seven parishes), seventy-five in the synod of Glasgow and Ayr (121 parishes), and in Dumfries the ministers of very slightly over half the parishes were deprived. Elsewhere the majority conformed—in Fife about one in three was deprived, in Lothian and the Borders rather fewer, and in the synods north of the Tay conformity was almost universal. The total number of deprivations was about 270, or a little more than a quarter of the ministers in the country, and with this figure some instructive comparisons can be made. Deprivations on such a scale far exceeded anything which had been known at the Reformation or on the revival of episcopacy under James VI, and even in the long covenanting ascendancy there had been a total of only about

---

20 *Lauderdale Papers*, I. 229-30.
21 Wodrow, I. xv.
22 Johnston of Wariston, *Diary*, III. 27, 61, 181.
23 Kirkton, pp. 138, 141-2, 297; Wodrow, I. 335; *Hind let loose*, p. 42.
24 Wodrow, I. 136, 207, 213-4, 226.

200 deprivations. On the other hand, in 1690, when presbytery was restored, more than half of the ministers of the country had to be deprived. At this stage, conformity was still the dominant note, and it is not difficult to find ministers who were appointed under Charles I, continued in office throughout the covenanting period and were still in office after the Restoration.[25] The tradition of a united church was still strong enough to curb secession, and some who were presbyterian in their opinions conformed because they would not " separate from the Church of God."[26] Moreover, the dislocation in Scotland after 1660 did not greatly exceed that in England, where the 2,000 puritan ministers deposed in 1662 amounted to about a fifth of the total number of ministers in that country. Arithmetic hardly supports the assumption that there was a peculiarly strong antipathy to episcopacy in Scotland.

The deprivations tell us nothing about lay opinion. Laymen, however, had never been much stirred on the issue of ecclesiastical polity, and the Restoration settlement did not obtrude the innovations in worship which had antagonised laymen earlier. On the other hand, the anti-clerical character of the settlement made a positive appeal to many laymen, who now had to endure the interference in politics of neither bishops nor ministers.[27] The nobles had not forgotten that in 1650 and 1651 peers of ancient lineage had been compelled to do penance on their knees before kirk sessions which disapproved of their political views,[28] and their customary anti-clericalism was now directed not so much against bishops as against ministers, especially as the ministers inducted since 1649 were men in whose selection they had had no voice:

> The nobility had been previously so much under the subjection of insolent churchmen that they were more willing to be subject to their prince than to any such low and mean persons as the clergy, which consisted now of the sons of their own servants and farmers.[29]

There were certainly some nobles whose sympathies were emphatically presbyterian and even covenanting: Cassillis, for

25 For a regional study which supports those general conclusions, see James Bulloch, " Conformists and nonconformists," in *Trans. East Lothian Antiq. and Field Naturalists' Society*, VIII. I have profited from a discussion with Dr Bulloch about the statistics for the country as a whole.
26 Wodrow, I. 189.
27 *E.g.*, Nicoll, pp. 204-5.
28 *Diary of John Lamont*, pp. 21, 25.
29 Mackenzie, *Memoirs*, pp. 159-60.

example, who acted " according to the laudable custom of his fathers "[30] in dissenting from the oath of supremacy in 1661 and voting against the act condemning conventicles in 1670, and Cathcart, Balmerino, Crawford, Bargany and Kirkcudbright. But not one of them was prepared to take up arms when the covenanters rose in revolt and so renew the combination of radical peers with fanatical ministers. In the rebellions of Charles II's reign the lower classes of the south-west acted for the first time on their own initiative, contrary to aristocratic leadership; after the covenant lost its appeal to the magnates, it survived as the rallying point of the humbler folk, and it was the " very mean persons " who were most obstinate.[31] If the reformed church, or the presbyterian church, did anything to break down the old social ties which had dominated Scotland in the past, it was done in this period, and not either at the Reformation or at the time of the National Covenant. The leadership of the nobility was displaced to some extent by the leadership of ministers, but mainly perhaps by the leadership of an idea. Of equal significance with the detachment of the nobility was the detachment now of the capital, which had taken the lead against Charles I but was acquiescent under Charles II. When an insurrection did break out in the south-west, in 1666, the rebels marched on Edinburgh but found that neither the city nor the surrounding countryside would give them any countenance, and an Edinburgh diarist was contemptuous of those " comonlie callit the Whigs," who " pretendit they died ' for God and the covenant'."[32]

The ecclesiastical disaffection with which the government had to deal arose initially from the deprivations. The displaced ministers were forbidden to preach or even to reside within twenty miles of their former parishes, and their places were taken by " curates." The " crew of young curates " have habitually been condemned, on the strength of a passage in Burnet's *History of his own Time*, as " the dregs and refuse of the northern parts . . . the worst preachers I ever heard, ignorant to a reproach, many of them openly vicious . . . a disgrace to their orders."[33] But the dispassionate pages of the *Fasti Ecclesiae Scoticanae* prove that Burnet's allegations about the youth and the poor educational standard of the curates are unfounded, and his slanders of the curates

[30] *Lauderdale Papers*, ii. 200n.   [31] *Lauderdale Papers*, ii. 96.

[32] Nicoll, *Diary*, p. 452.   [33] Burnet, *Own Time*, i. 269.

should be read with his description of the presbyterian ministers: " a grave, solemn sort of people. Their spirits were eager and their tempers sour. . . . They had a very scanty measure of learning, . . . of a very indifferent size of capacity, and apt to fly out into great excess of passion and indiscretion."[34] However, the prejudice against the curates was such that " the people in most of the parishes would not receive angels if they commit the horrid crime of going to presbyteries and synods,"[35] and the experiment could only embitter feeling. When some of the people showed signs of preferring the illegal ministrations of their outed ministers, an act of parliament (July 1663) imposed heavy fines on all persons who declined to attend worship in their own parish churches. The fines were exacted—in the absence of any other executive instrument—by the military, and troops were quartered on delinquents until they paid. Troops were also used to break up illegal meetings for worship. After England went to war with Holland, in 1665, the fear of a rising in conjunction with the Dutch led to more severe repression, but the result was to produce a rising, though when it came (in November 1666) it started almost fortuitously and was on a trifling scale. Sir James Turner, commander of the forces in the south-west, was surprised and captured in Dumfries by a band of whigs, whose success soon swelled their numbers to about 3,000 men. They marched through Ayrshire and Lanarkshire and made for Edinburgh. Hampered by the weather, pursued by Sir Thomas Dalziel, weakened by defection and disagreement, and discouraged by the indifference of the countryside, they yet held on as far as Colinton, when they fell back, to be defeated at Rullion Green (28 November). Of the prisoners who refused to take the oath of allegiance, about thirty were hanged, others banished to Barbados.

The experiment was next made of a policy of conciliation. In August 1667 the army was disbanded except for two troops of lifeguards and eight companies of foot, and in October an amnesty was issued to all save about sixty who had been involved in the rising, on condition only that they would swear not to bear arms against the king again. Conciliation in an ecclesiastical sense could take one of two forms—comprehension within the

---

[34] Burnet, *Own Time*, I. 264-6, cf. p. 59. Burnet's animosity against the Scottish ecclesiastical establishment comes out in the criticism printed in *S. H. S. Misc.*, II.

[35] *Lauderdale Papers*, II. 217.

national church or toleration outside it. The leading advocate of comprehension was Robert Leighton (1611-84), Bishop of Dunblane since 1661, who proposed that provincial synods should have power to censure bishops, that in diocesan synods bishops should have no negative voice and that any minister should be allowed to protest that he submitted to the bishop only for the sake of order and regarded him as no more than the chief of the presbyters. Leighton was chosen to supersede the unyielding episcopalian Burnet in the archbishopric of Glasgow, but the government preferred to experiment with a kind of toleration rather than with comprehension. The first indulgence (June 1669) resulted in the restoration of forty-two presbyterian ministers to their parishes, and a second, in 1672, allowed some ninety more of them to preach; these indulged ministers served under certain restrictions, but were not obliged to renounce their preference for presbyterian government. One result of the indulgences was to split the presbyterians: while the more moderate ministers accepted the indulgences, and many of the gentry welcomed the return of their old pastors, opposition was stimulated by ministers who had been banished to Holland after 1662, and hatred of the indulgences was instilled into the lower classes. The party who declined to accept the indulgences now denied the validity of episcopalian ordination,[36] rejected the preaching and the sacraments of the indulged,[37] and began to conduct their own ordinations in order to maintain a succession of covenanted clergy. The disbanding of the bulk of the army, and the generally milder attitude of the authorities, also had the result of facilitating conventicles, which spread from the south-west into Fife and the Lothians and became aggressive in pro-selytising among people who had previously been content with the ministrations of the authorised clergy. Therefore, even while the phase of conciliation continued, there had to be a proclam-ation (1669) fining heritors on whose lands conventicles were held, an act of parliament (1670) imposing fines on unlicensed ministers and their congregations and the death penalty on preachers at field conventicles, and another statute (1672) making baptism by lawful ministers compulsory and illegal ordination punishable by banishment or imprisonment.

In 1673 conciliation was succeeded by renewed repression,

[36] *Hind let loose*, p. 253; *Informatory Vindication*, p. 54.   [37] Kirkton, p. 334.

and Burnet was restored to Glasgow, while Leighton resigned and withdrew from Scotland altogether. In 1675 letters of inter-communing began to be issued against conventiclers, putting them under boycott or ostracism. It was already the law that heritors and masters should be responsible for the conformity of their tenants and servants, and in 1677 heritors were required to sign bonds for the loyal behaviour of all persons residing on their lands. Such an obligation could not be undertaken by many landholders in the west. When the heritors of Ayrshire and Ren-frewshire were warned that they must either devise means for the suppression of conventicles or have them put down by force, they declared that the suppression of conventicles was beyond their power and recommended toleration. As conventicles were each year becoming larger and more military in their character, it was increasingly clear that the ordinary means of preserving order and securing obedience to the law were going to break down. In July 1678 a convention of estates voted a sum of £1,800,000, chiefly for the purpose of suppressing conventicles, but it became clear that the lawfulness of paying the " cess " to raise this sum would be contested. Besides, the local militia was obviously untrustworthy in the disaffected areas, and the regular forces might easily prove inadequate should the masses of conventiclers once band themselves together into a central organisation. The administration hit on the extraordinary device of the " Highland host " (actually over a third of it con-sisting of Lowland militia), which was quartered on the disaffected districts in 1678.

This measure exacerbated feeling, and, as conventicles now concentrated into larger assemblies which never wholly dispersed, it was obvious by the spring of 1679 that an outbreak could not be long delayed, even before stimulus was given by the murder of Archbishop Sharp of St Andrews on 3 May.[38] Sharp, a native of the conservative north-east and a graduate of the episcopalian university of Aberdeen, had never been a fervent covenanter and during the Cromwellian period had emerged as a leader of the resolutioners. In the critical months of 1660 he was in London as a representative of that party, and with his background he found it congenial enough to give way to the drift towards

[38] There was an engagement between a party of dragoons and a conventicle at Lesmahago at the end of March (*Lauderdale Papers*, III. 162).

episcopacy. His compliance brought him the primacy, but to many he was a Judas who had betrayed the cause. His murderers encountered him by chance on Magus Moor, where they put him to death with ferocious brutality in his daughter's presence. They then fled to the west and, with the conventiclers who were massed there, framed the Rutherglen Declaration (29 May) against all violations of the covenants from the Engagement onwards. On 1 June an armed conventicle at Drumclog defeated a force under John Graham of Claverhouse (1648-89), who, after serving in France and Holland, had in the previous September been appointed captain of one of three troops of horse commissioned to deal with the situation in the south-west.

The successful insurgents were at once joined by large numbers and were able to enter Glasgow, but instead of organising their forces they spent their time in wrangling. While there were moderates who upheld the king's authority and craved only a free parliament and assembly, the extremists would collaborate with none who did not repudiate the indulgences and they would not acknowledge an uncovenanted government. The rebels were routed by the Duke of Monmouth, an illegitimate son of Charles II, at Bothwell Brig (22 June). There was a brief interlude of milder measures after the battle, for Monmouth, the champion and favourite of English dissent, secured an indemnity and a new indulgence, authorising house conventicles. The majority of the prisoners, after an imprisonment in Edinburgh,[39] were allowed to return home on promising not to bear arms again, and only a minority who refused were shipped off for the West Indies, most of them to perish in the Orkneys on the way. Presently, however, Monmouth was replaced by the Duke of York, the king's Roman catholic brother, who reverted to the policy of repression.

The main body of covenanting dissent had been broken by doses of concession and repression, but a section under Donald Cargill, Richard Cameron and Hackston of Rathillet (one of Sharp's murderers) remained in arms and in the Sanquhar Declaration (22 June 1680) disowned the king. Their defeat at Airds Moss (22 July 1680) removed Cameron by death on the field and Hackston by capture and execution. Cargill, the sole remaining field preacher, excommunicated the king, the Duke of

---

[39] For the place and conditions of their imprisonment, see W. Moir Bryce, *Old Greyfriars Church*, pp. 48, 112-5.

York and leading Scottish politicians and contended that this was a purely ecclesiastical matter for which he could not be called to account before any civil tribunal. Cargill was executed in 1681, but the Cameronians, styling themselves the " anti-popish, anti-prelatic, anti-erastian, anti-sectarian, true presby-terian Church of Scotland," preserved their organisation until they found a new leader in James Renwick, who ministered to them from 1683 until his execution in 1688. They considered themselves to be justified in what might be called " preventive murder,"[40] and they carried on a guerilla warfare against those whom they believed to be seeking their lives. The " presbyterian Hildebrandism " of the Cameronians may have been the logical sequel to Melville's doctrine of the two kingdoms, but their antithesis of " King Charles " and " King Jesus " was a false one : the true antithesis was between crown and parliament on one side and, on the other, an ecclesiastical faction which dis-regarded any opinion but its own. One contemporary who was favourable to the presbyterians thought the Cameronians under a " delusion, which seemed to be a sort of madness,"[41] and another commented, " O, whither shall our shame go, at such a height of folly are some men arrived."[42] A recent writer, also of strong presbyterian bias, concurs :

> They fought for something which no government could accept and which was abhorrent to most Scotsmen. . . . It was madness . . . . It should have been treated as madness.[43]

Possibly the government showed little sense of proportion in harrying this intransigent remnant, even though they would not save their lives when they could do so by abjuring their Declar-ations or even by saying " God save the king." But the atrocities of the " killing time " have been exaggerated,[44] and it must be

[40] This principle was enunciated in the *Apologetical Declaration* (1684) and the *Informatory Vindication* (1687).   [41] Burnet, *Own Time*, II. 295.
    [42] Law, *Memorials*, p. 161.   [43] J. M. Reid, *Kirk and Nation*, pp. 191, 195.
    [44] It has been demonstrated, for example, that " Bloody Clavers " used his exten-sive powers sparingly and that the number of lives he took did not exceed ten. And, although the two female " Wigtown Martyrs " were certainly condemned to be drowned, that they were in fact drowned has not yet been conclusively demonstrated, for no strictly contemporary or eye-witness accounts of the execution have ever come to light, and what purport to be descriptions differ in some material particulars. See Mark Napier, *The case for the crown in re the Wigtown martyrs* (1863), A. Stewart, *History Vindicated in the case of the Wigtown martyrs* (1867), and Napier, *History rescued, in answer to ' History Vindicated '* (1870).

remembered that the coercion used against those " solemn-leaguers " was no more severe than the coercion which they themselves would have applied had they been in power.

> There must have been many quiet, old-fashioned folk in the land, who, casting back their memories to the days after Philiphaugh, saw in the change the slow grinding of the mills of God. In one respect the later persecution, bad and indefensible as it was, fell short of the grossness of the earlier, for its perpetrators in their evil work did not profane the name of the meek gospel of Christ.[45]

If the ecclesiastical opposition was on limited issues and among sections of the nation restricted both socially and geographically, opposition of a quite different kind was aroused by several features in the conduct of the nation's secular affairs. Fiscal policy caused irritation, if nothing more, in a period when the economy was struggling to recover from serious dislocation: thus, a grant of £480,000 from customs and excise in 1661 was said to be " the ruin of the people," and duties imposed later on French salt, brandy and tobacco raised prices and " provoked the body of the people."[46] But such exactions were the more unpopular because the government was in the hands of men notorious for their greed and corruption. Lauderdale's own record was far from reputable. It was held against him that he made the office of king's commissioner in Scotland a permanent one, which he enjoyed year after year at a cost to the nation, so it was said, of £18,000 sterling;[47] he received a gift of the Cromwellian fort at Leith and then blackmailed Edinburgh into buying it from him for £5,000 sterling; he arranged that the crown should purchase the Bass Rock for £4,000 from one of his friends, and then had the profits of the island bestowed on himself. But worse than Lauderdale were some of his associates, including his second wife, who became the channel through which government patronage was distributed—for a consideration. Lauderdale's brother, Charles Maitland of Haltoun, who became treasurer depute, general of the mint and a lord of session, not only abused his position to advance the interests of his own clients, but was ultimately convicted of " embezzlements of the mint and coinage "[48] as well as of perjury. One example of sharp

---

45 John Buchan, *Montrose* (World's Classics edn.), pp. 318-19.
46 Burnet, *Own Time* (1823), II. 19.   47 *Lauderdale Papers*, III. 19.
48 *Lauderdale Papers*, III. 229.

practice concerned the earldom of Caithness: John Campbell of Glenorchy, a supporter of Lauderdale, was a principal creditor of the sixth earl, from whom he obtained a conveyance of the latter's dignities, lands and heritable jurisdictions; on the earl's death, Glenorchy was created Earl of Caithness, to the exclusion of the rightful heir. Somewhat similarly, on the death of the first Earl of Dundee, in 1668, the claims of the lawful heirs to the property and title were set aside in the interests of Haltoun, and it appears that the Register of the Great Seal was mutilated in order to conceal the terms of the original patent of the earldom.[49] A swindle of a different kind was done to James Mitchell, who, when indicted for an attempt to murder Archbishop Sharp in 1668, confessed the crime on promise of his life, but was subsequently executed because the promise was denied. Again, Baillie of Jerviswood, on trial for complicity in the Rye House Plot of 1683, was fined £6,000 by the privy council and then—by an irregularity which startled contemporaries—tried afresh by the court of justiciary on the same charge and sentenced to death. Any pretensions of the judicial bench to integrity vanished when, in 1677, the king insisted that all commissions should be *durante beneplacito*, and in 1682 an act against regalities was denounced as making the king in person " master of the whole justice and property of the kingdom."[50] From 1667 to 1681 the office of chancellor was held by the Earl of Rothes, who admitted his own unfitness, through " ignorance," for the office.[51] Contemporaries, like Sir James Stewart of Goodtrees in *An accompt of Scotland's grievances by reason of the duke of Lauderdale's ministrie* (?1674), were able to present a picture of a regime in which Lauderdale and his nominees feathered their nests by dubious means and controlled the judicature—to which " ignorant and insufficient men " were appointed—in such a way that appeals for justice were in vain.[52] Goodtrees was, as it happened, associated with the extreme left-wing of the presbyterian party,[53]

[49] *Dudhope Peerage: proceedings before the committee for privileges* (H.M.S.O., 1952), pp. 21-5.

[50] Burnet, *Own Time*, II. 298.   [51] *Lauderdale Papers*, II. 1.

[52] Stewart, *An accompt*, p. 20; Wodrow, I. app. lix.

[53] Stewart was part-author of *Naphtali, or the wrestlings of the Church of Scotland* (1667), which was answered by Andrew Honeyman, Bishop of Orkney, in *A survey of Naphtali*. Stewart replied with *Jus populi vindicatum*, which shows the association of ecclesiastical and political agitation.

but political and ecclesiastical grievances were connected to the extent that the prevalent corruption showed itself also in some of the proceedings against conventiclers. Thus Sir James Turner, for example, had little regard for the law when he exacted quartering money for his troops or when he imposed fines, and an inquiry led to his dismissal in 1668. Equally, in the early 1680s, when it was possible to take proceedings against anyone suspected of having been in contact with the Bothwell Brig rebels, every petty tyrant could exert pressure and exact fines.[54]

Actions of the administration were again and again challenged as not merely corrupt, but unconstitutional. The very core of the system of government was attacked in complaints that the powers now vested in the commissioner violated the constitution:[55] " For God's sake let us but have a trial of securing the peace and quiet of the country without a commissioner, having a chancellor and the old way of government."[56] The administration came into conflict with the bulk of legal opinion on the issue of the legality of appeals to parliament, when such an appeal was made from a decision which the court of session had reached after the intervention of Lauderdale in person (in his capacity as an extraordinary lord of session). In 1674 a petition by the convention of royal burghs for the repeal of certain acts was condemned as seditious.[57] Here again some of the anti-covenanting proceedings fitted into the general pattern, for commissions to the army to live at free quarters in time of peace were held to be contrary to the constitution.

Consequently, there were many appeals to " fundamental laws." The political opposition appealed to " the fundamental laws of the nation";[58] the ecclesiastical opposition suggested that real " authority " pertained to those who had " the fundamental laws of the land on their side."[59] On the other hand, the " fundamental laws of the kingdom " were cited in defence of the prerogative,[60] and the imposition of the covenants was held to have been " against the fundamental laws and liberties " of the subjects.[61] It was even more significant that Sir George Mackenzie of Rosehaugh, upholder of the prerogative as he was, held that

[54] E.g., *Melrose Regality Records* (S. H. S.), III. 22 ff.   [55] *Lauderdale Papers*, III. 19.
[56] *Ibid.*, II. 45.   [57] Burnet, *Own Time*, II. 48-9.
[58] *Lauderdale Papers*, III. 38.   [59] *Hind let loose*, p. 595.
[60] *Lauderdale Papers*, III. 105.   [61] Mackenzie, *Memoirs*, p. 64.

it was unlawful for a king, with or without parliament, to act against the fundamental laws of the kingdom. And, far though the Cameronians were from being friends to either liberty or democracy, there were elements in their thought in accord with the constitutionalism of the time: when they said of Charles II that he had " inverted all the ends of government "[62] they were using a phrase which was to find its way into the constitutional manifesto of the Revolution of 1689, the Claim of Right.

The fact was that Scottish political affairs were taking on a new character and that the nation was being introduced to what may be called ministerial government, for real authority lay with ministers as it had not done under James VI and Charles I. As the ministries were responsible in law to the king, the opposition could appeal to him, so that rival factions competed with each other by way of solicitation at court. Middleton, Charles II's first commissioner, made difficulties for himself through his own rashness, but he also lacked the full confidence of the king, who was much under the influence of Lauderdale, the secretary, in London. Middleton tried to eliminate Lauderdale through the " billeting affair," in 1662. The king was induced to agree to the exclusion from an act of indemnity of twelve persons to be named by parliament; at the suggestion of Sir George Mackenzie of Tarbat, an associate of Middleton, it was agreed that each member of parliament should write out anonymously his own list of twelve and that the twelve who were most frequently named should be excluded, and Middleton so arranged matters that Lauderdale's name was among the twelve. On Lauderdale's representations Middleton was then accused of conspiring to deprive the king of his servants, and in March 1663 he lost the commissionership, which went to Rothes, a closer friend of Lauderdale. Rothes worked with Archbishop Sharp, and the repression of presbyterians at this stage was consonant with the influence at court of Clarendon, the English chancellor, for it was the era of the " Clarendon Code " against English nonconformists. Lauderdale disapproved of the repression, but even if he had had sufficient influence to change policy he preferred to wait until the Pentland Rising discredited the policy of Rothes and Sharp.

In 1667 Rothes lost the offices of commissioner and treasurer

[62] *Informatory Vindication*, p. 40.

and was made chancellor, to the disappointment of Sharp. The treasury was put into commission, with a majority of Lauderdale's friends and supporters among the commissioners, and Lauderdale himself became commissioner when parliament next met, in 1669. Tarbat, Middleton's old ally, went out of office, and two friends to conciliation were brought in—the Earl of Tweeddale, who had sat in Cromwell's parliaments, had voted against the execution of Guthrie in 1661, and was speaking of an indulgence as early as 1667, and the Earl of Kincardine, who had been opposed to the restoration of episcopacy and in 1669 favoured " a qualified toleration."[63] When there was a reversion to repression, in 1674, Kincardine and Tweeddale were dispensed with, but Lauderdale remained in power until after Bothwell Brig and was not actually dismissed until 1681.

Apart from the jockeying of individuals and groups for the king's countenance, parliament itself became so plainly a platform for the opposition that Scotland may be said to have served an apprenticeship in something like parliamentary government in this " restoration " era. The revival of the committee of articles had been opposed in 1661, and it never recovered the control which it had exercised before 1638. When Lauderdale came as commissioner to the parliament of 1669, he had instructions to deal for a union with England, the act of supremacy, the establishment of a militia and measures of conciliation in the church. There was opposition of one kind or another to every item in this programme, for ecclesiastical extremists of both sides were opposed to the act of supremacy, highflying episcopalians were opposed to conciliation, and few were in favour of either a union or a militia. However, it was still possible so to manage parliament that the grumbling did not seriously embarrass the government, though it was a novelty that the house insisted on returning one measure to the committee of articles for amendment.[64] During the session of 1672, William Moir, member for Kintore, urged that before parliament approved the cess, members should be given time to consult their constituents, and he was imprisoned "for some words tending to the subversion of the constitution of parliament."[65] In the course of that same year, several nobles seem to have appealed to the Duke of Hamilton to become leader of a regular

[63] *Lauderdale Papers*, II. 126.   [64] *Ibid.*, II. 151.
[65] *A. P. S.*, VIII. 63; cf. *Source Book of Scottish History*, III. 252, 501.

opposition. This duke was the son of the Marquis of Douglas, and in his own right Earl of Selkirk, but he had married the heiress of the first Duke of Hamilton and was made Duke of Hamilton for life. He had therefore been antagonised by the proposed union of 1669, with its threat to his family's interest in the Scottish crown, and he was lukewarm to repressive measures against the presbyterians, for his estates lay in the disaffected areas and his wife was an enthusiastic presbyterian. By the time parliament opened in 1673 there was in existence a " club " or " party " in which Queensberry and Rothes were associated with Hamilton. It was significant of the change from the days when parliament had been no more than a docile registrar that Lauderdale was instructed to " endeavour to remove any just clamour " on account of certain fiscal measures,[66] but the opposition did not wait for evidence of concessions.

> When the parliament was opened, the king's letter was read, desiring their assistance in carrying on the war with Holland. . . . Hamilton moved that the state of the nation might be first considered that so they might see what grievances they had. . . . And then, as it had been laid, about twenty men, one after another, spoke to several particulars.[67]

" Warm debates arose in the house," a member asked " whether this was a free parliament or not " and Sir Patrick Hume of Polwarth and others " spoke with abundance of freedom and plainness."[68]　Lauderdale, who had to face this aristocratic opposition at a time when he had lost the support of most of the burgess estate, thought that the parliament showed " such a spirit as I thought never to have seen here."[69]　The government in effect acknowledged defeat, for parliament was first adjourned, then dissolved, and did not meet again until 1681.

After the adjournment, the opposition, deprived of their parliamentary platform, sent Hamilton and the Earl of Dumfries to court, to complain that Lauderdale, Haltoun and their friends engrossed all the profitable offices.[70]　In 1676 Kincardine, who lost his place on the council because of his opposition to Lauderdale, went to London to protest against that minister's

---

[66] *Lauderdale Papers*, III. 1.

[67] Burnet, *Own Time* (1823), II. 33-4; Mackenzie, *Memoirs*, pp. 256-7; *Lauderdale Papers*, II. 242 ff.　　[68] Wodrow, I. 364.

[69] *Lauderdale Papers*, II. 241.　　[70] Wodrow, I. 364, cf. p. 379.

rule,[71] and in 1678 Hamilton and others were again appealing to
the king against the ministry.[72] There was also co-operation
with the English opposition: the English whigs professed to
see in Lauderdale a second Wentworth, proposing to bring an
alien army into England, and therefore encouraged the agitation
in the parliament of 1673/4; later, a Scottish whig like Baillie
of Jerviswood was in communication with the English faction
under Monmouth and Russell which tried to bring about the
exclusion from the throne of the king's Roman catholic brother,
James, Duke of York, and there were plans for an insurrection
in Scotland at the time of the Rye House Plot in 1683.

Most of the features which had characterised Scottish politics
since 1660 disappeared after 1681, for, although Charles II lived
until 6 February 1685, policy in Scotland was directed mainly in
the interests of his brother. The Duke of York was in Scotland
for a time in 1679 and again from 1680 to 1682, and acted as his
brother's commissioner to the Scottish parliament. He obtained
an act ensuring that his hereditary rights would not be prejudiced
by his religion; and by the Test Act all office-bearers in church
and state and all electors and members of parliament were obliged
to take an oath acknowledging the Confession of Faith of 1560,
accepting the royal supremacy, renouncing the Covenants and
all leagues and meetings to treat of any matter of church or state,
and forswearing all endeavours to make any alteration in civil
or ecclesiastical government. This oath could hardly be taken
without qualification by any conscientious man: the Confession
of 1560, though never abrogated, was obsolete and little known;
some thought that Confession inconsistent with the terms in which
the royal supremacy was acknowledged; others asked how they
could swear to maintain the government of the church if the king,
in virtue of his supremacy, could alter it at will. Convinced
presbyterians could not accept the royal supremacy, but a considerable number of the parish clergy, too, refused to take the oath
and suffered deprivation. The Test Act was also the means of
effecting the ruin of the Earl of Argyll. This earl, though a son
of the covenanting marquis, was not himself a covenanter or
even a presbyterian, but he had made many enemies, for his
restoration to his father's estates, in 1669, had been prejudicial
to those who had claims on them, including the strongly royalist

[71] *H. M. C. Report*, xv. pt. viii, 217.   [72] Burnet, *Own Time*, ii. 136-7.

MacLeans, against whom Argyll carried on a private war for the acquisition of Mull, Morvern and Tiree. The Duke of York, suspicious of Argyll's aggrandisement, and aware that his own policy of ingratiating himself with Highland chiefs would be advanced by the overthrow of Argyll, was influenced by the earl's enemies to argue that his consent to take the Test Oath only " in so far as it was consistent with itself " was treasonable. Argyll was sentenced to death, but escaped to Holland.

In that country the leaders of both English and Scottish disaffection gathered, and the opportunity of James's accession was seized on for risings by Monmouth in England and Argyll in Scotland. But Monmouth's expedition was delayed, and Argyll's effort (May 1685) was a fiasco. The government had made preparations against him in his own country and had swept off the whigs already in custody to the security of Dunnottar; besides, the Cameronians would not collaborate with one who was not himself a covenanter. Argyll was captured in Renfrewshire, to be put to death in virtue of his conviction in 1681. The fact was that James's accession went all but unquestioned and he had the loyalty of the nation as a whole. Parliament, in granting him the excise in perpetuity, expressed in the most fulsome terms its belief in hereditary absolute monarchy:

> This nation hath continued now upwards of two thousand years in the unaltered form of our monarchical government, under the uninterrupted line of one hundred and eleven kings, whose sacred authority and power hath been upon all signal occasions so owned and assisted by Almighty God that our kingdom hath been protected from conquest, our possessions defended from strangers, our civil commotions brought into wished events, our laws vigorously executed. . . . These great blessings we owe in the first place to divine mercy, and, in dependence on that, to the sacred race of our glorious kings and to the solid, absolute authority wherewith they were invested by the first and fundamental law of our monarchy.

Political opposition in parliament and council was quiescent, and ecclesiastical opposition had been effectively broken. The south-western shires had been harried afresh since 1681, with a view to the imposition of the Test Act as well as the punishment of all who had been associated with rebels and all who did not attend church. Many of the indulged ministers, too, were turned out on the ground that they had violated the conditions imposed on them. And, at a time when the Cameronians had little more than a nuisance value, James's parliament declared it treason to own the National Covenant " as explained in the year 1638 " and made attendance at a conventicle punishable by death.

To his second parliament, in 1686, James offered free trade with England in return for the relief of Roman Catholics from the laws against them. There was strong opposition in the committee of articles, and indignation in the estates. The decision of the house was to write to the king to the effect that the estates would go as far as their consciences allowed, " not doubting that your majesty will be careful to secure the protestant religion established by law."[73] This amounted to a rebuff, and parliament was first adjourned (June) and later dissolved. On this issue of toleration, the usually subservient parliament had opposed and defeated the crown. James had chosen to raise what was probably the only issue that could bring down his throne.

As parliament had failed him, he had to proceed by other means. For one thing, attempts could be made to gain converts, partly by restricting royal favour to those of the king's persuasion. Certainly, without conversions on a large scale, Scotland was not going to become a Roman catholic country or the king find enough co-religionists to act as his agents, for in 1677 an envoy from Rome had reported that there were only 2,000 Romanists between the Moray Firth and the Solway, and even those were concentrated in Dumfriesshire and the highlands of Aberdeen and Banff.[74] Among James's early converts were the Earl of Perth, the chancellor, and his brother, Lord Melfort, a secretary of state. The Earl of Moray, another secretary, showed such signs of moving in the same direction that he became commissioner in 1686, although he did not declare himself until 1687. On the other hand, Queensberry, a firm protestant, lost the commissionership and was also removed from the treasury, which was put into commission with Perth as principal commissioner. The command of Edinburgh Castle was given to the Duke of Gordon, a Romanist. Apart from the pressure which the king could put on officials, attempts were made to impress others by turning the nave of the

---

[73] *A. P. S.*, VIII. 581.
[74] A useful assessment of " Roman Catholicism in Scotland in the reign of Charles II " was contributed by D. MacLean to *Scot. Church Hist. Soc. Records*, III. 43-54.

abbey of Holyrood into a Roman catholic chapel royal; a Jesuit school at Holyrood offered free education; and a Roman catholic printing press was established. In spite of all, very little progress was made, as a report by Perth in February 1688 shows:

> There have been very few conversions of late. Some few ministers, exemplary men, have come in, many of the ordinary sort, but few in towns. The ministers and university men are so wild and furious . . . that the people take their asseveration for full proof of their veracity. . . . Others here would have us believe they are our friends, who really are our most dangerous enemies, especially some in the army, the hundredth man in which is not a Catholic, and we have scarce any officers of that persuasion.[75]

As parliament had declined to countenance the king's plans, he intimated in August 1686 that he would proceed by prerogative to grant freedom of worship to Roman catholics in private houses. Six months later he went further, by a proclamation which granted toleration to Roman catholics and Quakers, provided that they did not worship in the fields, make processions in the high streets of royal burghs or invade protestant churches. At this stage James was still unwilling to extend concessions to the presbyterians, and his proclamation was accompanied by a letter inveighing against " those enemies of Christianity, . . . the field conventiclers, whom we recommend you to root out with all the severities of our laws."[76] In June 1687, however, by a second proclamation, all the king's subjects were allowed " to meet and serve God after their own way, be it in private houses, chapels, or places purposely hired or built for that use."[77]

James's grant of toleration transformed the ecclesiastical situation. Before this point, the hopes of a restoration of the presbyterian system had seemed extremely remote, and the many Scots who had a preference for presbyterianism, without being fanatical, had become conformers, acquiescing in the existing regime and attending the parish churches. Now it was all different. In any parish a presbyterian preacher could open a meeting house, in free competition with the parish minister, who was apt to find his congregation dwindling. The presbyterians grew in strength, refugees returned from Holland, there was once again an active presbyterian party which began to develop a

75 H. M. C., *Stuart Papers*, I. 30-1.
76 Wodrow, II. App. cxxviii.   77 *R. P. C.*, ser. III., XIII, 156-8.

regional organisation which would provide a possible alternative to the establishment. Presbyterianism had again become a cause with a future.

Apart from the handful of Roman catholics, the king had the support of few notables except some unprincipled politicians like the Earl of Breadalbane, Mackenzie of Tarbat and Sir John Dalrymple; Dalrymple's father, Sir James, had resigned his office of lord president rather than take the Test Oath, but Sir John came to terms with James in 1686 and was appointed lord advocate in place of Mackenzie of Rosehaugh, who, upholder of monarchy as he was, refused to concur in the king's policy and was dismissed in May 1686, to be reinstated only in February 1688. The strength of opposition in the council was shown by the refusal of three members, including Hamilton, to sign the letter acknowledging the king's proclamation of toleration. Even stronger was the opposition of the ecclesiastical establishment, and two bishops were deprived for their stand against the king. While presbyterians took advantage of the indulgence, they had no illusions about the king's motives, and James, without gaining their support, lost that of the episcopalians, who saw their position undermined however they looked at the royal proceedings—whether they were directed towards the toleration of presbyterians or towards the fostering of papistry. The people at large were moved by their deep-rooted fear of Rome, especially where they saw the apparatus of Roman catholic worship installed. As early as January 1686 the celebration of mass in the house of Lord Chancellor Perth had caused a riot in Edinburgh —the first sign of disaffection in the capital since 1660. It had never been possible to raise more than a small minority of the Scottish people to arms on the cry of " No prelacy," but there was now a nation-wide revulsion against James VII on the cry of " No popery."

Yet there were no indications of any readiness on the part of the Scots by themselves to initiate a revolution, even when the permanence of the regime seemed to be assured by the birth of a son to James's queen on 10 June 1688. The Revolution was made in England and imported to Scotland. And even when a revolution did begin in England, with the invasion of William of Orange and the flight of James, Scotland was slow to move. The presbyterians had gained toleration, and were not likely to act

except in favour of a government which would give them supremacy; the episcopalians knew that James's dynasty had in the
main been friendly, and hesitated to throw it over. Some part
in the events which led to the flight of James was, however,
played by Scottish exiles who had gathered at William's court
in Holland—Patrick Hume of Polwarth, Gilbert Elliot of Minto,
Sir James Stewart of Goodtrees, Baillie of Jerviswood the younger,
the minister William Carstares, Gilbert Burnet the historian, and
the elder Stair. The character of the political opposition which
had been developing since 1660 was reflected in a proclamation
which William issued to the people of Scotland on 10 October
1688, before he left Holland, for it was an adaptation of the
English proclamation issued on the same day and it laid its emphasis on the unconstitutional nature of James's proceedings but
was silent about ecclesiastical affairs (except, of course, the threat
of popery). Such a proclamation was not in itself likely to stir
the Scottish people, but when news reached them of William's
landing at Torbay (5 November) and the events culminating in
the flight of James (23 December), it was at once apparent that
the fabric of the Scottish administration was ripe for collapse.
James had called the Scottish army to England, and there was
no force at the disposal of the council to maintain order. In the
south-west, therefore, covenanting mobs arose and rabbled
the curates. In Edinburgh a mob arose, drove the Jesuits from
Holyrood, sacked the chapel royal and desecrated the tombs of
members of that line of over a hundred kings which the majority
of the Scots were now prepared to displace.

20

SCOTLAND IN THE LATER
SEVENTEENTH CENTURY

Two elements in historical judgment have combined to produce a distorted assessment of Scotland's achievements under the restored monarchy. For one thing, a very proper emphasis on the benefits to Scotland of the union of 1707 has militated against a search in earlier times for the beginnings, or at least the antecedents, of the great economic changes of the eighteenth century. Secondly, the preoccupation of so many historians with controversies over ecclesiastical polity has led to the neglect of cultural and constitutional, as well as economic, developments.

Under the restored monarchy there was enough freedom from serious disturbance to allow the readjustment of the economy after the dislocation caused in the 1640s and 1650s, but there was not a mere return to the *status quo ante* in economic affairs any more than in political or ecclesiastical affairs. The novelty, it must be said, did not come to any great extent from government policy, which merely revived the principles of James VI. It was, for example, a familiar measure when in 1661 the privileges of native Scots were extended to foreigners brought in to teach methods of manufacture. Again, very much as the estates had appointed a committee on manufactures in 1623, so in 1661 five members from each estate were appointed to form a council of trade, with power to enforce regulations about manufactures and to found companies, and twenty years later there was a committee of the council for the encouragement of trade and manufactures. Commercial policy was still the restraint of the export of raw materials and of the import of manufactured goods: thus in 1661 the export of linen yarn, hides and wool was forbidden, and in 1681 the import of stockings, shoes and articles made of wool, cotton or lint, was forbidden; on the other hand, both in 1661 and 1681 the import of raw materials and the export of manufactured goods were exempted from duty.

Manufactures were, however, now encouraged less by patents and monopolies to individuals than by the formation of joint-stock companies. Among the industries assisted in this way were soap-making and sugar-refining, the manufacture of glass, paper, hardware, pottery, rope and gunpowder. As in Jacobean times, special efforts were made to foster the production of cloth, and with good reason, at a time when Scottish soldiers had actually to be clad with imported material. A number of cloth-works were established—and did within a few years produce military uniforms[1]—but it was as true of them as of most manufactures that they made only moderate progress behind protective tariffs and that they were not adequate to make Scotland self-sufficient. The industry which most clearly expanded was that of linen cloth, and already, as home-grown flax was insufficient in amount, much flax was being imported. By the end of the century linen may well have been " the most noted and beneficial " of Scottish industries.[2] It certainly provided one of the most conspicuous exports, for between one and two millions ells were exported to England each year, accounting for between a third and two thirds of the value of all the exports to England.

While manufactures were a little more conspicuous than they had been, the economy of the country was still essentially rural. Yet the agrarian pattern was steadily changing. Although the first published works on Scottish husbandry did not appear until shortly after 1688,[3] there were already Scottish farmers who approached their work thoughtfully and critically.[4] Improvements in productivity were being brought about by the use of

1 The company founded in 1681 to operate the New Mills at Haddington is the best-known venture of the period, but deserves note chiefly because of its surviving records (printed by the S. H. S.).   2 T. Morer, *Account of Scotland* (1702), p. 4.

3 James Donaldson, *Husbandry anatomized, or an enquiry into the present manner of tilling and manuring the ground in Scotland* (1697); *The Countreyman's rudiments: or, An Advice to the farmers in East Lothian how to labour and improve their ground*, by A. B. C. [? James, second Lord Belhaven] (1699).

4 Alexander Fenton, " Skene of Hallyard's Manuscript of Husbandrie," in *Agric. Hist. Rev.*, XI. PT. II. 65-81.

lime[5] and other means, and tillage was being extended at the expense of pasture. Statutes passed in 1661, 1669, 1685 and 1686 facilitated the simplification of boundaries between estates and the erection of fences or dykes to protect crops and plantations. Scotland became, more than before, an exporter of grain: in 1685, which happened to be a year of good crops in Scotland and poor ones in the Baltic, over 103,000 bolls were shipped from harbours between the Tay and the Dornoch Firth, largely to Norway.[6] The contribution of cattle-raising to the economy was altering too, for exports of skins and hides were declining, partly because more leather was being manufactured at home but mainly because the export of live cattle to England was substantially increasing. The export of skins to the Baltic was only half as great after 1660 as it had been before 1640, whereas nearly 20,000 Scots cattle are said to have passed through Carlisle in 1662, and that number was sometimes exceeded in later years.[7] Among all exports, cattle probably came next to linen in value by the time of the Revolution. Most of the cattle and much of the linen went overland to England, and among sea-borne exports, coal was probably the most important. Its production continued to increase, until it could be said that Scotland was famed beyond all other countries for its export of this commodity.

The pattern of Scottish trade and of the Scottish economy generally was being affected more and more, for both good and ill, by Anglo-Scottish relations. English wars with continental powers had affected Scottish trade even before the personal union, for Scottish traders had been apt to find themselves debarred during wartime from the ports of England and her allies and harassed on their peaceful occasions by the ships of the warring powers, but it was worse for them after their king became king of England. Scotland had no navy to defend her ships, and apart from actual captures and sinkings there was great loss to trade by delay and interruption. The first signs of a break in the old economic ties with France had come during the Anglo-French war of 1626-9, when restraint of imports to Scotland from France caused great perturbation among Scottish merchants. England did not go to war with France again until 1689, but one of the casualties of the strongly protectionist policy now pursued

---

[5] *E.g.*, Chambers, *Domestic Annals*, II. 398.
[6] Smout, *op. cit.*, pp. 207, 210.   [7] Smout, *op. cit.*, pp. 213, 217-18.

by France was the traditional Scottish trading privileges in that
country, confirmed for the last time in 1646 and abolished in 1663.
Charles II had his wars with Holland (1665/7 and 1672/4), and
their detrimental effect on Scottish commerce caused much
temporary distress.[8]

Tension between England and Scotland themselves had often
arisen in the past from the whole trend of economic legislation.
However, the king and the council had hitherto exercised a
restraining hand on English legislation as well as on Scottish, and
indeed trade regulations had been a matter for council rather
than parliament; but after 1660 the English parliament was less
subject to guidance from the crown and less likely than the king
and council to give consideration to Scottish interests. English
attempts to curb Scottish exports caused many complaints, and
the Scots on their side tried to exclude English manufactures in
order to foster their own. Economic tension had much to do
with the failure of the union negotiations of 1669-70.

There was also friction in the matter of shipping, arising from
the Navigation Acts. By an English act of 1661, no goods were
to be brought into England except in English ships or ships of
the country of origin. The act also largely governed trade with
America, for it laid down that no goods were to be conveyed to
or from the colonies except in English ships; besides, sugar,
tobacco and certain other commodities were not to be shipped
from the colonies except to England or other English colonies.
On the narrower issue of shipping, Scotland retaliated with an
act (1661), laying down that, so long as Scottish ships were
excluded from the English and Irish trade, imports to Scotland,
if not brought in Scottish ships or ships of the country of origin,
must pay double customs. On the issue of colonial trade,
hankerings after a Scottish colony persisted, and in 1660 Charles
II authorised his commissioner to encourage plantations.[9]
Nothing came of it except Scottish settlements within the bounds
of English colonies—one planted, on Quaker initiative, in East
New Jersey, in 1684, and a colony of refuge for covenanters
established at Stuart's Town, South Carolina, in 1684 and turned
out by the Spaniards two years later.

However, in spite of the English exclusive policy, a certain
trade between Scotland and the plantations did develop,

8 *Lauderdale Papers*, 1. 211-3, 226, 279.   9 *Lauderdale Papers*, 1. 40.

sometimes legitimately by special licence or by way of an English port, more usually by illicit means.[10] Clearance papers could be forged, colonial ships could call at Scottish ports on their way between England and the colonies, load Scottish goods, and land them in America on the strength of their English clearance papers. In the colonies as well as in Scotland public opinion was largely against the enforcement of the regulations, some of the colonial officials were lax or collusive, and in parts of the long North American coast evasion of control was easy. There were already, too, a number of Scots settled in the colonies, and they welcomed their compatriots, who were in any event readily received by Americans who found that they could undersell the English merchants. There was also a certain amount of American trade by way of Ireland. The main Scottish exports were woollen and linen cloth, stockings, hats and beef; the imports were tobacco, sugar (for refining in Scotland), furs and skins. By the 1680s Glasgow was receiving six or seven American cargoes a year, and in 1693 it was said that twelve ships loaded sugar and tobacco in the plantations and returned direct to Scotland. In all, seventy-five transatlantic voyages are fully documented before 1707, thirty-two from the West Indies, forty-three from the North American mainland, and the imports to Scotland from America, especially of tobacco, were showing signs of a rapid increase.[11]

Trade with America was thus beginning, and, despite protective measures, trade with England flourished, though with fluctuations, until England was probably the most important market for Scottish exports and a more important source than ever before for imports. At the same time, the traditional Scottish commerce across the North Sea went on with only minor modifications. Timber still came from Norway, iron from Sweden, flax and hemp from Danzig and Königsberg, while from France and the Netherlands came wines, fine textiles, a wide range of luxury goods and a great variety of manufactured articles. The concept of the " staple " survived, and the staple exports were defined afresh in 1669 as skins, hides, woollen textiles, salmon, tallow and beef, but the " staple " port in the Netherlands—still at Campvere, except from 1667 to 1676, when it was at

[10] G. L. Beer, *The Old Colonial System*, PT. I, VOL. I (1912), pp. 85-91; L. F. Stock, *Proceedings and debates of the British parliaments respecting North America*, II (1927). 110-2.
[11] Smout, *op. cit.*, p. 177.

Dort—was no longer dominant, partly because Rotterdam and other more northerly Dutch ports were developing, partly because the pattern of Scottish exports had changed: woollen cloth, for example, was of diminishing importance, while coal, on the other hand, was not a staple export. Yet, while trade had broken its medieval bondage to the staple port, it was still true in the 1680s that about a third, perhaps more, of Scottish trade was with the Netherlands. So far as the Baltic was concerned, less grain came from there than of old, for Scotland was increasingly self-sufficient, and the number of Scottish ships passing through the Sound seldom approximated to the figures before 1638. The export of salt, which had grown so promisingly early in the century, fell away as countries like Holland and Norway turned rather to the Biscay area for supplies.

Scottish trade was in normal times carried on mainly in ships built in the Netherlands, or sometimes in Norway, but owned by Scotsmen, for the carriage of goods in foreign-owned (though not foreign-built) vessels was discouraged by the Navigation Act of 1661. During the Dutch wars, it was safer for neutral ships to carry cargoes to Scottish ports, and the percentage of foreign ships entering Leith rose sharply for a time; on the other hand, the Scots themselves did a certain amount of carrying, especially during the period 1673-9, when Dutch, French, Danes and Swedes were all at war. The vessels operating to and from Scottish ports had to be small, and rarely exceeded 100 tons, for Scotland had no rivers which were navigable but non-tidal and, owing to the great rise and fall of the tides around most of the coast, most Scottish harbours dried out with an ebb, in days when the construction of long quays or of docks was beyond the capacity of engineers. Efforts were made to serve shipping by the construction of harbours of refuge at Stonehaven and Peterhead, by frequent assistance from the convention of royal burghs towards the improvement of harbours and by the enterprise of individuals like the Earl of Winton, the Duke of Hamilton, Lord Wemyss and Sir Robert Cunningham of Auchinharvie, who constructed or developed harbours at Port Seton, Bo'ness, Methil and Saltcoats, mainly for the export of their coal and salt. The number of vessels owned by Scots doubled, so it was claimed, from 1668 to 1681.[12]

12 *R. P. C.*, SER. III, VII. 671.

While the economy was still essentially rural, burghs were becoming more conspicuous, and the changing pattern of the economy had its effect on the prosperity and relative importance of the various burghs. Since 1603 Edinburgh was no longer the seat of a permanent royal court, but it remained the regular meeting place of the parliament, the privy council and the central law courts. Yet the fact that it retained, and even slightly increased, its pre-eminence among Scottish burghs,[13] until it sometimes paid 40 per cent of the total assessment on the burghs, was due largely to the fact that its port, Leith, and some other Firth of Forth ports, remained the chief centre of continental trade, especially with the Low Countries, and that French wine imports, particularly, centred on Leith. Elsewhere on the east coast, the ports were in a less flourishing condition. The royal burghs of Fife, which had paid 9 per cent of the burghal taxation in 1612, paid only 3 per cent in 1705. The Firth of Tay area also declined in importance, because it lacked the coal which was now a main export, and Dundee took a long time to recover from its treatment at the hands of Montrose and Monck, so that its percentage of the assessment declined from 11 in 1612 to 4 in 1705. Aberdeen, which had driven quite a profitable trade in plaiding, suffered when the export of cloth declined, although the export of knitted stockings was some compensation.[14]

But if the east coast, except the Firth of Forth, was declining, Glasgow and the Clyde area were becoming ever more prosperous. During the century the royal burghs in the Clyde basin doubled their contribution to taxation, and Glasgow's share rose from 4 per cent to 20 per cent; Glasgow's place among the Scottish burghs had been fifth in 1594, and was second (though still a very poor second) by 1670. A variety of industries developed in Glasgow as part of the drive for the encouragement of manufactures— sugar refining, printing, coalmining, the manufacture of soap, cloth, rope, hardware and paper—and old industries like tanning expanded. At Greenock, too, there were factories for curing red herring and for manufacturing soap. Part of the expansion in

13 The proportions fixed for the levying of the militia in 1645 suggest that if Edinburgh had about 30,000 inhabitants, Dundee had about 11,000, Aberdeen about 10,000, Perth and Glasgow about 6,000.
14 Smout, *op. cit.*, CH. VII and Table I.

this area was a consequence of the achievements of James VI, which had facilitated an increased trade with the west Highlands and with Ireland—especially Ulster, with which coal and manufactured goods were exchanged for agricultural produce. But already before 1700 the American trade was beginning to have a noticeable effect. As a port, Glasgow itself was still hampered by the shallowness of the Clyde, but the harbour at Port Glasgow, lower down the river, was founded in 1662.

One of the most striking developments of the period was the great increase in burghal activity outside the royal burghs, with the incidental result that statistics showing the relative importance of burghs within the royal group are no longer an index of the economy of the country. Nearly as many burghs of barony received charters between 1661 and 1707 as had obtained them in the whole preceding century.[15] While some of those burghs of barony were mere "parchment burghs," reflecting only the megalomania of their patrons, others, especially the ports in the upper Forth area, rapidly became places of real importance. In addition to actual burghs, many non-burghal markets and fairs were authorised. This is significant in a general way of the expanding economy of the country, but significant also of the determination of the nobility and gentry not to be left out of economic, any more than political, developments. The nobility and gentry were in fact heavily committed in several branches of commerce and industry; on the other hand, it was still the case that the ambition of a prosperous merchant in Edinburgh or Glasgow was to acquire a landed estate, and rigid class distinctions were as weak as ever.

In this situation, inroads were made on the ancient rights of the royal burghs. So recently as 1633, a statute[16] had ratified the privileges of the "free royal burghs," which, in return for bearing their share of taxation, enjoyed important monopolies, each within its own "precinct." Their burgesses alone had the right to engage in foreign trade and to retail wines; foreigners had to buy and sell only within the burgh walls; fish, wool and hides could be sold only there, and all cloth had to be carried there to be finished. Royal burghs persistently strove to prevent burghs of regality and barony from infringing their trade monopolies, and

[15] G. S. Pryde, *Court Book of Burgh of Kirkintilloch* (S. H. S.), lxxix ff.
[16] *A. P. S.*, v. 42.

also to restrict the activities of crafts in the " unfree " burghs, but their efforts were no longer successful. It was, therefore, appropriate that a statute of 1672, while reserving to the royal burghs trade in foreign goods such as wine, wax, silks, spices and dyestuffs, liberated from restrictions the export of the produce of the kingdom and made the non-royal burghs free to export their own manufactures and to import articles necessary for tillage, building or their own manufactures.[17] These sweeping concessions were modified by acts of 1681 and 1690, but even so the burgesses of non-royal burghs retained the right to trade in the native commodities of the kingdom and to retail foreign commodities, provided that they had bought them from freemen of royal burghs.

There were in this period intellectual, as well as economic, achievements which made lasting contributions to the life of the nation. In the sphere of law, a landmark was the publication in 1681 of *The institutions of the law of Scotland,* by Sir James Dalrymple, first Viscount Stair, for this, unlike earlier " Practicks," was a treatise at once philosophical and practical, based on principles derived from a study of the sources of Roman law and the Dutch and French commentators thereon, as well as an examination of statutes, case law, canon law and divine law. " It represents a serious attempt to erect Scots Law into a philosophical system."[18] Another compilation of *Institutions* came in 1684 from Sir George Mackenzie of Rosehaugh (1636-91), best known as " bluidy Mackenzie " because it fell to him, as king's advocate, to conduct prosecutions of covenanters. But Mackenzie deserves better to be remembered for another achievement—the promotion of the Advocates' Library, now the National Library of Scotland, founded in 1682, when Mackenzie was dean of the faculty of advocates. Mackenzie was a man of prolific literary output, for he wrote fiction, philosophy, politics and memoirs as well as law. It was characteristic of the time that the study of history received official recognition in the appointment of the first historiographer royal in the early 1660s.

Religion was overshadowed by ecclesiastical politics, but it was not quite effaced, and in the north-east, where something

17 *A. P. S.,* viii. 63.
18 Balfour, *Practicks* (Stair Soc.), i. xxxix; cf. A. H. Campbell, *The structure of Stair's Institutions* (1954).

of the tranquillity of the days of the " Aberdeen Doctors " returned, Henry Scougal, son of the Bishop of Aberdeen, wrote *The life of God in the soul of man* (1677), which long enjoyed recognition as a religious classic. Bishop Leighton, who was temperamentally aloof from the controversies of " the times," and preferred to concentrate on " Jesus and eternity," published nothing in his lifetime, but was influential as a scholar, a university teacher and a preacher.

When there was a court—albeit of a high commissioner and not a king—at Holyrood, the drama enjoyed a certain amount of influential patronage. Scottish dramatists wrote plays which were successful in London as well as in Edinburgh, while, on the other hand, Dryden's plays were produced at Holyrood. There was a "theatre or comedy house" in Edinburgh in 1669,[19] and Sir John Foulis of Ravelston records in his diary seven visits to " the play " in as many months, in 1672.[20] To this period belongs also the first book of secular music printed in Scotland—*Cantus, songs and fancies . . . both apt for voices and viols*,[21] a product of the music-school of Aberdeen.

Scientific studies enjoyed an unusual vogue among men of fashion, and much important work was done by Scots like Sir Robert Moray, first president of the Royal Society of London. James Gregory, professor of mathematics at St Andrews from 1668 to 1674, devised improvements in the telescope, explored new fields of mathematics, and planned an observatory which would have been far in advance of anything yet known in Britain.[22] He subsequently became professor of mathematics at Edinburgh, where he was succeeded by his nephew, David, who became a skilled exponent of Newtonian physics and was later professor of astronomy at Oxford. George Sinclair published his *Natural Philosophy improven by new experiments* at Edinburgh in 1683. Sir Robert Sibbald (1641-1722), physician to Charles II and geographer of Scotland in 1682, president of the Edinburgh Royal College of Surgeons in 1684 and professor of medicine at Edinburgh in 1685, had a plan for the collection of material for a survey of Scotland which anticipated the plan of the *Old Statistical Account*

19 *Justiciary court records* (S. H. S.), i. 304.

20 Cf. also J. McKenzie, " School and university drama in Scotland," in *S. H. R.*, xxxiv. 103-21, and *Edinburgh Burgh Records, 1665-81.*

21 It went through three editions, in 1662, 1666 and 1682.

22 H. W. Turnbull (ed.), *James Gregory tercentenary memorial volume* (1939).

a century later, but only a few of the necessary regional descriptions were ever completed.[23] However, his *Scotia illustrata* appeared in 1684. Work in cartography continued, for between 1682 and 1688 John Adair, with the help of a privy council grant, drew a series of country maps, and he received further encouragement to enable him to produce a series of maps of the coastline. Medical studies, too, progressed. The Royal College of Physicians in Edinburgh was established in 1681 and three professors of medicine appointed at Edinburgh University in 1685. The ancillary study of botany had its beginnings in the Physic Gardens which appeared in Edinburgh from 1656 onwards and foreshadowed the Royal Botanic Garden.

There were many other gardens, some of them devoted to the cultivation of such fruits as apricots, figs and peaches, others designed merely for the adornment of the mansion-houses which they adjoined. Horticulture was becoming something of a science, and in 1683 there appeared *The Scots Gardener*, by J. Reid, " in two parts. The first is contriving and planting gardens, orchards, avenues, groves; with new and profitable ways of levelling; and how to measure and divide land. The second of the propagation and improvement of forrest and fruit-trees, kitchen herbes, rootes and fruits, with some physical hearbs, shrubs and flowers." The planting of trees, too, progressed. The ninth Earl of Argyll, like his father, the marquis, was a great planter who imported seeds from London; on the Breadalbane estates, the tradition of Duncan Campbell of Glenorchy continued, for limes were introduced to Taymouth in 1664; and larch—the tree which was to be planted by the million in the following century—appeared in an Edinburgh Physic Garden in 1683. In the 1660s, Sir Archibald Cockburn of Langton was planting and enclosing so extensively that public roads had to be diverted to meet his convenience.[24]

The mansion-houses to which some of the gardens belonged were themselves becoming ever more luxurious and splendid, and the last signs of fortification disappeared from the dwelling-house in this period. Leslie House (1661) was the last fortified house to be built, and the purely residential dwelling prevailed, in

---

[23] F. P. Hett (ed.), *The memoirs of Sir Robert Sibbald* (1932). Cf. *Spottiswoode Society Misc.*, I. 313-50; Andrew Symson, *A large description of Galloway, 1684* (1823).
[24] *R. P. C.*, SER. III, II. 31, 48.

buildings like Caroline Park near Granton (1685-96), Kinross House (1684-95), and Drumlanrig (1679-89). The Earl of Strathmore remarked in 1677 that castellated houses " truly are quite out of fashion, as feuds are, . . . the country being generally more civilised than it was of ancient times."[25] In the towns, too, finer houses were appearing, and the aspect of the capital was much improved in the last quarter of the century by extensive rebuilding of houses in a style which substituted stone fronts for the old timber fronts and by such a new edifice as the Exchange (to the plans of Sir William Bruce, architect of Charles II's reconstruction of Holyroodhouse), but many of the " stately buildings " of recent construction were swept away by the great Parliament Square fire in 1700.[26] For internal fittings to adorn the mansions there seems to have been some competition among the house-builders. In 1671, when Lauderdale was reconstructing Thirlstane Castle, he wrote, " as to the marble chimneys, I am far advanced, for I have bargained for six already, . . . and three of them are fairer than any I see in England, . . . two I have paid for this day, much finer than my Lord Chancellor's, larger and cheaper above a fourth than his."

In an essentially rural economy, where each community, and very often each family, could be self-sufficient, communications had been of little importance. Well constructed and properly maintained roads were unknown in Scotland until after this period, but it may be significant of the growing complexity of the Scottish economy, and perhaps also of the tendency to decentralise trade, that during the seventeenth century the government was impelled to give an attention to roads which was quite novel. There had been acts on highways in 1617, 1641 and 1655, and in 1669 came an act which remained in operation until the nineteenth century. The sheriff and the justices of the peace were made the local road authority, with power to convene all tenants and cottars and their servants to bring horses and carts to repair the highways and to give their labour thereon for up to six days in each of the first three years ensuing and for up to four days each year thereafter, under penalty of fine. Beyond the " statute labour," provision was made for assessing the heritors. to the amount of 10s. per £100 of valued rent.[27] This legislation

---

25 Quoted Cruden, *The Scottish Castle*, p. 151.
26 *B. O. E. C.*, XXIV. 137, 151; XXIX. 111 ff. 27 *A. P. S.*, VII. 574.

was widely disregarded, and all the indications are that roads remained poor. There were cart tracks connecting inland burghs with the nearest ports and connecting Edinburgh with some of the surrounding countryside. There were also two longer cart routes—Edinburgh to Glasgow by Linlithgow and Stirling, and Leith to the Leadhills. Stage coaches were tried out occasionally between Edinburgh and London, for example in 1652 and 1658, and also over the much shorter routes from Edinburgh to Haddington and to Glasgow, but it is unlikely that a permanent service was achieved by any of those ventures. However, carriages plying for hire were quite regular in Edinburgh after the Restoration,[28] and there was quite a number of private coaches throughout the country, apparently for utility and not merely for prestige. Archbishop Sharp " rode through Fife in coach " in 1663,[29] and it was while driving in his coach that he met his death; " their great men often travel with coach and six," we are told by an English visitor.[30] Yet the normal means of human transport was undoubtedly by horseback, and goods were more commonly carried on sledges, in creels or by pack-horses, than by cart. There had long been a greater interest in bridges than in roads, for bridges were useful for all forms of transport, and besides, as a bridge might save life, bridge-building and repair continued, after the Reformation as before it, to be regarded as a legitimate object of pious charity.[31] But in the late sixteenth century and throughout the seventeenth official encouragement by parliament or council stimulated or encouraged local efforts, not infrequently by authorising the exaction of tolls. The government took action in favour of bridges in many parts of the country, from Galloway to Aberdeen and Inverness and into Perthshire, and in more remote parts of the country there could still be local effort— for instance, the gentlemen of Sutherland rebuilt the bridge of Brora in 1619.[32] The post between Edinburgh and London was speeded up under Charles I, so that it took only six days, but it seems unlikely that before 1660 there was a regular postal service anywhere within Scotland. In 1662, however, posts were established to Portpatrick, a horse-post to Aberdeen followed in 1667,

28 *Domestic Annals*, II. 218, 247, 358-9.   29 Lamont, *Diary*, pp. 165-6.
30 Morer, *op. cit.*, (1715 edn.), p. 24.
31 *E.g.*, *R. P. C.*, II. 497; Lamont, *Diary*, p. 80.   32 *Earldom of Sutherland*, p. 8.

and a foot-post to Inverness in 1669. On the whole, therefore, there were clear intimations that regular and easier communications were going to extend to all the more accessible parts of the country, though little provision was yet made for traffic through the central and west Highlands.

If an official interest in roads was one indication not only of the growing complexity of the Scottish economy but also of a concern on the part of the administration for the welfare of society, another such indication is given by the history of poor relief, which until the late sixteenth century had been almost wholly a matter for individual or corporate piety. How far the Reformation may have destroyed or weakened ecclesiastical institutions which were still doing effective work for the poor it would be hard to determine,[33] but there is no doubt of the resolution of the reformers that their church should take its responsibilities to the poor more seriously than its unreformed predecessor had latterly been doing. It is significant of the new emphasis that former ecclesiastical property, in movables like sacerdotal vestments as well as in buildings like the friaries in Aberdeen and Dundee, were now turned over to the benefit of the poor.[34] Existing hospitals, too, were either maintained or re-founded with fresh endowments from old ecclesiastical revenues. Besides, the first Book of Discipline had been emphatic that "every several kirk must provide for the poor within the self,"[35] and, at a time when neither church buildings nor clerical stipends were a charge on the giving of congregations, church collections, as well as monies accruing from " mortifications " or bequests, from fees paid at baptisms, marriages and burials, from the fines exacted from delinquents who were " disciplined " by the kirk session, and from other sources, were all available for the benefit of the poor. Almost at once after the Reformation, however, provision had been made for reliance on something more than voluntary offerings and casual income, for in 1574 a statute allowed magistrates to assess the inhabitants of any parish for the maintenance of the poor, and while this was not widely applied there were instances of assessment, if only for limited periods. Neither the church nor the state believed in helping the able-bodied poor, or unemployed, and while solicitude was expressed for " the poor and

---

[33] Cf. *Essays on the Scottish Reformation*, pp. 121, 127, 128.
[34] I. B. Cowan, *Blast and Counterblast*, pp. 35-6.   [35] Knox, II. 290.

impotent," the " strang and idle beggar " was to be discouraged or even punished.

An act of 1672 was the foundation of the Scottish poor law until 1845. It revived the principle of assessment, by laying down that the poor fund of any parish could be supplemented by a levy, half on heritors, half on tenants or occupiers. An old concept, embodied in an act of 1535, that the responsibility for a pauper rested with his parish of origin, lay behind a clause to the effect that paupers who were licensed to beg must confine themselves to their parish of settlement (that is, where they had been born or where they had resided for three years without receiving relief). But if the impotent poor could beg, the able-bodied poor were to be forced to work. Statutes of 1661 and 1663 had already ordered heritors to provide for the instruction in textile processes of poor children, vagabonds and idle persons, and had allowed manufacturers to seize idle vagrants for forced labour and to receive payment from the parish of their origin by an assessment.

As the legislation on roads and poor relief indicates, local government, in anything like the sense in which we are familiar with it, was in effect the creation of the seventeenth century. The new office which most readily attracts attention is that of justice of the peace, and it is true that justices were given certain administrative duties, not least in the supervision of road construction and maintenance. But the most important and enduring office created in local government in the seventeenth century was that of the commissioner of supply, which was an offshoot of the growth of taxation and its increasing scope. The taxes raised in the 1640s for the levying of war against the king required new valuations of property, and those valuations, at first made—in default of secular organs of local government—by the presbyteries, were later made by commissioners specially appointed in each shire.[36] Similar arrangements were revived after 1660, and it was in that period that the term " commissioner of supply " became established. Almost at once the potentialities of the commissioners for purposes other than raising money were realised, and in 1669 they were associated with the justices of the peace for road administration. With ever-extending functions, they remained the most important officers in Scottish local government until so late as 1889, when the county council first appeared.

[36] In the burghs the magistrates acted as commissioners.

Very much as the commissioner of supply acted in the shire, the heritors acted in the parish. The heritors, as owners of lands and also, according to the intentions of Charles I, of teinds, had the obligation put upon them to maintain the minister, the church and the manse. It was not going very much farther, in logical sequence, to make them responsible for the erection of schools and the payment of schoolmasters. According to the education act of 1633 they were merely to advise the bishops in laying an assessment on the parish for education, but in 1646 the duty of making an assessment was laid directly on the heritors, and the same provision was made in the act of 1696, which remained the legislative basis of parochial education until 1872. The next thing was to bring the heritors into poor law adminis- tration, and this was done by acts of 1663 and 1672. In connexion with both education and poor relief the heritors worked in close conjunction with the kirk session, and the membership of the two bodies not infrequently overlapped.

It is noticeable that many pieces of machinery set up in the late sixteenth century or the seventeenth lasted until the nineteenth or later; the court of justiciary, as organised in 1672, was not reorganised until the nineteenth century; justices of the peace have had a continuous existence since their establish- ment by James VI, though with varying powers; the commissary courts and the commissioners of supply operated until the nine- teenth century, the heritors until the twentieth; seventeenth century legislation on poor relief, education and road-making was legislation which continued without much amendment until well into the nineteenth century. Plainly, developments in administration were among the many enduring achievements of the seventeenth century.

None of those administrative institutions was " democratic " or " representative " in a modern sense, for justices of the peace were nominated, heritors and commissioners of supply held office by a property qualification; election played no part in parish or county government until well into the nineteenth century. Yet significant changes had taken place. The basis of local government was much broader now than it had been when the only local officials were heritable sheriffs and lords of regality, and the machinery of government no longer depended on a hand- ful of magnates, for lesser men were holding the new offices.

Besides, the administration was much more closely related now to the central government, if only because of its direction by an ever-increasing bulk of legislation and its integration into the system for the collection and expenditure of public revenues. There was now an institutional cohesion and unity in the country which had been lacking before: it no longer depended on the person of the king, for the organs of government operated in the absence of the king and the nation had in fact developed an institutional as well as an emotional unity when it made war on the king. Attachment to the royal line was no longer an essential element in preserving national integrity, and it had become a matter mainly of sentiment. All parts of the country now shared many things besides the monarchy: a uniform system of government had been introduced everywhere, the laws were generally obeyed as they had not been a century before. Admittedly, the Highlands, or part of them, were not yet fully integrated with the rest of the country, and strange things were still to happen there. But it would have seemed ludicrous by 1688 should a landlord in Lowland Scotland have proposed to call out his dependents either to pursue a feud or to challenge the crown. Opposition to the government, as well as government itself, was increasingly finding expression through constitutional machinery, and when revolution came it came not by violence but by a vote in a convention.

BIBLIOGRAPHY

The more specialised books and articles cited in footnotes are in general omitted from the Bibliography.

The place of publication is not given except for older and rarer books. Neither date nor place is given for publications of clubs and societies.

A list of the contractions used in this volume is printed on pp. ix-x.

I. GUIDES AND WORKS OF REFERENCE

The period is covered in two volumes of the *Bibliography of British History*, that on the Tudor period by Conyers Read (2nd. edn., 1959) and that on the Stuart period by Godfrey Davies (1928); Scotland receives fuller treatment in the former than in the latter. The most comprehensive lists of books are to be found in A. Mitchell and C. G. Cash, *Contribution to the Bibliography of Scottish Topography* (S. H. S.), of which VOL. I is arranged topographically and VOL. II topically; there is a continuation in P. Hancock, *A Bibliography of Books on Scotland, 1916-50* (1960). As guides to printed sources, C. S. Terry, *A Catalogue of the Publications of Scottish Historical and kindred Clubs and Societies . . . 1780-1908* (1909), and its continuation to 1927 by C. Matheson (1928) are indispensable. They are supplemented by the *Hand list of Scottish and Welsh Record Publications*, by P. Gouldesbrough, A. P. Kup and I. Lewis (Brit. Records Association, 1954) and by the official list of *Record Publications* (H.M.S.O.). M. Livingstone, *A Guide to the Public Records of Scotland* (1905), lists the original records in the Register House, which are described by J. M. Thomson, *The Public Records of Scotland* (1922); lists of accessions to the Register House since 1905 are in *S. H. R.* from VOL. XXVI. As a key to the valuable material in the *Historical MSS. Commission Reports*, C. S. Terry, *An Index to the Papers Relating to Scotland* (1908), is no substitute for the indexes to the individual reports. Many private collections of papers have in recent years been deposited in the Register House, and the National Register of Archives (Scotland) has accumulated reports on many which still remain with their owners.

For early printed books, H. G. Aldis, *A List of Books printed in Scotland before 1700* (Edin. Bibliog. Soc.), can be supplemented and checked by the following: A. W. Pollard and G. R. Redgrave, *A Short-Title Catalogue of Books printed in England, Scotland and Ireland, 1475-1640* (1926, repr. 1946); Donald Wing's similar catalogue for 1641-1700 (1945-51);

R. R. Steele, *A Bibliography of Royal Proclamations . . . 1485-1714* (1910), VOL. II of which contains the Scottish proclamations; and the British Museum's *Catalogue of the Thomason Tracts* (2 vols., 1908).

Among specialised guides to sources, *Sources and Literature of Scots Law* (Stair Soc.), is indispensable for many branches of Scottish history. W. R. Scott, *Scottish Economic Literature to 1800* (1911), is continued and supplemented in three articles on the bibliography of Scottish economic history by W. H. Marwick in *Econ. Hist. Rev.*, III. 117-37, 2nd Ser., IV. 376-82 and XVI. 147-54.

Down to 1625, A. Dunbar, *Scottish Kings* (2nd. edn., 1906), is indispensable for chronology, besides being a handy guide to sources. The *Handbook of British Chronology* (Royal Hist. Soc., 2nd. edn.) gives lists of kings, bishops, officers of state, dukes, marquesses and earls.

Scottish biographical information is well represented in the *Dictionary of National Biography*, but use should also be made of Robert Chambers, *Biographical Dictionary of Eminent Scotsmen* (3 vols. 1868-70, and other edns.). *The Scots Peerage*, by J. B. Paul (9 vols., 1904-14) gives genealogical information about the vast number of the inhabitants of Scotland who were related in some way to noble families. The essential guide to writings on Scottish families is M. Stuart and J. B. Paul, *Scottish Family History* (1929); J. P. S. Ferguson's slighter *Scottish Family Histories* (1960) includes more recent books. There is no printed guide to Scottish portraiture, and information on this subject should be sought from the National Portrait Gallery in Edinburgh.

The clergy of the reformed church are briefly biographed in *Fasti Ecclesiae Scoticanae* (7 vols., 1915-28; VOL. VIII, 1950, contains additions and corrections). University graduates are the subject of volumes issued by the New Spalding Club for Aberdeen, the Maitland Club for Glasgow, the Bannatyne Club for Edinburgh and the Scottish History Society for St Andrews.

The following are devoted to the holders of specific offices: G. Brunton and D. Haig, *Senators of the College of Justice* (1832); G. W. T. Omond, *The Lord Advocates of Scotland* (2 vols., 1883); and S. Cowan, *The Lord Chancellors of Scotland* (2 vols., 1911).

The most useful topographical guide is F. H. Groome, *Ordnance Gazetteer of Scotland* (1882-5 and later edns.), which presents in convenient form a vast amount of information on history, geography and statistics. W. J. Watson deals with *The Celtic Place-Names of Scotland* (1926), but there are no other authoritative works on place-names except some regional studies. H. R. G. Inglis, J. Matheson and C. B. B. Watson provide a guide to *The Early Maps of Scotland* (2nd edn., 1936). Libraries, museums and similar repositories both in Edinburgh and throughout the country have collections of early maps and plans.

W. A. Craigie, *A Dictionary of the Older Scottish Tongue* (1933-   ), has now progressed more than half-way through the alphabet.

II. GENERAL

(a) Sources

Among record sources, the following official publications require no comment: *The Acts of the Parliaments of Scotland* (12 vols., 1814-75); *The Register of the Privy Council of Scotland* (36 vols. in three series [1545-1689], 1877-1933); *Rotuli scaccarii regum Scotorum: The Exchequer Rolls of Scotland* (VOLS. XIV-XXIII [1513-1600], 1894-1908); *Compota thesaurariorum regum Scotorum: Accounts of the Lord High Treasurer of Scotland* (VOLS. V-XI [1515-66], 1904-16); *Registrum magni sigilli regum Scotorum: the Register of the Great Seal of Scotland* (VOLS. III-XI [1513-1668], 1883-1914); *Registrum secreti sigilli regum Scotorum: the Register of the Privy Seal of Scotland* (VOLS. I-VII [1488-1580], 1908-65); and *Accounts of the Masters of Works* (VOL. I [1529-1616], 1960). Of the acts of the parliaments alone has printing been completed for the whole of this period; the other series are printed only as far as the dates shown above, but further volumes of the *Treasurer's Accounts, Register of the Privy Seal,* and *Masters of Works' Accounts* are in preparation.

The records of criminal justice, important for both political and social history, are so far printed in R. Pitcairn, *Ancient Criminal Trials in Scotland* [1488-1624] (3 vols., Bannatyne and Maitland Clubs), S. A. Gillon, *Selected Justiciary Cases, 1624–50* (Stair Soc.), and W. G. Scott-Moncrieff, *Records of the Proceedings of the Justiciary Court, Edinburgh, 1661-78* (2 vols., S. H. S.).

Among the many burgh records printed for this period, more than local importance attaches to the *Extracts from the Records of the Burgh of Edinburgh* (5 vols. [1403-1589] by Scot. Burgh Rec. Soc.; further vols [to 1701] by the Town Council) and the *Aberdeen Council Letters* [1552-1675], ed. L. B. Taylor.

In the absence of a *corpus* of archives of the Scottish secretary's department, it is necessary to rely for foreign correspondence mainly on the archives of other countries, especially England. T. Rymer, *Foedera* (20 vols., London, 1704-35; 17 vols., London, 1727-9), is still of value in this period, but the series of printed volumes of state papers from the Public Record Office form the most important single source. Down to 1547 the state papers relating to Scotland are calendared in the *Letters and Papers, Foreign and Domestic, of the reign of Henry VIII* (1862-1910); some were printed *in extenso* in *State Papers of King Henry VIII* (1830-52). In 1547 there begins the *Calendar of State Papers relating to Scotland and Mary, Queen of Scots,* which continues to 1603 (1898-1965) and includes items from other repositories besides the Public Record Office. Supplementary information is to be found in two specifically

Scottish collections, *The Border Papers* (2 vols., 1894-5) and *The Hamilton Papers* (2 vols., 1890-92), as well as in the *Calendars of State Papers* of the Foreign, Venetian, Spanish and Roman series and the *Calendar of State Papers, Domestic.* Some state papers of the period are printed in old collections like *Sir Ralph Sadler's State Papers* (ed. A. Clifford, 2 vols., 1809), P. Forbes, *A Full View of the Public Transactions in the Reign of Elizabeth* (2 vols., 1740-1), P. Yorke, Earl of Hardwicke, *Miscellaneous State Papers* (2 vols., 1778), S. Haynes and W. Murdin, *State Papers* (2 vols., 1740-59). The last of those collections is from the Cecil papers at Hatfield, which have been calendared by the Historical Manuscripts Commission.

For correspondence and papers in French archives, there are the works of A. Teulet: *Inventaire chronologique des documents relatifs à l'histoire de l'Écosse conservés aux archives du royaume à Paris* (Abbotsford Club), *Papiers d'état* (Bannatyne Club, 3 vols.) and [in effect a later edition of *Papiers d'état*] *Relations politiques de la France et de l'Espagne avec l'Écosse au xvie siècle* (5 vols., Paris 1862).

Selected items of record material and comparable documents are printed in the *Miscellanies* of the Maitland, Abbotsford and Bannatyne Clubs and in Sir William Fraser's volumes on the history of Scottish noble families. It should be emphasised that these published items represent a barely significant proportion of the masses of documents in private hands and in various repositories.

R. Chambers, *Domestic Annals of Scotland from the Reformation to the Revolution* (2 vols., 1859; other edns.), gives excerpts from both narrative and record sources.

(b) Secondary works

A general history on a substantial scale is seldom, if ever, entirely superseded, and use may still be profitably made of the older *Histories of Scotland* by P. F. Tytler (9 vols., 1828-43 and later edns.), J. H. Burton (9 vols., 1853, 1867-70 and later edns.), P. H. Brown (3 vols., 1899-1905) and A. Lang (4 vols., 1900-7). The *New History of Scotland*, by W. Croft Dickinson and G. S. Pryde (2 vols., 1961-2) is not expansive on the sixteenth century and is slight on the seventeenth, but certain chapters in VOL. I, dealing with late medieval life, are important; outstanding is Chapter XXV, on " Burgh life in the fifteenth and sixteenth centuries." Older histories of England are in the main unhelpful, even for Anglo-Scottish relations, but two exceptional pieces of work are F. W. Maitland's chapter on " The Anglican Settlement and the Scottish Reformation " in *Cambridge Modern History*, II, and Sir R. Lodge's treatment of Scotland in VOL. VIII of the *Political History of England* (Longmans). The Oxford History is more valuable, especially J. D. Mackie, *The Earlier Tudors*, and J. B. Black, *The Reign of Elizabeth*.

The most coherent account, on a substantial scale, of most of the period, is W. L. Mathieson, *Politics and Religion: a Study of Scottish History from the Reformation to the Revolution* (2 vols., 1902). *A Source Book of Scottish History*, ed. W. Croft Dickinson, G. Donaldson, and I. A. Milne (3 vols., 2nd. edn., 1958-61) gives documents and extracts with connecting commentaries. D. Nobbs, *England and Scotland, 1560-1707* (1952), has many suggestive thoughts.

Attention must always be given to the *Scottish Historical Review* (discontinued 1929, resumed 1947); there are general indexes to VOLS. I-XII and XIII-XXV.

The only book professing to be a general economic and social history is J. Mackinnon, *The Social and Industrial History of Scotland . . . to the Union* (2 vols., 1920-1); and I. F. Grant, *Social and Economic Development of Scotland before 1603* (1930), covers the sixteenth century. Two recent scholarly studies enlarge on parts of the period: S. G. E. Lythe, *The Economy of Scotland in its European Setting, 1550-1625* (1960), and T. C. Smout, *Scottish Trade on the eve of Union* (1963).

On the Highlands, the best general book is A. Cunningham, *The Loyal Clans* (1932), an important study of Highland history in relation to government policy. D. Gregory, *History of the Western Highlands and Isles of Scotland from . . . 1493 to . . . 1625* (1836, 1881), is thoroughly documented. W. C. Mackenzie, *The Highlands and Isles of Scotland* (1937; rev. edn. 1949) is especially useful for the sixteenth century.

An Introduction to Scottish Legal History (Stair Soc.) is the best general guide to the history of the law and law courts.

On the church, J. Cunningham, *The Church History of Scotland . . . to the Present Century* (2 vols., 1859; 2nd edn., 1882), and J. H. S. Burleigh, *A Church History of Scotland* (1960), are convenient summaries from the presbyterian point of view. G. Grub, a moderate and accurate episcopalian, wrote a more substantial and fully documented *Ecclesiastical History of Scotland* (4 vols., 1861). The *History of the Catholic Church in Scotland* was written from the Roman catholic viewpoint by A. Bellesheim and translated by D. O. H. Blair (1887-90); a new work on this subject is overdue.

III. THE REIGN OF JAMES V

In addition to the general record sources, the *Acts of the Lords of Council in Public Affairs, 1501-54*, a selection by R. K. Hannay from the Acta Dominorum Concilii (1932), is especially important for the minority. The sederunts of the council, which are indispensable for an understanding of the positions of individuals and factions, are not printed, but are available in typescript in the Register House; material of similar significance comes from the remissions, respites and escheats in the *Register of the Privy Seal.*

The most important collections of foreign correspondence are the *Letters of James V* (ed. R. K. Hannay and Denys Hay, 1954), the *Letters and Papers of Henry VIII* and (for the first years of the reign) the *Flodden Papers* (S. H. S.). *The Pittodrie Papers* (Spalding Club Misc., II) are those of Sir Thomas Erskine, the secretary, but add nothing of substance.

In the absence of internal correspondence and similar material which would reveal men's thoughts, the interpretation of events and an understanding of the state of opinion must be almost wholly a matter of inference, for the following contemporary or near-contemporary narratives, while they contain many suggestive passages, do not in themselves furnish ground for more than conjecture. R. Lindsay of Pitscottie, *The History of Scotland* (S. T. S. and other edns.) is over picturesque. John Lesley, *De origine, moribus et rebus gestis Scotorum* (1578; trans. Bannatyne Club and S. T .S.) is the work of a servant of Queen Mary who became a Roman catholic *émigré*, and must be used with caution, less because of any bias than because when it can be tested it often proves inaccurate. The bias of George Buchanan, *Rerum Scoticarum historia* (1582; trans. J. Aikman, 4 vols., 1827), was political and literary rather than religious. *A Diurnal of Remarkable Occurrents that have passed within the Country of Scotland* (Bannatyne and Maitland Clubs) is more revealing than Lindsay, Lesley or Buchanan. There is a contemporary French account of the life of James V in *Miscellanea Scotica* (1818-20), IV.

There are some important sources for ecclesiastical history: A. Theiner, *Vetera Monumenta Hibernorum et Scotorum historiam illustrantia* (Rome, 1864); R. Richardson, *Commentary on the Rule of St. Augustine* (S. H. S.); *Rentale Dunkeldense* and *Rentale Sancti Andree* (S. H. S.); and *St. Andrews Formulare* (2 vols., Stair Soc.)

The reign has not attracted much attention from recent historians, and most of the writings on it are anterior to the publication of important sources. The most detailed account of the minority is still that by John Pinkerton, *The History of Scotland from the Accession of the House of Stuart to that of Mary* (2 vols., 1797), but although Pinkerton used the English state papers he neglected other sources. A good deal of ground was covered by John Herkless and R. K. Hannay in VOLS. II, III and IV of *The Archbishops of St. Andrews* (5 vols., 1907-15), using largely the *Letters and Papers.*

There are the following specialised studies: M. W. Stuart, *The Scot who was a Frenchman* [Albany] (1940); E. Bapst, *Les mariages de Jacques V* (Paris 1889); R. K. Hannay, *The College of Justice* (1933); J. D. Mackie, " Henry VIII and Scotland," in *Trans. Roy. Hist. Soc.,*

4th ser., xxix. 93-114; and G. Dickinson, " Some Notes on the Scottish Army in the first half of the sixteenth century," in *S. H. R.*, xxviii. 133-45. Some of the material on Border history was collected in W. A. Armstrong, *The Armstrong Borderland* (1960).

iv. Queen Mary and the Reformation

The general series of records, official correspondence and state papers listed in section 2 are supplemented by *Foreign Correspondence with Marie de Lorraine* (ii vols., S. H. S.), *The Scottish Correspondence of Mary of Lorraine* (S. H. S.), *Mission de Beccarie de Pavie . . . en Écosse, 1543* (ed. G. Dickinson, 1948), *Two Missions of Jacques de la Brosse* [1543, 1560] (S. H. S.), *Papal Negotiations with Mary, Queen of Scots* (S. H. S.) and *A Letter from Mary, Queen of Scots, to the Duke of Guise, Jan. 1562* (S. H. S.). Many of the papers so industriously collected by Robert Keith and printed in his *History of the Affairs of Church and State in Scotland* (1734; and Spottiswoode Soc.) have now been printed elsewhere, but his work is still essential.

The fairly voluminous correspondence, especially with Mary of Guise, is such that from the beginning of this reign we have a knowledge of men's thoughts and motives which makes it easier to assess the contemporary narratives, including Buchanan, Lesley and the *Diurnal* (p. 407). Buchanan's chapters on Mary's personal reign are translated and analysed by W. A. Gatherer in *The tyrannous reign of Mary Stewart* (1958). John Knox's *History of the Reformation in Scotland* (2 vols. ed. D. Laing, 1846-8, and W. Croft Dickinson, 1949) is all-important, but it may be conjectured that had it not been written Knox's place in the history of the time would have been less conspicuous, for other men's writings have little to say of him. The *Historical Memoirs of the Reign of Mary, Queen of Scots*, by Lord Herries (Abbotsford Club) is the work of a staunch Marian. The *Memoirs of his own Life*, by Sir James Melville of Halhill (Bannatyne and Maitland Clubs), recount the doings and saying of a courtier and diplomat as recollected in his old age and are, like Knox's *History*, coloured by the writer's self-importance. On the English side, John Hayward's *Annals of the First Four Years of the Reign of Elizabeth* (Camden Soc.) are of interest for the English expedition of 1560.

Knox's *History* is a literary classic, but written in the author's acquired English rather than in Scots. For Scots literature which illuminates the history of the time we turn to the *Works* of Sir David Lindsay (4 vols. S. T. S., and other edns.) and *The Complaynt of Scotland* (E.E.T.S.). On the other hand, the following non-record sources for ecclesiastical history are also of literary significance: the *Gude and Godlie Ballatis* (S. T. S. and ed. D. Laing, 1868), which reveal the popular theology of the early, Lutheran, phase of the Scottish Reformation; Ninian Winzet, *Certaine Tractates for Reformatioun of Doctryne and Maneris* (Maitland Club; S. T. S.), the work of a schoolmaster who saw the need for reform but detected the weaknesses and inconsistencies in Knox's position; and Archbishop Hamilton's *Catechism* (ed. T. G. Law, 1884).

The most important pre-reformation ecclesiastical records,[1] including the legislation of the councils of 1549, 1552, and 1559, are in *Concilia Scotiae: Ecclesiae Scoticanae Statuta* (Bannatyne Club), translated by David Patrick (S. H. S.). Post-reformation record begins with the *Register of the Kirk Session of St. Andrews, 1559-1600* (2 vols., S. H. S.), which incorporates the proceedings of the court of the superintendent of Fife, and *Accounts of the Collectors of Thirds of Benefices, 1561-72* (S. H. S.), which elucidate the financial situation. It is a great obstacle to a full understanding of the early history of the reformed church that the official records of the general assembly are not extant before 1638. The *Acts and Proceedings of the General Assemblies* [1560-1618] (Bannatyne and Maitland Clubs, 3 vols.) consist of a partial reconstruction from unofficial transcripts. Later records of the assembly are printed as follows: *Records of the Kirk of Scotland . . . from the year 1638* [to 1654] (ed. A. Peterkin, Edin., 1838) and *Records of the Commissions of the General Assemblies* [1646-52] (3 vols., S. H. S.). Many printed records of local church courts are listed in *Sources and Literature of Scots law* (p. 403); the originals are now very largely in the Register House.

Secondary works are heavily concentrated on biography, and especially the biography of Queen Mary. D. H. Fleming, *Mary, Queen of Scots, from her birth to her Flight into England* (1897, 1898), is outstanding for its documentation. Antonia Fraser, *Mary, Queen of Scots* (1969), is the best biography. T. F. Henderson wrote on *The Casket Letters* (1889, 1890), as did Andrew Lang, in *The Mystery of Mary Stuart* (1901, 1904, 1912). R. K. Hannay's " The Earl of Arran and Queen Mary," in *S. H. R.*, XVIII. 258-77, threw fresh light on the Hamilton interest. Among the voluminous writing on the Kirk o' Field mystery, the works of R. H. Mahon (*Mary, Queen of Scots: a study of the Lennox narrative* [1924], *The indictment of Mary, Queen of Scots* [1923] and *The tragedy of Kirk o' Field* [1930]), advanced the theory of a conspiracy against Mary.

Maurice Lee's *James Stewart, Earl of Moray* (1953) is outstanding as " a political study of the reformation in Scotland." Mary of Guise deserves a better biography than that by E. M. H. McKerlie (1931). Thomas McCrie's *Life of John Knox* (1811 and many later edns.) was a remarkable work of research for its time and should still be used, but Eustace Percy's *John Knox* (1937) is acknowledged the best biography. P. Hume Brown's *George Buchanan* (1890) is a standard work, R. F. Gore-Browne's *Lord Bothwell* (1937) a spirited defence. Information about many of the personalities of the period is assembled in Karl Pearson, " The skull and portraits of Henry Stewart, Lord Darnley," in *Biometrika*, XX. 1-104.

[1] In addition to those listed above, p. 407.

The recent scholarship which has gone into the English history of the period is not to be ignored, especially J. E. Neale, *Elizabeth I and her Parliaments* (2 vols., 1953-7) and Conyers Read, *Mr. Secretary Cecil and Queen Elizabeth* (1955).

Ecclesiastical history has attracted some important non-biographical work. D. H. Fleming, *The Reformation in Scotland* (1910), is, within its scope, exhaustive and meticulous, despite the author's strong protestant prejudice, and his *Critical Reviews* (1912) also contains much of value. W. Murison, *Sir David Lyndsay* (1938), is a study of the pre-reformation church. G. Donaldson, *The Scottish Reformation* (1960), and Duncan Shaw, *The General Assemblies of the Church of Scotland* (1964), examine ecclesiastical organisation, while reformed worship is dealt with by William McMillan, *The Worship of the Scottish Reformed Church* (1931), and G. B. Burnet, *The Holy Communion in the Reformed Church of Scotland* (1960). These are all works of sound scholarship. Several articles from the *Innes Review* were reprinted in *Essays on the Scottish Reformation* (ed. D. McRoberts, 1962). Some important material relating to the counter-reformation is surveyed by Ludwig Hammermayer, " Deutsche Schottenklöster, Schottische Reformation, Katholische Reform und Gegenreformation," in *Zeitschrift für bayerische Landesgeschichte*, Bd. 26, heft 1/2.

v. The Reign of James VI

(*a*) *Sources*

The various printed collections of English state papers (pp. 404-5) remain important as far as 1603, but thereafter the English records have little to offer, though the *Calendar of State Papers, Domestic* is not to be ignored. The following collections have official correspondence and state papers for this reign: *Registrum honoris de Morton* (Bannatyne Club); *Correspondence of Robert Bowes* (Surtees Soc.); *Warrender Papers* (2 vols., S. H. S.); *Letters and Papers of Patrick, Master of Gray* (Bannatyne Club); *Original Letters of Mr. John Colville* (Bannatyne Club); *Secret Correspondence of Sir Robert Cecil with James I* (ed. Lord Hailes, Edin. 1766); *Correspondence of King James VI of Scotland with Sir Robert Cecil* (Camden Soc.); *The Earl of Stirling's Register of Royal Letters* (ed. C. Rogers, 2 vols., 1885); *Royal Letters . . . relating to the Colonization of New Scotland* (Bannatyne Club); *State Papers . . . of Thomas, Earl of Melrose* (2 vols., Abbotsford Club); *Letters and State Papers during the Reign of James VI* (Abbotsford Club); *Original Letters relating to the Ecclesiastical Affairs of Scotland . . . 1603-25* (2 vols., Bannatyne Club); *Report on the Events and Circumstances which produced the Union of the Kingdoms of England and Scotland* (ed. [J. Bruce], 2 vols., [London 1799]); *Memorials and Letters relating to the History of Britain in the Reign of James the First* (ed. David Dalrymple, Lord Hailes, 1762, 1766); *Correspondance diplomatique de B. de S. de la Mothe-Fénélon* (7 vols., Bannatyne Club). Some papers relating to the Highlands, 1607-25, are in *Highland Papers*, III (S. H. S.).

Among the important contemporary narratives are Richard Bannatyne, *Memorials of Transactions in Scotland, 1549-73* (Bannatyne Club); *The Historie and Life of King James the Sext* (Bannatyne Club); and Michel de Castelnau, *Memoires* (ed. J. le Labourer, 3 vols., Paris, 1731). In a reign when political and ecclesiastical events were peculiarly intermingled, the church histories of David Calderwood (8 vols., Wodrow Soc.) and John Spottiswoode (3 vols., Spottiswoode Soc.) are essential for their facts as well as for the light they throw on the presbyterian and the episcopalian attitude respectively, and Calderwood is very largely a collection of original documents. The *Diary* of James Melville, nephew of Andrew Melville (Bannatyne Club; Wodrow Soc.), is valuable for ecclesiastical history and also contains useful social material.

Some collections of Roman catholic material extend over this reign and later years: *Narratives of Scottish Catholics under Mary Stuart and James VI* (1885, 1889) and *Memoirs of Scottish Catholics during the XVIIth and XVIIIth Centuries* (2 vols., 1909), both edited by William Forbes Leith; "Narratives of the Scottish Reformation," in *Innes Rev.*, VII. 27-59, 112-21; Gilbert Blackhall, *Breiffe Narrative of the Services done to Three Noble Ladyes* (Spalding Club); Cathaldus Giblin, *Irish Franciscan Mission to Scotland, 1619-1646* (1964); and *The Blairs Papers, 1603-60* (ed. M.V. Hay, 1929), which deals mainly with Scots colleges abroad. T. G. Law's edition of *Catholic Tractates of the Sixteenth Century* (S. T. S., 1901) contains much of interest.

(b) Secondary Works

D. H. Willson, *King James VI and I* (1956), is the best general account of the whole reign, but is less favourable to James than a student of Scottish administration is bound to be. Anglo-Scottish relations down to 1590 are dealt with at length in Conyers Read, *Mr. Secretary Walsingham and the Policy of Queen Elizabeth* (3 vols., 1925), and after 1603 some of the interaction of English and Scottish affairs may be followed in S. R. Gardiner, *History of England . . . 1603-42* (10 vols., 1883-4).

Among specialised studies, R. S. Rait and A. I. Cameron, *King James's Secret* (1927), deals with James's attitude to his mother's execution; James's Continental negotiations are the subject of writings by J. D. Mackie—"Scotland and the Spanish Armada," in *S. H. R.*, XII. 1-23, "The Secret Diplomacy of King James VI in Italy," in *S. H. R.*, XXI. 267-83 and *Negotiations between James VI and I and Ferdinand I, Grand Duke of Tuscany* (1927); and the relations of James and his queen with the pope are covered by A. O. Meyer, *Clemens VIII und Jakob I von England* (Rome, 1906).

The only political biography is Maurice Lee's important *John Maitland of Thirlestane* (1959). Thomas McCrie, *Andrew Melville* (2 vols., 1819, and later edns.), is the fruit of research in a wide range of sources bearing on many aspects of ecclesiastical and educational history. None of the other important clerics of the period have found biographers except Patrick Forbes, Bishop of Aberdeen (W. G. S. Snow, 1951). The solitary Roman catholic martyr, John Ogilvie, a Jesuit executed for treason in 1615, was biographed by W. E. Brown (1925).

On Border history, and Anglo-Scottish relations on the frontier, George Ridpath, *Border-history of England and Scotland* (1776), is still a standard work, and D. L. W. Tough, *The last years of a frontier* (1928), is masterly, but with them may be read H. M. Wallace, " Berwick in the Reign of Queen Elizabeth," in *E. H. R.*, XLVI. 79-88, J. Graham, *Condition of the Border at the Union* (1902, 1907), a work based on Lord Muncaster's MSS. in *H. M. C. Report*, X, PART IV, and Penry Williams, " The Northern Borderland under the Early Stuarts'," in *Historical Essays presented to David Ogg* (1963). For Irish history the standard works are Richard Bagwell, *Ireland under the Tudors* (3 vols., 1885-90), and *Ireland under the Stuarts* (3 vols., 1909-16), but the following deal specifically with Scoto-Irish relations and with the plantation of Ulster: G. A. Hayes McCoy, *Scots Mercenary Forces in Ireland* (1937), Andrew McKerral, " West Highland Mercenaries in Ireland," in *S. H. R.*, XXX. 1-14, G. Hill, *An Historical Account of the Plantation of Ulster* (1877), and *An Historical Account of the MacDonnells of Antrim* (1873), and R. Dunlop, " Sixteenth Century Schemes for the Plantation of Ulster," in *S. H. R.*, XXII. 51-60, 115-26, 199-212. For works on the Highlands, see p. 406.

VI. ECONOMIC, SOCIAL AND CULTURAL HISTORY

(a) Sources

There is no other branch of Scottish history on which, despite the abundance of material, so much groundwork still requires to be done. Among the basic sources are the Records of Testaments, the court books of regalities and baronies, burgh records and notaries' protocol books. For lists of those which are printed, reference may be made to the *Hand list* by Gouldesbrough *et al.* and to the *Sources and Literature of Scots Law* (pp. 402-3). The unprinted MSS. are mainly in the Register House, though some burgh records are preserved locally. The *Records of the Convention of Royal Burghs* were ed. by J. D. Marwick (6 vols., 1866-90).

Accounts of Scotland by foreign visitors are important, but they have perhaps been relied on too much because of their availability in print and their frequently racy character. Extracts from the more important were collected in *Early Travellers in Scotland* (1891), by P. H. Brown, who also edited some of the " Tours " separately. W. Lithgow's *The Totall Discourse of the Rare Adventures* [etc.], published at London in 1614, was printed again in 1632 and 1906. A " Journey through England and Scotland made by Liupold von Wedel in the years 1584 and 1585 " is in *Trans. Roy. Hist. Soc.*, 2nd ser., IX. 223-70. Donald Monro's important *Description of the Western Isles of Scotland* (1549), frequently reprinted, was edited by R. W. Munro (1961).

Extracts from contemporary Scottish narratives are given in J. G. Fyfe, *Scottish Diaries and Memoirs, 1550-1746* (1928), and extracts from diverse sources in P. H. Brown, *Scotland before 1700* (1893), and Chambers, *Domestic Annals* (p. 405).

Other useful social material is to be found in *The* [Glamis] *Book of Record* (S. H. S.); *Correspondence of Sir Robert Kerr, first Earl of Ancram, and his son William, third Earl of Lothian* (ed. D. Laing, 1875); *Diary and General Expenditure Book of William Cunningham of Craigends* (S. H. S.); *The Account Book of Sir John Foulis of Ravelston, 1671-1707* (S. H. S.); and the seventeenth-century letters in E. D. Dunbar, *Social Life in former days, chiefly in the Province of Moray* (2 vols., 1865-6).

Among the sources specifically relating to commerce, the *Ledger of Andrew Halyburton* (ed. C. Innes, 1867) contains the Book of Customs of 1612; the statistics of the Baltic traffic are printed in N. E. Bang and K. Korst, *Tabeller over Skibsfart og Varetransport gjennem Oeresund, 1497-1660* (2 vols. [1497-1660 and 1661-1783], Copenhagen, 1906-33 and 1930-53); the *Compt Buik of David Wedderburne* (S. H. S.) gives the shipping lists of Dundee, 1580-1618, and with it may be read W. McNeill, " Papers of a Dundee Shipping dispute," in *S. H. S. Misc.*, x. *The Journal of Thomas Cunningham of Campvere* (ed. E. J. Courthope, 1928), covers the years 1640-54.

For Scots abroad, there are *Papers illustrating the History of the Scots Brigade in the service of the United Netherlands* (3 vols., S. H. S.), and *Papers relating to the Scots in Poland* (S. H. S.).

Reports on the State of Certain Parishes in Scotland in 1627 (Maitland Club) give information about education and other matters.

(b) Secondary Works

No history of Scottish agriculture has seriously attempted to deal with this period. T. B. Franklin, *A History of Scottish farming* (1952), has only a few paragraphs on it. D. McDonald, *Agricultural writers . . . 1200-1800* (1908), while not dealing to any extent with Scotland, has valuable reproductions of illustrations of old implements.

On commerce, Lythe and Smout (p. 406) cover large parts of the period, and T. Keith's *Commercial Relations of England and Scotland, 1603-1707* (1910), is a most useful little book. An essentially medieval story is brought to its conclusion in John Davidson and Alexander Gray, *The Scottish Staple at Veere* (1909), and M. P. Rooseboom, *The Scottish Staple in the Netherlands* (1910).

In the history of industry, there has been a fair amount of writing on the traditional crafts and allied subjects, e.g., J. D. Marwick, *Edinburgh Guilds and Crafts* (Scot. Burgh Rec. Soc.), H. Lumsden and P. H. Aitken, *History of the Hammermen of Glasgow* (1912, 1915), H. Lumsden, *History of the Skinners, Furriers and Glovers of Glasgow* (1937); several articles in the *Book of the Old Edinburgh Club;* and *The Records of the Trades House of Glasgow* (ed. H. Lumsden, 1910). On the new industries of the seventeenth century, there is little save the writings of W. R. Scott: " The Fiscal Policy of Scotland before the Union," in *S. H. R.*, I [dealing with the protective system and its effect on manufactures, especially after 1660]; " Scottish Industrial Undertakings before the Union" and "The Woolcard Manufactory at Leith," in *S. H. R.*, II; and *The Constitution and Finance of English, Scottish and Irish Joint Stock Companies* (3 vols., 1910-12). On " heavy industry " the standard works are J. U. Nef, *The Rise of the British Coal Industry* (1932), and H. R. Schubert, *History of the British Iron and Steel Industry* (1957).

The subject of *The Scot Abroad* is surveyed generally but inadequately by J. H. Burton (1881), and there are the following special studies: Francisque Michel, *Les Écossais en France, les Français en Écosse* (2 vols., 1862); W. Forbes Leith, *The Scots Men-at-arms and Life-guards in France* (2 vols., 1882); T. A. Fischer, *The Scots in Eastern and Western Prussia and Hinterland* (1903), *The Scots in Germany* (1902) and *The Scots in Sweden* (1907); and G. P. Insh, *Scottish Colonial Schemes* (1922).

The fullest general survey of social history is C. Rogers, *Social Life in Scotland from Early to Recent Times* (3 vols., Grampian Club). Various aspects are dealt with in John Warrack, *Domestic Life in Scotland*, 1488-1688 (1920), G. F. Black, *A Calendar of Witchcraft Cases in Scotland*, 1511-1727 (1938), S. Maxwell and R. Hutchison, *Scottish Costume* (1958), J. T. Dunbar, *History of Highland Dress* (1962), and A. Cormack, *Poor Relief in Scotland* (1923)—the last an inadequate work on an important subject. J. B. Paul, " Social Life in Scotland in the Sixteenth Century," in *S. H. R.*, XVII. 296-310, drew attention to the value of notaries' protocol books.

The most recent accounts of Scottish literature are to be found in the volumes of the Oxford History of English Literature; C. S. Lewis, in his volume on *English Literature in the Sixteenth Century* (1954) gives generous space to Scotland. An attempt to assess *The Scottish Tradition in Literature* was made by Kurt Wittig (1958), but not all would agree with his conclusions. Most of the verse, and some of the prose, of the period, has been printed by the Scottish Text Society, in volumes with full scholarly apparatus.

On the intellectual activity of the later part of the seventeenth century, H. W. Meikle, *Some Aspects of Later Seventeenth Century Scotland* (1947), is a sound, though brief and not exhaustive, survey.

For book production, use should be made of Aldis (p. 402), R. Dickson and J. Edmond, *Annals of Scottish Printing* (1890), and W. S. Mitchell, *History of Scottish Bookbinding* (1955).

With the exception of J. Grant, *History of the Burgh and Parish Schools of Scotland* (1876), which deals only with burgh schools, none of the published books on school education is satisfactory for this period, and several are no less than mischievous, owing to their preoccupation with the statute of 1696, which in fact did little at the time to improve the situation. The universities have been better served, by J. M. Anderson, *The University of St Andrews* (1878, 1883), R. G. Cant, *The University of St. Andrews* (1946), J. D. Mackie, *The University of Glasgow* (1954), R. S. Rait, *The Universities of Aberdeen* (1895) and Alexander Grant, *The University of Edinburgh* (2 vols., 1884). Relevant articles include John Durkan, " The Beginnings of Humanism in Scotland " in *Innes Rev.*, IV. 5-24, M. F. Moore, " The Education of a Scottish Nobleman's Sons in the Seventeenth Century," in *S. H. R.*, XXXI. 1-15, 101-15, and C. P. Finlayson, " Illustrations of Games by a Seventeenth Century Edinburgh Student," in *S. H. R.*, XXXVII. 1-10.

The standard works on architecture are D. Macgibbon and T. Ross, *Castellated and Domestic Architecture of Scotland* (5 vols., 1887-92), and *Ecclesiastical Architecture of Scotland* (3 vols., 1896-7). Important recent books are George Hay, *The Architecture of Scottish Post-Reformation Churches* (1957), and Stewart Cruden, *The Scottish Castle* (1960). The *Reports* and *Inventories*, county by county, published by the Royal Commission on Ancient and Historical Monuments, are authoritative.

Other branches of culture are dealt with in H. G. Farmer, *A History of Music in Scotland* (1947); Ian Finlay, *Scottish Crafts* (1948), *Art in Scotland* (1948) and *Scottish Gold and Silver Work* (1956); and J. W. Small, *Scottish Woodwork of the Sixteenth and Seventeenth Centuries* (1878), which deals with the detail of a number of articles of furniture and some panelling.

The Scottish coinage is the subject of works by E. Burns (3 vols., 1887), R. W. Cochran-Patrick (2 vols., 1876) and I. H. Stewart (1955).

For the titles of the many valuable local histories which contribute to economic, social, and cultural history, reference may be made to Mitchell and Cash and to Hancock (p. 402).

VII. THE CONSTITUTION

There are no sources on legislature and executive beyond the records mentioned on p. 404. The authoritative account of the parliament is R. S. Rait, *The Parliaments of Scotland* (1924), but Rait exaggerated the subservience of parliament. Other works are *The Scottish*

Parliament, its Constitution and Procedure, 1603-1707, by C. S. Terry (1905), *The Estate of the Burgesses in the Scots Parliament*, by J. D. Mackie and G. S. Pryde (1923), W. B. Gray, " The Judicial Proceedings of the Parliaments of Scotland," in *Juridical Rev.*, XXXVI. 135-51, and " Constitutional Position of the Scottish Monarch prior to the Union," in *Law Quart. Rev.*, XVII. 252-62. The complicated electoral law of the Scottish counties is the subject of Thomas Thomson's *Memorial on Old Extent* (Stair Soc.). A classic on the Scottish constitution is A. V. Dicey and R. S. Rait, *Thoughts on the Union* (1920). T. Pagan is the authority on *The Convention of the Royal Burghs* (1926).

On the history of the judicature, there are the following sources additional to those mentioned on p. 404: Jacques Makgill and Jean Ballenden, *Discours particulier d'Écosse* . . . *1559* (Bannatyne Club), a description of the financial and legal system, with special reference to the law of treason; H. Bisset, *Rolment of Courtis* (3 vols., S. T. S.), a compilation of the forms of civil action in the early seventeenth century; *The Old Minute Book of the Faculty of Procurators in Glasgow, 1668-1758* (ed. J. S. Muirhead, 1948); and *Justiciary Records of Argyll and The Isles, 1664-1705* (Stair Soc.).

In addition to Hannay's *College of Justice* (p. 407), use may be made of A. J. G. Mackay, *The Practice of the Court of Session* (2 vols., 1877-9); A. R. G. McMillan, *The Evolution of the Scottish Judiciary* (1941); " The Judicial System of the Commonwealth of Scotland," in *Juridical Rev.*, XLIX. 232-55; and R. D. Melville, " The use and Forms of Judicial Torture in Scotland," in *S. H. R.*, II. 225-49.

VIII. THE REIGN OF CHARLES I

(a) Sources

Some important bibliographical work was done by J. D. Ogilvie: bibliographies of the Glasgow assembly and the Bishops' Wars in *Glasgow Bibliog. Soc. Records*, VII. 1-12, XII. 21-40; bibliography of the Resolutioner-Protestor controversy in *Edin. Bibliog. Soc. Publications*, XIV. 57-85; " The National Petition, October 18, 1637," *ibid.*, XII. 105-31, " The Aberdeen doctors and the National Covenant," *ibid.*, XI. 73-86 and " The cross petition, 1643," *ibid.*, XV. 55-76.

Some of the collections of state papers noted in Section V, especially Stirling's *Register*, are relevant to this reign also.

There are a number of important contemporary and near-contemporary narratives, some containing original documents: the presbyterian John Row, *Historie of the Kirk of Scotland* (Maitland Club and Wodrow Soc.); *The Historical Works of Sir James Balfour* (4 vols., 1825), including his " Annales "; three episcopalian narrators: J. Gordon,

History of Scots Affairs (3 vols., Spalding Club), John Spalding, *History of the Troubles* (2 vols., Bannatyne and Spalding Clubs), and Bishop Henry Guthrie, *Memoirs* (1702 and other eds.); and the royalist R. Menteth, *The history of the Troubles of Great Britain . . .1633-50* (French edn., Paris, 1661, trans. London 1735). Clarendon's *History of the Rebellion* (6 vols., 1888), throws light on Charles I's Scottish policy, and the *Works* of Laud (9 vols., 1847-60) include, besides valuable narratives, the *Canons* of 1636. G. Donaldson, *The Making of the Scottish Prayer Book of 1637* (1954), prints preparatory drafts as well as the text ultimately issued.

For the events leading to, and following, the National Covenant, special importance attaches to the *Diary of Archibald Johnston of Wariston* (S. H. S.: 3 vols. *plus* part of VOL. XXVI of the Society's publications); *A Relation of Proceedings . . . from August 1637 to July 1638*, by John Leslie, Earl of Rothes (Bannatyne Club); and *A Large Declaration concerning the Late Tumults* (1639)—the official defence of the king's policy, composed by Walter Balcanquhal, Dean of Durham. The following collections are important for several years from 1637-8 onwards: Gilbert Burnet, *The Memoir of James and William, Dukes of Hamilton* (1852); *The Hamilton Papers* (Camden Soc.), which consists of items not printed by Burnet; and *The Letters and Journals of Robert Baillie* (3 vols., Bannatyne Club). The principal sources for the period of Scottish intervention in the English civil war and the Montrose episode are: *Papers Relating to the Army of the Solemn League and Covenant, 1643-7* (2 vols., S. H. S.); *The Diplomatic Correspondence of Jean de Montereul and the Brothers de Bellièvre* (2 vols., S.H.S.); *Short Abridgment of Britane's Distemper* (Spalding Club); G. Wishart, *The Memoirs of James, Marquis of Montrose* (ed. Simpson and Murdoch, 1893); *Memorials of Montrose and his Times* (Maitland Club); and " Documents relating to the Massacre of Dunaverty, 1647," in *Highland Papers*, II (S. H. S.).

There are certain sources containing matter of general interest for this period and later: *Memorialls, or The Memorable Things that fell out . . . from 1638 to 1684*, by Robert Law (ed. C. K. Sharpe, 1818); *Memoirs of Sir Ewen Cameron of Locheill* (Abbotsford and Maitland Clubs); *Life of Mr. Robert Blair* (Wodrow Soc.). Maidment's *Historical Fragments* contains several seventeenth-century memoirs and journals, especially of the period 1644-60.

(b) Secondary Works

For a period when English and Scottish affairs were so closely intermingled, the works of English historians are especially useful, notably S. R. Gardiner, whose *History of England* (p. 411) is continued in his *History of the Great Civil War* (3 vols., 1886-91; 4 vols., 1893), and C. V. Wedgwood, *The King's Peace* (1955), *The King's War* (1958), and " Anglo-Scottish Relations, 1603-40," in *Trans Roy. Hist. Soc.*, 4th Ser., XXXII. 31-48. David Mathew, *Scotland under Charles I* (1955), an attempt at a new approach, is unsuccessful but contains suggestive ideas.

On the complex matter of the act of revocation and the settlement of the teinds, the standard work is J. Connell, *A Treatise on the Law of Scotland respecting Tithes* (2nd. edn., 2 vols., 1830); cf. Masson's introduction to *Register of the Privy Council*, 2nd. ser., I. Simplified accounts of this subject are apt to mislead.

The covenanting struggle, in all its phases, has stimulated historical writing, and there are a good many works in which hagiography outweighs scholarship. The following, though some show partisanship on one side or the other, represent serious work; J. K. Hewison, *The Covenanters* (2nd. edn., 2 vols., 1913); J. Willcock, *The Great Marquess: Life and Times of Archibald, . . . Marquess of Argyll* (1903); M. Napier, *Memoirs of the Marquis of Montrose* (2 vols., 1856); John Buchan, *Montrose* (1928); R. Gilmour, *Samuel Rutherford* (1904); R. L. Orr, *Alexander Henderson* (1919); J. A. Inglis, *Sir John Hay, " the incendiary "* (1937); and C. S. Terry, *The Life and Campaigns of Alexander Leslie* (1899).

IX. THE CROMWELLIAN INTERLUDE

(a) Sources

Many of the vital documents were printed in four volumes issued by the Scottish History Society: *Charles II and Scotland in 1650*, *The Cromwellian Union*, *Scotland and the Commonwealth* and *Scotland and the Protectorate*. Official records, and some other material, are of course to be found in English collections, especially *Acts and Ordinances of the Interregnum, 1642-60* (edd. C. H. Firth and R. S. Rait, 3 vols., 1911) and *The Clarke Papers: Selections from the Papers of William Clarke, Secretary to the Council of the Army . . . and to General Monck* (4 vols., Camden Soc.). Thomas Carlyle's *Oliver Cromwell's Letters and Speeches* was edited by S. C. Lomas (3 vols., 1904).

Miscellaneous sources are: *Letters from Roundhead Officers written from Scotland* (Bannatyne Club); *In Defence of the Regalia: being Selections from the Family Papers of the Ogilvies of Barras* (1910); accounts of Glencairn's rising in *Miscellanea Scotica*, IV (Glasgow, 1820), and in John Gwynne, *Military Memoirs of the Great Civil War* (ed. Sir W. Scott, 1822); *Register of the Consultations of the Ministers of Edinburgh* (2 vols., S.H.S.); *Report upon the Settlement of the Revenues of Excise and Customs in Scotland a.d. 1656*, by R. Tucker (Bannatyne Club).

Two important diaries span this period and the early years of Charles II's reign: *A Diary of Public Transactions* [1650-1667], by J. Nicoll (Bannatyne Club), which contains many documents, not least on the union " negotiations " of 1651-2; and *The Diary of Mr. John Lamont of Newton, 1649-71* (Maitland Club), which, although largely concerned with personalities, throws many sidelights on life in Fife. A " Diurnal of Occurrences in Scotland, 1652-4 " is in *Spottiswoode Soc. Misc.*, II. 173-208.

(b) Secondary Works

The only secondary works to be added to those already mentioned in the preceding section are C. H. Firth, *The Last Years of the Protectorate* (1909) and *Cromwell's Army* (1902 and later edns.,), and W. S. Douglas, *Cromwell's Scotch Campaigns* (1899). The emergence of Quakerism in Scotland during the English occupation is noted in G. B. Burnett, *The Story of Quakerism in Scotland* (1952).

x. The Reigns of Charles II and James VII

(a) Sources

Earlier writers on the period relied much on Robert Wodrow, *The History of the Sufferings of the Church of Scotland* (2 vols., 1721-2; 4 vols., 1828-30), but many of the papers he so industriously transcribed are now available in the *Register of the Privy Council*, and the Sharp letters of 1660 which he printed are supplemented in *Consultations of the Ministers of Edinburgh* (S. H. S.), II. 193 *et seq.* However, both Wodrow's *Sufferings* and his *Analecta* (4 vols., Maitland Club) contain a mass of material in support of the presbyterians' case. The voluminous correspondence of Lauderdale is scattered through several publications: *The Lauderdale Papers* (3 vols., Camden Soc.), which includes letters of most of the leading figures of the time; *S. H. S. Miscellany*, I, V and VI; *Letters from Lady Margaret Kennedy to Lauderdale* (Bannatyne Club); and *Letters from Archibald, Earl of Argyll, to Lauderdale* (Bannatyne Club). Other collections of letters and papers are: *Letters addressed by Prelates and Individuals of High Rank in Scotland . . . to Sancroft, Archbishop of Canterbury* (ed. W. N. Clarke, 1848); *Annals and Correspondence of the Viscount and the first and second Earls of Stair* (ed. J. M. Graham, 2 vols., 1875); *Letters . . . to George, Earl of Aberdeen, Lord High Chancellor of Scotland, 1681-4* (Spalding Club); *Seafield Correspondence* [1685-1708] (S. H. S.); *Papers of the Earls of Marchmont, 1685-1750* (ed. G. H. Rose, 3 vols., 1831).

Among contemporary narratives, Gilbert Burnet's *History of his Own Time* (2 vols., 1724-34, and later edns.) must be used with caution, for Burnet was the husband of a daughter of the strongly presbyterian house of Cassillis and he wrote to justify the Revolution of 1688-9 and the attitude of his patron, William of Orange. James Kirkton, author of *The Secret and True History of the Church of Scotland*, was a presbyterian who found an anti-covenanting editor in C. K. Sharpe (1817). Sir George Mackenzie of Rosehaugh, the lord advocate, was a prolific writer, who defended the prerogative in *Jus Regium* (1684) but also left important *Memoirs of the Affairs of Scotland* (ed. T. Thomson, 1821). The *Memoirs of Sir John Clerk of Penicuik*, (S. H. S.) begin in 1676 but are of value mainly for the period after the Revolution. *Chronological Notes of Scottish Affairs from 1680 till 1701* (ed. Sir W. Scott, 1822), *Historical observes of memorable occurrents in Church and State* [1680-86], *Historical Notices of Scottish Affairs* [1661-88] (both Bannatyne Club), and *Journals . . . with Observations, 1665-76* (S. H. S.), all by Sir John Lauder, Lord Fountainhall, give the views of a temperate presbyterian. The *Memoirs of Great Britain and Ireland* [1681-92], by Sir J. Dalrymple, were published in 2 vols. in 1771-3 and in 3 vols. in 1790. *A Memoir Touching the Revolution in Scotland* was written by Colin Lindsay, Earl of Balcarres, for James VII (Bannatyne Club).

The following memoirs and diaries are of less importance for the general course of history: Sir James Turner, *Memoirs* [1632-70] (Bannatyne Club); *Diary of Alexander and James Brodie* [1652-85] (Spalding Club); *Narrative of Mr. James Nimmo, a Covenanter, 1654-1709* (S. H. S.); *Memoirs of the Rev. John Blackadder* [presbyterian minister] (ed. A. Crichton, 1832); *Memoirs of Mr. William Veitch and George Bryson* [presbyterians] (ed. T. McCrie, 1825); and *Journal of the Hon. John Erskine of Carnock, 1683-7* (S. H. S.).

The Cameronian position is expounded in A. Shields, *Hind let loose* (1687 and later eds.), and M. Shields, *Faithful Contendings Displayed* (ed. J. Howie, 1780).

Highland Papers, I (S. H. S.), contains papers relating to the dispute of the MacLeans of Duart with Argyll, 1670-80.

(b) Secondary Works

The leading politicians have in the main been served by biographers who wrote adequately if without distinction: W. C. Mackenzie, *Life and Times of John Maitland, Duke of Lauderdale* (1923); Andrew Lang, *Sir George Mackenzie* (1909); C. S. Terry, *John Graham of Claverhouse, Viscount of Dundee* (1905); J. Willcock, *A Scots Earl of Covenanting Times . . . Archibald, 9th Earl of Argyll* (1907); A. Robertson, *The Life of Sir Robert Murray* (1922); A. Fergusson, *The Laird of Lag* [Sir Robert Grierson] (1886); and A. J. G. Mackay, *Memoir of Sir James Dalrymple, first Viscount Stair* (1873). The ecclesiastics have not fared so well, but R. H. Story, *William Carstares* (1874), and D. Butler, *Robert Leighton* (1903), are serviceable. T. Stephen, *Archbishop Sharp* (1839), is quite inadequate. The covenanters, of course, have had their hagiographers, like P. Walker, in *Six Saints of the Covenant, Peden, Semple, Welwood, Cameron, Cargill and Smith* (ed. D. H. Fleming, 2 vols., 1901 and earlier edns.) and A. Shields, in *The Life and Death of . . . James Renwick* (1724); these lives and others are collected in *Biographia Presbyteriana* (1827).

The most useful non-biographical studies are the following: C. S. Terry, *The Pentland Rising and Rullion Green* (1905); J. R. Elder, *The Highland Host of 1678* (1914); W. R. Foster, *Bishop and Presbytery: the Church of Scotland, 1661-1688* (1958)—a fully documented study of ecclesiastical administration; and T. Maxwell, " Presbyterian and Episcopalian in 1688," in *Scott. Church Hist. Soc. Rec.*, XIII. 25-37, a discussion of the respective strengths of the two parties.

ADDENDA

Three important new works of reference have appeared since this volume was first published: D. E. R. Watt, *Fasti Ecclesiae Scoticanae Medii Aevi ad annum 1638* (1969); Ian B. Cowan, *The Parishes of Medieval Scotland* (S. R. S.); and G. S. Pryde, *The Burghs of Scotland* (1965). A second edition of Godfrey Davies, *Bibliography of British History:Stuart Period, 1603-1714*, revised by Mary F. Keeler, was published in 1970. There are no outstanding additions to printed source material, but T. C. Smout, *A History of the Scottish People, 1560-1830* (1969), breaks new ground as a work of synthesis in general history, and several of Sir James Fergusson's essays (collected in *The White Hind* [1963] and *The Man behind Macbeth* [1969]) lead their reader into fascinating and rewarding by-ways. Border history has been given a completely new look by T. I. Rae in *The Administration of the Scottish Frontier, 1513-1603* (1966). A central aspect of economic history is dealt with in the monumental two volumes of Mark L. Anderson, *History of Scottish Forestry* (1967), which, though subject to a good deal of criticism in detail, open up this subject as never before. To the works on education must be added D. B. Horn, *A Short History of the University of Edinburgh* (1967), which is especially valuable on the antecedents and early days of the university. Two outstanding books on buildings and visual art are John Dunbar, *The Historic Architecture of Scotland* (1966), and M. R. Apted, *The Painted Ceilings of Scotland* (H.M.S.O.).

GENEALOGICAL TABLE

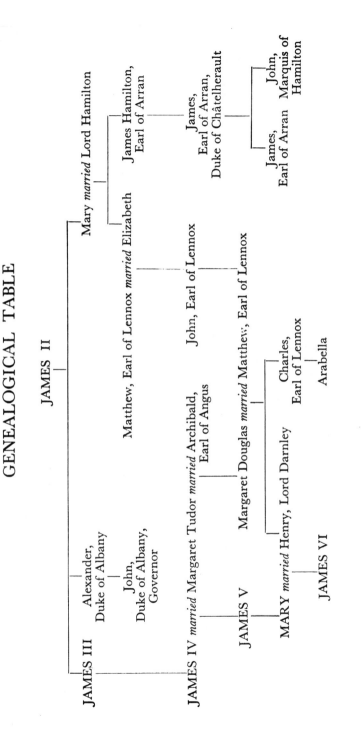

JAMES II

JAMES III
- Alexander, Duke of Albany
- John, Duke of Albany, Governor

JAMES IV *married* Margaret Tudor *married* Archibald, Earl of Angus

JAMES V

MARY *married* Henry, Lord Darnley

JAMES VI

Mary *married* Lord Hamilton

James Hamilton, Earl of Arran

Matthew, Earl of Lennox *married* Elizabeth

John, Earl of Lennox

James, Earl of Arran, Duke of Châtelherault

James, Earl of Arran

John, Marquis of Hamilton

Margaret Douglas *married* Matthew, Earl of Lennox

Charles, Earl of Lennox

Arabella

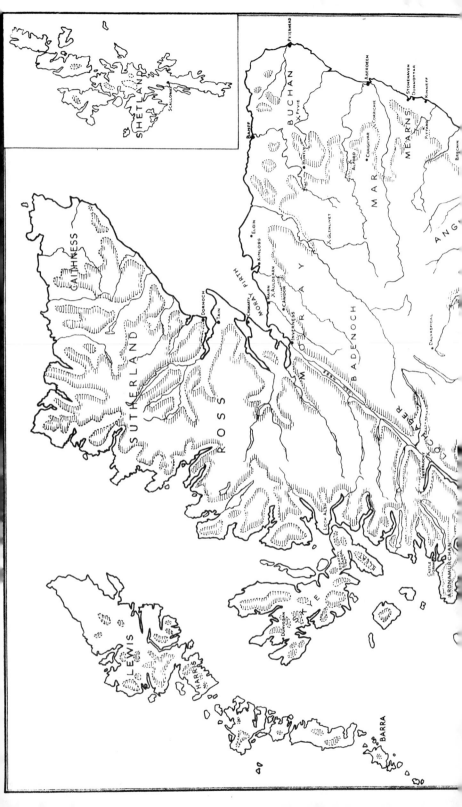

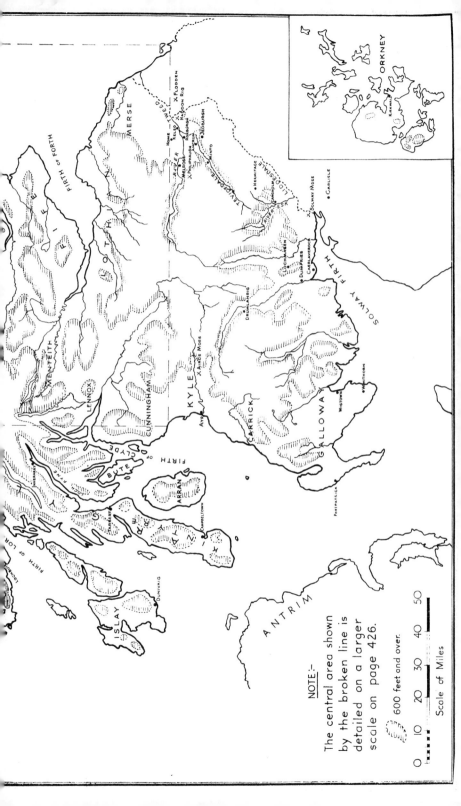

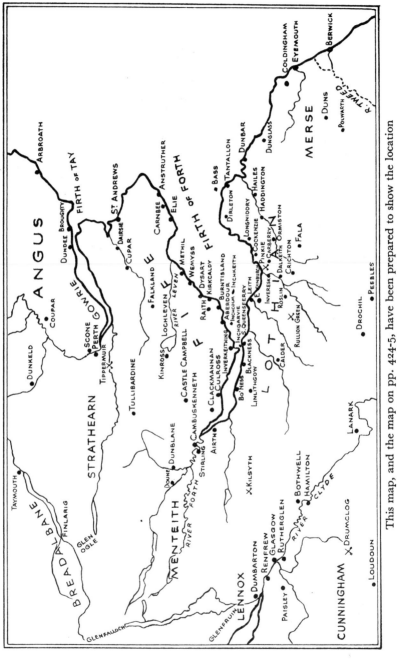

This map, and the map on pp. 424-5, have been prepared to show the location of all places mentioned in the text.

INDEX

Abbots, in parliament, 8, 276-7.

Aberdeen, 6, 108, 112, 189, 190, 204, 208, 268, 273, 334, 351, 391, 397; attitude to Reformation, 101; opposition to Covenant, 319, 323, 325.
bishopric of, 15, 136.
Bishops of, *see* Dunbar, Gavin, Elphinstone, William, Forbes, Patrick, Gordon, William *and* Stewart, William.
friaries in, 398.
Psalter, 269.
University of, 266-7.

Aberdeenshire, Reformation in, 26.

Aberdour Castle, 271.

Adair, John, cartographer, 395.

Adamson, Patrick, Archbishop of St Andrews, 181.

Advocate for the poor, 56.

Advocates' Library, 393.

Agriculture, 238-42, 386-7.

Airds Moss, battle of, 371.

Albany, Dukes of, *see* Stewart, Alexander *and* John.

Alexander, Sir William, Earl of Stirling, secretary, 218, 329; his Nova Scotia scheme, 254-5; poet, 269-70; his "turners", 303.

Alford, battle of, 334.

Allen, Cardinal William, 176.

Alyth, 343.

America, trade with, 251, 351-2, 388-9, 392.

Ancram, Earl of *see* Kerr, Robert.

Ancrum, battle of, 71, 73.

Angus, Reformation in, 26-7.
Earls of, *see* Douglas.

Anne of Denmark, Queen of James VI, 186, 217, 259, 273; crowned, 192; criticised by ministers, 194; her dowry, 301.

Annexation, Act of (1587), 193, 205.

Anstruther Easter, church of, 274.

Antrim, 228, 252.

Apparel, act on (1609), 235; of clergy, 151, 306-7.

Arbroath, abbey of, 77, 81, 173, 220, 297.

Arbuthnot, Alexander, printer, 260.
Alexander, principal of King's College, Aberdeen, 266-7.

Architecture, 271-4, 395-6.

Ardnamurchan, 229, 333.

Argyll, 13, 72.
Bishop of, *see* Hamilton, James.
Earls of, *see* Campbell.

Armada, Spanish, 185, 192.

Arminianism, 305-6.

Armstrong, family of, 50.
Johnnie, 50.
Simon, 62.

Arran, Earls of, *see* Hamilton, Stewart.
isle of, 72.

Articles, Committee of, 284-6, 307, 327, 359, 377.

Atholl, Earl of, *see* Stewart.

Auldearn, battle of, 334.

Ayr, 119, 251; Reformation in, 93; fort at, 346.

Ayrshire, Reformation in, 27, 338.

Ayton, Sir Robert, poet, 259.

Bailies of ecclesiastical properties, 136.

Baillie, George, younger, of Jerviswood, 384.
Robert, of Jerviswood, 374, 379.
William, General, 334, 338.

Balcarres, Lord, and Earl of, *see* Lindsay.

Balfour, Sir James, of Denmilne, 262.
Sir James, of Pittendreich, parson of Flisk, 120; clerk-register, 122; his part in Darnley murder, 126-7; his *Practicks*, 261-2.
Sir Michael, of Mountquhanie, 78.

Balmerino, Lord, *see* Elphinstone.

Baltic, trade with, 248-9, 251*n*, 252-3, 351, 389-90.

Bancroft, Richard, 192; Archbishop of Canterbury, 204.

Banff, 282.

Barbados, transportation to, 350.

Bargany, Lord, *see* Hamilton, John.

Baronies, 5.

Barons, in parliament, 102, 278-9; in general assembly, 199-200, 320.

Barton, Robert, of Over Barnton, 36, 42.

Bass Rock, 343, 373.

Bassandyne, Thomas, printer, 260.

Bastie, Antoine d'Arces, seigneur de la, in Scotland, 18, 35.

Beaton, David, on diplomatic missions, 26, 39, 49; Archbishop of St Andrews and cardinal, 59-60; chancellor, 63, 68; imprisoned, 64-5; legate, 68; leads anti-English party, 15, 69; in control of affairs, 71-2, 76; murdered, 28, 74-5; 51, 82, 130, 136.

James, Archbishop of Glasgow and of St. Andrews, chancellor, 32, 35-6, 38-9; deprived of great seal, 40; opposed Angus, 40; his importance, 42; 44, 47, 82.

James, Archbishop of Glasgow, 81; in France, 103, 112, 153; supported Mary, 161, 174, 176; ambassador of James VI, 189.

Mary, 79.

Beggars' Summons, 91-2.

Bellenden of Auchnoule, family of, 218.

John, his *History*, 259.

Berwick-on-Tweed, 29, 37, 91, 96, 99, 215, 323.

Treaty of, 98.

Pacification of, 324.

Bible, in vernacular, 22, 64-5, 69, 77.

Bishops, in 1560, 102; after 1560, 103, 144; in reformed church, 147-8, 168, 198-9, 202; office condemned, 178, 198, 322, 324;

Bishops (*Continued*)
office revived, 205; consecretion, 206, 364; Jacobean, 221-2; Caroline, 299, 307, 354; in 1638, 314-22; in 1661, 363.

in parliament, 8, 276-7, 281, 284, 286, 327.

in privy council, 290, 299, 359.

" Black Acts ", 181, 198, 215.

Blackness Castle, 65, 78, 81.

Blaeu's Atlas, 257.

Blantyre, priory of, 221.

Blood relationship in Scottish society, 12-13, 151-2.

Blois, Treaty of, 165.

Boleyn, Anne, 23-5.

Bonds of manrent, 14.

Bo'ness, 252, 390.

Bonot, M., bailie of Orkney, 86.

Book of Common Order, 118, 141-3, 208-9, 263.

Book of Common Prayer (of England), 90, 94, 141-3, 208-10, 306, 364; (of Scotland, 1637), 270, 308-11, 322.

Book of Discipline, First, 102, 104-5, 143-4, 147, 263, 265-6, 297, 398.

Second, 199, 320.

Bordeaux, 251-2.

Borders, under James V, 50, 60-1; under Morton, 167; under James VI, 227-8; under Cromwell, 348.

Borthwick Castle, 123, 130.

Bothwell Brig, battle of, 371.

Bothwell, Earls of, *see* Hepburn, James *and* Patrick, *and* Stewart, Francis.

Adam, Bishop of Orkney, 129, 131, 161, 232; his kinsmen, 219.

Boulogne, Treaty of, 29.

Bowes, Sir Robert, 59, 177.

Boyd, Robert, 5th Lord, 121, 165, 168.

Breadalbane, 13.

Earls of, *see* Campbell.

Brechin, Bishop of, *see* Whitford, Walter.

Breda, negotiations at (1649), 340.
Bridges, 6, 397.
Brig o' Dee, action at, 189.
Broghill, Lord, 353, 355.
Brora, 258, 397.
Broughty Castle, 76, 78, 81, 86.
Broun, George, of Colstoun, 78.
Bruce, Alexander, 2nd Earl of Kincardine, 377-8.
    Edward, Commendator of Kinloss, 220.
    Sir George, 246.
    Robert, minister of Edinburgh, 192, 203.
    Sir William, architect, 396.
Buchanan, George, 14, 114; quoted, 10, 58, 123; his political thought, 146, 187; tutor of James VI, 172, 187.
Burgesses, attitude to Reformation, 27, 134, 137; attitude to Covenant, 323; in parliament, 8, 277-8, 281-2, 284, 286; in convention of estates, 287; in general assemblies, 105-6, 199-200, 320.
Burghs, ferms paid by, 5; courts of, 5, 225; baronial and royal, 11, 291, 392-3; influence of crown and nobles in, 12, 281-2; their place in economy, 10-12, 238, 245-6, 251-2, 347-8, 391-2; in Highlands, 228, 247; population of, 238; schools in, 262 ff.
Burnet, Alexander, Archbishop of Glasgow, 359, 369-70.
    Gilbert, historian, 384.
Burntisland, 252, 274.
Busso, Francisco de, 120.
Bute, 70, 72.

Caerlaverock Castle, 72, 272.
Caithness, 4, 233.
    Bishops of, see Forbes, Alexander, and Stewart, Robert.
    earldom of, 374.
    Earls of, see Sinclair and Campbell.

Calderwood, David, historian, 261.
Callendar, Earl of, see Livingstone, James.
Calvert, Sir George, 255.
Calvinism, 139, 305.
Cambuskenneth, abbey of, 134.
Cameron of Lochiel, 348.
    Richard, covenanting preacher, 371.
Cameronians, 371-2, 376, 380-1.
Campbell, family of, 13-4, 229-30, 319; of Glenorchy, 13, 321.
    Alexander, Bishop of Brechin, 86.
    Archibald, 4th Earl of Argyll, under James V, 51, 54; in minority of Mary, 15, 63, 66, 70, 73, 78-9; his attitude to Reformation, 86, 89, 90.
    Archibald, 5th Earl, as Lord Lorne signed First Band, 89; attitude to Reformation, 86, 93, 100; opposed Darnley marriage, 118, 121-2; part in schemes against Darnley, 124; Marian, 158-9, 161, 164-6, 168; died, 167.
    Archibald, 7th Earl, 193, 229, 230, 232.
    Archibald, 8th Earl and 1st Marquis of Argyll, as Lord Lorne, privy councillor, 299, 318; his part in the covenanting rebellion, 319, 327-30; defeated by Montrose, 334; opposed Engagement, 338; his attitude to Charles II, 341-2; executed, 361.
    Archibald, 9th Earl of Argyll, and Test Act, 379-80; his rebellion, 395.
    Colin, 3rd Earl of Argyll, 35-6, 38-41, 43, 50.
    Colin, 6th Earl of Argyll, 169-70, 174-5, 180.
    Colin, of Glenorchy, supported Reformation, 93.
    Colin, of Glenorchy, 270-1.
    Donald, Abbot of Coupar, 86.
    Duncan, of Glenorchy, 243, 258.
    James, Earl of Irvine, 255.

Campbell
John, of Glenorchy, 346.
John, Earl of Caithness and of Breadalbane, 374, 383.
John, of Loudoun, 1st Earl of Loudoun, 299, 307, 311n, 312-3, 328-30, 338, 350.
Campbeltown, 229, 247.
Campvere, 24, 389.
Canaries, trade with, 252.
Carberry, encounter at, 8, 130-1, 158.
Carbisdale, battle of, 340.
Cargill, Donald, covenanting preacher, 371-2.
James, botanist, 257.
Carlisle, 20, 70, 227.
Carlos, prince of Spain, 115-6.
Carnegie, David, of Culluthie, 217n.
Caroline Park, 395.
Carstares, William, 384.
Carthusian monks, 134.
Casket Letters, 128, 157, 160.
Cassillis, Earls of, 136; see also Kennedy.
Castle Campbell, 13.
Castles, 6, 9, 10.
Cateau-Cambrésis, Treaty of, 91.
Catharine of Aragon, 23, 25.
de Medici, 45, 104.
sister of Henry of Navarre, 185.
Cathcart, Lord, 367.
Cattle trade, 387.
Cecil, William, secretary of state, 30, 91-2, 95-6, 99, 103, 112, 160.
Chancellor, office of, 283, 375.
Chapel Royal, 270.
Charles I, birth, 296; character and aims, 295-6, 299, 308-10, 325; policy in Borders and Highlands, 227, 231; opposition to, 305 ff.; campaigns against covenanters, 323-5; in Scotland, 306-7, 328-9; Scottish loyalty to, 213; surrenders to Scots, 335-6; beheaded, 340.
Charles II, accepted as king, 213, 340; crowned, 342; in exile, 356; policy, 282, 286; work at Holyrood, 214.

Charles
V, Emperor, 17, 19, 20, 23-7.
IX, King of France, 115.
Archduke, 115.
Charlotte, daughter of Francis I, 19.
Charteris, John, of Cuthilgurdy, 15.
" Chaseabout Raid ", 12, 118-9.
Châtelherault, Duke of, see Hamilton, James.
Chichester, Sir Arthur, 229.
Chisholm, William (I), Bishop of Dunblane, 87, 103.
William (II), Bishop of Dunblane, 120, 161, 189.
Christian IV, King of Denmark, 253-4, 271.
Church, crown rights in, 4; wealth and power, 12, 132; privileges, 52; policy of James V towards, 54; abuses in, 81-2, 133 ff.
buildings, 10-12, 73, 133, 135, 273-4.
courts, 6, 46, 103, 145.
reformed, organisation of, in 1560, 103, 105, 113, 141; legislation in favour of, 102-3, 112, 128, 145; worship and order, 141-3; endowment, 111-2, 125, 143-4, 147-8, 150-1, 168, 296-8; relations with state, 105-6, 113, 125, 146, 149-50, 178, chapter 11, 359.
Clans, structure of, 13, 231-2.
Classes, Act of, 339, 342.
" Cleanse the Causeway ", 35.
Clement VII, Pope, 45-7.
Clergy, social status of, 12, 150-2, 221-2; see also Ministers.
Cloth-making, 244, 250, 386, 389-90.
Clyde, River and Firth of, 4, 70, 247.
Coaches, 397.
Coal industry, 246, 390.
Cockburn, Sir Archibald, of Langton, 395.
John, of Ormiston, supporter of Reformation, 28, 78, 86, 179.
Cockenzie, 252, 258.
Code of Canons, 309, 314, 322.
Coldingham, priory of, 57, 191.

College of Justice, foundation of, 46-8; *see also* Court of Session.

Collegiate churches, 11-12, 134.

Colonisation, 252-5, 357, 388.

Colquhoun, family of, 232.
John, of Luss, 53.

Colville, Sir James, comptroller, 42, 52, 53.

Commissary courts, 145, 400.

Commissioner, King's, to parliament, 283, 373, 375.

Commissioners of supply, 399-400.

Commonwealth, government of, 343 ff.

Confession of Faith of 1560, 102, 105, 153, 379.
of 1616, 305.

Confirmation by bishops, 207, 211, 364.

Conformity of clergy after Reformation, 152; under James VI, 210; after 1660, 365-6.

Constant moderators, 205.

Convention of estates, 287.
of royal burghs, 291.

Corn, export of, 241, 387.

Coronation oath, 146, 313.

Corrichie, battle of, 112.

Councils of Scottish Church, pass reforming legislation, 81-2, 90-1.

Court of Session, 42, 46-8, 55-6, 235, 288, 291, 303.

Courts of High Commission, 226, 322.

Covenanters, prepare to oppose Charles I, 319, 322; pack Glasgow assembly, 320-1; success against king, 325; divisions among, 326 ff.; after 1660, chapter 19.

Cowper, William, Bishop of Galloway, 261.

Craig, John, physician, 257.
Sir Thomas, jurist, 244, 262.

Craigievar Castle, 271.

Craigmillar Castle, 123, 126.

Crail, 49.

Cranston of Smailholm, 40.
William, 3rd Lord, 349-50.
Sir William, 227.

Crawford, Earls of, *see* Lindsay.

Crichton Castle, 123, 272.

Crichton, Alexander, of Brunstane, supporter of Reformation, 28; plotted against Cardinal Beaton, 74, 78; rehabilitated, 86.
George, Bishop of Dunkeld, 47.
Robert, Bishop of Dunkeld, 103, 161.
Robert, Lord Sanquhar, 223.
William, Jesuit, 175-6, 185, 189.
William, Earl of Dumfries, 378.

Cromarty, 230.

Cromwell, Oliver, quoted, 241, 350; invaded Scotland, 338-9, 341; quarrels with his parliaments, 345.
Richard, 345, 346n.

Crops, 240-2.

Cross petition, 330.

Crown matrimonial, 88-9, 120.

Crown revenues, 5; *see also* Finance.
rights in church appointments, 4, 135, 140.

Culross, 246.

Cumbernauld Bond, 328.

Cunningham, Alexander, 5th Earl of Glencairn, signed First Band, 89; supported revolution of 1559-60, 93; summoned to trial, 121; restored to favour, 122.
Cuthbert, 3rd Earl of Glencairn, 32, 40.
Sir Robert, of Auchinharvie, 390.
William, 4th Earl of Glencairn, (Master of G.), 52; in pro-English party, 15, 64, 68-9, 72-3, 80, 86.
William, 6th Earl of, 174, 179.
William, 9th Earl of, 346, 350, 358.

Cupar, 93.

Customs, 5, 301, 360, 373.

Dairsie, church of, 273.

Dalkeith, castle or palace of, 65, 272, 319, 323, 344.

Dalnaspidal, 346.

Dalrymple, Sir James, lord president, 383, 393.

Sir John, lord advocate, 383.

Dalziel (or Dalyell) of Carnwath, family of, 350.

Sir Thomas, 368.

Danelourt, Sebastian, 120.

Davidson, William, chemist, 257.

Davison, William, secretary of state, 176, 182, 184.

Deacons, office of, in reformed church, 142, 150, 309, 364.

Deane, Richard, major-general, 349.

Deer, abbey of, 220.

Denmark, trading and other contacts with, 22, 185, 253-4, 271-2.

Dick, William, of Braid, 323.

Dickson, David, minister, 311n, 312.

Dieppe, 48, 89, 92, 251.

Dirleton, church of, 273.

Discipline in reformers' programme, 140-1; in practice, 150, 225-6.

Donald Dubh, claimed lordship of Isles, 72.

Gorm of Sleat, 51.

Donibristle, 189.

Doon Hill, 341.

Douglas, family of, 12, 31, 45, 49, 52, 179, 350.

Archibald, 5th Earl of Angus, 31.

Archibald, 6th Earl of Angus, married Margaret Tudor, 31; driven from Scotland, 32; a regent, 34-5; associated with English faction, 37-9; held James V in captivity, 40-1; chancellor, 40, 42-3, 50; besieged in Tantallon, 9, 13, 41; exiled, 41, 54; returned, 64; in minority of Mary, 68-73; at Pinkie, 77; 79.

Archibald, 8th Earl of, associated with ultra-protestant faction, 174, 178-80, 187, 190.

Archibald, of Glenbervie, 13.

Archibald, uncle of 6th Earl of Angus, treasurer, 40.

Archibald, agent of James VI, 184.

Douglas

Gavin, Bishop of Dunkeld, 32-3, 36-7.

George, brother of 6th Earl of Angus, 40, 64, 73.

Hugh, of Longniddry, 28, 78.

James, 3rd Earl of Morton, 53, 68.

James, 4th Earl of Morton, gave bond to Mary of Guise, 86; signed First Band, 89; not involved in Moray's rebellion, 119 and n; his part in Riccio's murder, 121-2, and in Darnley's, 126-8; with confederate lords, 131; head of king's party, 165; his regency, 166-70, 181, 187, 281; deprived of office, 171; resumed control, 171-2; executed, 173; relations with Elizabeth, 176-7; his buildings, 271.

James, of Drumlanrig, 40.

James, of Parkhead, 40, 52.

James, 2nd Earl of Queensberry, 350.

John, rector of St Andrews University, 110.

Jonet, Lady Glamis, executed, 52.

Margaret, daughter of Angus and Margaret Tudor, 68; married Lennox, 70; 117, 119n.

Sir Robert, of Lochleven, 15, 53.

Sir William, of Lochleven, 179.

William, 10th Earl of Angus, 189.

William, Earl of Morton, 350.

William, Earl of Selkirk and Duke of Hamilton, 350, 377-9, 383, 390.

William, 3rd Earl of Queensberry, 378, 381.

Drake, Francis, 183.

Drama, 203, 268-9, 394.

Drochil Castle, 271.

Drumclog, battle of, 371.

Drumlanrig, 396.

Drummond, James, Lord Madertie, 218n.

James, Earl of Perth, 381, 383.

John, 1st Lord Drummond, 31, 33.

Drummond
  John, Earl of Perth, 350.
  John, Earl of Melfort, 381.
  William, of Hawthornden, 214, 258-60, 262, 326.
Drury, Sir William, 163, 166.
Dudley, John, Earl of Warwick, 29.
  Robert, Earl of Leicester, 116.
Dumbarton, 11, 35, 69-70, 75, 79, 108, 159, 163-4, 173, 323, 343, 346.
Dumfries, 76, 119, 368.
  Earl of, see Crichton, William.
Dun, Patrick, physician, 257.
Dunbar, 11, 93, 121, 123, 129, 130, 139, 251; French garrison in, 35, 39, 48, 78, 81, 87, 99; battle of, 341.
  Earl of, see Home, George.
  Gavin, Archbishop of Glasgow, chancellor, 40, 44, 46-7, 55, 77.
  Gavin, Bishop of Aberdeen, 39.
Dunblane, Bishops of, see Chisholm, William, and Leighton, Robert.
Dundee, 10, 65, 68, 76, 202, 251, 268, 334, 343, 391; Reformation in, 22, 27, 92-3; friaries in, 398.
  Earl of, see Scrimgeour, John.
Dunfermline, 271, 273, 296.
  Earl of, see Seton.
Dunglass, 79.
Dunkeld, Bishops of, see Crichton, George and Robert, and Douglas, Gavin.
Dunnottar, 343, 380.
Duns Law, 323.
Dury, John, minister, 179.
Dysart, 98.

East Lothian, reforming thought in, 27-8, 78.
Edinburgh, 60, 70-1, 76, 88, 101, 113, 119, 179, 191, 200, 203, 210, 222, 260, 272-3, 275, 278, 324, 339, 341, 371, 373, 395-6; place in economy, 11-12, 251-2, 301,

Edinburgh (Continued)
  351-2, 391; provosts of, 11, 35; disturbances in, under James V, 35, 39; attitude to Reformation, 65, 90, 94, 95, 97, 109-110; in campaign of 1559-60, 93-4, 97; riots in, (1596) 195, 201, (1637) 311 ff., (1686) 383, (1688) 384; relations with Charles I, 303-4; attitude after 1660, 367.
  Bishop of, see Forbes, William.
  Castle of, 57, 99, 164-6, 271-2, 319, 342.
  Kirk o' Field in, 125-8, 268.
  Schools in, 265, 268-9.
  Treaty of, 29, 99-100, 103, 108, 114.
  University of, 267-8, 305.
Education, 134, 149, 262-9, 400.
Edward, Prince, later Edward VI, 26, 28, 64, 83.
Eggs, trade in, 235.
Eglinton, Earls of, see Montgomery.
Eilean Donan Castle, 51.
Elders, in reformed church, 90, 142, 149, 200, 320-1, 339-40.
Elgin, 226.
Elie, 251.
Elizabeth, Queen of England, 30; succeeded, 91-2; relations with lords of the congregation, 95-6, 103; with Earl of Arran, 104; with Mary, 107-8, 113-7; attitude to Darnley marriage, 118-9; to king's and queen's parties, 159-66; to Morton, 167, 176-7; to Lennox, 176-7; to Ruthven Raid, 179-80; to Arran, 181-2; to Francis, Earl of Bothwell, 192; criticised by ministers, 194-5.
Elliot, Gilbert, of Minto, 384.
Elphinstone, James, 1st Lord Balmerino, 217n, 220-1.
  James, 2nd Lord Balmerino, 307-8, 311n, 312-3, 329.
  John, 3rd Lord Balmerino, 367.
  William, Bishop of Aberdeen, 32.
Engagement, 336-8, 357, 362.

England, relations with, 17-30; under James V, 36-8, 45, 48, 55, 59-60; in Mary's minority, 64, 67, 69-72, 75-8, 80, 83-4; in 1559-60, 91, 93, 95, 98, 103; in first covenanting period, 329 ff., 336 ff.; under Commonwealth, chapter 18; *see also* Elizabeth.

League with (1585-6), 182-3.

trade with, 250-1, 253, 352, 386-9.

union with, proposed (1669), 357*n*, 377-8.

Erections, 219-21, 296-7.

Erik, King of Denmark, 115.

Errol, Earls of, *see* Hay.

Erskine, Alexander, Master of Mar, 171.

John, 5th Lord, 15.

John, 6th Lord, 1st Earl of Mar, held Edinburgh Castle, 97, 99; regent, 165-6.

John, 2nd Earl of Mar, 171, 179-80, 187, 220.

John, Lord (1620), 245.

John, of Dun, reformer and superintendent of Angus, 27, 85, 93; signed First Band, 89; commissioner to France, 89.

Thomas, of Haltoun, secretary, 42, 45-6.

Esk, River (Solway), 60.

River (Musselburgh), 76.

Excise, 353, 360.

Exhorter, office of, 142.

Exports, 240-1, 247-8, 386-7, 389-90.

Eyemouth, 79, 87, 251.

Fala Muir, muster at, 26.

Falkland, 93, 243*n*; palace of, 6, 57, 60, 191.

Ferdinand, Archduke, 115.

Ferrara, Duke of, 115.

Feu charters of church lands, 136, 144-5, 239.

Fife, burghs in, 10-11, 391; Reformation in, 27.

Finance, 5, 43-4, 46, 56-8, 87, 169-70, 228, 234, 300-303, 352-3, 360, 373.

Finlarig Castle, 270, 343.

" First Band ", 89.

Fisher, Bishop John, 25.

Fisheries, 247.

Fleming, James, 4th Lord, 80.

John, 2nd Lord, 18.

John, 5th Lord, 122, 159.

John, Earl of Wigtown, 222.

Malcolm, 3rd Lord, 64, 66.

Mary, 79.

Flodden, battle of, 17.

Forbes, Alexander, Bishop of Caithness, 233.

Alexander, 11th Lord, 254.

John, Master of, 37, 52, 62.

John, of Corse, 261.

Patrick, Bishop of Aberdeen, 267.

William, Bishop of Edinburgh, 306.

Forfeitures, 5, 56, 216, 349.

Forman, Andrew, Archbishop of St Andrews, 34.

Forth, Earl of, *see* Ruthven, Patrick.

River and Firth of, 4, 247.

Fort William, 247.

Foulis, Sir John, of Ravelston, 394.

Thomas, burgess of Edinburgh, 252.

Fowler, T., 120.

William, poet, 259.

France, relations with, 17-30; under James V, 36-8, 45, 48-9; in Mary's minority, 68, 70-2, 75-8, 80-1, 83-4; chapter 6; 108.

Scottish privileges in, 48, 88-9, 249, 387-8.

Scots soldiers in, 254.

trade with, 246-9, 387-91.

Francis I, King of France, 18, 20-1, 24-6, 28, 39, 45, 48-9.

II, King of France (as Dauphin), 78-9; 95, 104.

Fraser, Andrew, of Muchalls, 222.

Frederick II, King of Denmark, 186.

Friars, 54, 134.

Fyvie, battle of, 334.

Gaelic, 258-9.
Galloway, bishopric of, 136.
Bishops of, *see* Cowper, William, Gordon, Alexander *and* Sydserf, Thomas.
Gardens, 272, 395.
Geddes, Jenny, 311.
General Assembly, antecedents and development, 104-6, 113, 146; organisation, 141, 199-200; under regents, 168; views of Melville and James VI on, 198, 200, 291; arrangements for summoning, 199; composition, 200, 320-1; meeting-places, 200-1, 204; in later years of James VI, 206-7, 308; under Commonwealth, 354.
General Bond, 230.
General Council, composition and powers of, 8, 287.
Germany, contacts with, 22.
Gillespie, Patrick, principal of Glasgow University, 355.
Glamis, Lady, *see* Douglas, Jonet.
Lord, *see* Lyon.
Glasgow, 10, 11, 33, 69, 98, 124-5, 159, 225, 268-9, 334, 371; general assemblies at, (1610) 205-6, (1638) 320-2; trade of, 351, 391-2.
archbishopric of, 77, 147, 178.
Archbishops of, *see* Beaton, James, Burnet, Alexander, Dunbar, Gavin, *and* Leighton, Robert.
cathedral of, 15, 273.
University of, 149, 266, 325.
Glass-making, 244, 386.
Glencairn, Earls of, *see* Cunningham.
Glencoe, 348.
Glenfalloch, 232.
Glenfruin, 232.
Glenlivet, battle of, 193.
Glenluce, abbey of, 136.
Glenlyon, 232.
Glenogle, 232.
Gonzolles, Anthony, 36.
Gordon, family of, 13-14, 102, 230, 350.

Gordon
Alexander, 3rd Earl of Huntly, 35-6, 41, 43.
Alexander, Bishop of Galloway, reformer, 93, 102; Marian, 161, 164.
George, 4th Earl of Huntly, 15, 44, 51, 59, 63, 66, 70; chancellor, 77, 79, 80, 86; attitude to Reformation, 93-4, 101, 107; relations with Mary, 108, 111; death, 112.
George, 5th Earl of Huntly, 119-20; supported Mary, 122, 124, 128, 130, 158, 159, 161, 164-6.
George, 6th Earl and 1st Marquis of Huntly, 174-5, 180; associated with Spanish intrigues, 185, 187, 189, 193.
George, 2nd Marquis of Huntly, 299, 319, 323, 326-8, 333, 335, 340.
George, 9th Earl of Huntly and 1st Duke of Gordon, 381.
George, Lord Gordon (1563), 112.
George, Lord Gordon (1644), 333-4.
James, parson of Rothiemay, 257.
Jean, Countess of Sutherland, 258.
Sir John, 111-2.
John, Earl of Sutherland, 112.
John, of Haddo, 333.
John, Viscount Kenmure, 306.
Sir Patrick, of Auchindoun, 189.
Robert, of Straloch, 257.
William, Bishop of Aberdeen, 102.
William, physician, 257.
Gouda, Nicholas de, Jesuit, 112, 175.
Gourlay, Norman, protestant martyr, 54.
Robert, burgess of Edinburgh, 252.
Gowrie Conspiracy, 203.
Graham, James, 6th Earl and 1st Marquis of Montrose, in covenanting movement, 320, 323-4, 327-9, 331; his campaigns, 333-5, 340, 359, 391; quoted, 214; 337.

Graham
John, 3rd Earl of Montrose, 180,
187; chancellor, 220.
John, of Claverhouse, 281, 371,
372n.
William, 2nd Earl of Montrose, 41.
William, Earl of Menteith and
Airth, 213.
Gray, Patrick, 4th Lord, 15, 53, 64,
72, 78.
Patrick, Master of, 182-5, 187.
" Great Tax ", 46, 136.
Greenock, 391.
Gregor, Clan, 231-2, 234.
Gregory, David, mathematician, 394.
James, mathematician, 394.
Greenwich, Treaties of, 67-8, 71, 75.
Grey, William, Lord, English com-
mander, 99.
Guise, family of, its influence in
France, 28, 99, 104, 114.
Duke of (1580), 175-6, 180.
Gunpowder Plot, 204.
Gustavus Adolphus, King of Sweden,
253-4.
Guthrie, James, minister, 342, 361.

Hackston, David, of Rathillet, 371.
Haddington, 60; English occupation
of, 29, 76, 78-9.
Earl of, see Hamilton, Thomas.
priory of, 65, 191.
Treaty of, 79.
Haddon Rig, 59.
Hailes Castle, 78, 123.
Hamilton, 96, 159.
family of, 66, 81, 88, 96, 158, 213.
Alexander, brother of Earl of
Haddington, 322.
Lord Claud, son of Châtelherault,
77; Commendator of Paisley, 83,
220; Marian, 165-6; forfeited,
173, 180; intrigued with Spain,
185, 187.
Lord David, son of Châtelherault,
77.

Hamilton
Gavin, coadjutor of St Andrews,
81, 97, 159.
James, 1st Earl of Arran, in
France, 18; place in succession,
31; under Albany, 32-6; relations with Angus, 39-41.
James, 2nd Earl of Arran, 51;
governor, 15, 63-4, 66-7; and
English alliance, 68-70; and
Beaton, 71-2, 75, 77; gained
to French policy and created
Duke of Châtelherault, 78-9;
loss of power and office, 81,
83-4; and Reformation, 92, 94,
96, 98, 104, 109; relations with
Huntly, 112; opposed Darnley
marriage, 118; in France, 121,
158-9; Marian, 161, 164-6;
death, 167.
James, 3rd Earl of Arran, 100;
his proposed marriage to Queen
Mary, 30, 66, 71; to Elizabeth,
67, 96, 103-4; to a French
heiress, 79, 83; in St Andrews
Castle, 68; in France, 78-9, 96;
relations with Mary in 1561,
107-9; insane, 109.
James, 3rd Marquis and 1st Duke
of Hamilton, 297, 299, 300;
king's commissioner, 317-24; relations with king and covenanters,
328-30; and Engagement, 336-
8; executed, 340.
Sir James, of Finnart, 54, 58.
James, nominated for archbishopric
of Glasgow, 77, 81n; Bishop of
Argyll, 102.
James, of Bothwellhaugh, 163.
James, Viscount of Claneboye,
252.
John, Commendator of Paisley, 66;
treasurer, 68; Bishop-elect of
Dunkeld, 75; Archbishop of St
Andrews, 77, 79; his reforming
councils, 81-2, 90; resigned
Paisley, 83; policy under Mary
of Guise, 86, 90; attitude to

Hamilton, John (*Continued*)
Reformation, 96, 102-3; imprisoned, 112, 119; restored to jurisdiction, 125, 129n; Marian, 158, 162; part in Moray's murder, 163; hanged, 147; 136.
Lord John, son of Châtelherault, (Earl of Arran, 1st Marquis of Hamilton) provided to Arbroath, 81, 83, 220; Marian, 158; forfeited, 173, 180; 187.
John, 2nd Lord Bargany, 367.
Patrick, Commendator of Fearn, protestant martyr, 22, 139.
Thomas, Earl of Haddington, 217n, 220, 221, 254.
William, Earl of Lanark, 328.
" Hamilton's Catechism ", 82.
Harlaw, William, preacher, 85.
Harvey, William, physician, 257.
Hay, Edmund, Jesuit, 175.
Francis, 9th Earl of Errol, 174, 189, 193.
George, 7th Earl of Errol, 15, 68.
Sir George, of Kinfauns, Earl of Kinnoull, 218, 245.
John, 4th Lord Hay of Yester, 50n.
John, 2nd Earl of Tweeddale, 358, 377.
Sir John, royalist, 326.
Henderson, Alexander, minister, 311n, 312-3, 329-30.
Edward, teacher in Edinburgh, 267.
Henry VIII, chapter 2; in minority of James V, 32-3, 37-8; relations with James V, 45, 49, 55, 59-60; proposal for English marriage for Queen Mary, 64-7; orders invasions of Scotland, 69-72; his policy of bribery, 72-4, 77.
Henry II, King of France, 28, 78, 81, 91, 95-6.
IV, King of France, 185.
Prince, birth and baptism of, 212-3, 270, 302n.
Hepburn, family of, 14, 102.
James, 4th Earl of Bothwell, intercepted English subsidy, 97;

Hepburn, James (*Continued*)
conspired with Arran, 109; supported Mary, 119-20, 122; part in schemes against Darnley, 124, 126-8; married Mary, 113, 128-9; flight after Carberry, 130-1, 157; death, 158, 162 and n, 217.
Lieut.-Col. James, 254.
John, marshal of France, 254.
John, prior of St Andrews, 32, 34.
Patrick, 3rd Earl of Bothwell, 41, 50, 53-4, 64-6, 73, 78, 122, 130.
Patrick, Bishop of Moray, 90n, 93, 94n, 102, 157.
Heriot, George, 252.
James, of Trabroun, 78.
Heritable jurisdictions, 5, 225, 299, 350.
Heritors, 400.
Hermitage Castle, 78, 123.
Herries, John, Lord, Marian, 160-1.
Hertford, Earl of, *see* Seymour, Edward.
" Highland Host ", 370.
Highland Line, 4
society, 13-14, 231-2.
Highlands and Islands, under James V, 50-2; under James VI and Charles I, 228-32, 392; under Cromwell, 348-9.
Hill, John, Cromwellian commander, 349.
History, writing of, 261, 393.
Holt, William, Jesuit.
Holyroodhouse, abbey of, 57, 232, 273, 306, 382.
palace of, 6, 57, 67, 95, 110, 123, 129, 130, 191, 209, 214, 301, 396.
Home Castle, 79.
family of, 14, 35-6, 40, 49.
Alexander, 3rd Lord, and Albany, 32-3.
Alexander, 5th Lord, Marian, 164.
George, 4th Lord, under James V, 39-41, 50; French pensioner, 73, 80.

Home
  Sir George, of Wedderburn, comptroller, 301.
  Sir George, of Spott, Earl of Dunbar, 218, 274.
  James, 3rd Earl of Home, 350.
  Sir Patrick, of Polwarth, 378, 384.
  Patrick, of Polwarth, 50.
Honeyman, Andrew, Bishop of Orkney, 374*n.*
Hope, Sir Thomas, Lord Advocate, 218, 262, 318-9.
Houses, 10, 251-2, 395-6.
Howard, Thomas, Duke of Norfolk, negotiated Treaty of Berwick, 98-9; relations with Mary, 160, 162, 165.
Hunsdon, Henry, Lord, 182.
Huntly, castle of, 272.
  Earls of, bailies of bishopric of Aberdeen, 136; *and see* Gordon.
Hurry, Sir John, General, 338.

Icolmkill, statutes of, 231.
Imports, 248-9, 389.
Inchcolm, 76, 220.
Inchgarvie, 35.
Inchkeith, 76, 80, 87, 98-9.
" Incident ", 328.
Indulgences, 369, 371, 380, 382.
Inveraray, 229, 334.
Inveresk, 79.
Inverkeithing, battle of, 342.
Inverlochy, battle of, 334; fort at, 346, 349.
Inverness, 112, 346, 398.
Iona, 230; *see also* Icolmkill.
Ireland, trading and other relations with, 228-9, 248-9, 392.
Iron, 248, 389.
Irvine, Earl of, *see* Campbell.
Islay, 52, 228.
Isles, Bishop of, *see* Knox, Andrew.
  lordship of, claimed by Donald Dubh, 72.

James I, 5-6.
  III, 8.

James
  IV, 4-6, 10, 22, 43; death, 17, 32-3.
  V, 3, 13, 19; birth, 31; coronation, 17; education, 44 and *n*; " erected " as king, 38; captive of Angus, 40-1; marriage proposals, 19-20, 23-5, 37, 44-5, 48-9; marriages, 49; ecclesiastical policy, 23, 25-6, 54-8, 68, 135, 140; domestic policy, 49-60; war with England, 26-7, 59-60; death, 27, 60-1, 63; character, 61-2.
  VI, 119*n*; birth, 122; baptism, 123-4; coronation, 131, 157; government in his name, 171-2; relations with Esmé Stewart, 172-3; attitude to his mother, 175, 184-5; in hands of Ruthven Raiders, 178-80; and English succession, 183-4; marriage, 185-6; political and ecclesiastical opinions, 186-9, 197-8, 214, 216-7, 236; association with Maitland of Thirlstane, 188; attitude to Roman catholic and protestant factions, 188-96; ecclesiastical policy, chapter 11, 296, 307; king of England, 213, 215, 236-7, 289-90; character and achievement, 214-5, 289; policy in Borders and Highlands and Islands, 227-33; economic views, 244, 246; intellectual interests, 256, 259, 268; his buildings, 271-2.
  VII, as Duke of York, 371, 379; policy as king, 281-2, 379 ff.
Jamesone, George, 270-1.
Jedburgh, 21, 79, 123.
Jesuit missionaries, 174.
Johnston, Archibald, of Wariston, 313, 316, 318-9, 321-2, 329, 332, 346*n*, 356, 361.
  Samuel, of Elphinstone, 246.
Johnstone, John, of that ilk, 50.
Joint-stock companies, 386.

Jonson, Ben, in Scotland, 260.

Judicial system, 5-6, 56, 223-5, 235, 288, 347-8, 374.

Justice-ayres, 5, 6, 52, 167, 223.

Justices of the peace, 224-6, 348, 400.

Justiciary, court of, 223-4, 288, 400.

Keith, George, 4th Earl Marischal, 180, 187, 220, 258; founded Marischal College, 257, 267.

William, 3rd Earl Marischal, 15, 41, 68, 73-4, 80.

Sir William, of Ludquharn, 222.

Kelso, 21, 87.

abbey of, 57, 86.

Kemp, Henry, of Thomastoun, 55.

Kenmure, Lord, see Gordon, John.

Kennedy, Gilbert, 2nd Earl of Cassillis, 39-40.

Gilbert, 3rd Earl of Cassillis, in English party, 15, 64, 68-9, 73-4, 80; treasurer, 86; in France, 89.

Gilbert, 4th Earl of Cassillis, 119; Marian, 162, 165.

John, 5th Earl of Cassillis, 222.

John, 6th Earl of Cassillis, 311n, 329, 332, 338, 346n, 367.

Quentin, Commendator of Crosraguel, 152.

Kerr, family of, 40, 71.

Andrew, of Fernihurst, 50.

George, 189.

Robert, Earl of Somerset, 186, 218.

Robert, Earl of Ancram, 300.

Robert, Earl of Roxburgh, 300.

Robert, 2nd Earl of Lothian, 223.

Sir Thomas, of Fernihurst, 176.

Sir Walter, of Cessford, 78.

William, 3rd Earl of Lothian, 322, 350.

Killigrew, Sir Henry, 166-7.

Killin, 343.

" Killing time ", 372-3 and n.

Kilsyth, battle of, 334.

Kin, in Scottish society, 12-13, 151-2.

Kincardine, Earl of, see Bruce, Alexander.

" Kindly tenants ", 13, 239.

King, James, of Birness and Dudwick, Lord Eythin, 253, 322.

Kinghorn, 98.

Earl of, see Lyon.

Kingship, 3-8, 101-2, 212-4, 277, 380, 401.

Kinloch, David, physician, 257.

Kinloss, abbey of, 134, 220, 239.

Kinmont Willie, 227.

Kinneff, 343.

Kinnoull, Earl of, see Hay, George.

Kinross House, 395-6.

Kintail, Lord, see Mackenzie.

Kintyre, 43, 51-2, 228-9, 252, 319, 334.

Kirk sessions, 103, 150, 207, 225-6, 363, 366, 400.

Kirkcaldy, 49, 252.

Sir James, of Grange, 74.

Sir William, a murderer of Cardinal Beaton, 74, 86; rebel (1566), 121; attitude to Marian party, 158, 162; held Edinburgh Castle, 164-6; executed, 166.

Kirkcudbright, John, 3rd Lord, 367.

Kirke, David, 255.

Kirkwall, 10, 272.

Knox, Andrew, Bishop of the Isles, 230.

Knox, John, 74, 152, 162, 268; preached at St Andrews, 76; sent to galleys, 76; returned to Scotland, 85-6, 89, 92; preached at Perth, 93; minister of Edinburgh, 94-5; attitude to Elizabeth, 95; attitude to Mary, 104, 109-10; approved Riccio murder, 122; at coronation of James VI, 131; approved of bishops, 148; in St Andrews, 164; returned to Edinburgh and died, 166; quoted, 14, 30, 90n, 91-2, 94n, 97, 98 and n, 101, 146, 315.

Lairds, attitude of, to Reformation, 27-8, 134, 137.

Lambert, John, Cromwellian general, 339, 342.

Lanark, Earl of, *see* Hamilton, William.

Land tenure, 10, 13, 239-40.

Langholm, 60.

Langside, battle of, 159.

Language, 258-9.

Lansac, M. de., 81.

Laud, William, Archbishop of Canterbury, 306, 308.

Lauder, 59, 79.

Lauderdale, Earls and Duke of, *see* Maitland.

Law, James, Bishop of Orkney, 233.

Learmonth of Dairsie, family of, 282.

Leather manufacture, 245.

Legal writings, 261-2, 393.

Legitimation, letters of, 53.

Leicester, Earl of, *see* Dudley.

Leighton, Robert, Bishop of Dunblane and Archbishop of Glasgow, 369-70, 394.

Leith, 49, 69, 70, 79, 92, 108, 186, 191, 251, 323, 341, 347; Reformation in, 22, 27; military operations at (1559-60), 94-5, 97-100; trade of, 273, 390-1; Cromwellian fort at, 346, 373.

Lekprevik, Robert, printer, 260.

Lennox, Earls of, 14, 15; *see also* Stewart.

Lent, 143, 240.

Leslie House, 395.

Leslie (*or* Lesley), Alexander, Earl of Leven, 322-3, 329, 332-3, 337-8.

Andrew, 5th Earl of Rothes, 121, 180.

David, General, 333-4, 337-8, 341.

George, 4th Earl of Rothes, 15, 41, 68.

John, 6th Earl of Rothes, 299, 307, 311, 313, 316, 320, 322, 328.

John, 7th Earl of Rothes, 358, 374, 376-8.

John, Bishop of Ross, 160-1, 165, 189.

Leslie

John, a murderer of Cardinal Beaton, 74.

Norman, Master of Rothes, a murderer of Cardinal Beaton, 74.

Leven, River, 98.

Earl of, *see* Leslie, Alexander.

Lewis, 228, 230, 252.

Liddell, Duncan, scientist, 257.

Liddesdale, 53, 60.

Lindsay, Alexander, 1st Earl of Balcarres, 346.

David, 8th Earl of Crawford, and his son, 53-4.

David, 10th Earl of Crawford, 130.

David, 11th Earl of Crawford, 174, 178, 180, 187, 189.

David, 1st Lord Balcarres, 257.

Sir David, author of *The Three Estates*, 54, 139, 227, 259.

John, parson of Menmuir, secretary, 217*n*, 258.

John, 17th Earl of Crawford, 358, 367.

Patrick, 6th Lord, 119, 121-2, 179.

Robert, of Pitscottie, 259.

Linen industry, 244, 250, 386, 389.

Linlithgow, 31, 40, 60, 65-6, 163, 205, 271.

friaries in, 94.

palace of, 6, 57, 63, 272.

Little, Clement, 268.

Liturgical position at Reformation, 142-3; changes under James VI, 208-10; under Charles I, 306-10.

Livingston, Sir James, of Brighouse, Earl of Callendar, 322, 338.

Mary, 79.

Lochaber, 328.

Lochgarry, action at, 346.

Lochiel, Cameron of, 348.

Lochleven, 131, 159.

Lochmaben, 60, 72.

Loch Ness, 349.

Lockhart, William, of Lee, 346*n*, 347.

Lords of the congregation, 89, 93-4, 102.

Lorges, seigneur de, 71-2.
Lorne, Firth of, 6.
Lothian, Earls of, *see* Kerr.
Louis XII, King of France, 18.
Louise, daughter of Francis I, 19.
Low Countries, relations with, 22-4.
   Scots soldiers in, 253-4.
   trade with, 248-9, 352, 388-91.
Lowland Scots language, 259.
Luffness, 79.
Lutheran influence in Scotland, 22-3, 82, 110, 139.
Lyon, John, 7th Lord Glamis, 72.
   Patrick, Earl of Strathmore, 396.
   Sir Thomas, Master of Glamis, 178, 180, 187, 217.

MacCulloch, John, physician, 257.
MacDonald of Clanranald, 72.
MacDonald (*or* MacDonnell) of Dunivaig and the Glens, 228, 230.
   of Sleat, 230.
   Alexander, of Islay, 50-1.
   Alisdair, 333-4.
   Donald, of Eilean Tioram, 231.
   Sir Donald, of Lochalsh, 33, 41.
   Randal, Earl of Antrim, 319, 323.
MacGill, David, of Cranston Riddell, Lord Advocate, 218.
   Sir James, provost of Edinburgh, 218.
   James, of Rankeillor Nether, clerk-register, 218.
   James, Viscount of Oxfuird, 218.
MacGregor of Glenstrae, 231-2.
MacIan of Ardnamurchan, 72, 229.
MacKay, Donald, 1st Lord Reay, 253-4, 322.
Mackenzie, Colin, 1st Earl of Seaforth, 230.
   George, 2nd Earl of Seaforth, 334.
   Sir George, of Rosehaugh, lord advocate, 375-6, 383, 393.
   George, Viscount Tarbat, 346, 376-7, 383.
   Kenneth, Lord Kintail, 230.
MacKinnon of Strathardle, 72, 230.

MacLean, family of, 50, 230, 380.
   of Coll, 231.
   of Lochbuie, 72, 230.
   Lachlan, of Duart, 33.
   Hector, of Duart, 50, 72.
MacLeod, Alasdair, of Dunvegan, 33.
   William, of Dunvegan, 72.
   Roderick, of Dunvegan, 231.
   of Lewis, 72, 230-1.
MacMoran, John, burgess of Edinburgh, 251, 273.
MacNeil of Barra, 72.
MacQuharrie of Ulva, 231.
Madeleine, daughter of Francis I, 20, 24-5; married James V, 49; died, 49.
Maitland, Charles, of Haltoun, 373-4, 378.
   John, of Thirlstane, Marian, 166; associated with Lennox and Arran, 173, 180, 183; secretary, 181; chancellor, 187-8, 191, 217.
   John, 1st Earl of Lauderdale, 243.
   John, 2nd Earl and 1st Duke of Lauderdale, 282, 285-6, 290, 330, 332, 396; secretary, 358-9, 376; commissioner, 377-9; corruption of his administration, 373-4.
   William, of Lethington, 85; secretary, negotiates with England, 92, 96, 98, 103, 114; attitude to Mary in 1561, 107-8; attitude to Spanish marriage project, 115; part in schemes against Darnley, 124, 126; 128; attitude to Marian party, 158, 160, 162, 164; death, 166.
Major, John, 22, 146.
Manufactures, 244-7, 352, 385, 391.
Mar, Earls of, *see* Erskine.
Margaret Tudor, Queen of Scots, tutrix to James V, 17; married Angus, 31; relations with Albany, Angus and Arran, 22, 32-3, 37-40; married Henry Stewart, 39; 43, 68.
Marignano, battle of, 19.
Marischal, Earls, *see* Keith.

Marriage law, at Reformation, 145.

Marston Moor, battle of, 333.

Mary of Guise, married James V, 25, 49, 57; opposed Arran (1543), 65, 69; relations with Earl of Bothwell and Cardinal Beaton, 66, 122, 130; attempt to seize power in 1544, 15, 70; reconciled with Arran, 71; her policy of conciliation, 79-80, 89; in France, 80; aims and character, 80; governor, 83-4; her policy as governor, 85-92, 101; "suspended", 97; death, 99.

Queen of Scots, born, 63; crowned, 68; proposed English marriage, 27, 64, 67, 75; French marriage, 28, 78, 88, 95; proposed marriage to Master of Hamilton (Arran), 71, 104; in Inchmahome, 78; in France, 79, 87, 96; claim to English crown, 30, 91, 99-100; proposal to depose, 95, 103; returned to Scotland, 104, 107-8; relations with Elizabeth, 107-8, 113-7; attitude to ecclesiastical situation, 108-14, 117-20, 124-5, 147, 162; life in Scotland, 113-4; foreign suitors, 115; married Darnley, 12, 117; relations with Riccio, 120-1; estranged from Darnley, 122; partiality for Bothwell, 122; in danger, 124; part in Darnley's death, 125-8; married Bothwell, 129-30; surrendered at Carberry, 8, 131; in Lochleven, 125n, 131, 157, 159; abdicated, 131, 157; her case at York-Westminster conference, 160; her supporters after 1578, 174; scheme for "association" with James, 179-80, 182; executed, 184; 203.

daughter of Henry VIII and Queen of England, 22, 24, 29, 30, 37, 83, 85, 91.

Queen of Hungary, 23-4.

daughter of Duke of Vendôme, 48-9.

Mass, hostility to, 133; legislation against, 102, 108-11; prosecutions for saying, 112, 153.

Mauchline, 338.

Maule, Patrick, 1st Earl of Panmure, 218n.

Maxwell, James, Earl of Dirleton, 218n.

John, 9th Lord, 223.

John, Bishop of Ross, 310-1.

Robert, 5th Lord, 41, 50, 54, 60, 64, 72-3.

Robert, 6th Lord, 80.

Robert, 8th Lord, Marian, 164; Earl of Morton, involved in Spanish intrigues, 173-4, 185, 227.

Robert, 1st Earl of Nithsdale, 305.

Mearns, Reformation in, 26.

Medici, Lorenzo de, 34.

Melfort, Earl of, see Drummond.

Melrose, 40, 57, 71, 73.

abbey of, 239, 273.

Melville, Andrew, his career and thought, 148-50, 168, 197-200; in exile, 181; at Queen Anne's coronation, 192; 193; lectured James VI, 194; banished, 204-5; educational work, 266-7.

James, of Carnbee, a murderer of Cardinal Beaton, 74.

James, diarist, quoted, 192, 269; banished, 205.

Sir John, of Raith, and his sons, 15, 78.

Robert, of Murdocairny, Marian, 166, 173; in Arran's administration, 180; ambassador to England, 184.

Menteith, Earl of, see Graham.

Menzies of Weem, 231.

Methil, 390.

Methven, Lord, see Stewart.

Middelburg, candidate for staple, 24, 34.

Middleton, John, Earl of, 338, 341-2, 346, 356, 359, 376.

Mines, under James V, 56-7, 58.

Ministers, appointment of, 141-2; moral and educational standards, 150, 263; social status, 150-2; stipends, 296-8, 304.

Mitchell, James, 374.

Moir, William, member of parliament, 377.

Monarchy, see Kingship.

Monasteries, 134.

Monck, George, General, 347, 357, 391.

Monmouth, James, Duke of, 371, 379-80.

Montgomery, Alexander, 6th Earl of Eglinton, 338, 350.

Hugh, 1st Earl of Eglinton, 32, 41, 66.

Hugh, 3rd Earl of Eglinton, 165, 175.

Hugh, of Braidstane, 252.

Robert, Archbishop of Glasgow, 178.

Montrose, 27.

Earls and Marquis of, see Graham.

Moray, Bishop of, see Hepburn, Patrick.

Earls of, see Stewart.

Sir Robert, 359, 394.

More, Sir Thomas, 25.

Morton, Earls of, see Douglas.

Mortuary dues, 56.

Morvern, 50, 380.

Mull, 50, 380.

Mure, Sir William, of Rowallan, 243.

Murray, Andrew, of Blackbarony, 218.

Sir David, of Gospertie, Lord Scone, 221.

Sir Gideon, of Elibank, treasurer depute, 218, 302.

John, Earl of Annandale, 218n.

Sir Patrick, of Geanies, 221n.

Sir William, of Tullibardine, comptroller, 119.

Music, 269-70, 394.

Musselburgh, 100, 341.

Myln, Alexander, Abbot of Cambuskenneth, 42, 47.

Walter, protestant martyr, 90.

Napier, family of, 12.

John, of Merchiston, 257.

Naseby, battle of, 334.

National Covenant, 264-5, 313 ff., 326-7, 335, 344.

Navigation Act (of Commonwealth), 352; (of Charles II), 388, 390.

Negative Confession, 178, 315, 319-20.

Nemours, Duke of, 115.

New Year's Day, 236.

Nithsdale, Earl of, see Maxwell.

Nobles, resources and power of, 7-9, 12, 14, 298-9; in parliament, 277, 281, 284, 286; attitude to churchmen, 12, 311, 337, 359, 366; attitude to other social groups, 12; attitude to Reformation, 137, 168; alienated from James V, 52-6, 60; antagonised by Mary, 120-1; under James VI, 216-25; antagonised by Charles I, 298-300, 307, 311; under Cromwell, 349-50; under Charles II, 358 ff., 392.

Norfolk, Duke of, see Howard, Thomas.

Northampton, Treaty of, 228.

Northumberland, Earls of, see Percy.

Norway, Scots soldiers in, 253.

trade with, 248, 387, 389-90.

Nova Scotia, 254-5.

Oath of Supremacy, 146, 167.

Ochiltree, Lord, see Stewart.

Octavians, 217.

Officers of state in parliament, 278, 280, 286.

Ogilvie, Sir George, of Dunlugus, 282.

James, 5th Lord, 111.

James, of Cardell, 111.

Orkney, 51, 60, 157, 186, 232-3, 235, 252, 288.

bishopric of, 304.

Bishops of, see Bothwell, Adam, Honeyman, Andrew, and Reid, Robert.

Otterburn, Adam, lord advocate, 42, 52.
Oysel, Henri Cleutin, sieur d', 81, 86, 93.

Painting, 270-1.
Paisley, 69.
  abbey of, 220.
Palaces, royal, 6, 57-8, 271, 396.
Papacy, relations with, under Albany, 33-4; under James V, 23, 25, 45-7, 52, 54, 135; in Mary's minority, 27-9, 68, 82, 87, 136; at Reformation, 102, 132, 140-1; of Mary and Darnley, 124.
Paper, manufacture of, 244, 386.
Parishes, before Reformation, 135, 143; reformers' plans for, 105, 142.
Parish registers, 234-5.
Parliament, composition, 8, 102, 276-82, 284; representation of reformed church in, 198, 201-2, 276-7; powers, 8-9, 288; procedure, 282-3, 285-6, 299-300, 307; king's commissioner to, 283, 375; opposition in, 286-7, 377-8; revolutionary changes, 327; under Commonwealth, 345-6; after 1660, 359-60, 377-8, 381.
Parsons, Robert, English Jesuit, 175-6.
Patronage, in church, 151-2, 199, 339, 363, 365.
Paul III, Pope, 47.
Paupers, attitude of, to Reformation, 138.
Pavia, battle of, 22, 39.
Peebles, 60.
Peerage, 217-21, 277.
Pentland Rising, 368, 376.
Percy, Henry, Earl of Northumberland, 54.
  Thomas, Earl of Northumberland, 163.
  Sir Henry, 92.
Perth, 11, 64, 78, 94, 162, 201, 203, 268-9, 333, 342; Reformation in, 27, 92-3; Cromwellian fort at, 346.

Perth
  Carthusian priory of, 93, 134.
  Earl of, see Drummond.
  Five Articles of, 209-10, 281, 286, 296, 305, 314, 322, 362.
  Pacification of, 166.
Peterhead, 251, 390.
Philip II, of Spain, 29, 115-6, 175.
Physicians, Royal College of, 395.
Pinkie, battle of, 28, 76, 77.
  House, 272.
Poetry, 259-60.
Philiphaugh, battle of, 334.
Poland, Scots in, 253.
Pont, Timothy, 257.
Poor relief, 398-9, 400.
Population of Scotland, 133, 238.
Portpatrick, 397.
Port Seton, 390.
Postal service, 215, 397-8.
Presbyterianism, rise of, 149-50, 168-9, 178, 181, 193, 199.
Presbyteries, development of, 178, 192-3, 198-9; operate with bishops, 207, 363.
Preston, battle of, 338, 359.
Preston Tower, 272.
Preston, Richard, Lord Dingwall, 218n.
Prestonpans, 252.
Primrose, Archibald, writer, 219.
  Archibald, clerk of privy council and clerk-register, 219.
  Gilbert, surgeon to James VI, 219.
  James, clerk of privy council, 219.
  James, physician, 257.
  Peter, minister, 219.
Pringle, Sir James, 243.
Printing, 260-1.
Privy Council, composition of, 8, 290-1, 359; relation to Committee of articles, 285-6; functions, 288-90.
Propaganda, of English, 77-8; at Reformation, 100-1; in reign of James VI, 215-6.
Protectorate, government of, 345 ff.

Protestant faction, in later 16th century, 173-4, 179-80, 190-1, 194-6.
Protestors, 353-6, 360-2, 365.

Queensberry, Earls of, *see* Douglas.
Queensferry, South, 273.

Raban, Edward, printer, 260.
Radcliffe, Thomas, Earl of Sussex, 163.
Ramsay, Alexander, 253.
David, 257.
Randan, M. de, 99.
Randolph, Thomas, English ambassador, 176-8, 183.
Rannoch, Moor of, 232.
Read, Alexander, physician, 257.
Reader, office of, 142, 150.
Recusancy, 148, 152.
Reformation, causes, 133 ff.; beginnings and progress, 22, 26-8, 54, 58, 64, 73-4, 77, 82, 85-6, 89-90; takes shape as revolution, 91 ff.; legislation in favour of, 102-3, 161; financial and administrative programme, 105; resistance to, 152-3; influence on language, 259.
Regalia, 58, 164-5, 343.
Regalities, 5.
Reid, J., *The Scots Gardener*, 395.
Robert, Commendator of Kinloss and Bishop of Orkney, 220-1, 267.
Reidswire, Raid of, 167.
Remissions and respites, 52-3, 167.
Remonstrance, Western, 342.
Remonstrants, 342; *see also* Protestors.
Renwick, James, Cameronian preacher, 372.
Rescissory Act, 362.
Resolutions, 342.
Resolutioners, 342, 353-6, 360-1, 365.
Restalrig, 99.
Revocation, Acts of, 5, 53; of Charles I, 296-8, 305.

Riccio, David, 120-1, 203.
Ripon, Treaty of, 325.
Roads, 396-7.
Robert II, 3, 213.
Roman catholicism, 152-3, 174, 220, 310, 381-2; *see also* Recusancy.
" Roman catholic " faction in late sixteenth century, 174, 188-94, 216, 220.
Roslin, 20.
Ross, Bishop of, *see* Leslie, John, Maxwell, John *and* Sinclair, Henry.
Rothes, Earls of, *see* Leslie.
Roubay, M. de, 86.
Rouen, Treaty of, 19-20, 24, 45.
" Rough Wooing ", 69-72.
Roxburgh, Old, 79.
Earl of, *see* Kerr, Robert.
Roytell, John, master of works, 86.
Rullion Green, battle of, 368.
Rupert, Prince, 341.
Russell, Sir Francis, 183.
William, Lord, 379.
Rutherford, Samuel, 311*n*, 316.
Rutherglen Declaration, 371.
Ruthven, John, 3rd Earl of Gowrie, 203, 257.
Patrick, 3rd Lord, (Master of R.), 78, 80; supported Reformation, 93, 119, 121-2.
Patrick, Earl of Forth, 254, 322.
William, 1st Lord, 40.
William, 2nd Lord, 15, 69, (Master of Ruthven) 281.
William, 4th Lord and 1st Earl of Gowrie, 173, 178-80, 190, 217.
Ruthven Raid, 178-80, 187, 198, 203, 216.
Rye House Plot, 374, 379.

Sadler, Sir Ralph, 64, 67-8, 72, 95.
St Andrews, 11, 28, 49, 69, 76, 93, 98, 201, 268, 282.
archbishopric of, 32-4, 77, 147.
Archbishops of, *see* Adamson, Patrick, Beaton, David *and* James.

St Andrews, Archbishop of, (*Continued*) Forman, Andrew, Hamilton, John, Sharp, James *and* Spottiswoode, John.
   castle of, 32, 68, 74-6.
   priory of, 57, 297.
   University of, 82, 134, 149, 208, 265-6, 325, 329.
St Bartholomew's Eve, massacre of, 165-6.
St John, Lord, *see* Sandilands, James.
Salt manufacture, 246-7, 258, 389.
Saltcoats, 390.
Sandilands, James, of Torphichen, 80; Lord St John, 103.
Sanquhar Declaration, 371.
   Lord, *see* Crichton, Robert.
Sasines, Register of, 234.
Scandinavia, trade with, 248-9; *see also* Norway, Sweden.
Schools, 263-5, 269.
Scone, 342.
Scott, family of, 71.
   Walter, of Branxholm, 53.
   Walter, of Buccleuch (temp. Jac. V), 40, 50.
   Walter, of Buccleuch (temp. Jac. VI), 227.
   Sir William, of Balwearie, 42.
Scougal, Henry, divine, 394.
Scougall, John, portrait-painter, 271.
Scrimgeour, John, Earl of Dundee, 374.
Seaforth, Earl of, *see* Mackenzie.
Sempill, Robert, 3rd Lord, 100.
   William, 2nd Lord, 66.
Sessions for civil justice, 6, 42; *see also* Court of Session.
Seton, 65.
   House, 272.
   Alexander, reforming preacher, 139.
   Alexander, alchemist, 257.
   Alexander, Earl of Dunfermline, chancellor, 217n, 220-1, 272.
   George, 5th Lord, 101, 122, 166, 173-5.

Seton
   George, 4th Earl of Winton, 390.
   Mary, 79.
   Robert, 2nd Earl of Winton, 258, 272.
Seymour, Edward, Earl of Hertford and Duke of Somerset, invaded Scotland, 27, 69-70, 72, 76; protector of England, 28; his propaganda, 77-8.
   Jane, wife of Henry VIII, 49.
Sharp, James, spokesman of Resolutioners, 355; Archbishop of St Andrews, 359, 370-1, 374, 376-7, 397.
Sheep, "rooing" of, 235.
Sheriffs, heritable, 5-6, 50n, 53.
Shetland, 60, 186, 232-3, 235, 252, 288.
Shipping, 251-2, 258, 388, 390.
Shire commissioners, in parliament, 278-81, 284, 286; in general assembly, 113, 199-200; in convention of estates, 287.
Sibbald, Sir Robert, 394.
Sinclair, George, Earl of Caithness, 174-5.
   George, scientist, 394.
   Henry, Bishop of Ross, 112.
   John, 9th Lord, 358.
   Oliver, of Pitcairns, 60.
Skene, Sir John, clerk-register, 217n, 262.
Soap manufacture, 245, 386.
Social structure, 7, 9, 12-14, 102, 151, 221-2, 350-1, 367, 392, 401.
Solemn League and Covenant, 331-2, 336-7, 344, 361-2.
Solway Firth, 20.
   Moss, battle of, 26, 60.
Somerville, Hugh, Lord, in pro-English party, 64, 73.
Spain, Mary's negotiations with, 115-6, 119-20; Darnley's dealings with, 124; Scottish Roman catholics and, 185, 189-90; trade with, 194, 248-9, 252.
Spanish blanks, 190, 192.

Spottiswoode, John, parson of Calder and superintendent of Lothian, 80.

  John, Archbishop of Glasgow and of St Andrews, 208, 210, 230, 261, 299, 306, 318, 325.

  Sir Robert, 299, 326.

Spynie, 157.

  Alexander, Lord, 254.

Staple, 44, 389-90; *see also* Middelburg, Campvere.

" Start ", 341.

Stewart, Alexander, Duke of Albany, 18.

  Alexander, Earl of Moray, 381.

  Andrew, 2nd Lord Ochiltree, 121.

  Andrew, 3rd Lord Ochiltree, 229-230.

  Arabella, 172.

  Archibald, 52.

  Charles, 5th Earl of Lennox, 158, 172.

  Esmé, seigneur d'Aubigné, Duke of Lennox, 172-3, 175-8, 187-8.

  Francis, Earl of Bothwell, 190-3, 256, 272.

  Henry, 1st Lord Methven, 39, 77.

  Henry, Lord Darnley, King of Scots, 12, 116-28.

  James, illegitimate son of James IV, Earl of Moray, 38, 40-1, 51, 54, 59-60, 63, 66, 70.

  James, illegitimate son of James V, Earl of Moray, 80, 86, 89, 128; and lords of the congregation, 93, 103; attitude to Mary in 1561, 107-10; relations with Huntly, 111; approved negotiations with Spain, 115; opposed Darnley marriage, 118-20; summoned to trial, 121; restored to favour, 122; part in schemes against Darnley, 124, 126; regent, 131, 157-63, 170; murdered, 163; 190.

  James, Earl of Arran, 173, 178-83, 187, 217, 256.

Stewart

  James, of Doune, 179, 220; Earl of Moray, murdered, 189-90, 193.

  Sir James, of Goodtrees, 374, 384.

  James, 4th Duke of Lennox, 297, 300, 350.

  John, Duke of Albany, 18; governor of Scotland, 19-22, 24, 31, 33-6, 43, 57; returned to France, 38; lost office, 39; Scottish agent on Continent, 45-6; death, 45.

  John, 3rd Earl of Lennox, 32-3, 36, 38-9, 40, 45.

  John, 4th Earl of Atholl, 120; supporter of Mary, 122, 161, 164; under Morton, 169-70, 177; 174.

  John, 5th Earl of Atholl, 190.

  John, Earl of Traquair, treasurer, 312-3, 318, 324.

  Lord John, illegitimate son of James V, 80, 191.

  Ludovick, Duke of Lennox, 182.

  Matthew, 4th Earl of Lennox, returned to Scotland, 65; in English party, 68-70, 72, 75, 117; married Margaret Douglas, 70; in England, 116, 120; after Darnley's murder, 128; regent, 163-5, 168.

  Patrick, Earl of Orkney, 233, 272.

  Lord Robert, illegitimate son of James V, 128; Commendator of Holyrood and Earl of Orkney, 232-3.

  Robert, Bishop of Caithness, in English party, 75, 80; supported Reformation, 102, 117; Earl of Lennox, 172-3.

  Walter, Lord Blantyre, 217*n*, 221.

  William, Bishop of Aberdeen, 47, 55.

Stirling, 17, 66, 70-1, 92-4, 96-8, 123, 165, 171, 183, 318, 342-3.

  castle of, 6, 31, 40, 57, 68, 180.

  chapel royal of, 270.

  Earl of, *see* Alexander, Sir William.

Stonehaven, 251, 258, 390.
Stornoway, 247.
Strathardle, 243.
Strathmore, Earl of, see Lyon.
Strathtay, 232.
Stratoun, David, of Lauriston, protestant martyr, 54.
Succession to the throne, 3, 30, 66, 158, 212-3.
Sugar refining, 245, 386, 389.
Sunday observance, 194, 269, 274, 348.
Superintendents, in reformed church, 105, 113, 140-1, 147.
Supremacy, royal, over church, 167, 206, 359.
Sussex, Earl of, see Radcliffe.
Sutherland, Earl of, 14; see also Gordon.
Sweden, Scots soldiers in, 253-4.
trade with, 248, 389.
Swinton, John, 347.
Sydserf, Thomas, Bishop of Galloway, 312.
Sym, Alexander, teacher in Edinburgh, 267.

Tain, 6.
Tantallon Castle, 9, 41, 60.
Tarbat, Viscount, see Mackenzie.
Taxation, 5, 56, 87-8, 101, 169-70, 301-3, 307, 352-3, 360, 370, 399.
of church, 46-7, 65, 87, 132, 136, 144.
Taymouth, 270-1, 395.
Teinds, 56, 138-9, 143-4, 240, 296-8.
Tenants, legislation in favour of, 14, 56, 144-5; their grievances, 138-9; attitude to Reformation, 138-9.
Test Act (1681), 281, 379-80.
Teviotdale, 54.
Theology of Reformation, 133, 139.
Thirds of benefices, 111, 144.
Thirlstane Castle, 396.
Throckmorton, Sir Nicholas, 159.
Timber, imports of, 243, 248, 389.

Tippermuir, battle of, 333.
Tiree, 50, 380.
Tobacco, 235-6, 389.
Toleration, 345, 354-5, 361, 369, 382.
Torphichen, preceptory of, 147.
Tower houses, 9, 271.
Trade, 246-52, 351-2, 357, 385-93.
Transportation, 350, 371.
Traquair, Earl of, see Stewart, John.
Trees, 243.
Trent, Council of, 27, 112, 153.
Triennial Act, 327.
Tulliallan, 252.
Turner, Sir James, 368, 375.
Tweed, River, 3, 21.
Tweeddale, Earl of, see Hay, John.
Tyndale, William, 22.

Udward, Nathaniel, 245-6.
Ulster, plantation of, 229, 252-3, 319.
Universities, 134, 265-8.
Urquhart, Sir Thomas, 258.

Valence, Bishop of (Jean de Monluc), 99.
Villemore, Bartholomew de, 80, 86.
Villiers, George, Duke of Buckingham, 186.

Wallace, Adam, 82.
Walsingham, Francis, 176, 180, 182, 184.
Wark Castle, 21.
Warwick, Earl of, see Dudley, John.
Watts, William, priest, 175.
Welwood, William, jurist and inventor, 258.
Wemyss, 245, 251, 252.
David, 2nd Earl of, 390.
John, of that ilk, 243.
Wentworth, Sir Thomas, Earl of Strafford, 323, 335n.
Westminster Assembly, 332.
Wharton, Thomas, Lord, English deputy-warden, 60.

Whiggamore Raid, 338-9.
Whitford, Walter, Bishop of Brechin, 326.
Whitgift, John, Archbishop of Canterbury, 181.
Whithorn, 6.
Wigtown, 136.
    Earl of, *see* Fleming, John.
" Wigtown Martyrs ", 372n.
William of Orange, 383-4.
Willock, John, protestant preacher, 85, 89, 95, 97; " bishop " and superintendent of Glasgow, 103, 110.
Winram, John, subprior of St Andrews, 80; superintendent of Fife, 110.
Winter, Sir William, English admiral, 98.
Winton, Earls of, *see* Seton.
Winyet, Ninian, Roman catholic apologist, 152-3.

Wishart, George, protestant preacher, 27, 74, 133.
    Sir John, of Pittaro, 27; collector of thirds, 119.
Witchcraft, 191, 354-5.
Wood, David, of Craig, comptroller, 55.
    Patrick, Edinburgh merchant, 252.
Wool, trade in, 250.
Worcester, battle of, 342, 359.
Wotton, Sir Edward, 182-3.
    Dr Nicholas, 99.
Wright, Michael, portrait-painter, 271.

York, conference at, 160.
Young, Patrick, scholar, 261.
    Peter, tutor of James VI, 172; an " Octavian ", 217n.

Zwinglian influence in Scotland, 82.